GREECE

P. de Franqueville/MICHELIN

Executive Editorial Director	David Brabis
Chief Editor	Cynthia Clayton Ochterbeck

THE GREEN GUIDE GREECE

Editor	Gwen Cannon
Principal Writer	Anne-Marie Scott
Production Coordinator	Allison M. Simpson
Cartography	Alain Baldet, Michelle Cana, Peter Wrenn
Photo Editor	Lydia Strong
Proofreader	Gaven R. Watkins
Layout & Design	Tim Schulz
Cover Design	Laurent Muller, Ute Weber

Contact Us:

The Green Guide
Michelin Maps and Guides
One Parkway South
Greenville, SC 29615
USA
☏ 1-800-423-0485
www.michelintravel.com
michelin.guides@us.michelin.com

Michelin Maps and Guides
Hannay House
39 Clarendon Road
Watford, Herts WD17 1JA
UK
☏ (01923) 205 240
travelpubsales@uk.michelin.com

Special Sales:

For information regarding bulk sales, customized editions and premium sales, please contact our Customer Service Departments:
USA 1-800-423-0485
UK (01923) 205 240
Canada 1-800-361-8236

One Team ...
A Commitment to Quality

There's just one reason our team is dedicated to producing quality travel publications—you, our reader. We want you to get the maximum benefit from your trip—and from your money. In today's multiple-choice world of travel, the options are many, perhaps overwhelming.

In our guidebooks, we try to minimize the guesswork involved with travel. We scout out the attractions, prioritize them with star ratings, and describe what you'll discover when you visit them.

To help you orient yourself, we provide colorful and detailed, but easy-to-follow maps. Floor plans of some of the cathedrals and museums help you plan your tour.

Throughout the guides, we offer practical information, touring tips and suggestions for finding the best views, good places for a break and the most interesting shops.

Lodging and dining are always a big part of travel, so we compile a selection of hotels and restaurants that we think convey the feel of the destination, and organize them by geographic area and price. We also highlight shopping, recreational and entertainment venues, especially the popular spots.

If you're short on time, driving tours are included so you can hit the highlights and quickly absorb the best of the region.

For those who love to experience a destination on foot, we add walking tours, often with a map. And we list other companies who offer boat, bus or guided walking tours of the area, some with culinary, historical or other themes.

In short, we test and retest, check and recheck to make sure that our guidebooks are truly just that: a personalized guide to help you make the most of your visit. After all, we want you to enjoy traveling as much as we do.

The Michelin Green Guide Team

PLANNING YOUR TRIP

INTRODUCTION TO GREECE

SYMBOLS

- **Tips to help improve your experience**
- **Details to consider**
- **Entry Fees**
- **Walking tours**
- **Closed to the public**
- **Hours of operation**
- **Periods of closure**

DISCOVERING GREECE

The Islands

HOW TO USE THIS GUIDE

Orientation

To help you grasp the "lay of the land" quickly and easily, so you'll feel confident and comfortable finding your way around, we offer the following tools in this guide:

- Detailed table of contents for an overview of what you'll find in the guide, and how it is organized.
- Map of Principal Sights showing the starred places of interest at a glance.
- Detailed maps of city centres, regions and towns.
- Floor and site plans of museums and cathedrals.
- Principal Sights ordered alphabetically for easy reference.

Practicalities

At the front of the guide, you'll see a section called "Planning Your Trip" that contains information about planning your trip, the best time to go, getting to and getting around the destination, basic facts and tips for making the most of your visit. You'll find driving and themed tours and suggestions for outdoor fun. There's also a calendar of popular annual events in the region. Information on shopping, sightseeing, activities for children, sports and recreational opportunities is also included.

LODGINGS

We've made a selection of hotels and arranged these lodgings within the cities, categorized by price to fit all budgets. For the most part, we selected accommodations based on their unique quality, their regional feel, as it were. If you want a more comprehensive selection of accommodations in Athens, see the red-cover *Michelin Guide Main Cities of Europe.*

RESTAURANTS

We thought you'd like to know the popular eating spots in selected cities and towns described in this guide. So we selected restaurants that capture the flavor of the area. Many of them feature regional specialties, though we're not rating the quality of the food per se. As we did with the hotels, we organized the restaurants within the Principal Sights and categorized them by price to appeal to all wallets. If you want a more comprehensive selection of eateries in Athens, see the red-cover *Michelin Guide Main Cities of Europe.*

Attractions

Contact information, admission charges and hours of operation are given for most attractions. Unless otherwise noted, admission prices shown are for a single adult only. Discounts for seniors, students, military personnel, etc. may be available; be sure to ask. If no admission charge is shown, entrance to the attraction is free. Within each Principal Sight, attractions wiithin a town or city are described first, sometimes in the form of a walking tour. Then come outlying sights and Excursions. If you're pressed for time, we recommend you visit the three- and two-star sights first—the stars are your guide.

STAR RATINGS

Michelin has used stars as a rating tool for more than 100 years:

★★★ Highly recommended
★★ Recommended
★ Interesting

SYMBOLS IN THE TEXT

Besides the stars, other symbols in the text indicate the nearest tourist information ; wheelchair access ; on-site parking ; sights to visit if time permits ; and sights of interest to children . See the map legend at the back of the guide for symbols appearing on the maps.
Throughout the guide you will find colored text boxes or sidebars containing anecdotal or background information.

Maps

All maps in this guide are oriented north, unless otherwise indicated by a directional arrow. See the map Legend at the back of the guide for an explanation of other map symbols. A complete list of the maps found in the guide appears at the back of this book.

Addresses, phone numbers, opening hours and prices published in this guide are accurate at press time. We welcome corrections and suggestions that may assist us in preparing the next edition. Please send your comments to:

Michelin Maps and Guides
Hannay House
39 Clarendon Road
Watford, Herts WD17 1JA
UK
travelpubsales@uk.michelin.com
www.michelin.co.uk

Michelin Maps and Guides
Editorial Department
P.O. Box 19001
Greenville, SC 29602-9001
USA
michelin.guides@us.michelin.com
www.michelintravel.com

Principal sights

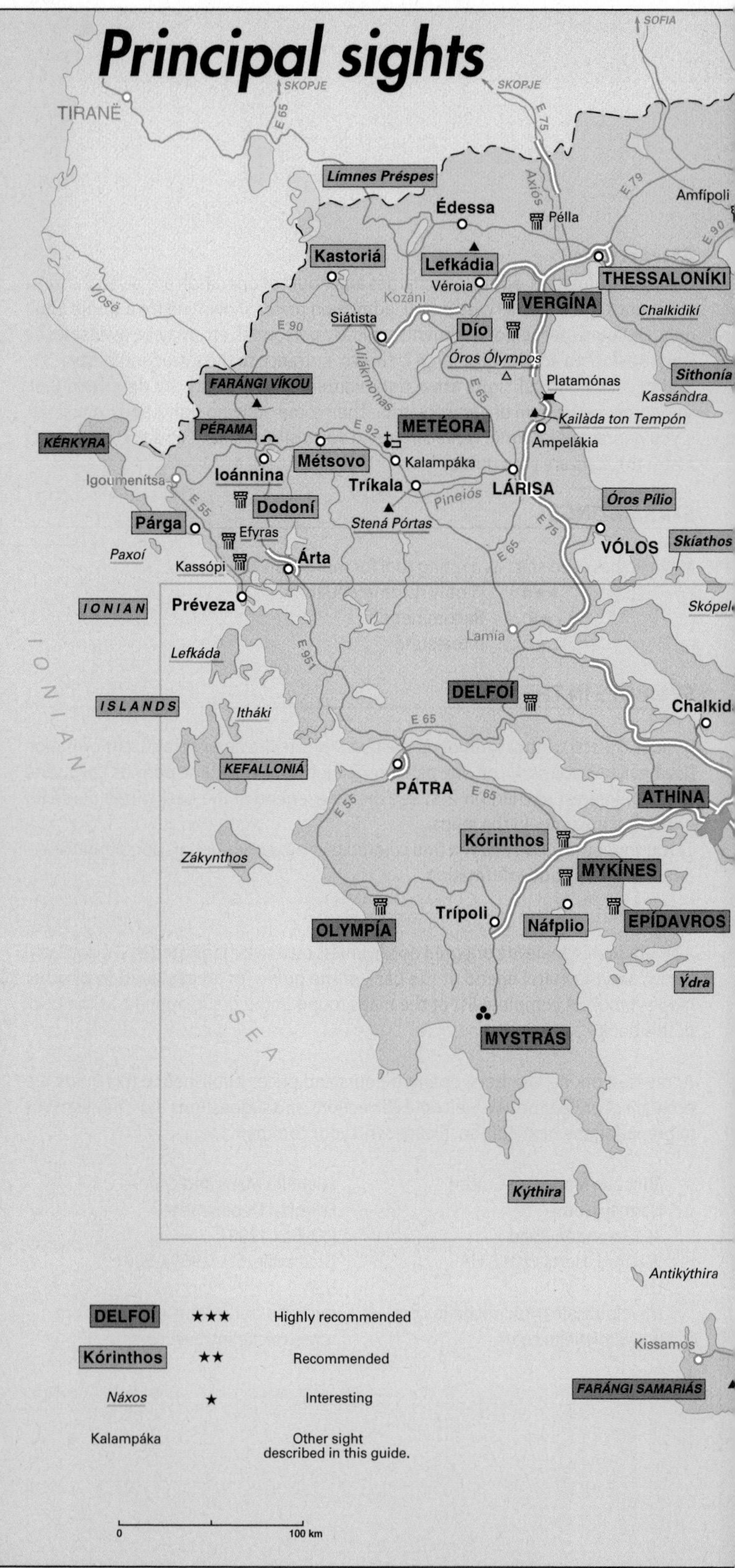

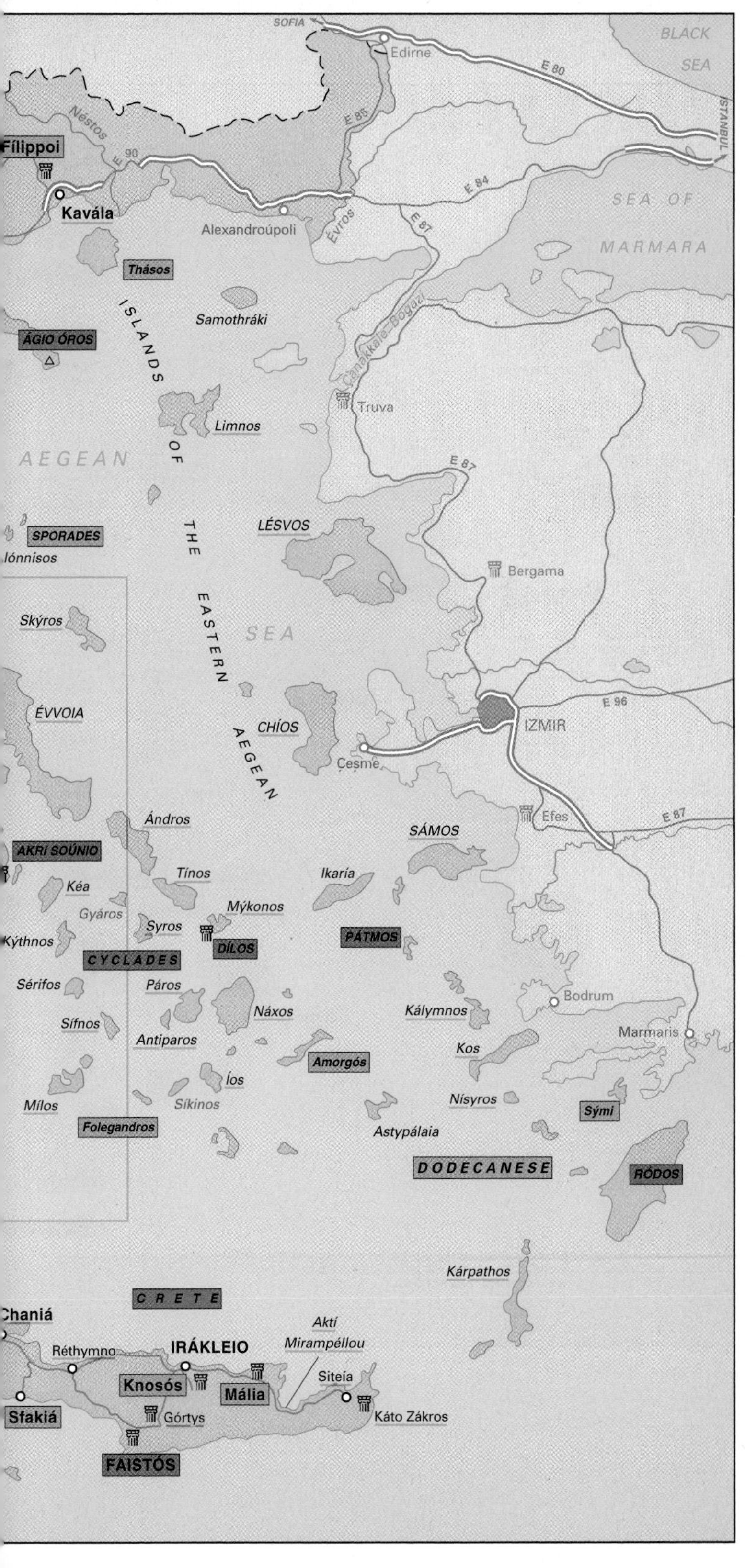

SOFIA
Edirne
BLACK SEA
E 80
ISTANBUL
E 85
Néstos
Fílippoi
E 90
Kavála
Alexandroúpoli
Évros
E 84
E 87
SEA OF MARMARA
Thásos
ISLANDS OF THE EASTERN AEGEAN
Samothráki
ÁGIO ÓROS
Çanakkale-Boğazi
Truva
Limnos
AEGEAN SEA
LÉSVOS
SPORADES
Alónnisos
Bergama
Skýros
ÉVVOIA
E 96
IZMIR
CHÍOS
Çesme
Efes
Ándros
SÁMOS
AKRÍ SOÚNIO
Tínos
Ikaría
Kéa
Mýkonos
Gyáros
Syros
Kýthnos
DÍLOS
PÁTMOS
CYCLADES
Sérifos
Páros
Náxos
Bodrum
Kálymnos
Sífnos
Antiparos
Marmaris
Amorgós
Kos
Íos
Nísyros
Mílos
Síkinos
Sými
Folegandros
Astypálaia
DODECANESE
RÓDOS
Kárpathos
CRETE
Chaniá
Aktí Mirampéllou
Réthymno
IRÁKLEIO
Siteía
Knosós
Mália
Sfakiá
Górtys
Káto Zákros
FAISTÓS

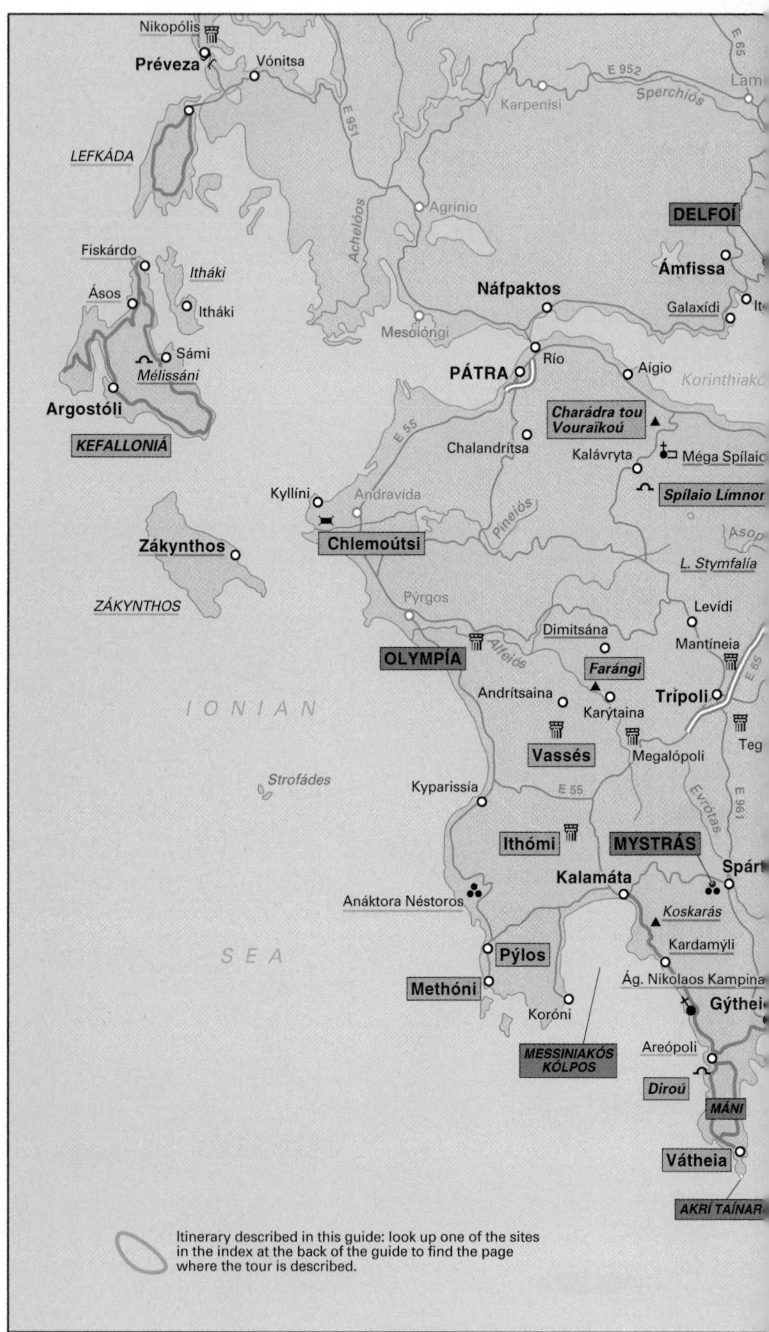
Nikopólis
Préveza
Vónitsa
LEFKÁDA
Karpenísi
E 952
Sperchiós
E 65
E 951
Agrínio
Achelóos
DELFOÍ
Ámfissa
Galaxídi
Fiskárdo
Itháki
Ásos
Itháki
Náfpaktos
Mesolóngi
Sámi
Mélissáni
Río
PÁTRA
Aígio
Korinthiakó
Argostóli
KEFALLONIÁ
E 55
Charádra tou Vouraïkoú
Chalandrítsa
Kalávryta
Méga Spílaio
Spílaio Límnon
Kyllíni
Andravída
Pineiós
Zákynthos
Chlemoútsi
L. Stymfalía
ZÁKYNTHOS
Pýrgos
Levídi
Dimitsána
Mantíneia
OLYMPÍA
Alfeiós
Farángi
Andrítsaina
Karýtaina
Trípoli
I O N I A N
Vassés
Megalópoli
Strofádes
Kyparissía
E 55
Evrótas
E 961
Ithómi
MYSTRÁS
Kalamáta
Anáktora Néstoros
Koskarás
Kardamýli
S E A
Pýlos
Ág. Nikólaos Kampinari
Methóni
Gýtheio
Koróni
Areópoli
MESSINIAKÓS KÓLPOS
Diroú
MÁNI
Vátheia
AKRÍ TAÍNARO
Itinerary described in this guide: look up one of the sites in the index at the back of the guide to find the page where the tour is described.

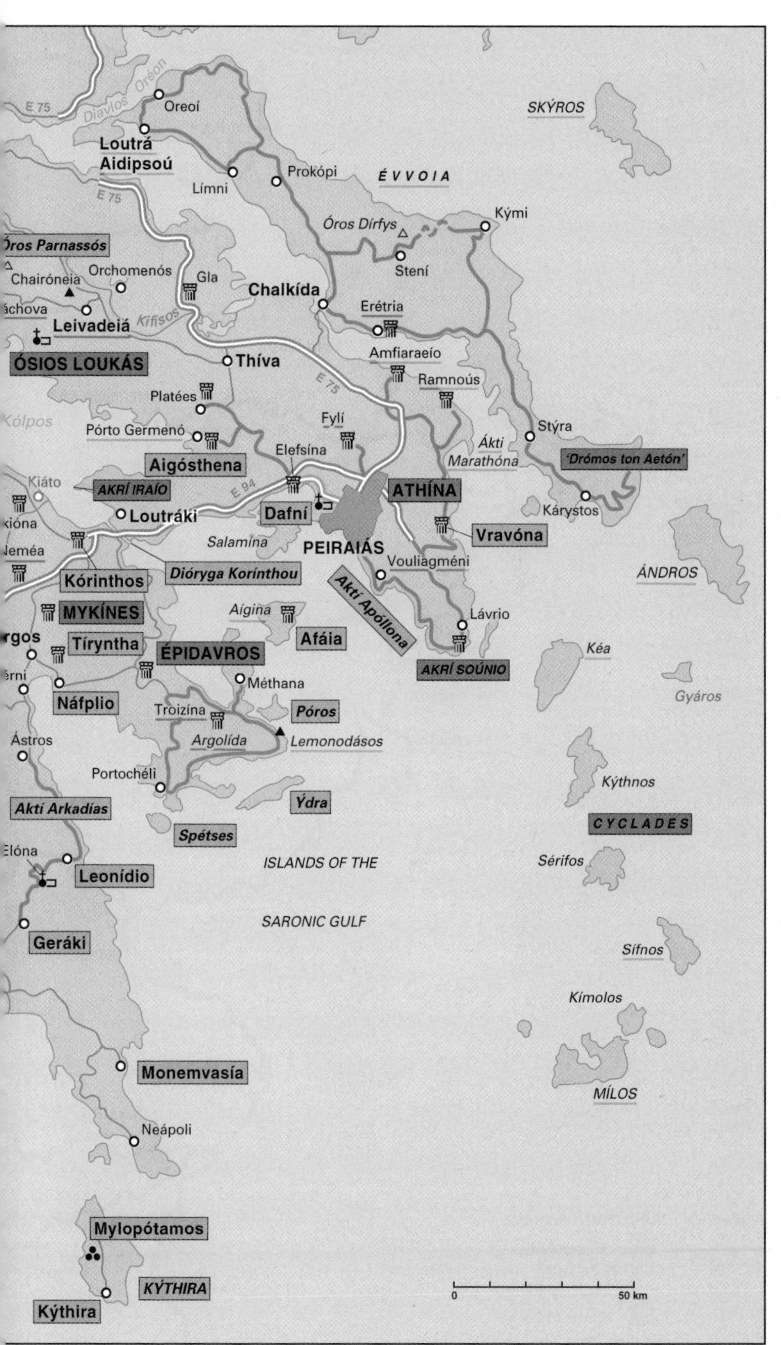

Oreoí
Loutrá Aidipsoú
Límni
Prokópi
ÉVVOIA
SKÝROS
Kými
Óros Dírfys
Stení
Óros Parnassós
Chairóneia
Orchomenós
Gla
Chalkída
Erétria
Leivadeiá
Kifisos
ÓSIOS LOUKÁS
Thíva
Amfiaraeío
Ramnoús
Platées
Pórto Germenó
Fylí
Elefsína
Stýra
Ákti Marathóna
'Drómos ton Aetón'
Aigósthena
Kiáto
AKRÍ IRAÍO
ATHÍNA
Kárystos
Loutráki
Dafní
Vravóna
Salamína
PEIRAIÁS
Vouliagméni
ÁNDROS
Kórinthos
Dióryga Korínthou
Aktí Apóllona
MYKÍNES
Aígina
Lávrio
Tíryntha
Afáia
ÉPIDAVROS
Kéa
AKRÍ SOÚNIO
Méthana
Gyáros
Náfplio
Troizína
Póros
Argolída
Lemonodásos
Ástros
Portochéli
Kýthnos
Aktí Arkadías
Ýdra
CYCLADES
Spétses
ISLANDS OF THE SARONIC GULF
Sérifos
Leonídio
Geráki
Sífnos
Kímolos
Monemvasía
MÍLOS
Neápoli
Mylopótamos
KÝTHIRA
Kýthira
0
50 km
E 75
E 94

Driving tours

TIRANA - SKOPJE
★★ Limnes Préspes
Édessa
Flórina
★★ Lefkádia
Véroia
Kastoriá ★★
1
Vjosë
E 90
★ Siátista
Kozáni
Aliákmonas
FARÁNGI VÍKOU ★★★
★ Monodéndri
★★★ PÉRAMA
METÉORA ★★★
Métsovo ★★
Kalampáka
★★ Kérkyra
E 90 - E 92
Ioannina ★
Achelóos
Dodóni ★★
Tríkala
E 92
Pineiós
Igoumenítsa
★★★ KÉRKYRA
E 55
Stena Pórtas ★
Éfyras ★
★★ Párga
Kassópi ★
Árta ★
Tavropós
★ Nikopólis
Préveza
E 952
Vónitsa
Sperchiós
IONIAN
Lefkáda
★ LEFKÁDA
Nydrí
Achelóos
Náfpaktos
E 55
E 65
Mesolóngi
CÉPHALONIE
PÁTRA
SEA
E 55
Andravída
Pineiós
ZANTE
OLÝMPIA ★★★
Pyrgós
Karýtaina
Andrítsaina
★★ Vassés
Megalópoli
Kyparissía
E 55
Alfeiós
Kalamáta
★ Anáktora Néstoros
Pýlos ★★
★★ Methóni
MESSINIAKÓS KÓLPOS ★★★
Northern Greece
1 : 750km/466mi
(6 days including 1 day in Thessaloníki and 1 day in Kastoriá)
2 : 700km/435mi
(4 days including 1 day in Thásos)
Central Greece : 1750km/1087mi
(11 days including 1 day in Kérkyra, 1 day in Ioánnina and its environs, and 1 day in Vólos and its environs)
Principal ancient sites : 900km/559mi
(7 days including 2 days in Athína and 1 day in Náfplio and its environs)
Southern Peloponnese : 1100km/683mi
(7 days including 3 days for the environs of Gýtheio)

SKOPJE
SOFIA
★★ Fílippoi
Kavála ★
ALEXANDROÚPOLI
E 79
Strymónas
Axiós
E 75
Amfípoli
Pélla
E 86
2
E 90
1
E 90
THESSALONÍKI ★★
Thásos ★★
Vergína ★★★
2
E 75
★★ Dío
Vourvouroú
Litochóro
Óros Ólympos ★
Platamónas ★
Sithonía ★★
Kailáda ton Tempón ★
LÍMNOS
AEGEAN
LÁRISA
SEA
E 75
VÓLOS
Óros Pílio ★★
E 65
SPORÁDES
Lamía
SKYRÓS
E 75
Ámfissa
DELFOÍ ★★★
ÉVVOIA
Gla
Kifisos
Galaxídi ★
ÓSIOS LOUKÁS ★★★
E 75
Korinthiakós
Eleftherès
E 962
Kólpos
E 65
ATHÍNA ★★★
E 94
★★ Dafní
★★ Kórinthos
Aktí Apóllona ★★
Asopós
MYKÍNES ★★★
E 65
Aígina
Árgos
Tíryntha ★★
AKRÍ SOÚNIO ★★★
Mantíneia
EPÍDAVROS ★★★
Náfplio ★★
Trípoli
Àstros
CYCLADES
Ýdra
Aktí Arkadías ★★
Spétses
MYSTRÁS ★★★
Leonídio ★★
Sparte
Elóna
E 961
Evrotas
Geráki ★★
Gýtheio
Areópoli ★
Monemvasía ★★
Diroú ★★
MÁNI ★★★
0
50 km
Vátheia ★★

Naoussa Port, Páros, Cyclades

C. Legrand/MICHELIN

PLANNING YOUR TRIP

WHEN AND WHERE TO GO

Driving Tours

See the Driving Tours map on p 12.
The suggested itinerary route maps at the beginning of this guide take into account the availability of accommodation along the way, the number of sites of interest, and the ease of travel along the route. Certain major sites do not have a convenient hotel; you may need to look for lodging in a nearby town of little interest to the visitor.

AROUND OLYMPOS

This itinerary explores the rugged peaks of northern Greece near the Albanian border. After seeing **Thessaloníki**, the second city of the country, head for the Macedonian tombs of **Lefkadia** (3-2C BC) before visiting the **Prespa Lakes** (a national park) and staying in the charming town of **Kastoriá**, situated on a peninsula. Travel through the mountains, dominated by Olympos, to reach **Lárissa**, the capital of Thessaly. Return along the coast with its fine beaches, making a point of stopping at the Ancient city of **Dío**.

NORTHERN GREECE

Starting in **Thessaloníki**, this itinerary takes in the fertile plains and valleys of Macedonia. The **Sithonia** peninsula is especially attractive with woodlands and beaches. To the north of **Kavála** is the site of **Fílipi,** founded by Philip II of Macedon and greatly expanded by the Romans. Then cross to the island of **Thássos** with its fine archaeological remains for the final leg of the trip.

CENTRAL GREECE

This long circuit through some of the most beautiful countryside in Greece is best started from **Athens**. Along the way visit the monastery of **Óssios Loukás**, **Delphi** (where the natural scenery is as breathtaking as the historical remains), and the island of **Leucas** (linked by a bridge to the mainland) with its white cliffs (don't miss **Nidri Bay**, sheltered by a series of small islands). After an overnight stay at **Párga**, take a ferry from Igoumenítsa to the idyllic beaches and Italian influences of **Corfu**. Returning to the mainland head east to **Ioánina**, capital of Epirus, from where the natural beauties of the area, such as the Perama cave and the Víkos gorge, and the archaeological splendour of **Dodona**, may be easily reached. Farther east are the gravity defying monasteries of **Metéora**. Return to Athens via Trikala and Vólos; the route hugs the coast back to the capital.

THE GREAT SITES OF ANTIQUITY

The main monuments of Classical Greece can be toured over the course of a week. Start in **Athens** with the Acropolis and its environs, and the big museums. Two days in the capital should suffice before taking to the road: the Ancient city of **Corinth**, **Mycenae** with its famous Lion Gate, the ramparts at **Tiryns**, **Epidauros** with its fine theatre, **Olympia** and the moving sight of its extensive remains. Return to Athens via **Patras** and the unparalleled **Delphi**, with its Sacred Precinct and interesting museum.

THE SOUTHERN PELOPONNESE

This programme takes in the main sites of the Peloponnese, including **Nauplion** with its fine citadel; close by are **Mycenae** and **Epidauros**. Continue to the attractive resort of **Leonidío** and then on to unspoilt **Monemvassiá**, before exploring the **Máni** peninsula. Returning northwards, visit **Mystra** and the stunningly situated **Pylos**, prior to continuing to the ruins of **Olympia**, and finally stopping to admire the breathtaking sight of the temple at **Bassae**.

THE CYCLADES

Eight days suffice to see much of the Cyclades. The itinerary begins in **Piraeus** before visiting **Syros**, **Tenos**, **Mykonos**, **Páros**, **Náxos**, **Íos** and **Santorini**. From Santorini the return journey can either be by plane to Athens or by boat to Piraeus; or extend the itinerary by going on to **Herakleion** in Crete before flying back to Athens.

Suggested Itineraries

ATHENS (3-6 DAYS)

This great city was one of the most beautiful places in Antiquity.

Day 1 – Top priority is a visit to the **Acropolis**, followed by a stroll through the **Plaka** district.

Day 2 – Visit the **National Archaeological Museum**, with its unparalleled examples of Classical art, followed by a trip to the **Agora** and the **Keramíkos cemetery**.

Day 3 – Don't miss the remarkable **Benaki Museum** and the **Museum of Cycladic Art**. Witness the changing of the guard before seeing the Olympieion, the National Gardens and Odós Ermou.

Days 4-6 – Rent a car to see the sights of the **Attica** peninsula, **Delphi**, **Mycenae**, **Epidauros** and **Nauplion**.

NAUPLION (3 DAYS)

In the eastern Peloponnese, Nauplion is an Ancient city situated on a peninsula. It is also an excellent base from which to visit the archaeological sites of Mycenae, Epidauros and Corinth.

Day 1 – Discover Epidauros and its stunning theatre, one of the great monuments of the Classical world.

Day 2 – A trip to Mycenae in the morning to admire the ruins of this great city founded in the second millennium BC; do not miss the famous Lion Gate. In the afternoon visit Corinth, remarkable for its citadel (Acrocorinth) and for its canal linking the Gulf of Corinth to the Saronic Gulf.

R. Cuzin/MICHELIN

Day 3 – Explore Nauplion itself, especially its citadel, and then finish your visit by relaxing at the beach.

GÍTHIO (3 DAYS)

This port on the Laconic Gulf is also the gateway to the Máni peninsula. With numerous good quality hotels, it is the ideal base from which to explore the southern Peloponnese.

Day 1 – Discover the wild mountains of the Máni peninsula and its villages such as Vathia.

Day 2 – Visit Sparta and then continue up Mount Taigetos to Mystra, which occupies a fine panoramic position.

Day 3 – Explore the gulf of Messenia with its many beaches. From here it is a short hop to the island of Kythera.

CORFU (4 DAYS)

This island is a garden of Eden in the Ionian Sea, close to the coast of Epirus and the shores of Albania. **Corfu Town** shows a strong Italian influence with its tiled roofs and cypress trees.

Day 1 – Wander through the streets of the old town, with its Baroque churches, museums and citadels.

Day 2 – Make an early start to walk to the tip of the **Kanoni peninsula** from where some of the finest landscape in Greece can be seen, before visiting the **Achilleion**, a villa built in the neo-Classical style for Sisi, Empress of Austria.

Day 3 – Discover the west coast of the island, including **Pelekas** (fine panoramic view) and **Paleokastrítsa Bay**.

Day 4 – Take a trip to the north of the island; near **Sidari** are numerous inlets and rocky promontories caused by erosion. Inland, the countryside is dotted with ancient olive groves.

SANTORINI (3 DAYS)

The best-known island of the Cyclades, Santorini is also one of the most beautiful. Formed by a partially submerged volcanic crater, its landscape is of a breathtaking beauty.

Day 1 – Visit **Thíra**, the principal town, and its environs before enjoying the sunset from the beautiful village of **Oia**.

Day 2 – Take a boat trip round the submerged crater and enjoy a swim.

Day 3 – Discover the archaeological sites of the island at **Akrotíri** and **Thíra** before ending the day with a visit to one of the fine beaches to the south.

CRETE (5 DAYS)

At the eastern end of Crete, the resort of **Ágios Nikólaos** is close to numerous places of interest, both natural and architectural.

Day 1 – Wander round the town, constructed on the shores of a lake.

Day 2 – Visit the tranquil island and peninsula of **Spinalónga**.

Day 3 – Explore the Ancient Minoan city of **Mália**, and the picturesque village of **Krítsa**.

Day 4 – Discover more of Crete by heading to **Ierápetra** and then turning west and following the coast before returning via Chersonisos.

Day 5 – Start early and head to **Vai** at the eastern tip of Crete, pausing at **Sitía** on the way. At Vai, the palm-fringed beach is especially beautiful. If there is time turn south to visit the Minoan palace at **Káto Zákros**.

RHODES (6 DAYS)

Rhodes is most easily reached by flying direct to the island. A six-day stay will allow time to discover not only Rhodes but also the beautiful neighbouring island of Sími.

Day 1 – Explore **Rhodes Town** with its citadel, which in the Middle Ages was one of the great bastions against the Turks.

Day 2 – Discover the east coast, making a point of visiting the town of **Lindos** and its medieval citadel.

Day 3 – Head for the rugged west coast with its many inlets which are ideal for a swim. Do not miss the fortress of **Monolithos** which dominates the landscape.

Day 4 – Travel into the mountains, where there are many small churches and vineyards.

Day 5 – Take a boat across to the island of **Sími**, whose neo-Classical town is one of the most beautiful in Greece.

Day 6 – Enjoy the beaches of Sími before returning to Rhodes.

When to Go

Spring in Greece is brief but idyllic, with the mountains and islands covered in wild flowers; the sea, however, can be chilly. The best time of year to visit is during the month of June, with pleasant temperatures and gentle breezes. Accommodations are also cheaper as there are fewer visitors than in high season. September offers similarly favourable weather, and sea temperatures at their peak. Autumn is mild until mid-November, although many hotels close at the end of October. Days then begin to shorten significantly, and downpours revitalise the landscape. Note that most Greeks do not travel abroad for their holidays and further swell the tourist numbers in high season. Hotels and restaurants are full, and prices double or even triple. In the Aegean, there are strong winds throughout the summer which offer some relief from the heat, but they can blow violently and make sailing difficult.

In winter, Greece is a nation of contrasts. In the north and at higher altitudes there is abundant snow, whereas the south and the islands remain mild. In January the average temperature is 11°C in Athens and 12°C in Herakleion. Skiing is available just two hours' drive from Athens, where on sunnier winter days it is possible to dine outside.

KNOW BEFORE YOU GO

Useful Web Sites

The Internet enables visitors to contact tourist offices, consult programmes and brochures, and make bookings on line.

www.gnto.gr
Greek National Tourist Office.

www.culture.gr
Web site of the Ministry of Culture, with lists of sites and museums, and numerous links; in English and Greek.

www.cultureguide.gr
Museum hours, exhibitions, lectures and public events; in English and Greek.

www.travelinfo.gr
Good source of information for the Cyclades, Dodecanese and Crete.

www.gtp.gr
Connection and timetable details for ferry services; links to operators' sites for booking.

www.ferries.gr
Schedules, connections and prices for ferry services from mainland Greece to the islands and Europe.

www.greek-tourism.gr
General information for travel to and from Greece.

www.phantis.com
Comprehensive search engine for all aspects of Greece.

www.greek-islands.org
Site created by a devotee of the Cyclades; good tips and addresses.

www.greek-islands.net
General information, reviews, links.

www.explorecrete.com
Links, blogs and general information about Crete.

Tourist Offices

TOURIST ORGANISATIONS

Greek National Tourist Organisation (GNTO), Elinikós Organismós Tourismoú (EOT)
Information and brochures on all regions of Greece are available from the following official tourist offices:

- 4 Conduit Street, **London** W1S 2DJ ☎ (020) 7495 9300; Fax (020) 7287 1369; info@gnto.co.uk; www.gnto.co.uk
- 645 Fifth Avenue, Olympic Tower, **New York**, NY 10022 ☎ (212) 421 5777; Fax (212) 826 6940; www.gnto.gr
- 1170 Place du Frère André, 3rd Floor, **Montreal**, H3B 3C6 ☎ (514) 871 1535; Fax (514) 871 1498.
- 1500 Don Mills Rd. Suite 102, **Toronto**, Ontario M3B 3K4 ☎ (416) 968 2220; Fax (416) 968 6533; grnto.tor@on.aibn.com
- PO Box R203, 37-49 Pitt Street, **Sydney**, NSW 2 000 ☎ (00612) 9241 1663, 9252 1441; Fax (00612) 9241 2499; hto@tpg.com.au

Local Tourist Offices
Local tourist offices generally supply information on accommodation, sightseeing and transport. The addresses and telephone numbers of these offices appear after the ℹ in the introduction section for each entry in the Discovering The Sights section.

Greece National Tourism Organization

International Visitors

GREEK EMBASSIES AND CONSULATES

United Kingdom
1A Holland Park, London W11 3TP ☎ (020) 7229 3850; Fax (020) 7229 7221; www.greekembassy.org.uk

USA
2217 Massachusetts Avenue NW, Washington, DC 20008 ☎ (202) 939 1300; Fax (202) 939 1324; www.greekembassy.org

Canada
80 MacLaren Street, Ottawa, Ontario, K2P 0K6 ☎ (613) 238 62 71/3; Fax (613) 238 5676; embassy@greekembassy.ca; www.greekembassy.ca

Australia
9 Turrana Street, Yarralumla, Canberra 2600 ☎ (62) 733 883; 733 158; Fax (62) 732 620; greekemb@greekembassy.au.org

EMBASSIES AND CONSULATES

Information on all embassies and consulates is available from the Ministry of Foreign Affairs ☎ (210) 36 11 058 (8am to 2pm).

- **Australian** Embassy and Consulate, Level 6, Thon Building, Kifisias & Alexandras Ave, Ambelokipi, Athens 115 23 ☎ (210) 870 4000; Fax (210) 870 4111.
- **Canadian** Embassy, 4 Odós Ioannou Gennadíou, 115 21 Athens ☎ (210) 727 3400; Fax (210) 727 3480
- **Irish** Embassy, 7 Leofóros Vass. Kon/nou, 106 74 Athens ☎ (210) 723 2771; Fax (210) 729 3383
- **New Zealand** General Consulate, 268 Kifissias Ave, 152 32 Halandri ☎ (210) 687 4700
- **South African** Embassy and Consulate, 60 Leofóros Kifissias, 151 25 Maroussi ☎ (210) 610 6645; Fax (210) 610 6640
- **USA** Embassy and Consulate, 91 Leofóros Vassilissi Sofías, 101 60 Athens ☎ (210) 721 2951
- **UK** Embassy and Consulate, 1 Odós Ploutárchou, 106 75 Athens ☎ (210) 727 2600

DOCUMENTS

A **passport** or (for EU residents) a valid **identity card** is required for a stay not exceeding three months.
A national driving licence is sufficient for citizens of EU member countries and for US drivers for up to 3 months but an international driving licence is necessary for other drivers. An international **green insurance card**, covering vehicles driven outside their country of origin and issued by the Motor Insurers Bureau, is required if you drive your own car in Greece; check with your insurance provider or www.mib-hellas.gr.

HEALTH

International visitors from EU countries should acquire a **European Health Insurance Card** which entitles the holder to urgent treatment for accident or unexpected illness. Nationals of non-EU countries should check that their insurance policy covers them for overseas travel, including doctor's visits, medication and hospitalisation in Greece (you may need to take out **supplemental insurance**). All prescription drugs should be clearly labelled; carry a copy of the prescription with you.

ACCESSIBILITY

Away from Athens, facilities for disabled travellers are limited, although the helpful and friendly nature of the Greeks can sometimes be relied upon to minimise any problems. Some ferries and aircraft serving the islands offer access for wheelchairs.

ANIMALS

An **international vaccination card** and a **certificate of good health** issued in the country of origin 15 days before departure, are required for all animals entering Greece.

GETTING THERE

By Air

There are daily flights to Athens from many cities by international carriers and by **Olympic Airlines**, the national air carrier of Greece (96 Leofóros Singrou, 117 41 Koukaki, Athens, ☎ (210) 92 69 111; reservations (210) 9 666 666; www.olympicairlines.com). Reserve well in advance, especially in summer. International flights also serve Herakleion, Rhodes and Thessaloniki.

Olympic Airlines Offices:

- 11 Conduit Street, **London** WS 2LP ☎ 0870 606 0460; Terminal 2, Heathrow Airport ☎ (020) 8745 7339 or 8759 5884; Gatwick Airport ☎ (01293) 535 353 or (01293) 502 469
- 125 Park Avenue, **New York** 10017 ☎ 800 223 1226 (toll free); oausa@olympicairlines.us
- 37-49 Pitt Street, Underwood House, Level 3, Suite 303, **Sydney**, NSW 200 ☎ (2) 9241 5173; management@olympic-airways.com.au.
- 1200 McGill College Ave, Ste 1250, **Montreal** H3B 4G7 ☎ (514) 878 3891; sales.yul@olympicairlines.ca
- 80 Bloor Street West, Suite 502, **Toronto**, OT M5S 2V1 ☎ (416) 920 2452; yyz@olympicairlines.ca

International Carriers:

British Airways:Reservations ☎ 0845 77 333 77; +00 44 191 490 7901 (from outside the UK); www.britishairways.com
Virgin Express: Reservations ☎ 0870 730 1134 (UK); ☎ +32 70- 35 26 37 (outside the UK); www.virgin-express.com
Delta Airlines: Reservations ☎ 800 241 4141 (in the US); ☎ 404 765 500 (outside the US; ☎ 0845 600 0950 (UK); www.delta.com

In summer there are charter flights from the UK to all or some of the following destinations:

Athens (new terminal)	Mykonos
Cephallonia	Patras
Corfu	Préveza
Chania (Crete)	Rhodes (Dodecanese)
Herakleion (Crete)	Sámos
Kalamáta	Santorini
Kavála	Skiáthos (Sporades)
Kos (Dodecanese)	Thessaloníki
Lemnos	Zakynthos
Lesbos	

By Train

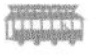

There are rail links from northern Europe to Athens changing at Munich, Cologne or Venice. For information apply to GNTO (EOT) or to Greek Railways (OSE),1-3 Odós Karolou, Athens ☎ (210) 529 77 77, www.ose.gr.

By Car

Travellers wishing to visit Greece by car from Western Europe are advised to travel by ferry from Italy. Crossings have become more popular and more frequent in recent years. From Italy, ports include Venice, Trieste, Ancona, Bari and Brindisi; ports in Greece include Corfu, Igoumenitsa, Patras and Piraeus. Reserve at least 2 months in advance in summer. For information, contact **www.greekferries.gr** or **www.ferries.gr**.

MAPS

For journey preparation and selection of your itinerary, refer to the listing of Michelin maps and plans at the back of this guide.

GETTING AROUND

Driving in Greece 

HIGHWAY CODE

The speed limit is 100kph (62mph) or 120kph (74mph) on motorways, 80kph (50mph) on trunk roads, and 50kph (31mph) in built-up areas. Seatbelts are compulsory. Drive with caution; Greece has the highest rate of fatal accidents in the EU.

The Greek road network, which now consists of over 117 000km (72 700mi) of roads, has improved considerably during the past 30 years. There are two motorways (with tolls) linking Athens to Patras and Thessaloníki. The other roads tend to be slow and winding because of the terrain and relief. There are still some unsurfaced local and regional roads which carry heavy traffic including buses. Roads are frequently under repair, and delays are inevitable as there are often no alternative routes.

Extra care is required in the country, as there are numerous flocks of sheep or goats as well as donkeys in mountain areas.

The roads are sometimes poorly signposted, although many of the signs are written in Roman as well as Greek lettering; the main sights are indicated in English. Off the beaten track, road signs are often rudimentary and are only in Greek; it's a good idea to familiarise yourself with the Greek alphabet.

The Greek Automobile Touring Club (ELPA) has about 40 offices throughout the country and runs a roadside breakdown service (OVELPA – ☎ 104) which is free to members of other national Automobile or Touring Clubs.

PARKING

There is no metered parking in central Athens and finding a space during the day can be difficult. The bus or metro is an easier way of getting around. Illegal parking can result in the confiscation of a number plate, returnable only upon payment of a fine.

ACCIDENTS

In the event of a road accident, a police officer must compile a report, a copy of which is given to the parties involved. Greece's many garages are usually well equipped to deal with incidents of minor damage.

PETROL/GAS STATIONS

These are frequent enough except on some mountain roads. The price of petrol tends to be less than in other European countries. Most service stations do not accept credit cards; wait for an attendant, as self-service is not available in Greece.

Rental Cars

It is possible to hire a car from rental offices in the cities and towns, at airports and railway stations, and at large hotels. Rentals are by the day; be sure the check the condition of the vehicle before signing the contract:

- **Avis** – www.avis.gr
- **Europcar** – www.europcar.com/gr
- **Hertz** – www.hertz.gr

Mopeds

Renting a moped requires a valid driving licence. Clarify with the hirer whether rental is for a 24-hour period or only for the duration of the day (this has caused some confusion in the past). Check the condition of the vehicle and fuel quantity. Request a crash helmet, as they are compulsory.

By Air 

The domestic airline network is extensive. Fares which are equal to a first-class boat ticket are good value. It is advisable to book early in season as domestic services are very popular with both Greeks and tourists, particularly during Greek public holidays. Some lines operate small planes which may suffer long delays in the event of strong winds and bad weather. Carriers include:

- **Olympic Airlines** – www.olympicairlines.com
- **Aegean Air** – www.aegeanair.com
- **Hellas Jet** – www.hellas-jet.com

By Boat

In general there is daily **ferry service** from Piraeus to the well-frequented islands with a weekly or twice-weekly service to the other islands. Vessels include large ferries, which are very dependable and travel all year even in rough weather; hydrofoils or catamarans (twice as fast as traditional ferries); and launches or caiques operate in season between the islands. *See the Address Books in the* Discovering Greece *sections for further information*.
Ships on the major routes have two, three or four classes. Tourist (C) class accommodation consists of a lounge fitted with armchairs and a bar-cafeteria, with easy access to the upper deck for a good view.
Timetables (which may vary from week to week, especially in mid-season) are available from tourist offices (GNTO/EOT) abroad and in Athens; they are published every month by the GNTO (EOT) and by the excellent Web site **Greek Travel Pages, www.gtp.gr.** The timetables of ships operated by private companies are sometimes unreliable. The list of services posted on information boards on the dockside is not always exhaustive; it is advisable to enquire in the offices of the different shipping-lines round the harbour.
Be aware that ferry crossings are always subject to delay or cancellation due to weather, so plan accordingly. It's best to return to Athens the day before your flight home, for example.
Tickets for all trips (ferries and hydrofoils) are issued in the shipping-line offices or at mobile counters on the dockside. Be sure to book in advance for car ferries in season and for berths on night ferries (Crete and Rhodes). The ferries are likely to be crowded during Greek public holidays.

D. Hée/MICHELIN

Piraeus Central Port Authority
☎ (210) 45 11 311/9.

For hydrofoil services:

- Ceres Hydrofoil Joint Service, 8 Akti Themistokleous, 18536 Piraeus ☎ (210) 428 0001; to know which boats are departing that day.

Information also available from:

- **Blue Star Ferries**, www.bluestarferries.com
- **Minoan Lines**, 98 - 100 Sygrou Ave, 117 41 Athens ☎ (210) 920 0020; www.minoan.gr

PLEASURE CRUISING

For the hire of yachts, motor cruisers and caiques, with or without crew, apply to the GNTO (EOT). The Cyclades and the Sporades Islands are the most popular for pleasure cruising. The Ionian Islands, protected from the wind, are less popular. The main moorings for pleasure craft are shown on Michelin map 737.

By Bus

The bus network is very extensive and the buses, some of which have air-conditioning, are a cheap and colourful way of exploring the country as they run to even the most remote places. Information is available at all bus stations. The OSE railway company also runs bus services to the provinces.

Information on services for the Athens region and intercity connections is available from local tourist offices and the GNTO (EOT). Intercity services are run by KTEL (a group of private bus companies). In principle, there are daily services with frequent express buses from Athens to the regional capitals.
The table below indicates the journey time from Athens:

Journey Times from Athens:	
Árgos	5hr
Cephallonia	8hr
Corfu	11hr
Corinth	1hr 30min
Delphi	3hr
Epidauros	2hr 30min
Ioánina	7hr 30min
Halkída	1hr 30min
Kalamáta	4hr 30min
Kavála	10hr
Lamía	3hr 15min
Monemvassiá	6hr
Nauplion	2hr 30min
Olympia	5hr 30min
Patras	3hr
Sparta	4hr
Thebes	1hr 30min
Thessaloníki	7hr 30min

By Train

The Greek railway system is not very extensive. Fares are inexpensive and trains run frequently, but travel is slower than by bus. There are ordinary trains and wagon-lits organised by the **Hellenic Railways Organisation (OSE)**.

The northern network links Athens *(Lárissa Station)* to Thessaloníki with branch lines to Halkída, Vólos, Tríkala and Kalambáka (Metéora), and north-west to Édessa and Kozáni; a line also runs from Thessaloníki to Alexandroúpoli and Orestiáda on the way to Istanbul in Turkey.
The southern network in the Peloponnese, which runs on a narrow gauge (982km – 610mi) links Athens *(Peloponnese Station)* to Kalamáta via Patras and Pírgos (branch line to Olympia), or via Árgos-Nauplion and Trípoli.
Some routes are very picturesque, especially the elevated section between Livadiá and Lamía (central Greece), which includes some impressive viaducts, and the rack railway through the Vouraïkós Gorge between Diakoftó and Kalávrita (Peloponnese).
Further information is available at the **GNTO** (EOT) or **OSE** stations or from:
Greek Railways (OSE),1-3 Odós Karolou, Athens ☎ (210) 529 77 77, www.ose.gr

By Taxi

Metered taxis can be hired at a taxi stand or will stop on request. Always ask the price before riding. Other passengers going in the same direction may share the taxi but rarely the cost. Drivers will stop to pick up passengers going in the same direction, so don't hesitate to hail a taxi that is not completely full. When paying it is advisable not to offer a high-value note but to give the right (or nearly right) amount in change. The driver may add a supplement to fares between Athens-Piraeus and Athens-airport. Taxis are yellow in Athens and grey or burgundy in the rest of the country.

WHERE TO STAY AND EAT

Where to Stay

Hotels are described in the Address Books within the Discovering the Sights section of this guide. Comfort, location, quality of service and value were our criteria when selecting establishments. All have been visited and carefully chosen. Note that in popular destinations such as Athens or Mykonos, it can be difficult to find good value accommodation. Always reserve well in advance in high season.

CATEGORIES

Our selection is divided into four price brackets: (under 65€ in large cities and high-demand areas; under 45€ elsewhere); (65€ to 100€ in large cities and high-demand areas; 45€ to 65€ elsewhere); (100€ to 160€ in large cities and high-demand areas, 65€ to 100€ elsewhere); and (more than 160€ in large cities and high-demand areas; more than 100€ elsewhere). These categories appear in the Legend on the cover flap.

ACCOMMODATION

The Greek hotel sector is well developed, offering everything from luxury hotels to rooms in private houses. Prices vary according to categories established by the GNTO (EOT). B and C class hotels are usually clean and reasonably comfortable; all rooms have facilities. D hotels are simpler but often have rooms with facilities. D and E hotels do not serve breakfast but there are usually cafés nearby.
The following price categories apply:

Luxury	€180 upwards
A	€130 to €300
B	€90 to €170
C	€60 to €135
D	€40 to €65
E	€25 to €50

This classification applies to establishments approved by the GNTO (EOT), which display a blue and yellow plaque, and a full list of prices. Details can be obtained from local tourist offices. Note that prices often halve out of season.

Hotels

Rooms are available by the night; credit-card details may be requested when the reservation is made. The Web site *www.greekhotel.com* offers a vast number of places to stay. If staying on the islands, tell your hotel on which ferry you will arrive and they may come to meet you.

Rooms in private houses

Outside large towns and resorts it is common to take a room in a private house, particularly on the Aegean Islands where the boats are met by homeowners offering rooms. Signs reading *Rooms* or *Domatia* are also found on the roadsides. You can also check *www.familyhotels.gr*, an excellent Web site with links to organizations arranging this type of accommodation. Breakfast is not normally included. Credit cards are not widely accepted.

Self-catering

A good value when travelling with a group of family or friends, this type of accommodation is generally of a high standard.

D. Hée/MICHELIN

Hostels

There are youth hostels throughout Greece. Holders of an International Youth Hostel Federation card should get a list from the International Federation or from the **Greek Youth Hostels Association**, 75 Odós Damareos, Athens, (210) 751 9530, y-hostels@otenet.gr

Where to Eat

Selected restaurants are described in the Address Books within the *Discovering Greece* sections of this guide. Ambiance, location, quality of cuisine and value were our selection criteria. Our selection is divided into four price brackets: (under 16€ in large cities and high-demand areas; under 14€ elsewhere); (16€ to 30€ in large cities and high-demand areas; 14€ to 25€ elsewhere); (30€ to 50€ in large cities and high-demand areas, 25€ to 40€ elsewhere); and (more than 50€ in large cities and high-demand areas; more than 40€ elsewhere). These categories appear in the Legend on the cover flap.

... AND DON'T FORGET

The Michelin Guide Main Cities of Europe

Updated annually, this includes numerous establishments in Athens with full details of price, standards of service and levels of comfort. Selections for inclusion are made after research and visits by Michelin experts. Hotels of an especially high standard are distinguished by a red symbol. The guide also lists a selection of restaurants; those offering truly remarkable cuisine are graded between one and three stars.

What to Eat

GREEK CUISINE

Restaurants in Greece cater to all tastes and budgets. **Tavernas** serve simple, inexpensive traditional cuisine. **Ouzeries** (and *mezedopólio*) are different from tavernas because their menus feature *mezédes* (savoury snacks) instead of cooked dishes. Restaurants *(estiatória)* offer both Greek and international cuisine, even elaborate specialised dishes.

Greeks rarely lunch before 1pm, and 9pm is the preferred dinner hour. Often listed on a blackboard, dishes in Greek restaurants can usually be chosen by diners direct from the kitchen. Greek cuisine relies heavily on numerous side dishes and starters, which tend to be served all at once (be sure to request otherwise if you want them served one after another). Meals are often concluded with fruit; for a proper dessert go to a *zaharoplastio* (patisserie); for coffee visit a *kafenion* (café).

SPECIALITIES

Starters

Dolmádes: vine leaves stuffed with meat and rice.
Tzatzíki: yoghurt with chopped cucumber and garlic.
Kokorétsi: spit-roasted offal sausages.
Melizanosaláta: aubergine purée with black olives.
Moussaká: aubergine and minced lamb with a béchamel sauce.
Piláfi: rice with tomatoes.
Taramosaláta: purée of fish roe and breadcrumbs or potatoes.

Soups

Psarosoúpa: fish soup.
Soupa avgolemono: broth with rice, egg and lemon.

Fish

Fish *(psari)* is served boiled *(vrasto)*, fried or grilled *(psito)*.
Garídes: prawns.
Glóssa: sole.
Ksifías: swordfish.
Kalamári: squid.
Oktapódi: octopus.
Sardéles: sardines.

Meat

Meat can be roasted, grilled *(sharas)*, boiled or braised *(stifado)*. The words

tis oras next to a dish mean that it will be cooked to the client's wishes; most dishes are prepared in advance.
Arni and *arnaki*: mutton and lamb.
Bifteki: minced beef.
Kirino: pork.
Kotopoulo: chicken.
Moshari: veal.
Soutzoukakia: meatballs, tomato sauce.
Souvlákia: meat on a skewer served with tomatoes and onions.

Vegetables

Agouria: cucumbers.
Domates gemistes: tomatoes with rice.
Domatosalata: tomato salad.
Fassolakia: beans.
Kolokinthakia: courgettes.
Melidzanes: aubergines.
Patates: potatoes.
Rízi: rice.
Salata horiatiki: classic Greek salad of tomatoes, cucumbers, oregano, onions, olives, green peppers and *féta*.

Cheese

Féta: goats' or sheep's cheese normally served with olive oil.
Graviéra: similar to Gruyère.
Kefalotiri: a sweeter version of Parmesan cheese.
Kasseri: Mild cheese similar to Cheddar.

Fruit

Eliés: olives (those from Vólos, Kalamáta and Amfissa are especially good).
Fraoules: strawberries.
Karpouzi: watermelons.
Kerassia: cherries.
Lemoni: lemons.
Peponi: melons.
Portokali: oranges.
Rodakina: peaches.
Sika: figs.
Stafilia: grapes.
Verikoko: apricots.

Desserts

Baklavá: millefeuilles with nuts.
Bougátsa: flaky pastry turnover with cream and cinnamon.
Halva: almond or sesame paste.
Kataífi: rolls of thread-like pastry with honey and walnuts or almonds.
Loukoumádes: mini doughnuts with honey and sesame or cinnamon.
Rizogalo: rice cake.

Snacks

Amigdolata: macaroons.
Kourabiedes: almond cakes.
Loukoum: pâté with sugar glaze.
Mezes: snacks, including olives, almonds, seafood, eggs, and cheese, best enjoyed with a glass of ouzo.
Omeletta: omelette.
Spanakópita: spinach in a pancake wrap.
Souvlakopita: grilled meat in a pancake wrap.
Tirópita: cheese in a pancake wrap.
Yaoúrti me meli: yoghurt with honey.

Drinks

Tap water is generally safe in Greece.
Frape: frothy coffee.
Granita: sorbet.
Lemonada: freshly pressed lemon drink or lemonade.
Pagoto: ice cream.
Portokalada: orangeade.

Apéritif

Ouzo is the national drink; aniseed-flavoured, it is either consumed neat or diluted with water.

Wine

Wine from the vat *(krassí híma)* is served in carafes or copper pitchers.

Coffee and liqueurs

Coffee is usually served with a glass of water. Greek coffee leaves a grainy deposit at the bottom of the cup which should not be consumed. Order it *gliko* (plenty of sugar), *metrio* (a little sugar), or *sketo* (no sugar).
Samian wine is normally drunk as a liqueur at the end of the meal, as is the Greek brandy **Metaxas**.
The Cretan **raki**, a very strong spirit (not to be confused with Turkish raki which is similar to ouzo), and **mastika**, a sweet resin drink from Chios.
For more information on Greek food and drink, see the section of the Introduction entitled "Greek Cuisine".

WHAT TO DO AND SEE

Outdoor Fun

A trip to Greece conjures up sea, sun and historical sites, and it is easy to forget that it is also a mountainous country with ideal winter sports weather at altitude. In many regions or islands, local tourist offices provide lists of the sporting activities available. Those looking for more specific information on a particular sport or activity should consult the appropriate federation.

CANOEING AND KAYAKING

Several organisations propose trips either to **Lake Kremastá** or **Lake Plastira** in Thessaly. For further information, contact the Federation of Canoeing and Kayaking or specialist agencies

- **Federation of Canoeing and Kayaking:** ☎ (210) 41 11 764 and (210) 41 12 195
- **Trekking-Hellas:** ☎ (210) 33 10 323, *www.trekking.gr*

GOLF

Golfers are well served with many courses on Corfu, Rhodes, and at Glífáda and Porto Carras. For further information contact the **Greek Golf Federation** at Glífáda ☎ (210) 89 45 9727.

SCUBA DIVING

This sport is strictly controlled to avoid theft of antiquities. For information, contact **Hellenic Centre for Scuba diving** (☎ (210) 41 21 708) or **Piraeus Diving Centre** (☎ (210) 46 34 297), or consult the webiste *www.greeka.com/greece/greece-diving.htm* Despite restrictions, it is possible to go on a cruise with special diving classes to enjoy the lovely underwater sights. Before going on your own, contact the **Underwater Archaeology Department** ☎ 30 1036 03 662 to find out which sites are authorised.

WHITE-WATER RAFTING

Trips varying in length from one week to three weekends are organised on different class rivers and are coupled with theoretical and practical lessons on site (essential). The most popular areas to practise this sport are Evritania (in the Karpensíssi region) or in Grevená and Arachtos (contact **Trekking-Hellas** ☎ (210) 33 10 323) as well as Evinos and in the Alfiós gorges.

CLIMBING AND MOUNTAINEERING

These activities are growing in popularity and provide an opportunity to have close contact with nature. And what could be more exciting than clambering over cliffs overlooking the Aegean Sea (well-maintained trails in Chios, Mílos, Kálimnos, Míkonos), the Kofinias peak in Crete, or happening upon a monk in meditation after climbing a rock in Metéora? Several associations organise relatively easy trips according to the number of participants. A number of agencies also offer day excursions or even longer trips. For information, contact:

- **Federation of Alpine Clubs**: ☎ (210) 36 45 904
- **Trekking-Hellas:** ☎ (210) 33 10 323, *www.trekking.gr*

WINTER SPORTS

Greek ski resorts have expanded rapidly, but they still lack the services provided by many large ski stations. They are nonetheless of high quality and most of them are relatively inexpensive. On-site lodging is still sparse, and it is often necessary to stay in villages far from the slopes. For information, contact the **Hellenic Ski Federation**, 7 Odós Karagiorgi Servias, 105 63 Athens ☎ (210) 32 04 182.

SAILING

Sailing is an excellent way to explore the beautiful Greek islands, provided that you are an expert sailor. Several agencies rent yachts equipped with a captain but you can also hire one individually through specialised organisations. For information contact the **Federation of Sailing**,51 Ákti Poseïdónos, Moshato, Athens, ☎ (210) 94 04 825.

Activities for Children 

In this guide, sights of particular interest to children are indicated with a Kids symbol. Some attractions may offer discount fees for children.

Calendar of Events

For exact dates apply to the tourist office.
In the Orthodox Church, Lent, Easter and Whitsun are fixed according to the Julian Calendar and may fall from one to four weeks later than in the Western church.

6 JANUARY (EPIPHANY)

Piraeus and other ports — Blessing of the sea and immersion of a cross, retrieved by swimmers.

FEBRUARY-MARCH

Patras — Carnival, the most important in Greece: procession of floats.
Athens — Carnival with masks and disguises.
Skíros — Carnival; costume procession; traditional dances.
Náoussa (Macedonia) — Carnival of the *Boúles*, masked dancers.

MONDAY BEFORE LENT

Athens — Popular songs and dances near the temple of Zeus; kite-flying competition.

G. Bludzin/MICHELIN

PALM SUNDAY AND HOLY SATURDAY

Corfu — St Spiridon's procession.

GOOD FRIDAY

Throughout Greece — Procession of the Epitáfios (image of Christ).

EASTER SUNDAY

Throughout Greece — Midnight mass outdoors.

EASTER WEEK

Kálimnos — *Voriatikí* (North Wind), a men's dance.

Mégara (Attica) — Local festival: traditional dances in costume.

23 APRIL (ST GEORGE'S DAY)

Skála (Cephallonia) — Local festival.

MAY

Lesbos — Animal sacrifices, horse racing, dancing, religious festival (*see LÉSVOS*).

21-23 MAY

Langadás (NE of Thessaloníki) and Agiá Eléni in Séres (NE of Thessaloníki) — Ritual ceremonies: the *Anastenarídes*, dance barefoot on hot coals holding icons of Saints Constantine and Helena.

29 MAY

Mystra — Commemoration of the death of Emperor Constantine Palaiologos on 29 May 1453.

MAY-SEPTEMBER

Athens — Folkloric dancing by the Dora Stratou company.

MID-JUNE-EARLY OCTOBER

Athens — Athens Festival: Greek drama, concerts, ballet.

SATURDAYS AND SUNDAYS, END JUNE-END AUGUST

Epidauros — Festival of Ancient drama.

MID-JUNE-EARLY OCTOBER

Patras — Cultural Festival.

END JUNE-END SEPTEMBER

Herakleion (Crete) — Festival.

19 JULY

Throughout Greece — Pilgrimages to peaks dedicated to St Elijah (Ilías).

JULY-AUGUST

Rethymnon — Renaissance Festival.
Delphi — Arts demonstrations.
Thássos — Ancient Drama Festival.

JULY-EARLY SEPTEMBER

Rhodes — Wine festival.

MID-JULY-SEPTEMBER

Rethymnon (Crete) — Wine festival.

AUGUST

Leukas — Arts and folk festival.

6 AUGUST

Corfu — Procession of boats to the isle of Pondikonísi.

11 AUGUST

Corfu — St Spiridon's procession.

12-15 AUGUST

Arhanés and Neápoli (Crete) — Festival of popular art; wine tasting.

AUGUST-SEPTEMBER

Patras — Wine festival.
Dodona — Performances of Ancient Greek drama.
Ioánina — Diverse performances.

B Kaufmann/MICHELIN

The first circle of tombs, Mycenae

15 AUGUST

Tenos — Pilgrimage to the miraculous image of the Virgin.

FIRST SUNDAY AFTER 15 AUGUST

Portariá (Mount Pelion) — Representation of a traditional country wedding.
Skiáthos — Procession of the Epitáfios (image of the Virgin).

LAST SUNDAY IN AUGUST

Kritsá (Crete) — Representation of a traditional country wedding.

END AUGUST-EARLY SEPTEMBER

Zakynthos — International Medieval and Popular Drama Festival.

SEPTEMBER

Thessaloníki — International Fair.
Xánthi — Carnival

14 SEPTEMBER

Préveli — Religious festival of the True Cross; pilgrimage.

OCTOBER

Thessaloníki — Film Festival.

OCTOBER-NOVEMBER

Thessaloníki — St Demetrios's procession; Dimitria festival.

8 NOVEMBER

Arkádi (Crete) — Parade and traditional dances in memory of the sacrifice of the defenders of the monastery.

30 NOVEMBER (ST ANDREW'S DAY)

Patras — Procession in honour of the patron saint of Patras.

24 AND 31 DECEMBER

Throughout Greece — Children sing *Kálanda* in the streets.

Shopping

Local dealers have succeeded somewhat in adapting items of traditional provenance to the tourist market...but beware. Most souvenirs marked "traditional" are mass-produced elsewhere. It's worth seeking out authentic items made locally.

WOOD

Some islands such as the **Northern Sporades** are renowned for their furniture, and in the Peloponnese there is a tradition of making objects in wood, especially in the town of **Vitína** between Tripoli and Olympia.

JEWELLERY

In the 1950s, **Ilias Lalaounis** introduced themes from Classical times into contemporary jewellery design. A goldsmiths' school was founded to train artisans in the necessary techniques. Since then, some extraordinary pieces drawing their inspiration from Minoan civilisation, Macedonia, Classical Greece and Byzantium have been created. When buying jewellery it can be difficult at first glance to distinguish between the mass-produced and the hand crafted, but the asking price should offer a good indication. In the areas popular with tourists there are many jewellery shops, most of which sell mass-produced items, which usually make for good-value souvenir items.

CARPETS AND TEXTILES

A legacy of Ottoman domination, there is a strong tradition of carpet weaving in **Thessaloníki**. Elsewhere in Greece, most notably in **Crete**, **Delphi** and **Epirus**, decorative textiles are made incorporating traditional

B. Morandi/MICHELIN

patterns handed down through the generations.

EVERYDAY OBJECTS

Ideal items to take home include *tavli* (game of Ottoman origin), *flitzanakia* (porcelain coffee cups), *keramika* (ceramic items from Siphnos, Rhodes and neighbouring islands), *bouzoukia* (the traditional stringed instrument), and the famous *kombolóï* (worry beads).

CULINARY SPECIALITIES

Those looking to take home some of the memorable flavours of Greece have a wide choice: honey, fig or cherry jam, Egina pistachios, Muscat from Sámos, or, of course, a bottle of ouzo or retsina. Greece's olive oil is world renowned; the most famous comes from Crete.

Discounts

BY TRAIN: ALL AGES

The Inter-Rail ticket allows the holder (must have been an EU resident for at least 6 months) to travel through 30 countries divided up into 8 geographical areas: zone G includes Italy, Slovenia, Greece, Turkey, and ferry travel between Italy and Greece. Those under 26 benefit from a reduced price. For details contact **Rail Europe Direct** ☎ 08705 848 848; www.raileurope.co.uk/inter-rail; or www.raileurope.com.

FOR YOUNGER TRAVELLERS

The International Student Identification Card (ISIC) entitles the holder to various travel-related discounts. Contact **STA Travel** ☎ 800 781 4040 (US); 08701 600 599. www.statravel.com

Books and Films

BOOKS

Art and Archaeology

The Glory that was Greece, JC Stobart, revised RJ Hopper, Sidgwick & Jackson, 1989.
The Mycenaean World: Cities of Legend, K Wardle and D Wardle, Bristol Classical Press, 1997
Minoan and Mycenaean Art, Reynold Higgins, Thames and Hudson, 1997.
Myths of Greece and Rome, Thomas Bulfinch, Viking Press, 1981.
A Handbook of Greek Art, Gisela Richter, Phaidon Press, 1987.
Non-Attic Greek Vase Inscriptions, Rudolf Wachter, Clarendon Press, 2001.
Linear B and Related Scripts, J Chadwick, British Museum Press, 1987.
Cycladic Art, J Lesley Fitton, British Museum Press, 1999.
The Elgin Marbles, BF Cook, British Museum Press, 1997.
The History of Greek Vases: Potters, Painters, Pictures, John Boardman, Thames and Hudson, 2001

Geography and History

Cultural Atlas of the Greek World, Peter Levi, Phaidon Press, Oxford, 1983.
The Spartans: An Epic History, Paul Cartledge, Channel 4 Books, 2002
The Ancient Olympic Games, Judith Swaddling, British Museum Press, 1999.
Lord Elgin and the Marbles, William St Clair, Oxford, 1998.
Ill Met by Moonlight, W Stanley Moss, Cassell Military, 1999.

B. Kaufmann/MICHELIN

The Flame of Freedom: The Greek War of Independence, 1821-1833, David Brewer, Overlook Press, 2003.
The Wound of Greece, P Sherrard, Rex Collings, 1978.
The Coming of the Greeks, Robert Drews, Princeton University Press, 1995.
The Greeks, HDF Kitto, Penguin, 1999.
Modern Greece: A Short History, CM Woodhouse, Faber & Faber, 1999.
The Greeks: Crucible of Civilization, Paul Carledge, BBC Consumer Publishing, 2001.

Travel Books; Literature

The Greek Islands, Lawrence Durrell, Faber & Faber, 2002.
Prospero's Cell (Corfu), Lawrence Durrell, Faber & Faber, 2000.
Reflections on a Marine Venus (Rhodes), Lawrence Durrell, Faber & Faber, 2000.
Roumeli: Travels in Northern Greece, Patrick Leigh Fermor, John Murray, 2003.
Máni: Travels in the Southern Peloponnese, Patrick Leigh Fermor, John Murray, 2003.
Deep into Máni, Journey to the Southern Tip of Greece, Peter Greenhalgh and Edward Eliopoulos, Faber & Faber, 1985.
The Cretan Runner, G Psychoundakis, translated by Patrick Leigh Fermor, Penguin, 1998.
Greek Myths, Robert Graves, Penguin, 1992.
Greek Gods and Heroes, Robert Graves, Random House, 1960.
A Crowded Heart, Nicholas Papandreou, Picador, 1999.
Eleni, Nicholas Gage, Harvill Press, 1997.
Dinner with Persephone, Patricia Storace, Granta, 1998.
The Magus, John Fowles, Vintage, 1997.
Captain Corelli's Mandolin, Louis de Bernières, Vintage, 2001.

General

Greek Food: An Affectionate Celebration of Traditional Recipes, Rena Salaman, Collins, 1993.
Cooking the Greek Way, Anne Theoharous, Mandarin, 1992.
Greece on Foot, Marc Dubin, Cordee, 1986.
Women in Ancient Greece, Sue Blundell, British Museum Press, 1999.

FILMS

Never on a Sunday, Jules Dassin, 1959. Set in 1950s Piraeus, the story of an encounter between a prostitute and an American trying to comprehend the mysteries of Greek society. Dassin's finest Greek film, here directing his future wife Melina Mercouri.

Stella, Michael Kakoiánnis, 1955. The film that launched Mercouri's career. A tender and tragic evocation of the post-war poverty experienced by so many in Greece. Also by the same director: *Electra*, 1962; and the famed *Zorba the Greek*, 1964, with Anthony Quinn, adapted from a novel by Kazantzakis.

Z, Costas Gavras, 1968. Charting the rise of the Far Right in Greece, this political thriller drew its inspiration from the Lambratis case, the assassination of a Left wing politician in the early days of the junta.

Eternity and a Day, Theo Angelópoulos, 1998. The work of this director, the only contemporary Greek film-maker with an international profile, has recurrent themes of identity, frontiers and memory running through it.

BASIC INFORMATION

Business Hours

Opening hours are idiosyncratic and vary from town to town, but the following can be taken as guidelines:

- In towns, shops are open from 9am-2pm on Mondays, Wednesdays and Saturdays, and from 9am-2pm and 5-8pm on Tuesdays, Thursdays and Fridays. On Sundays, bakeries and drinks retailers are open, in some cases until 8pm.
- In tourist villages, shop opening hours vary widely. In summer, some shops stay open until 10pm or later all week.

Throughout the day and for much of the night, chilled cabinets are available for the purchase of drinks outside restaurants and bars.

MUSEUMS

Visiting times for museums and monuments are given throughout this guide, and are subject to change.

MUSEUMS AND ARCHAEOLOGICAL SITES

Generally speaking these are open between April and October from 8am to late afternoon or early evening. They are closed on Mondays and public holidays. Between November and March, opening hours tend to be 8.30am-3pm. For more specific information, consult www.culture.gr

CHURCHES

Parish churches are open daily, in the mornings and late afternoons. The larger churches tend to stay open all day. The numerous private chapels are usually closed, as are some establishments of historical significance (usually for their preservation). These may be visited on the feast days when they are opened for services, or by application to the tourist office.

Electricity

The voltage is 220ac, 50 cycles per second; the sockets are for two-pin plugs. It is therefore advisable to take an adaptor for hairdryers, shavers, computers, etc.

Emergencies

General police services: ☎ 100
Tourist police services: ☎ 171
Ambulance services: ☎ 166
Emergency: ☎ 112

Money

The unit of currency is the **euro** which is issued in notes (€5, €10, €20, €50, €100, €200 and €500) and in coins (1 cent, 2 cents, 5 cents, 10 cents, 20 cents, 50 cents, €1 and €2).

BANKS

Banks are usually open Monday to Friday, 8am-2.30pm or 2pm. Most branches operate on a numbered ticket system so be sure to obtain a ticket on arrival.

CREDIT CARDS

Payment by credit card is widespread in the cities and larger resorts but often not accepted on the islands or off the beaten track.

NOTES AND COINS

The designs on euro banknotes were inspired by European architecture. Windows and gateways feature on the front of the notes, and bridges on the reverse, symbolising openness and cooperation. Euro coins have one face common to all 12 countries in the Eurozone, and a reverse side specific to each country.

Notes and Coins

The euro banknotes were designed by Robert Kalinan, an Austrian artist. His designs were inspired by the theme "Ages and styles of European Architecture." Windows and gateways feature on the front of the banknotes, bridges feature on the reverse, symbolising the European spirit of openness and co-operation. The images are stylised representations of architecture typical of each period, rather than specific structures.

Classical

Baroque and Rococo

Romanesque

19C Iron and glass

Gothic

Renaissance

20C Modern

Euro coins have one face common to all 12 countries in the European single currency area or "Eurozone" (currently Austria, Belgium, Finland, France, Germany, Greece, Ireland, Italy, Luxembourg, The Netherlands, Portugal and Spain) and a reverse side specific to each country, created by their own national artists.

Euro banknotes look the same throughout the Eurozone. All Euro banknotes and coins can be used anywhere in this area.

TRAVELLERS CHEQUES

The safest way to carry money around, cheques are widely available from American Express, Thomas Cook, Visa, Travelex, Citicorp (Canada) and other providers. Some establishments may charge a small commission when accepting them. Although very common in the cities and larger resorts, they are not widely used in quieter parts of Greece. All banks, however, will accept them.

Mail

Post offices can be recognised by their yellow **ELTA** signs displaying the figure of Hermes. They are usually open Monday to Friday, 7.30am-2pm. In the bigger branches a numbered ticket system operates. In addition to standard mail, the Greek postal service offers an express service.

Newspapers

Most foreign papers are available the day after publication. Alternatively, *Athens News* (printed in English, on sale in the capital and major tourist resorts) reports on local stories.

Public Holidays

1 January – New Year's Day.
6 January – Epiphany. All coastal towns and villages hold a blessing-of-the-sea ceremony.
First Monday in Lent (variable, celebrated 41 days before the orthodox Easter)
25 March – Independence Day and Feast of the Annunciation, marked by military parades in Athens and Thessaloníki, and children's parades throughout Greece.
Easter – Good Friday sees processions in many towns. The Resurrection is celebrated at midnight on Saturday with fireworks. On Easter Sunday, it is traditional to eat roast lamb. The Monday is also a public holiday.
1 May – Labour Day.
15 August – Feast of the Assumption.
28 October – Ohi Day, with military parades, marks Greece's defiance of Italian territorial demands in 1940.
25-26 December – Christmas.

Telephone

The **OTE** offices are generally open from 8am to 2pm Monday-Friday There are telephone booths in the streets and also at newspaper stands *(períptera)*. Telephone cards can be purchased from the OTE offices or in kiosks.

DOMESTIC CALLS

Since November 2002 a new system has been in force; all numbers are 10 digits long and start with a 2. Since January 2003, all mobile numbers have been prefixed by a 6.

INTERNATIONAL CALLS

To ring a foreign number directly from Greece, dial **00** followed by the country code, the city or district code and the person's number.
162 Information on calling abroad
169 Instructions for international calls (English, French)
161 Announcements on telephone calls abroad

International dialling codes:
6 for Australia
64 for New Zealand
1 for Canada
44 for United Kingdom
353 for Ireland
1 for United States of America
When telephoning Greece from abroad dial **00 30**.

Time

Greece is two hours ahead of the United Kingdom; only one time zone applies across the country.

Tipping

Although not compulsory, it is customary to leave a tip at the end of a meal. When using taxis, the normal procedure is to round up the bill in the driver's favour.

Conversion Tables

Weights and measures

1 kilogram (kg)	2.2 pounds (lb)	2.2 pounds
1 metric ton (tn)	1.1 tons	1.1 tons

to convert kilograms to pounds, multiply by 2.2

1 litre (l)	2.1 pints (pt)	1.8 pints
1 litre	0.3 gallon (gal)	0.2 gallon

to convert litres to gallons, multiply by 0.26 (US) or 0.22 (UK)

1 hectare (ha)	2.5 acres	2.5 acres
1 square kilometre (km²)	0.4 square miles (sq mi)	0.4 square miles

to convert hectares to acres, multiply by 2.4

1centimetre (cm)	0.4 inches (in)	0.4 inches
1 metre (m)	3.3 feet (ft) - 39.4 inches - 1.1 yards (yd)	
1 kilometre (km)	0.6 miles (mi)	0.6 miles

to convert metres to feet, multiply by 3.28 . kilometres to miles, multiply by 0.6

Clothing

Women			
Shoes	35	4	2½
	36	5	3½
	37	6	4½
	38	7	5½
	39	8	6½
	40	9	7½
	41	10	8½
Dresses & Suits	36	4	8
	38	6	10
	40	8	12
	42	12	14
	44	14	16
	46	16	18
Blouses & sweaters	36	08	30
	38	10	32
	40	12	14
	42	14	36
	44	16	38
	46	18	40

			Men
40	7½	7	Shoes
41	8½	8	
42	9½	9	
43	10½	10	
44	11½	11	
45	12½	12	
46	13½	13	
46	36	36	Suits
48	38	38	
50	40	40	
52	42	42	
54	44	44	
56	46	48	
37	14½	14,5	Shirts
38	15	15	
39	15½	15½	
40	15¾	15¾	
41	16	16	
42	16½	16½	

Sizes often vary depending on the designer. These equivalents are given for guidance only.

Speed

kph	10	30	50	70	80	90	100	110	120	130
mph	6	19	31	43	50	56	62	68	75	81

Temperature

Celsius (°C)	0°	5°	10°	15°	20°	25°	30°	40°	60°	80°	100°
Fahrenheit (°F)	32°	41°	50°	59°	68°	77°	86°	104°	140°	176°	212°

To convert Celsius into Fahrenheit, multiply °C by 9, divide by 5, and add 32.
To convert Fahrenheit into Celsius, subtract 32 from °F, multiply by 5, and divide by 9.

Some hilltop monasteries of the Metéora
H Champollion/MICHELIN

INTRODUCTION TO GREECE

NATURE

The combination of sea and mountains, the many peninsulas and deep bays all contribute to Greece's unusual geography; no stretch of coastline is far from a mountain.

Topography

A MOUNTAINOUS PENINSULA AND THOUSANDS OF ISLANDS

Lying at the southern end of the Balkan peninsula, Greece is a mountainous country with a land mass of 131 944km^2/50 944sq mi (a little over half the size of the United Kingdom). Its geography gives it a feeling of vastness, the mainland broken up by mountain ranges, and its many islands scattered across the sea. A total of 1 000km separate Corfu from Kastéllorizo, and the eastern end of Crete is 800km from the northern boundaries of Thrace.

The country, with its highest point at Mount Olympos (2 917m/9 577ft), presents a fragmented and complex topography, with numerous peaks over 2 000m (notably Mount Smólikas in the Pindus range at 2 637m, Mount Parnassos at 2 457m, Mount Ida on Crete at 2 456m, Mount Taíyetos in the southern Peloponnese at 2 407m, and Mount Falakró in Macedonia at 2 182m).

The country's geology forms two main zones. In the east, an ancient primary substratum has been raised by movements of the earth's crust: this includes the mountain ranges of Thrace and Macedonia, Mounts Olympos and Pelion, and Euboia; the Aegean Islands are traces of a continent (the mythical Atlantis) submerged at the end of the Tertiary era by earthquakes. Volcanic activity is still evident, especially on Níssiros in the Dodecanese, and Santorini in the Cyclades, where a catastrophic eruption was the most likely cause of the disappearance of the Minoan civilisation.

In the west, a tertiary chain, the Balkan Dinaric Alps, continues south to form the spine of Greece, composed mainly of karst, a limestone rock eroded by running water to form caves, chasms and swallow-holes *(katavóthres)*. This mountain range includes the peaks of the Pindus, **Mount Parnassos** (2 457m/8 061ft), the Peloponnese and terminates in the mountains of Crete.

CONTINENTAL GREECE

Central Greece and Euboia

The heart of historic Greece, **Attica** is a promontory consisting of low hills and plains. Population density is high, even outside the Athens metropolitan area.

H Champollion/MICHELIN

The mountainous terrain of Epirus

Breathtaking views over the caldera of Santorini

To the north of Attica, between Mounts Parnes and Parnassos, lies **Boeotia**; its main towns, Thebes and Livadiá, are important agricultural markets. The land once flooded to form Lake Copaïs is now a huge cotton plantation.
The island of **Euboia** (Évia) lies parallel to the east coast of the Attic peninsula to which it is linked by a bridge. Like the mainland, it is very mountainous.
Phocis, the region lying between Boeotia and Etolía, is dominated by Mount Parnassos with its ski resorts; to the west lies the lake formed by the dam on the Mórnos, which supplies water to Athens. Phocis is particularly famous for the sanctuary at Delphi and the sea of olive trees which fills the Ámfissa basin.
Etolía on the west coast comprises a cool mountainous district clothed with holm oaks round the huge reservoir, Lake Trihonída, and the River Ahelóos expanding into the Agrínio basin; the gleaming lagoon at Messolónghi (salt marshes) lies on the north coast of the Gulf of Patras.
The wooded highlands of **Eurytania** in the north of central Greece are still impenetrable in parts. Karpeníssi, dominated by Mount Timfristós, is the main town in the region, where forestry is the principal activity. On the western boundary with Etolía lies the vast Kremastón reservoir formed by the dammed waters of the River Ahelóos, which has a great energy production capacity.
To the northeast of Phocis, the region of **Pthiotis** is largely agricultural and is bisected by the beautiful Sperhiós Valley. The only large town, Lamía, is an important road and rail junction.

Peloponnese

The **Peloponnese**, linked to Attica by the Isthmus of Corinth (now breached by the Corinth Canal), is a mountainous peninsula made up of high peaks, inland basins caused by subsidence and irrigated coastal plains.
The eastern coastal plain is known as the **Argolid**. To the north lies a fertile coastal strip between the mountains and the gulf of Corinth; this area comprises **Corinth** (east) and **Achaia** (west).
Patras, which is the third largest city in Greece and an important centre for wine merchants, is also a popular port.
Down the west coast extends the verdant agricultural plain of **Elis**.
The southern coast is split into three promontories: the longest, an extension of the Taígetos massif, is **Máni**, a wild limestone region. Taígetos is flanked by two alluvial plains: **Lakonía** and **Messinía**.
At the centre of the Peloponnese lie the pasturelands of **Arcadia** (between 600m and 800m/1 968ft and 2 625ft above sea level), home to the town of Tripoli.

Epirus

Between the Ionian Sea and the western border of Thessaly rise the mountains of **Epirus**; the landscape is majestic and harsh, furrowed by valleys and gorges. The capital, **Ioánnina**, is situated by a lake. To the northeast rise the limestone heights of Zagória. To the south extends the plain of Árta.

Thessaly

Thessaly, which has two main centres at Lárissa and the port of Vólos, is

composed of a rich agricultural basin, watered by the River Piniós and surrounded by high peaks: Pindus, Olympos, Pelion and Timfristós. The region is cold and damp in winter and very hot in summer.

At the foot of Mount Pelion lies the port of Vólos providing maritime communications. Road and rail links with Macedonia to the northeast pass through the famous Vale of Tempe at the foot of Mount Óssa; the road to Ioánina and Epirus in the northwest climbs over the Métsovo Pass (1 705m/5 594ft), the highest road pass in Greece. As it rises into the Pindus range the road passes the curious pillars of rock created by erosion which are known as the Metéora.

Macedonia

This vast province stretches along the border with Albania and Bulgaria. At the centre of the province lies the alluvial plain of the River Axiós, also known as the Vardar. East of the mouth of the Axiós lies the port of **Thessaloníki** (Salonica), the capital of Macedonia and the second largest city in Greece.

Chalcidice (Halkidikí), the region southeast of Thessaloníki, consists of three wooded peninsulas, the most easterly of which is the site of the famous monasteries of Mount Athos.

The country farther east round Kavála is composed of broad valleys and inland depressions overlooked by high plateaux and Mount Pangaion with its famous gold mines. In the mountains

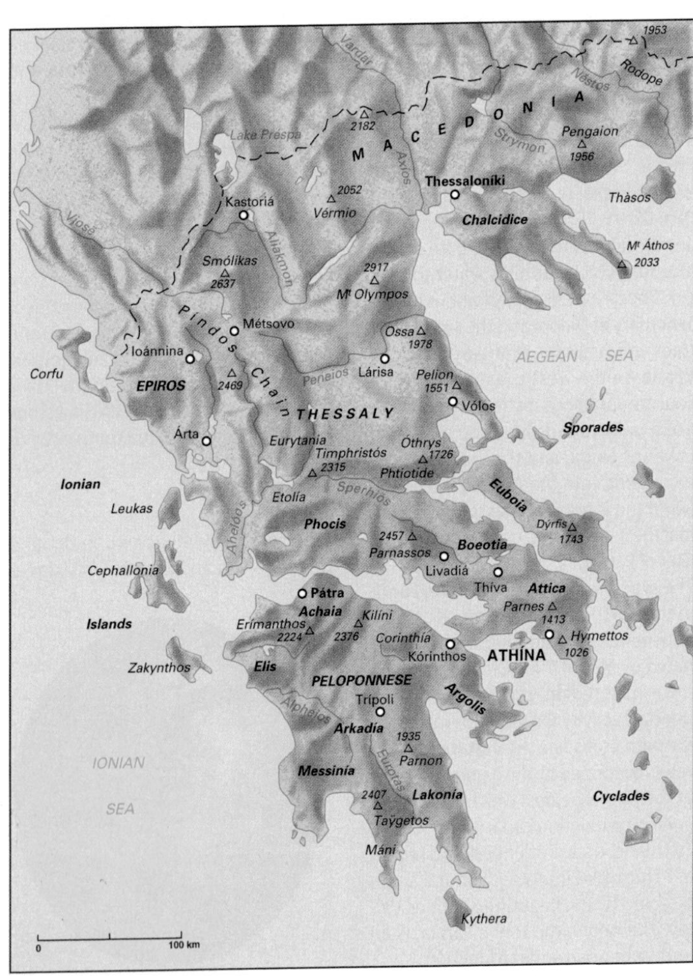

of western Macedonia there are some fine lakes, particularly Préspa, a nature reserve on the border with Albania.

Thrace

Reunited under the Greek flag after the Second World War, Thrace is the easternmost province of mainland Greece, flanked by Bulgaria and Turkey. The country consists of hills and cultivated plains. There is still a Muslim minority particularly round Komotiní, Álexandroúpoli and Souflí where Turkish is taught in primary schools.

C Legrand/MICHELIN

Fisherman, Port of Siphnos

THE SEA AND THE ISLANDS

The sea is never far away in Greece; its long coastline is extended by countless bays and gulfs. The lack of tide, the transparent blue water and the excellent visibility are favourable to navigation.

Ionian Islands

Strung out in the Ionian Sea off the west coast of Greece and not far from Italy, these islands are as Latin as they are Greek. There are seven main islands: Corfu, Paxós, Leukas, Cephallonia, Ithaca, Zakynthos, also known as Zante, and Kythera which falls within the Attica administrative region and lies off the southern tip of the Peloponnese.

Aegean Islands

Although some form part of regions administered from the mainland, these islands strung out towards Turkey are a world apart from the rest of Greece.
In the Cyclades and the Dodecanese the cuboid houses under their dazzling whitewash contrast starkly with the barren rock-strewn land. Close to the Turkish coast, the Dodecanese is a group of 12 islands, the principal one being Rhodes. The islands of the northern Aegean – Lemnos, Lesbos, Chios and Sámos – are green and fertile.

Crete

Dominated by three mountain ranges, and ringed by fabulous beaches, Crete is the largest island in the Greek archipelago. Although the north coast is relatively flat, sheer cliffs plunge into the sea along the south of the island.

EUROPE'S MOST MEDITERRANEAN COUNTRY

The Greek climate is hot in summer and mild in winter (except in the mountains). Inland, particularly in northern Greece, the climate is more continental: stifling in summer, cold in winter, with some areas experiencing sudden and heavy rainfall. At altitude, snow is frequent between November and April

The national parks

Greece has 10 National Parks, covering a total area of 69 000ha/170 500 acres, established to protect flora and fauna: the Prespa Lakes (Macedonia), Mount Olympos (Thessaly and Macedonia), the Pindos Chain (Epiros), Mount Parnassos (central Greece), Cape Sounion (Attica), Mount Ainos (Cephallonia), the Samaria Gorge (Crete), the Vikos Gorge (Epiros), and Mount Oitis (Phocis). They are sparsely populated, and camping, touring by car, picking flowers, and hunting are forbidden. Each of these unspoilt areas is ecologically important for its local flora, fauna or geology. The Prespa Lakes, for example, have more than 30 species of rare birds; the Samaria Gorge, aside from its natural splendour, has the only wild goats left in Europe; Mounts Olympos and Parnassos have rare and beautiful plants.

Bathed in brilliant light, the islands of the Aegean are exposed to the prevailing wind, which blows from the north. In winter it is known as the *voriás* but in spring and summer it becomes the *meltémi* which can blow for two or three days at a time, roughening the sea but refreshing the air. The sea temperature is warm and swimming is possible everywhere between May and October; the water is warmest in September.
Average temperatures (January and July, degrees Celsius): Athens 12 and 32, Corfu 10 and 25, Herakleion 11 and 27, Lesbos 9 and 26, Rhodes 13 and 27.

A LAND OF VILLAGES

In the mountains of the north the building style, typified by stone houses with sloping roofs, has not changed for centuries. Greece's most beautiful villages, are found on the islands of the Aegean. Most of them have a port or a landing place called *skála* (steps) in a sheltered bay, a town called *hóra* (place) on a hill out of reach of marauders and a fortified site *(kástro)*, which may have begun as an Ancient Greek acropolis and subsequently became a castle or citadel.

Flora

Greece boasts over 6 000 botanical species, of which about 600 are unique to Greece including 130 in Crete alone. Here in the land of Dionysos, the vineyard is ubiquitous, either cultivated for winemaking (as in the Peloponnese, Attica, Macedonia, Sámos, Euboia, Crete and Santorini) or grapes.
Cultivated trees are found on farmland, in the plains and on the lower slopes of the hills, grown in plantations: olives more or less everywhere up to 600m/1 969ft, citrus fruits on irrigated land, almonds in sheltered spots and mulberries, figs and pomegranates.

M Janvier/MICHELIN

Rock rose (Cistus ladaniferus), Myrtle

M Janvier/MICHELIN

Olive trees

ABC of Greek flora

Acanthus: Curved, jagged leaves are often represented in Classical architecture.

Almond tree: Widely cultivated in the plains and valleys; early pink blossom.

Bougainvillea: Climbing plant with vivid clusters of flowers.

Holm oak: Evergreen oak growing in calcareous soil below 800m/2 620ft.

Cistus: Dark-green foliage contrasts with its white or pink flowers.

Juniper: Purplish berries are a favourite of birds like quails and blackbirds.

Lentisk: Dense evergreen foliage with small round fruits which turn black when ripe; smells strongly of resin.

Myrtle: White flowers and blue-black berries symbolise passionate love.

Olive tree: Twisted trunk and silvery foliage; a symbol of Greece since Antiquity.

Aleppo pine: Found on calcareous coastal slopes, this tree has light foliage, a twisted trunk and grey bark.

Tamarisk: Small tree often found on the fringes of beaches.

HISTORY

The origins of Greece are buried in legend, and it can be difficult to determine where myth leaves off and reality begins. The nation's complex and turbulent history was born of many waves of invasion and conflict: the city-states of the Classical period; the empires of Macedonia and of Rome; and the long period when Greece virtually disappeared within the Byzantine and Ottoman empires before finally taking its place as an independent European nation.

Antiquity

Although Greece was definitely inhabited from the Palaeolithic period (around 40000 BC), it was not until the Neolithic period (around 6000 BC) that settled communities established themselves, as is evident from excavations in Epirus, Macedonia and Thessaly. It was the Bronze Age (3000 BC), however, that was to witness the development of civilisation, founded largely on a common Indo-European language.

LEGENDARY ORIGINS

In his poem *Works and Days*, **Hesiod** (second half of 8C BC) laid down a chronology associating metals with the generations who had lived before. If the golden age was lost in time, the age of silver corresponded to the Neolithic period (6000-2600 BC), while the age of bronze witnessed the Ionian and Achaean invasions (2600-1500 BC). Hesiod's own period (the Archaic era) was the age of iron.

H Champollion/MICHELIN

Cyclopean walls, Mycenae

R Mattes/MICHELIN

Minoan fresco

The myth of the Flood

According to legend, Zeus sent a great flood to punish the impious people of the Bronze Age. Only two were saved: Deucalion, son of Prometheus, and his wife Pyrrha, who had been advised by Prometheus to ride out the flood in an Ark. After nine days and nights, the vessel came to rest in the mountains of Thessaly. Zeus sent Hermes to make the survivors swear their fidelity to him. Deucalion asked for companions, and the two survivors were told to throw the bones of their mother over their shoulders. Their mother being the earth, they threw stones as instructed. Deucalion's stones became men, and Pyrrha's became women.

Deucalion and Pyrrha had many children, including Helen whose sons were Doros, Xouthos and Eole; Xouthos in turn fathered Achaeos and Ion. Thus the main groups of invaders – Dorians,

Aolians, Achaeans and Ionians – were legitimised in mythology.

THE MYCENAEANS (1600-1100 BC)

While a culture had developed in Crete which used a pictogram script known as **Linear A** (which subsequently evolved into the syllabic **Linear B** script, finally deciphered in 1952), continental Greece was being settled by groups of Caucasian origin: the **Ionians** and **Aeolians** (around the beginning of the second millennium), and later the **Achaeans** (c 1600 BC); this last group settled in

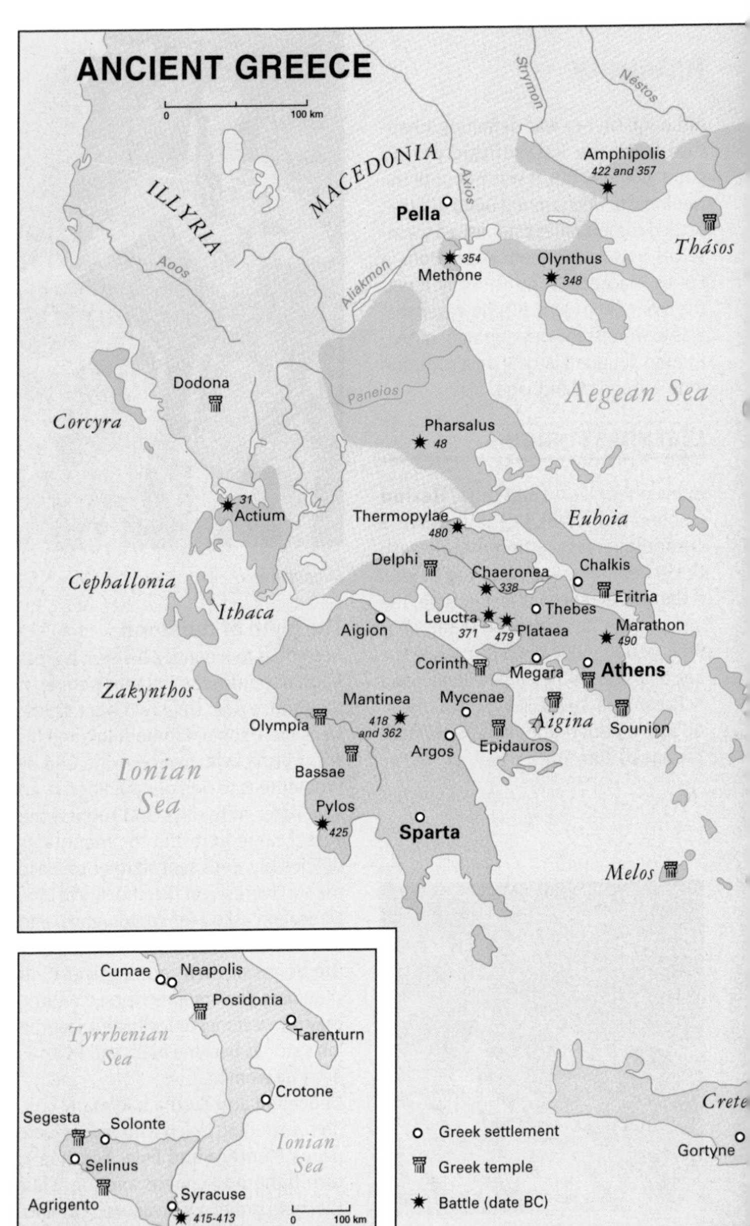

the Peloponnese. This era witnessed the establishment of fortified settlements centred on a *megaron*, administered by the *anax* (king). Society was dominated by a military aristocracy. This **Mycenaean** culture, of which much is known (both from the works of **Homer** and from archaeological evidence), used the Linear B script to record commercial transactions, practised ancestor worship and were able to work in non-ferrous metal. It's likely that their common language allowed communities to cooperate, as evidenced by colonisation of Crete (15C BC) and Rhodes, and the sack of Troy (around 1230 BC).

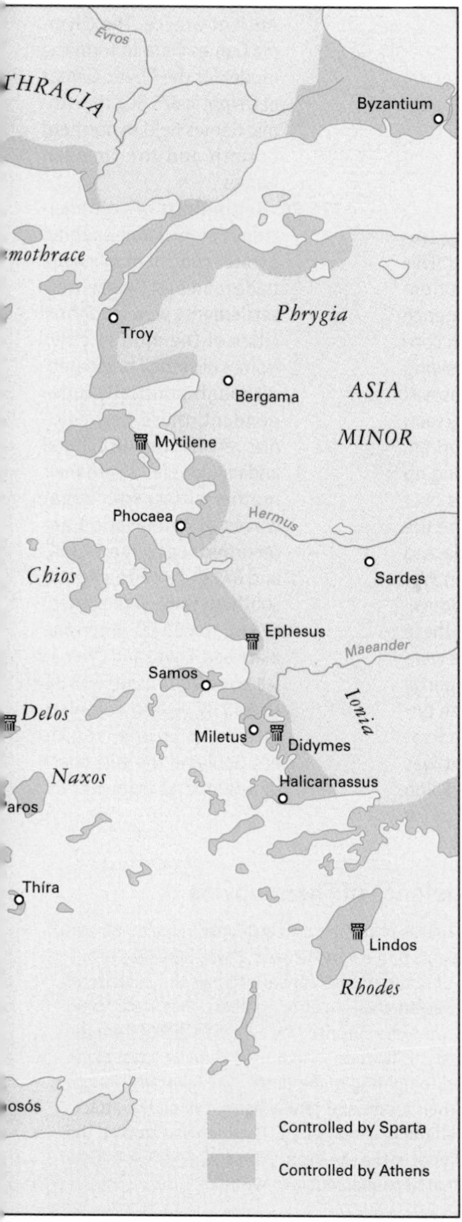

THE DARK AGE (LATE 12C-EARLY 8C BC)

According to Thucydides, author of the *History of the Peloponnesian War*, the end of Mycenaean culture was caused by the arrival of the **Dorians**, a new wave of invaders originating from the valleys of the Danube. Driving out the established inhabitants, the Dorians brought with them iron, ceramic wares and the first identifiable sacred sites. Over the course of the 9C and 8C BC, the Phoenician alphabet was adapted to become the Greek alphabet, engendering a literary civilisation with a common language. Within a few decades, the great epics the *Iliad* and the *Odyssey* were to be written.

THE ARCHAIC ERA (MID-8C-6C BC)

This period was a cultural reawakening, with the development of political institutions centred on the *polis*, a spirit of commercial dynamism which fuelled colonisation throughout the Mediterranean world, and eventually a religious apogee, ample evidence of which exists in the holy places (Olympos, Delphi, Epidauros) and temples of this date.

Plutarch (1C) relates how "Theseus had a grand plan to gather together all the

Cycladic idol (Louvre, Paris)

peoples of Attica in one great city, creating one state for one people." This structure, increasingly prevalent from the 8C BC, resulted in the emergence of autonomous **city states**, each constituting an urban settlement presiding over its surrounding lands. Árgos was probably the first of these, but they soon proliferated to include Sparta, Corinth, Thebes and Athens. This parcelling up of land led to incessant disputes over territory. From such conflict came the Lelantine War (between Halkída and Eretria in Euboia), the Messenian War (between Sparta and her neighbours), and many others. Over the years these societies evolved (although there were exceptions to this rule, such as Sparta) from royalties, to oligarchies, then tyrannies, before emerging as democracies. An important development was the emergence of legislators like Solon of Athens. Their contribution did much to assuage unrest among ordinary citizens who were concerned by the arrogant ambitions of the aristocracy. This was also a fundamental reason for the emergence of tyrant rulers, many of whom established dynasties.

September 776 BC Inauguration of the **Olympic Games**. This date represents a key milestone in the chronology of Ancient Greece. The Olympic Games were to form the model for the Phytic Games at Delphi (c 675 BC), the Isthmic Games held in northern Corinth and the Nemean Games.

c 775 BC Beginnings of colonisation. Colonisation enabled greater control of maritime trade routes for Greece. New settlements were daughter cities of the mother cities from which they originated. Although politically independent, these new colonies retained strong cultural and religious links with their mother cities. Four great waves of colonisation are recorded: between 775 BC and 675 BC, when Sicily and southern Italy were settled; 675 BC to 600 BC, when the Black Sea, Egypt and Cyrenaica were colonised; 600 BC to 545 BC, when colonists arrived in Etruria, southern Gaul and the east coast of Spain; and from 545 BC

The heroic defence of Thermopylae

The narrow defile of Thermopylae was protected by a wall built in the 6C BC and is the main access between Thessaly and central Greece. It was here that Leonidas deployed his meagre force of Spartans and Thebans to halt the advance of Xerxes' 130,000 Persian troops. Despite their superior numbers, they were not to succeed. Although the Greek forces were surprised by a Persian attack from the rear, Leonidas ordered the bulk of his force to withdraw and made a last stand with just 800 soldiers committed to fighting to the death. The Spartans "fought with their swords, their hands, their teeth" and took a heavy toll on the attacking Persians, who finally prevailed but at a heavy cost. Thermopylae entered the annals of Greek legend. A monument at the site bears the inscription "Go, tell the Spartans, thou who passest by, that here obedient laws we lie".

Treasury of the Athenians, Delphi

onwards when Thrace and the islands were colonised.

c 750 BC Homer's epics, the *Iliad* and the *Odyssey*, are written.

c 740 BC Lelantine and Messenian wars.

621-620 BC Edict of Draco in Athens lays down legislative framework to deal with criminal acts.

594-593 BC Archonate of Solon introduces social reforms and political structures.

560-510 BC Tyranny of Pisistratos and his sons.

508 BC Reforms of Cleisthenes.

THE CLASSICAL PERIOD: THE TRIUMPH OF ATHENS (5C BC)

This was a bloody time in Greek history, starting with the revolt against Persian domination in the Ionian colonies, which was followed by the Persian Wars, and later in the century the long Peloponnesian War. Between these two great conflicts, however, Athens was to experience a golden age of artistic and political pre-eminence.

499-494 BC Revolt of the Ionian Greeks. A contingent of Athenians destroy Sardes, the Persian capital. Miletus is sacked in reprisal and the Ionian cities are obliged to swear allegiance to the Persian king Darius.

492 BC First Persian War.

490 BC Darius lands in eastern Attica, but is defeated by the Athenians at Marathon.

482 BC Themistocles builds a fleet of 200 triremes to defend Athens.

481 BC Formation of the League of Corinth: at the request of Athens, the Greek states (except Thessaly and Boeotia) form an alliance under the command of Sparta.

480 BC Second Persian War. Darius's successor, Xerxes, triumphs over Leonidas's heroic Spartans at Thermopylae. The Persians burn down the Acropolis but are subsequently checked by the allied Greek states.

478 BC Formation of the League of Delos. The cities of the Ionian and Aegean unite with Athens against the Persians. Each city contributes towards a common war chest to maintain an army and navy.

454 BC Transfer of the League's treasury from Delos to Athens.

449-448 BC Peace of Callias ends the Persian Wars: autonomy of the Greek cities of Asia Minor is recognised by Persia.

446 BC Thirty Years Peace agreed between Athens and Sparta.

444-428 BC Pericles at the forefront of Athenian affairs: affirmation of democracy, strengthening

Pericles (Pius-Clementine Museum, Vatican City

SCALA

Discobolos, National Roman Museum, Rome

of naval power, and a vibrant political scene.

431-404 BC Peloponnesian War. Athens' attempt to spread her power results in Corinth and other cities of the isthmus appealing to Sparta. War is declared and the lengthy struggle which ensues involves the whole Greek world. Athens is finally defeated in 404.

404-403 BC Tyranny of the Thirty: rule by oligarchy until democracy re-established in 402 BC.

MACEDONIAN HEGEMONY AND HELLENISTIC GREECE (4C-3C BC)

Under the watchful eye of the Persian Empire, Sparta and Thebes vied for supremacy in the aftermath of the Peloponnesian War.The intervention of the kingdom of Macedonia brought greater stability; this was the prelude to the reign of Alexander the Great and his empire which was to extend to the Indus and the foothills of the Himalayas.

399 BC Socrates is condemned to death.

395-387 BC Corinthian War. Thebes occupied by the Spartans (382 BC). Peace negotiated under the auspices of Artaxerxes II of Persia.

377 BC Formation of the second League of Delos: Athens and other cities unite against Spartan hegemony. Unlike the first such coalition, Athens is not able to impose her wishes unilaterally.

376 BC Reorganisation of the Boeotian League centred on Thebes. Theban hegemony under Pelopides and Epaminondas. After the defeat of the Spartans at Leuctra (371 BC), the Boeotians invade the Peloponnese, ravage Sparta and occupy Messenia.

356 BC Mausolus, Statap of Caria in Asia Minor, forms an alliance including Chios, Rhodes and Byzantium, destroys the Athenian fleet, and forces Athens

Heroes, citizens and mercenaries

From the Homeric wars to the Macedonian conflicts, war is an omnipresent feature of Greek life, marked by evolving strategies and tactics. The first big development came in the 7C BC with the emergence of the phalanx, which allowed troops to advance in tight formation with their weapons drawn. Composed of infantry troops known as hoplites armed with a javelin or sword, and protected by a shield, helmet, leather breastplate and gaiters, the phalanx is in stark contrast to the concept of the aristocratic mounted warrior, as depicted in the *Iliad*, in quest solely of individual glory. Philip of Macedon added archers and javelins throwers, and developed the *sarissa*, a steel-tipped pike which could be as long as 5m/5.5yd. Full-time soldiers in the pay of the king, Macedonian troops were to incorporate Greeks among their ranks, as well as using mercenaries when necessary.

Detail from Battle of Alexander and Darius, mosaic (National Archaeological Museum, Naples)

to accept the independence of the rebel Aegean cities.

356-336 BC Philip II of Macedon conquers the territories neighbouring his kingdom. Exploiting the disarray among the city states, he advances into central Greece and defeats the Athens-Thebes coalition at Chaeronea (338 BC). Demosthenes, who had worked tirelessly to foil the Macedonian invaders, railed against his fellow citizens: "It is shameful, a slur on your reputation, that of Athens and of your ancestors, to allow Greece to become enslaved." Philip negotiated a treaty with Athens that was more generous than in the case of other Greek states; he did, however, appoint himself commander-in-chief of the Hellenic League, the alliance formed to tackle the Persian threat. In 336 BC, Philip was assassinated at Pella.

336 BC Alexander, son of Philip, is acclaimed king by the army. Conflict with neighbouring northern states, and the Theban revolt (335 BC).

334-323 BC Alexander's Asian campaigns fulfil his father Philip's ambitions. The young king's army sweeps across Asia Minor, defeating the Persians at Granicus. After conquering the cities of the south and west coasts, he stops at Gordium, where he severs the famous knot (according to legend, whoever achieved this feat would become master of all Asia). Halicarnassus was taken, before Darius and the Persians were defeated at Issus (333 BC). The Phoenicians were next to crumble before Alexander, after Tyre was besieged (332 BC). Egypt was added to his dominions (Alexandria was founded in 331 BC) before Alexander crossed the Tigris and Euphrates, defeated Darius again at Gaugamela and annexed Babylon and Susa. Persepolis was destroyed, Media and Parthia were then conquered and by 329 BC Alexander's army had reached Bactria. Crossing the Indus in 326 BC, Alexander reached his furthest point, before his troops' unwillingness to proceed obliged him to retrace his steps. In 324 BC he married Roxane of Bactria, and then set about building a fleet to conquer Arabia. This ambition, however, was cut short by his death on 13 June 323 BC.

323 BC The compromise of Babylon: Alexander's generals divide up the empire between themselves and conflict ensues among them. The Antigonid dynasty become rulers of Greece. Various alliances are formed, either to fight Macedonian control, or to preserve a pan-Hellenic status quo.

280-275 BC **Pyrrhus**, king of Epirus, aids Tarentum against Roman expansionism and wins a number of victories.

279-278 BC Delphi attacked by the Gauls.

228 BC Athens expels the Macedonian garrison from Piraeus.

227 BC Cleomenes III of Sparta implements reforms.

212 BC Fall of Syracuse to Rome.

ROMAN GREECE (2C-1C BC)

After Philip V of Macedon (221-179 BC) had supported Hannibal in the Second Punic War, Rome began to take an interest in the Hellenic world which had developed from the empire of Alexander. Having defeated Philip V at Cynoscephalae, Rome declared the freedom of Greece in 196 BC. In fact, the Greeks recovered only part of their independence under Roman control. The continuing intervention of Rome in Greek affairs led in 146 BC to a rebellion by the Achaean League headed by Corinth, which was laid waste by the Roman legions. The various city leagues were then broken up and Greece came under Roman occupation, which subsequently spread to the rest of the Hellenic world; this was annexed completely after the triumph of Augustus over Anthony and Cleopatra at Actium in 30 BC. In 27 BC the Romans united the Greek lands to form a single province, the province of Achaia. Some cities were given the status of free cities (eg Byzantium), while others had federated or allied status.

COMING OF THE BYZANTINE EMPIRE (1C-4C AD)

Although the Greek city states lost power and prestige, **Hellenism** flourished and Greece retained its cultural, literary and artistic influence. No doubt this was largely due to the political and religious tolerance practised by the Romans, for whom Greece held a strong fascination (the Emperor Hadrian visited Athens three times). Administration was largely in the hands of the local population and the practice of the Greek religion was permitted. This relative autonomy granted by Rome gradually created two spheres of influence in the Roman Empire: on the one hand a Greek East combining the Greek world proper and the Hellenistic areas of Asia Minor, and on the other a Latin West.

From the 3C AD, Greece, in common with the rest of the Empire, had to face barbarian invasions, which were more successfully resisted by the eastern part of the Empire than the western part. These dangers made Rome's loss of influence more palpable and in 330 the **Emperor Constantine** made Byzantium, a former Greek colony on the Bosphorus, the capital of the Empire. Initially called New Rome, the city was soon to bear the name **Constantinople** in his honour.

In 380, during the reign of **Theodosius the Great**, Christianity became the official religion, pagan cults were banned, and in 393 the Olympic Games were abolished. In order to resist the barbarian invasions in its western part, he divided the Empire at his death in 395 between his two sons: Arcadius inherited the East and Honorius the West. Constantinople remained the capital of the Eastern Empire.

Life in the 5C BC

Prior to the 6C BC there is very little documentary evidence to help historians reconstruct daily life. From this date onwards, however, there is ample material: ceramic wares, written texts, coinage and other archaeological finds. The most data has been gathered for Athens and Attica, Sparta, Thebes and Boeotia, more than enough to give a clear picture of daily life in Classical times.

Attica's population numbered between 250 000 and 300 000. Sparta, covering a larger but harsher territory, had slightly fewer inhabitants. Around 150 000 lived in the Theban province of Boeotia. Excluding Macedonia and the colonies of Asia Minor and greater Greece, the total population was close to 2 000 000.

BEHIND THE FAÇADES

The great legends give the impression of a society of luxurious villas, streets paved with marble, rigorous order and impeccable cleanliness. The reality, however, was rather different. One visitor observed: "The city has no water supply, and signs of its decrepitude are everywhere." To conclude, he stated: "it is difficult to believe that this place is truly Athens." Although the great monuments such as the Acropolis or the Agora were very elegant sites, the rest of the city was a dirty, malodorous mass of confused streets and alleys. The first real town planner was **Hippodamos of Miletus** (mid-5C BC) who introduced a more ordered approach. To him is attributed the reconstruction of Piraeus (as decreed by Themistocles) and Miletus, among other projects.

Houses were built in adjoining terrace fashion, separated by thin dividing walls (so thin that when the Thebans attacked the Plataea in 431 BC, the inhabitants fled their attackers by knocking through

SCALA

Athena building the Trojan Horse (Archaeological Museum, Florence)

ALINARI

The Goddess Athena and her animal symbol, the owl (National Archaeological Museum, Athens)

the walls from house to house). In Athens, the poor lived in cave dwellings carved into the hillsides. The more prosperous lived in houses, each built around a central courtyard, sometimes embellished with a portico and a well. In areas of dense habitation, some houses were divided up into numerous apartments, each rented to a separate family. Flooring was usually plain earth at ground level, with wood boards used for the upper storeys. Windows were small and doors opened directly into the street.

FOOD AND CLOTHING

Although the Greeks had been able to tell the time accurately from the 5C BC, the ordering of the days was largely dictated by meals. Breakfast (usually corn or barley bread soaked in wine) was eaten at dawn. Lunch at noon was a light affair, with supper as the main meal of the day. Away from mealtimes, there would be trips to the market, and for more prominent citizens, involvement in public affairs.

A ubiquitous feature of the Greek diet was the *maza*, made from barley flour. Fish and game were also common; meat, though, was reserved for sacrificial purposes. The many Greek states had differing attitudes towards food, from the austere Spartans (who existed almost exclusively on a diet of black gruel) to the opulent Boeotians (whose gluttony was widely observed). In addition to water, the Greek drank goats' milk, and, of course, wine, often diluted with sea water or flavoured with thyme or cinnamon. Certain Greek wines, notably those from Lesbos, Chios and Thasos, were highly regarded and exported throughout the Mediterranean. Wine flowed freely at Greek banquets (symposia) where diners, served by slaves, reclined at low tables and ate with their hands.

Evening meals would often be preceded by a bath (at the public bathhouse, at home for the better off, or indeed in the river for the austere Spartans). Beards were the norm (until the reign of Alexander the Great at least), hair was cut short in Athens and usually dispensed with altogether in Sparta. Women had elaborate hairstyles and wore make-up.

Clothing was similar in style across the social classes, although the better off had theirs made of finer fabrics. A short tunic *(chiton)* fastened at the shoulders was the norm; on more formal occasions a larger cloak *(himation)* was also worn. Women wore a longer tunic garment fastened with a belt at the waist.

CRADLE TO GRAVE

According to Greek literature, courtesans were for pleasure, concubines for the fulfilment of everyday needs, and wives for the production of legitimate heirs and the running of the household. The Athenian wife lived a secluded existence (unlike Sparta's women, who scandalised the world with their relative freedom), in the company of her mother-in-law and other female members of the family, and played no part whatsoever

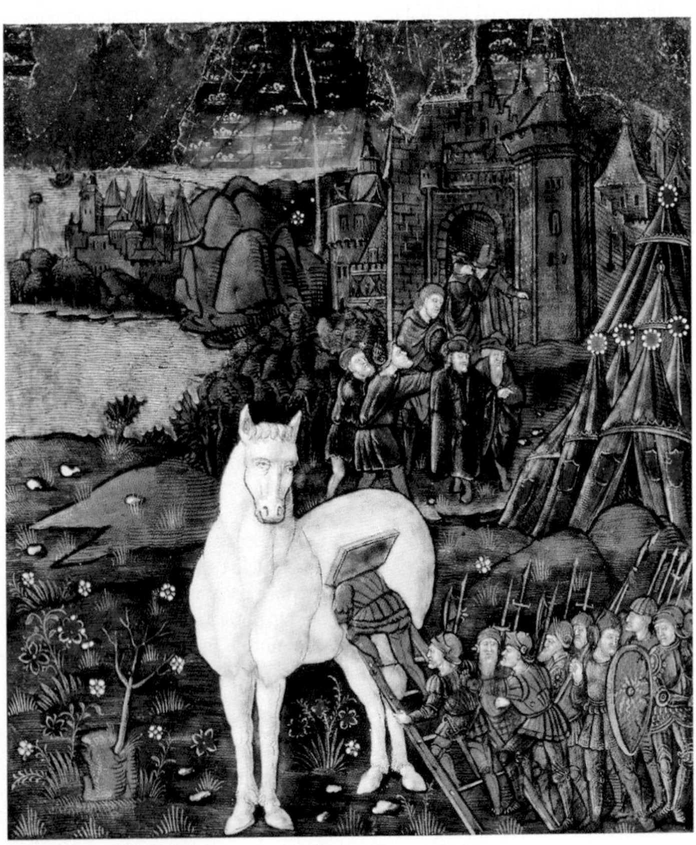

J.-G. Berizzi/RMN

Greeks hiding in the Trojan Horse, enamel, 1530 (Louvre, Paris)

H Lewandowski/RMN

Banqueting scene, 6C BC crater (Louvre, Paris)

in public life. Dedicated to procreation alone, few marriages were based on romance. The emphasis on breeding a strong next generation was particularly accentuated in Sparta, where ruthless weeding out of the weak was practised. Babies deemed in any way deficient were thrown to their deaths over a cliff. Those who were fit and healthy underwent a rigorous upbringing: at the age of seven they were taken from their mothers and entered state academies where they learnt the martial skills necessary for Sparta's continued military pre-eminence. This training culminated in a period of living wild in the forests at which point the young Spartans were expected to hunt down and kill a slave to prove themselves. Young Athenians, on the other hand, received a wide and cultivated education which included the study of grammar and music. Those who sought further education could then become pupils of one of the seats of learning founded by the philosophers, such as Plato's Academy or Aristotle's Lyceum.

All Greeks were duty bound to assist and care for their parents; failure to do so could result in loss of civil liberties or even imprisonment. The elderly were an object of veneration. Funeral rites were complex, involving ceremonial purification, mourning and processions; both burial and cremation were practised.

WORK AND PLEASURE

The 5C BC saw a decline in the economic importance of agriculture and a corresponding increase in the importance of manufacture and trade. Money replaced bartering, the **drachma** becoming a universal currency as Athens' power grew. Status in society, however, remained largely dictated by the role played by

H Lewandowski/RMN

Tanágra figurine (Louvre, Paris)

the individual rather than based on personal wealth.

Manufacture and trade were highly diversified, with potters, linen merchants, food producers and many other retailers in the city markets. Industrial activity such as mining was well established, with some operations functioning 24 hours a day; the ready availability of large numbers of slaves facilitated this and, indeed, all aspects of life for the Greeks.

For free citizens, there was plenty of time for relaxation. In Athens there were 152 public holidays a year, days dedicated to games, hunting, fishing and theatrical events.

Byzantine Greece

In the late 4C AD, the eastern territories of the Roman Empire included the Balkans, modern Greece, Asia Minor and Egypt. Greek, the language of the Church and the vernacular of the peoples of the eastern Mediterranean, gradually superseded Latin as the official language. Thus a totally Hellenised empire emerged which was to perpetuate the traditions of Rome long after the fall of the western empire in 476.

RELIGIOUS CONFLICT AND EXTERNAL THREATS

AD 395 Division of the Roman Empire between the sons of Theodosius: a Latin empire in the west, and a largely Greek empire centred on Constantinople (formerly Byzantium) in the east.

451 **Council of Chalcedon**: confirmation of the position of the Patriarch of Constantinople as second only to the Pope.

476 The last western emperor is deposed by Odoacer. **Constantinople** becomes sole capital of the empire.

Byzantium was a theocratic empire, where the emperor (known by the Greek title of basileus from the 7th century onwards) and patriarch exercised interdependent functions (symbolised by the twin-headed eagle, Byzantium's emblem), the former as protector of the empire's status as the ultimate manifestation of God's kingdom on earth, and the latter as guardian of the Christian faith. Doctrinal issues were of concern to everyone in society, since not only did such matters jeopardise the chances of the individual soul's entry into heaven, but they could also threaten the very fabric of society. Indeed, the history of Byzantium is largely dictated by religious debates.

Throughout its thousand-year existence, the empire was under constant threat of invasion. From the west came barbarians, Normans, Franks and Venetians; from the north the Slavs, who occupied mainland Greece and the Peloponnese from 6C to 8C; from the east the Persians, the Arabs and finally the Turks. The erosion of the empire over time resulted in shortages of food, manpower

H Champollion/MICHELIN

Christ Pantocrator (Daphne Monastery)

and revenue, so necessary for the operation of the vast bureaucratic machine which Byzantium had become. The Byzantines were fine soldiers, but just as importantly they used diplomacy skilfully, paying off one group of aggressors while receiving tribute monies from other adversaries. They also spread Christianity, converting their northern neighbours, the Slavs.

527-65 Reign of Justinian I. In 529 he closed the great Athenian seats of learning, the Academy and the Lyceum, suspecting them of propagating paganism. He retook Italy from the Ostrogoths and a large part of Spain from the Visigoths, but the barbarians invaded Thessaly and reached the Isthmus of Corinth. During his reign the Corpus Juris Civilis legal texts were compiled, subsequently known as the Justinian Code.

532-37 Construction of Hagia Sophia in Constantinople.

580 onwards Slavic invasion: siege of Thessaloníki and occupation of the Peloponnese.

610-41 Reign of Heraclius. Defeated the Persians, and saw off the Avar siege of the capital (626), but could not prevent the conquest of Syria and then Egypt by the Arabs (636).

717-41 **Reign of Leo III** the Isaurian, who, in 726, forbade the cult of icons and ordered their destruction (iconoclasm); he also stemmed Arab expansionism.

Phototravellers/MICHELIN

Icon of St George

754 Iconoclast Council of Hiera.

783 Victory of Staurikos over the Slavs, who were subsequently defeated at Patras (805).

805 Decree by Basil II consecrating Mount Athos to monastic life. The first monastery erected in 963.

813 The Bulgars lay siege to Constantinople.

827 Crete falls to the Arabs.

19 March 843 Affirmation of orthodoxy and rehabilitation of icons.

856-87 and 877-86 Patriarchate of Photius who sought to convert the Slavs, sending out the missionaries Cyril and Methodius, pioneers of the Cyrillic alphabet.

860 The Russians attack Byzantium, laying siege to Constantinople.

904 Fall of Thessaloníki to the Arabs.

The Latin empire of Constantinople

A college of six Venetians and six Frenchmen elected Baldwin of Flanders emperor. With the exception of Epiros, Greece was divided along feudal lines: the Venetians took the islands and the main coastal sites, while the French and Lombards controlled the bulk of the mainland. The Emperor Baldwin held Constantinople, which he shared with the Venetians, Thrace and the adjacent parts of Asia Minor, After his death, he was succeeded by his brother Henry of Flanders, then by Peter and Robert de Courtenay, and finally by Baldwin II de Courtenay in 1261.

961 Crete recaptured from the Arabs by Nicephoras Phocas, who, in 969, also takes Antioch.

1001-14 Basil II campaigns against the Bulgars: in the narrow defile of Clidion the Byzantines inflict a heavy defeat on Samuel's Bulgar army.

1032 Recapture of Édessa, an important centre of icon manufacture.

c 1050 Michael Psellus reintroduces the study of philosophy at the University of Constantinople. Through his pupils he was to exert enormous influence on Byzantine thought and is seen as a proto-humanist.

1054 Schism between the Catholic and Orthodox Churches.

1071 Battle of Mantzikert: the Byzantines are defeated by the Turks, marking the beginning of Ottoman expansionism.

1081-85 The Comnenus dynasty: through their oligarchic rule, neglect of the army and imprudent expenditure, they heralded the decline of the empire.

FROM THE CRUSADES TO THE OTTOMANS

The Crusades were unleashed in the east by 11C and 12C Popes on the pretext of aiding the Byzantines in their efforts to recover the Holy Land from the Muslims; the Franks, however, were clearly more interested in carving out territory for themselves and the Venetians saw commercial opportunities aplenty.

BNF Paris

The siege of Rhodes, 1480

1185 Thessaloníki taken by the Normans.

1204 Constantinople taken on the pretext of resolving the issue of succession to the imperial throne. On 13 April, the troops of the Fourth Crusade sack the city, desecrating its churches.

This event and the subsequent occupation, aggravated no doubt by the stark doctrinal differences between the Catholic and Orthodox Churches, served to intensify Greek hostility towards the west.

This Latin incursion into the Byzantine world brought with it feudal structures: a Latin empire around Constantinople was established, encompassing Thrace and the northwest of Asia Minor (1204-61); the kingdom of Macedonia, taking in Thessaloníki and Macedonia (1204-24); central Greece was carved up into baronies, and the Peloponnese became the principality of Achaia. Confronting this Latin hegemony were three independent states preserving the Greek traditions: the empire of Nicea (1204-61), the despotic State of Epirus (1205-1318), and the empire of Trebizond (1204-1461), geographically isolated to the east of what is now modern Turkey.

ALINARI

Emperor John VIII Paleologos by Antonio Pisanello (Bargello National Museum, Florence)

1249 Foundation of Mystra. Originally a simple defensive fort, it became a leading centre of cultural and spiritual affairs under the influence of the philosopher George Gemistos Plethon.

1261 The emperor of Nicea, Michael VIII Paleologus, recaptures Constantinople, and over subsequent years part of the Peloponnese is retaken. The despotic State of Morea is founded at Mystra in 1348; it is to last until 1460.

1331 Nicea captured by the Turks.

Late 14C Exodus of Byzantine academics and intellectuals to the west: Manuel Chrysolaras to Florence, where he taught Greek language and literature, and George Ermonymos to Paris, where he taught Erasmus.

The Principality of Morea

The prince of this state was styled Duke of Achaia, who had 12 barons as his principal vassals. The first rulers were from Champagne; originally in the hands of Guillaume de Champlitte, it then passed to the Villehardouin family before becoming property of the Anjou-Sicily dynasty in the person of Charles I of Anjou, brother of King Louis IX of France. After the Byzantines retook Constantinople in 1261, they gradually won back the Peloponnese. The princes of Morea, whose story is told in the *Chronicle of Morea*, also held sway over the duchies of Thebes and Athens, which had devolved to the La Roche, who were succeeded by the Brienne. When Gautier de Brienne and his knights were killed at the Battle of Kephisos in 1311, the duchy fell into the hands of the Catalans; from there it passed in 1388 to the Acciaiuoli, Florentines allied to the Anjou-Sicily dynasty.

H Champollion/MICHELIN

St Pantaleon Monastery, Mount Athos

The spread of Greek ideas contributed to the development of humanism.

1439 Council of Florence: proclamation of an alliance between Catholic and Orthodox Churches (subsequently condemned by Patriarch Gennadius II Scholarius in 1456).

29 May 1453 Constantinople finally falls to the Ottomans, despite the valiant efforts of the last emperor Constantine Paleologus, who waited in vain for assistance from the west.

1460 Mystra taken by the Turks.

Ottoman Domination and Independence

For four centuries, Greece formed part of the Ottoman Empire. The Turks inherited the Byzantine machinery of government and ruled their dominions firmly. During this era there was a revival in Hellenistic sentiment, which was to reach its climax in a bloody struggle for independence, drawing in other European nations and giving birth to a modern state.

TWO CENTURIES OF CONQUEST

It would be wrong to imagine the Turks descending as a horde upon the empire of Byzantium. Their process of conquest started in the Balkans in the 14C, peaked with the capture of Constantinople in 1453, and was not concluded until 1669, when Herakleion was captured from the Venetians, who continued to maintain a presence in the Ionian Islands, notably Corfu, until the 18C.

1444-81 Reign of Mehmet II who, after taking Constantinople, conquers eastern Greece.

1456-75 Fall of the Duchy of Athens, Boeotia, Lesbos, Halkída in Euboia, and Sámos.

1480 Siege of Rhodes; the Knights of St John successfully defend the island against the Turks.

Phototravellers/MICHELIN

Murad Reis Mosque, Rhodes

Mehmet II's heirs continue his expansionist strategy, taking the Peloponnese and numerous islands, gaining mastery of the eastern Mediterranean.

1500 Sack of Naupacte.

1522 Suleiman the Magnificent takes Rhodes and the Dodecanese.

1537 onward Nauplion, Monemvassía and the Aegean Islands fall to the Ottomans. Only Timos, under Venetian control, remains unconquered. The former corsair Khair al Din, originally from Lesbos, now Suleiman II's grand admiral, defeats Charles V's fleet off Prévesa.

1566 Capture of Chios.

1571 Cyprus taken. **Naval Battle of Lepanto**; Don John of Austria and the Venetians defeat the Turkish fleet, thereby curbing Ottoman expansion.

1669 The fall of Herakleion ends Venetian control of Crete.

Organisation of the Ottoman Empire

The Turks allowed Christians and Jews to worship freely, but as non-Muslims their status was inferior; known as *raïas*, their continued existence was deemed necessary in order to meet the empire's manpower requirements.

Large towns were administered by **pashas**; smaller towns and villages were ruled by **agas**. The government exacted heavy taxes from the Muslim and non-Muslim communities alike, but the latter had to perform all sorts of additional duties imposed by the local rulers in the rich agricultural regions. According to Ottoman law, all lands belonged to the sultan, who often delegated their administration to his great generals. They acted as tax gatherers, keeping large amounts of revenue for themselves.

The harshest aspect of the occupation, especially during the first 200 years, was the abduction of young boys. The strongest were chosen to serve as mercenary soldiers, **Janissaries**, the sultan's personal guard. The brightest were raised in the harem and became devoted government officials. Some Christians converted to the Islamic faith to escape poverty. Many more took refuge in the harsh, wild mountains where the Turks hardly ventured and succeeded in forming prosperous and largely autonomous communities.

From the 17C **Phanariots**, natives of the Phanar district in Constantinople, who were often descendants of the Byzantine imperial families, were appointed as governors *(hospodar)* of the Romanian provinces, as interpreters *(dragoman)*

SCALA

The Battle of Lepanto (Correr Museum, Venice)

for the sultan and often as ambassadors to the western powers. Many of those Christians who could afford to leave chose exile; this Greek diaspora was to make a significant contribution towards the emergence of humanism in the west, and keep alive Hellenic aspirations which would subsequently lead to an independent Greece.

After the fall of Byzantium, the sultan not only confirmed the authority of the **Patriarch of Constantinople** in religious matters, but also appointed him as temporal leader *(ethnarches)*, responsible for the internal affairs of all the orthodox communities throughout the empire. He was also answerable to the Turkish authorities for the loyalty and good behaviour of the Christian population. In spite of, or perhaps because of, this dual function, the **Orthodox Church** succeeded in maintaining the Greek religion, language and traditions in these difficult times. The monasteries, in particular those on Mount Athos, the Metéora and Patmós, were the principal centres of Greek culture.

E Slatter/HEMISPHERES

Statue of Bouboulina, Spetsae

THE STRUGGLE FOR LIBERTY

There had been revolts in the 17C, but it was in the 18C that a feeling of nationalism began to develop with the full support of the Orthodox Church. Meanwhile, the Venetians continued to maintain a strong presence in the eastern Mediterranean; in 1687 they retook the Peloponnese and the island of Aigina. Following the Treaty of Karlowitz, the Ottomans ceded Morea to Venice.

It was from outside Greece, however, that the strongest impulses came. Among émigré Greeks there were numerous secret societies which raised funds and laid plans to bring an end to Ottoman occupation. The largest was the **Filikí Etería**, founded in Odessa in 1814 by **Alexander Ypsilantis**, aide-de-camp to the Russian Tsar. These socie-

Heroes of the struggle for independence

Lascarína Bouboulína (1771-1825): Originally from Spetsae, she fought the Turks at sea and in the Peloponnese.

Márkos Bótzaris (1771-1826): Of Souliot origin, he led the defenders of Missolonghi and was killed near Karpeníssi.

Germanós (1771-1826): He blessed the standard of Greek independence at the monastery of Agía Lávra, and preached the cause at Patras on 25 March 1821.

Constantinos Kanáris (1790-1877): A fire-ship expert, later a politician.

Giorgios Karaïskakis (1780-1827): Leader of the *palikares* on the mainland; he was killed at the Battle of Phaleron near Athens.

Theodore Kolokotrónis (1770-1843): Originally from the Peloponnese, he inflicted the first major defeat upon the Turks in the Dervenáki Gorge in 1822.

Ioannis Makriánnis (1797-1864): A native of Thessaly and military leader. His memoirs are a precious and picturesque testimony of the popular uprising.

Andréas Miaoúlis (1769-1835): Sailor who fought numerous battles against the Turkish navy between 1822 and 1825.

Greece on the Ruins of Missolonghi, Delacroix

ties consisted of merchants and civil servants like the **Phanariots** (natives of the Phanar district in Constantinople), ship owners from the islands and businessmen, bankers and writers living in Greece or abroad, where they were influenced by the ideals of the Age of Enlightenment and later of the French Revolution.

In the mountains, bands of **klephts** (the word literally means robber in Greek) began to harass the Turks; they were joined by the militia *(armatoles)*, composed of Greek citizens armed by the Turks to fight the rebels but who took up their cause.

The intellectuals of the secret societies and the rebels of the mountains had little in common except a desire to overthrow Ottoman rule; there was no clear agenda as to how it should be replaced, with some favouring a republic, others a monarchy. The hunger for liberation, however, was the factor which overrode all others.

THE GRAND REVOLUTION

1797 End of the Venetian Republic. The Ionian Islands come under French control.

1800 Ionian Islands taken by Russia and handed over to Turkish rule.

1807 Treaty of Tilsit – Ionian Islands revert to French control.

1809 The British occupy the Ionian Islands, except Corfu which resists occupation until 1814.

1818 Ionian Islands declared independent, under a British protectorate. Greek confirmed as the official language.

The first uprisings begin in the Danube districts in 1821, but a lack of wider support results in failure.

25 March 1821 The Metropolitan of Patras, **Germanós**, raises the flag of revolt, a white cross on a sky-blue background, against Sultan Mahmoud II at the Agía Lávra Monastery near Kalávrita. The revolt spreads throughout the Peloponnese, into Epirus, ruled by Ali Pasha, and to the islands

Ibrahim Pasha, Viceroy of Egypt (Museum of the Chateau de Versailles)

Lord Byron (Pierpont Morgan Library, New York)

of the Saronic Gulf; 40 000 Turkish troops are massacred. This was the start of the War of Independence, also known as the **National Revolution**. By 1822 **Theodore Kolokotrónis** and his troops were in total control of the Peloponnese.

1 January 1822 Unilateral declaration of independence. The provisional government under Alexandros Mavrocordato is established at Missolonghi. Following the insurrection on Sámos, the Turks massacre 20 000 men, enslaving their women and children. Discord between the provisional government and Kolokotrónis in the Peloponnese, with a second assembly being established at Kranidi.

1823 New government in place, first under Petros Mavromichalis, and subsequently Georgios Coundouriotis.

1825 End of civil war between monarchist and republicans. Turkish victory at Modon; the troops of Mehmet Ali, Sultan of Egypt, ravage Morea.

Having failed to storm **Missolonghi**, the Turks besiege the city in April 1822. In 1824 **Lord Byron** visits the city and resolves to do everything in his power to help the cause of Greek independence, but he dies prematurely the following year. The city falls in 1826 and the resultant loss of life has a great impact in Europe.

1826 St Petersburg protocol; Britain and Russia decide to intervene to enforce an armistice "without however taking any part in the hostilities". The allied fleet goes to parley with the Turkish fleet anchored off Chios (Híos) in Navarino Bay and ends up destroying it.

1827 National assembly convenes and proposes a republican government headed by a president to hold office for seven years, and the election of a chamber of deputies. Subsequently the London convention upholds the St Petersburg protocol. The Ottoman Empire refuses to comply and its fleet is blockaded, then destroyed, by the allies in October that year.

1828 John Kapodístrias becomes governor of Greece, reorganising the state and army, but his republican leanings alienate many.

1829 Treaty of Adrianople grants autonomy to Greece.

1830 Treaty of London; Greece's independent status recognised by the Great Powers.

9 October 1831 Assassination of John Kapodístrias.

1832 Exploiting a clause in the Treaty of London, the allies decide on a monarchy for Greece and ask Otto von Wittelsbach to become king.

Democracy and a European Identity

OTTO I AND GEORGE I

1833-62 Reign of **Otto I** of Bavaria.

1834 Athens becomes capital of independent Greece. Foundation of first state university in 1837.

1854 Crimean War. Greece sides with Russia, provoking an Anglo-French attack on Piraeus.

1863-1913 Reign of **George I** of Denmark, a constitutional monarch along the British model.

1864 The **Ionian Islands**, British possessions since 1814, become part of Greece. Proclamation of a new liberal constitution: George I declared 'King of Greeks'.

1881 Congress of Berlin: Greece recovers Thessaly and most of Epirus.

1882-93 Construction of Corinth Canal.

1896 First modern Olympic Games.

1908 Elefthérios Venizélos proclaims the unification of Crete with Greece.

1912-13 **Balkan Wars**. Macedonia and Epirus liberated from the Turks by the Greek army.

After **John Kapodístrias**, the prime minister, was assassinated in 1831, the Great Powers (Russia, Britain and France) imposed an absolute monarchy upon Greece, in the shape of a Bavarian prince, **Otto I**, who was not even 18 years old at the time of his accession. A Catholic himself, his wife (also Catholic) was vehemently opposed to Orthodoxy, and he presided over a cabinet made up of Bavarian ministers and a German speaking court. A coup on 3 September 1843 forced him to choose a Greek cabinet and approve a constitution. Even so, as the king continued to intervene in political life, the wave of liberal opposition – secretly supported by the British who disliked the king's close relationship with Russia – culminated in a second coup and Otto was deposed.

On 6 June 1863 Prince William of Denmark (1845-1913), suggested by Britain as a possible candidate for the throne, accepted the crown and became king with the title of **George I**. For its part, Britain gave up its protectorate of the Ionian Islands, which restored Greek territorial integrity. The role of the new dynasty was in fact to bring Greek policy into line with that of the British in eastern Europe. Pressure from an increasingly influential middle class led the new king to grant a more liberal constitution in 1864, then to introduce parliamentary government in 1875.

The main problem, however, remained the territorial issue, as significant areas of Greek population were still under Turkish occupation. In 1866 the king backed a Cretan uprising against the island's Ottoman overlords but, lacking support from the big powers, he had to leave the island in the hands of the sultan. When the Russo-Turkish war began in 1877, Greece invaded Thessaly but, although the Treaty of San Stefano recognised the independence of Serbia, Romania and Bulgaria, it maintained Turkish rule in Macedonia. It was not until 1881 and the Congress of Berlin that Thessaly became part of Greece. In March 1896 Crete, with the support of Greek volunteers, again rebelled against the sultan. The Greek government landed troops there in February 1897 and an army commanded by

Corinth Canal

the Crown Prince Constantine invaded Macedonia, where it was defeated. The mediation of the big powers led to the signature in December of the Treaty of Constantinople, which granted Crete autonomy under the rule of the king's second son, Prince George.

Dissatisfied with the lack of territorial recovery, discontent developed and was aggravated by the Balkan crisis. The first sign of this potent nationalism occurred in 1908, when the Cretan **Elefthérios Venizélos** (1864-1936) proclaimed the unification of Crete with Greece. An army revolt in 1909 forced the king to call on Venizélos to form a government in 1910. The aim of Venizélos was to unite all territories with Greek populations and to reorganise the administration, army and economy. In 1911 he gained approval for a new constitution with better guarantees for individual freedoms. In 1912, together with Bulgaria, Serbia and Montenegro, he founded the **Balkan League**, which declared war on Turkey on 18 October. Greece invaded Macedonia, and in November took Thessaloníki, where King George was assassinated in March 1913. The London Conference in May 1913 put an end to this first conflict, but the arguments over the partition of Macedonia started a second one, with Bulgaria this time fighting its former allies. The Treaty of Bucharest in August 1913 sanctioned the annexation of southern Macedonia, southern Epirus and most of the Aegean Islands by Greece, as well as her sovereignty over Crete, but gave northern Macedonia to Serbia. In the same year, the Council of Florence ceded northern Epirus to the newly formed state of Albania. Even today, territorial issues remain hotly debated.

WAR FOLLOWS WAR

1913 Constantine I comes to the throne.

1914-18 First World War. Greece brought into the war by Venizélos on the side of the Allies. Thrace and Smyrna awarded to Greece in 1919.

1917 Abdication of Constantine I; his younger son Alexander I succeeds him.

1919-22 New Greco-Turkish conflict; the **Great Catastrophe**. After the defeat of the Greek army, 1.5 million ethnic Greeks from Asia Minor become refugees.

1920 Following a referendum, Constantine returns to the throne.

1922 Constantine abdicates again in favour of his elder son George II.

1923 Treaty of Lausanne redraws Greece's frontiers: Turkey takes Smyrna, Italy the Dodecanese, and Britain the island of Cyprus.

25 March 1924 Declaration of a republic; Admiral Coundoriotas elected president.

1935 After a number of coups, a monarchist government is elected; following a referendum George II returns to the throne.

1936-41 Dictatorship of General Metaxas.

1940-41 Italian troops invade Epirus on 28 October 1940. The Greek army repulses this attack, pushing the Italians back into Albania.

1941-44 German occupation.

When war broke out in 1914, the Greek government was split between the patriots with Venizélos at their head and the Germanophiles grouped around King Constantine I (1868-1923), brother-in-law of Kaiser Wilhelm II. Venizélos suggested that the king should align himself with the Allies but he was forced by the king to resign in March 1915. Returned to power by the electors, Venizélos tried to make a secret pact with the Allies but again the king demanded his resignation. The army then gave its backing to the prime minister and together they formed a republican government at Thessaloníki in September 1916. The king then started to form partisan battalions, so the French occupied Thessaly and demanded his abdication. Venizélos returned to Athens in June

1918. The new king, **Alexander I** (1893-1920), asked him to form a government and on 15 September aligned himself with the Allies. In the Treaties of Neuilly (1919) and Sèvres (1920), Greece gained eastern Thrace and the Smyrna region of Asia Minor came under its administration.

Then Britain, playing on Venizélos's imperialist ambitions, caused the Greek leader to start a new war with Turkey by annexing the Smyrna region. This proved very unpopular and brought about the downfall of Venizélos at the polls in November 1920, immediately after the death of the king. A plebiscite followed, recalling Constantine I. Abandoned by its allies, Greece was unable to hold out for long against the Turks. Military failures led to Constantine's second abdication in September 1922, in favour of his son **George II** (1890-1947), and to the evacuation of Asia Minor and the tragic forced emigration of the ethnic Greeks living there. This massive influx of new population could only aggravate an already difficult economic situation. The elections returned the Venizélos party to power and the King preferred to abdicate (in December 1923). A republic was proclaimed on 25 March 1924 and confirmed by a plebiscite. It experienced numerous crises, with a succession of alternating dictatorships and republican union governments. July 1928 saw the return of Venizélos as head of government until his resignation in 1932. Numerous domestic problems accentuated the political divide between the Right and the Communist Left. Consequently a further coup in March 1935, supported by Venizélos himself, abolished the republic; a plebiscite soon restored the monarchy and reinstalled George II. The king asked **General Metaxás** to form a government, although, to all intents and purposes, he acted as dictator until his death in 1941. With the king's agreement, Metaxás abolished the constitution, dissolved parliament and adopted Fascist policies. Greece had, however, felt threatened by the annexation of Albania by Italy under Mussolini. When in October 1940 Italy demanded free passage for its troops, Greece rejected the ultimatum and came over to the British side. The Italians crossed the border into Greece but the Greek army succeeded in pushing them back towards Albania. German troops then came to Mussolini's aid. The king fled first to Crete and then, under British occupation, to Cairo; Greece was divided between the Italians, Germans and Bulgarians. Resistance groups, in particular the fiercely Marxist National Liberation Front (EAM), waged active guerrilla warfare against the occupiers with ever-increasing support among the population. The Russian offensive in Romania caused the Germans to evacuate Greece in October 1944. The king, George II, had meanwhile set up a government in exile under Papandréou, and promised not to return until there had been a plebiscite.

THE CIVIL WAR AND ENTRY INTO EUROPE

1947-49 Civil war.
1952 Greece joins NATO.
1953-63 Period of conservative governments under Pagagos and **Konstandínos Karamanlís**.
1967-74 Dictatorship of the Colonels.
1974 Referendum decides in favour of a republic.
1981 Greece joins the EEC, subsequently the European Union.
2004 Athens hosts the Olympic Games.
2006 The Council of the European Union names Patras, Greece the European "Capital of Culture" for 2006.

As the Germans evacuated Greece to the north, the British army was disembarking at Piraeus. The British were particularly worried about the influence exerted by the EAM and asked in vain that their partisan army should be disarmed. In the elections of March 1946, massive abstentions on the part of the republicans gave the victory to the royalists, who pressed forward with a plebiscite which came out in favour of the return of the king. When he died soon after, he was succeeded by his brother, **Paul I** (1901-64). While the Treaty of Paris of February

1947 gave the Dodecanese Islands to Greece, the interior of the country faced an extremely critical situation since the left-wing parties refused to support the monarchy. In December 1947, with Soviet support, General Márkos formed a provisional government of Free Greece and took refuge in the mountains of the north; from there he waged a guerrilla campaign against the royalist government. The civil war lasted until October 1949 and was ended only by the capture, with the help of the United States, of the rebels' main stronghold in the Grámmos Mountains.

The ensuing elections were a victory for the moderate parties but successive governments up to 1963 were, in fact, controlled by extreme right-wing forces, which in effect formed a parallel government. The emergency laws passed at the time of the civil war were never repealed and remained in force. When the elections of 1963 gave power to the democratic parties, **Giórgos Papandréou** (1888-1968) was asked to form a government; however, the positions he adopted were not always in line with US policy, and the extreme right in Greece saw in his premiership a threat to their privileges. Badly advised, the young King **Constantine II** (b 1940) disagreed with his head of government, who resigned. This gave rise to a political crisis, in the course of which every attempt to form a legitimate government failed. When the elections held in 1967 failed to produce the parliamentary majority expected by the extreme right, a **junta** led by a number of colonels, who did not even represent a majority within the army, took power in the name of the king.

The colonels set up a regime based on terror; opponents were dragged before a military court and either imprisoned or deported. Constantine II tried to remove the colonels in a coup but failed; he left Greece on 13 December 1967. A new constitution restricted individual freedom and gave excessive powers to the army. The hostility of the majority of the population steadily increased and, in spite of some measures intended to give an illusion of liberalisation, such as the deposition of the king and proclamation of the republic in July 1973,

J Malburet/MICHELIN

demonstrations against the regime grew in scale. The colonels responded by proclaiming martial law and setting up special courts, but in 1974, because of the Cyprus crisis and squabbles within the junta, those in power were obliged to call on **Konstandínos Karamanlís**, leader of the right-wing parties and an opponent of the regime. He abolished all the institutions of dictatorship and reintroduced the constitution of 1952, with the exception of the clauses relating to the monarchy. Fundamental liberties were restored, political parties legalised, and the main figures involved in the dictatorship brought to justice. The referendum of 8 December 1974 decided in favour of a **republic**, and a new constitution was promulgated in June 1975.

Since then, the return to democracy has been clearly demonstrated by the alternation in power of right- and left-wing parties, and further reinforced by Greece's membership of the EEC, which it joined in 1981. Greek political life continues to be dominated by relations with its neighbours, especially Turkey, whose entry into the European Union (as at 2003) it opposes, Macedonia (in 1992 Greece refused to recognise the republic of this name formed from part of the former Yugoslavia, which also laid claim to part of the Greco-Macedonian heritage), and Albania.

ART AND CULTURE

The influential role of Classical Greek arts and architecture is undisputed. The emergence of modern Greece after the long period of Turkish and Ottoman rule has brought many artists, writers, filmmakers and musicians to the forefront of Greek culture, among them the Nobel-prizewinning poets Giórgos Seféris and Odysséas Elitis, the filmmakers Mihális Kakoiánnis and Theo Angélopoulos, the plastic artist Takis, and singers Nana Mouskouri and Maria Callas.

Architecture

CONSTRUCTION TECHNIQUES

The chief building material was stone: limestone tufa (often shell limestone), and marble from the quarries on Pentelikon, Thássos and Náxos. The stone blocks were quarried with a pickaxe and extracted with the aid of metal or wooden wedges; the latter soaked to make them expand. Often the blocks were then shaped on the spot into architectural elements: columns, capitals, models of statues.

The blocks were removed from the quarry down a slipway constructed so as to have a regular gradient. Weighing on average five tonnes, the blocks were loaded onto wooden sledges which were lowered on ropes hitched round fixed bollards. The blocks were then transferred to carts or drays drawn by bullocks for transport to the building site.

R Corbel/MICHELIN

Rectangular Bonding

R Corbel/MICHELIN

Trapezoidal bonding

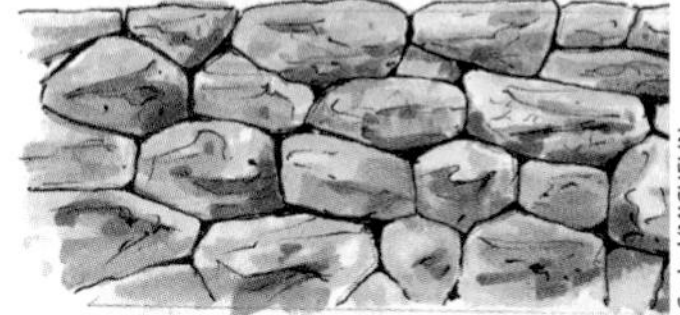
R Corbel/MICHELIN

Cyclopean bonding

B Pérousse/MICHELIN

Temple of Aphaia, Aigina

On the site the rough or prepared blocks were unloaded with the aid of levers and rollers and sent to the workshop to be dressed or decorated (fluting, moulding) or carved (capitals, pediments and metopes). The blocks were raised into position with a block and tackle and hoist or derrick. The dressed stones, which were placed one upon another without mortar, were held in place by H or N clamps. Wooden or metal pins were used to secure the piles of drums which made up a column: the holes which held them can still be seen. Stone columns received a coat of stucco.

In large-scale constructions the blocks of stone were cut and placed in various ways according to the purpose and period of the building and the means and time available. No bonding material was used. This gives Greek stonework an almost unrivalled aesthetic and functional value. The **Cyclopean** style of construction, rough but sturdy, is to be found in some **Mycenaean** structures, especially at Tiryns. Polygonal bonding was used in all periods, often for foundations; at first the blocks were rough hewn, then came curved surfaces and finally flat ones. Trapezoidal bonding, with varying degrees of regularity, was widespread in the 4C BC. Rectangular bonding, which occurred in all periods, was used most frequently in the Classical period.

MYCENAEAN PERIOD (1550-1100 BC)

The Mycenaean palace stood within a fortified city *(acropolis)* surrounded by Cyclopean walls, so-called because legend said they had been built by giant masons, the **Cyclops**.

The palace itself had a simple and logical plan: one entrance, a courtyard with the throne room on one side preceded by a vestibule and the main reception rooms on the other. The largest room was the **megaron** with four columns supporting the roof and surrounding the central hearth; it served both domestic and religious purposes. Beyond lay the private apartments of the king and queen, usually furnished with baths.

The best examples of Mycenaean palaces are Mycenae, Tiryns, Chios and Gla.

The dead were buried on the edge of the city in three different sorts of graves: a pit grave, a rock sepulchre or a circular domed chamber (*thólos*) with an entrance passage *(drómos)*. The skilled craftsmanship of the objects found in these **tombs** indicates that the princes who were buried in them were astonishingly rich; for many years the graves were known as 'Treasuries'. The best examples of Mycenaean graves are at Mycenae, Chios, Vapheio, Peristéria in the Peloponnese and Orchomenos in Boeotia.

TEMPLES (700 BC ONWARDS)

The temple was the dwelling place of the god or goddess to whom it was dedicated and housed his or her statue; some temples were dedicated to more than one divinity. Thought to represent the architectural ideal, they are essentially a blend of structural simplicity and harmonious proportions. The proportions were governed by the module, the average radius of the column, which determined the height since the column was the basic element in the elevation of a building.

In some buildings the architects departed from rigid verticals and horizontals to correct optical distortion. The horizontal entablatures were slightly bowed, making the centre imperceptibly higher than the ends; each column was inclined towards its inner neighbour as it rose, the angle of incline increasing from the centre of the colonnade towards the outer corner.

Sculpted figures, often didactic, were placed on the secondary architectural features: the tympanum *(pediment)* and the metopes *(architrave)*.

The temples were painted: the background was generally red with the prominent features in blue to form a contrast. These brilliant colours made the stone or white marble sculptures stand out. A gilded bronze colour was used to pick out certain decorative motifs such as shields or *acroteria*.

H Champollion/MICHELIN

Kore (Acropolis Museum, Athens)

H Levandowski/RMN

The Sophocléenne, 330 BC (Louvre, Paris)

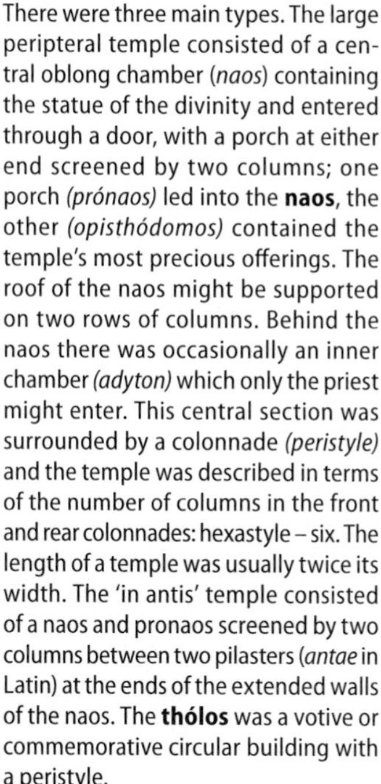

There were three main types. The large peripteral temple consisted of a central oblong chamber (*naos*) containing the statue of the divinity and entered through a door, with a porch at either end screened by two columns; one porch *(prónaos)* led into the **naos**, the other *(opisthódomos)* contained the temple's most precious offerings. The roof of the naos might be supported on two rows of columns. Behind the naos there was occasionally an inner chamber *(adyton)* which only the priest might enter. This central section was surrounded by a colonnade *(peristyle)* and the temple was described in terms of the number of columns in the front and rear colonnades: hexastyle – six. The length of a temple was usually twice its width. The 'in antis' temple consisted of a naos and pronaos screened by two columns between two pilasters (*antae* in Latin) at the ends of the extended walls of the naos. The **thólos** was a votive or commemorative circular building with a peristyle.

The main elements of a temple were the base *(stylobate)*, the columns, the entablature supporting a wooden roof frame covered with tiles and a pediment at either end. The articulation of these elements gave rise to the orders.

Developed on the mainland among the Dorian people, the **Doric** Order was the most common style in Greece from the 7C onwards. The columns, which had 20 flutes, rested directly on the stylobate without bases; the capitals were plain. The entablature consisted of three parts one above the other: the architrave, the frieze and the cornice; the frieze was composed of metopes, panels often carved in high relief, alternating with triglyphs, stone slabs with two vertical grooves. The triangular pediments were sculpted with scenes in high relief and also adorned with decorative motifs *(acroteria)* at the angles. Along the sides above the cornice were sculpted ornaments *(antefixa)* which served as gargoyles.

The Ionians who had settled in Asia Minor in the 5C BC created the **Ionic** Order, which was considered a feminine style; its delicate grace and rich ornament contrasted with the austere strength of the Doric Order. Its main characteristics are tall slim columns with 24 flutes resting on moulded bases and crowned by capitals in the form of a double scroll; an entablature consisting of an architrave, a continuous sculpted frieze and a cornice decorated with egg and dart and leaf and dart moulding; a pediment with acroteria shaped like palm leaves at the angles. The best example is the **Temple of Athena Nike** in the Acropolis.

Invented in Corinth in the 5C BC the **Corinthian** Order did not spread until the 4C BC; it was very popular in the Roman period. It is a derivative of the Ionic Order and its chief distinction is the scroll capital almost entirely covered in curled acanthus leaves. The best examples are the **Olympieion** and **Hadrian's Arch** in Athens and the **Temple of Octavian** in Corinth. The capital was invented by **Kallimachos**, a sculptor and contemporary of Pheidias; he is thought to have been inspired by a basket filled with flowers.

THEATRES

Nearly all religious sites in Ancient Greece included a theatre originally designed for the Dionysiac festivals that included hymns or dithyrambs, which later developed into tragedy.

The original wooden structures were later built of stone and from the 4C BC comprised:

- a central circular area *(orchestra)* where the chorus performed round the altar of the god and the actors wearing the appropriate masks acted their parts;
- tiers of seats (*koilon* or *theatron*) extending round more than half the orchestra to form the segment of a circle; the first row of seats was reserved for the priests and officials; a promenade *(diázoma)* ran round between the upper and lower tiers of seats. The audience reached their seats from above, from the diázoma or through passages *(parodos)* leading into the orchestra;
- a proscenium *(proskenion)*, a sort of portico forming a backdrop, and a stage *(skene)*, originally a storeroom. In the Hellenistic period the stage was incorporated into the performing area; the back wall improved the acoustics.

Odeons were covered theatres, which became very numerous in the Roman period.

The major theatres are in Athens, Delphi, Árgos and Epidauros and Dodona.

Art

ARCHAIC PERIOD (700-500 BC)

In the 7C BC the Greek world began to produce its first full-size statues, strange, rigid figures made of wood *(xoanon)*, with ecstatic expressions inspired by Asiatic, particularly Egyptian, models.

In the 6C BC two well-known and distinctive types of statue were produced: the **kouros**, a naked young man, and the **kore**, a young woman dressed in a tunic, Doric peplos or Ionian chiton. The figures, which were life size or larger, were sometimes made of bronze, like the Piraeus Apollo discovered in 1959, but more often of limestone *(poros)* or marble and then painted with vivid colours.

The high reliefs, carved in stone and also painted, mostly come from pediments and are impressive for their realistic and expressive appearance; the bronze sculptures are more stylised.

The Acropolis Museum in Athens has an important series of Archaic figures (*kouroi* and *korai*, high-relief pedimental sculptures, moscophoroi); the National Museum displays the **Warrior of Marathon** and several *kouroi* including the kouros of Sounion, the oldest known (600 BC), and the kouros of Anávissos;

Jockey from Artemision (National Archaeological Museum, Athens)

the **Piraeus Apollo** (late 6C BC) is to be found in the Piraeus Museum.

Other examples typical of Archaic art are the stone Gorgon from the Temple of Artemis in Corfu (Corfu Museum), the marble frieze from the Siphnian Treasury and two kouroi representing Cleobis and Biton (Delphi Museum).

CLASSICAL PERIOD (500-300 BC)

There was a transition period, marked by the **Charioteer of Delphi** (475 BC), where the figure turns slightly to the right and takes his weight on one hip; passing through two distinct phases, Classical statuary then freed itself from the rigid frontal stance.

In the idealistic phase (5C BC) Greek sculpture reached its height in the work of **Polykleitos** and **Pheidias**. The former established a standard model, the **canon**. The latter created an ideal standard of beauty composed of strength, majesty and serenity in the delicately carved lines of his marble figures: his genius is expressed in the Parthenon sculptures (Acropolis Museum, British Museum, Louvre); unfortunately the famous chryselephantine (gold and ivory) statue of Zeus at Olympia was destroyed.

Other typical works of the period include **Athena Mourning** in the Acropolis Museum and *Poseidon* from Artemision in the National Museum.

During the 'naturalist' phase (4C) majesty gave way to grace and the female nude made its appearance. Artists began to compose from nature giving their figures expressive faces; the best known are Skopas, Lysippos and Praxiteles who produced tall figures such as the Hermes of Olympia. The *Apollo Belvedere* (Vatican) also dates from this time as do the great bronzes in the Athens Museum: the *Ephebe* from Antikythera and the *Athena* and *Artemis* in the archaeological museum in Piraeus.

Tanágra in Boeotia produced the famous funerary figurines in terracotta.

H Champollion/MICHELIN

Gold cup found in a tomb at Peristéria, Pylos

HELLENISTIC PERIOD (300-100 BC)

Sculpture began to be influenced by expressionism and orientalism. Realism, sometimes excessive, was used to express not only pain but also movement as in the *Laocoon* (Vatican) and the *Victory of Samothrace* (Louvre); at the same time it could produce the beautiful serenity of the *Melos Aphrodite (Venus de Milo)*. Artists took delight in representing old people and children, such as the bronze jockey from Artemision in the National Archaeological Museum, Athens.

PAINTING AND CERAMICS

Except for the Minoan frescoes in Crete or Thíra (Santorini) and the Hellenistic funerary paintings in Macedonia (*see VÉRIA*) few examples of Ancient Greek painting have survived. In fact, although painting played a major role in the decoration of sculptures and monuments, it was less important as an art form in its own right and the works of the great painters of the 4C BC – Zeuxis and above all Apelles, Alexander the Great's favourite artist – have not survived the passage of time. For a knowledge of Greek painting one must study the decoration of pottery on the many vases which have come down to us.

The ornamentation painted on vases is one of the major sources of information about Greek religion and civilisation.

These vases had specific functions: the *pithos* was used for storing grain, the *amphora* for the storing and transport of oil or wine. The *pelike*, *krater* and *hydria* were used as jars for oil, wine and water respectively. The *oinochoë* was used as a jug for pouring water or wine into a kantharos; the *kylix* was a drinking cup and the *rhyton* was a vessel shaped like

H Champollion/MICHELIN

Dionysos mosaic (Isthmian Sanctuary Museum, Corinth)

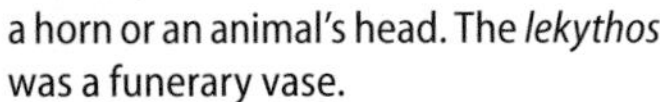

H Champollion/MICHELIN

Gold necklace, 510 BC (Archaeological Museum, Thessaloníki)

a horn or an animal's head. The *lekythos* was a funerary vase.

Styles developed in step with the great artistic periods; there were several types.

Creto-Mycenaean vases (1700-1400 BC): scenes of flora and fauna treated with great freedom and decorative sense.

Typical examples: octopus amphora; Phaistos krater (Herakleion Museum); Santorini vases (National Museum in Athens).

Archaic vases (1000-600 BC): geometric style in the Cyclades and Attica with large kraters or amphorae decorated with dotted lines, the key pattern, checks, lozenges and sometimes animals; orientalising style in Rhodes and Corinth where small vessels were decorated with oriental motifs: roses, lotus sprays, sphinxes and deer.

Typical examples: amphorae from the Kerameikos and the Dipylon (National Museum in Athens); perfume flasks (Corinth Museum).

Black-figure vases (600-480 BC): subjects for decoration drawn from mythology or history: silhouettes in black painted on a red ochre ground.

Typical examples: krater showing Herakles and Nereus (National Museum in Athens).

Red-figure vases (480-320 BC): subject for decoration not only mythological (so called 'severe' style – 5C BC) but also familiar and more light-hearted: scenes and figures drawn in detail and accentuated by a black or white ground (lekythoi).

Typical examples: krater from Kalyx and lekythoi from Erétria (National Museum in Athens).

Intellectual Pursuits

A new cultural age dawned with Homer's great epics; these were soon followed by Hesiod, then the great historians and tragedians of the 5C BC. At the same time, intellectuals were trying to understand the world, nature and humankind: physics, mathematics, medicine and philosophy all have their roots in Greece.

THE FIRST STORYTELLERS

Two poets are identified with the origins of Greek literature: **Homer** (late 9C to mid-8C BC), although there is little firm evidence of his existence and many believe his oeuvre to be the work of various authors, and the peasant poet **Hesiod** from Boeotia (late 8C BC), of whom more is known from the contents of his work.

Homer's two great epics are the *Iliad* and the *Odyssey*, which include some of the most famous characters of the Greek imagination. The *Iliad* does not simply recount the story of the Trojan War; it focuses on the anger of Achilles and how it jeopardises the whole of the Greek attack on Troy. Less warlike in tone, the *Odyssey* recounts a long journey during which the hero Ulysses has to overcome many dangers before returning home to his love. Both are tales of the struggles of man, but the gods play significant roles, siding with one party or another.

Hesiod recounts the origins of the gods and their conflicts in the *Theogony*; his other great poem, *Works and Days*, traces the origins of humankind and depicts a rustic ideal.

ORIGINS OF THE THEATRE

There is convincing evidence to suggest that Greek theatre derives from religious rituals associated with the cult of Dionysos, whose places of worship formed the backdrop for the first plays.

It was in Attica in the 5C BC that the theatre began to come into its own, with the appearance of the first purpose-built structures.

Malburet/MICHELIN

Aristotle (National Archaeological Museum, Athens)

The pioneer of Greek tragedy is believed to be Thespis (6C BC); three great names, however, were to dominate in the following century: **Aeschylus** (525-455 BC), whose life coincided with the rise to greatness of Athens, focused on the frailties of men and gods alike as his main theme; **Sophocles** (497-406 BC), who lived at the time of Athenian pre-eminence, dwelt upon the notion of humanity and the liberty of man; and **Euripides** (480-406 BC), who looked beyond a society dominated by deities, produced an oeuvre characterised by psychological and ideological issues.

In the field of comedy, **Aristophanes** (445-386 BC) was a wry observer of politics and society, who did not hesitate to

Cycladic Art and Idols

The brilliant civilisation that flourished at the end of the 3rd millennium BC in the Cyclades left behind a great deal of artistic evidence. This included painted and engraved ceramics, jewellery, elaborate weapons, but, above all, astonishing marble statuettes, the famous Cycladic idols, whose function remains shrouded in mystery. They mainly represent women, arms crossed over naked bodies, with oval, flat and perfectly smooth heads and only a nose protruding. Less common forms include musicians, flautists or harpists sitting cross-legged. These surprisingly modern art works, with their perfect proportions, bold curves and acute sense of stylisation, influenced many 20C artists, especially the Cubists.

combine vulgarity and farce with serious philosophical comment. In the late 4C BC, **Lysander** (342-293 BC) produced comical works which blended intrigue with sentimentality.

HISTORY

As tragedy was to treat the happenings of the past from a dramatic perspective, so history was to attempt to record bygone events factually. The pioneer historians of the 5C BC worked to transcribe the mythical past and bear witness for future generations.

Herodotus (mid-5C BC) is generally acknowledged to be the first historian. An avid traveller, he gathered vast amounts of information on his journeys for his work on the history of the Persian War. **Thucydides**, a few years younger than Herodotus, produced a history of the Peloponnesian War; this relied on analytical methods (notably eyewitness accounts) explained by the author at the beginning of the work, which have a remarkable modernity. In the 4C BC **Xenophon**, a pupil of Socrates, produced historical works which were narrative rather than analytical in style.

PHILOSOPHY

Tracing its origins to the outer limits of the 6C Hellenistic world, philosophy sought to explain the mysteries of the universe without resort to myth. The earliest philosophers were active at Miletus in Asia Minor: among them was *Thales*, who looked for general principles governing the cosmos.

It was with **Socrates** (470-399 BC) that philosophy began to make its mark; he endeavoured to lay bare the falsehoods distorting public opinion, refute the claims of politicians and reveal their ignorance. He left no written documentary evidence, but his pupil Plato (428-347 BC) ensured that his ideas would survive and thrive.

In his *35 Dialogues*, **Plato** used the same analytical methods as his teacher to denounce the violence, immorality, injustice and disorder prevalent at the time.

Aristotle (384-322 BC) was Plato's pupil but his pragmatic ideas represented a departure, drawing their inspiration from reality rather than abstract concepts. He distinguished between the different disciplines, identifying logic,

SCALA

Companions of Ulysses blind the Cyclops (Villa Giulia National Museum, Rome)

Alcibiades: portrait of an opportunist

Born into a great Athenian family, raised by Pericles, and a friend of Socrates, Alcibiades was handsome, rich, eloquent and intelligent. His flamboyance made him a magnet to women and men alike, he spent lavishly and dazzled all and sundry with the success of his racing stables. However, his escapades also earned him many enemies. Accused of irreverence to the gods, he fled to Sparta and betrayed Athens by revealing the city's weak points and sealing an alliance with Persia. However, kept at arm's length by the Spartans, Alcibiades betrayed them in turn, finally managing by way of intrigue, disavowals and clever speeches to return to Athens as a saviour. But he lost his credibility following the defeat of the Athenian fleet at the Battle of Notium (406 BC) and was removed from office. He eventually took refuge in Phrygia, where the Spartans had him assassinated.

The chorus

The various genres in Classical theatre were set pieces; the chorus, manifestation of the city, selected its members from the leisured classes of society, and was directed by a professional dramatist. The development of tragedy can be traced through the titles of works: collective names such as *The Persians*, *The Choephori* and *The Eumenides*, or more frequently, titles focusing on a principal character such as *Electra*, *Hercules* and *Iphegenia*. As time went on, Athens lost its splendour and this was reflected in the theatre: choruses shrank in size. In Aeschylus' time a chorus was just two people, and in the age of Sophocles three. By the time of Euripides, the chorus had disappeared altogether.

B Chabrol/MICHELIN

rhetoric, ethics, politics and physics in their own right.

Men like Thales and **Pythagoras** are seen as the fathers of mathematics, but their achievements also included discoveries in astronomy and physics. Other philosophers also made great discoveries, such as **Hippocrates** (c 460-377 BC), whose work in the field of medicine was to remain the backbone of the subject until the Middle Ages.

Numerous philosophical schools were active between the 4C and 2C BC: the Epicureans, the Stoics, the Cynics and the Sceptics. Philosophy's basic tenet, which was the nature of the individual, was in contrast to the traditional social structure of the city state and served to hasten its demise.

TWILIGHT OF HELLENISM

The intellectual life of Greece fascinated the Romans, who drew upon it for inspiration in many spheres. History became increasingly recognised and respected with the work of Polybius (c 207-130 BC), Diodorus and most notably **Plutarch** (46 BC-AD 125). Geography was developed as a subject by Strabo (64 BC-c AD 22), and subsequently Pausanias (2C AD), whose work includes the earliest travel guides. Finally, it is worth noting that the Evangelists spread the Christian gospel in the Greek language.

SCALA

Theatrical mask (National Archaeological Museum, Athens)

Literature and Language

Although the Greek language has been spoken without interruption through the ages, it has undergone changes to adapt to the times.

LINGUISTIC CHANGES

Throughout the Ottoman period, the patriarchate preserved a formal Greek speech which was used by the elite, while the majority of the population spoke various dialects. Dimitrios Katardzis (1730-1807) was the first public figure to propose a policy of teaching and promoting a correct form of the language to the general population. Subsequently **Adamántios Koraïs** (1748-1833) adopted a simple and sober form of the educated language (*katharévoussa*), enriched it and brought it up to date. This was used as the official language, appearing in administrative documents, the press, and in schools. The language used by the ordinary people, known as demotic, remained unchanged by these developments. After the Second World War, the socialist press began to print their newspapers in demotic Greek as a reaction against the bourgeois sentiments of other papers. In 1974, demotic Greek was recognised as the official language of the country, although certain official documents still employ the formal style. Thus the law followed the lead of the country's authors, who for many years had written their books in the language of the people.

S. Sauvignier/MICHELIN, Reproduced with permission. Librairie Desmos Paris

S Sauvignier/MICHELIN-reproduced with permission Librairie Desmos, Paris

A LITERARY RENAISSANCE

The Ionian School

In the Ionian Islands, the Greek uprising inspired the first neo-Hellenic poetry. Originally from Zakynthos, **Andréas Kálvos** (1792-1867) holds an important place in the history of Greek literature because of his publication of 20 odes in two volumes in Geneva and Paris in Greek and French: *La Lyre* (1824) and *Odes Nouvelles* (1826). The leader of this 'Ionian School' was another native of Zakynthos, **Dionysios Solomós** (1798-1857); he blended romantic feelings with Classical rigour. Part of his *Hymn to Liberty*, translated into English by Rudyard Kipling, is now the Greek national anthem.

The romanticism of the Athens School and contemporary movements

As Europe's intellectuals encouraged the Greek uprising, so Greece's authors drew upon foreign works for their inspiration: *The Prince of Morea* (1850) by Rangravis, for example, shows the influence of Sir Walter Scott. The unbridled romanticism of the **Athens School** is characterised by a reactionary chauvinism mixed with foreign influences from writers such as Musset and Byron.

The memoirs of **Yannis Makriyannis** (1797-1864), a peasant who took up arms to fight for liberation from the Ottomans, provide an insight into the realities of the struggle of ordinary people against the occupiers, and have an essential humanity untainted by preoccupation with stylistic issues.

Another important figure in 19C Greek literature is **Emmanuel Roidis** (1836-1904), author of *Pope Jean* (1866), a stylishly satirical work which defied the romantic status quo.

THE 1880 GENERATION

Poetry

As a reaction to the often mediocre realism of the Romantics, Symbolism became popular. A pioneer of the new style was **Ioánnis Papadiamantópoulos** (1856-1910), who wrote in the French language under the pseudonym **Jean Moréas**; a classic Symbolist poet/author, his themes were vanity, glory, solitude and old age. **Kóstas Palamás** (1859-1943), a leading light of the Athenian School, also adopted Symbolism. Other important names include **Koromikles Drossinis** (1859-1951), who loved myths and stressed the folklore element, and **Ángelos Sikelianós** (1884-1951), a lyrical poet-philosopher with a lively imagination.

On the margins of the symbolist movement was **Constantine Caváfy** (1863-1933), an educated though private man, who was born in Alexandria in 1863, spent seven years in England in his youth and returned to Alexandria in 1885. His widely translated verse reflects two worlds: contemporary Alexandria and Ancient Greece.

Prose

John Psichári (1854-1929), who lived in Paris for many years, contributed to the pre-eminence of the demotic language in Greek literature and also wrote several novels. The 1880 generation's prominence increased when they took over the review *Hestia*, and from 1881 Palamás and Drossinis were regular contributors. **Nikólaos Politis** (1852-1921) became the principal figure in this group; he specialised in folklore and made an important contribution to the evolution of modern Greek culture.

Geórgios Vizyinós (1849-96) was one of the first writers to launch out into new fields. Most of his themes are connected with Thrace, his birthplace, and with the study of contemporary manners. Initially he published collections of poetry (*My Mother's Sins* and other stories available in English).

Aléxandros Papadiamántis (1851-1911) was one of the great classical writers of Greek prose. His novels describe the humble and often tragic lives of fishermen and peasants in elegant but comprehensible language (*The Murderers* is translated into English).

Andréas Karkavitsas (1865-1922) was the author of several volumes of short stories, his best containing vivid descriptions of his period.

Constantinos Theotókis (1872-1923) was influenced by the great Russian novelists. He devoted himself to Greek politics. Most of his works, some of which appear in English, have a social orientation and some are very touching.

NEO-HELLENIC LITERATURE

Poetry

Geórgios Seféris (1900-71), influenced by Symbolism, expressed his anguish in confronting existence with poems imbued with an evocative power. He was awarded the Nobel Prize for literature in 1963. **Odysséus Elýtis** (1911-96) reveals through his surrealist poetry

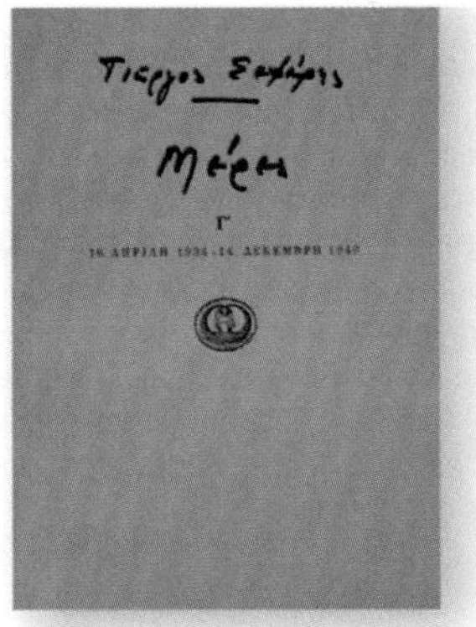

S Sauvignier/MICHELIN-reproduced with permission Librairie Desmos, Paris

the sacred feeling Greeks have for their natural environment: the land, the sea and above all the light. He was awarded the Nobel Prize in 1979. In his poems, **Iánnis Rítsos** (1909-90) blends the commonplace with the imaginary, invoking memory, exile and death.

Prose

Outstanding writers translated into English include **Strátis Mirivílis** (1892-1969), **Iánnis Skaribas** (1893-1984), who wrote several works including a bitter and amusing novel set in the 1930s, **Thanássis Petsalis-Diomidis** (1904-95), who deserves a place in Greek literature, **Ilias Venézis** (1904-73), an imaginative writer and a humanist, who expressed his thoughts in clear and elegant phrases, **Ángelos Terzákis** (1907-61), the author of several remarkable works, **Mihális Karagátsis** (1908-60), a born storyteller, endowed with a great creative imagination, which is reflected in his vast output of stories and novels, and **Níkos G Pentzikis** (1908-92), an exponent of the interior monologue, who believed in the power of speech. Finally, **Vassilis Vasilikos** (b 1934) deserves a mention; his screenplay for the film *Z* won a Palme d'Or at the Cannes film festival.

Mythology

Gods who mixed with men, watching over them, sharing their feelings, their sorrows as well as joys; such are the divinities who inhabited the Greek pantheon. This interweaving of mortal and immortal forms the inspiration for the religion of Ancient Greece.

What the modern world understands as Classical religion involved a series of rituals performed in specific locations or in private involving persons of status. These well-defined rites commemorated divinities or heroes whose exploits form a complex and remarkable web which we call **mythology**. Originally a purely oral tradition, this series of tales came to be recorded in writing, starting with Hesiod's *Theogony*.

The impiety of Socrates?

In Classical Greece, where religion was founded on practicality rather than dogma, the accusation of impiety was a serious one. Numerous philosophers suspected of questioning the accepted beliefs were banished and some, like Socrates, were condemned to death for having corrupted society's youth. The charges levelled at Plato's teacher stated that "Socrates is guilty of not believing in the deities in which the city believes, and of proposing new gods". In reality, it was fear of his philosophical teachings and their potential impact upon the State's political cohesion, rather than any spiritual considerations, which prompted his demise. As ever in Greece, behind the façade of religion lurked the machinations of politics.

ORIGINS

Unlike biblical tradition, which presupposes a god outside and above the world, the Greek creation myth involves a separation of primitive forces from which the gods were born.

From **Chaos**, a chasm of darkness, emerged **Gaia**, the earth, mother of all, and then Eros. To the Greeks, Chaos was neuter, Gaia feminine, and Eros masculine; between them, they constituted the three primitive forces. Also to emerge from Chaos were Erebe, total darkness, and Nyx, the night, who begat Ether, light, and Hemera, the day. Gaia then begat Ouranos, the sky, and Pontos, the oceans. Ouranos and Gaia went on to have numerous offspring, including Kronos and Rhea who were parents to the principal Olympian gods: **Zeus**, **Hera**, **Hestia**, **Demeter** and **Poseidon**. These divinities and other major gods and goddesses lived in majesty on Mount Olympos hidden in the clouds with Zeus the thunderer at their head. There was also a host of lesser divinities: local gods, Egyptian and Syrian gods, demi-gods born of the love affairs between the greater gods and mere mortals, and heroes; they all peopled an ever-growing pantheon where divinities from the Creto-Mycenaean period gradually became confused with the great gods whose cult was reduced to catering for special needs.

Religious celebrations took various forms depending on the purpose of the ceremony, which could be adjusted for individual circumstances and used for initiation. The complex **mysteries** which made use of symbolic objects such as representations of sexual organs were supposed to bring eternal salvation and ensure an afterlife; the most famous were performed at **Eleusis** (Elefsína). Another purpose of the ceremonies was to foretell future events, and so the faithful also came to consult the **oracles**, replies which the gods sent through the medium of the priests. The sanctuary of Apollo at **Delphi** (Delfí) is famous for the predictions made there by the **Pythia**. The rites could, of course, involve the whole community, and the most important ceremonies took place on the occasion of particular festivals. They were accompanied by activities which for us today have no connection with religion, such as poetry competitions or games and sporting events. The athletic and horse-riding competitions also had an aspect of initiation, since the winner (for example at the **Panhellenic Games** held annually at Olympia) received a

TAP

Poseidon (National Archaeological Museum, Athens)

The role of the Gods

(Latin names in brackets)

Name	*Sphere*	*Attributes*
Aphrodite *(Venus)*	Amorous love	Doves, shells
Apollo *(Apollo)*	Light, the arts	Lyre, arrows, laurel, sun
Ares *(Mars)*	War	Helmet, arms and armour
Artemis *(Diana)*	Chastity, hunting	Bow and quiver
Athena *(Minerva)*	Wisdom, arts and crafts	Shield, helmet, owl, olive branch
Demeter *(Ceres)*	Farming, motherly love	Ear of wheat, sceptre, scythe
Dionysos *(Bacchus)*	Wine, joy	Vine, thyrsus, goat, panther
Hades *(Pluto)*	Underworld	Throne, beard
Hephaïstos *(Vulcan)*	Fire, metal	Anvil, hammer
Hera *(Juno)*	Marriage (Zeus's wife)	Peacock, diadem
Hermes *(Mercury)*	Commerce, eloquence	Winged sandals and helmet, caduceus, ram
Hestia *(Vesta)*	Family hearth	Fire
Poseidon *(Neptune)*	Sea and storms	Trident
Zeus *(Jupiter)*	King of gods and the world	Eagle, sceptre, thunder

Athena (National Archaeological Museum, Athens)

sacred olive branch brought by **Herakles** (Hercules). The cult of **Dionysos** was accompanied by choruses, originally not written down, which are considered to have been the origin of all forms of theatre, whether tragedy, comedy or satire (the Satyrs were the companions of Dionysos). The prayers were usually accompanied by an offering: libations of milk or wine, and cakes and fruit placed before the altar. In return for a favour from the god a commemorative stele or a small votive statue would sometimes be promised. For a more important request animal sacrifice was used, part of which was burnt on the altar and the rest divided between the priests and the faithful. There were also purification rites with the purpose of cleansing the persons or objects considered impure by sprinkling them with water.
The temple *(hieron)*, dedicated to the god or goddess, stood within a sacred precinct *(témenos)* which was entered by a grand gateway *(propylaia)*. Purified with consecrated water, the worshippers entered the precinct and proceeded along the sacred way past the treasuries, small buildings for the reception of offerings, the semicircular bench seats *(exedra)* and the votive offerings (inscriptions, statues) which also surrounded the temple. The altar, where the libations were poured and the animals were sacrificed, stood in the open in front of the temple. After the sacrifice the people entered the temple vestibule to see the statue of the divinity through the open door of the inner chamber (*naos*).

Byzantine Orthodox Church

Actively involved in state politics, eastern Christianity evolved through numerous heresies and schism with Catholicism into Orthodoxy, strictly interpreting the teachings of the Gospels. Close to the ordinary people, it is ever present in the landscape through its countless churches and monasteries. Fundamental to the faith is the cult of images and relics; the domes of its churches have since the earliest times been decorated with beautiful mosaic work by anonymous artists seeking to glorify God.

HERESY, SCHISM AND RECONCILIATION

It is impossible to dissociate the Hellenisation of the Eastern Empire and its conversion to Christianity. Just as **Hellenism** was gaining ground, the Christian religion was spreading throughout the territory. In the early days of Christianity, its adherents were only united on a few articles of faith and worship. Its evolution was marked by the gradual growth of an internal hierarchy with the creation of bishops and archbishops. When in 380 Theodosius the Great made Christianity the official religion and outlawed pagan cults, his intention was to consolidate the temporal structure of the empire by insisting on its spiritual unity. But the distance between **Rome**, the religious capital and Constantinople, the political capital, made communication between the emperor and the head of the Church difficult. So **Constantinople** was raised to the status of metropolis, the same title as Rome, by a Council of 381, a decision confirmed and reinforced by the Council of Chalcedon in 451, which gave Constantinople primacy throughout the east. Although the link between the emperor and the patriarchate in Constantinople and the dependence of the one on the other was confirmed, the Church of Rome maintained its supremacy over ever more vast territories beyond the control of the eastern emperor and insisted ever more firmly on its divine right to rule, inherited from its first bishop, St Peter.

Differences of interpretation between the two Churches also came to the surface. In addition, numerous heretical sects were popular: **Arianism** followed the tenets laid down by the early-4C Alexandrian bishop Arius (Christ's divinity was secondary to that of God); the **Nestorians** adhered to the teachings of the 5C bishop Nestorius (Christ was simply a man, not God made man); the **Monophysites** (5C-6C), on the other hand, emphasised Christ's divinity rather than humanity. All these sects were condemned at the Council of Ephesus in 431, and again at the Council of Chalcedon 20 years later, but their influence remained strong in some regions of the empire. More important was the issue of **iconoclasm**, promoted by Emperor Leo III from 726 with the aim of bringing the eastern peoples back into the Orthodox fold; this required the destruction of all images (icons and other representations of the godhead). The long internal conflict resulting from this prohibition also aggravated the divisions between the eastern and western churches. Iconoclasm was finally abandoned in 843, and icons have remained a prominent feature of Orthodox worship to this day.

In the temporal sphere, the crowning of Charlemagne as emperor of the west by the Pope in 800 made him a usurper in the eyes of the Byzantines, who regarded their emperor as the sole legitimate heir to the Roman Empire. In the religious field the main subject of dispute was the Filioque issue (the use in prayer of the doctrine that the Holy Ghost proceeds from the Father and the Son). Despite many attempts to restore unity, a gulf gradually opened up between east and west, between Orthodoxy and Roman Catholicism. The final break came in 1054 when the Patriarch of Constantinople, Michael Cerularius, and Pope Leo IX excommunicated one another.

SCALA

Emperor Constantine

The Crusades brought to Greece Roman Catholic monks, especially **Cistercians**, whose task it was to work towards oecumenism ('union'). At the same time, the critical situation in which the empire found itself meant it had to seek a rapprochement with Rome, already indispensable in view of the capture of Constantinople by the **Crusaders** in 1204. The plan was to take on more concrete form with the **Council of Lyon**

J.-P. Neil/MICHELIN

(1274), held by Pope Gregory X in the presence of the Latin Emperor Baldwin II de Courtenay and the Byzantine Emperor Michael VIII Paleologos, who accepted the conditions laid down by Rome. The plan failed because of the opposition of the populations involved.
A second attempt to achieve oecumenism in Greece was made in 1438 at the **Council of Florence**, which brought together Pope Eugenius IV, the Emperor John VIII Paleologos, Cardinal Bessarion and the philosopher Gemistos Plethon. After agreement had been reached on the Filioque clause, the condition of dead souls, the primacy of the Pope and the freedom of liturgical practices, the act of union was signed by the majority of the Orthodox priests present, but this propitious project was wrecked by the Turkish invasion of Greece in 1461.

MONASTIC PRESTIGE

The strictly hierarchical eastern clergy had at its head the patriarch, chosen by the emperor from a list of three candidates put forward by the Synod, composed of senior clergy drawn from the aristocracy. The position was as important as that of any of the great offices of State. At the other extreme, the local clergy, usually peasant-priests, performed an administrative role in the villages of the empire. Their role was more functional than spiritual. The ordinary population, whose zeal focused on images and relics, looked to the monastic communities for religious guidance.
The earliest monks were hermits who sought out the isolation of desert life. It was St Pacomas who developed a new means of withdrawal from society by bringing together communities of monks to live in monasteries. Geographically, visually and spiritually, monasticism came to occupy centre stage in Greek life. The monk was cast in the role of holy man, whose wisdom was in demand as much for practical advice as for religious guidance. Unsurprisingly, the tombs of exceptional examples of such figures became local sites of pilgrimage, often marked by the construction of a church or monastery. Every

SCALA

Virgin and child (Benáki Museum, Athens)

detail of their lives was perpetuated through oral tradition, thereby creating characters of legendary status, and their relics were invested with miraculous powers.
As with icons, relics were perceived to be sacred and became objects of unparalleled veneration. Around such items grew up cult places of worship which made the monasteries rich, incurring the resentment of the temporal authorities who realised, however, that relics, unlike icons, could not be banned.

CHURCH DOMES AND THE APOGEE OF MOSAICS

The confluence of Roman civilisation and the traditions of Asia Minor give rise to a distinctive Byzantine style most clearly expressed in religious architecture. Certain features are ubiquitous, such as the centralised plan and the dome decorated to resemble the heavens (the ability to construct domes on rectangular structures was the great architectural triumph of the age).
Inheriting the layout of Classical buildings, early Christian churches (5C-6C) were preceded by an atrium. The design was either a basilica (a nave and two aisles), or on a Greek cross layout, with an imposing dome at the centre and galleries for women worshippers. Only the ruins of such churches remain

in Greece (at Philippi, Lechaion in Corinth, and Thessaloníki).

A second golden age of architecture (9C-12C) saw the construction of many more churches, often small in scale but of perfect proportions, built to a cross-in-square design, most striking when viewed from the exterior. These buildings, usually entered through a narthex, have domes resting on drums to give them greater height, and are decorated with low-relief carvings, marble and mosaic work. Fine examples may be seen at Daphne, Óssios Loukás in Boeotia, Néa Moní on Chios and Agía Sophía in Monemvassía.

Renaissance under the Palaeologues (13C-16C)

More elaborate schemes combining basilica and Greek cross characteristics, multiple domes and increased fresco decoration were the features of this period, as can be seen in the churches of Thessaloníki (Holy Apostles, St Catherine's), Árta, Kastoriá and Mystra.

Churches were ornately decorated with polychrome marble pavements, frescoes (13C onwards), and mosaics which used gold and warm colours to capture the imagination of the viewer. The subject matter was strictly defined by religious dogma: in the dome, Christ Pantocrator (the Creator) surrounded by archangels, Apostles and Evangelists; the Virgin Theotokos (Mother of God) or Galactophroussa (Suckling the Christ Child) between the archangels Michael and Gabriel in the apse; scenes from the life of Christ or the Virgin, usually following the sequence of feast days rather than chronological order. Some of the finest Byzantine mosaics may be observed in the monasteries of Daphne, Néa Moní on Chios and Óssios Loukás.

Alongside these dazzling works of art, the tradition of **icon** painting and its significance to the eastern Christian tradition must be considered. Painted on wood, these images are displayed in churches on the iconostasis, the screen dividing the nave from the sanctuary, but are equally common in private homes. Objects of veneration once accused of bordering on the idolatrous, their purpose was confirmed by the Council of

Phototravellers/MICHELIN

Interior of Ágios Georgios church, Lakki, Crete

Nicea in 787 ("God the Son is the living icon of God the Father").

Among the commonest subjects of icon painting are the Hetoimasia, depicting an empty throne from which God will oversee the Last Judgement, the descent of Christ into Limbo, the Dormition of the Virgin, and the three angels dining at Abraham's table. The archangels Michael and Gabriel are often depicted at the head of celestial armies; the most venerated saints are the hierarchs or Doctors of the Church, namely John Chrysostom, Basil and Gregory of Nazianzus. Other popular saints include John the Baptist (known as Prodomos, the forerunner), George (depicted slaying the dragon), Andrew of Patras, Demetrios of Thessaloníki, Michael, Nicholas, Athanasios, Cyril and Pantaleon, the two Theodores, Cosmas and Damian, and Pantaleon and Hermolaos who were known as the 'penniless saints' as they practised medicine without charging fees.

Art and Cinema

Contemporary Greek culture has had only limited impact abroad. Although certain actors and directors have become international names, Greek film remains firmly on the art-cinema circuit rather than in the mainstream.

AN ARTISTIC TRADITION OPEN TO MANY INFLUENCES

The accession to the throne of Otto of Bavaria in 1832 heralded the arrival of foreign artists who taught at the College of Fine Arts, founded in 1843. They influenced numerous Greek artists; other Greek painters studied abroad, notably in Munich, where **Nikifóros Lítras** (1832-1904), who concentrated on painting scenes from daily life and portraiture, spent time. Another famous name in Greek painting of this period was **Konstandínos Volonákis** (1839-1907), who made his name as a marine artist, although his *Munich Circus* exhibited at the National Gallery in Athens shows a move towards Impressionism. In all spheres of art, the second half of the 19C in Greece bore the stamp of officially approved academicism.

At the turn of the century art in Greece underwent an important evolution under the influence, in painting, of **Konstandínos Parthénis** (1878-1967), who followed the path of Impressionism and Fauvism and taught at the College of Fine Arts, and of the sculptor **Konstandínos Dimitriádis** (1881-1943), who was inspired by Rodin. They opened the way for Greek art to embrace modern forms and the most advanced movements of the time, as seen in the work of the expressionist painter **Giórgos Bouziáni** (1885-1959), cubist **Níkos Gíka** (1906-94), and surrealist **Níkos Engonópoulos** (1910-85).

After the Second World War, Greek art flourished again, following two principal directions. Together with the search for a true Greek spirit, of which the main exponent was **Iánnis Morális** (b 1916), there developed a strong movement concerned with contemporary forms. Its most notable members were the abstract painters **Aléxandros Kontópoulos** (1905-75), **Krístos Lefákis** (1906-68) and **Iánnis Spyrópoulos** (1912-90), and the sculptors **Giórgos Zogolópoulos** and **Akilleús Apérgis**. Although on the one hand there is a clear return to representative art, notably with the painter **Iánnis Gaitis** (1923-84) and the sculptor **Giórgos Giorgiádis**, those Greek artists working in a contemporary vein are ever more closely linked with the various Western artistic movements, many of them working abroad.

In addition to figures such as **George Candilis** (1913-1995), the architect who designed the urban development at Toulouse-le-Murail and also worked in Berlin, and **Mario Prassinos** (1916-1985), well known for his pointillist works in

Océan Films

Eternity and a Day, 1998

The legendary couple of Greek cinema

Jules Dassin was born in 1911 in the USA; he began his career in New York and in barely three years achieved fame with four major films: *Brute Force* (1947), *The Naked City* (1948), *Night and the City* (1949), and *Thieves' Highway* (1950). After making *Riffi* (1955), a thriller set in Paris, he met Melina Mercouri and made her an international star with roles in *Never on Sunday* (1960); they married in 1960.

Born in 1923, Melina Mercouri began her career in theatre, then appeared in Kakoiánnis's film *Stella* (1954). Her reputation was established with roles in *Phaedra* (1962), *Topkapi* (1964), *Promise at Dawn* (1971) and *A Dream of Passion* (1977), all by Jules Dassin. She was also a popular singer, before becoming involved in politics as an ardent opponent of the regime of the Colonels. This forced her into exile for a time, but she returned to become Minister of Culture in the subsequent Socialist administrations between 1981 and 1989 and again from 1993 until her death in New York a year later. The couple acquired legendary status among young Greeks, who were captivated by her beauty and courage, and by his charm.

black and white and the cartoons he produced for the Aubusson weavers, two names have gained international recognition. **Iánnis Kounellis** (b 1936) lives and works in Italy, where he has been active in the **Arte Povera** movement; after offering performances and installations, he has taken a more minimalist line which purports to be close to poetry in its original form. Panayótis Vassilákis, known as **Takis** (b 1925), has been living in Paris since 1954. His name is associated with technology in art, with his research into magnetism using constructions of metal rods, indicator lights and electromagnets, and making musical clocks.

FAMOUS NAMES

The theme of many of the films made between 1946 and 1949 was wartime resistance, but as they were divorced from their social context they lack objective comment. There were also several comedies, the most daring being *The Germans are Back* by **Alekos Sakellarios**, which pleaded for national unity at a time when the government was actively anti-Communist. The scenario used the return of the Germans to promote reconciliation among the divided Greeks.

The dominant influence during the 1950s was **Italian neo-realism**. In 1953 **Mihális Kakoiánnis** made *Sunday Awakening*, a neo-realist comedy, the first of many remarkable films including *Stella* (1955), *Electra* (1961), *Zorba the Greek* (1964), *The Trojans* (1971), and *Iphigenia* (1977). Around the same time *Magic City* and *Serial Killer* (1956) appeared, masterpieces by the Cretan film-maker **Níkos Koúndouros**.

In the 1970s Greek cinema reflected a social and political approach. **Theo Angelópoulos** produced a historical trilogy covering 1936 to 1977, followed by *Alexander the Great* (1980) which won awards in Venice, *Voyage to Kythera* (1984), which won the prize for best scenario at the Cannes Festival in 1984, *The Bee-keeper* (1986) and *Foggy Landscape* (1988), which won nine international prizes. More recently he made *The Glance of Odysseus* (1995), for which he won the Grand Prix at the Cannes festival. He was awarded the Palme d'Or in 1998 for *Eternity and a Day*, a deeply moving meditation on the passage of time, opportunities missed and vanished hopes.

Arts and Traditions

For centuries the political situation in Greece ensured that a large number of traditions and practices with roots going back to Ancient Greece were preserved, but rural folk traditions have now almost entirely disappeared because of the combined effect of modernisation of agriculture and the revolution in means of communication, which has brought the villages out of isolation.

CRAFTS

During the last decade a craft revival has been promoted by government organisations and private associations. Schools and workshops have been set up throughout the country and about 100 workshops produce **carpets** in beautiful designs, reviving the making of *flokáti* from shaggy wool, which was formerly widespread in Thessaly. In the country practically all households had a loom in the past and **weaving** is still a common pursuit. The methods, materials (wool, silk or cotton) and designs (floral or geometrical) vary from region to region; bags, cushions and bedspreads are the most common articles produced.

Embroidery, which enhances garments, curtains and bed valences, is highly decorative and red is usually the dominant colour; the floral designs denote the oriental influence of Greeks from Asia Minor; in Epirus, Skíros and Crete, scenes from everyday life are also included. Weavers and lacemakers are often seen at work on their doorstep. **Ceramics** remain a male preserve except for decoration. Huge jars made in Crete, Attica and the western Peloponnese that were used in the past to store oil or cereals now serve as garden ornaments. The richly decorated glazed pottery found in the eastern Aegean Islands and Rhodes recalls the influence on Greek art of Asia Minor. Skíros has beautiful decorative plates; Aigina and Siphnos have produced high-quality pottery for centuries.

Wood carving remains a special tradition in Epirus, Skíros, Thessaly and Crete (pews, iconostasis, wedding chests). Votive offerings and painted shop signs are popular forms of naïve art.

TRADITIONAL DRESS

Traditional dress is hardly worn except for patronal festivals or feasts of the Virgin (processions), at weddings, during the carnival or, in a simpler form, on market day. The women are resplendent in embroidery and chased ornaments chiefly displayed on their bodices and skirts. A few men still wear the heavy pleated **kilt** *(foustanélla)*, which

M Guillochon/MICHELIN

Traditional dress (Nauplion Folk Museum)

is the uniform of the soldiers *(évzoni)* of the Guard, as well as the **pompom shoes** *(tsaroúhia)*. Local costumes are most common at Métsovo in Epirus, on Leukas, in the northern Sporades, in the Peloponnese, on Kárpathos and Astipálea in the Dodecanese and also in Crete; women spinning are often to be seen in the country districts. Costumes are also displayed in the museums of traditional art such as those of Nauplion, Thessaloníki, Chios and Athens.

MUSIC AND DANCE

Popular music is played at festivals and other ceremonies (weddings and funerals), in the cafés and squares. On these occasions the traditional instruments are used: the **bouzoúki**, a sort of lute with a very long neck, three or four pairs of strings, and a shrill tone imported from Asia Minor, the **baglamás**, which is a small bouzoúki, the **Cretan lyre** (*lyra*), a three-stringed viol played with a bow, the **sandoúri**, which is played by striking its steel strings with small hammers, and the **Epirot clarinet**. There are also

B Chabrol/MICHELIN

Musicians celebrating the Feast of the Assumption, Amorgós

various rustic wind instruments, such as the **floiéra**, a transverse flute from Epirus, the **dzamára**, a straight pipe, and the **pipiza**, a kind of high-pitched oboe.

These instruments accompany singers, whose plaintive style owes much to oriental music: the **kléftikos** attributed to the **klephts** in the War of Independence and the famous **rebétika** dramatic accounts of the terrible conditions in the urban slums or the search for an impossible love. The greatest exponent of rebétika was **Vassilis Tsitsanis** (1915-84), who succeeded in transcribing them in a very pure form.

After 1945 Greek music was radically changed. Composers turned to the traditional forms for rhythm and melody and began to take an interest in rebétika. The leading lights in this musical renewal, who had different techniques but both exhibited the same attachment to popular Greek music, were **Mános Hatzidákis** (1925-94) – romantic, lyrical and elegant *(5 laîkos zografies, O megálos eroticós, I epochi tis Melissanthis)* – and **Míkis Theodorákis**, with his passion for social problems (*Axion Esti*, a setting of extensive extracts from the verse work of this name by **Odysséas Elítis**, Romiosini, Canto General, film music for *Zorba the Greek* and *Z*).

In mentioning this folk-inspired music, we must not forget that several composers working in a more experimental vein also did much to put Greek music on the map, notably **Níkos Skalkóttas** (1904-49) and **Ioánnis Xenákis** (b 1922).

Some dances are of oriental origin such as the *zembétiko*, improvised by a man on his own, or the *hassápiko*, the butchers' dance, performed by men who lay their hands on one another's shoulders. Others such as the Cretan *pendozáli* imitate war; a clarinet accompanies the *mirológia*, funeral dances and dirges, often improvised and danced in turn to the point of exhaustion by the women taking part in the wake (Máni and Crete). The national dance, *kalamatianós*, is danced in a ring and recalls the sacrifice of the Souliot women. The lively *sirtáki* devised for the film *Zorba the Greek* is aimed more at tourists (its name was even invented outside Greece); it was based on the *hassápiko*. The list would not be complete without the *anastenária*, a dance with a constantly accelerating rhythm performed in Macedonia and Thrace in May on St Constantine's Day, in which the dancers achieve a trance-like state.

THE COUNTRY TODAY

Travellers to Greece expect to discover and enjoy the country's intriguing traces of past civilisations. In doing so, they encounter the Greeks of today, a warm and welcoming people who are remarkably friendly and open to visitors. Who are they, the Greeks of today, and how do they live? Answers lie not just in the past, but in the present: in Greek music, crafts and popular arts, and in the delectable Greek cuisine.

Population

Today's Greece, with a population of about 11 million, comprises nine administrative regions made up of 53 districts or *nomi*; some of these are vast and almost void of people, others cover a tiny area but are crammed with inhabitants. The Athens metropolitan area, composed of the two *nomi* of Athens and Piraeus, continues to extend its sprawl and is now home to around a third of all Greek citizens; Thessaloníki in Macedonia has a population of 700 000. At the other extreme, an exodus from agriculture means that the mountain areas and some of the islands now have less than 10 inhabitants per km^2.

R Mattes/MICHELIN

Economy

Greece remains a predominantly rural country, especially in Boeotia, Macedonia, Thessaly and Thrace. Farms are generally small (except in the north); the main crops are olives, citrus fruits, maize, cotton, sugar beet, barley and rice. Agriculture and associated activities employ around 20% of the workforce; half this number work directly in farming.
Greece has several hydroelectric and thermal power schemes. There is an active bauxite mining industry around Mount Parnassos (the raw material is used to make aluminium); the building sector is also significant to the economy.
The nation's two greatest sources of income are merchant shipping and tourism. Greek shipping is world class, with over 3 200 vessels registered. The tourist industry, evident everywhere across the country, accounts for 17% of GDP. With nearly 20 million visitors a year (2006), Greece has more tourists than inhabitants. The excellent weather, warm sea, beautiful countryside and countless historic sites account for this success.
Greece joined the European Union in 1981 and is part of the European single currency area or 'Eurozone' (*see Notes and Coins*). The organisation of the Olympic Games held in 2004 has led to substantial modernisation of the country's infrastructure, with aid from the European Union.

Food and Drink

The Greek soil seems to have been blessed by the gods, who since Antiquity have ensured a plentiful supply of grapes for wine, olives for oil, goat's and sheep's milk for cheese. The influence of the Venetian occupation can still

Phototravellers/MICHELIN

be tasted in the cuisine of the Ionian Islands, while the flavours of the Ottoman Empire remain in the sweet pastries and the use of spices. The island of Crete in particular is renowned for its supremely healthy dishes.

DISHES

Greek cuisine is simple but full of flavour. The main elements are Mediterranean: olive oil, tomatoes, lemons, herbs and aromatic spices (oregano, mint, sesame). The pastries and cakes, which are very sweet and flavoured with honey and cinnamon, evoke the Orient. Authentic but inexpensive Greek dishes are to be found in the tavernas and some more modest restaurants *(estiatório)* in the towns and the country.

A favourite aperitif and the national drink is a colourless aniseed spirit *(ouzo)*, served in tiny glasses accompanied by a glass of water or diluted in a glass of water which turns cloudy.

Aperitifs are usually accompanied by *mezédes* or *meze*. These include vine leaves stuffed with meat and rice *(dolmádes)*, spit-roasted offal sausages *(kokorétsi)*, aubergine purée with black olives *(melidzanosaláta)*, yoghurt with chopped cucumber and garlic *(tzatzíki)*, purée of fish roe and breadcrumbs or potatoes *(taramosaláta)*, rice with tomatoes *(piláfi)*, stuffed tomatoes, peppers and aubergines *(gemistá)*.

When in season, melons and watermelons are popular starters, as is the famous Greek salad, which contains tomatoes, cucumbers, feta cheese, onions and olives, all generously doused in olive oil.

L Campion/MICHELIN

Octopus being dried

Main courses are usually selected from a board or direct from the kitchen. If you want your dishes to arrive in sequence rather than all at once, it is best to specify this. On the coast, fish dishes are weighed prior to cooking and sold at cost per pound. It is sadly not uncommon now for frozen fish to be used; this should be described as such *(katepsigmenos)* on the menu. The staple seafood dishes include prawns *(garídes)*, swordfish *(ksifías)*, squid *(kalamári)*, octopus *(oktapódia)*, and sardines *(sardéles)*.

The food resources of mainland Greece are ample: in Thessaly and the Pelopon-

The perfect moussaka

Serves 6

Ingredients: 1kg aubergines (eggplants), 1 large onion, 2 cloves of garlic, 400g minced lamb, 1 glass of white wine, 4 tomatoes, 1 bunch of parsley, olive oil, butter, salt, pepper, a little flour, grated cheese.

Slice the aubergines into long thin slices and flavour them with salt and pepper; leave for 1 hour. Soften the chopped onion and garlic in butter before adding the minced lamb and 4 tablespoons of water. Cook for 5 minutes on a low heat, stirring regularly. Add the chopped and peeled tomatoes, parsley and wine, and flavour with salt and pepper. Cover and simmer for 15 minutes. Sprinkle the aubergines with flour, then fry lightly in olive oil before draining on paper towels. Line a greased dish with half the aubergines, then add the meat and tomato mixture before covering with the remaining aubergines. Sprinkle with grated cheese before placing in a pre-heated oven at 180°C / 350°F until golden.

nese there are countless orchards and farms producing tomatoes, aubergines, pistachios, chestnuts and olives. Pelion is renowned for its meat and especially game sausages. Against this backdrop, it is easy to forget that Greece is essentially a frugal country. Dishes are predominantly seasonal, and meat can be roasted, grilled or fried. Vegetable dishes are often stuffed or fried.

The Greeks eat a lot of cheese. The best known is goat's or sheep's milk cheese *(féta)* which may be served with olive oil and olives; also popular is a sort of Gruyère *(graviéra)* and a mild cheese similar to Cheddar *(kasséri)*.

Desserts tend to be eaten separately, often as a mid-afternoon snack. These include millefeuilles with walnuts or almonds and cinnamon *(baklavá)*; rolls of thread-like pastry with honey and walnuts or almonds *(kadaïfi)*; mini doughnuts with honey and sesame or cinnamon *(loukoumádes)*; flaky pastry turnover with cream and cinnamon *(bougátsa)*; almond or sesame paste *(halva)*.

WINES AND SPIRITS

With its dry, warm climate and limestone or volcanic soil Greece is an excellent country for producing wine; the main wine regions are the northern Peloponnese, Attica, Crete, Rhodes and Sámos. Twenty-six regions now have recognised status as winemaking districts. Elsewhere matters are less strictly controlled, and the wine is sold under the name of the grower or a cooperative. The best-known Greek wine is probably *retsina*, a white wine to which pine resin has been added as a preservative; served chilled as it usually is, it is very refreshing without being heavy.

Among the unresinated wines *(aretsínato)*, some have earned a particular reputation: the full-bodied reds from Náoussa in Macedonia, the fruity reds from Neméa in the Argolid, the scented rosé from Aráhova near Delphi, the well-rounded dry white wines of Hymettos and Palíni in Attica, the sparkling dry white wine of Zítsa in Epirus, the white wines of Chalcidice, which preserve their quality well, and the popular white wines of Achaia (Demestica, Santa Laura, Santa Helena).

In the islands there are the generous reds and rosés from Crete, dry whites from Lindos in Rhodes, the heady and scented wines from the Cyclades, particularly Náxos and Santorini, and from the Ionian Islands: Zakynthos (Verdéa, Delizia), Cephallonia (Róbola, fruity and musky) and Leukas (Santa Maura).

Greek coffee is always drunk with a glass of water. It has a strong aromatic flavour.

Samian wine can be drunk as a liqueur; **Métaxas** is the brand name of Greek brandy. Cretan *rakí* is a fruit brandy, and *mastíka* a sweet liqueur flavoured with mastic gum.

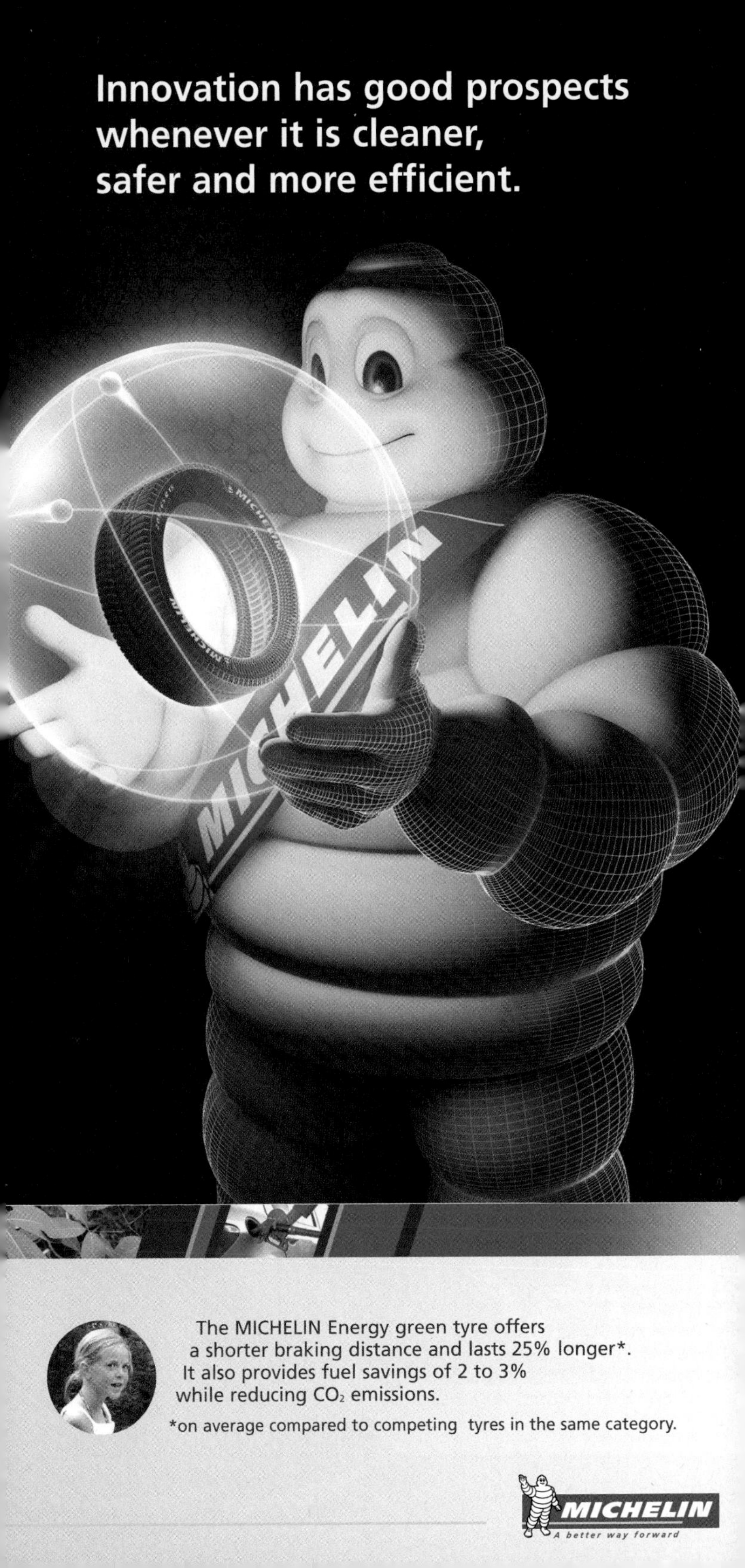

Theatre ruins, Dodona, near Ioánnina

R. Mattes/MICHELIN

ÁGIO ÓROS★★★

MOUNT ATHOS – Αγιο Οροζ

POPULATION 2 262

Mount Athos (the Holy Mountain) is covered with forests (oaks, chestnuts and pines) culminating at the southern tip in Mount Athos, 2 033m/6 670ft high. Since the 9C the peninsula has been a centre of Orthodox monasticism. This forbidding place has many treasures, but opens its doors to few travellers.

- **Orient Yourself:** The mountain lies 36km/85mi southeast of Thessaloníki, 161km/101mi south of Kavála, on the easternmost peninsula of Chalcidice.
- **Don't Miss:** The monastery of Megistis Lavras and its superb treasury.
- **Organizing Your Time:** One-day boat tours around the Holy Mountain are available for those barred from visiting the mountain itself (*see Address Book*).
- **Also See:** Halkidikí

Address Book

For coin categories, see the Legend on the cover flap.

ACCESS

Mount Athos is closed to tourists and women. Only visitors able to demonstrate religious or academic motives are allowed; the minimum age for applicants is 21. Contact the **Pilgrim Office of Holy Mount Athos**, *9 Odós Engnatia, Thessaliníki;* ☎ *(031) 861 611*. The daily limit for permits is 10 for foreigners so book well in advance; religious holidays are best avoided altogether. Once a permit is secured, book accommodation at the monastery where you wish to stay. Keep the acknowledgement of your reservation to show at the office in Ouranópoli, where you collect the entry permit (25€) which allows stays of up to 4 days. Access is by boat from Ouranópoli at 9am to Dáfni.

Boat excursions skirt the coast of Mount Athos; **passengers must be appropriately dressed**.

During the season these excursions leave from Ouranópoli, Órmos Panagías on the Sithonía peninsula, and Thássos.

WHERE TO EAT

Karidas – *Ouranópoli* – ☎ *(23770) 71 180*. A taverna on the harbour offering a wide selection of reasonably priced fish dishes.

WHERE TO STAY

Akrogiali – *Ouranópoli, 100m/110yd from the bus stop, on the left by the sea* – ☎ *(23770) 71 201 – 18rm*. Comfortable rooms if a little monastic; ideal if preparing for life on Mount Athos. Some rooms with sea view. No breakfast.

Makedonia – *Ouranópoli, take the second street on the left after the Akrogiali (same management)* – ☎ *(23770) 71 085, fax (23770) 71 395 – 18rm*. A comfortable, quiet hotel 100m from the sea.

Xenios Zeys – *Ouranópoli, in the main street on the sea side* – ☎ *(23770) 71 274, fax (23770) 71 185 – 20rm*. This small hotel represents good value for money. Ask for a room with a sea view. Breakfast extra.

Xenia – *outskirts of the village* – ☎ *(23770) 71 412, fax (23770) 71 362 – 20rm*. A very pleasant, quiet and comfortable hotel with its own beach. The service is good, but prices are high (although heavily discounted out of season). Breakfast is included and half-board is available.

WHAT TO BUY

Icons – painted by the monks, these icons can be bought in Ouranópoli and Kariés.

A Bit of History

The first community *(lávra)* of monks dates from AD 963 when **St Athanasius of Trebizond** was encouraged by the Emperor Nikephoros Phocas to found the monastery of the Grand Lavra. Other communities were established from the 13C onwards, and by the 16C there were 30 000 monks in about 30 monasteries.
Today there are around 1 472 monks in about 20 monasteries; the majority are Greek. Since the 10C, Mount Athos has existed as a kind of Orthodox monastic republic, the capital of which is Kariés.
The major monasteries were usually arranged round a courtyard and fortified with towers. The walls of the churches and refectories are decorated with frescoes; the most beautiful were painted by artists such as M Panselinos (14C), Theophanes the Cretan, Zorzio and Frango Kastellanos (16C). The libraries, which are often housed in the keep, contain upwards of 10 000 ancient manuscripts.

Sights

The monasteries mentioned here are the most famous or the most easily visited. They all close at sunset.

Símonos Pétras

The lofty 14C monastery with its row upon row of wooden balconies occupies a spectacular site on the western face of the mountain. Founded by St Simon (13C), it was extended in the 14C by a Serbian prince, and was extensively restored in the 19C.

Ágiou Dionissíou

This monastery (16C) was founded on a rocky site overlooking an inlet on the west coast. The church and refectory are decorated with remarkable frescoes dating from the 16C by Zorzio the Cretan and from the 17C. The library contains a 7C crypt.

Megístis Lávras

The oldest (AD 963) and the largest (around 100 monks) of the monasteries on the Holy Mountain is situated near the end of the peninsula.
Athanasius, the founder, is buried in the 10C-11C church beneath the huge dome. The refectory walls are covered with **frescoes**, also 16C, by Theophanes the Cretan. The **library** contains 5 000 volumes. The monastery's treasury includes rare and precious pieces including the crown and robes of the Emperor Nikephoros Phocas.

H Champollion/MICHELIN

Dochariou Monastery

Ivíron

This 10C monastery, which was originally dedicated to St John the Baptist, is hidden in a hanging valley overlooking the sea and surrounded by olive and pine trees. The church is 11C; a chapel contains the miraculous icon of the Mother of God of the Gate (Panagía Portaítissa) (10C). The library possesses many illuminated manuscripts (11C to 13C), and the **treasury** is among the finest on Mount Athos.

Vatopedíou

This huge monastery was established in 980, and was fortified early in the 15C. The 15C bronze entrance doors came from Agía Sophía in Thessaloníki; the mosaic is a remarkable piece of 11C work. The treasury boasts some rare gold reliquaries and a 15C jasper cup on an enamelled silver base. The library is well stocked with ancient manuscripts including a 12C copy of Ptolemy's *Geography*.

B Kaufmann/MICHELIN

Fresco, Vatopedíou Monastery

AIGIO

Αιγιο

POPULATION 21 255

This pleasant resort on the south bank of the Gulf of Corinth, makes a good base from which to visit the spectacular Vouraïkós Gorge.Aigio is located 39km/26mi east of Patras and 103km/64mi west of Corinth. Nowadays the town's activity mainly centres around the port, which is linked to Ágios Nikólaos on the opposite side of the gulf by a daily ferry service.

Visit

While in the village, stop by the **Archaeological Museum** (*open Tue-Sun 8.30am-3pm (Wed until 9pm in winter, 11pm in summer); ☎ (26910) 215 17)* to see objects excavated from digs in the region are pleasingly displayed in chronological order. Note especially the handsome terracotta vases, tools and jewelry. Also worth a stop is the **Museum of Folklore and History** (*☎ (26910) 621 06/233 77)* where objects of daily life offer glimpses of days gone by.

Vouraïkoú★★

The gorge can be reached either by train from Diakoftó to the southeast of Aigio, or by a scenic road from Trapeza (19km/12mi southeast of Aigio) which leads to Kalávrita (30km/19mi).

From the heights of Mount Aroánia, which rises to 2 340m/7 677ft, the River Vouraïkós flows down into the Corinthian Gulf some 50km/30mi to the north. Along the way it has worn a deep channel through the limestone rock, creating a fantastic gorge. The Decauville **narrow-gauge railway**, which was built late in the last century between **Diakoftó** on the coast and **Kalávrita**, is a particularly bold feat of engineering. It runs for 22km/nearly 14mi along a vertiginous route, through tunnels, along overhangs, across bridges and viaducts and on a rack in certain sections where the incline is steeper than 7%. Since 1962 diesel engines have replaced the old steam locomotives.

On leaving Diakoftó station the train crosses the foothills of Aroánia, passing through vineyards and orchards before entering the gorge between high sheer cliffs which are riddled with caves. The railway line crosses from one side to the other high above the racing torrent.

Zahloroú *(26km/16mi from Diakoftó)* lies on a natural terrace overlooking a narrow basin. The charming little station is half hidden in the trees between the rock face and the stream *(tavernas, small hotel)*. From there it is up a winding path (*2hr there and back*) to the monastery of Méga Spíleo *(also reachable by road)*.

The train continues to the terminus at Kalávrita (*see KALÁVRITA*).

A Bit of Advice

Narrow-gauge railway: Four trains per day, with additional services in summer, taking 1hr 5min. Arrive at least 15min before departure if you want a seat (those directly behind the driver are the best). Buy your return ticket in advance and check departure time of return train.

WHERE TO STAY

Chris-Paul – *Diakoftó, in the centre of the village – ☎ (26910) 41 715, www.chrispaul-hotel.gr– 25 rm.* This comfortable hotel 80m from the station (with a swimming pool) is a good place to stop for the night. .

Méga Spíleo★

22km/13mi from Diakoftó.

The monastery of Méga Spíleo ('great cave'), which attracts many pilgrims, appears at the foot of a bare rock face on a wild **site**★★ deep in the magnificent landscape of the Vouraïkós Valley, at an altitude of 924m/3 030ft.

It was founded in the 8C by two hermits, Simeon and Theodore. The monastery reached its apogee in the Middle Ages under the Palaeologi, the despots of Mystra. The conventual buildings, which burned down in 1934, have been rebuilt.

The rock church (17C) occupies the great cave from which the monastery takes its name. There is a beautiful door of embossed copper (early 19C. A recess harbours the miraculous image of the Virgin, attributed to St Luke.

A small **museum** houses a collection of liturgical ornaments and objects, carved crosses, manuscripts, old books and icons. The treasury is full of reliquaries, icons and Byzantine manuscripts, some of which date from the 9C.

The guests' refectory and the household rooms (bakery, cellar) are also open.

H Champollion/MICHELIN

On board the narrow-gauge railway, Vouraïkoú

AKTÍ ARKADÍAS★★

ARCADIAN COAST

MICHELIN MAP G-H 11 – ARGOLID – PELOPONNESE.

The isolated east coast of the Peloponnese, forming the foothills of the Mount Párnonas (Parnon) range, has long been overlooked by tourists. The area has become more accessible thanks to a new road along the winding coastline of the Argolic Gulf. It offers a succession of views across the gulf to the Argolid peninsula and the island of Spetsae.

- **Orient Yourself:** From Argos, take the Lerne road 32km/20mi south to Astros. 50km/31mi separate Astros from Leonídio. There are few service stations, so fill your tank before you leave.
- **Organizing Your Time:** The drive takes about two hours.
- Kids **Especially for Kids:** Swimming in the Argolic Gulf!
- **Also See:** Árgos, Náfplio, Spárti, Trípoli, Spétses.

A Bit of History

A literary and pictorial myth – Inhabited by followers of Pan, god of shepherds, Arcadia represented a pastoral idyll to the Ancients, affording its people a life of ease in stark contrast to the toil that was the lot of most Greeks.

From the 1C BC it became fashionable in Rome to aspire to the simple pleasures of Arcadian life. Against this backdrop Virgil wrote the *Bucolics* (42-39 BC); later, during the Renaissance, the same inspiration was to produce *Arcadia* by Iacoppo Sannazzaro (1455-1530). Painters were equally captivated, including Guercino and most famously Nicolas Poussin (*The Shepherds of Arcadia*, c 1640).

Excursions

50km/31mi, allow 2hr.

Ástros

Ástros is an agricultural centre specialising in the cultivation of fruit trees.

The **Archaeological Museum** displays finds from excavations at the site of the Villa of Herodes Atticus (*see below*). On view are some beautiful Greek and Roman sculptures, marble heads, Roman ceramics, inscriptions and architectural elements. *Open Tue-Sun 8.30am-3pm. 2€. ☎ (27550) 22 201.*

For coin categories, see the Legend on the cover flap.

GETTING ABOUT

In summer there are regular hydrofoil services from Zéa Marina in Piraeus and Kythera, with stops including Paralía Tiroú, Pláka, Kyparissi and Monemvassiá. Allow at least 4 hours for the trip. Contact: **Dolphin Sea Lines** ☎ (210) 42 24 775-7, fax (210) 4173 559; or **Hellas Flying Dolphins** ☎ (210) 41 17 341, fax (210) 41 71 190

WHERE TO STAY

Hotel Apollo – *Paralía Tiroú, by the sea to the south of the village – ☎ (27550) 41 393 – 12rm.* A clean hotel of recent construction. Kitchen facilities available. The most pleasant rooms overlook the sea.

Hotel Dionysos – *Pláka port, Leonídio – ☎ (27570) 22 383 – 16rm.* A quiet and well-maintained hotel. Very popular and thus advisable to book well in advance.

Villa of Herodes Atticus

Visit on request at the Archaeological Museum. Located 4km/2.5mi from Ástros on the road to Tegéa and Trípoli (at Eva Dolianon Kynourias), near the Loukos Monastery.
The excavations at the site of the magnificent residence have unearthed remains that are now on display in the museums of Ástros and Trípoli.

Monastery of Loukos

4km/2.5mi east of Ástros (signposted).
Built in the 12C, the monastery's Byzantine church, is decorated with beautiful 17C frescoes. Farther on to the left of the same path lie the ruins of a Roman aqueduct built in the 2C to supply Herodes Atticus's villa.

Parálío Ástros

This small seaside resort has the longest sandy beach along this coast; it is situated on promontory below the remains of an Ancient citadel refurbished by the Franks.
Return to Astros and take the road south to Leonídio; beyond Ágios Andréas it passes above several inlets which are suitable for bathing (lovely pebble beaches).

Tirós★

Hydrofoil landing stage.
This old town, which spreads out like a fan among terraced olive groves, is bypassed by the new road running along the coast below through the little resort of **Paralía Tiroú** *(several hotels).*
Beyond Tirós a corniche road offers beautiful views across the sea to **Spetsae**.

Sambatikí★

The narrow road that winds down to the car park requires great caution.
Attractive site in a curving bay protected by a watchtower; lovely pebble beach with crystal-clear water and fishing boats. The road runs high up above Leonídio Bay and the fertile coastal strip.
The river mouth is flanked by two small beaches: Lékos and **Pláka** *(tavernas; guest-houses; hydrofoil landing point).* Nearby is the peaceful seaside resort of **Poúlithra**; a lovely place for walks and a starting point for trips out to the mountain villages.

Kiparíssi

Hydrofoil landing stage. A picturesque little port *(fish tavernas)* situated in a pleasant bay.

Leonídio★★

Timeless and peaceful (at least out of season), the little town of Leonídio extends from the bank of its river to a high red cliff. It has a certain old-world charm: a 12C fortified house and old rough-cast houses with balconies and Saracen chimneys.
Walk to the far end of the town for a view (near the ruined tower) over the site and the coastal basin down to the sea.
Farther inland *(32km/20mi there and back)* along the road to Géraki lies the **Elóna Monastery** huddled against the rocks on a wild **site**★ overlooking a narrow valley; it safegurads a miraculous icon of the Virgin, supposedly the work of Saint Luke.

H Champollion/MICHELIN

On the road to Leonídio

The road beyond the monastery is magnificent, but very rough in places, as it continues to **Kosmás**, a charming mountain village with a beautiful church over a main square shaded by enormous 100-year-old plane trees and lined with cafés and tavernas; and **Geráki** (see SPÁRTI), from where one can reach **Gíthio**.

ARÁHOVA★

Αραχοβα

POPULATION 3 703

MICHELIN MAP 737 G 8 – BOEOTIA – CENTRAL GREECE.

This small mountain town on the southern flanks of Mount Parnassos above the Pleistos Ravine is a popular winter resort for skiers, and makes a good base from which to explore the surrounding area. The narrow main street abounds with cafes, restaurants and shops; and a lovely view★ extends from the terrace of the Agios Georgios church.

- **Orient Yourself:** To the northwest of Athens; once over the Aráhova Pass on the traditional road from Livadiá (44km/28mi) to Delphi (10km/6mi), you'll be enchanted by the lovely view down onto the site of the town.

Visit

Koríkio Ándro (the Corycian Cave) and Óros Parnassós (Mount Parnassos) are about 45km/27mi (about 2hr 30min) from Aráhova. Take the road towards Delphi; turn right towards Lílea. After 11km/7mi, just beyond Kalívia, turn left (sign 'Chat Tours') into a narrow stony track which winds uphill for 5km/3mi. It's best to turn off after the first

Address Book

For coin categories, see the Legend on the cover flap.

WHERE TO EAT

Aráhova is well known for its culinary specialties: sample the *loukanika* (sausages), *formaeia* (cheese) and honey while you're here.

Parnassos – *Next to Hotel Santa Marina.* A small, simple local restaurant, good quality, a bit off the tourist trail.

Taberna Karaouli – *Next to Hotel Lykoreia.* Traditional cuisine in a vast dining room with bay windows overlooking the valley.

WHERE TO STAY

Nostos – *In the town centre – ☎ (22670) 31 385, nostos@otenet.gr – 15rm.* The proprietor offers a minibus to take guests sightseeing in the area. Excellent value.

Lykoreía – *Turn right 300m out of town on the Delphi road – ☎ (22670) 31 180/321 32 – 28rm.* Comfortable, discreet little hotel; terrace overlooking the valley. Closed Jul-Aug.

Villa Filoxenia – *Follow signs to the right along the road to Delphos – ☎(22670) 310 46, bkatsis@filoxenia-arahova.gr – 16 studios.* Welcoming traditional house; spacious rooms all with wooden balconies.

TAKING A BREAK

Syros Formaela, the cheese used to make *saganaki*, can be found in the excellent shop in the centre of town.

EVENTS AND FESTIVALS

For three days starting on the evening of 22 April, the town holds a festival in honour of St George, including a procession, feasts, dances and sports.

H Champollion/MICHELIN

Aráhova

2km/1.25mi onto the side road leading to a car park; 5min on foot to the cave.

Koríkio Ándro★★

The cave is high above the sea and very extensive. In Antiquity it was devoted to **Pan**, the shepherd god, a horned and bearded deity. The cave was already in use in the Neolithic and Mycenaean periods. Subsequently it was used as a refuge. One can penetrate right into the cave which has good natural light and a few stalactites.

From the threshold there are views towards Parnassos, the Pleistos Valley and the Bay of Itéa.

The Muses

Parnassos, which is often under snow or enveloped in clouds, was thought to be the home of **Apollo** whose main sanctuary was nearby, and of the nine **Muses**: Clio (History), Euterpe (Music), Melpomene (Tragedy), Thalia (Comedy), Terpsichore (Dancing), Urania (Astronomy), Erato (Elegy), Polyhymnia (Lyric poetry) and Calliope (Epic poetry).

Óros Parnassós★★ (Mount Parnassos)

The road follows the hanging valley of Kalívia where sheep are pastured. After about 15km/9mi turn right into a good road which climbs through a mountain landscape of pine trees to a chalet belonging to the Athens Ski Club and continues to Liákoura (2 457m/8 061ft), the highest peak of Parnassos.

Climbing this peak takes about 1hr 30min on foot there and back. On rare clear days, there is a superb panorama of a large part of Greece from the Peloponnese to Mount Athos. Four-wheel drive vehicle trips are also available.

The impenetrable Parnassos massif is still home to wolves; it was the base of the local *klephts* during the **Greek War of Independence** and served again after the Second World War as the stronghold of the ELAS resistance movement which survived there until 1949. There is also extensive **bauxite** mining.

Excursions

Livadiá★

34km/22mi east of Aráhova.

Livadiá, the capital of Boeotia, lies at the mouth of the gloomy Erkínas (Hercyna) Gorge, thought in Antiquity to be the entrance to the Underworld. During the Turkish occupation it became Greece's second most important city after Thessaloníki.

H Champollion/MICHELIN

The humpbacked bridge at Erkínas Gorge

It is a lively town, and an industrial centre. The **upper town** is graced by white houses dating from the 18C and the 19C, little shops shaded by broad awnings and tavernas where *souvláki* and cherry conserve, the local specialities, are served.

Park the car in the square in the centre of the modern lower town and take one of the streets leading to the upper town.

Erkínas Gorge★★

Walk upstream, leaving the great square tower to the right. An old humpbacked stone bridge spans the river.

On the east bank the spring of **Mnemosyne** (Remembrance) flows into a pool where niches for votive offerings have been carved out of the cliff face. A passage not far away leads to what is thought to be the spring of **Lethe** (Oblivion).

Continue up the gorge, deep into the rocky mountain. There are fine views of the fortress and the Jerusalem hermitage.

Return to the square tower, which is at one end of the fortress's outer wall, and turn left into a path that follows the line of the wall past a beautiful Byzantine church with an apse and a dome.

From the **Kástro**★ crowning Mount Agiios Ilias, there is a spectacular **view**★★ over gorge, mountains and town.

The village of **Herónia** *(14km/9mi north of Livadiá)* is home to a grand marble **lion** commemorating those who died in the Battle of Herónia in 336 BC. There is also a small **Archaeological Museum** *(☎(26100) 95 270).*

Orhomenós

14km/9mi northeast of Livadiá.

Orchomenos, which had been the capital of the Minyans in the prehistoric era, was the rival of Thebes in Antiquity. It is now a small country town on the edge of what was formerly a huge marsh known as **Lake Copaïs (Kopaïda)**. At the end of the 19C, a network of canals was created to channel the water south towards the **River Kifissós**. Over a period of years nearly 200km^2/77sq mi of land was reclaimed. The ruins of Ancient Orchomenos and the Church of the Dormition of the Virgin face each other on the Kástro road at the eastern outskirts of the modern town.

Ancient ruins

On the left of the theatre is the path leading into the **Treasury of Minyas**★ a huge Mycenaean *thólos* tomb similar to the Treasury of Atreus at Mycenae. The roof has fallen in but the huge blue marble lintel is still in place over the door, and the inner chamber has retained part of its original ceiling decoration.

The acropolis *(1hr on foot there and back)* gives a fine **panorama**★ over Orchomenos and the Copaïc region. Remains of old walls and temples are visible.

Kimísseos Theotókou★

The Byzantine **Church of the Dormition of the Virgin**, which dates from the 9C, belonged to a monastery built on the site of a temple dedicated to the Graces *(charities)*. In the 13C the monastery passed to the Cistercians, who altered the church and the conventual buildings.

Inside the church is an unusual Byzantine paved floor. There are Greek inscriptions and many Byzantine stones sculpted with symbolic motifs along the exterior wall.

ARGOLÍDA★

POPULATION 105 770

MICHELIN MAP 737 G 10, H 10-11 – PELOPONNESE.

This peninsula, which separates the Saronic and Argolic Gulfs, is composed of limestone hills, some forested; the coastal plains are planted with citrus orchards. The little ports and sheltered creeks for bathing which are dotted along the shore were formerly accessible only by sea, but now there is a coast road serving the modern hotels and resorts offering attractive views of the islands of Póros, Hydra, Dokós and Spetsae. To get to the peninsula, take the E94 motorway from Athens; exit at Corinth and follow signs for Porós or Spétses.

Driving Tour

Starting from Portohéli at the southern end of the peninsula, this 216km/135mi circuit leads back to Kósta, looking out towards Spetsae. Allow 1 day.

H Champollion/MICHELIN

Olive groves, Argolída

Portohéli

Well sheltered in its attractive bay, Portohéli (the name means 'eel port') is a fishing village and port for Spetsae . To the north, where Aliïs once stood *(signposted)*, traces of the base of an acropolis (dating from 700 BC) can be seen.

Kranídi

This beautiful village of stone houses is set in pleasant surroundings. The Church of Agía Triáda boasts some magnificent 13C frescoes, and nearby stand the monasteries of St Anne, Panagias tis Pantanassas and Agion Anargiron (11C).

▸ *Turn left just after Kranídi.*

Koilada

This little fishing village occupies a lovely setting with some very inviting beaches nearby, particularly the one at **Korakia**. A footpath in the mountains to the north leads to Fraghti Cave, which was inhabited as early as the 8th millennium BC.

▸ *Head back towards Kranídi and turn left onto the road to Ligourió.*

Beyond **Foúrni**, a dirt track on the right *(signposted)* leads past the Church of Agion Anargiron to the northern entrance to the wild and secluded **Katafyki Gorge**.

Craters of Dídima

Just past the village of Dídima lies a vast crater on the mountainside to the left. According to local tradition it was formed by a meteorite and dates from the 19C. A dirt road suitable for cars *(sign 'pros spilia')* leads to a larger crater which is not visible from the road. Steps lead down a tunnel to a little chapel built by the people of a neighbouring village in thanksgiving for a narrow escape.

▸ *Continue towards Ligourió. Just before Trahiá turn right to Fanári.*

Beyond **Fanári**, clinging to the steep hillside, a corniche road descends the cliff face providing spectacular **views**★ of the Saronic shoreline and the **Méthana peninsula** which ends in Mount Helóni (743m/2 438ft), an extinct volcano.

▸ *7km/4.5 miles beyond Kaloní turn left towards Méthana.*

The road crosses the neck of land leading to the former volcanic island of Méthana. Just before Méthana there is an attractive view of the town and the harbour.

Méthana

There is a boat service from Piraeus to Méthana, where traces of a 4C BC fortress have been found. It is a seaside resort and spa featuring warm sulphurous waters.

Vathí

This fishing village is tucked away in a small bay. Farther north along the coast road, a footpath heads off through the forest to the remains of the surrounding wall of the ancient acropolis of Méthana *(300m/330yd from the road)*. Continuing northwards, the road provides some magnificent bird's-eye **views**★ of the sea before plunging into the forest on the way to **Kaïméni Hora**. This deserted village stands at the foot of a volcanic cone, whose summit *(access by footpath in poor condition)* affords magnificent views of the wild and beautiful countryside.

▸ *Return to Méthana by the same road, and at the crossroads on the mainland turn left towards Galatás; after 2km/1.25mi turn right (sign) into a minor road leading to Trizína (formerly Damalas).*

Go through the village and follow the signs 'Acropolis of Trizína' turn right into a minor road (sign 'Diavologéfira' and 'Antiquities'). At a junction near a Roman bridge bear right and continue for 1.5km/1mi along a track past two churches (after the second church the track is in poor condition for 700m/765yd). Sign 'Sanctuary of Hippolytos, Asclepieion, Episkopi'.

Trizín★

On the left of the road are the scanty remains of the shrine of Hippolytus and, on the right, those of an *asklepieion*, a sanctuary to **Asklepios**, the god of healing. A short distance away stand the ruins of a Byzantine church and a bishop's palace. Return to the junction and turn right at the Roman bridge, continuing to a Hellenistic tower, part of an Ancient fortress; the upper section dates from the Middle Ages. Continue to the end of the road. A 5min walk leads to the lower end of the **Devil's Gorge**★ and to the Devil's Bridge, '**Diavologéfira**', a natural rock formation linking both sides of the gorge. The path runs west to the top of the cliffs where an Ancient acropolis, a sanctuary to Pan, and the 13C fort of Damalet stood.

Return to the road to Galatàs.

Galatàs

Magnificent **views**★★ of the straits and Póros Island.

Head for Ermióni.

Lemonodássos★

On the coast opposite Póros Island there is a huge lemon grove of about 30 000 trees covering a gentle slope above **Alíki** beach. *Park the car beside the road near the sign by a chapel.* From there walk up the hill *(30min on foot there and back)* through the scented lemon grove which is irrigated by narrow channels of running water. The path *(sign 'Pros Kéntron Cardássi' or 'Restaurant Cardássi')* soon reaches the Cardássi taverna; attractive view of Póros Island.
The coast road to Ermióni affords many fine views of Hydra and Dokós through the ubiquitous olive groves. Pass **Plépi**★, an attractive resort with small harbour.

Ermióni

Seat of a Byzantine bishopric, the town is now a resort and sheltered fishing port. *Regular services to Hydra.*

Continue along the coast road bearing left at the fork to Kósta, an attractive modern resort. Ferry to Spetsae and coastal vessels to Hydra.

ÁRGOS

Αργοσ

POPULATION 24 239

MICHELIN MAP 737 G 10 – ARGOLID – PELOPONNESE.

Árgos, the oldest city in Greece according to the Ancients, is today an unremarkable modern city. The capital of the Argolid of Classical times, its population was as large as that of Athens; there are many important reminders of its great past, including its striking theatre, its Roman baths and archaeological museum.

- **Orient Yourself:** Árgos is just south of Mycenae, 135km/84mi southwest of Athens, and 48km/30mi southwest of Corinth. The city is dominated by a rocky peak upon which the citadel sits; the settlement fans out beneath it and on a lesser hill, the Aspis. Seek accommodation in Nauplion or along the coast, where the choice of hotels and restaurants is better.

A Bit of History

Perseus, hero of the Argolide – Árgos was founded by an Egyptian, Danaos, father of the famous Danaids. Later the city came under Perseus and his descendants. Perseus' origins are mired in myth. As the story goes, the nymph Danae was imprisoned by her father, King Acrisius, in order to thwart a prophecy that her son would kill his grandfather. But the god Zeus visited her in a shower of gold, fathered **Perseus**, and brought mother and son to safety on the island of Seriphos.
After heroic feats including the slaying of the Gorgon Medusa (a mythical creature with snakes for hair and the power to turn onlookers to stone), Perseus arrived in Árgos. The grim prophecy was fulfilled when Perseus , competing in the ceremonial games, threw the discus, hitting the king on the head and killing him. Refusing to accede to Acrisius's throne, Perseus became king of Tyrinth instead.

Changing fortunes – Throughout the Archaic period the city dominated the northeast of the Peloponnese in rivalry with Sparta. During the Classical period it supported a brilliant civilisation which produced a school of sculptors in bronze including **Polykleitos**, second only to Pheidias.

ÁRGOS	
Bouboulinas	2
Danaou	3
Fidonos	5
Filellinon	7
Makariou	9
Metaxa	10
Nikitara	13
Vas. Kon/nou	14
Vas. Sofias	15

Argos was supplanted in importance by Nauplion under the Franks. The town was burned during the War of Independence and rebuilt on a grid plan. Today it is a communications centre and a market for the agricultural produce of the coastal plain.

Visit

Arheótites (Ancient ruins)★

Southwest along the road to Trípoli. Open Tue-Sun 8.30am-3pm. (27510) 68 819. 2€ (joint ticket with museum: 3€). The Agora is usually closed to the public.

Excavations reveal evidence of activity on this site going back 5 000 years.

By the western entrance to the site is an Ancient road leading to a theatre, to the left of which are the remains of a large building. Roman **baths** were built here in the 2C; there are traces of mural paintings and mosaics (partly covered up).

The **theatre**, which dates from the 4C BC, was one of the largest in Greece; the terraces could accommodate 20,000 spectators. To the left of the theatre are the remains of an odeon (2C-3C AD). Farther south are the ruins of the Sanctuary of Aphrodite and the foundations of a 5C BC temple. On the opposite side of the road are the remains of the **agora**, which dates from the 4C BC.

Finds from the site and from Lerní are handsomely displayed in the **Archaeological Museum** (*open Tue-Sun 8.30am-3pm; 2€*).

Outskirts

From Agis Petros square take the Mycenae (Mikínes) road and then head up the road which winds up to the citadel.

Lárissa Citadel★

Open Jul-Oct Tue-Sun 8.30am-3pm.

The Deirás Gap separates Aspís Hill (traces of a sanctuary to Apollo and a fortress; fine view of the citadel) from Lárissa Hill. The citadel on this wild, isolated but very beautiful site was completed by the Franks in the 13C-14C on the foundations of an Ancient acropolis. The building now consists of an outer wall with towers and the castle itself. The water cisterns are impressive. There is a fine **view**★★ of the plain of Argolis stretching from the mountains to the Gulf of Nauplion.

8km/5mi northeast of Árgos. From the centre take the road to Corinth; bear right after the river bed (sign 'Inahos', 'Prósimna'). In Inahos continue straight ahead (sign 'Ireon'); in Hónikas (11C Byzantine church) take the road to Mycenae (Mikínes) and then continue for 2km/1.5mi along a minor road (sign 'Ancient Ireo').

H Champollion/MICHELIN

Lárissa Citadel

Iréo★

The sanctuary, which was consecrated to Hera, the tutelary goddess of fertile Argolis, was already in existence in the Mycenaean period. Discovered in 1831, the ruins occupy a magnificent solitary **site★★** above the plain of Árgos.

On the first terrace stand the bases of the columns which formed a 5C BC portico (stoa); at the back, built of limestone blocks, is the retaining wall of the second terrace, which was the platform for a Classical temple (late 5C BC). The sculptures are on display in the Athens Museum. On the upper terrace are the massive lower courses of an Archaic Doric temple (early 7C BC), which burned down in 423 BC.

The cult of Hera was still celebrated on this spot in Roman times: Roman baths have been found on the west slope, and Hadrian made a gift of a jeweled peacock (Hera's symbol).

▸ *9km/5.5mi southwest of Árgos. Take the road to Trípoli. After 5km/3mi turn right into a track which leads to the Erássinos spring.*

Kefalári

The river gushes from a cave consecrated in Antiquity to **Pan** and **Dionysos**; a sanctuary stands on the terrace above. In summer the cool shade of the huge plane trees and the tall poplars is particularly welcome *(open-air cafés).*

ÁRTA★

Αρτα

POPULATION 19 435

MICHELIN MAP 737 D 6 – EPIROS.

A small town situated on a bend in the River Árahthos and dominated by a 13C citadel built on much earlier foundations, Árta was the former capital of the Despotate of Epiros; it has some fine examples of Byzantine architecture. Árta lies in the south of Epiros, 77km/48mi south of Ioánina, 97km/61mi northeast of Préveza.

Visit

Bridge★

The 17C humpbacked bridge over the Árahthos on the edge of Árta (Ioánina road) is celebrated for its elegant curve and its wide arches alternating with smaller ones, which ease the flow of water when the river is in spate.

Panagía Parigorítissa★

Near Skoufá Square. Open Tue-Sun 8.30am-3pm. 2€.

The great Church of the Virgin Comforter (13C), with its six domes, was inspired by the churches of Constantinople. The interior is surrounded by galleries for women *(gynaecea).* The central dome is raised on three stages of projecting columns ; the base is supported

For coin categories, see the Legend on the cover flap.

WHERE TO STAY

Cronos – *Platia Kilkis – ☎ (26810) 22 211, fax (26810) 73 795 – 55rm.* Comfortable air-conditioned rooms; well placed for visiting Árta.

Byzantino – *On the Préveza road, 47042 Filothei – ☎ (26810) 52 205, fax (26810) 52 116 – 53rm.* Comfortable modern hotel with a swimming pool and tennis courts.

SHOPPING

The town is a centre for citrus-fruit farming, but there is also a craft market selling embroidery and *flokatia*.

H Champollion/MICHELIN

Humpbacked bridge over the Árahthos

on squinches of an unusual type, seen elsewhere only at St Theodore's Church in Mistrás.
There is an **archaeological museum** in the neighbouring building.

Agía Theodóra

Off the main street heading toward the citadel. *Open daily 7am-1pm; 5-8pm.*
The church houses the tombe of Theodora, wife of the despot Michel II.

Outskirts

Rogoús Fortress

15km/9.5mi west of Árta, near the village of Néa Kerassoús on the Préveza road. Above a bend in the **River Loúros** stand the ruins of this Ancient fortress (late 5C BC), impressive for its size and state of preservation. Fine polygonal stonework. The frescoes in the little church are in somewhat poor condition.

Monastery of Vlahérna

3km/1.9mi northeast of Árta. Ask for the key at the kiosk.
The 13C church on a basilical plan features noteworty frescoes *(damaged).*

ATHÍNA★★★

ATHENS – Αθινα

POPULATION 745 714 (GREATER ATHENS 3 042 469)

MICHELIN MAP 737 I 9 – ATTICA.

The attractive site, the brilliant light, the beauty of the Ancient monuments and the quality of the museums all contribute to the pleasure of visiting Athens, the city of Athena, the cradle of Western civilisation. Athens also has many Roman, Byzantine and neo-Classical remains, and certain districts, such as the old Bazaar, have an enticing oriental flavour. With a population of 3 million, Athens today is also a modern metropolis. In recent years the city undertook an ambitious programme of improvements in preparation for hosting the 2004 Olympic Games.

26 Vas. Amalias (near Síndagma Square). *(21033) 10 392, www.gnto.gr*

- **Orient Yourself:** Athens is close to the Saronic Gulf and port of Piraeus, where ferries and hydrofoils offer service to most of the Greek islands. The new Athens airport is located at Markopoulos (27km/17mi southeast of the city). The main historic areas of Plaka and Monastiráki lie north of the Acropolis. From there the immense modern city spreads forth, scored by wide, busy avenues.
- **Parking:** Traffic can be infernal in Athens, especially at rush hours; it's best to park your car quickly and move about on foot or by public transportation. There's a large underground garage on Odós Rizari near the Ethniki Pinakothiki.
- **Don't Miss:** The Acropolis; a stroll through the Plaka district; the National Archaeological Museum, the museum of Cycladic Art and the Benaki Museum.
- **Organizing Your Time:** It's possible to hit the highlights of Athens in two days, but a stay of five days or longer would be much better, particularly if you want to visit the outskirts.
- Kids **Especially for Kids:** The zoo in the National Garden; the Museum of Popular Musical Instruments.
- **Also See:** Attica, Kórinthos, the Saronic Gulf Islands.

A Bit of History

Ancient Athens

Birth of Athens – The Acropolis was built on a natural defensive site consisting of a steep-sided hill, the approaches protected by two rivers – **Kifissós** *(west)* and **Ilissós** *(east)* – with a circle of hills forming outposts. Athens is thought to have been founded by Cecrops, the king of a prehistoric race. Erechtheos, a descendant of Cecrops, established the cult of Athena, the goddess who was associated with the olive and the owl: the cult was practised on the site where the Erechtheion now stands.
Aigeus's son, **Theseus** (12C or 11C BC), made Athens the capital of a coherent state covering present-day Attica and afforded great importance to the processions in honour of Athena, called the Panathenaia. In his reign the city was scarcely larger than the Acropolis.

Athens in her glory (6C-5C BC) – After the great urban reforms introduced by **Solon** and the enlightened dictators, Peisistratos and his sons (561-510), the city developed extensively. A new circuit wall was built enclosing the Areopagos hill northwest of the Acropolis, as well as the two agoras of Theseus and Solon. At

Office National Hellénique de Tourisme

Aerial view of Athens, with the Acropolis in the background

Address Book

GETTING TO AND FROM ATHENS

BY AIR - Athens International Airport (E. Venizelos) is located at Markopoulos, 27km/17mi southeast of the city.

The simplest way to get to the centre of Athens is via the **metro** from the airport (Aerodromio) station. Trains depart every 30min to Syntagma and Monastiraki stations, which connect to other metro lines. 6€. If returning to the airport via metro, note that not all trains go all the way to the airport; be sure that Aerodromio is the ultimate destination indicated on the sign at the head of the train.

Suburban trains link the Aerodromio station to the Larisa station with stops at Nerantziotissa near Maroússi. Departures every 30min. 6€.

Allow one hour or more to travel from the airport to the centre of Athens by **bus** or **taxi**. Buses from the airport terminate at Ethniki Amyna underground station (bus X 94), Síndagma Square (X 95) or Piraeus (X 96). They operate seven days a week and every 10 minutes during the day; check schedules for nighttime frequency. A ticket to or from the airport costs 2.90€ (3€ with transfer) and is available from ticket kiosks and bus and underground stations. For more information: www.oasa.gr

Car rental agencies are located in the lower level arrival hall.

BY TRAIN (OSE) – Two stations are linked by underground line 2: **Lárissa Station**, *31 Odós Deligiani, ☏ (21052) 97 777* for northern and eastern Greece (Thebes, Larisa, Thessaloníki) and **Peloponnese Station**, *3 Odós Sidirodromon, ☏ (21051) 31 601*, for the southwest of the country. There is also a train station at Piraeus. For general information and reservations (at least two days before departure), contact **OSE**, *6 Odós Sina, ☏ (21052) 97 313.*

BY BUS (KTEL) – There are 3 main bus terminals in the centre of Athens:

Terminal A or KTEL Kifissou, *100 Odós Kifissou, ☏ (21051) 50 785 / 24 910*: for the Peloponnese, Etolía, Epiros, Macedonia and the Ionian Islands.

Terminal B or KTEL Liossion, *260 Odós Liossion, ☏ (21083) 17 147/53*: for central Greece, Eubea and Thessaly.

KTEL Attica, *Pedio Areos, to the north of the National Museum, ☏ (21082) 13 203/(21088) 43 250*: Sounion, Lávrio, Rafína, Marathon, Markópoulo and Thessaloníki.

BY BOAT– The port at Piraeus is accessible from Athens by the metro line 1 (green line; 20min from Monastiraki station) or by bus X 96 from the airport.

GETTING AROUND ATHENS

BY METRO – Consisting of 3 lines and recently expanded, the Athens underground network is certainly the easiest way to get around the principal tourist sites (Acropolis, Síndagma, Monastiráki, Omónia, Thissío, Piraeus). It runs every day from 5am till 11.30pm. A one-use ticket costs €0.90, but you can buy a ticket good for one day 2.90€, or one week 10€ covering the whole public transport network (bus, trolley bus, trams and metro). Be sure to validate your ticket before boarding. Maps and information available in English at ticket counters or at *www.ametro.gr.*

BY BUS AND TROLLEY – There are 320 bus routes in Athens. Information and maps are available from the OASA office, *15 Odós Metsovou*, behind the National Archaeological Museum. Tickets, priced from €0.45, are also available from the office.

TRAMS – The tramway links the centre of Athens with western Attica (Faliro, Agios Kosmas).

SUBURBAN TRAINS – Lines connect to the underground network at Aerodromio, Doukissis Plakentias (line 3) and Neratziotissa (line 1) stations.

TAXI – Radio Taxi, Athens, *☏ (21092) 179 42.*

TOURS – An easy, if less scenic means of getting from place to place, the **Sightseeing Public Bus Line** departs from the National Archaeological Museum every 30min and passes by 20 touristic sights; visitors alight at will, visit the sights and continue on the next convenient bus. Ticket 5€, valid 24hrs.

LODGING IN ATHENS

Hotel options can be rather expensive in Athens, especially during the high season (April-October). Prices can nearly double during holidays (Easter) or special events. Internet reservations generally result in the best prices.

See area Address Books for specific recommendations.

EVENTS AND FESTIVALS

Athens Festival – *39 Odós Panepistimíou (Odós Venizelou) – ☎ (21032) 21 459, www.hellenicfestival.gr.* The festival is held from May to September at the foot of the Acropolis in the **Odeon of Herodes Atticus** and the **Lycabettos Theatre**. International and national companies perform plays, operas, concerts, ballets, contemporary and traditional dancing, and Classical tragedies; also concerts of jazz, rock and Greek music. Tickets available at the office *(above)* or at the door just before the performance.

Traditional dance – *Dora Stratou Theatre. Information: 8 Odós Scholiou, in Plaka – ☎ (21032) 443 95 (9am-4pm); 13€.* Performances take place every evening May–September at 9.15pm (Sundays, 8.15pm) on Philopappos hill.

SHOPPING AND STROLLING

For tourists the centre of Athens is **Síndagma Square** with its large hotels, travel agencies, banks and cafés. Bars and nightclubs crowd the side streets. Women's dress shops line **Odós Ermoú**.

Southwest of Síndagma Square lies **Pláka**; in the evenings tourists throng the souvenir shops in **Odós Adrianóu** and **Odós Pandrassou** and the tavernas blare *bouzoúki* music.

Pláka merges into **Monastiráki**, an old Turkish bazaar, now a sort of flea market, particularly on Sunday mornings.

Northeast of Síndagma Square lies **Kolonáki**, a wealthy, elegant district with **luxury shops**: fashion, antiques, jewellery, galleries, and gourmet foods.

Síndagma Square is joined to Omónia Square *(northwest)* by two busy shopping streets, **Odós Stadíou** and **Odós Venizélou**.

Lively **Omónia Square** bustles with the shops of tradesmen and artisans. Running south, Odós Athinas passes through the **Kendrikí Agorá**, a huge covered market which sells a fascinating and astonishing variety of foodstuffs.

On fine evenings Athenians stroll in Síndagma or Omónia Squares, in the Kolonáki district or in the Zapio Garden, where they dine or attend the popular musical entertainment. **Lycabettos** *(café-restaurant)* has a magnificent view south over Athens, and Pedío Áreos is known for its **open-air cinemas**.

the same time various municipal undertakings were being carried out in the lower town: public buildings, a water system, sewers and roads. The first coins were struck bearing the effigy of Athena and the owl; the Lyceum and the Academy—famous gymnasia surrounded by gardens—were established.

When **Kleisthenes** rose to power in 508 BC he organised Athens into a direct democracy. Legislative power was exercised by an assembly of the people *(Ecclesia)* which met three or four times a month on the Pnyx; a Senate *(Boule)* of 500 members which was subordinated to the Assembly; and a tribunal *(Heliaia)* comprising elected magistrates and juries chosen by lot. Executive power was exercised by the archons and the strategi; the latter were in command of the army.

Following the Persian Wars in 479 BC, Themistocles, the victor of the Battle of Salamis, gave orders for the construction of the wall which bears his name; he also built the 'Long Walls', a fortified corridor linking Athens and Piraeus.

In the **Age of Pericles**, that great Athenian statesman devoted himself to the reconstruction of Athens with the advice of the sculptor Pheidias. An overall plan was drawn up for the Acropolis, and the Propylaia, the Parthenon, the Erechtheion and the Temple of Athena Nike were constructed. Almost the whole area within the walls was covered by brick houses.

Athens in decline (4C-2C BC) – The Peloponnesian War (431-404), in which Athens was defeated by Sparta, marked the beginning of a decline in the moral sphere which is illustrated by the death of the philosopher **Socrates**.

Despite the exhortations of the great orator **Demosthenes**, the Greeks failed to agree on a concerted policy, and after the Battle of Chaironeia (338 BC) Athens became subject to Philip of Macedon, who was succeeded by Alexander the Great.
Secure under Macedonian 'protection', which lasted until the end of the 3C BC, the Athenian municipal authorities embarked on public works of embellishment: the theatre of Dionysos and the choregic monument of Lysicrates.
The Hellenistic period, which began with the death of Alexander (323 BC), was marked by the division of the Macedonian Empire into several kingdoms. Athens vegetated; only the building of a few porticoes and gymnasia, in the reigns of the kings of Antioch and Pergamon, reveal the city's continuing intellectual power.

Conquered by Rome (1C BC-4C AD) – The political independence of Athens came to an end in 86 BC when the city was captured by **Sulla** and the walls were razed. Nonetheless the 'Roman peace' enabled Athens to retain its leadership in cultural affairs in the Mediterranean world; the Romans carried away or copied her works of art, imitated her citizens' way of life and sent their sons to Athens to complete their education. In the 1C BC a temple to Rome and Augustus (Naós Rómis ke Avgoústou) was built on the Acropolis hill and a Roman forum and a hydraulic clock, known later as the 'Tower of the Winds', were built at the foot; a covered theatre (Odeon) was built on the old agora.
In AD 53 Christianity was brought to Athens by **St Paul** who preached the gospel and exalted the 'unknown god' on the Areopagos.
Later, in the 2C AD, the **Emperor Hadrian**, who cherished all things Greek, completed the temple of Zeus (Olympieion) begun by Peisistratos, built a library and aqueducts and a new district east of the Acropolis protected by a wall. Herodes Atticus, a wealthy Athenian, constructed a theatre (Odeon), which still bears his name, on the southern slope of the Acropolis, and a splendid white-marble stadium on the east bank of the Ilissós.

Byzantine, Medevial and Ottoman Athens

Rise of Christianity (5C-13C) – Following the Germanic invasions in the middle of the 3C the Roman Empire was split in two in 395, with Athens in the eastern part ruled by the emperor residing in Byzantium (Constantinople). The Edict of Milan in 313 allowed Christians to practise their religion legally and their proliferation from the 5C to the 7C led to the suppression of the schools of philosophy and the establishment of basilicas in the Parthenon and other pagan temples. The majority of the Byzantine churches date from the 9C and often incorporated fragments of Ancient buildings; many have survived.
Until the late 12C when Athens was sacked by the Saracens, it was a flourishing city with a stable population protected by the castle on the Acropolis.

Dukes of Athens (13C-15C) – The Fourth Crusade, which captured Constantinople in 1204, caused Athens to fall into the hands of the Frankish knights who also held Thebes. Athens passed to a family of Burgundian origin, the **La Roche**. During their tenure Athens was raised to a duchy by Louis IX of France (1260).
The Franks fortified the Acropolis and altered the Propylaia to form a palace guarded by the Frankish Tower, which stood until it was demolished in 1875. The Frankish domination of Athens to an end in 1311 after the Battle of Kephisos.
The Catalans then occupied the region but established their stronghold in Thebes In 1387 Athens was captured by a Florentine, Nerio Acciaiuoli. After a brief Venetian interlude from 1394 to 1403 the Acciaiuoli reigned until 1456, when they were obliged to submit to the Turks who had captured Constantinople three years earlier.

Athens at its lowest ebb (1456-1821) – Sultan Mahomet II, the Turkish ruler, granted a certain degree of autonomy to Athens and allowed several churches to be built; in the 17C the Turks even permitted the Jesuits and Capuchins to found monasteries. The Acropolis was fortified to form the kernel of the Turkish fortress; in 1466 the Parthenon was converted into a mosque with an adjoining minaret; the Propylaia was used as a powder magazine and the Erechtheion housed a harem.

Venetian troops laid siege to Athens in 1687; during the bombardment a powder magazine on the Acropolis exploded, causing grave damage to the Parthenon. The Turks surrendered but recaptured the town a year later.

From then until independence Athens was a town of about 10 000 to 15 000 inhabitants living on the northern slopes of the Acropolis hill. The city began to attract many visitors from Western Europe. In 1762 **'Athenian' Stuart** and Revett published the first volume of "an accurate description of the Antiquities of Athens." Richard Chandler, who visited Athens some 10 years later, remarked that it was "to be regretted that so much admirable sculpture as is still extant... should be all likely to perish..." **Lord Elgin**, British Ambassador in Constantinople at the time, is famous for his acquisition of marble sculptures.

Athens, Capital of Greece

Independence (1821-34) – On 25 April 1821 the Athenians rose in rebellion and occupied the town except for the Acropolis, which held out until 10 June. A counter-attack in 1826 enabled the Turks to capture Missolonghi and to lay siege to Athens.

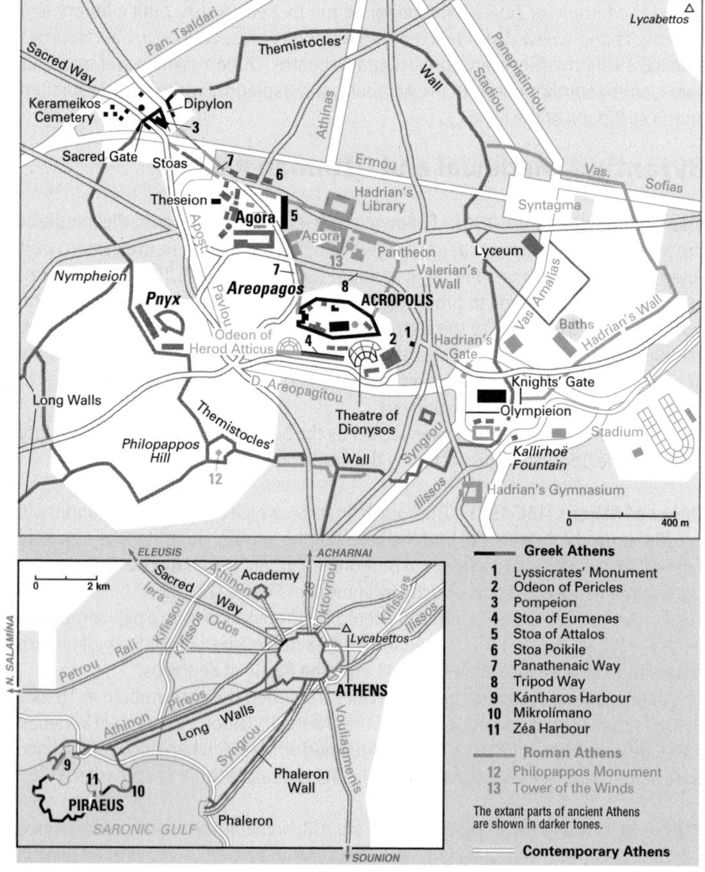

The Greek troops were forced to surrender on 24 May 1827. Eleven months of fighting and bombardment had devastated the town.
Although the War of Independence ended in 1829, the Acropolis remained in Turkish hands until 1834 when Athens succeeded Nauplion as the capital of the new State of Greece; the population numbered barely 4 000.

First neo-Classical era (1834-1900) – In 1832 the Great Powers imposed on Greece a German king, the young **Otto of Bavaria**, son of Ludwig I of Bavaria.
In the reign of Otto and Queen Amalia, a policy of great works was inaugurated under the aegis of the Bavarian architect, Leo von Klenze. A new town with straight streets was traced out in a triangular area based on Odós Ermoú with Odós Pireós (Panagí Tsaldári) and Odós Stadíou forming the two sides and meeting in Omónia Square. In 1861 the population of Athens had reached 41 298.
Many of the buildings from this period were in the neo-Classical style. The main German contributions were the Royal Palace, the University, the Academy and the Observatory. **Kleanthes**, a Greek architect, worked more on houses for private clients: the Duchess of Plaisance's residence in Ilissia *(see Byzantine museum)* and his own house in Pláka.

Expansion (after 1900) – When the Greeks from Smyrna in Asia Minor were expelled by the Turks in 1922, a wave of refugees settled in Athens, mainly in the district north of Piraeus. The city has continued to expand. The lower slopes of Lycabettos have been covered by the elegant Kolonáki district; the Ilissós now runs underground beneath a broad highway, and the outer districts of detached houses now extend from Kifissiá in the north to Fáliro (Phaleron) in the south. After the Second World War new buildings were concentrated along Leofóros Venizélou. The Hilton Hotel and the American Embassy by Gropius, the Athens Tower at Ambelókipi, and the more recent Olympic Stadium at Maroússi are the most striking constructions.
In the early 1980s, measures were put in place to protect and restore the traditional buildings of Pláka and the city centre. Part of Pláka and many streets in the centre are pedestrianised and planted with trees; the problem of atmospheric pollution remains an issue which the authorities continue to tackle.

Sights

Ancient Athens

Metro station Acropoli (red line), bus no. 230 from Sindagma Square or trolleys 1, 5 or 15 (Makrigiani stop). Walk along Leofóros Dioníssou Areopagitou which passes the Theatre of Dionysos and the Odeon of Herodes Atticus. The area has recently been transformed into an archaeological park, a vast pedestrianised area with a new museum housing the collections currently in the Acropolis Museum *(scheduled completion 2007)*.

Théatro Dioníssou★★ (Theatre of Dionysos)

Open daily 8am-2.30pm. 2€ (Sun no charge). (210) 32 24 625.
The first stage to be built on this spot was set up in the 6C BC, followed early in the following century by a real theatre equipped with wooden terraces, where the great Classical dramas were played: *The Persians* by Aeschylus, *Oedipus Rex* by Sophocles, *Medea* by Euripides and the *Wasps* by Aristophanes. The present stone structure (4C BC), provided 17 000 seats. It was restored early in the 19C.
Beyond the remains of a temple to Dionysos and a portico lies the stage of the theatre. Its foundations date from the 4C BC but it was rebuilt under Nero (1C AD): the sculptures at the front of the stage date from this period. The terraces (4C BC) are partially preserved; they rose as high as the monument to Thrasyllos, 30m/98ft. In the first row were the seats reserved for individuals, bearing the names of the those who occupied them in the 2C AD.

J Malburet/MICHELIN

Odeon of Herodes Atticus

From the top there is a good view of the site; on the left are traces of the **Odeon of Pericles**, a covered theatre.
There is nothing left but the pedestal of the **Mnimío Thrassílou (Choregic monument of Thrasyllos)**, a votive monument set up by Thrasyllos a chorus-leader *(choregós)* in 4C BC, in honour of Dionysos, who was worshipped in the cave *(below)*.

Asklipiío

A long terrace west of the upper part of the Theatre of Dionysos bears the remains of two sanctuaries to Asklepios (Aesculapius); one dates from the 4C BC *(east)* and the other *(west)* from the 5C BC.
Below the Asklepieion, facing south, is the **Stoa of Eumenes**, built in the 2C BC by **Eumenes II**, king of Pergamon; the **facade**★ is especially noteworthy.

Odío Iródou Atikoú★ (Odeon of Herodes Atticus)

Not open except for performances.
The Odeon (161 BC) was built by Herodes Atticus in memory of his wife. The **façade**★ is fairly well preserved. It can accommodate 6 000 spectators and today hosts performances of the Athens Summer Festival.
From the Odeon, a path leads to the Beulé Gate and thence to the Acropolis.

Acropolí★★★

Open daily 8.30am-2.30pm, 7pm in summer. Closed public holidays; museum closed Mon mornings. 12€ ticket good for four days allows entry to all Acropolis sites plus the Theatre of Dionysos, the Ancient Agora, the Olympieion, the Roman Agora and the Keramíkos Cemetery. ☎ (21032) 10 219.
The artistic climax of Greek architecture, the Acropolis stands on the summit of a steep rock platform. Covering an area of 4 ha/just under 10 acres, it dominates the lower town by 100m/329ft.
The Acropolis comprises traces of construction from various periods dating back to the second millennium BC (Mycenaean period), but the principal buildings are all in white Pentelic marble and belong to the Age of Pericles (5C BC). The 1981 earthquake, coupled with air-pollution problems in recent years, has made it necessary to take steps to protect the stone and to replace the remaining sculptures with copies.
The entrance to the Acropolis is known as the **Píli Beulé** (Beulé Gate) since it was discovered in 1853 by French archaeologist Ernest Beulé. Beyond is a flight of steps, flanked by the Temple of Athena Nike *(south)* and a pedestal of grey Hymettos marble *(north)*, the Mnimío Agrípa, which in about 15 BC supported the quadriga (four-

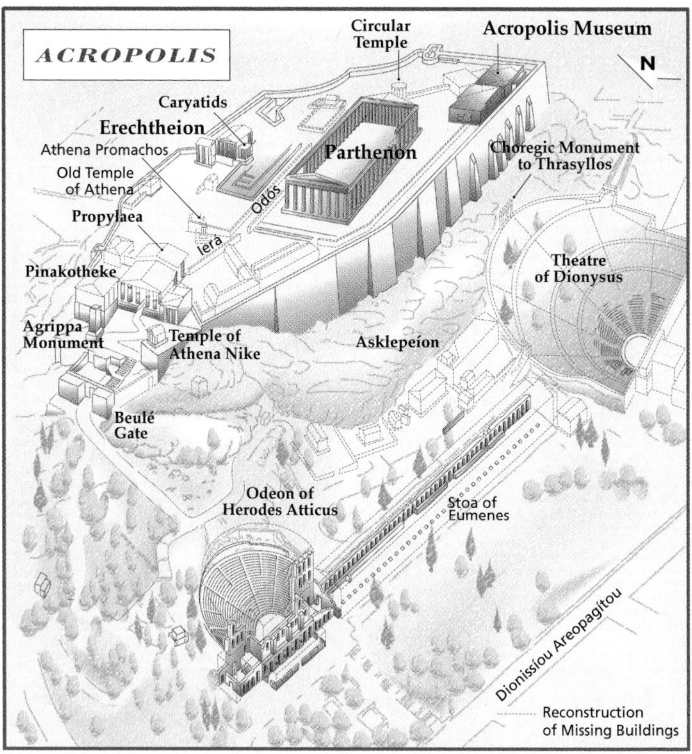

horse chariot) of Agrippa. Before the Roman period the entrance to the Acropolis was below the Temple of Athena Nike; it consisted of a steep ramp continuing the Sacred Way (*Ierá Odós*) along which the Panathenaic processions made their way up to the temple. A projecting terrace north of the Agrippa monument gives a good view of the three hills to the west: Philopappos, the Pnyx and the Areopagos.

Propílea★

The marble steps are very slippery.

The monumental gates to the Acropolis, the **Propílea**, were built by the architect Mnesikles. From the 12C to the 15C they were adapted as a palace. The Turks reinforced the gates with bastions, and it was not until 1836 that the Propylaia were stripped of their military accretions.

On passing through the Propylaia, one comes face to face with the graceful silhouette of the Erechtheion *(left)* and the majestic golden pile of the Parthenon *(right)*. Opposite the Propylaia stood the **Prómahos Athiná** (9m/30ft high), an impressive warrior figure of Athene, designed in bronze by **Pheidias** to commemorate the Athenian victory over the Persians.

Parthenonás★★★

This Doric temple was constructed by **Iktínos** under the direction of Pheidias in the Age of Pericles. The Parthenon was dedicated to Athena, whose statue by Pheidias, adorned the sanctuary. Pheidias was also responsible for the sculptures decorating the pediments, friezes and metopes.

The statue of Athena was removed to Constantinople in the Byzantine period and destroyed in 1203. The Parthenon was converted into a church and richly decorated

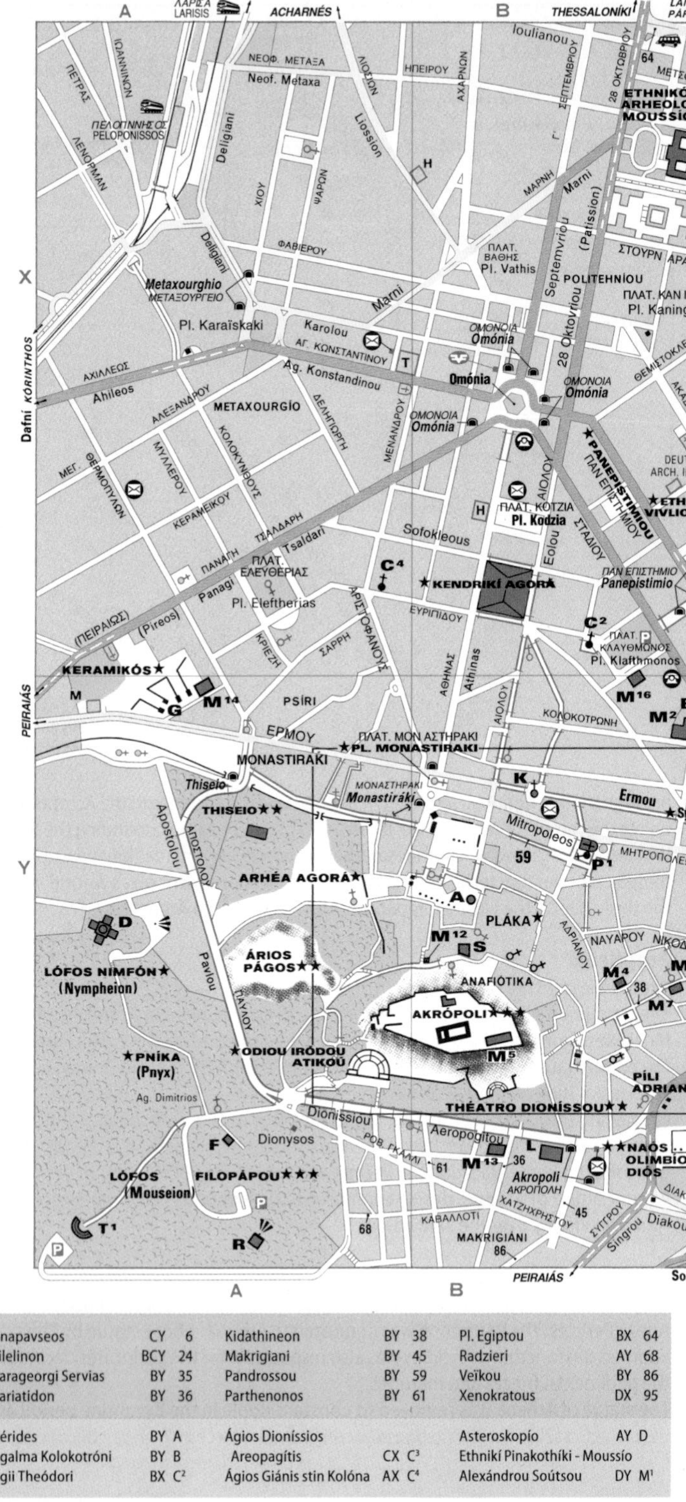

Anapavseos	CY	6	Kidathineon	BY	38	Pl. Egiptou	BX	64
Filelinon	BCY	24	Makrigiani	BY	45	Radzieri	AY	68
Karageorgi Servias	BY	35	Pandrossou	BY	59	Veïkou	BY	86
Kariatidon	BY	36	Parthenonos	BY	61	Xenokratous	DX	95

Aérides	BY	A	Ágios Dioníssios			Asteroskopío	AY	D
Ágalma Kolokotróni	BY	B	Areopagítis	CX	C[3]	Ethnikí Pinakothíki - Moussío		
Ágii Theódori	BX	C[2]	Ágios Giánis stin Kolóna	AX	C[4]	Alexándrou Soútsou	DY	M[1]

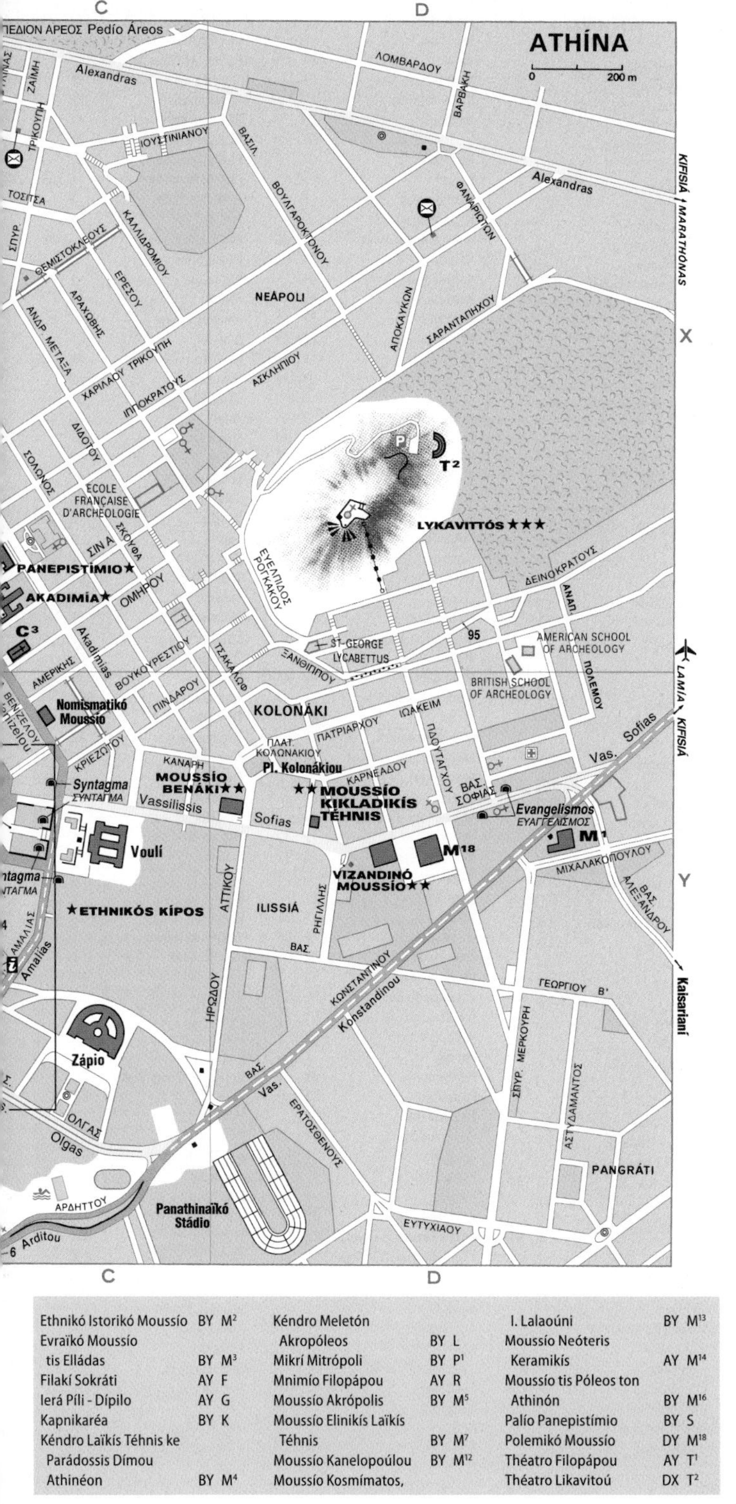

Ethnikó Istorikó Moussío BY M²	Kéndro Meletón Akropóleos BY L	I. Lalaoúni BY M¹³
Evraïkó Moussío tis Elládas BY M³	Mikrí Mitrópoli BY P¹	Moussío Neóteris Keramikís AY M¹⁴
Filakí Sokráti AY F	Mnimío Filopápou AY R	Moussío tis Póleos ton Athinón BY M¹⁶
Ierá Píli - Dípilo AY G	Moussío Akrópolis BY M⁵	Palío Panepistímio BY S
Kapnikaréa BY K	Moussío Elinikís Laïkís Téhnis BY M⁷	Polemikó Moussío DY M¹⁸
Kéndro Laïkís Téhnis ke Parádossis Dímou Athinéon BY M⁴	Moussío Kanelopoúlou BY M¹²	Théatro Filopápou AY T¹
	Moussío Kosmímatos,	Théatro Likavitoú DX T²

ATHÍNA

Street	Grid	No.
3-Septemvriou	BX	
A. Theochari	Z	
Adrianou	BY	2
Ag. Filipou	F	4
Ag. Konstandinou	AX	
Aharnon	BX	
Ahilleos	AX	
Akadimias	BCX	
Akti Kondili	Z	
Akti Koundouriotou	Z	
Akti Miaouli	Z	
Akti Themistokleous	Z	
Alexandras	CDX	
Amerikis	CXY	
Anapavseos	CY	6
Anapiron Polemou	DXY	
Apokafkon	DX	
Apostolou Pavlou	AY	
Arahovis	CX	
Arditou	CY	
Áreos	F	8
Aristofanous	AX	
Asklipiou	DX	
Ath. Diakou	BY	
Athinas	BXY	
Athinon	UV	
Athinon	Z	
Bouboulinas	CX	
Deligiani	AX	
Deligiorgi	AX	
Dexipou	F	13
Didotou	CX	
Diogenous	F	15
Dionissiou Areopagitou	ABY	
Dioskouron	F	16
El. Venizelou	CXY	
Eolou	BXY	
Epaminonda	F	20
Eratosthenous	DY	
Erehtheos	F	22
Ermou	F	
Ethn. Andistasseos	Z	
Evangelistrias	G	23
Evelpidos Rongakou	DX	
Fanarioton	DX	
Favierou	AX	
Filelinon	G	24
Flessa	G	25
Fokionos	G	27
Galanou	G	28
Georgiou	Z	
Geronda	G	29
Gounari	Z	
Hadzihristou	BY	
Harilaou Trikoupi	CX	
Hatzikiriakou	Z	
Herefondos	G	30
Hiou	AX	
Iera Odos	V	
Ifestou	F	32
Ioulianou	AX	
Ioustinianou	CX	
Iperidou	G	33
Ipirou	ABX	
Ipokratous	CX	
Ir. Politehniou	Z	
Irakleiou	U	
Irodou Atikou	DY	
Kalidromiou	CX	
Kanari	CY	
Kapnikareas	F	34
Kapodistriou	U	
Karageorgi Servias	F	35
Kariatidon	BY	36
Karneadou	DY	
Karolou	AX	
Kavaloti	BY	
Kekropos	G	37
Keramikou	AX	
Kidathineon	BY	38
Kifissias	U	
Kifissou	V	
Kiristou	F	40
Klepsidras	F	42
Klesovis	Z	
Kolokinthous	AX	
Kolokotroni	BY	
Kriezotou	CY	
Liossion	AX	
Lissikratous	G	43
Lissiou	F	44
Lomvardou	DX	
M. Hatzikiriakou	Z	
Makri	BY	
Makrigiani	BY	45
Markou Avriliou	F	47
Marni	ABX	
Meg. Alexandrou	AX	
Menandrou	AX	
Messogion	U	
Metsovou	BX	
Mihalakopoulou	DY	
Mitropoleos	F	49
Monis Asteriou	G	52
Navarhou Nikodimou	G	53
Neof. Metaxa	AX	
Nissou	F	55
Normanou	F	56
Omiridou Skilitsi	Z	
Omonia	BX	
Paleologou Benizelou	FG	58
Pandrossou	BY	59
Panepistimiou	BX	
Panos	F	60
Parthenonos	BY	61
Patission	BX	
Patr. Ioakim	DY	
Pedío Áreos	CX	
Pelopida	F	62
Petrou Rali	V	
Pikilis	F	63
Pindarou	CY	
Pireos Panagi Tsaldari	AX	
Pl. Anexartissias Vathis	BX	
Pl. Egiptou	BX	64
Pl. Eleftherias	AX	
Pl. Eth. Antistasseos Kodzia	BX	
Pl. Kaningos	BX	
Pl. Karaïskaki	AX	
Pl. Klafthmonos	BX	
Pl. Kolonakiou	DY	
Pl. Mitropoleos	G	65
Pl. Monastiráki	F	
Ploutarhou	DX	
Polignotou	F	66
Possidonos	V	
Pritaniou	F	67
Psaron	AX	
Radzieri	AY	68
Rigilis	DY	
Rovertou Gali	AY	
Sahtouri	Z	
Sarandapihou	DX	
Selei	G	70
Singrou	BY	
Skoufa	CX	
Sofokleous	ABX	
Solonos	CX	
Sotiros	G	72
Souri	G	73
Spir. Merkouri	DY	
Spir. Trikoupi	CX	
Stadiou	BXY	
Stournara	BX	
Stratonos	F	74
Syntagma	CY	
Thalou	G	76
Themistokleous	BCX	
Theotiki	Z	
Thermopilon	AX	
Thespidos	FG	77
Thoukididou	G	81
Tossitsa	CX	
Trikoupi	Z	
Tripodon	G	84
Tsakalof	DXY	
Tsangari	G	85
V. Athanasiou	Z	
Varvaki	DX	
Vas. Alexandrou	DY	
Vas. Amalias	CY	
Vas. Georgiou B'	DY	
Vas. Konstandinou	DY	
Vas. Olgas	CY	
Vas. Sofias	CDY	
Vas. Sofias	Z	
Vassiliou Voulgaroktonou	DX	
Veïkou	BY	86
Vironos	G	88
Voukourestiou	CXY	
Vouliagmenis	V	
Vrissakiou	F	90
Xanthipou	DXY	
Xenokratous	DY	
Zaïmi	CX	
Zani	Z	

Sight	Grid	Ref.
Aérides	F	A
Ágalma Kolokotróni	BY	B
Agía Ekateríni	G	C
Ágii Anárgiri	F	C[1]
Ágii Apóstoli	F	
Ágii Theódori	BX	C[2]
Ágios Dioníssios Areopagítis	CX	C[3]
Ágios Giánis stin Kolóna	AX	C[4]
Ágios Ioánis o Theológos	F	C[6]
Ágios Pávlos (Anglikanikí Eklissía)	G	C[5]
Akadimía	CX	
Akrópoli	F	
Aktí	Z	
Arhéa Agorá	F	
Arheologikó Moussío	Z	M[21]
Ários Págos	AY	
Astériou	V	
Asteroskopío	AY	D
Averoff	V	
Dafní	U	
Dzamí Fetiye	F	E

Ethnikí Pinakothíki - Moussío Alexándrou Soútsou	DY	M[1]
Ethnikí Vivliothíki	BX	
Ethnikó Arheologikó Moussío	BX	
Ethnikó Istorikó Moussío	BY	M[2]
Ethnikós Kípos	CY	
Evraïkó Moussío tis Elládas	G	M[3]
Filakí Sokráti	AY	F
Ierá Píli - Dípilo	AY	G
Kaisarianí	V	
Kapnikaréa	F	K
Kastéla	Z	
Kendrikí Agorá	BX	
Kéndro Laïkís Téhnis ke Parádossis Dímou Athinéon	G	M[4]
Kéndro Meletón Akropóleos	BY	L
Keramikós	AXY	
Kifisiá	U	
Lófos Filopápou	AY	
Lófos Nimfón	AY	
Lykavittós	DX	
Megáli Mitrópoli	G	P
Metamórfossis	F	
Mikrí Mitrópoli	G	P[1]
Mikrolímano	Z	
Mnimío Filopápou	AY	R
Mnimío Lissikrátous	G	
Mnimío Lórdou Vírona	G	R[1]
Monastiráki	AY	
Mouseío Design 20ou aióna	U	M[24]
Moussío Akrópolis	F	M[5]
Moussío Benáki	CDY	
Moussío Elinikís Laikís Keramikís	F	M[6]
Moussío Elinikís Laïkís Téhnis	G	M[7]
Moussío Elinikón Moussikón Orgánon	F	M[8]
Moussío Frissira	G	M[10]
Moussío Goulandrí Fissikís Istorías	U	M[23]
Moussío Kanelopoúlou	F	M[12]
Moussío Kikladikís Téhnis (Idrima N.P. Goulandrí)	DY	
Moussío Kosmímatos, I. Lalaoúni	BY	M[13]
Moussío Neóteris Keramikís	AY	M[14]
Moussío tis Póleos ton Athinón	BY	M[16]
Naftikó Moussío	Z	M[22]
Naós Olímbiou Diós	G	
Nomismatikó Moussío	CY	
Odío Iródou Atikoú	F	
Omónia	BX	
Óros Ymitós	V	
Palío Panepistímio	F	S
Panathinaïko Stádio	DY	
Panepistímio	CX	
Peiraiás	V	
Píli Adrianoú	G	
Pláka	BY	
Pníka	AY	
Polemikó Moussío	DY	M[18]
Romaïkí Agorá	F	S[1]
Soúnio	BY	
Stoá Atálou	F	
Syntagma	CY	
Théatro Dionissou	F	
Théatro Filopápou	AY	T[1]
Théatro Likavitoú	DX	T[2]
Thiseio	AY	
Tíhos Kónonos	Z	
Vivliothíki Adrianoú	F	V
Vizandinó Moussío	DY	
Voulí	CY	
Zéa	Z	

with frescoes and mosaics. After eight centuries of Orthodox worship, the Franks styled it St Mary of Athens, in the Roman rite.

The Turks converted the Parthenon into a mosque and built a minaret at the south-west corner. The building still retained the majority of its sculptures before the explosion of the powder magazine in 1687 destroyed many of them and brought down the Parian marble roof slabs, the walls of the naos and 28 columns.

Since 1834 efforts have been made to restore the structure, particularly the re-erection of the colonnades, a difficult operation known as **anastylosis**, which was carried out by Greek archaeologists after the First World War.

Exterior

The Parthenon rests on a marble stylobate and is surrounded by a peristyle of 46 fluted columns (8 at the ends and 17 down each side).

The pediments were decorated with painted sculptures against a blue background. The east pediment showed the Birth of Athena, fully armed, from the head of Zeus in the presence of the Sun (Helios) and the Moon (Selene) who are driving their chariots. The west pediment represented the Quarrel between Athena and Poseidon for possession of Attica; two very damaged pieces have survived.

The Doric frieze consisted of the usual triglyphs alternating with 92 metopes showing sculpted battle scenes against a red ground: the Battle between the Giants and the Olympian Gods *(east)*, the Battle between the Lapiths and the **Centaurs** *(south)*, the Battle between the Greeks and the **Amazons** *(west)* and the Siege of Troy *(north)*. Only a few of the original metopes still exist: there are 15 in the British Museum, one in the Louvre in Paris and several others in the Acropolis Museum.

The shields which were presented by Alexander the Great were attached to the architrave.

Interior

Closed to the public.

The east portico *(prónaos)* where the offerings were placed led into the sanctuary through a door 10m/33ft high. The inner chamber (naos) contained a gigantic **statue of Athena** (12m/39ft high). Behind the naos there was another chamber housing the treasure of the Delian League which was under the leadership of Athens.

Elgin Marbles

When **Lord Elgin** arrived in Constantinople as British Ambassador to the Porte (the central office of the Ottoman government in Constantinople) he obtained permission from the Sultan to make copies and models of Ancient buildings and to remove any interesting pieces. His agents in Athens induced the local Turkish authorities to allow pieces of sculpture to be removed from the temple itself. Elgin's purpose in acquiring his collection of Antiquities had been to improve artistic taste and design in Britain. His expenses, which he had hoped to recover from the government, made him bankrupt and he was finally forced to sell his collection to the British Museum at half the cost of obtaining it.

The wall enclosing the naos and the Parthenon was decorated on the outside with the **frieze of the Panathenaia**; this famous band of sculpture, which contained 400 human figures and 200 animals, depicted the Panathenaic procession. About 50 pieces, the best preserved, are displayed in the British Museum; a few others can be seen in the Acropolis Museum.

Traces of a Turkish minaret can be seen near the south corner of the west portico. Casts of the majority of the Parthenon sculptures can be seen at the Acropolis Interpretation Centre.

▶ *Cross the area between the Parthenon and the Erechtheion: look for traces of the foundations of the earlier Temple of Athena (Arhéos Naós Athinás) built in the early 6C BC and destroyed 100 years later to make room for the Erechtheion.*

Eréhthio★★★

This little Doric and Ionic temple, which was completed in 407 BC, incorporated several existing shrines, including those to Athena, Poseidon, Erechtheos and Cecrops, kings of Athens.

The famous southern portico faces the Parthenon. It is known as the Kariátides, the **Porch of the Caryatids**, because it is supported by six statues of young women. The figures are copies; one of the originals is in the British Museum; the others are on display in the Acropolis Museum. The eastern portico opens into the sanctuary that contained the oldest statue of Athena, which was made of olive wood.

From the viewpoint in the northeast corner of the site there are dramatic **views**★★ over the Roman town *(east)* (Hadrian's Arch, Temple of Zeus), down into the old district of Pláka *(north)* and over the suburbs to the northeast of Athens surrounded by the Parnes, Pentelikon and Hymettos ranges.

Porch of the Caryatids

J Malburet/MICHELIN

▶ *Make for the Acropolis Museum tucked away in a hollow in the rock.*

Acropolis Museum ★★★

Open Tue-Sun 8am-7pm, Mon 11am-7pm (2.30pm in winter). ☎ (210) 32 36 665. In 2007 the museum will transfer its collections to a new, larger space. Highlights of the collection which may be on view are described below.

The Acropolis Museum contains the sculptures and other objects found during the excavation of the Acropolis. You'll find 7C and 6C BC pediments or fragments of pediments, some in tufa as opposed to marble, as was common during the period. There is a beautiful fragment of a marble quadriga (four-horse chariot); the Pediment of the Olive Tree or of Troilus; and above all the **Moscophoros**, a painted marble statue with eyes originally of glass paste, a votive statue of about 570 BC; and a headless *kore* in white marble, the oldest of those from the Acropolis (between 580 and 570 BC).

The museum possesses an important collection of statues of young women (**kore** in the singular, **korai** in the plural) in coloured marble (6C BC). The peplos *kore* is attributed to Phaidimos, the earliest known Attic sculptor; also by him are an extraordinarily life-like dog, a lion's head and a smiling horseman (a copy; the original, known as the Rampin Horseman, is in the Louvre).

Note also 8-7C BC ceramics in the geometric style, and four statues from the pediment (c 525 BC) of the old Temple of Athena; Athena is recognisable, brandishing a lance. Among other remarkable works are the *kore* by Antenor, of great refinement, from the end of 6C BC, the statue of Nike (Victory) in flight dating from about 500 BC, and the *kore* with the dove. Try not to miss the famous **Athena mourning**, a 5C votive relief, and a young man's head in marble from Pheidias' studio.

Reconstructions of the **Parthenon pediments** include Birth of Athena, Quarrel between Athena and Poseidon. Some sculptures were removed from the temples for preservation: the Panathenaic procession from the Parthenon, and items from the Temple of Athena Nike including the figure of Nike (Victory) undoing her sandal before offering a sacrifice. Several of the famous caryatids from the Erechtheion are displayed behind a protective glass screen.

▸ *On leaving the museum walk along the southern edge of the Acropolis hill: interesting views down over the theatres of Dionysos and Herodes Atticus).*

Naós Athinás Níkis★★★

The **Temple of Athena Nike**, which was formerly known as the Temple of Nike Apteros (Wingless Victory), stands on a projecting bastion west of the Propylaia. A small but graceful Ionic temple (late 5C BC), it consisted of a chamber (naos) between two porticoes supported on monolithic columns. The badly damaged exterior frieze comprises a few original pieces (east and south sides); the rest are copies.

▸ *Leave the Acropolis by the Beulé Gate and bear right to the Areopagos.*

Áríos Págos★ (Areopagos)

Theseus's enemies, the Amazons, camped on this limestone hill and consecrated it to Ares, god of war. Another legend says that **Orestes**, who was being pursued by the **Furies**, was judged here. **St Paul** is thought to have preached at Areopagos when he converted the senator who was to become St Dionysius the Areopagite, the first Bishop of Athens.

Fine **view** of the Acropolis and of the Greek agora and Roman forum below.

▸ *Return to Leofóros Dionissou Areopagitou. Those braving the climb to Philopappos Hill and the Pnyx will be rewarded with stunning views.*

Lófos Filopápou★★★ (Philopappos Hill)

Paths start near the Dionysos restaurant. In Antiquity Philopappos Hill was dedicated to the Muses and bore the name Mouseion. The path climbs past Ancient troglodyte cave-dwellings; one was long thought to be **Socrates' prison**. The hill is dominated by the **Philopappos monument** (AD 116) commemorating a benefactor of Athens. There are spectacular **views**★★★, of the Acropolis, Athens, Hymettos and the plain of Attica. The Philopappos Theatre on the west face of the hill presents performances of traditional dances.

Pníka★

The **Pnyx** forms a sort of amphitheatre, where the Assembly of the people *(Ecclisía)* met between the 6C and the 4C BC. Many famous orators, such as **Themistocles**, **Pericles** and **Demosthenes**, spoke here. From the terrace there is a splendid **view**★★★ of the Acropolis; sound and light shows are held here during the summer.

Lófos Nimfóna★

The **Nympheion**, the Hill of the Nymphs, is scattered with traces of dwellings and offers a view of the Parthenon. The hill is crowned by an observatory, a neo-Classical building which was completed in 1957 with the addition of a seismology station.

Return to the foot of the Acropolis and follow Apostolou Pavlou, which skirts the base of the hill. Cross the railroad tracks; a bridge over the tracks leads to the Agora.

Arhéa Agorá★ (Agora)

Open Tue-Sun, 8am-7pm, Mon 11am-7pm. 4€ (ticket also valid for museum entry). ☎ (21032) 10 185.

The agora, which is now a confused jumble of ruins, was originally a rectangular open space covering about 2.5ha/6 acres and divided diagonally by the Panathenaic Way, which ran past the Altar of the Twelve Olympian Gods from which the distances to other Greek cities were measured. The space was enclosed within buildings, temples and shops arranged in a long portico (stoa) where citizens gathered.

The Romans encroached on the open space with buildings such as the Odeon of Agrippa and the Temple of Ares. Under the Byzantines a district grew up around **Ágii Apóstoli** (the Church of the Holy Apostles – late 10C AD).

The **thólos**, which dates from about 470 BC, was a round building where the 50 senators *(prytaneis)* met to take their meals; the standard weights and measures were also kept here. To the north of the *thólos* stood the **Metroon** (Mitróo), the Temple of the Mother of the Gods, behind which stood the Bouleuterion, the Senate house;

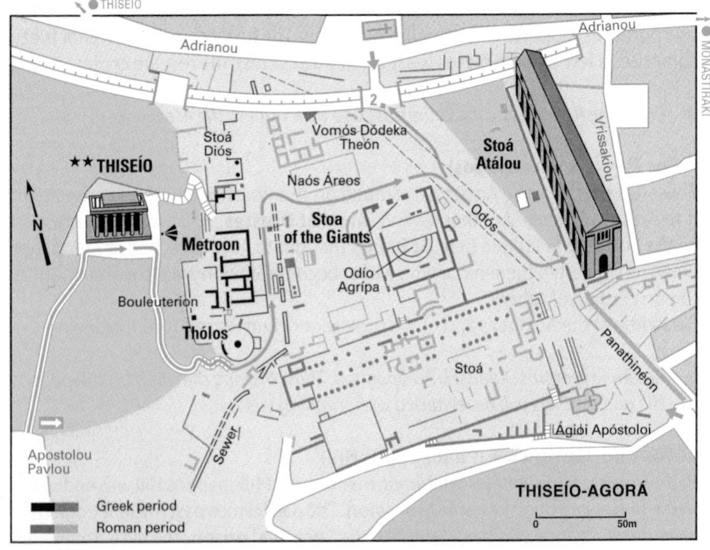

beyond the Metroon stood the Temple of Apollo Patroos and the Stoa of Zeus. Only the foundations of these buildings remain, but there are also traces of a great drain which passed to the east of them and of pedestals for statues: one of them bears the likeness of the Emperor Hadrian (**1**).
The **Stoá Atálou**, which was built in the 2C BC by Attalos, king of Pergamon, has been reconstructed. It is a long two-storey building which displays the articles found during the excavations in the agora. The external gallery displays the Apollo Patroos (4C BC), and the interior gallery contains objects from everyday life in Antiquity. Near the entrance in Odós Adrianóu there is a mosaic reconstruction showing the agora as it was in Antiquity.

Thisío★★ (Theseion)

This 5C BC Doric temple, one of the best preserved in the Greek world, stands on a mound dominating the agora, the centre of Athenian public life in Antiquity. Known since the Middle Ages as the Theseion, it is, in fact, the **Hephaisteion** mentioned by Pausanias, the Temple of Hephaïstos, god of smiths and metalworkers.
In the Byzantine period the temple was converted into a church; under the Turks it became the burial place of Englishmen and other Protestants. The last service was held in 1834; it then housed the first collections of the National Museum.
The stone Hephaisteion, older and smaller than the Parthenon, was originally painted. The deteriorated sculptures of the external frieze recall the exploits of Herakles (Hercules) and Theseus. The east portico with its marble coffered ceiling still in place leads into the naós (5C AD). The temple terrace offers fine views of the agora, the Monastiráki district and the Acropolis.

Walking Tours

On the northern slopes of the Acropolis old Athens lives on in the Pláka and Monastiráki, the only districts in the capital evoking the atmosphere of Athens in the Middle Ages or during the Turkish occupation. The conservation of the old buildings and the exclusion of traffic have greatly enhanced the charm of the area. Farther to the north lie sights dating from the neoclassical period, the first decades of independent Greece.

Pláka★★ 1

Circuit from Sindagma Square. 1 day.
Pláka consists of picturesque and peaceful narrow streets and alleys opening out into tiny squares and terraces linked by steps. There are a few Byzantine churches tucked in between the old houses. Here and there one catches a glimpse of the city or the Acropolis. The broader streets below the slope are thronged with shops and inexpensive guesthouses.
After dark Pláka comes alive with nightclubs and tavernas. Crowds tarry late into the night, savouring the Greek cuisine with glasses of *retsina*, listening to the music, and dancing the modern *sirtáki*.

▸ *From the southwest corner of Síndagma Square take Odós Mitropóleos.*

On the left under the arcade of a modern building is the tiny Chapel of **Agía Dínami** (17C). The street opens into a square, Platía Mitropóleos: the Orthodox cathedral, is known as the **Megáli Mitrópoli** (Great Metropolitan) and dates from the 19C.

Mikrí Mitrópoli★★

The **Small Metropolitan**, dedicated to the Virgin who answers prayers swiftly (Panagía Gorgoepíkoos), is a charming 12C Byzantine church built on the Greek cross plan with a dome.

Incorporated in the external walls are many decorative pieces from an earlier age: between the two Corinthian capitals flanking the façade stretches an unusual Ancient frieze (4C BC) showing the months and the signs of the zodiac. The cross with a double bar and the arms of the La Roche and De Villehardouin families *(pediment)* were added in the Frankish period (13C).

PLÁKA

Rues

Street	Square	No.
Adrianou	F	2
Ag. Filipou	F	4
Áreos	F	8
Dexipou	F	13
Diogenous	F	15
Dioskouron	F	16
Epaminonda	F	20
Erehtheos	F	22
Evangelistrias	G	23
Filelinon	G	24
Flessa	G	25
Fokionos	G	27
Galanou	G	28
Geronda	G	29
Herefondos	G	30
Ifestou	F	32
Iperidou	G	33
Kapnikareas	F	34
Karageorgi Servias	G	35
Kekropos	G	37
Kidathineon	G	38
Kiristou	F	40
Klepsidras	F	42
Lissikratous	G	43
Lissiou	F	44
Markou Avriliou	F	47
Mitropoleos	F	49
Monis Asteriou	G	52
Navarhou Nikodimou	G	53
Nissou	F	55
Normanou	F	56
Paleologou Benizelou	FG	58
Pandrossou	F	59
Panos	F	60
Pelopida	F	62
Pikilis	F	63
Pl. Mitropoleos	G	65
Polignotou	F	66
Pritaniou	F	67
Selei	G	70
Sotiros	G	72
Souri	G	73
Stratonos	F	74
Thalou	G	76
Thespidos	FG	77
Thoukididou	G	81
Tripodon	G	84
Tsangari	G	85
Vironos	G	86
Vrissakiou	F	90

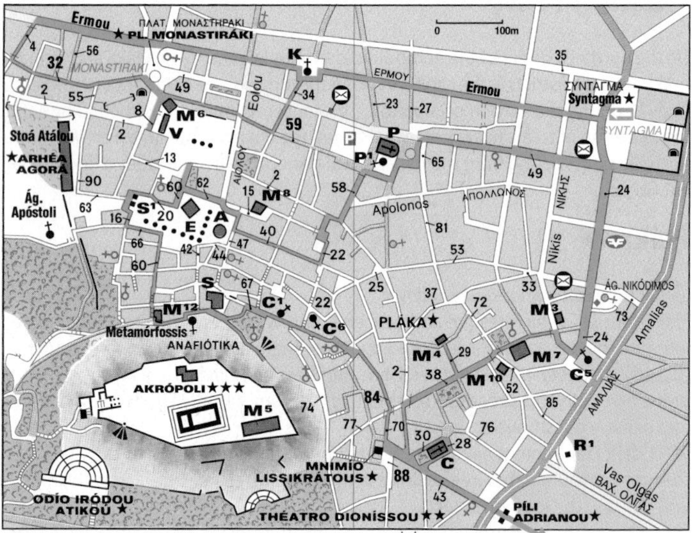

Sight	Square	Key
Aérides	F	A
Agía Ekateríni	G	C
Ágii Anárgiri	F	C^1
Ágios Ioánis o Theológos	F	C^6
Ágios Pávlos (Anglikanikí Eklissía)	G	C^5
Dzamí Fetiye	F	E
Evraïkó Moussío tis Elládas	G	M^3
Kapnikaréa	F	K
Kéndro Laïkís Téhnis ke Parádossis Dímou Athinéon	G	M^4
Megáli Mitrópoli	G	P
Mikrí Mitrópoli	G	P^1
Mnimío Lórdou Vírona	G	R^1
Moussío Akrópolis	F	M^5
Moussío Elinikís Laikís Keramikís	F	M^6
Moussío Elinikís Laïkís Téhnis	G	M^7
Moussío Elinikón Moussikón Orgánon	F	M^8
Moussío Frissira	G	M^{10}
Moussío Kanelopoúlou	F	M^{12}
Palío Panepistímio	F	S
Romaïkí Agorá	F	S^1
Vivliothíki Adrianoú	F	V

Pláka Address Book

For coin categories, see the Legend on the cover flap.

WHERE TO EAT

Platanos – *4 Odós Diogenous. Closed Sunday evenings.* Eat in the shade of eucalyptus and plane trees. Classic Plaka taverna; a local haunt.

Sholarhio to Geraini – *14 Odós Tripodon. Open for lunch.* Large assortment of delicious *mezes* served under a vine-covered pergola.

Xinou, *4 Odós Angelou Geronda. ☎ 32 21 065. Closed on Saturdays and Sundays.* Good food, pleasant setting in a courtyard, with live music.

O Glikis – *Odós A. Gerondas.* A local institution; note the grand wooden bar. Excellent *mezes.*

Tou Psara – *16 Odós Erehtheos. Open for lunch.* Charming and unique setting and delicious cuisine. One of the best restaurants in Pláka.

Ermeion – *15 Odós Pandrossou and 7 Odós Mnissikleous, in an arcade.* Elegant atmosphere,refined cuisine and service. Try the swordfish (lemon and olive sauce) and baklava.

Diogenes – *Platía Lissikratous.* Calm, pleasant atmosphere in which to sample a drink or a variety of house specialities.

WHERE TO STAY

Kimon – *27 Odós Apollonos – ☎ (21033) 14 658 – 14rm.* Satisfactory rooms; good views of the Acropolis from the pretty terrace.

Adonis – *3 Odós Kodrou – ☎ (21032) 49 737 – 26rm.* Situated in the heart of Pláka, this comfortable hotel has superb views of the Acropolis from its terrace bar. Rooms without air-conditioning cost less.

Acropolis House – *6-8 Odós Kodrou – ☎ (21032) 22 344, htlacrhs@otenet.gr – 19rm.* This neo-Classical hotel has every modern comfort. All **non-smoking** (rare in Greece!). Rooms without air-conditioning cost less.

Metropolis – *46 Odós Mitropoleos – ☎ / fax (21032) 17 469, (21032) 17 871, www.hotelmetropolis.gr – 22rm.* Clean, comfortable hotel in a pink building with flower-filled balconies. No breakfast. Rooms without en-suite facilities cost less.

Omiros – *15 Odós Apollonos – ☎ (21032) 35 486, www.omiroshotel.gr – 37rm.* Modern, comfortable hotel. Enjoy views of the Acropolis over breakfast on the pleasant terrace.

Niki – *27 Odós Nikis – ☎(21032) 209-13 – 21rm.* Discreet, quiet hotel in a narrow street off Sindagma Square.

Adrian – *74 Odós Adrianóu – ☎ (21032) 21 553, (reservations ☎ (21052) 034 91), www.douroshotels.com – 22rm.* A comfortable little hotel in the heart of Pláka. Beautiful, shady terrace with views of the Erechtheion.

Plaka – *7 Odós Kapnikareas – ☎ (21032) 227 06 (res.), www.plaka-hotel.gr – 67rm.* Recently renovated, with comfortable rooms (ask for one with a view of the Acropolis). Beautiful terrace with wonderful views.

Byron – *19 Odós Vironos – ☎ (21032) 30 327, www.hotel-byron.gr – 22rm.* Recently modernised, comfortable hotel, well-situated and and with a welcoming ambience; Acropolis view.

Hermes – *19 Odós Apollonos – ☎ (21032) 35 514, www.hermeshotel.gr – 45rm.* Every one of the spacious guestrooms has a balcony. Comfortable, well-designed and equipped; in-house travel agent; gameroom for kids.

TAKING A BREAK

Nikis – *Odós Nikis. From Síndagma Square, take the first right off Odós Ermou.* Close to the shops of Odós Ermou, this calm street café is the perfect place for a coffee break.

Kidathinaion – *Platia Filomoussou Etairas/Odós Kidathnieon.* An old-style local hangout on a lively square, perfect for people-watching.

Nefeli – *24 Odós Panos and Odós Aretousas.* Charming views of the palm trees of the Agora from the little tables of this café set along Odós Dioskouron, particularly at dusk when the sun sets on the Hephaisteion.

SOUVENIRS

Browse the shops along Odós Kidathinaion and Adrianou for leather, statuettes, ouzo and honey.

▶ *Take Odós Erehthéos and Odós Kirístou.*

Hammam Abid Effendi

No. 8. Open Wed-Sun 9am-2.30pm.

Exhibitions of contemporary art are presented in the shadowy light and echoing acoustics of these restored Turkish baths.

▶ *Walk around the Tower of the Winds and continue down Odos Diogenous.*

Museum of Popular Musical Instruments

Kids *1-3 Odós Diogenous. Open Tue-Sun 10am-2pm (Wed 12-6pm). No charge. ☎ (21032) 501 98.*

Look and listen (headphones at each display) to a fascinating collection of some 600 traditional musical instruments from the 18C to the present day.

Romaikí Agorá (Roman Forum)

Walk round in an anti-clockwise direction *(Odós Diogénous and Odós Pelopida)* passing an old 16C mosque, the **Fetihie Cami**, with domes and an attractive columned porch. On your left you'll see the **Tower of the Winds**★ **(Aerides)**, an octagonal tower of white marble dating from the 1C BC. It was built to house a hydraulic clock, supplied by the Klepsidra spring on the north slop of the Acropolis hill.

On the west side stands the monumental **Forum gateway** (AD 2), which gave access to the forum proper; the interior court has been excavated.

▶ *Walk around the agora by Odós Epaminonda, then Dioskouron, and finally left on odós Polignotou. Follow Odos Panos to the right as it begins the steep climb up the north flank of the Acropolis; turn left on Odos Theorias.*

H Champollion/MICHELIN

The Tower of the Winds, a tower built to house a hydraulic clock

Housed in a fine 19C residence, the **Moussío Kanelopoúlou**★ *(corner of Odós Theorias and Odós Panos; open Tue-Sun 8.30am-3pm; 2€; ☎ (21032)123 13)* is a fine collection of Ancient ceramics, Tanágra figurines, busts of Sophocles and Alexander, jewellery, Byzantine icons and popular works of art.

A little way along on the right stands the small **Church of the Transfiguration** (Metamórfossis) which dates from the 12C-14C;it rises above the semi-rural district of Anafiótika, founded by refugees from Anaphe in the Cyclades.

Below and to the north of the church lies the **'Old University' (Palió Panepistímio)** (19C) which was originally the house of the architect **Kleanthes**.

▶ *Turn right and continue for 100m/110yd up an alleyway which climbs above the Anafiótika quarter.*

A fine **view**★★, especially beautiful at sunset, unfolds over the roofs of the old quarters, beyond to the town centre, southeast to Hymettos, south to the columns of the Olympieion at the far end of the National Garden (Ethnikós Kípos), and north, to the slope of Pentelikon; to the east the town stretches to the foot of Mount Parnes.

Continuing along Odós Pritaniou, the **Church of Ágii Anárgirii** (17C) is on the left, in the courtyard of the Convent of the Holy Sepulchre. Farther on stands the 12C Chapel of St John the Evangelist (Ágios Ioánnis o Theológos). Bear south to join **Odós Tripódon** linking the Theatre of Dionysos to the *Agorá*.

Mnimío Lissikrátous★ (Lysicrates' Monument)

The only survivor of the votive monuments in Odós Tripódon was erected in 334 BC. The monument was used as a library and was known as the **Lantern of Demosthenes** since tradition wrongly asserted that the great orator had worked there. The rotunda-like structure escaped the turmoil of the War of Independence and was restored in 1845.

Farther east on the far side of a shady square stands **St Catherine's Church** (Agía Ekateríni); it was built in the 13C but has been altered several times since.

Proceed along Odós Lissikratous to Leofóros Amalias.

Píli Adrianoú★ (Hadrian's Arch)

The arch dates from c 131 BC, and bears an inscription in the frieze indicating that it divided the Greek city from Hadrian's new Roman city (Hadrianopolis), which extended from the present-day Leofóros Amalias as far as the River Ilissós. A short distance from the gate stands a monument to Lord Byron.

Naós Olímbiou Diós★★ (Olympieion)

Entrance at the top of Avenue Vassillis Olgas. Open daily 8.30am-3pm. 2€. (21092) 26 330.

There are only a few traces beyond Hadrian's Arch of the temple to Zeus which was one of the largest in the Greek world. As early as the 6C BC this site was chosen for a colossal temple, not completed until AD 132 under the Emperor Hadrian. Of the 84 original marble columns only 15 remain. Even today the Corinthian columns are impressive because of their width and height.

Make for Odós Kidathinéon; turn left to reach Odós A. Hatzimiháli .

At no. 6, the **Centre for Popular Art and Traditions** (*open Tue-Fri 9am-1pm and 5-9pm, Sat-Sun 9am-1pm; no charge*) presents collections of weaving and embroidery, along with costumes, musical instruments and agricultural implements.

Return to Odós Kidathneon and turn right on Odós Monis Asteriou.

At no. 3, the **Frissirias Museum**★ (*open Tue-Fri 10am-5pm, Sat-Sun 1am-5pm; 6€*) mounts rotating displays of works from its collection of some 3500 paintings of the human figure by well-known Greek and international artists.

Return to Odós Kidathneon.

The **Museum of Green Folk Art**★ (*Kids no. 17; open Tue-Sun 9am-3pm; 2€*) features traditional costumes, household objects and objects related to cultural traditions such as shadow theater and Dionysian rituals.

Turn left into into Odós Nikis.

The **Jewish Museum of Greece**★ (*no. 39, on the right; open Mon-Fri 9am-2.30pm, Sun 10am-2pm; ring bell for access; 5€*) traces the 2 000-year history of Jewish presence in Greece.

Turn north into Odós Filelínon to visit the **Russian Church of St Nicodemus** (Ágios Nikódimos), an 11C building with a dome, which was altered in the last century.

Monastiráki 2

This was the centre of the Turkish town with the bazaar and the souks as well as the main mosques and administrative buildings. Now it is a popular commercial district incorporating the Athens flea market.

From Síndagma Square, head down **Odós Ermoú**, *a busy shopping street.*

Kapnikaréa

The church, which is attached to the University of Athens consists of two adjoining chapels: the one on the right dates from the 11C; the other dates from the 13C.

Walk south down Odós Kapnikaréas and turn right into Odós Pandróssou.

Odós Pandróssou★

Thronged with busy crowds, this street resembles a market, complete with awnings and pavement stalls. There is an amazing range of articles for sale.
On the left was the entrance to the bazaar, set up in the ruins of Hadrian's Library.

Platía Monastiráki★

This square, with its frippery goods displayed on open-air stalls, is the heart of the old Turkish district and one of the liveliest attractions of Athens. The church, **Pandánassa** (17C) originally belonged to the convent from which the square takes its name.

Dzistaráki Mosque

Open Wed-Mon, 9am-2.30pm. 2€. ☎ (21032) 42 066.
At the junction of Odós Pandróssou with Odós Áreos stands the former Dzistaráki Mosque (1759); it has lost its minaret but it was skilfully restored in 1975 to house the **Museum of Traditional Greek Ceramics** *(open Wed-Mon 9am-2.30pm; 2€).*

Monastiráki Address Book

For coin categories, see the Legend on the cover flap.

The lively (and newly trendy) **Psiri** district north along Odós Ermou, centred around Platia Iroon, bustles with cafés and restaurants.

WHERE TO EAT

Naxos – *Psiri, Odós Christokopidou, at the foot of the church. Mezedopolio. Open for lunch.* Delicious fish *mezes.*

Platía Iroon – *Psiri, 1 platía Iroon. Mezedopolio. Open evenings only.* Tables available on the square. Over 30 *mezes* to choose from.

WHERE TO STAY

Tempi – *29 Odós Eolou – ☎ (21032) 13 175/42 940, tempihotel@travelling.gr – 24rm.* Very well situated in a pedestrianised street near the Agia Irini church. Simple, but with a welcoming air. No breakfast.

Cecil – *39 Odós Athinas – ☎/fax (21032) 17 079, info@cecil.gr – 40rm.* Set in a beautiful, neo-classical building, recently renovated. Some of the charming guest rooms are noisier than others (ask for a room on the little back street). Welcoming atmosphere.

Attalos – *29 Odós Athinas – ☎ (21032) 12 801 – www.attalos.gr – 78rm.* Beautiful roof terrace; clean and comfortable rooms. View of the Acropolis from the balconies.

TAKING A BREAK

Metropol – *Platia Mitropoleos.* Old-fashioned café; tempting pastries. A great place to stop for a mid-day treat.

Pottery and porcelain from the different regions are pleasantly displayed in the setting of a Muslim place of worship with its *mihrab* and its galleries.

Vivliothíki Adrianoú (Hadrian's Library)

Odós Áreos. The destruction by fire of the bazaar in 1885 made it possible to investigate the remains of Hadrian's Library built in 132 BC. It was an impressive rectangular building with a peristyle of 100 columns, restored in the 5C AD.
The entrance façade on Odós Áreos is quite well preserved, particularly the Corinthian colonnade. It is about half the length of the original façade.

Return to Monastiráki Square and continue westwards along **Odós Iféstou**, *running on from Odós Pandrossou. As in Antiquity, it is occupied by metalworkers and takes its name from Hephaïstos, god of the forge. At the end, take Odós Astingos to Odós Ermou and continue to Odós Agiion Asenaton.*

At no. 22 you'll find the annex of the famed **Benaki Museum of Islamic Art** *(open Tue-Sun 9am-3pm; 9pm Wed; 5€; no charge Wed).* The terrace offers nice views of the Keramíki Cemetery. Inside there are ceramics, jewellry, decorative arts and arms arranged in chronological order or four floors.
Retrace your steps to Odós Melidoni to nos. 4-6, location of the **Museum of Contemporary Ceramics** *(open Mon, Thu, Fri 9am-3pm; Wed 9am-8pm; Sat 10am-3pm; Sun 10am-2pm; closed Wed; 2€)* dedicated to the study of traditional and modern ceramic items of daily life.

Retrace your steps to Odós Ermou.

Ierá Píli ke Dípiloa★

The **Sacred Gate** was built at the same time as Themistocles' wall (5C BC) and marks the beginning of the Sacred Way to Eleusis. The **Dipylon**, from the same period, was the main entrance to Athens.The Panathenaic processions started here.

Keramikós Cemetery★

48 Odós Ermou. Open daily 8am-7pm. Closed Mon, Nov-Mar. 2€ (ticket also valid for museum entry). ☎ (21034) 63 552.
The **Kerameikos**, the largest **cemetery** in Athens, was situated outside the wall of the Ancient city. From the 6C BC the graves were marked with gravestones and statues. The site has yielded some handsome finds now displayed in the National Museum; a few statues and stones have been left in place.
Leaving the **museum** on the left descend the path (South Way) that leads to the best-preserved part of the cemetery: tombs dating from the 4C BC to the 1C AD. Turn left into the West Way, lined by tombs erected in the 4C BC. On the corner there is a tomb with a low relief (moulding) of a cavalryman fighting: this is Dexileos, who was killed in 393 BC in the war against the Corinthians. Look for the tomb of Dionysos, the treasurer (bull standing on a pillar); the monument to Lysimachides, the archon (a dog). On the other side of the West Way stands the famous gravestone of Hegeso (moulding); the original is in the National Museum. On the south side are the gravestone of Antidosis, which was painted, and the vase *(lekythos)* of Aristomachos.

Sindagma Square to Omónia Square 3

Platía Sindágmatos★

Síndagma Square (Constitution Square) is in the elegant part of Athens that attracts many tourists. The east side is filled by the former royal palace, built for Otto I of Bavaria, which became the **Parliament (Voulí)** in 1935.
In front, before the monument to the Unknown Soldier, stand two **soldiers** *(évzoni)*, dressed in the distinctive kilt and pompom shoes. At appointed times they emerge

from their boxes to perform a sort of military ballet. Try to visit on Sundays at 11am when the ceremony is conducted with additional military personnel.

J Malburet/MICHELIN

Panepistimíou★

Return to Síndagma Square, north side.
This is University Avenue, which is lined with luxury hotels, large terraced cafés, restaurants and smart boutiques. **Schliemann's House** is a large private house known as the 'palace of Troy' (Iliou Mélanthron) which the brilliant German archaeologist had built in 1879; it now houses the **Numismatic Museum** *(no. 12; open Tue-Sun 8.30am-3pm; 3€)* with a noteworthy collection of 600 000 coins and medals, including some of the earliest ever made).
A little farther on stands the Roman Catholic Cathedral of **St Dionysius the Areopagite** (Ágios Dionisis Areopagitis).

Panepistímio, Akadimía, Ethnikí Vivliothíki★ (The University, Academy and National Library)

These three 19C buildings in white Pentelic marble form an architectural group in the neo-Classical style. The **University** in the centre is the oldest; it was designed by Christian von Hansen, the Danish architect, and built between 1837 and 1864. To the right, the **Academy** was designed by von Hansen's brother Theophilos in the style of an Ionic temple. On the left, the **National Library**, which contains 500 000 volumes and 3 000 manuscripts.
Continue on to **Platía Omónia** (Concord Square) with its noise, crowds and hawkers, particularly in the evening. From here go left along Odós Athinas to **Platía Kodziá**, the centre of Athens in the second half of the 19C. The National Bank of Greece (Ethnikí Trápeza tis Eládos) on the east side was founded in 1842. About 500 Ancient tombs have been found in the centre of the square, just outside the city walls.

Follow Odós Eolou (pedestrian street) to the market.

Kolonáki Address Book

For coin categories, see the Legend on the cover flap.

WHERE TO EAT

To Kioupi – *4 Platía Kolonakíou. Open Sun-Fri, 11am to 7pm.* A local instituti-tion since 1929. Family-style dishes served up quickly; friendly atmosphere.
Athinaïkon – *2 Odós Themistokléous (near Omónia Square) ☏ (210) 38 36 485. Open for lunch.* Traditional marble tables; aura of Athens during the 1930s. Spend the hottest part of the day sampling *mezes* in air-conditioned comfort.
O Andreas – *18 Odós Themistokleous (in a little street to the right off Omónia Square). Open for lunch; closed Sun.* Try the delicious fish *mezes* with ouzo or white wine.

WHERE TO STAY

Athinea – *9 Odós Vilara, pedestrian street off Agios Konstantinou – ☏(21052) 455 81.* – Very simple, comfortable hotel; excellent value.
Pythagorion – *28 Odós Agio Konstandinou – ☏(21052) 811 14 – www.bestwestern.com/gr/pythagorionhotel.* Well-kept rooms, some with balconies.

Ethniki Agorá★

Athens' **National Market** (closed Sun) is a spectacular sight with its vendors, goldsmiths and money changers on the north side (Odós Sofokléous). From the south side of the market go west along Odós Evripidou to nº 72 where stands the **Chapel of St John of the Column** (Ágios Ioánnis stin Kólon), much sought after for curing fevers.

Odós Stadíou

Street parallel to Panepistimíou.

At its start this is a shopping street; halfway along on the south side is **Platía Klafthmónos** (Wailing Square). In the west corner stands the 11C **Church of the Sts Theodore** (Ágii Theódori), the oldest in Athens. The small neo-Classical mansion (1834) southeast of the square was the residence of the Greek royal family from 1836 to 1842; it now houses the **City of Athens Museum** (*open Wed-Sun 10am-2pm, Sat-Sun 9am-1.30pm; 5€*) highlighting daily life in Athens during the reign of King Otto.
At no. 13 stands the **National Historical Museum**★ (*open Tue-Sun 9am-2pm; 3€*) housed in the former Parliament building and highlighting the history of modern Greece from the fall of Byzantium in 1453 to the end of the Second World War.

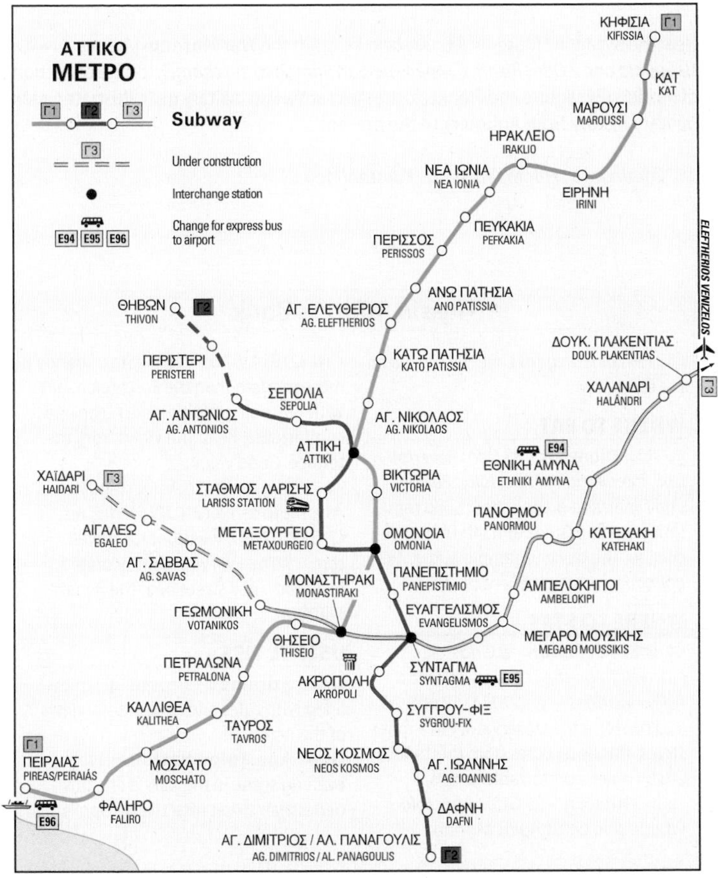

Around Mount Lycabettos★ 4

Leave Sindagma Square by Vassilissis Sofias, left of the Parliament.

Grand avenue Vassilissis Sofias, ranging the National Garden, is lined with embassies, bank headquarters and several important museums, notably the Benáki Museum, the Museum of Cycladic Art and the Museum of Byzantine Art *(see descriptions below)*.

Platía Koloniakíou

Kolonáki Square, ringed with luxury shops, cafés and restaurants, is at the centre of the elegant Kolonáki district. The streets are lined with the smartest shops in Athens.

Likavitós★★★ (Lycabettos)

Access by funicular (at junction of Aristipou and Ploutarchou; bus no. 60 stops in Odós Kleomenous below the funicular): departs every 30min from 9am-3am. Return ticket 4€.
According to legend, Athena dropped Mount Lycabettos (Wolves' Hill) from the heavens to provide the setting for the Acropolis. The summit is crowned by a chapel dedicated to St George; the adjacent terraces offer an admirable **panorama** of the city of Athens, the Acropolis, the sea coast at Piraeus and the major mountain peaks.

Descend back to Vassilissis Sofias.

Near the Byzantine Museum *(see below)* stands the **War Museum** *(Avenue Vassilissis Sophia and 2 Odós Rizari; open Tue-Sun 9am-2pm; no charge)*. Its fine collection of models (Byzantine and Frankis fortresses), arms and military gear illustrate Greek military history from Antiquity to the present.

Continue to Leofóros Vassilissis Konstantinou.

Thissío Address Book

For coin categories, see the Legend on the cover flap.

WHERE TO EAT

Dionysos – *43 Odós Rovertou Gali, intersection of Apostolou Pavlou and Dionissiou Areopagitou.* Solid reputation for fine Greek and international cuisine. The place to sample authentic *dolmades* or the excellent *baclava.*

WHERE TO STAY

Erechtheion – *8 Odós Flamarion on the corner with Odós Agias Marinas – ☎ (21034) 59 606/26, – 22rm.* Near the Observatory in a quiet street, this hotel dates from the 1960s. Clean, quiet, comfortable rooms.

Thission – *25 Odós Apostolou Pavlou and Odós Agias Marinas – ☎ (21034) 67 634/55 – 25rm.* Slightly more modern than the Erechteion, but with noisy air-conditioning. Clean and comfortable. Beautiful views from the terrace. Good value.

Jason Inn – *12 Odós Agion Assomaton – ☎ (21032) 51 106, res. (21052) 02 491, www.douros_hotels.com – 57rm.* Every comfort, situated in a residentail street near the Benaki Museum.

USEFUL TIPS

Odós Adrianóu – Pedestrian streets lined with cafés and restaurants; views of the Acropolis.

Odós Apostolou Pavlou – Lively evening scene in the bars along this pedestrian street near the Acropolis

Ethnikí Pinakothíki – Moussío Alexándrou Soútsou★

No. 50, Leofóros Vas Konstandinou. Open Mon-Sat, 9am-3pm, Sun 10am-2pm. Closed Tue. 6.50€. ☎ (21072) 359 37.

This excellent museum presents a comprehensive panorama of Greek painting. The first level, devoted to the different periods in Hellenic art since its inception, presents18C works from the Ionian Islands and19C canvases of the Munich School; pride of place goes to the remarkable works by Domenico Theotocopoulos **(El Greco)**. The upper floor is devoted to contemporary Hellenic painting. You'll see works by **Konstantinos Parthenis**, influental in the development of 20C Hellenic art, and by **Nikos Engonopoulos** (surrealism), **Nikos Chazikyriados-Ghika** (Cubism).

Stádio

Avenue Konstandinou.

The **stadium** stands on the site of its Ancient predecessor laid out in the 4C BC and rebuilt by Herodes Atticus in AD 144. In 1896 it was rebuilt on its original plan for the modern Olympic Games. From the top of the white marble terraces, which can accommodate 70 000 spectators, there is a view of the National Garden and the Acropolis.

National Garden★(Ethnikós Kípos)

Kids Open 8am-9pm in summer.

The former royal garden was remodelled in 1840 and is a pleasant stroll. There are some 500 species of trees and plants, a **botanical museum** and a small zoo. Adjoining the National Garden to the south is the **Zappeion Park (Zápio)**, very popular with Athenians, particularly in the evenings. The **Zappeion Hall** is a pleasant neo-Classical building (1888) now used for exhibitions.

Visit

The Major Museums of Athens

Ethnikó Arheologikó Moussío★★★

44 Odós 28-Oktovriou. Metro stop Viktoria (green line), or bus no. 200. Open Tue-Sun, 8am-7pm, Mon 12.30-7pm. 12€. ☎ (21082) 177 17.

The **National Archaeological Museum**, one of the richest of its kind in the world, is devoted to Ancient art from the Neolithic period to the Roman era and displays the major works of art from the Greek archaeological sites, except for Macedonia, Delphi, Olympia and Crete.

Neolithic and Cycladic Antiquities

Idols, notably the idol of the Goddess with child *(Kourotrophos)* and a seated male idol, ceramics originating in Thessaly in particular, and jewellery (earrings) from Polióhni similar in style to finds from Troy.

Vases and stylised marble idols with rounded contours originating in the Cyclades. The shape and decoration of the vases, especially the examples from Filakopí (Melos), recall the Santorini ceramics.

Office National Hellénique de Tourisme

Mask of Agamemnon

Mycenaean Antiquities (16C-11C BC)

Finds from the excavations conducted at Mycenae since 1876 by Schliemann and his successors. Notable among the exhibits are the **'mask of Agamemnon'**, the famous funerary mask of an Achaean king discovered by Schliemann in the Mycenae acropolis (5th tomb in the 1st circle) and believed by him to be the mask of Agamemnon; bronze daggers with blades encrusted with gold, silver and enamel (Mycenae, same tomb); and a hexagonal wooden box covered with embossed gold plate showing lions pursuing deer (same tomb).
Also from Mycenae are: a **flask** *(rhyton)* used for libations in the shape of a bull's head, in silver with gold horns and muzzle and a gold rosette; a shallow vessel, like a sauceboat, in the shape of a duck made of rock crystal; and a woman's or sphinx's head in limestone painted to pick out the features in vivid colours. In addition there are two admirable **gold cups** discovered at Vafió near Sparta, and a seal ring depicting spirits offering libations to a goddess holding a cup (Tiryns Treasury).

Geometric and Archaic art (10C-6C BC)

The main attraction is the huge geometric *amphora* dating from the mid-8C. The **'Dipylon Head'** belonged to a funerary *kouros* standing on a tomb. The huge votive *kouros* from Sounion once stood in front of the first temple to Poseidon.
Kouroi or *korai* from the Cyclades and Attica, include the crowned *kore* Phrasikleia, and the statue of Winged Victory from Delos. Note also the very fine *kouros* found at Volomandra in Attica. Other artefacts of the same period include the funerary *stele* of Aristion, the **'warrior of Marathon'**, sculpted by Aristokles. An unusual tombstone shows a 'running hoplite' or a Pyrrhic dancer.
In addition there is a superb funerary *kouros* from Anávissos in Attica (520 BC). The statue of Aristodikos, one of the later *kouroi*, shows the transition from Archaic to Classical art. Two bases of statues discovered in Themistocles' wall are decorated with low reliefs showing youths *(ephebes)* practising physical exercises.
Among the tombstones and votive tablets there is a votive relief in honour of a girl named Amphotto holding an apple (c 440 BC); also the Attic relief of the ephebe crowning himself, found at Cape Sounion.

Classical art (5C-4C-3C BC)

Masterpieces include the extraordinary bronze **Artemision Poseidon** c 460-450 BC; and the **Eleusinian Relief** (c 440-430 BC).
Among the numerous funerary *steles* stands the great Myrrhine *lekythos*. Note also the Classical sculptures and votive reliefs; worth seeing are the relief dedicated to Hermes and the Nymphs, a second dedicated to Dionysos, and the copies of the original Classical 5C and 4C BC statues, in particular the Parthenon Athena, a lost work by Pheidias. The astonishing **Horse and Jockey of Artemision** is a 2C BC Hellenistic bronze.
The Karapános collection consists of figurines and various small bronze items from 8C BC to 3C BC. The most remarkable are those from the Sanctuary of Zeus at Dodona

TAP

Athletes exercising (low relief)

(Epiros). Note the little statue of Zeus, a horse and a statuette of an armed man. Also worthy of note is the interesting series of 4C BC sculptures from the Temple of Asklepios (Aesculapius) at Epidauros (attractive *acroteria*).
Finally, four remarkable works attract attention. A high relief of a horse held by a slave comes from a 2C BC funerary monument found in Athens in 1948 near Lárissa station; this realistic work shows the transition from Classical to Hellenistic art. The **Ephebe of Antikythera**, a statue in bronze of 4C BC, shows Paris offering the apple *(missing)* to Aphrodite. A stone head of Hygeia is attributed to Skopas. The bronze Ephebe of Marathon (4C) may have come from the School of Praxiteles.
It is impossible to miss the colossal and dramatic statue of **Poseidon** of Melos (2C BC); also worthy of note are two bronze portraits: a philosopher's head (3C BC), and a man's head (c 100 BC) excavated on Delos.
The "little refugee" statue of a child wearing a cape and holding a dog was found at Smyrna in 1922 and brought back to Athens when refugees from Asia Minor were arriving in Greece. Note the group with Aphrodite, Eros and Pan (c 100 BC) and a marble statue of the goddess Artemis, both found on Delos.

Roman Art
The period is represented by works from various Greek schools from the 1C BC to the 3C AD, the heyday of the Roman empire. Portraits of the emperors include a bronze statue of Octavion Augustus, and a bust of Hadrian.

Bronzes
Works in bronze include smaller sculptures dating from as early as the 8C BC; jewellery, vases, figurines and votive offerings.

Egyptian antiquities (5000 BC to 1C BC)
Dating from the pre-Dynastic to the Ptolemaic period, the collection comprises 7 000 items and is the fourth most important of its kind in Europe.

Santorini Frescoes and Ceramics
These magnificent frescoes discovered in the 1970s on Santorini, depict life on the island in the 16C BC. Note the one showing a naval battle framed in a frieze containing numerous figures, various types of vessel, and a villa.

Ceramics
Among the most precious pieces are the funerary *krater* of the Dipylon type found near the Kerameikos cemetery, the Nessos Amphora and the four *kraters* from Melos, a *krater* showing Herakles (Hercules) struggling with Nereus and white-ground funerary *lekithoi*.

Moussío Benáki★★ (Benáki Museum)
Kolonáki district. 1 Odós Koumbari, via Vassilis Sofias Avenue. Metro stop Syntagma. ☎ (21036) 710 00. Open daily 9am-7pm (until midnight Thu); Sun 9am-3pm. Closed Tue. 6€.
This museum, devoted mainly to Greek and oriental art, houses the collection of **Antonis Benáki** (1873-1954), a wealthy patron of the arts. Further enriched by later bequests, the museum has been expanded and remodelled. The collections of Ancient art, which reveal aspects of cultural life, are displayed in chronological order, from prehistoric times to the present, and highlight the continuity of Greek civilisation and traditions.

First Floor (Rooms 1 to 12)
This covers the period from prehistory to the post-Byzantine era, includes a fine series of **gold objects** (3200-2800 BC), Hellenistic jewellery, and vases and idols from Alexandria.

Examples of Coptic art include two **portraits from Fayyum** (2C-3C AD); there is a remarkable series of **icons** on subjects such as *The Hospitality of Abraham* which is of superb quality (late-14C), *St Demetrios* (15C), a fine *Transfiguration* (or Evangelismos tis Theotokou, 16C); also on display are a superb icon depicting St John and two youthful works by El Greco: the *Adoration of the Magi* (1560-65) and *St Luke* (1560).

Second floor (Rooms 13 to 27)

This focuses on the development of Hellenism under foreign domination, and contains a large collection of regional **costumes**, traditional jewellery and embroidery, and some beautiful pieces of **gold work** from islands in northern Greece.
Don't miss the two 18C reception rooms from Siátista and Kozáni in Macedonia.
Works of religious art bear witness to the unifying role of the Orthodox Church during the occupation. On display are some beautiful **icons** *(Room 25)*, including an extraordinary composition by Th. Poulakis (Crete, 17C), a pictorial synthesis of the Hymn to the Virgin and the Last Judgement.

Third floor (Rooms 29 to 32)

Here the spotlight is on pre-War of Independence economy and society as well as the Age of Enlightenment in Greece. Fine musical instruments, vessels and tools.

Fourth floor (Rooms 33 to 36)

Greece during the 20C is the focus, with objects such as the Constitution signed in 1844 by King Otto, personal items (including a gold seal) belonging to the poet Dionysios Solomós, and copies of the first printed works of the poets Geórgios Seféris, Odysséus Elýtis, Ángelos Sikelianós and Andréas Embiricos. There are also works by Konstandínos Parthénis, Níkos Engonópoulos, and the composer Nikos Skalkotas.

Moussío Kikladikís Téhnis★★

Kolonáki district, 4 Odós Neofytou Douka. Open Mon, Wed-Fri, 10am-4pm; Sat, 10am-3pm. Closed Tue and Sun. 3.50€. ☎ (21072) 283 21/3.
The private collection of **NP Goulandris** provides the major part of the exhibits in the **Museum of Cycladic Art**, which illustrates the development of Greek art over a period of 3 000 years.

First floor

A total of 230 objects produced by the Cycladic island civilisation – Ancient Cycladic I (3300-2700 BC), Ancient Cycladic II (2800-2300 BC) and Ancient Cycladic III (2400-2200 BC) includes marble and pottery vessels, and marble **idols**.

Second floor

Among the 300 works illustrating Ancient Greek art are: Minoan and Mycenaean artefacts; a fine collection of vases with red and black figure decoration, in particular an Attic bell *krater* (430 BC) and a *lekythos* (560-550 BC); the Lambros Evtaxias Collection of **bronze vessels** (8C BC-1C AD) including a *kados* from Thessaly; jewellery and clay vases from Skíros (1000-700 BC); south Italian fish plates (4C BC); glass perfume flasks; a fine collection of Boeotian terracotta

J Malburet/MICHELIN

Statuette, Museum of Cycladic Art

The Story of a Community

The first Jewish community was founded in Thessaloníki in the early 3C BC; other settlements followed shortly after in Corinth and Sparta. These communities, although keeping their own tradition, were soon influenced by Hellenic culture. The Jews within the Byzantine Empire were known as Romaniotes, as the Empire and its people saw themselves as successors of the Roman Empire. Under the Turks, Jewish communities spread to the large cities of the Ottoman Empire. Sultan Bayazid II invited the Sephardic Jews expelled from Spain and Portugal in 1492 to settle in Thessaloníki, Constantinople, Edirne and Smyrna in the midst of the Romaniote communities.

At the beginning of the Second World War, the Jews fought with great heroism at the Battle of Epiros. During the German occupation, 87 per cent of the Jewish population was murdered, thus virtually wiping out a 2 000 year-old tradition. Today the Jewish community of Greece numbers about 5 000.

and female idols with bird faces from the same area (590-550 BC); marble sculpture and funerary reliefs.

New wing

Accessed through the garden. Built in the neo-Classical style in 1895, this building hosts temporary exhibitions.

Vizandinó Moussío★★ (Byzantine and Christian Museum)

Kolonáki district, 22 Vassilis Sofias Avenue. Open Tue-Sun, 8.30am-3pm. 4€. ☎ (21072) 315 70. The museum is currently undergoing renovation.
This engaging museum offers a look at artistic development from the end of Antiquity through the fall of the Byzantine empire, with a fascinating look at the origins of Christian art. Note the reconstructions of two early churches and a remarkable collection of **icons**; also frescoes and illuminated manuscripts.

Outskirts

Southwest of Athens

Pireás (Piraeus)

10km/6mi southwest of the centre of Athens. Access by metro (Peiraias, line 1) or by car along Odós Piréos or Leofóros Singroú (the latter is less direct but quicker).
Lively and cosmopolitan, Piraeus (pop 476 304) is the principal port of Greece; it was chosen in Ancient times as the port of Athens because of its exceptional situation: It was **Themistocles** in c 493 BC who decided to move Athens' harbour to Piraeus. The new town was linked to Athens by the Long Wall, which formed a fortified corridor. In the Age of Pericles the town was rebuilt according to a grid plan. In 85 BC the Romans sacked Piraeus and set it on fire. The designation of Athens as the capital, however, and the opening of the Corinth Canal in 1893 brought a commercial revival.
The modern **port** consists of Piraeus harbour, Herakles harbour, the Eleusinian Gulf and the two small harbours, Zéa and Mikrolímano. From Piraeus to Eleusis the coast is lined with commercial installations; it is Greece's largest industrial complex.

Zéa★

In Antiquity this round bay was a large port for triremes; traces of boat-sheds are visible today. The waterfront is lined with fish restaurants and tavernas.
The fine **Archaeological Museum**★ *(31 Odós Kariloau Trikoupi; temporarily closed for renovation)* features well-known works including the Piraeus **Apollo**, a splendid Archaic *kouros* (c 525 BC), probably the oldest known Greek statue; the Piraeus **Athena,** c 340 BC;

two bronze statues representing **Artemis**; a reconstruction of a sanctuary from the Classical period; and the **Kallithéa Monument**★, an impressive 7m/23ft-high tomb.
The **Naval Museum** *(Quai Themistokleous; open Tue-Fri 9am-4pm, Sat 9am-1.30pm; closed Aug; 2€)* illustrates the history of navigation in Greece from Antiquity to the Second World War.

Mikrolímano★
Like Zéa, Mikrolímano was a harbour, today lined by fish tavernas. The harbour lies at the foot of **Mounychia Hill** (Kastéla), 87m/285ft high. From the neighbourhood of the open-air theatre there is a fine view of Piraeus, the coast and the Saronic Gulf.

Aktí
The **coast road** round the peninsula gives attractive views of the port and the coast. There are traces of the sea wall (Tíhos Kónonos) built by Konon in the 4C BC. Near the public garden at the western end of the peninsula stands the tomb of **Andreas Miaoúlis**, a famous Hydriot admiral.

Northeast and east of Athens

Kifissiá★
14km/8.75mi northeast of Athens. Metro stop Kifisiá (line 1).
Kifissiá is an elegant residential town at the foot of Mount Pendeli, pleasantly cool and fresh in summer because of its altitude, its water and its trees. The lower town features relaxed tavernas and the public park; the elegant upper town boasts avenues of plane trees, 19C villas and luxury hotels and restaurants.

Goulandris Museum of Natural History★
13 Odós Levidou. Housed in an elegant 19C villa, the museum has attractive displays. The **herbarium** contains 200 000 plant varieties from the Mediterranean basin.

20C Design Museum
12km/7mi northeast of Athens, in Maroússi; metro Maroussi (line 1). 4-10 Odós Patmou. Open Sun-Fri 9am-6pm, Sat 11am-3pm.

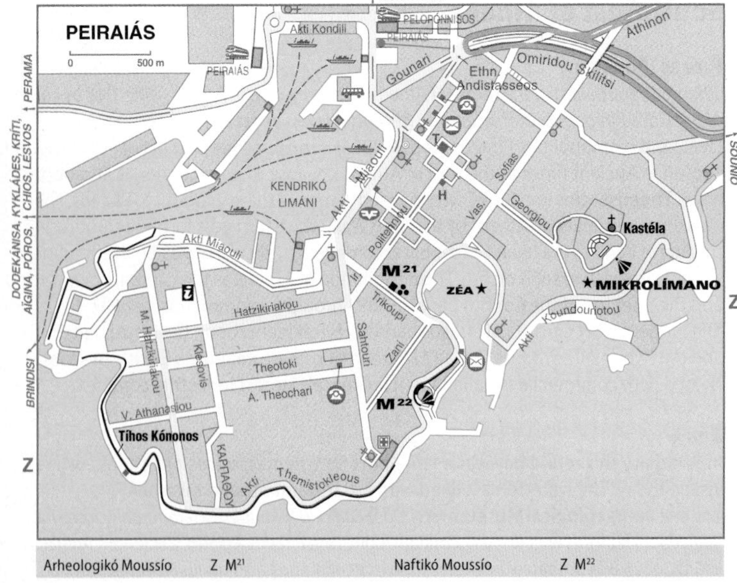

Excellent displays of furniture and works by such renowned contemporary designers as Hoffmann, Mies Van der Rohe, Le Corbusier, Mackintosh, Dali, etc.

On the flanks of Mount Hymettos★★

9km/5.5mi east of Athens. Beyond Kessarianí (bus terminus) the road climbs up the verdant slope. After 3km/2mi the Kessarianí Monastery appears on the right.

Kessarianí Monastery★★

Open Tue-Sun 8.30am-3.30pm. 2€. ☎ (21072) 36 619. The silent, serene monastery (11C) was dedicated to the Presentation of the Virgin; it is now deconsecrated.

A recess in the outer wall of the monastery on the east side of the first courtyard contains the famous Ram's Head Fountain, a sacred spring in Antiquity that was celebrated by the Latin poet Ovid in his *Ars Amatoria*.

Ancient fragments dot the inner **courtyard**. In the Middle Ages the 11C building *(left)* was the monks' bathhouse. The adjoining wing has a gallery at first-floor level serving the monks' cells.

The church (11C; the narthex and the side chapel were added in the 17C) is decorated with **murals**: those in the narthex date from 1682; those in the church itself are probably 18C. Opposite the church are the **convent buildings**.

Leave the monastery on this side and take the path up through the trees (15min on foot there and back) to a sanctuary southeast of the monastery.

Peiraiás Address Book

For coin categories, see the Legend on the cover flap.

WHERE TO EAT

⊖ **To palió tou katsíka** – *171-173 Odós Ypsilántou, near Zéa Marina. Closed Sun.* Updated traditional taverna; a good place to try local cuisine.

⊖ **Tá ennéa Adélphia ('The 9 brothers')** – *48 Odós Sotíros. From Zéa Marina, go up Odós Lambrákis to the first street on the right; in a tiny square.* This local favourite has a wide choice of well-prepared Greek dishes.

⊖⊖⊖ **Ziller** – *Zéa Marina.* One of the best of the fish restaurants clustered near the small port. Choose the dining room overlooking the port on fine days.

WHERE TO STAY

⊖ **Eva** – *2 Odós Notará – ☎ (21041) 701 10.* Pleasant new hotel, small but comfortable rooms (the quietest on the 6th floor). No breakfast.

⊖ **Zacharato** – *Corner of Odós Notará and Odós Evangelistrias – ☎ (21041) 78 830 – 59rm.* Opposite Hotel Eva, an older establishment but clean and comfortable.

⊖⊖ **Anita-Argo** – *23-25 Odós Notará – ☎ (21041) 21 795, www.hotelargoanita.com – 57rm.* Modern hotel behind the metro station. Ask for a room on one of the upper floors overlooking the street. Minibus service to the harbour. Free parking.

⊖⊖ **Phidias** – *198 Odós Kontouriotou – ☎(21042) 964 80/961 60/672 20, www.hotelphidias.gr – 26rm.* New, comfortable hotel off Zéa Marina. Charming welcome.

⊖⊖ **Lília** – *Marina Zea (Passalimani) – 131 Odós Zeas – ☎ (21041) 79 108, info@liliahotel.gr – 20rm.* Small, quiet hotel in an attractive street overlooking the marina. Recently renovated. Ask for a room overlooking the street (the others face a blank wall). Ideal base from which to explore Piraeus. Free shuttle service to the harbour.

⊖⊖⊖ **Poseidonio** – *3 Odós Charilaou Trikoupi – ☎(21042) 866 51/6, hotelp@otenet.gr – 49rm.* Recently renovated hotel with comfortable rooms. No restaurant, but room service is available.

⊖⊖⊖ **Noufara** – *45 Odós Iroon Politehniou – ☎(21041) 155 41/3 – 49rm.* Same proprietor as the Poseidonio, but located along the main avenue of Piraeus, near the square.

Here there are traces of a 10C church built on the foundations of a palaeo-Christian basilica; a 13C vaulted Frankish church; and a chapel dedicated to the Archangels. Fine views of Athens, Attica and the Saronic Gulf.

Mount Hymettos★★

Continue up the road past the 11C **Asteri Monastery**. There are views of Athens and the Saronic Gulf as far as the Peloponnese to the west, and of the Attic peninsula (Mesógia), its eastern shore and Euboia to the east. The summit is prohibited *(military zone)*, but in Antiquity it was crowned by a statue of Zeus. The Hymettos range, which rises to 1 026m/3 366ft, extends north-south for about 20km/12.5mi.

▶ *From Kessarianí head straight on past the monastery to rejoin the main road, then head in the direction of Lavrio/Sounion.*

Vorres Museum

In Peania, Odós Diadochou Konstandinou. ⓒ*Open Sat-Sun 10am-2pm.*
A fine collection of post-war Greek art; rooms furnished in traditional Greek style.

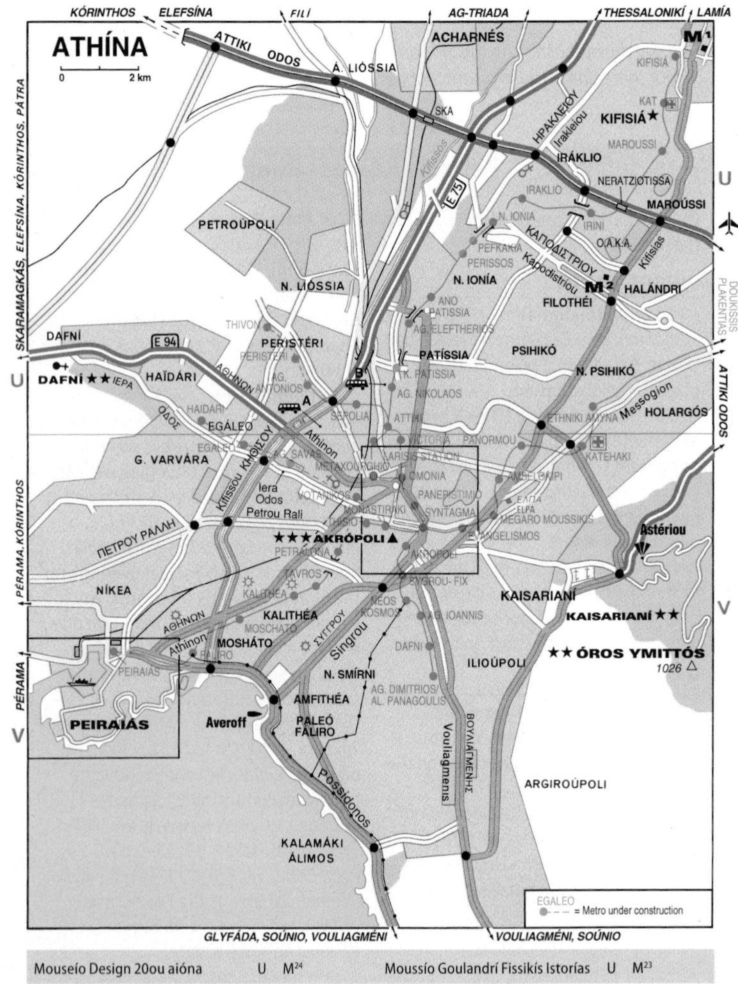

Mouseío Design 20ou aióna U M24 Moussío Goulandrí Fissikís Istorías U M23

ATTICA

POPULATION 3 598 007
MICHELIN MAP 737 H-J 9-10.

The southernmost tip of continental Greece, Attica juts out into the Aegean Sea. Of the timeless landscapes described by poets and travellers, there remains woefully little. The mainland section, covering 2 600km^2, makes up about one-fortieth of Greece, but is home to nearly half the population. The ceaseless expansion of Athens has made most of the peninsula an urban and industrial area but, as the cradle of Greek civilisation, it boasts some of the most interesting museums and sites in the country. *In Athens; 26 Odós Amalias, near Sindagma Square.*

- **Orient Yourself:** Attica is composed of the peninsula up to its border with Boeotia, the islands of the Saronic Gulf, Hydra, Spetsae, and Kythera. The E 75 motorway runs through it, starting from Athens.
- **Don't Miss:** Cape Sounion at sunset
- **Organizing Your Time:** Factoring in some beach time, you can explore the coast in two days (overnight at Cape Sounion). If time is limited, a day or less for excursions from Athens.
- **Also See:** Athína, Évia, Kéa

A Bit of History

Granary of the Ancients, and covered with olive groves, the region also had lead mining and marble quarries. Today's industry (refineries, metalworks, chemical plants, textile manufacturers etc) produces two-thirds of the nation's wealth, but at considerable cost to the environment of the area.

Address Book

For coin categories, see the Legend on the cover flap.

WHERE TO EAT

Tavernas and fish restaurants abound in villages all along the Apollo coast. On the east coast, look for restaurants in Rafina and Pórto Ráfti.

WHERE TO STAY

Kyani Akti – *Pórto Raftí, 40 Agias Marinas – ☎(22990) 864 00 – 25rm.* Small hotel at a reasonable price; open all year. A charming spot.

Calypso Motel – *Anavysos – ☎ (22910) 60 170 – 66rm.* Rooms in the main building and in bungalows (with air-conditioning) next to a calm bay.

Xenia Ilios – *Anavysos – ☎ (22910) 37 024 – 104rm.* A hotel-management school open Jun—Sep. Good service; comfortable rooms overlook the sea. Full- or half-board options.

Aegon – *Below the Temple of Poseidon, at Sounion – ☎ (22920) 39 200 – 89rom.* This hotel is the closest to the temple at Sounion. Recently renovated; fine location; rooms overlook the beach.

Mont Parnes – *Aharnés – ☎ (210) 24 69 111, fax (210) 24 60 768 – 39rm, 6 suites.* Mountain hotel exudes bygone splendour. Spacious rooms with marble bathrooms, spectacular views. Casino.

Mare Nostrum – *Vravrona, Club Med, on the seafront – ☎ (22940) 71 000 – 300rm.* Recently renovated, this is one of the few hotels on the east coast. It offers games, activities, shops, etc, as well as a nearby thalassotherapy centre.

SPORT AND LEISURE

For information contact the *Greek Federation of Climbing Clubs, 5 Odós Milioni, Athens, ☎ (210) 36 45 904, fax (210) 36 44 687.*

Driving Tours

1 The Apollo Coast to Cape Sounion★★

65km/41mi round trip. From Athens, take the fast road to Elenikó airport which then goes on to the coast.

Glifáda

This sizeable resort just 14km/9mi from Athens comprises a beach, a marina and an 18-hole golf course.

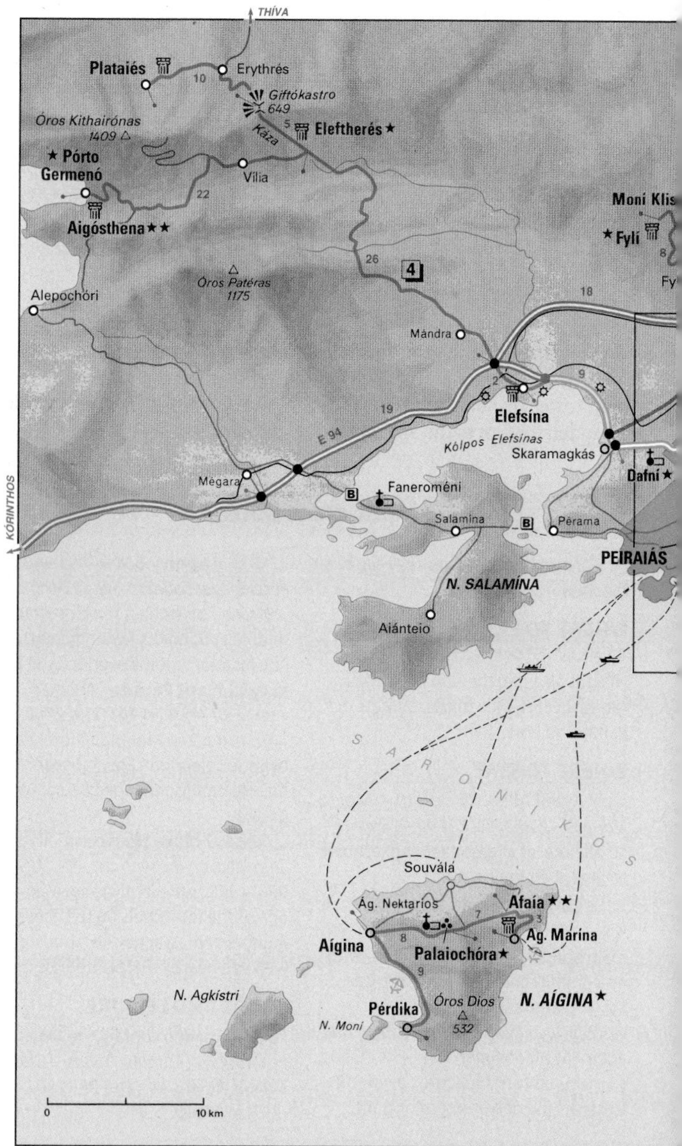

The road passes through **Voúla** *(beach) and* **Kavoúri***, skirting small bays.*

Vouliagméni★

An elegant resort pleasantly situated at the head of a deep inlet, Vouliagmeni offers beaches, safe moorings and several hotels. From the southern headland beyond the harbour there is a fine **view** of the coast extending south towards Cape Sounion. The road continues to **Várkiza** and then to **Lagoníssi**, another summer resort. The dramatic coastline features views of the Saronic Gulf and the **isle of Patroclos**.

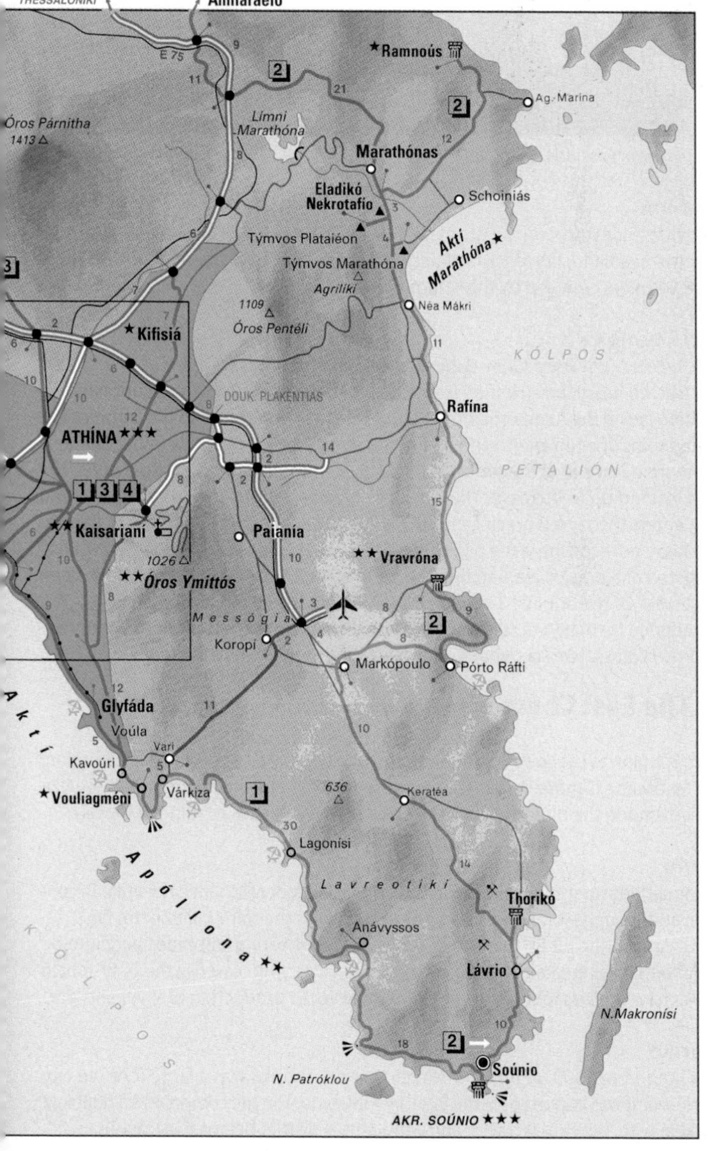

R Cuzin/MICHELIN

The Temple of Poseidon, Sounion

Sounion
A small seaside resort on the site of the Ancient town and port of Sounion. In an inlet near the headland, dry-dock facilities for two triremes have been found. **View**★ of Cape Sounion, crowned by the columns of an Ancient temple.

Ákri Soúnio★★
Open every day from 10am-dusk. €4. ☏ (22920) 39 363.
The "sacred headland" (Homer) is the outpost of Attica, occupying a commanding position facing the Aegean Sea and the Cyclades at the entrance to the Saronic Gulf. Famed ruins of a temple to the god of the sea crown the precipitous headland.
The marble **Temple of Poseidon** (440 BC) was a Doric building with a peristyle. The path leading up to it crosses the wall, which enclosed the Ancient acropolis, and then enters the sacred precinct at the point where the original gate stood, flanked by a large portico where the pilgrims assembled. The entrance façade *(facing east)* consisted of a portico leading into the *naós,* of which the corner pillars have been preserved. Of the original 34 columns of the peristyle, 16 remain.
Abandoned for many years, the temple was restored in the 19C. Excavations uncovered two colossal Archaic *kouroi*, which are now in the Athens Museum.

2 The East Coast *160km/100mi from Sounion to Ramnoús.*

From Sounion to Lávrio the road winds its way along the east coast of Cape Sounion. The landscape is more verdant than on the western side; villas and hotels are dispersed among the pine and olive trees above little beaches nestling in the bays.

Lávrio
This small industrial town and mineral port lies at the foot of Mount Lavreotíki. Recent excavations suggest mining activity here as early as the third millennium BC.
It was early in the 5C BC that the deposits of silver-bearing sulphides began to be exploited, bringing wealth and power to Athens. Extraction ceased in the 2C BC, but In 1864 a new process for treating the mineral restored production of silver and zinc.

Thorikó
Inhabited from 2000 BC until the Roman period, Thorikó was a large fortified city where wood was imported for the foundries in Lávrio. The site comprises a 5 000-seat **theatre** with elliptical terraces, and a residential district below an acropolis.

Return to Lávrio to rejoin the Athens road. Beyond **Keratéa** *it enters the Messógia, a sparsely inhabited plain. At Markópoulo, join the road towards Vravróna and Pórto Ráfti and continue 8km/5mi to the entrance to the archaeological site of Brauron.*

Vravróna★★

In Ancient times the **Brauron** sanctuary was a place of pilgrimage dedicated to Artemis Brauronia. According to legend, Agamemnon's daughter Iphigenia, who had escaped being sacrificed, returned with the sacred statue of Artemis to found the sanctuary. It was served by young priestesses, called 'bears' in honor of Artemis' mascot and dedicated to the goddess at the age of seven.

H Champollion/MICHELIN

Detail of a votive sculpture from the Sanctuary of Artemis Brauronia

Sanctuary

Open Tue-Sun 8.30am-3pm. 3€. ☎ (22990) 27 020.
Beyond a 6C AD basilica *(left)* is the sacred fountain that flowed into a stream spanned by a 5C BC bridge.
On the right, below St George's Chapel (15C), are the foundations of the Temple of Artemis (5C BC); behind in a crack in the rock is the 'Tomb of Iphigenia'. Opposite was the grand peristyle courtyard, which was flanked on three sides by the 'parthenon'; part of the colonnade has been re-erected.

Museum

500m/550yd from the sanctuary. Open Tue-Sun, 8.30am-3pm. €3.
This displays geometric vases (9C-8C BC), a low-relief votive sculpture showing the figures of Zeus (seated), Leto, Apollo and Artemis (5C BC) and particularly a series of ravishing statuettes or marble heads of little 'bears' (4C BC): the *'Bear with a bird'* and the *'Bear with a hare'* are masterpieces.

Return to Markópoulo via **Pórto Ráfti**, *a seaside resort, and the port of the Messógia (Limáni Messogéas).*

At the mouth of the bay there is an island crowned by a colossal Roman marble figure of a man sitting cross-legged; it is popularly called the tailor *(ráftis)* and was probably used as a leading mark.

Marathon Coast★

Rafína

Ferries for Euboia and the eastern Cyclades leave from Rafína, a commercial and fishing harbour. Fish tavernas line the waterfront and the beach.

Take the coast road which passes a series of beaches, then rejoin the main road at Néa Makri; after 5km turn right onto the road to Marathon.

Marathon Battlefield

Open Tue-Sun and public holidays 8.30am-3pm. 3€ (site and museum). ☎ (22940) 55 155.

The Battle of Marathon

In 490 BC a Persian fleet sent from Asia Minor to quell the Greek rebellion anchored in the Gulf of Marathon and prepared to march on Athens. Camped on the lower slopes of Mount Agriliki, some 8 000 Greek defenders faced 20 000 Persians.

Under General Miltiade the Athenians surrounded the Persians, inflicting heavy casualties and forcing them to retreat. It is traditionally believed that the Persians lost 6 400 men, against Greek casualties of just 192.

Legend has it that, victory assured, Miltiade dispatched Pheidippides, a messenger, to Athens with the news. Pheidippides ran to Athens where, after announcing the victory, he collapsed from exhaustion and died.

The 'marathon' of the first modern Olympics in 1896 was run over 40km/25mi, the distance between Marathon and Athens. The official distance for marathons is now set at 26mi and 385yd as laid down at the 1908 London Olympics; this corresponds to the distance between Windsor Great Park and White City Stadium, the start and finish points for the event on that occasion.

The stretch of coastal plain south of Marathónas was the scene of the famous battle (490 BC) described by Herodotus. Isolated in the plain is the **Marathon Barrow** commemorating the defenders who died in battle. At the foot is a reproduction of the gravestone of the Soldier of Marathon (original in the National Museum in Athens). From the top there is a fine view of the plain, and the surrounding mountains.

▸ *Return to the main road and 1km/0.5mi farther north turn left to the Barrow of the Plataians. Immediately on the right stands a hangar covering a cemetery.*

The **Helladic cemetery** is proof of Ancient human occupation of the plain of Marathon. The tombs (2000 BC) contain perfectly preserved skeletons. The **Barrow of the Plataians** covers the graves of Platalans who died at Marathon.
The **museum** contains an interesting collection of primitive objects from the Helladic and Mycenaean periods: funerary urns; statuettes; helmets and weapons.
Near the museum is a Helladic and Mycenaean cemetery.

▸ *Return to the main road continuing north; just before Marathon turn right to the pleasant beach at Shiniás (beautiful pine grove) and Ramnoús.*

Ramnoús★

Open daily 8.30am-6pm. 2€. ☎ (22940) 63 477.
The ruins of Ancient Ramnoús lie in a remote valley running down to the sea. Here lie the foundations of two Doric temples. One is dedicated to Themis (6C BC). The other temple (5C BC) contained a famous effigy of Nemesis, goddess of Punishment and Divine Retribution (now displayed in the British Museum in London).
Continue down the path to the site of the ruined acropolis (4C BC). There are traces of the enclosing wall, a small theatre, buildings and a citadel. Fine views extend over the wild and rocky coast; the position of the Ancient lower town can be surmised.

▸ *Rejoin the E 75 motorway and head north towards Chalkida. Turn off at Malakasa and follow the signs for Skala Oropou/Amfiaraío.*

Amfiaraío

Open Tue-Sun 8.30am-3pm. 2€. ☎ (22950) 62 144.
In a narrow peaceful valley, lie the ruins of a sanctuary (4C BC) dedicated to **Amphiaraos**, King of Árgos; he was also a seer and healer whose cult developed in these remote parts as did the cult of Asklepios in Epidauros.

To the right of the path was the temple, with the base of the cult statue and the offering table in the centre; in front of the temple was a huge altar. On the other side of the path is the 'Statue Terrace'; the pedestals date from the Roman period. Beyond was the portico *(abaton)* where the sick lay down to sleep. Note the feet of the supports for the marble bench which ran the whole length of the portico. Farther on was the theatre (3 000 seats) where the votive festival (Amphiaréa) took place.

3 North of Athens, towards Filí★ (Phyle Fortress)

56km/35mi there and back. Leave Athens by Odós Liossíon, which follows the railway to Néa Lióssia and then Áno Lióssia. Beyond the village of Phyle the road starts to climb Mount Parnes. Turn right at one of the bends into a road (sign 'Moní Klistón').

Moní Klistón (Convent of the Gorge)

The convent (14C) of nuns takes its name from its spectacular **position**★ above a deep gorge riddled with caves, some of which were occupied by hermits.

The road continues upwards past the track (right) to the Plátani Kriopigí taverna; soon after turn left to reach Phyle Fortress.

Filí★

In an empty landscape the ruins of **Phyle Fortress** command one of the passes between Attica and Boeotia. Considerable sections of the enclosing wall are still standing; it was built in the 4C BC of huge rectangular blocks up to 2.70m/over 8ft thick and reinforced with several towers.

4 West of Athens *Around 90km/56mi*

Dafní★★ (Daphne Monastery)

The monastery was severely damaged in the 1999 earthquake and remains closed to the public. Check with the Athens Tourist Office or ☎(21058) 115 58 for information.

Just at the motorway to Corinth, at the foot of a wooded hill, stands Daphne Monastery, renowned for its church and mosaics, which are some of the finest in Greece. Climb the slopes to the west for a fine view of the whole complex: the primitive gateway, the walls including a section dating from the 5-6C, the cloisters and the church.

The peaceful paved **cloisters** are flanked on the east side by a typically Cistercian arcade. Under the western arcade are ducal sarcophagi. Fragments of stonework were discovered in the crypt.

The domed **Byzantine church** was built over the crypt in the 11C and enlarged in the 13C by the Cistercians.

There is a fine view from the cloisters of the south front of the church.The narthex, which is crenellated, must have been built on the model of Citeaux; the tombs of the Dukes of Athens were placed here. The pointed arches of the west front and traces of a groined vault suggest the inspiration of Burgundian architecture.

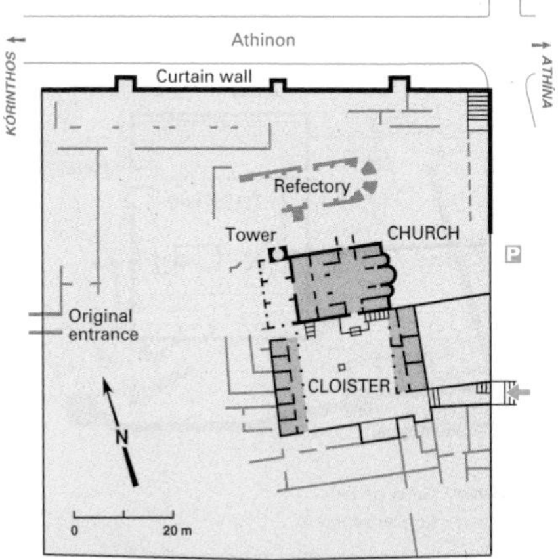

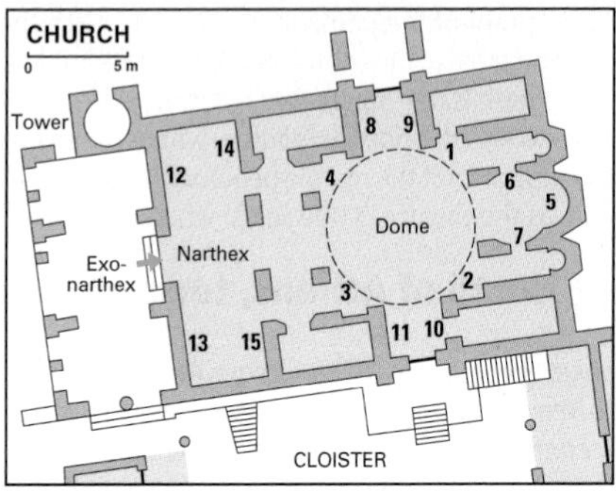

On the north side of the church beyond the square tower are the remains of the 11C refectory. The elevation of the church and the dome can be admired; the small windows date from the 11C; the others are probably 13C.

Inside, the church is magnificently decorated with late-11C **mosaics**★★ against a gold background, which are remarkable for their delicacy of line and colouring. The scene, are arranged according to the theological concepts of the period.

- in the dome, Christ Pantocrator, surrounded by the 16 Prophets; in the squinches, the Annunciation (**1**), the Nativity (**2**), the Baptism (**3**) and the Ascension (**4**) of Christ;
- in the apse, the Virgin Mary (**5**) flanked by the Archangels Michael (**6**) and Gabriel (**7**);
- in the transept arms, gospel scenes including the Birth of the Virgin, the Entry of Christ into Jerusalem (**8**) and the Crucifixion (**9**) *(north transept)*, the Adoration of the Magi, Christ rising from the dead (**10**), doubting Thomas (**11**) *(south transept)*;
- in the narthex, the Betrayal by Judas (**12**) and a scene from the legend of Joachim and Anne (**13**) are opposite the Last Supper (**14**) and the Presentation of the Virgin in the Temple (**15**).

Elefsína

Open Tue-Sun 8.30am-3pm. 3€ (site and museum). ☎ (210) 55 43 470.

The sanctuary at Eleusis, where the fertility cult of the 'great goddesses' Demeter and Persephone was celebrated, was one of the great shrines of Antiquity. It was linked to Athens by the Sacred Way. The sanctuary lies against a low hill topped by an acropolis overlooking Eleusis Bay and Salamis Island. Part Greek and part Roman, the ruins convey a great sense of history, despite modern-day pollution.

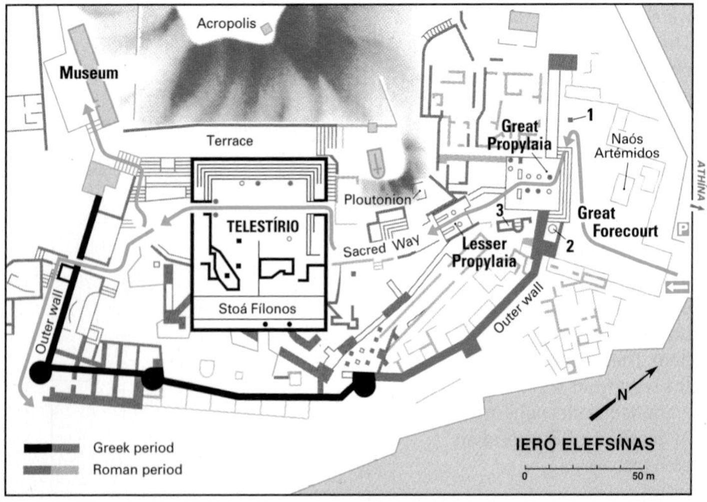

The Eleusinian mysteries

In mythology, it was at Eleusis that Demeter found her daughter, Persephone, who had been abducted by Hades, king of the underworld, near Lake Pergusa in Sicily. Keleos, king of Eleusis, gave the goddess hospitality and in return she gave the king's son the first grain of wheat and showed him how to make it bear fruit. .
The secret rites of the fertility cult, known as the 'Eleusinian mysteries', were celebrated until the 4C BC, and took place during a great festival in the autumn. Themes included the union of Zeus and Demeter – a sign of fertility; the legend of Persephone detained in the world of the dead for six months – symbol of annual dormancy and rebirt; and the journey to the underworld – man's final destiny.
The dramatist Aeschylus was born at Eleusis in c 525 BC.

Great Forecourt

2C AD. The square, which is paved with marble, was laid out in the Roman era. Near the site of a Temple to Artemis *(Naós Artémidos)* is the colossal medallion bust of the Roman Emperor Antoninus Pius (1) from the pediment of the **Great Propylaia**.
To the left of the entrance is the Kallichoron well (2) (6C BC). Inside are traces of the Roman sewer *(cloaca)* (3). To the right are parts of the architrave of the **Lesser Propylaia** (1C BC) decorated with symbolic ears of corn.
The Sacred Way, which was paved by the Romans, leads past caves on the right hollowed out of the hillside to symbolise the entrance to the underworld; at the base on a triangular terrace stands a little temple, the Ploutonion, which was dedicated to Hades.

Telestírio

The Telesterion at the heart of the sanctuary was a majestic building. It has been refashioned many times and retains traces of every period. The ground floor consisted of a huge room that could accommodate about 3 000 people. A paved portico, the portico of Philo (Stoá Fílonos), runs along the southeast front.
From the terrace, cllimb the steps to reach the museum overlooking the Bay of Eleusis and Salamis Island.

Museum

Sculptures from the site are on view in the museum. There is also a reconstruction of the sanctuary in its heyday. The courtyard contains a horse's head dating from the Hellenistic period, and a sarcophagus from the Roman era.

On leaving Elefsína (Eleusis) bear right into the Thebes (Thíva) road, which climbs gently towards the Kithairon mountain range forming the border between Attica and Boeotia. Continue past the turning (left) to Vília; the ruins of ***Eleutherai*** *(Eleftherés) are soon visible on a rock spur to the right.*

Eleftherés★

Park near a disused petrol station and taverna and return to the path (left) which leads up to the fortress (30min on foot there and back).
Eleutherai Fortress stands on a desolate site, exposed to the wind, commanding the way over the Kithairon range at the southern end of the Káza Pass.
The walls were built by the Athenians in the 4C BC. The parapet walk is quite well preserved, particularly on the north side; views of Attica.

Continue by car to the ***Giftókastro Pass*** *(649m/2 129ft), where there is a magnificent view westwards over Mount Kithairon and northwards over the fertile Boeotian plain. A short distance away are the ruins of Plataia.*

Plateés

Only a few traces remain of the Ancient city of **Plataia**; they lie on a sloping terrace at the foot of the north face of Mount Kithairon (Kitherónas). There is a fine view of the Boeotian plain. Northeast of the site by the River Assopós, the **Battle of Plataia** took place in 479 BC and ended the Persian Wars.
On the right of the road from Erithrés, just outside the modern town, are the Ancient ruins, in particular traces of the 5C-4C BC circular walls.

▶ *Return downhill to the turning (right) to Vília.*

The road runs through the pleasant little town of **Vília** *(hotels, restaurants)*—past the military road *(right)* leading to the summit of Mount Kithairon (1 409m/4 623ft)—and winds down through stands of Aleppo pines to the bay of Pórto Germenó.

Pórto Germenó★

This quiet seaside resort (the beach is huge) is pleasantly sited in a bay at the eastern end of the Gulf of Corinth.

Egósthena★★

Access by the narrow coast road.
Above the olive groves stands a well-preserved acropolis, a good example of Greek military architecture in the late 4C BC. The enclosing wall is strengthened with posterns, huge lintels and high towers.
In the 13C **Aigosthena Fortress** was restored by the Franks – there are traces of a monastery – and linked to the seashore by two fortified walls enclosing the lower town; part of the northern wall survives.

DELPHI – Δελφοι

POPULATION 2 481

MICHELIN MAP 737 G 8 – FOKÍDA – CENTRAL GREECE.

In Antiquity Delphi was one of the most important religious centres; the Sanctuary of Apollo, situated above the River Pleistos gorge against the backdrop of Mount Parnassos, attracted hordes of pilgrims who came to consult the oracle. Now it is tourists who come here in droves to explore these mysterious ruins. *11 Odós Apollonos and 12 Odós Pávlou & Friderikis (at the top of a flight of steps). Open daily except Sun and bank holidays, 8am-3pm. ☎ (22650) 82 900.*

- ▶ **Orient Yourself:** Perched high on the mountainside, Dephi lies 160km/99mi northwest of Athens via Thebes and Livadía. The archaeological site is near the road, about a kilometre before the modern village. Hotels line the two principal streets which run one-way in each direction.
- **Parking:** Lots near the site and at the village entrance.
- **Don't Miss:** The theatre, the museum and the thólos.
- **Organizing Your Time:** The site is steep; plan at least one (tiring!) day.
- **Also See:** Aráhova

A Bit of History

Gaia, earth goddess – Mythology relates that Delphi was founded by Zeus. By the second millennium BC Delphi was already a place of worship dedicated to the earth goddess (Gaia) and her daughter Themis, who was said to reside at the bottom of a fault, guarded by her son, the snake Python.

The oracle – A hymn attributed to Homer tells how the god Apollo in 750 BC killed the Python and took his place, giving oracles through a priestess known as the Pythia (later called the Delphic Sibyl).

The priestess (always a woman over 50 whose life was beyond reproach) would go into the temple and enter a trance, delivering ambiguous replies in hexameter verse in response to questions put by pilgrims. The Pythia seems to have been well informed in politics; in turn she favoured Xerxes during the Persian invasions, then Athens, Sparta and Thebes in the 4C BC, then Philip of Macedon and Alexander the Great, whom she proclaimed invincible, and finally Rome.

The sanctuary itself was served by two high priests, a steward, a treasurer, five priests, of whom Plutarch was once one, and several acolytes, who attended the Pythia.

Enduring importance – During its heyday as a pan-Hellenic sanctuary, Delphi attracted pilgrims from all over the Greek world, from Spain to the Black Sea. Despite fire, earthquakes and pillaging, Delphi was still thriving under the Emperor Hadrian in the 2C AD. It was finally closed in 381 by the Byzantine Emperor Theodosius the Great. Delphi then became a Christian site. In the early 6C it was laid waste by the Slavs.

Visit

Open Apr–Oct, daily 8am-7pm; Nov–Mar, daily 8.30am-3pm. 6€ (site and museum 9€; museum only 3€; 8.30am-3pm). No charge Sun from 1 Nov to 31 Mar and the first Sun of the month except Jul-Sep, 6 Mar, 18 Apr, 18 May, 5 Jun and last weekend in Sep. ☎ (22650) 82 312.

A pedestrian path links the village with the sanctuary of Apollo, situated along the road to Aráhova. Above the museum, cross the road and follow the path to the entrance.

The Ancient ruins range down the mountain side below two roseate rock faces, the Phaidriades. Between them is a deep cleft from which emerges the Kastalian Spring.

B. Kaufmann/ MICHELIN

Delphi Theatre

The view to the south overlooks the River Pleistos winding round the foot of Mount Kírphis towards the coastal basin and the bay of Itéa.

Ieró Apólona★★★

It is a short walk uphill to the agora, which precedes the Sanctuary of Apollo.

Agora

Traces of brick houses and baths from the Roman period are visible above the agora. Down one side ran an Ionic portico with shops for pilgrims; a few of the columns survive. Fragments from a palaeo-Christian church are displayed (**1**) in the far corner. Four steps lead to the main entrance to the **sacred precinct** (*témenos*). The wall encloses a trapezoidal area of which the lower part contains votive offerings and the **Treasuries**, small temples erected by the Greek city states to receive the offerings made by their citizens.

Sacred Way

The Sacred Way leads up to the Temple of Apollo; the paving dates from the Roman period. It is lined with **votive offerings**; on the right stands the base of the bull of Corcyra (**2**). Again on the right is the votive monument of the Arcadians (**3**) next to that of the Lakedaimonians; on the left the votive monument of Marathon, followed by the monument of the Argives. These monuments, what little is left of them, testify to the rivalry between the Greek cities.

Address Book

For coin categories, see the Legend on the cover flap.

Aráhova, a mountain village 13km/8mi to the east of Delphi, offers options for accommodation and food.

WHERE TO EAT

Lekaria – *Odós Appollonos.* Delicious dishes (try the lamb or the saganaki sausage) served on a terrace overlooking the gulf.

WHERE TO STAY

Thólos – 31 *Odós Apóllonos* – ☎ *and fax (22650) 82 268 – 17rm.* Clean rooms, near the church. Breakfast served on the terrace next door (magnificent view). Open mid-Mar to end of Oct, Fri-Sun only in winter, (closed Nov).

Pan and **Artemis** – *Loutraki – Odós Pávlou & Frideríkis, between the bus station and the Post Office* – ☎ *(22650) 82 294 – 25rm.* Two traditional establishments; modest, attractive rooms.

Iníohos – *19 Odós Pávlou & Frideríkis* – ☎ *(22650) 82 710,www.delphi-hotels.gr – 23rm.* This reliable hotel has clean, stylish rooms with balconies.

Galaxa – *Galaxidi, Odós Eleftherías & Kennedy, near the sea* – ☎ *(22650) 41 620; in Athens* ☎ *(210) 65 22 092 – 18rm.* Small hotel in a former sea captain's house. Serene, family atmosphere and immaculate rooms.

Argo – *Galaxidi, on a street perpendicular to the harbour* – ☎ *(22650) 41 996/42 100 – 18rm.* Recently built, all-white building with marble floors. Small, pleasant rooms. Home-made cakes and jams at breakfast.

SHOPPING

Crafts – Carpets, cushions and curtains made of woven cotton; a good selection at Níkos Giannópoulos in the upper part of the town.

Antiques – *Odós Apóllonos 56* – Superb selection of traditional objects (pottery, old signs, fabrics), albeit at high prices.

EVENTS AND FESTIVALS

The inhabitants of Delphi hold an **Easter parade** for which they dress in traditional costume, and cook mutton kebabs.

Performances (drama, poetry) in fine weather)in the sanctuary stadium.

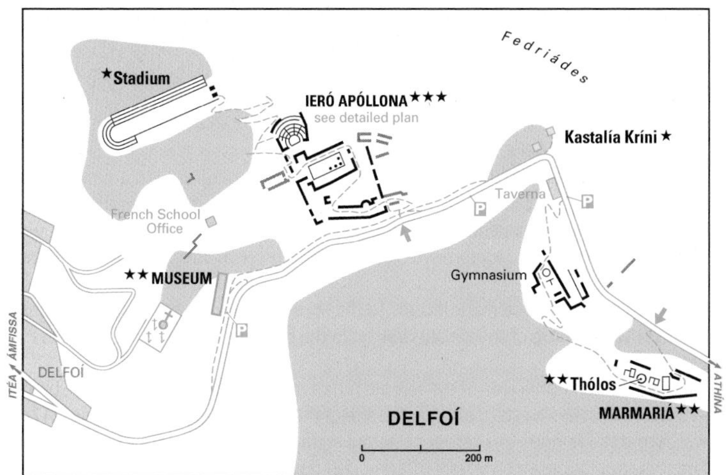

The Sacred Way then passes between the foundations of two semicircular structures erected by the Argives; to the right was the monument of the king of Árgos (**4**), built in 369 BC; it was decorated with 20 statues of the kings and queens of Árgos.

The first **treasury** is that of Sikyon (**5**); the bases remain (6C BC). Beyond stands the wall of the **Treasury of Siphnos** (**6**), built of marble in about 525 BC. In the southwest corner stood the **Treasury of Thebes** (**7**); the tufa foundations are visible. Nearby are the foundations of the Treasury of the Boeotians and a limestone version of the *omphalos* (**8**).

The **Treasury of the Athenians**★ *(Thisssavrós Athinéon)* is a Doric building (490-480 BC) in white Parian marble, decorated with sculptures illustrating the battle between the Greeks and the Amazons *(in the museum)*. Inscriptions on the walls, base and terrace are in honor of the Athenian victory at Marathon.

After the Treasury come the sparse ruins of the **bouleurterion** (**9**) (the Senate of Delphi), followed by a pile of rocks (**10**) marking the site of the early Delphic oracle; behind the rocks stood the Sanctuary of the Earth goddess, Ge or Gaia. Farther on are the fallen drums of an Ionic marble column (**11**), a gift from the Naxiots in about 570 BC.

The polygonal wall (6C BC) retaining the terrace on which the Temple of Apollo is built is inscribed with more than 800 Acts granting slaves their freedom during the Hellenistic and Roman periods. Three columns of Pentelic marble mark the Stoa of the Athenians (**12**) which dates from about 480 BC

At this point the Sacred Way crosses a circular area *(halos)* where processions to the temple formed; note the handsome Ionic capital (**13**) and the curved seat *(exedra)* for the priests. On the edge of this area stood the Treasury of the Corinthians; nearby under the Sacred Way a cache of precious objects *(in the museum)* was discovered in 1939.

The Sacred Way rises steeply; the circular pedestal *(right)* bore the **Tripod of**

G Gautier/MICHELIN

Treasury of the Athenians

Plataia (**14**), now in Constantinople. On the left are the foundations of the great **Altar to Apollo** (**15**) which dates from the 5C BC.
The huge stone pillar (**16**), to the right of the temple façade, bore an equestrian statue of Prusias (2C BC), King of Bithynia in Asia Minor.

Temple of Apollo★★

The existing ruins date from the 4C BC. It was a Doric building with a peristyle; a half dozen of the columns have been re-erected. A statue of Homer stood in the portico. The *naós* at the centre of the temple was furnished with altars and statues; beyond was the crypt *(adyton)* where the Pythia sat near the *omphalos* and the tomb of Dionysos.
The views from here are magnificent. To the south the temple columns stand out against the backdrop of the Pleistos Valley. To the northwest rise the perfect curves of the theatre.
Parallel with the uphill side of the temple runs a retaining wall, or **'Iskégaon'**, built in the 4C BC; at the western end, on the site of the votive offering of Polyzalos (**17**), was found the famous Charioteer of Delphi *(in the museum)*.
The rectangular base of a votive offering (**18**) has preserved the dedicatory stone on the back wall on the left.

Theatre★★

Dating from the 4C BC, the theatre could seat 5 000 spectators. From the top row there is a marvellous **view**★★★ down over the sanctuary ruins, across the Pleistos Valley to Mount Kírphis.
The gangway *(diázoma)* running round the theatre halfway up continues westwards as a path winding up the hillside to the Stadium; very fine views of the site of Delphi *(30min on foot there and back)*.

To reach the stadium, take the path to the left of the theatre (steep climb).

Stadium★

Before the first stone seating was built in the 3C BC the stadium was surrounded by earth terraces buttressed by a polygonal wall. In the 2C AD it was altered by Herodes Atticus, who built the present terraces to seat 6 500 people and erected a monumental **gateway**. The starting and finishing lines are still in place.

Museum★★★

Open daily 8.30am-3pm. 3€. No charge on Sun from 1 Nov to 31 Mar and the first Sun of the month except Jul-Sep, 6 Mar, 18 Apr, 18 May, 5 Jun and last weekend in Sep. ☎(22650) 823 12.
This museum displays to good effect the works of art excavated at Delphi.
At the top of the steps stands a conical block of marble, a Hellenistic copy of the famous **omphalos**★ (navel) which was kept in the Temple of Apollo and was supposed to mark the centre of the world.
The **Hall of the Siphnian Treasury** is devoted to Archaic sculpture (6C BC). In the middle stands the winged Sphinx of the Naxiots flanked by two caryatids from the Treasuries of Knidos and Siphnos. Around the walls are pieces of the marble frieze from the **Siphnian Treasury**★; the sculpted decoration was brightly painted.
In the next room are two huge **kouroi**★, (6C BC) depicting twins from Árgos who died of exhaustion after pulling their mother's chariot for 45 *stadia* (just under 5 miles).
In the **Hall of the Bull** you'll find cult objects discovered beneath the Sacred Way. The principal item is an Archaic **bull**★ dating from the 6C BC; also several gold panels from a statue, and a statuette in ivory of a god taming a fawn. Bronzes include an incense burner held by a young girl dressed in a *peplos* (5C BC).
In the **Hall of the Athenian Treasury** there are sculpted metopes *(damaged)*, which date from the Archaic period; the head of Theseus *(left)* is very fine.

A magnificent group of **three dancers**★★ in Pentelic marble stands on an acanthus column; the dancers are bacchantes or Thyiads, priestesses of Dionysos. Against the wall are the statues from the Monument (4C BC) of Daochos II. Note the figure of the athlete Agias; it is probably a copy of a bronze by Lysippos.

The Charioteer of Delphi

Office National Hellénique de Tourisme

The **Charioteer of Delphi**★★★, the jewel of this museum's collection, is one of the most beautiful Greek statues from the late Archaic period (478 BC). The figure was part of a bronze votive offering representing the winning quadriga (four-horse chariot) in the Olympic Games of 473 and 474. The noble, life-size figure wears the victor's headband.

A showcase in the same room displays a white **libation cup** (5C BC) showing Apollo seated, wearing a crown of laurel and holding a tortoise-shell lyre. Note also the marble **statue of Antinoüs** (2C AD), a favourite of Hadrian.

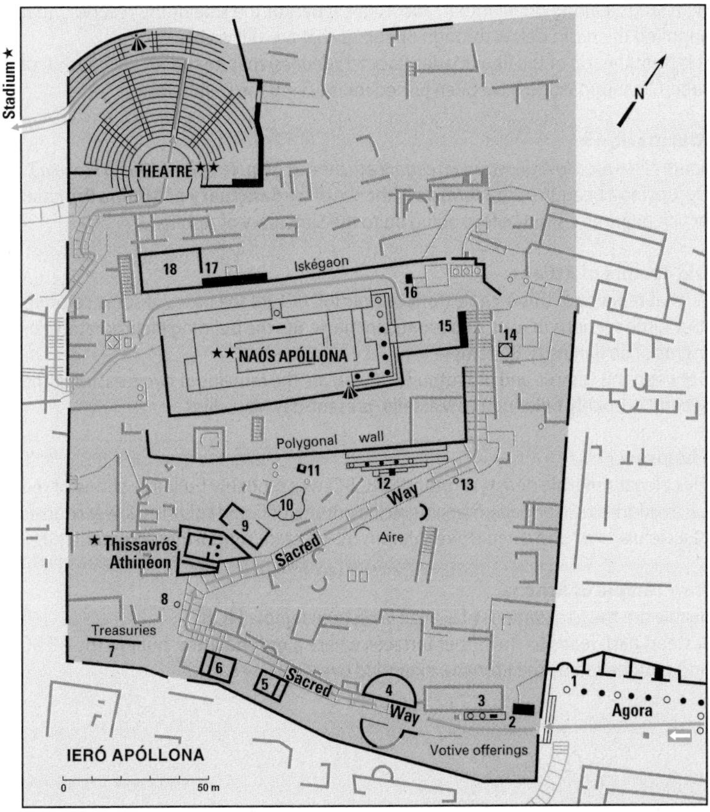

B Kaufmann/MICHELIN

The Thólos of Delphi

Kastalía Kríni★

The **Kastalian Spring** wells up at the end of the wild ravine dividing the Phaidriades Rocks. Here the pilgrims performed ritual ablutions to purify themselves before entering Apollo's Sanctuary.

Remaining are a huge Archaic paved basin, a longer basin hewn out of the rock with steps leading down into it, and above it part of the side of the reservoir that supplied the basin below through openings that are still visible.

It is from the top of the Phaidriades Rocks *(Fedriádes)* that **Aesop** (6C BC), author of fables, is supposed to have been hurled for mocking the Delphians.

Marmariá★★

South of the road to Aráhova; main entrance to the east (sign 'Temple of Athena Pronaia').

Occupying a beautiful site, Marmariá is the site of the **Sanctuary of Athena Pronaia,** which pilgrims visited before going on to the Sanctuary of Apollo.

Old Temple of Athena

All that remains of this Archaic Doric temple (6C BC) are the bases of some columns and some sections of wall. Abandoned in the 4C BC, the building incorporated elements of an earlier 7C BC temple.

Between this temple and the rotunda *(thólos)* are the remains of two treasuries; the second probably belonged to Massalia, present-day Marseilles.

Thólos★★

This elegant marble peristyle rotunda (4C BC) was probably built as a shrine of the earth goddess (Ge or Gaia). Remains include drums of fluted columns, lower courses of a circular wall and three Doric columns (re-erected) supporting an entablature.

New Temple of Athena

Visible are the foundations of a small limestone temple (4C BC).

A steep path leads to the upper terraces where a **gymnasium**, built in the 4C BC and remodelled by the Romans, extended over two levels.

Outskirts

Itéa

17km/11mi to the southwest.

The road descends the slopes of the Pleistos Valley into the coastal plain, which belonged to the Sanctuary of Apollo and was the setting of the Ancient racecourse. The famous olive groves here are aptly referred to as a **sea of olives**★. Together with recent plantations on the slopes of the Pleistos Valley they number some 400 000 olive trees; harvesting begins in September. The olive mills are powered by the waters of the Pleistos.

Itéa is a bathing resort and port at the head of Itéa Bay. It was chosen by the Allies in 1917 as the base town on the supply route which ran to the eastern front. To the east of Itéa lay the Ancient port of Delphi, Kirra; there are traces of an Ancient jetty.

Galaxídi★

33km/21mi southwest via Itéa.

Fine view of the Bay of Itéa. Galaxídi is a charming old town with a sheltered harbour, which until early this centuryrivalled Syros *(see SÍROS)*. The fine stone houses with their balconies suggest former days of wealth; in the 19C Galaxídi traded throughout the Mediterranean. A small **Maritime Museum** evokes the port's past glories. The **cathedral** at the top of the town contains a beautiful 19C carved-wood iconostasis.

Ámfissa

20km/12mi northwest.

The rival of Delphi in Antiquity, Amphissa is built against the curved slope at the head of the valley. Known as Salona in the 13C, it was the seat of a Frankish domain taken by the Turks in 1394. Its fortress, formerly called Château de la Sole, was erected on the site of the old acropolis that can still be traced; there are remains of the keep, the living quarters and a 13C round tower. Fine views of the town and of the valley.

ARHÉA EPÍDAVROS★★★

ANCIENT EPIDAUROS – Απχ. Επιδαυροσ

MICHELIN MAP 737 H 10 – ARGOLÍDA – PELOPONNESE.

The elegance, perfection of design and quality of conservation at the Theatre of Epidauros cannot be overstated and were already acknowledged in Antiquity. It was the jewel in the crown of the Sanctuary of Aesculapius, the god of medicine; from all over Greece people came to consult the oracle here. Its ruins occupy an isolated site of gently rolling hills carpeted with pine trees and oleanders.

- **Orient Yourself:** 68km/43mi south of Corinth, 30km/19mi east of Nauplion. Note that there are three places named Epidauros: the villages of Néa Epídavros and Paleá Epídavros (near the sea), and Arhéa Epídavros, the Ancient site, also known as Askilipio.
- **Parking:** Large lot next to the road from Nauplion (signs from Ligourio).
- **Don't Miss:** The theatre
- **Organizing Your Time:** Plan at least two hours to visit the site.
- **Also See:** Árgolida, Árgos, Mikínes, Náfplio, Tírintha.

A Bit of History

The power to heal – According to legend, **Asklepios**, a son of Apollo, was trained by centaurs in the healing arts, becoming so proficient that he was able to resuscitate the dead, drawing the ire of Zeus and Hades. Jealous of a power reserved for the gods, Zeus sent a thunderbolt to strike Asklepios dead and his body was buried at Epidauros.

From the 6C BC Asklepios became the object of a cult of healing, which reached its greatest intensity in the 4C BC. The great Greek doctors, even the famous **Hippocrates** of Kos, claimed authority from him.

Asklepios is generally represented as a bearded figure leaning on an augur's wand accompanied by the magic serpent; these elements later came to be included in the **caduceus**, the doctor's emblem.

The Epidauros treatment – Supplicants would proceed through stages of sacrifice and purification before sleeping in a sacred dormitory *(abator)*. They might be cured instantly or Asklepios might appear to them in dreams, which the priests would translate into treatment, accompanied by exercises, relaxation, baths or intellectual pursuits. This explains the importance given to the theatre and the sports facilities and to the Asklepian Games, held every four years. The people expressed their gratitude with the sacrifices and votive offerings. Under the Romans, thaumaturgy gradually yielded its place to a more scientific form of medicine. Late in the 5C AD a Christian basilica was built on the site of the Ancient sanctuary.

Epidauros languished until the beginning of the 19C. In 1822 the independence of Greece was proclaimed in the theatre. In 1881 Greek archaeologists, assisted by the French School in Athens, began to work on the site.

Sights

From the car park a path leads through the trees to the archaeological site. Open Apr–Oct: daily 7.30am-7pm; Nov–Mar 7.30am-5pm. 6€. ☎ (27530) 23 009 or (27530) 22 666.

Theatre★★★

Outstanding for the beauty of its setting, its magnificent lines and harmonious proportions, the theatre (4C) is set into the north slope of Mount Harani facing the valley sacred to Asklepios. In 1954 it was restored to accommodate modern produc-

B Kaufmann/MICHELIN

Theatre of Epidauros

tions of the Ancient repertory as well as musical recitals.

The theatre, which can accommodate 14 000 spectators, consists of 55 rows divided by a promenade *(diázoma)* into upper and lower sections. The circular orchestra, where the chorus performed, is marked at the centre by the base of the altar to Dionysos. On the north side of the orchestra are the foundations of the stage and the proscenium incorporating an arch that supported the scenery.

It is worth climbing the steps between the rows of seats to appreciate the structure's contours and proportions. The performance could be heard and seen perfectly from every seat; have someone whisper or rustle a piece of paper in the centre of the orchestra to demonstrate.

The view from the top is very fine, particularly in the early evening when the sacred valley of Asklepios lies peacefully in the shelter of the surrounding hills.

In the **museum** *(closed Mon morning)* you'll find unusual *stele* bearing inscriptions, a collection of Roman medical instruments and a partial reconstruction of the rotunda using authentic elements).

EVENTS AND FESTIVALS

Epidauros Festival – Held in July and August; the great plays of Classical Greece are performed at 9pm on Fridays and Saturdays; be sure to book well in advance. Tickets may be purchased here three hours before performances, ☎ (27530) 22 026; or at the tourist office in Nauplion, Odós 25 Martiou, ☎ (27520) 24 444; also in Athens from the **Athens Festival Box Office**, 4 Odós Stadiou, ☎ (210) 322 14 59.

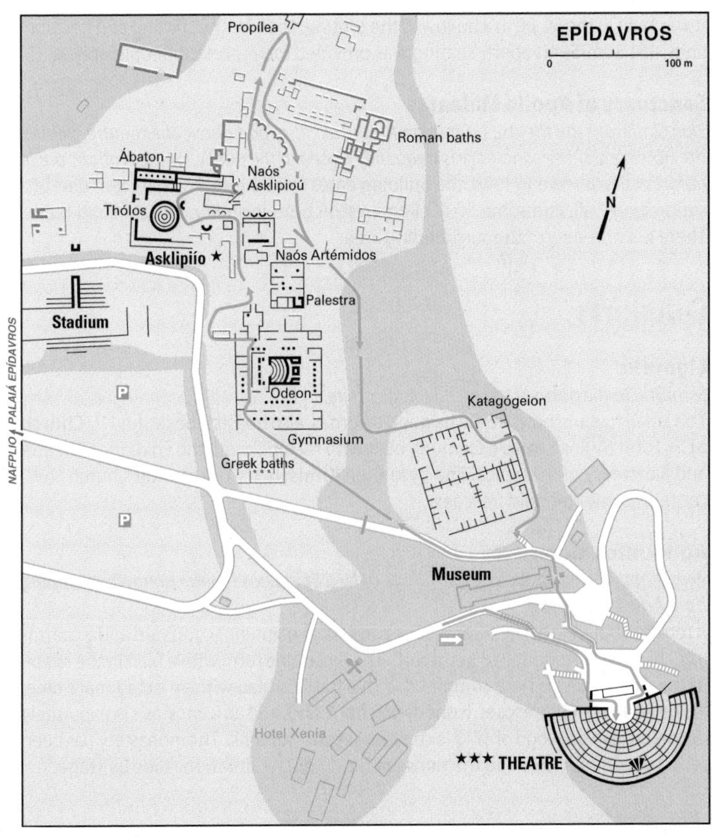

Asklipiío★ (Sanctuary of Asklepios)

From the theatre, pass the museum to reach the **gymnasium***; the central part of it was converted into an odeon by the Romans. Descend the ramp, which led up to the main entrance to the gymnasium, passing the remains of the* **palaestra**.

To the northwest are the foundations of the Temple of Artemis, Naós Artémidos (late 4C BC), which has been partially reconstructed in the museum.

In the Sanctuary of Asklepios, the main monuments are surrounded by a wall that confined the sacred serpents.

An outline of rectangular foundations marks the site of the **Naós Asklipioú**, a small Doric temple with a raised peristyle. It contained a statue of Asklepios seated on a throne, a baton in his right hand and his left resting on the head of a serpent. South of the temple are the remains of the sacrificial altar.

More foundations belong to the famous rotunda *(thólos)* which was built in the 4C BC by the architect of the theatre, **Polykleitos the Younger**, as a mausoleum for the hero Asklepios. The rotunda was sumptuously decorated with different-coloured marbles, paintings and finely sculpted motifs, some of which are on display in the National Archaeological Museum in Athens.

To the north of the rotunda and the temple are the foundations of the dormitory where the sick slept in the hope that Asklepios would appear to them in a dream.

Beyond are traces of the foundations of the monumental entry *(propylaia)* to the sanctuary built in the 4C BC.

On the north side are traces of a huge 4C BC hotel *(katagógeion)* comprising 160 rooms arranged round four courtyards.

Stadium

It was built in the 5C BC in a hollow in the ground. Look for the starting and finishing lines, 181.30m/594ft apart. Seating was provided for important people only.

Sanctuary of Apollo Maleatas

3km/2mi from the theatre (30min on foot). Take the road above the theatre, behind the Hotel Xenia. The sanctuary is frequently closed to the public, as excavations are in progress. Discovered in 1928, the building dates from the 4C BC; there are ruins of a supporting wall, and some 2C AD Roman structures including a cistern and baths. There is a fine view of the surrounding area.

Outskirts

Ligourió

5km/3mi to the north of the archaeological site.

This small town, renowned for its good tavernas, also boasts a beautiful 11C **Church of St John** (Ágios Yannis o Elemon), built with material from the Epidauros Theatre and Sanctuary of Asklepios. The Byzantine **Kimissis tis Theotokou** Church (16C) contains some splendid frescoes.

Agnountos Monastery

7km/4.5mi northeast, before the village of Néa Epídavros (on the right when coming from Arhéa Epídavros).

A fortified building of the 6C and 8C, it consists of an interior courtyard and a charming 11C church, remodelled in the 14C. The Byzantine form with a plan in the shape of the Greek cross is here combined with a basilica plan with an octagonal dome. Inside there are 13C frescoes, icons dating from 1759, and an iconostasis in exquisitely decorated carved wood of 1713 (a copy, for security reasons). The monastery has been reoccupied since 1980 and the nuns are tackling its restoration stage by stage.

Paleá Epídavros

9km/5.5mi northeast of the Ancient site. Small fishing village and resort with several fish tavernas at the end of a picturesque valley.

At the end of the road running along the seashore, a path through a citrus orchard leads to a recently discovered small theatre from the time of Alexander the Great *(10min on foot, turn right at the junction).*

ÉVIA★

EUBOIA – Ευβοια

POPULATION 205 500

MICHELIN MAP 737 H I7, I-J 8, J-K 9 – ÉVIA – CENTRAL GREECE.

The largest of the Greek islands after Crete, Euboia lies off the coast to the east of Boeotia and Attica, one hour from Athens. A bridge at Halkída spans the Evrípos Channel from the mainland. Euboia's landscapes are beautiful and varied: wooded mountains and fast-flowing rivers in the north, wild, rocky inlets on the east coast, and sandy beaches and plains on the west coast. Moreover, the island has some fine Ancient sites. *SET-kosmos, 7 Karistos Square, Karistos, western side of the main esplanade. ☎ (22240) 26 200/25 700, fax (22240) 29 011, set@hlk.forthnet.gr*

Driving Tour

The South of the Island 1 *625km/391mi departing from Halkída.*

Halkída (Chalkis)

The capital of Eubola and very popular with tourists, Halkída is a port, an agricultural market and industrial centre. The modern seafront sports hotels and cafés.

Halkída was one of the most dynamic cities of Ancient Greece. Her powerful fleet allowed her to establish colonies in Thrace and Macedonia in the 8C BC. The colonists who settled there named the region Chalcidice and went on to found other settlements in Italy and Sicily.

From the 13C to the 15C the Venetians developed an important commercial centre here. In 1470 the town fell to the Turks but remained a lively trading centre. In 1688, 15 000 Venetian soldiers tried to recapture the town.

The Church of **Agía Paraskeví** is in the second street on the left coming from the bridge. The church is Byzantine in origin and rests on Ancient columns of cipolin marblel. It has fine mosaics and a marble iconostasis. Not far away in the small square *(Platía Kóskou)* there is a disused mosque and a Turkish fountain; the small alleyways are lined by traditional houses with wooden balconies.

The **Archaeological Museum**★ contains fine pieces from the prehistoric, Hellenistic and Roman periods. Note the funerary stele (4C BC) depicting a young athlete and his dog *(13 Venizelou; open daily, 8.30am-3.30pm. 2€; (22210) 76 131).*

Returning towards the bridge, note the ruined **Karababá Fort** (1686) across the water. From the west bastion, there is a fine **view**★ of Halkída, the Evrípos and the Bay of Aulis *(south).*

▶ *Leave Halkída and head towards Néa Artaki and Psachna, where the route bears right in the direction of Attali and Stení, and climbs the slopes of Mount Dyrfis.*

Stení

32km southeast of Halkída. Stení is a cool and shady mountain resort; its chalets are built on either side of a mountain torrent. There are many walks in the forests of which cover the slopes of Mount Dírfis *(allow 2hr 30min if planning to climb to the summit).* The view of the sea and the island is breathtaking.

Follow the road to Metochi 21km/13mi away. From there, a well-surfaced road leads to Kími (another 20km/12mi away) via Vitala.

Kími

The little town of Kími developed from the Ancient town of Kyme, whose inhabitants founded Cumae near Naples in Italy. The town stands on a rocky plateau overlooking the Aegean Sea towards the island of Skíros.

A fine old house has been turned into a **Museum of Folk Art** (Laografikó Moussío), featuring crafts, costumes and furniture *(between the village and the port; open 10am-1pm and 5-7.30pm).*

From Kími head back towards Lepoura (35km/22mi), passing through Koniastres and Monodryio.

Beyond **Lepoura**, the south of the island unfurls; the route becomes steeper as it winds around arid mountains; white windmills dot the landscape.

Stíra

41km from Lepoura. The village on the slopes of Mount Klióssi is known for its marble quarries and its beach at **Néa Stíra** down below on the coast; to the east stood the mighty Frankish castle of Lármena.

'Drómos ton Aetón'★★★

Between Stíra and Káristos (about 30km/18.5mi) the **Eagles' Road** runs along a ledge on the southwest coast of Euboia. Birds of prey hover over the hillsides, which offer splendid views down over Marmári and across the bay to the Petalií Islands.

Káristos

This is a summer resort with a port for fishing boats and ferries (from Rafína). Mount Óhi, which rises behind the town, was already being quarried in Antiquity for its green cipolin marble. To the east of the quay are the remains of a 14C Venetian fortress, the Bourzi. Opposite is a small **archaeological museum** *(open Tue-Sun, 8.30am-3pm; 2€; ☎ (22240) 25 661).*

On the top of Mount Folí stand the ruins of a huge castle, called **Castel Rosso** (Red Castle) because of the colour of the stone.

From Káristos the coast road leads to the southeast tip of the island (Platanistos, Komito), taking in some beautiful inlets and wild beaches.

Head back on the same road as far as Lepoura, then follow directions to Velos. From there, take the minor road to the ruins of Dístos.

Dístos (Ruins)

Isolated on flat, open ground by a little lake lie the ruins of Ancient Dystos. The 5C BC walls are of polygonal construction with strengthened square towers.

B Chabrol/MICHELIN

Return to Velos, then take the coast road (heavily developed) to Aliveri and Amarynthos. Continue to Erétria.

Erétria★

Erétria was for many years the rival of Halkída for possession of the rich Lelantine (Lefkandí) Plain. There are several traces of the **Ancient city**, which was extensive and prosperous. The main ruins lie to the north, including vestiges of a **gymnasium** and a fairly well-preserved **theatre** (3C BC) at the foot of the acropolis with the foundations of a **Shrine to Dionysos** nearby.
A little to the east is the **House of the Mosaics**, a 4C BC villa centred on an open courtyard surrounded by a peristyle. The reception rooms on the north side were decorated with magnificent mosaic pavements depicting mythological scenes

Address Book

For coin categories, see the Legend on the cover flap.

GETTING ABOUT

BY BOAT
Ferries serve **Marmari** from **Rafína** *(6-8/day);* **Eretria** from **Skala Oropou** *(every 30min from 5am to 10pm in summer*). From **Arkitsa** to **Loutra Edipsou**: *(every 30min from 7am to 8.30pm)*. Other ferries also connect the mainland to numerous ports on the west coast: Glifa to Agiokambos, Agia Marina to Néa Stira.
A hydrofoil operates from **Kimi** to **Skiros** *(1-2/day; ☎ (22220) 22 022).*

BY PLANE
From Athens three times a day. Other flights from Thessaloníki and Lesbos.

WHERE TO EAT

Kissos – *Stení, on the left hand side of the road – ☎ (22280) 51 226/51 227.* A large restaurant; several terraces and a wide range of reasonably priced dishes.
O Plátanos – *Límni, under the only plane tree on the quayside.* Pleasant shaded terrace, popular with locals. Specialities include grilled and fried fish. Efficient family management. Open weekends only, out of season.
Cavo d'Oro – *Káristos, Párados Sahtóuri (an alleyway at right angles to the quayside beyond the esplanade).* Traditional taverna serving copious meat dishes in sauces. Menu only in Greek.
To Kalámia – *at the start of the beach, Káristos.* Nice taverna close to the water and off the tourist trail. Traditional cuisine, tasty and inexpensive.
To Ástro (Ioánnou Brothers' Taverna) – *3.5km/2.2mi south of Límni in a hamlet on the water – ☎ (22270) 31 487/32 426.* The place for a romantic dinner; meals are served on the large terrace in a charming setting. Classic dishes offering variety and quality.

WHERE TO STAY

Límni Hotel – *Límni, south of the quayside – ☎ (22270) 31 316/31 748, – 27rm.* Comfortable, good-value hotel, away from the bustle of the harbour. Most rooms have sea views.
Hotel Stení – *Stení – ☎ (22280) 51 221- – 35rm.* Comfortable rooms which are well kept, quiet and spacious, with attractive wood panelling and fine views of the valley.
Corali Hotel – Kimi, *300m/330yd south of the harbour, 150m/165yd up and to the right – ☎ (22220) 22 212/22 002, info@coralihotel.gr – 22rm.* Quiet, spacious and comfortable rooms with balconies.
Karystion Hotel – *Kárystos, 3 Kriezótou, at the eastern end of the quay, after the "Bourzi" – ☎ (22240) 22 391/22 191, karistio@otenet.gr – – 39rm.* Modern, tasteful, comfortable hotel; professional service. Ask for a west-facing room so you can enjoy the sunset from your terrace. Excellent breakfast served on the garden terrace.
Hotel Apartments Iliathídes – *Amárinthos, on the main road, north of the town by the Shell station. – ☎ (22290) 37 605/37 215 – 16rm.* Spacious and comfortable apartments with kitchens and views of the port. Friendly management; no breakfast.

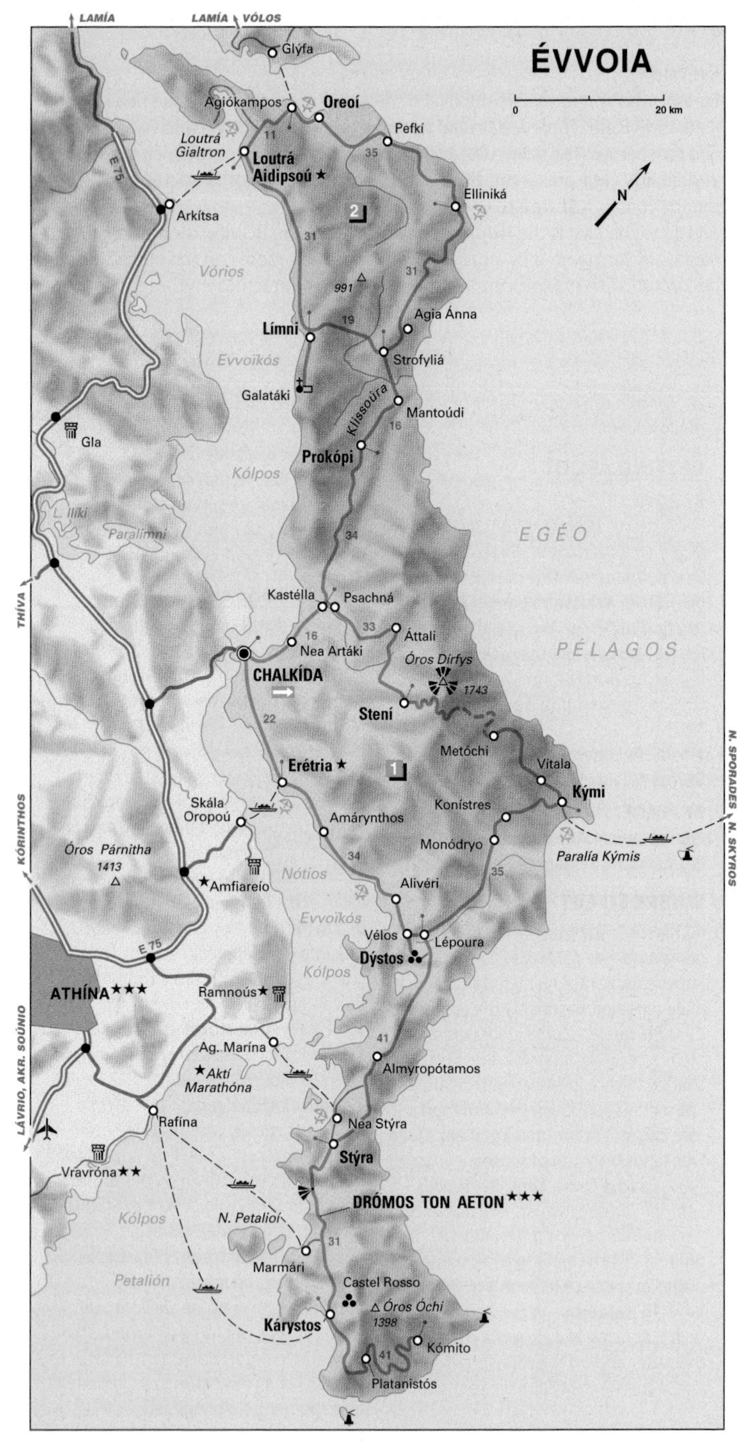
ÉVVOIA
0
20 km
N
LAMÍA
LAMÍA
VÓLOS
Glýfa
Agiókampos
Oreoí
Pefkí
Loutrá Gialtron
Loutrá Aidipsoú ★
Arkítsa
Ellinikä
2
Vórios
991
Agia Ánna
Límni
Strofyliá
Evvoïkós
Galatáki
Klissoúra
Mantoúdi
Gla
Prokópi
Kólpos
L. Iliki
Paralímni
EGÉO
THÍVA
Kastélla
Psachná
Áttali
Nea Artáki
CHALKÍDA
PÉLAGOS
Óros Dírfys
1743
Stení
Metóchi
N. SPORADES
N. SKYROS
Erétria ★
1
Vítala
Kými
KÓRINTHOS
Skála Oropoú
Amárynthos
Konístres
Monódryo
Paralía Kýmis
Óros Párnitha
1413
★Amfiareío
Nótios
Alivéri
Evvoïkós
Vélos
Lépoura
Dýstos
Kólpos
ATHÍNA★★★
Ramnoús★
LÁVRIO, AKR. SOÚNIO
Ag. Marína
Almyropótamos
★Aktí Marathóna
Rafína
Nea Stýra
Stýra
Vravróna★★
DRÓMOS TON AETON★★★
Kólpos
N. Petalioí
Marmári
Petalión
Castel Rosso
Óros Óchi
1398
Kárystos
Kómito
Platanistós

(*open Tue-Sun, 8.30am-3pm, 2€.*) Be sure to stop in at the Archaeological Museum to see 6C BC **sculptures of Theseus and Antiope** from the ruins of Erétria, and items from neighbouring sites at Lefkandi and Chiropolis (*open same hours as House of Mosaics; ticket admits to both sites*).

Return to Halkída, 22km/14mi to the west.

The North of the Island 2 *350km/219mi departing from Halkída.*

Between Halkída and Loutra Edipsou the countryside is green and mountainous, and has some of the most beautiful scenery in Greece. There are also some undiscovered beaches to enjoy. Leave Halkída heading towards Néa Artaki. Continue north beyond Kastella. Prokópi is 52km/33mi from Halkída.

Prokópi

South of Mandoúdi, deep in the picturesque **Klissoúra Valley** lies Prokópi, formerly known as Achmet Aga. The banks of the stream which runs through the valley are covered by luxuriant vegetation: planes, poplars, walnuts and oleanders.

Continue to Mandoúdi and Strofylia, where the route bears left towards Limni, 19km/12mi away.

Limni

This pretty fishing village is perched on the mountainside; houses hanging out over the sea. From here, walk to the isolated convent of **Galataki** (fine 16C frescoes in the catholicon) at the far end of the promontory to the south of the village.

Returning from Limni take the coast road leading to Loutrá Edipsoú.

Loutrá Edipsoú★

This was a very fashionable spa in Antiquity; Sulla, Augustus and Hadrian came here to take the waters. Beyond the pump room on the east side of the town are the hot springs with their sulphurous vapour; some of the water tumbles into the sea by a little beach, **Loutrá Gialton**, some 15km/9mi to the west. From Loutrá Edipsoú it is possible to return to the mainland (boats to Arkitsa).

Head back towards Agiokambos (ferry to Glyfá) and Oreí.

Shortly before Oreí is a pleasant beach overlooked by a tower on an islet, which is the perfect spot for a swim.

Oreí

From the port (numerous cafés and restaurants) there are fine views across the Oreí Channel to Mount Óthris on the mainland and the entrance to the Vólos Gulf.

The north and northeast of the island are its most inaccessible areas. From Oreí take the main road back to Peffki and Elinika (fine beaches). Before reaching Strofilia, where the route heads back towards Halkída, stop in the peaceful village of Agia Anna.

HALKIDIKÍ★

CHALCIDICE – Χαλκιδικι

POPULATION 104 894

MICHELIN MAP 737 I-J 4, I 5 – HALKIDIKÍ – MACEDONIA.

The Strymon Gulf and the Gulf of Thessaloníki, coupled with a depression forming two large lakes, delineate the northern boundary of the peninsula of Chalcidice, located 60km/37mi southeast of Thessaloniki. To the south, it extends outwards in three promontories: Kassándra, Sithonía and Mount Athos. The last of these is dedicated to monasticism; the other two offer more earthly pleasures; the many miles of fine beaches are virtually deserted.

Excursions

Sithoná Peninsula★★

Round-trip of 109km/68mi along attractive coastline.
Sithonía boasts many natural beauty spots: forests of sea and umbrella pines, fine sandy beaches, deep fjords with sheer rock walls. The coast road runs past many beautiful sites, becomes a corniche road along the cliffs and offers extensive views particularly east to Mount Athos, although the summit is often shrouded in clouds.

Órmos Panagías

Picturesque hamlet in a rocky bay.

Sárti

Small cultivated coastal plain running down to a sandy bay.

Cape Drépano★

Rocky promontory deeply indented with many inlets extending into fjords, particularly at **Koufós** and round **Kalamítsi**★.

Address Book

For coin categories, see the Legend on the cover flap.

WHERE TO EAT

Chrístos – *Néos Marmarás, Sithonía – ☎ (23750) 71 211. On the left of the bay facing the sea (entrance difficult to see).* A vast selection of fish and seafood served indoors or on the raised terrace.

Filaktos – *Koufos, Sithonía – ☎ (23750) 51 280.* Terrace dining; ideal spot to try grilled sardines.

Kyaní Aktí – *Paralía Nikítas – ☎ (23750) 22 908.* Pleasant restaurant by the beach serving fresh fish dishes.

WHERE TO STAY

Marmarás – *Sithonía, Néos Marmará – ☎ (23750) 72 184 – 15rm.* Comfortable hotel with balconies overlooking the sea. Breakfast not included.

Zeus – *Kassándra, Afytos – ☎ (23740) 91 132 – 20 apartments.* Good décor, fully equipped; garden with pool.

Pórto Koufós – *Sithonía, Pórto Koufós – ☎ (23750) 51 207 – 26rm.* Situated opposite the bay. Comfortable rooms with balconies. Breakfast.

TAKING A BREAK

Dodoni – *Néos Marmarás, near the Christos restaurant.* Some of the finest ice cream in Greece.

Pórto Koufós★

The port and beach are magnificently located in a protected inlet.

Toróni Bay★

The long sandy beach of this idyllic bay curves gently south into a tiny peninsula which bears the remains of an Ancient fortress and palaeo-Christian basilicas. Beyond Toroni, the coast has some beautiful unspoilt **beaches**★.

Pórto Carrás

Developed by the oil tycoon, John C Carras, this seaside resort centres on two imposing hotels, a charming seaside village with a harbour, a golf course, tennis courts, a casino, a riding stable etc.

From the Sithoná Peninsula, you can continue east along the coast to get to Mount Áthos.

Kassándra Peninsula

60km/37mi south of Thessaloníki, then a round trip of 118km/73mi to make a complete tour of the peninsula.

This peninsula is less wooded and less attractive than Sithonía, but it is more fertile and more densely populated. The isthmus has been breached by a canal at Néa Potídea, the site of Ancient Poteidaia. There are pleasant beaches and a number of hotels especially at **Saní, Kalithéa, Agía Paraskeví** and (most notably) **Palioúri**, which lies at the southern end looking across a bay to the Sithonía peninsula.

Olynthos

5km/3mi to the east of Nea Moudania, turn left. Open Tue-Sun, 8.30am-3pm. 2€.

The rare geometric layout laid down by Hippodamus of Miletus is visible, with main artery roads crossing at right angles forming (some black and white mosaic work remains; don't miss the one depicting Bellerophon).

Petrálona

12km/8mi to the east off the road from Thessaloníki to the peninsula; turn left towards Néa Silata and left again to Elaiochoria. Open daily 9am-1 hr before sunset. 5€. (22373) 71 671.

The **cave of Kókines Pétres** (the Red Stones) is known to palaeontologists for the discovery of a Neanderthal skull and fossils of prehistoric animals. Only 2km/1.25mi may be visited. There is a small museum with a selection of finds.

HLEMOÚTSI★★

CHLEMOUTSI – Χλεμουτσι

MICHELIN MAP 737 D 9 – ILÍA – PELOPONNESE.

The largest and best preserved citadel in the Peloponnese, the famous castle of Clermont is a masterpiece of medieval defensive architecture. It lies in the west-facing region between Kyllini and Andravida, which was the base of the Franks in Morea from the 13C to the 15C. The area bears many monuments and other reminders from this time.

- **Orient Yourself:** The fortress lies 75km/47mi southwest of Patras and 60km/38mi northwest of Olympia, on the Kilíni peninsula overlooking the islands of Cephallonia and Zákinthos.
- **Don't Miss:** The fortress and its wonderful panoramic view.
- **Organizing Your Time:** Plan an hour for the visit
- **Also See:** Olimbía, Pátra, Kefalonía, Zákinthos

A Bit of History

Completed in 1223, the Clermont (Chlemoutsi) fortress was the most imposing in Morea. It bears the modifications made by its various possessors over the centuries: the Angevins of Naples (late 13C); the despotic Palaiologi (1427); and the Turks (1460). It was significantly damaged in 1827 by the forces of Ibrahim Pasha.

Visit

Castle

6km/4mi from Kástro. Open Tue-Sat, 8am-8pm, Sun and bank holidays 8am-2.30pm. No charge. ☎ (22610) 95 033.

The fortress consists of an outer court and the castle proper, which is built on a polygonal plan.

Address Book

For coin categories, see the Legend on the cover flap.

WHERE TO EAT

Castello – *Kástro, in the town centre.* A shady terrace and good-quality cuisine: beef in filo pastry, grilled meats that melt in the mouth, home-made taramosaláta, all washed down with a pleasant, slightly smoky white wine.

WHERE TO STAY

Catherine Lepida – *Kástro, in the town centre on the left going up – ☎ (26230) 95 224, in winter ☎ (26230) 95 444.* Renovated in 1998, these five large studios are quiet, cheerful and well equipped (good kitchens).

Paradise – *on a minor road between Kástro and Kilíni – ☎ (26230) 95 209.* A pleasant modern establishment; garden with trees. Water-skiing and parascending can be arranged.

Arcoudi – *Loutra Kylinnis, slightly out of the way by woodland – ☎ (26230) 96 480, www.arcoudi-hotel.gr.* Pleasant, comfortable spot near the beach. Play area for kids.

EVENTS AND FESTIVALS

Festival of theatre, dance and music; held in the castle during July and August.

SHOPPING

In Kástro there is a shop called **Camara**, in a street which descends on the left from the town centre, which sells attractive pottery.

JP Naïl/MICHELIN

Hlemoútsi's castle walls

The **outer court** was the domain of the servants. There is a fine view of the walls of the castle; originally the round towers were some 6m/20ft higher than the walls.
A plaque placed at the entrance to the **castle** recalls that **Constantine XII Palaiologos**, the last Byzantine Emperor, lived here for five years and died in the Battle for Constantinople, which was taken by the Turks on 29 May 1453.
The impressively large vaulted entrance is flanked *(left)* by the 2-storey chapel, and *(right)* by a vast structure also with two storeys.
At the centre of the castle is a hexagonal court where jousts and other kinds of entertainment were held. Surrounding it are vast halls built against the outer curtain wall, which is up to 8m/26ft thick in places.
From the terraces atop the curtain wall there is a splendid **panorama**★★ of Zakynthos *(west)* and the other Ionian Islands *(northwest)*; the coast by Missolonghi *(north)*; the plain of Elis *(east)*, which is bordered to the north by Mount Skólis and Sandoméri; the valley of the River Piniós *(east)*, the mountains of Arcadia *(southeast)* and Cape Katákolo *(south)*.

Outskirts

Kilíni (Kyllene)

6km/4mi north of Chlemoutsi. A seaside resort (Olympic Beach) and a sheltered harbour make up the modern town of Kyllene. The **Ruins of Clarence**, famed in the Middle Ages, include a few traces of the Clarence citadel; there is a fine view of the coast and the islands (*1.5km/1mi by car along the coast to the northwest then 10min on foot from a farm up to a bluff marked by a concrete post).*

Moní Vlahernón

On leaving Kilíni heading eastwards, turn right in the hamlet of Káto Panagía into a narrow road (sign); follow for 2km/1.25mi. The road enters a verdant but deserted valley containing the **Vlacherna Monastery,** named for a famous church in Constantinople dedicated to the Virgin. The monastery was built in the Byzantine period (12C), it may at one time have served as a Cistercian community and bears the hallmarks of French Gothic architecture.

Loutrá Kilínis

7km/4mi south of Chlemoutsi.
This spa, set in a beautiful eucalyptus forest, uses the waters of several springs to treat respiratory ailments, and has developed into a seaside resort best known for the long stretch of sand called **Golden Beach**.

IOÁNNINA★

Ιεαννινα
POPULATION 57 000
MICHELIN MAP 737 D 5 – IOÁNNINA – EPIROS.

Standing on the shore of Lake Pamvotis, the capital of Epiros is a dynamic modern city. Ioánnina serves as a convenient base from which to explore the Pérama Cave, the site of Ancient Dodona, and, a little farther away, the mountain village of Metsovo and the extraordinary Zagória district. Three major roads provide access to the city: the E 92, E 90 and E 951. *39 Odós Dodonis, ☏ (26510) 411 42. Open Mon-Sat, 9am-1pm, and 5.30-8.30pm in summer.*

A Bit of History

'The Lion of Ioánnina' – In the 15C, Ioánnina came under Turkish control. The city rose to prominence in the late 18C under the rule of **Ali Pasha**, who was appointed by the Turkish Sultan in 1788. An adroit political maneuverer, Ali formed alliances with Greek partisans and European nations, playing all sides in an effort to become independent of the Sultan. For more than 30 years he exercised almost sovereign power over western Greece and Albania. Despite his reputation for cruelty, Ali Pasha exercised tolerance toward Christians, and Ioánnina developed into an important centre for Greek culture.

Alarmed at his power, the Sultan in 1820 besieged the citadel of Ioánnina for 15 months. Ali Pasha was eventually killed by the Turks in 1822; his head was put on display in Ioánnina and then sent as a trophy to the Sultan.

Visit

Froúrio★★

The huge fortress dominating the lake was originally constructed in the 11C but was restored in the early 19C during the reign of Ali Pasha, whose palace stood atop the rock.

The northern end of the fortress, **Aslán Dzamí**★, includes the attractive Aslan Aga Mosque (1619) with its slim pointed minaret. The building has been converted into a **Municipal museum** displaying items illustrating the history of the town.

H Champollion/MICHELIN

Typical building in Ioánnina, situated next to the lake

The embroidered costumes and archaeological finds are remarkable. *Open daily, 8am-8pm; 8am-6pm in winter. ☎ (26510) 26 356; 3€.*
From the terrace there are very fine **views**★★ of the lake and mountains. Below the mosque stands the former Turkish Library roofed with several little domes; farther west is the Old Synagogue, a reminder that in the 19C there were nearly 6 000 Jews in Ioánnina.

Address Book

For coin categories, see the Legend on the cover flap.

WHERE TO EAT

To Koumanio – *Ioánnina, Platía Georgíou* – Simple, quality Greek cuisine (grills, spit roasts).
To Mánteio Psistariá – *Ioánnina, Platía Georgíou.* Same category and fare as the previous entry, but a bit livelier.
Límni – *Odós Papágou.* The last restaurant but one in this row; delicious *bekrí mezzé* (beef in tomato sauce).
Es Aei – *Ioánnina, Odós Koundouriótou 50 – ☎ (26510) 34 571.* In an old mansion,this restaurant is known for refined, creative cooking (try the *'Es Aei'*, a tasty plate of cheeses and kebabs).

WHERE TO STAY

Hotel Tourist – *Ioánnina, Odos Kolleti 18 – ☎(26510) 250 70, www.hoteltourist.gr – 29rm.* Clean, bright rooms near the citadel; excellent value. No breakfast.
Philyra – *Odós Paleologou 18, in the citadel – ☎(26510) 835 60, ppapadias@tee.gr – 5rm.* Renovated stone building; spacious, comfortable studios.
Astoria – *Ioánnina, Odós Paraskevopoúlou 2 – ☎ (26510) 207 55, fax (26510) 784 10 – 16rm.* Recently renovated, comfortable rooms.
Palladion – *Ioánnina, 1 Odós Nóti Bótsari – ☎ (26510) 25 856, www.palladion.gr – 125rm.* High standards of comfort and competent English-speaking management. The view of the lake from the upper floors is stunning. Prices negotiable out of season; good value.
Kastro – *Ioánnina, Odós Paleológou 57 – ☎/fax (26510) 22 866, ritzan@otenet.gr – 7rm.* In an old house, a charming hotel. Comfortable rooms.
Olympic – *Odós Melanidis w – ☎ (26510) 222 33, www.hotelolymp.gr – 54rm.* Luxury hotel with charming rooms; lake views from the top floor.
Egnatia – *Main street, Metsovo – ☎ (26560) 41 263, www.hit360.com/egnatia – 32rm.* An attractive reception area and clean, comfortable rooms. The owner is an avid hiker and offers advice on treks.
Guest House – *Koukouli, main square – ☎ (26530) 710 70, www.amelio.gr – 10rm.* Pretty *pensione* in 3 traditional houses. Comfortable rooms, warm welcome, advice on area hikes.
Monodendri Katerina – *Monodendri – ☎ (26530) 71 300, www.monodendrihotel.com– 10rm.* A magnificent 17C property, a fine restaurant. Plenty of charm, but bathrooms are not en suite.
Nikos Tsoumanis – *Megalo Papingo – ☎(226530) 418 93, www.tsoumnik.gr – 6rm.* Spacious rooms, some with kitchenettes; bikes available.

WHAT TO BUY

Market – *Odós Papafilou,* mornings except Sun.
Antiques – *Ioánnis Kariofilis – Odós Paleológou, in the citadel – ☎ (26510) 36 047.* Antique jewellery.
Crafts – *Métsovo, main square and streets.* Boutiques with wooden items, traditional fabrices.

TAKING A BREAK

Walking – *Robinson Expeditions – 8 Odós Merarchias – ☎ (26510) 74 989.* This agency specialises in the Zagória Valley (hiking, mountain bike, climbing, paragliding).
WWF Centre – *☎ (26530) 410 71 – www.papigo.gr – 10am-5.30pm, Fri-Sat, 11am-6pm; closed Wed.* Information on the flora and fauna of the region, and on the Voidomatis coast, the cleanest stretch of coastline in Europe.

EVENTS AND FESTIVALS

Don't miss the Zitsa **wine festival** in late August (28km/18mi from Ioánnina).

In the **Inner Citadel** there is another mosque, the Fetiye; in front of it is the tomb of Ali Pasha. To the right is the former seraglio, now home to the **Byzantine Museum** (*open Tue-Sun 8am-5pm; 3€*), with early Christian and Byzantine sculpture, pottery, manuscripts, post-Byzantine icons and silverware.

Límni Ioannínon (Limni Pamvotis)★★

Boats to the island (10mn) depart from Mavili Square every 30mn 7am–11.30pm in summer, 7am–10pm in winter.

Still known as Lake Pamvótis, Ioánnina Lake has a remarkable island (**Nisi Ioannínon**★★), home to five Byzantine monasteries and a fishing village.

The lake collects the waters flowing down from Mount Mitsikéli to the north, and its level varies according to the seasons and the outflow of the swallow-holes *(katavóthres)* worn through the soft limestone round the shore.

On disembarking, walk through the village to admire the tiled roofs of its houses.

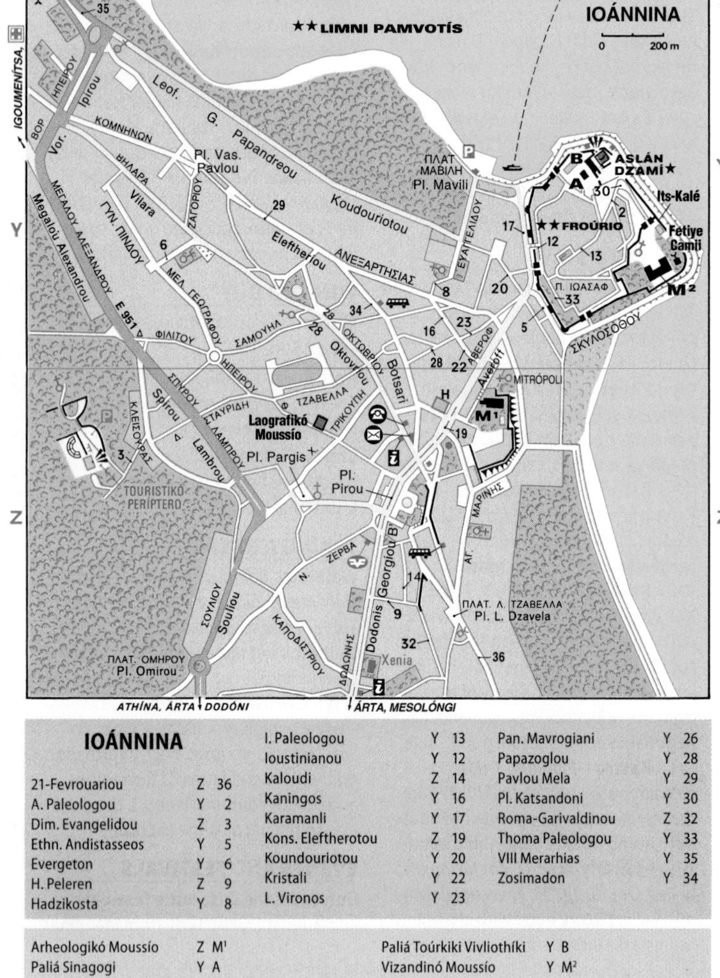

IOÁNNINA

Street	Grid	No.
21-Fevrouariou	Z	36
A. Paleologou	Y	2
Dim. Evangelidou	Z	3
Ethn. Andistasseos	Y	5
Evergeton	Y	6
H. Peleren	Z	9
Hadzikosta	Y	8
I. Paleologou	Y	13
Ioustinianou	Y	12
Kaloudi	Z	14
Kaningos	Y	16
Karamanli	Y	17
Kons. Eleftherotou	Z	19
Koundouriotou	Y	20
Kristali	Y	22
L. Vironos	Y	23
Pan. Mavrogiani	Y	26
Papazoglou	Y	28
Pavlou Mela	Y	29
Pl. Katsandoni	Y	30
Roma-Garivaldinou	Z	32
Thoma Paleologou	Y	33
VIII Merarhias	Y	35
Zosimadon	Y	34

Sight	Grid	Ref.
Arheologikó Moussío	Z	M1
Paliá Sinagogi	Y	A
Paliá Toúrkiki Vivliothíki	Y	B
Vizandinó Moussío	Y	M2

Monastery of Pandeleímonas

This 16C foundation is the best known of the island's monasteries: the house where Ali Pasha was killed by the Turks (now a museum) is located here *(open daily, 8am-10pm in summer, 9am-8pm in winter. 2€).*
Beyond is the **Monastery of St John the Baptist** (Ágios Ioánnis Pródromos) with its 16C church and a cave that contained an Ancient hermitage.

Monastery of the Philanthropiní

Also known as Nikólaos Spanós, this monastery on the other side of the village was built on a hill in the 13C, but altered in the 16C. The church is decorated with remarkable 17C **frescoes**★.

Monastery of Stratigópoulos

Also known as Nikólaos Dílios, it dates from the 11C; the church is decorated with beautiful 16C **frescoes**★.

Kostas Frontzos Museum of Folk Art

Open Tue-Sat 8am-3pm. ☎ (26510) 780 62.
Furniture, jewellery and traditional costumes from the 19C and 20C.

Outskirts

Pérama Cave★★★

6km/3.75mi to the north. Open daily, 8am-8pm, 5pm in winter. 6€. Guided tour (45min) along a route of 800m/880yd.
This remarkable cave extends for about 1km/0.5mi and covers an area of 14 800m²/5 714sq mi. Most of the caverns are lit to enhance the splendid colored limestone concretions. Formations include stalagmites and stalactites, excentrics, curtains, low walls and pools. The bones and teeth of cave bears have been discovered here. From the exit, superb **views**★★ extend over Ioánnina.

From the cave, drive east along the road to Métsovo to see extensive **views**★★ down over the valley, the lake and the town of Ioánnina.

Dodóni★★ (Dodona)

21km/13mi south. From Ioánnina take the road to Árta (E 951), after 8km/5mi turn right. Open every day, 8am-7pm, 5pm in winter. 2€. ☎ (26510) 82 287.
Situated in a high, fertile valley, Ancient Dodona grew out of a sanctuary initially dedicated to the goddess Dione, and later Zeus. A famous oracle flourished here from the second millennium BC until the 4C BC. Although not as important as that at Delphi, the Dodona oracle was renowned throughout Greece; Croesos and Alexander the Great both consulted it, and it was referred to in the *Odyssey*.
Along the road to the site, magnificent **views**★★ extend back over the Ioánnina basin; to the southwest Mount Tómaros rises to 1 974m/6 476ft

Ruins

Part of the walls still exists. Beyond the entrance lie the remains of the **stadium** (late 3C BC) indicated by traces of the terraces of seats.
First constructed in the late 3C BC, the **theatre**★★ is one of the largest and best preserved of Ancient Greece. Under the Romans it was transformed into an arena for gladiatorial and animal combats.
Beyond the theatre are the foundations of an **assembly hall** *(bouleuterion)* and a little Temple to Aphrodite. Next come the remains of the Sanctuary to Zeus Naios which included the precinct of the oracle. Finally, look for traces of a Byzantine-period **basilica**.

Métsovo★★

53km/33mi east of Ioánnina on the E 92.

Métsovo is admirably situated in a mountain combe just below the highest road pass in Greece (Katara, alt 1 705m/5 594ft), which marks the border between Epiros and Thessaly. In summer the little resort town offers offering bracing walks in the forest; sports opportunities abound in winter.

Architecture and tradition are a large part of Métsovo's charm. It's common to see old women in traditional costume and peasants riding mules. Métsovo cuisine is celebrated for its cheese, trout and wine.

In the village centre there is a vast open space shaded by huge plane trees; nearby is the Church of **Agía Paraskeví**, which contains a flamboyand 18C **iconostasis**★.

Follow the main street and turn left into a narrow street near the petrol pump.

This leads to the **Tosítsa Foundation Museum of Folk Art**★, housed in the Tosítsa family residence in the heart of the old quarter. Note the carved woodwork interior; the rooms are furnished with fine carpets and embroidered textiles and decorated with gold ornaments, beaten copperwork and icons. The huge reception room is particularly impressive with its divans and its monumental samovar. *Open Fri-Wed, 9am-1.30pm and 4-6pm. Guided tour: 30min (door locked during tour). 3€. (026560) 410 84.*

Return to the main square and take the path on the right of the Bank of Greece.

The **Avéroff Gallery** has an interesting collection of 19C and 20C Greek paintings. *Open Wed-Mon, 10am-4pm and 10am-6.30pm 15 Jul-15 Sep. €3.*

Ágios Nikólaos★

45min excursion from Métsovo.

The restored Monastery of St Nicholas features a nice display of icons in the narthex. In the church, note the 16C-17C frescoes and the iconostasis. The conventual buildings contain the monks' cells and the school.

Excursions

The Zagória★★ *80km/49mi there and back. Allow one day.*

From Ioánnina take the road to the airport which follows a valley dominated to the east by Mount Mitsikéli. Turn right at Asfaka into a narrow tarred road, which climbs towards Vítsa.

In the heart of a mountainous region incuding the Timfi massif (2 497m/8 190ft) and a small section of the northern Pindos, the Zagória seems to occupy a something of a time warp. The natural habitat is undisturbed; the traditional architecture (grey-stone houses with projecting upper storeys, churches with painted interiors, old 'Turkish bridges') survives, and residents adhere to a traditional way of life.

Part of the region falls within the Vikos-Aoos National Park, an area of forests and pasture where bears and wolves still roam. At this elevation, winter snowfall is heavy and frequent.

In these wild mountains, Greek troops defied the advancing Italian forces when they invaded from Albania in November 1940.

Before reaching Vítsa, 10km/6.25mi after turning off the main road, take the narrow tarred road to the right.

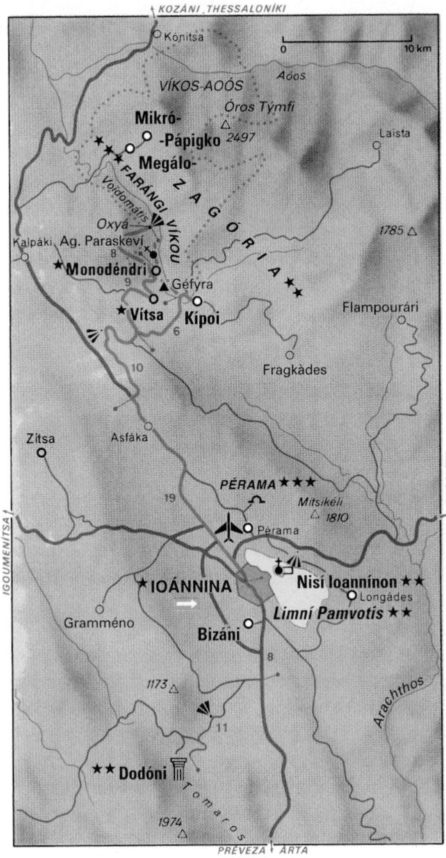

The route leads to a very unusual **bridge** *(géfira)* with three arches (1814) downstream from Kípi, the administrative centre of the Zagória country.

Return to the Vítsa road.

Vítsa★

The town is built on a picturesque site; most of the houses are in the traditional style. Excavations have discovered evidence of a settlement here from the 9C BC to the 4C AD.

Take the minor mountain road to Monodéndri, 3km away.

Monodéndri★

This is a picturesque village of stone houses with shingle roofs and a fine church with an external gallery typical of the Zagória region.

Take the narrow road (600m/660yd long) on the far side of the village, which leads to the Monastery of Agía Paraskeví and, on the way back to Monodéndri, the Víkos Gorge. *Allow a day if returning via Víkos.*

Farángi (or Harádra) Víkou★★★ (Víkos Gorge)

The grey stone buildings of the Monastery of Agía Paraskeví cling to the rocks directly above a precipitous drop into the Voldomátis River gorge 1 000m/3 281ft below. From the monastery, a path winds down the face of the cliff past terraces and caves that sheltered for *klephts* and hermits. It reaches a platform overlooking the confluence of the Voidomátis and a neighbouring mountain stream.

There is another magnificent **view**★★★ of the gorge from the hamlet of **Osía**, which can be reached by a narrow forest road *(7.3km/4.5mi)* from Monodéndri.

Near the square in Monodéndri a path leads down to the bottom of the gorge (45min) and to the village of Víkou, which is a 5hr walk in the shadow of the cliffs.

Head towards Kónitsa, take the Kalpaki road and after several miles turn right in the direction of Aristi.

Megalo Papigko and Mikro Papigko

These are two beautiful and undiscovered villages which deserve a visit. **Megalo Papigko** has retained its character, tranquillity and historic buildings.

Mikro Papigko, a little farther on, has an attractive church and produces good wine. Take a stroll through its streets; there are many pleasant walks in the vicinity.

KALAMÁTA

Καλαματα

POPULATION 49 550

MICHELIN MAP 737 F 11 – MESSINÍA – PELOPONNESE.

This ancient Frankish city, once capital of Messenia, was almost totally destroyed in the 1986 earthquake and now offers little in the way of sights. It remains a busy town, however, with a thriving daily produce market, and is an ideal base from which to explore the area. *Two offices; one at 6 Odós Polyvriou (2nd floor, ☎ (27210) 22 059, detak@otenet.gr (Open Mon-Fri 8am-2.30pm); another at the airport (closed Sun).*

Orient Yourself: Kalamata is located 169km/106mi southwest of Corinth and 61km/38mi west of Sparta, on the Gulf of Messinía.

Visit

Proceed via Odós Faron, passing through Ipapandis Square with its church, and continue as far as the entrance on Odós de Villeardouin.

Kástro

The Frankish castle (13C) stands on a rocky eminence overlooking the coastal plain on the site of the Ancient acropolis. All that remain are traces of the 13C keep and the circuit walls. From the terrace there is a view of Kalamáta and the Gulf of Messinía.

Bazaar

Shops surround a teeming daily produce market in the old town between the Benaki museum and the double Church of the **Holy Apostles** (chancel originally a 10C Byzantine chapel).

Address Book

For coin categories, see the Legend on the cover flap.

WHERE TO EAT

I Psaropoúla – *Kalamáta, Leofóros Navarínou 14.* Taverna on the water overlooking a small fishing port. Excellent grilled fish and *kokorétsi* (kebabs).

Symposium – *Koroni, main street – ☎ (27250) 22 385.* Popular hangout with good fish and grilled meat. Rooms available upstairs *( )*.

WHERE TO STAY

Rex – *Kalamáta, 26 Odós Aristoumenous – ☎ (27210) 27 492, www.rexhotel.gr – 42rm and two suites.* Illustrious hotel with an air of bygone splendour. Luxurious.

Elite – *Kalamáta, on the jetty, corner of Odós Vérga and Leofóros 2 Navarínou – ☎ (27210) 22 434, www.elite.com.gr – – 57rm and 87 bungalows.* Pleasant new hotel; bright, clean, comfortable rooms with balconies overlooking the beach. English-speaking staff.

TAKING A BREAK

Igloo – *Kalamáta, Leofóros Navarínou, opposite the Bank of Greece.* One of the best ice-cream parlours in town.

SHOPPING

Household linen made of **cotton** or **silk**, woven, embroidered or dyed by the nuns at the Monastery of St Constantine and St Helen.

EVENTS AND FESTIVALS

International dance festival, held from late-June to mid-July in the theatre at the foot of the fortress.

Kalamáta is not only the capital of the fertile region of Messenia (Messinía) but also an agricultural market celebrated for its black olives, dried figs, honey and sesame cakes, and *raki*.

Benaki Archaeological Museum

6 Odós Papazoglou. Open Tue-Fri 8am-2.30pm, Sat-Sun 8.30am-3pm. 2€. (27210) 262 09.

Housed in a handsome Venetian-style residence, the museum presents artefacts from the Bronze Age to the Roman period from various sites in Messinía.

Sights

City of Epaminóndas

25km/15mi northwest of Kalamáta. Once through modern Messinía, follow the Mavromáti road. The site of Ithómi (signposted 'Ancient Messene') is on the left on leaving the village. Turn onto the unsurfaced road which heads down to the ruins. Open daily 8.30am-6.30pm. No charge. (27240) 51 201.

Messene★★

The ruins of Ancient Messene lie against a majestic backdrop of mountains dominated by **Mount Ithómi**; at the centre stands the modern village of Mavromáti. Destroyed by Spartans, Messene was rebuilt by **Epaminóndas**, who defeated the Spartans at Leuktra (371 BC). Excavations are in progress on the site at the time of publication and new finds are constantly being made.

Stop in at the **Folklore and History Museum** *(Odós Kiriakou; Open Tue-Sat 9am-1pm; Sun and public holidays 10am-1pm; 2€; (27210) 284 49).*

Circuit Wall★★

The circuit wall (over 9km/5.5mi long), which dates from the 4C BC and was well known in Antiquity, turned the town into a sort of fortress. The best-preserved section is on the north side around the Arkadia Gate.

Follow the Ancient road (wheel ruts) out beyond the gate for a view of the ramparts; several tombs have been found in this area.

B Kaufmann/MICHELIN

View of the Messenian Gulf

Asklepieion★

A path leading off the road northwest of Mavromáti descends to the remains of a small theatre, the fountain of Arsinoë and a sanctuary dedicated to Asklepios (Aesculapius) *(sign 'Ithómi, Archaeological site'; about 30min on foot there and back).*
The excavations have uncovered the foundations of a temple to Asklepios from the Hellenistic period. As at Epidauros, next to the sanctuary there is a theatre *(ecclesiasterion)*; adjoining this are the council chamber *(bouleuterion)* and the Propylaia.
To the west lay the **Temple of Artemis Orthia**; the statue of the goddess (in the museum) is attributed to the famous sculptor Damophon.
To the south of the Asklepieion lay the Hellenistic public baths(included a swimming bath fed by terracotta pipes) and the Hierothysion (temple).
Farther south are the remains of a stadium and its palaestra, as well as vestiges of a large Doric funerary monument.

Lakonia Gate

From Mavromáti drive up to the Lakonia Gate to see a fine view of Mount Éva; below lies the new Voulkáno Convent.

Archaeological Museum

Open daily 8.30am-3.30pm. 2€. (27240) 512 01. Between the Arkadia Gate and the village of Mavromáti.
Worth a stop to to see architectural elements, sculptures, and a model of the Asklepieion.

Mount Ithómi

798m/2 618ft. From the Lakonia Gate a steep path (1hr 30min on foot there and back) climbs up past the remains of a temple to Artemis to the Ancient citadel of Ithómi.
At the summit is the old Voulkáno Convent (8C). Magnificent **views**★★ of Messene, the region of Messenia and the southern Peloponnese.

Outskirts

Koróni

52km/33mi southwest of Kalamáta, on the west coast of the Messenian Gulf.
The white houses of Koróni (called Coron by the Franks) are scattered over the slope of a promontory that protects a charming little port. A castle surmounts the high point at the end of the promontory and a long beach skirts the southern shore.

Excursions

The West Coast of the Messanian Gulf★★★

The magnificent 80km/50mi of road between Kalamáta and Areópoli, climbing high into the western foothills of the Taígetos chain, provides views of the indented eastern shoreline of the gulf (many quiet inlets ideal for bathing).
The road passes through a varied landscape: fairly austere in the south but more hospitable farther north, where cultivated basins alternate with terraced hillsides.

Koskarás Defile★

The river has created a gorge spanned by a bold, modern bridge. Park the car and climb down a short way to admire the design and the site.
Leaving the Kámbos basin, presided over by the medieval ruins of **Zarnáta Castle**, the road climbs then drops to Kardamíli, giving bird's-eye **views**★★ over the Kardamíli basin and the coast.

Kardamíli★

Kardamíli is an unpretentious resort and fishing port protected by a fortified islet; its old houses and churches cluster on the banks of a mountain stream. The best-known church is St Spiridon (13C) in the old quarter of Kardamíli (Ano-Kardamíli).
The land behind Kardamíli, now planted with olive trees, was once guarded by **Beaufort Castle** which was built by the Franks on an isolated site.

From Kardamíli it is possible to make a detour on foot to the Viros Gorge. Allow 6hr extra and take good shoes and a supply of water.

Harádra tou Viroú (Viros Gorge)

The hike is easier starting from Tséria (6km/4mi northeast of Kardamíli), taking a track on the right from there. The splendid hike involves first descending to the bottom of the gorge and then climbing out again up a track leading to Exohóri. Continue along the same path, and after reaching the monasteries of Sotíras and Likaki return to Ano-Kardomíli.

Resume the itinerary from Kardamíli.

Stoúpa

Fine , pink-pebbled beach, good for swimming.

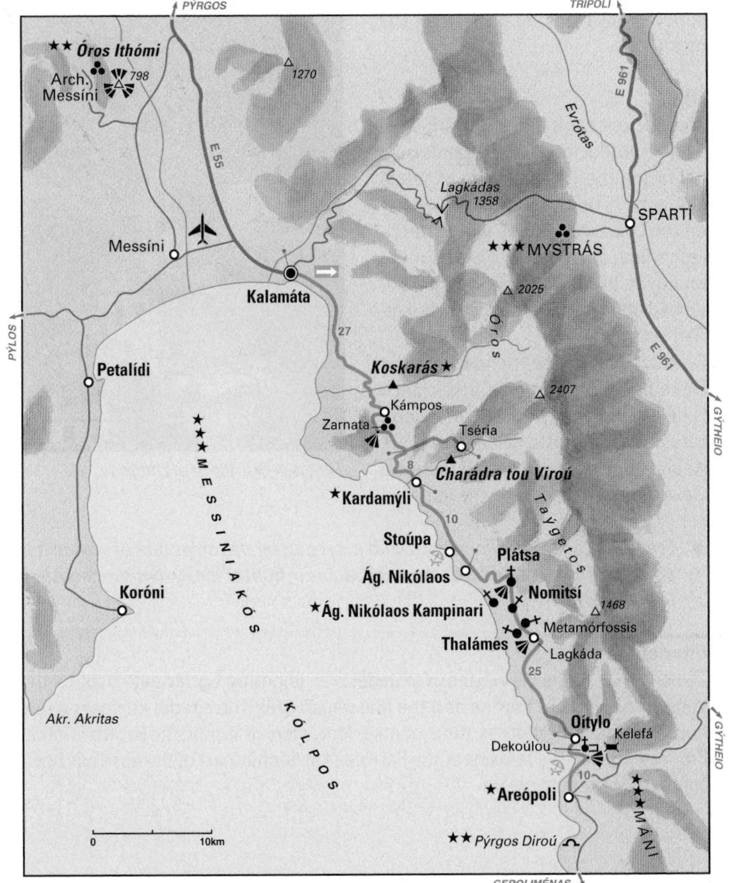

Ágios Nikólaos
Little fishing village with small tavernas by the sea.

Plátsa
Several Byzantine churches worth visiting, superb view of the gulf.
Just before a cluster of pine trees an admirable **view**★★★ opens out over the whole of the Messenian Gulf.

Ágios Nikolaos Kambinari★
About 1km/0.5mi before Nomitsí on the right.
This little chapel (10C) stands among the olives and cypresses on the terraced hillside facing Koróni across the Messenian Gulf.

Nomitsí
Beside the road through the village stands the Anárgiri Chapel, a rare example of a cruciform plan within a square, decorated with frescoes.
In an enclosure on the left side of the road between Nomitsí and Thalámas stands the Church of the Transfiguration (Metamórfossis) which dates from the 11C; unusual capitals carved with Byzantine motifs (peacocks, cockerels etc); traces of frescoes.

Thalámas
13C Church of St Sophia. At **Langáda**, with its church and towers, there are superb views looking down over the gulf.

Ítilo
The Ancient capital of the Máni, now a wine-producing centre, stands on a hill facing the Turkish castle of Kelefá (16C and 17C) inland and a sheltered bay on the coast (Néo Útilo), where Napoleon's fleet anchored in 1798 en route for Egypt. In the 17C it was the port of embarkation for those Maniots who settled in Corsica.
On the slope below the road lies the Dekoúlou Monastery (18C); the church is decorated with frescoes and wood carvings (iconostasis, baldaquin).
As one approaches **Areópoli** there are views of Kelefá Castle on the left.

JP Nail/MICHELIN
Towers in the village of Langáda

Leave the car in the village and climb a steep street and steps (out of season it is possible to go by car as far as the small square in front of the Byzantine monastery in the citadel).

Citadel
The entrance to the very extensive citadel is an imposing Gothic gate built by the Venetians. Views of Korone and the Messenian Gulf. The citadel encloses a few houses, former storehouses, the Byzantine Monastery of St John the Baptist (Timiou Prodromou) and the remains of the Basilica of St Sophia; part of the apse has been converted into a chapel.

KALÁVRITA

Καβαϖρυτα

POPULATION 1 747

MICHELIN MAP 737 F 9 – ACHAIA – PELOPONNESE.

This attractive town is situated in the heart of a mountainous wooded district. It is linked to the Achaean coast by a well-known narrow-gauge railway which follows a spectacular route.

- **Orient Yourself:** Kalávrita is located 72km/45mi southeast of Patras by mountain road and 47km/29mi south of Aigio small ski resort on the northern slopes of Mount Helmos.

Visit

- *Just beyond the village on the road to the Agía Lávra Monastery, turn left onto a dirt track (signposted) and walk up to the fortress (15min).*

Kástro tis Orias

Remains of the Frankish fortress can be seen on the hill. Beautiful view of the surrounding area.

- *From the road to Pátras, take the 1st turn to the left.*

Monastery of Agía Lávra

7km/4.5mi southwest of Kalávrita. Open daily 10am-1pm and 3-4pm. (29620) 223 63.

The 17C church here has earned a place in history: here, on 25 March 1821, **Germanós**, Archbishop of Patras, raised the standard of revolt against the Turks in the War of Independence.

Outside is a tree-shaded terrace where Germanós stood when addressing the crowd. The monastery buildings now house a **museum** containing manuscripts, icons, gold and silver ware, and souvenirs of the War of Independence.

Above the monastery a path *(sign 'Paleón Monastírion'; 30min on foot there and back)* leads to the original hermitage where the monks lived until 1689.

Excursion

- *Head east out of Kalávrita, towards the ski resort. After 7km/4.25mi, turn right towards Klitoría.*

The 'Cave of the Lakes'★★

An underground river has carved 1 980m/2 166yd of galleries out of the limestone, forming caverns that contain 13 lakes on three levels.

Entrance to the cave is via a man-made tunnel that leads to the second level and the so-called 'Room of the Bats'. In summer, the drop in the water level reveals basins that are separated by saw-tooth barrages up to 4m/13ft high, and cave walls blanketed in stalactites and stalagmites.

The temperature remains a constant 13-15°C/55-59°F. In the Neolithic period (4200-3000 BC), the cave served as a dwelling and storage area, place of worship and burial ground. Excavations have uncovered animal bones and human skeletons, as well as scales dating from the Neolithic and Protohelladic periods.

The road to Klitoría passes through a magnificent **region**★★ covered with forests of plane trees and crystal-clear streams brimming with trout: a wonderful place for a walk.

KARÍTENA

Καριταινα

POPULATION 271

MICHELIN MAP 737 F 10 – ARCADIA – PELOPONNESE.

This picturesque medieval town is built into the curve of a hillside and dominated by an imposing Frankish castle. The villages in this isolated area, composed of the beautiful landscapes of the Alfiós and Loússios Gorges, retain their traditional building styles (stone roofs, wooden balconies). From the modern bridge there is a spectacular view★★ of the site of Karítena.

- **Orient Yourself:** Karítena is located 56km/35mi west of Trípoli by the Megalópoli road and 107km/69mi southeast of Olympia. The Megalópoli crosses the River Alfiós by a modern bridge which overshadows its 15C predecessor.

Visit

Medieval bridge

Built by the Franks in the 13C, and subsequently restored in the 15C; four of its six original arches remain. One of the pillars of the structure houses a small chapel.

Address Book

For coin categories, see the Legend on the cover flap.

WHERE TO EAT

Ta Aidónia – *Vitína ☎ (27950) 222 24, www.taidonia.gr.* The best restaurant in town. Enjoy goat *('katzíki')* with oregano and lightly resinated white wine while sitting in the shady garden.

Taverna 1821 – *Stemnitsa, near the main square. ☎ (27950) 815 18.* Traditional Greek dishes at good value, served in a large dining room.

WHERE TO STAY

Epicurios Apollo – *Andrítsena, main square – ☎ (26220) 22 840 – 6rm.* Large comfortable rooms; a good place to stay. Book in advance.

Maria – *300m/330yd from the station, in a pedestrian street to the right of the main square – ☎ (26920) 22 296 – 11rm.* A quiet, small hotel offering simple, though clean and pleasant, accommodation.

Dimitsána – *Dimitsána – ☎ (27950) 31 518 – 30rm.* Outskirts of the village, this refurbished hotel has pleasant heated rooms overlooking the valley. Dining either on the terrace or indoors. Prices rise by a third in winter.

Menalon Art – *Vitína, on a quiet square not far from the town centre – ☎ (27950) 22 200 – 50rm.* This relatively recent establishment is one of the best hotels in the area and certainly the friendliest. It also has the most interesting decor, since the owner also runs an art gallery.

TAKING A BREAK

Tsigouri –*Andritsaina, up the steps leading to the main square.* An old-fashioned taverna with blackened *'briki'* (coffee pots), oilcloths and a friendly landlady who also keeps the keys to the Ethnographic Museum.

SPORT AND LEISURE

Outdoor pursuits – In season, skiing and other winter sports are the main attraction. Walkers will also appreciate the many mountain trails in the area. Contact **Club Alpin** (☎ *(21067) 53 14, www.alpinclub.gr*) for information on treks and trips.

Village

Below is the 17C Church of Our Lady (Panagía) with a square stone belfry and, on the way up to the castle, Ágios Nikólaos, a small post-Byzantine church.

JP Nail/MICHELIN

Castle★

The feudal castle (1254) was the stronghold of a powerful Frankish barony. During the War of Independence Kolokotrónis defied Ibrahim Pasha from here. Only the ruins of the residence of the lord of the castle remain against the south wall, but several cisterns have been preserved *(beware of falling)*. From the top there are extensive **views**★★ of the gorge *(west)*, the Megalópoli basin *(east)* and Mount Líkeo (Lykaion) *(south)*.

Outskirts

Andrítsena

29km/18mi west of Karítena.

Andrítsena is a charming market town, with old wooden houses and craft workshops lining the streets where goats, donkeys and pigs roam at will. The charming main square has a café and a fountain shaded by a plane tree.

Among the peaks bordering Elis to the east is Mount Líkeo (Lykaion); it was a primitive sanctuary to Zeus, involving human sacrifice and ritual cannibalism, before the establishment of the magnificent **Temple of Bassae**★★.

Near the Trani fountain (18C), you'll find the **Folk Museum** *(open Tue-Sun 10am-1.30pm)* with displays of fabrics and costumes. Andritsaína also boasts a magnificent historical **library** of 25 000 volumes.

Ruins of Megalopolis

15km/9mi southeast of Karítena. 1km before Megalópoli on the right. No charge.

The Ancient city of Megalopolis was built between 371 and 368 BC by Epaminóndas as part of his plan to contain Sparta. It was the native city of Philopoimen (253-

JP Nail/MICHELIN

Remains of a Temple to Asklepios, Gortys

183 BC), the 'last of the Greeks', who sought to maintain Greek unity in the face of the Roman expansion, and of the historian Polybios (204-122 BC).

Thersilion

The huge assembly hall was designed to hold the 'Ten Thousand', the representatives of the Arcadian League. The 67 pillars were placed so that almost all those present could see the speaker.

Theatre

The theatre, the largest in Greece, could accommodate about 20 000 spectators; the acoustics were excellent. The lower rows are well preserved.

Excursion

Villages and Monasteries of the Loússios Gorge★★

30km/19mi from Karítena to Kefalari.

The Loússios, a tributary of the Alfiós, is a spectacular geographical feature forming the backdrop for numerous monasteries and villages.

Gortys

12km/7.5mi north of Karítena; signposted from the junction near Ellinikó.

On this beautiful, remote **site**★ liethe remains of a Temple to Asklepios and surrounding wall, and the bases of some buildings and baths.

Stemnitsa

This attractive mountain village on the slopes of Mount Menalon was an important metalworking centre in Byzantine times and the tradition is still alive today. In 1821, the village was the capital of the Greek rebellion for 15 days and the first National Assembly sat in the 15C Zoodohou Pigis Church. There are 18 churches here, the most important ones being the Three Hierarchs, St Nicholas (14C frescoes) and Panagía Mpafero (12C). A beautiful carved stone bell tower adorns the main square. You can also visit the local **Folk Art Museum** *(in the old Hadzi building)*, with icons, traditional costumes, ceramics and wood carvings.

▸ *Before entering Dimitsána, turn left and follow the winding road 8km/5mi down into Loússios Gorge.*

Agiou Ioánnou Prodrómou Monastery

A few monks still live in this 11C monastery built next to a vertical rock face in a beautiful, isolated **setting**★. The tiny church houses some frescoes.

Philosóphou Monastery

Opposite the Agiou Ioánnou Prodrómou Monastery.

The old monastery has been abandoned in favour of a new building, situated on the west bank next to the Byzantine Church of Naos Panagias and its 17C frescoes.

Dimitsána

25km/15mi north of Karítena on the road to Trípoli.

Buried at the heart of the Peloponnese is the old medieval city of Dimitsána, which is built on a spectacular **site**★★ overlooking the Loússios Valley.

In the 18C it was a centre of the independence movement; its secret schools were attended by patriots such as Germanós. You can visit the **Ecclesiastical Museum**, with its collection of religious art; also the House of the Patriarch.

Aimyálon Monastery
Bbeautiful monastery, built beneath the rock; 17C frescoes in the church.

Ipethrió Moussío Hydrokinissis★
4km/2.5mi south of Dimitsána. Open Wed-Mon, Apr-Oct, 10am-2pm and 5-7pm; winter 10am-4pm. 1.50€. ☎ (27950) 31 630.
The **Open-Air Water-Power Museum** shows how the forces of the local rivers have been harnessed in the region, and demonstrates various manufacturing processes.

KASTORIÁ★★

Καστορια
POPULATION 14 813
MICHELIN MAP 737 E 3 – MACEDONIA.

The history of Kastoriá is inextricably linked to that of the Balkans and Central Europe. Renowned for its furriers, it maintains much of its traditional charm; known as the 'town of a hundred churches', it has many fine examples of Byzantine architecture. Kastoriá lies at the neck of a peninsula jutting out into the picturesque waters of a lake bearing the same name. Close by are the Prespa Lakes, a protected area of great natural beauty.

- **Orient Yourself:** Kastoriá is located 209km/131mi west of Thessaloníkí and virtually on the frontier with Albania and Macedonia.
- **Don't Miss:** Byzantine churches and traditional houses; the Prespa Lakes.
- **Organizing Your Time:** Plan a 2-day visit.

A Bit of History

For some 600 years Kastoriá has been a centre of the fur industry. Exemption from import tax on the pelts, and particular skill in working with skins enabled local workshops to produce coats and wraps for export to Constantinople and to the capitals of Central Europe. The goods are now exported directly to Western cities. The local furriers buy pelts mainly from America and Scandinavia, but there are also mink and wolf farms on the outskirts of town. Workshops are dotted about the town, and skins stretched out on frames and drying in the sun are to be seen on the pavements.

Panagía Koubelídiki

JP Nail/MICHELIN

Sights

Byzantine churches★★
About 50 survive, some dating from the 10C. The churches are beautifully decorated with frescoes and sculptures. To visit them, inquire at the **Byzantine Museum** (*open Tue-Sun 8.30am-3pm; no charge; ☎(24670) 267 81*), which offers

a good introduction to the town's religious heritage; on view are fine icons and other artworks dating from the 14C-17C.

Panagía Koubelídiki★

Near the school. Built in the mid-19C and dedicated to the Virgin, it is the only domed church in Kastoriá with a tall drum, hence its name, from a Turkish word *(kouben)* meaning drum. The narthex vaulting bears the Holy Trinity, which is rarely represented in the Byzantine tradition.

Ágios Nikólaos Kasnídzis (St Nicholas of Kasnitsis)

Below Platía Omonia. The exterior of this small 12C church was partly decorated with frescoes; traces are visible above the apse. 12C frescoes in the nave.

From Platía Omonia, head down Odós Manolaki and turn left into an alley.

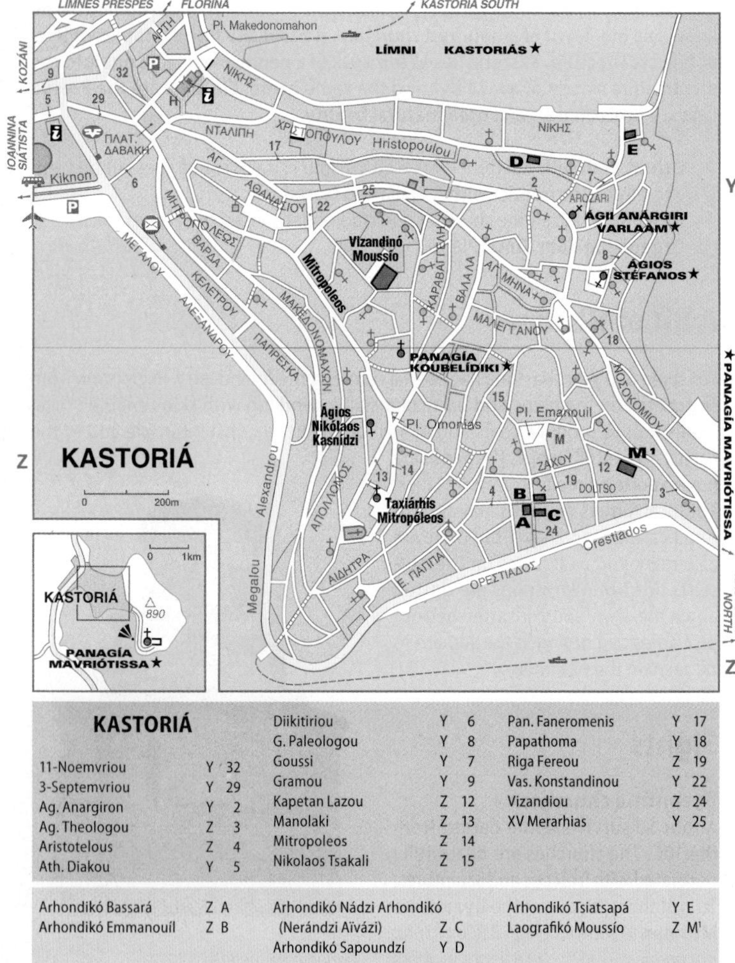

KASTORIÁ

Street			Street			Street		
11-Noemvriou	Y	32	Diikitiriou	Y	6	Pan. Faneromenis	Y	17
3-Septemvriou	Y	29	G. Paleologou	Y	8	Papathoma	Y	18
Ag. Anargiron	Y	2	Goussi	Y	7	Riga Fereou	Z	19
Ag. Theologou	Z	3	Gramou	Y	9	Vas. Konstandinou	Y	22
Aristotelous	Z	4	Kapetan Lazou	Z	12	Vizandiou	Z	24
Ath. Diakou	Y	5	Manolaki	Z	13	XV Merarhias	Y	25
			Mitropoleos	Z	14			
			Nikolaos Tsakali	Z	15			

Sight			Sight			Sight		
Arhondikó Bassará	Z	A	Arhondikó Nádzi Arhondikó (Nerándzi Aïvázi)	Z	C	Arhondikó Tsiatsapá	Y	E
Arhondikó Emmanouíl	Z	B	Arhondikó Sapoundzí	Y	D	Laografikó Moussío	Z	M[1]

Taxiárhis Mitropóleos

The 9C Metropolitan Church of the Taxiarchs (leaders of the heavenly host), the Archangels Michael and Gabriel, contains capitals from an early-Christian basilica that previously stood on the site. Inside, the east walls still bear traces of 9C frescoes.

Ágios Stéfanos★ (St Stephen's)

Northeast, Odós Paléologou.

The vaulting of the lofty nave (9C) is painted with 12C frescoes. In the rest of the church, the 9C frescoes have been preserved. A stairway leads to a women's gallery, a unique feature in Kastoriá (St Ann's Chapel).

Ágii Anárgiri Varlaám★

Odós Vitsiou, not far from Ágios Stéfanos.

High up above the lake, the church (10C) is among the largest in Kastoriá and is dedicated to the 'holy penniless ones', the physicians who practised medicine without charging fees *(anárgiris)*. Inside most of the frescoes are 11C or 12C, but an earlier 10C layer is visible in some parts of the church.

Address Book

For coin categories, see the Legend on the cover flap.

WHERE TO EAT

Swan – *Kastoriá, 1 Odós Thomaídos.* Excellent value; very good trout and grilled meats; the lake can smell rather unappetising though.

Omonoia – *Kastoriá, 97 Odós Mitropóleos, near Platia Omónia.* Small restaurant, simple and inexpensive. A good spot to eat after visiting the nearby churches.

Nostalgia – *Kastoriá, 2 Odós Nikis, opposite the landing stage – ☎ (24670) 22 630.* Grilled meat and fish dishes in a quiet setting facing the lake.

Mavriotissa – *Kastoriá, near the monastery*. Popular spot serving fish and beef dishes on an attractive terrace shaded by plane trees.

Taverna Kostas – *Psarádes, on entering the village.* A warm welcome and reasonably priced fish dishes.

WHERE TO STAY

Europa – *Kastoriá, 12 Odós Agíou Athanassíou – ☎ (24670) 23 826 – 36rm.* A good hotel near Platía Daváki; well-kept, clean, comfortable rooms.

Psarádes – *Psarádes – ☎ (23850) 46 015 – 16rm.* A modern and comfortable hotel on the other side of the bay, facing the village. Breakfast not included.

Ágios Achílios – *island of Ágios Achílios – ☎ (23850) 46 601.* This guesthouse is a solid traditional-style building and has a pleasant lounge with fireplace.

Pension Filoxenia – *Kastoriá, in a quiet part of town to the northeast of the centre (follow signposts) – ☎ (24670) 22 162 – 9rm.* Guesthouse on the lakeside to the north. All rooms are clean, pleasant, and have balconies; fine views.

Ágios Germanós – *Ágios Germanós, right of the village square – ☎ (23850) 51 397 – 11rm.* Two traditional buildings provide spacious and comfortable accommodation with central heating. Diners eat in a room looking onto the courtyard; good breakfast.

Aiolis – *Kastoriá, 30 Odós Agíou Athanassíou – ☎ (24670) 21 070 – 14rm.* Occupying a colonnaded building on the corner, this luxurious hotel is extremely comfortable and offers first-class service.

EVENTS AND FESTIVALS

From 6-8 January, a colourful carnival takes place during the **Ragoutsaria**.

The first weekend in August, the village of Nestorio (20km from Kastoriá) has a series of concerts as part of the **River Festival**.

Old Houses★

A few handsome, tower-like houses *(arhondiká)* in the typical Macedonian style, built in the main in the 17C and 18C for the rich local furriers, add to the charm of the quarters near the peninsula.

There are two of these old houses in the north Arozari quarter near the lake: the **Sapoundzís Mansion** (Odós Hristopoulou) and **Tsiatsapás Mansion**. Most are situated in the Doltso district south of the town and, in particular, in Odós Vizandiou south of Platía A Emanouíl: the **Nadzis**, **Emanouil** and **Bassarás Mansions**. Farther along, near the peninsula, the restored Nerándzis Aïvázis mansion is now the **Museum of Folk Traditions**★, giving a good picture of Macedonian family life in bygone days *(Odós Kapetan Lazou; open daily 10am-6pm; .80€)*.

Excursions

Límni Kastoriás★ (Kastoriá Lake)

Tour of the peninsula: 9.2km/5.5mi

At the start of the drive; there are lovely views of the southern part of the town and of the traditional flat-bottomed boats with raised prows. Not far from the Monastery of the Virgin *(2.5km/1.5mi)* the road widens. Fine view of the lake.

Panagía Mavriótiss★★

Macedonian-style monastery building. The exterior south wall of the Church of the Virgin (Panagía), which dates from c 1000, is decorated with 13C frescoes *(under cover)*; there are 12C frescoes on the east and west walls of the nave.

Return to Kastoriá by the same route *(drive carefully as cars on the return journey do not have right of way)* or continue round the peninsula *(one-way road from the monastery)* to the north side of the town and the small harbour.

Límnes Préspes★★ (Préspa Lakes)

64km/40mi. From Kastoriá take the Flórina road north.

Beyond the town *(about 5km/3mi)* a fine **view**★★ unfolds. Beyond a pass the road skirts the wooded valley of the Ladopótamos River. After 35km/21.5mi turn off the Flórina road and bear left towards the lakes and Lemós. After a saddle (low ridge) the road affords a splendid **view**★★ of the Little Préspa Lake.

Mikrí Préspa★ (Little Préspa Lake)

The lake, which extends southwest into Albania, was designated as a national park in 1974 together with the Greek section of the Great Préspa Lake.

An abundant fauna thrives in the reed beds around Little Préspa, including pelicans (also the white species), cormorants, egrets, herons and cranes. There are two islands: on the larger, Ágios Ahílios, are several Byzantine churches including the 11C Church of St Achilles. There are boat trips to the islands and to bird-watching posts from **Makrolímni** *(4km/2.5mi from the junction)*.

The main road skirts the little lake, and at the junction at the far end a road on the right leads to the village of **Ágios Germanós** with its 11C domed church and fine frescoes, at the foot of Mount Varnóus (Peristéri – 2 156m/7 074ft).

Megáli Préspa★ (Great Préspa Lake)

The lake lies in three nations: Albania, Macedonia and Greece.

The village of **Psarádes** with its traditional houses with wooden balconies *(hotel, guesthouses)* overlooks a deep bay on the other side of the peninsula *(9.5km/6mi farther on)*. On the Greek side excursions by motor launch take visitors to the rugged cliffs and caves (in particular the cave of the Panagía Eleoússa) painted by hermits in the 14C and the 15C. Good **views**★ of the Albanian shore and mountains.

Siátista★

59km/36.75mi southeast of Kastoriá; 30km/18.5mi west of Kozáni.

Formerly renowned for its wine and leather, Siástista joined the fur trade in the early 20C. In the upper town, Hóra, most of the Macedonian-style 18C mansions *(arhondiká)*, are in the care of the archaeological department housed in the **Neranzópoulou Mansion**★, which has painted ceilings and stained-glass windows. Farther down the street are **Manoúsi Mansion** and **Poulkídi Mansion**, splendidly decorated with painted walls and ceilings. The **Hatzimiháli Kanatsoúli Mansion** at 430 Odós Mitropoleos, near the belltower, is still inhabited.

KAVÁLA★

Καβαλα

POPULATION 60 802

MICHELIN MAP 737 K 2 – EASTERN MACEDONIA.

Dominated by the Turks from 1380 to 1913, Kavála still has an oriental air. It is a lively town built on the shores of a broad bay. In Antiquity it was the port of Philippi; it retained its importance through the Classical and Byzantine periods, as evinced by its majestic ruins. **EOT** *Eleftherias Square,* ☎ *(25106) 205 66/331011.* *Open daily 10am-2pm, 6-9pm.* *Closed Sun.*

- **Orient Yourself:** Kavála is 175km/109mi northeast of Thessaloniki on the Aegean coast; airport 30km/19mi to the west on the Xanthi road.

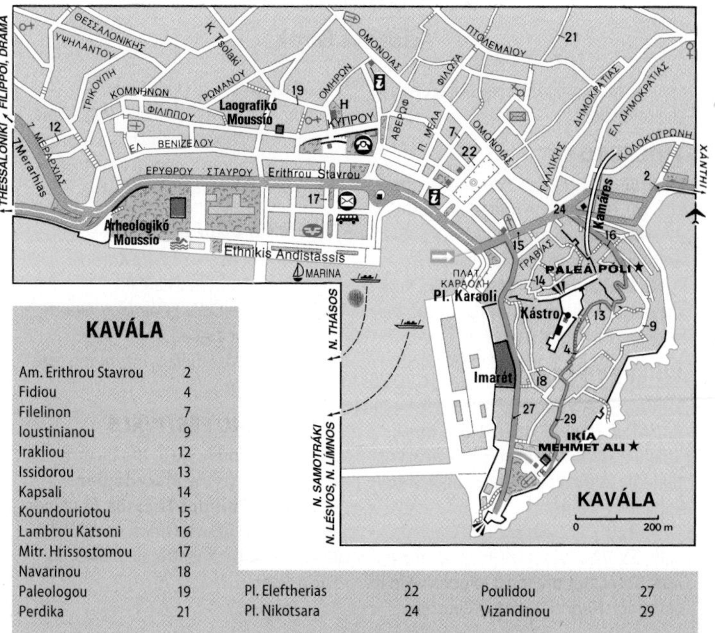

KAVÁLA

Am. Erithrou Stavrou	2	Pl. Eleftherias	22	Poulidou	27
Fidiou	4	Pl. Nikotsara	24	Vizandinou	29
Filelinon	7				
Ioustinianou	9				
Irakliou	12				
Issidorou	13				
Kapsali	14				
Koundouriotou	15				
Lambrou Katsoni	16				
Mitr. Hrissostomou	17				
Navarinou	18				
Paleologou	19				
Perdika	21				

A Bit of History

First a colony founded by Thássos and later (called Neapolis) the main port of Philippi, Kavála was an important settlement throughout the Classical period. St Paul passed through with Silas on his way from Asia Minor to Philippi.

In the Middle Ages the town was called Christoupolis. Raids on the city were undertaken first by Normans, and then the Ottomans, who conquered it in 1391. In the 16C it was called Bucephalos, after Alexander the Great's horse; this is probably the origin of its present name Kavála. In 1913, the city was ceded to Greece and in 1922 it became home for 25 000 ethnic Greek refugees from Asia Minor.

Today it is an industrial centre and the hub of the Macedonian tobacco export business. The old district huddles on a rocky promontory crowned by a citadel, and the modern town extends westward along the harbour.

Visit

▸ *Starting from* **Platía Karaolí**, *a charming shady square, walk up the narrow street, Odós Poulídou, which passes the Imarét (right).*

Within the ramparts lies the picturesque old town; its narrow streets and steps wind between the Turkish houses with their tiny courtyards and flowering balconies.

Imarét

This is an unusual group of Muslim style buildings founded by Mehmet Ali as an almshouse, run by Islamic monks (dervishes) for 300 poor men. Today it is a luxury hotel.

Ikía Mehémet Áli

This 18C house was the birthplace of Mehmet Ali, son of a wealthy Albanian tobacco merchant. It is now owned by the Egyptian Government.

Address Book

For coin categories, see the Legend on the cover flap.

WHERE TO EAT

Apiko – *29 Odós T Poulídou (in the citadel).* Good-value grilled fish dishes.
Antonia – *Odós T Poulídou.* Popular with the locals for its fish dishes.
Ta Plakakia – *4 Odós Dorianis, near the port.* Excellent seafood, but can be overrun with tourists.

WHERE TO STAY

Giorgo Alvanos – *35 Odós Anthémiou – ☎ (25102) 81781 – 8rm.* Small, traditional house in the heart of Panagía (difficult parking); small, simple well-kept rooms.
Nefeli – *50 Odós Erithroú Stavroú – ☎ (25102) 27 441 – 94rm.* A comfortable hotel, but the most expensive in its category. Negotiate out of season.
Oceanis – *32 Odós Erithroú Stavroú – ☎ (25102) 21 981 – 168m.* This seven-storey luxury hotel has a rooftop pool with stunning view. A haven of peace amid the hustle and bustle.

TAKING A BREAK

Café Nikitoros – *42 Platia Karaoli.* Engaging, traditional café.
Café Imaret – *Odós T Poulídou.* Good for a coffee, or a salad.
Flyboat – *Odós Ethnikis.* Intriguing café aboard a yacht.

EVENTS AND FESTIVALS

During July and August, the theatre at Philippi hosts the **Macedonian Festival of Philippi-Thássos**. Bookings at the Kavála Tourist Office, ☎ *(25102) 22 425*, or at the theatre, ☎ *(25105) 16 470, 6-9pm.*

The wooden partitions and the layout are typical of a Turkish dwelling, with the stable and kitchen on the ground floor. The second-floor harem is fitted with *moucharabies*, wooden lattices that enable one to see out without being seen.
An extensive **view**★★ from the tip of the promontory extends over the harbour, the town and the bay as far as Thássos Island.

D Pazery/MICHELIN

Walk through the old Turkish quarter, Odós Vizandinóu and Odós Fidíou, past a mosque and up to the Kástro, the citadel.

Kástro

Open daily 8am-9pm (4pm Nov-Mar). 1.50€.
The citadel stands on the site of an Ancient acropolis and is surrounded by Byzantine ramparts, with views of Kavála. Prisons and a cistern lie within the ramparts.

Kamáres Aqueduct★★

Spannng the depression between the modern town and the old town, the aqueduct was built in the 16C by Suleiman the Magnificent to supply the Kástro with water from local springs.

Archaeological Museum

Odós Ethnikis Antistatis. Open Tue-Sun 8am-3pm. 2€. (25102) 223 35.
This modern museum covers eastern Mascedonia from the Neolithic period to the Roman Empire. On view you'll find colossal Ionic capitals from the Sanctuary of Parthenos, and fine examples of gold **Hellenistic jewellery**.

Municipal Museum

4 Odós Filipou. Open Tue-Sun 9am-1pm.
An interesting collection of Greek contemporary and folk art, highlighted by works of the painter and sculptor Polygnotos Vagis (1894-1965).

Excursions

Amfípoli

88km/55mi southwest of Kavála. Open every day, 8am-7pm. No charge.
The Ancient city of **Amphipolis** lay near the mouth of the **River Strymon** and **Mount Pangaion** (Pangéo), known as the 'holy mountain'.
Amphipolis was officially founded as an Athenian colony in the 5C BC, and it prospered during the Macedonian and Roman periods, when Mark Antony set sail from here to do battle against Octavian at Actium. St Paul passed through around AD 50, marking the beginning of the city's palaeo-Christian era, and it was still an important centre during the Byzantine period.

The Lion

On the left of the road from Thessaloníki, just before the bridge over the Strymon, stands a huge marble lion. It resembles the lion of Chaironeia, although it is later, dating from the end of the 4C BC.

After crossing the bridge over the Strymon, take the road to Séres (left); after 1.5km/1mi turn left to the modern village of Amfípoli and then left again towards the church; after 0.5km/547yd a path to the right leads to the ruins.

Ruins

The prosperity of the city is evident from the monumental buildings decorated with mosaic floors and wall paintings. The recently-discovered Hellenistic **walls** are 7m high in places; they stretched for 7km and included towers, gateways and bastions. The northern section gives visitors a good picture of how things looked.

The most surprising feature is the **bridge** constructed from wooden beams, parts of which show posts standing out from the structure as a result of having dried out. On the plateau, not far from what was probably the agora, are traces of palaeo-Christian basilicas: **mosaics** of birds.

Archaeological Museum

Open Tue-Sun 8am-7pm (Wed 11pm in summer); Mon noon-7pm. 2€. ☎ (23220) 324 74.

Finds from the site include gold **Hellenistic jewellery**, Roman sculpture, a silver ossuary and gold-leaf **diadem**.

Ruins of Fílipi★★

15km/9mi northwest of Kavála. Open daily 8am-7pm. 2€. Sitting in the fertile Macedonian plain is the site of the Ancient city of Philippi. Founded in 360 BC, it was renamed four years later in honour of **King Philip II of Macedon**. It is the most important archaeological site in eastern Macedonia.

In 49 AD, St Paul began preaching in Philippi; he was denounced and imprisoned for a time. But Christianity spread rapidly, as Paul witnessed on his return six years later. St Paul's Epistle to the Philippians was probably sent from Rome in AD 64.

The ruins now visible date mostly from the Roman and early Christians era; the main vestige of the Macedonian city is the theatre by the acropolis, and the walls. The Romans modified the layout, and the original heart of the settlement (forum, temples, market, palaestra) did not revive until the 6C and 7C.

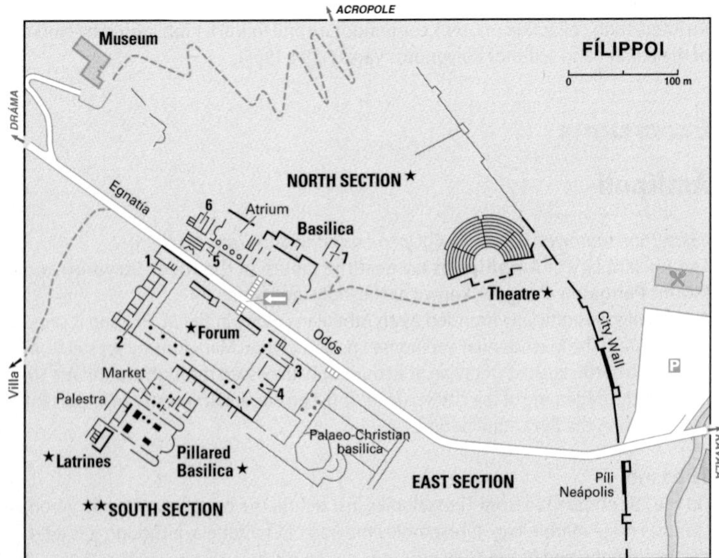

A Decisive Victory

After the assassination of Julius Caesar in 44 BC, his murderers, Brutus and Cassius, fled east with their forces and occupied the country east of the Adriatic. Antony and Caesar's nephew, Octavian, marched against the Republican partisans and met them west of Philippi in October 42 BC. After various engagements, Antony and Octavian gained the advantage; Cassius and Brutus committed suicide.

Later, veterans of the victorious army were settled in Philippi, which was granted the status of a Roman colony, giving the inhabitants the same rights as the Romans in Italy. The city prospered thanks to its location, its proximity to the gold mines of Mount Pangaion and the fertility of the surrounding countryside.

East Section

The entrance to Philippi from Kavála is through the Píli Neápolis (Neapolis Gate), The section of the wall running north climbs up to the Greek acropolis.
The area between the walls and the forum is still being excavated. There are traces of a large **palaeo-Christian basilica** *(limited access)* which was built, exceptionally, on an octagonal plan similar to St Vitale in Ravenna, a baptistery and a bishop's palace.

South Section

Access by steps from the modern road. The **Via Egnatia**, which is the first level below the modern road, formed the main street *(decumanus maximus)* of Roman Philippi; on the left of the steps are the ruts worn by the wagons which plied the road.

Forum★

At the centre is a large, marble-paved court. Down the north side runs the Via Egnatia; the other three sides were bordered by steps and porticoes leading to the main municipal buildings. The west side is bordered by traces of a temple (**1**) and administrative buildings; in the southwest corner stands an unusual upturned **marble table** (**2**): the different-sized cavities in it are thought to have been used for measuring; farther on at the foot of the second column of the south portico there are holes in the ground for the game of marbles. The east side was bordered by another temple (**3**) incorporating fluted columns and a library (**4**).

Market

On the far side of the street lay the market composed of shops and a hall supported on columns, some of which have been re-erected. Between them on the paving stones are the marks of various games.

Pillared Basilica★

Begun in the 6C, the basilica was never finished because it proved impossible to construct a dome to cover such a large building. The huge pillars speak to the ambitious nature of the building. On the north side, towards the forum, are traces of a baptistery and a chapel that housed the bishop's throne. There are a few traces of the **Roman palaestra** (2C AD) byond the narthex.

Latrines★

Contemporary with the *palaestra* and situated below the southwest corner is a huge public latrine; most of the original marble seats and water ducts are still extant.

North Section★

Climb up to the terrace for an extensive view southwest to Mount Pangaion.

Basilica with atrium

It was built in the 6C, but was probably destroyed by an earthquake soon afterwards. There are still traces of the steps that descended into the confessional, which housed the relics beneath the high altar.

Saint Paul's prison

Below the basilica, at road level, is the Roman crypt (**5**), which by the 5C had come to be considered as the prison where St Paul was detained.
Higher up rear the massive blocks of the foundations of a Hellenistic temple (**6**); the Byzantines converted them into a cistern.
The path to the theatre passes at the foot of some little **rock sanctuaries** (**7**), recesses hollowed out of the rock.

Theatre★

The shell-shaped hollow in the lower slopes of the Acropolis hill contained a great theatre (4C BC); it was converted in the Roman period as an arena, which dated back to the 4C BC but was refurbished by the Romans in the 2C AD for gladiatorial and animal combat.

KÓRINTHOS★★

CORINTH – Κορινθοζ

POPULATION 36 555

MICHELIN MAP 737 G-H 9 – KORINTHÍA – PELOPONNESE.

Extensive remains, an impressive acropolis and the port of Lechaion all recall the golden age of 'wealthy Corinth', Cosmopolitan and dissolute, it was one of the busiest trading cities in Antiquity. Corinth is well placed for trips along the coast of the Gulf of Corinth, and for exploring other Classical sites farther inland.

- **Orient Yourself:** Located 85km/53mi west of Athens along the E 94 motorway, Corinth lies at the end of the isthmus separating the Gulf of Corinth and the Saronic Gulf. The ancient city is 8km/5mi away by the E 65 motorway. Near the entrance, a road to the left leads to Acrocorinth.
- **Don't Miss:** The Ancient city; the view from the Heraion Headland
- **Organizing Your Time:** The ancient city takes a least a day to visit.
- **Also See:** Mikínes, Náfplio, Tírintha, Arhéa Epídavros

A Bit of History

According to legend, one of Corinth's early kings was **Sisyphos**, a mortal whose cunning ways drew the ire of Zeus. Jealous, the god condemned Sisyphos to carry a rock up a steep slope in Hades, only to have it tumble back to the bottom over and over again, for all eternity.
Corinth occupies an eminently favourable position at the crossroads of the land and sea routes linking Attica and the Peloponnese, the Ionian and the Aegean Seas. High on a hill, its almost impregnable acropolis controlled movement in all directions on the isthmus of Corinth in Ancient times.

A strategic site – Only 6km/3.75mi wide, the isthmus was the site of fortification works as early as the Mycenaean period, and plans were laid to dig a shipping canal across the ithsmus. Nero began such a project in AD 67, but left it unfinished.
In those days the isthmus was more densely inhabited than it is now, and there were three ports on its coastline. From 582 BC the Isthmian Games, second only to the Olympic Games, were held here every two years in honour of Poseidon

An opulent city – In the Archaic era Corinth prospered and became a major trading centre dealing in wheat from Sicily, papyrus from Egypt, ivory from Libya, leather from Cyrenaica, incense from Arabia, dates from Phoenicia, apples and pears from Euboia, carpets from Carthage and slaves from Phrygia.
The **Corinthian capital** (an architectural feature) is thought to have been invented here in the 5C BC by the sculptor **Kallimachos**. The Corinthians produced pottery for export as well as bronze, glass and purple-dyed cloth; their naval shipyards launched the first *triremes*. In the 4CBC the city led Greece in the **League of Corinth** under Macedonian rule.
Corinth also gained renown for its courtesans *(hetairai)* and priestesses *(hierodules)* engaged in sacred prostitution in the precincts of the Temple of Aphrodite.

Corinth, a Roman colony – Corinth was sacked In 146 BC; the precious metals on the city's statues eventually ended up on the baldaquin in St. Peter's basilica in Rome. In 44 BC Julius Caesar founded a new town on the ruins of Ancient Corinth. It became the capital of Roman Greece and a destination for commerce and tourism.
Beginning in AD 51 **St Paul** spent 18 months here; in his Epistle to the Corinthians he castigated the shameless behaviour of the citizens. The Jewish priests had Paul tried in the agora, but he was acquitted.
Following the rule of Hadrian, who erected many buildings and an aqueduct to bring water from **Lake Stymphalos**, Corinth declined thanks to earthquakes and invasions. Only the acropolis retained a certain importance as a military stronghold.

Address Book

For coin categories, see the Legend on the cover flap.

WHERE TO EAT

Tássos – *Old Corinth, centre of the village.* A typical taverna with great ambience: souvláki being grilled, friendly staff and local music.
Marínos – *Old Corinth, at the guest-house of the same name.* An excellent taverna with tables laid out beneath the trees. Set menu (wine included).

WHERE TO STAY

Marínos – *Old Corinth, in the first street on the right after the Tássos taverna – ☎ (27410) 31 209 – 25rm.* A large house, not luxurious, but with a friendly welcome. Quiet rooms in the pavilion.
Le Petit France – *Loutraki, 3 Odós Botsari, to the right of the main road – ☎ (27440) 22 401, lepetitfrance@yahoo.com – 15rm.* Centrally located but shielded from the noise, this hotel is run by a Franco-Greek couple and offers a warm welcome and clean, spacious rooms.
Agelidis Palace – *Loutraki, 19 Odós G. Lekka, towards the northern end – ☎ (27440) 26 695 – 43rm.* This 1920s palace is in a class of its own. Huge rooms, some with balconies.
Kalamaki Beach – *Isthmia – ☎ (27410) 37 331 – 76rm.* Large international hotel on the beach. Spacious rooms with terraces. Price includes half-board.

TAKING A BREAK

At Posidonia, to the left of the bridge west side of the canal, the **café-taverna Diolkos** offers fine views of the canal. The bar Posidonio, on the right, is the ideal place to watch the sunset.

H Champollion/MICHELIN

The ruins of Acrocorinth

Excavations and the opening of the canal – During the Turkish occupation Ancient Corinth disappeared under urban development. Excavations began in 1896 and uncovered a jumble of ruins, mostly Roman.
Around this time the project to create a canal across the ithsmus was resurrected. Work began in 1882, and was completed in 1893. The **Corinth canal**★★ permanently altered the shipping routes, and enabled Piraeus to become the major port of Greece.

Visit

Modern Corinth

The modern town grew up after two earthquakes decimated the area, the second one in 1928. Laid out on a linear grid plan, the city offers little of interest but is a useful base from which to explore the area. Worth a stop is the **Historical and Folk Museum** *(close to Eleftério Venizélou Square; open Tue-Sun 8am-1pm; 1.50€)*, to see its fine collection of traditional costumes, embroidery and finely worked silver jewellery.

Arhéa Kórinthos★★ (Ancient Corinth)

7km/4.5mi southwest of the modern town. Take the motorway towards Tripoli; after 6km follow the signs for the Ancient site. Park in the car park; the main entrance is on the west side of the archaeological site. It is also possible to reach the site from the Lechaion road. Allow 2hr. Open 1 Apr-30 Oct, daily 8am-7pm (11pm on Wed); 1 Nov-31 Mar, daily 8am-5pm (9pm on Wed). 6€ (Sun no charge). (27410) 31 207.
Inhabited since Neolithic times, Corinth has a vast array of archaeological material, although the visible remains date from the Roman period.
Start from the **Naós Oktavías**, the Temple of Octavian, a Roman building from which three fine Corinthian capitals have been re-erected.

Archaeological museum

The collections include most of the objects discovered from excavations on the site, including fine **Archaic ceramics** with oriental decoration, and examples of Roman mosaics.

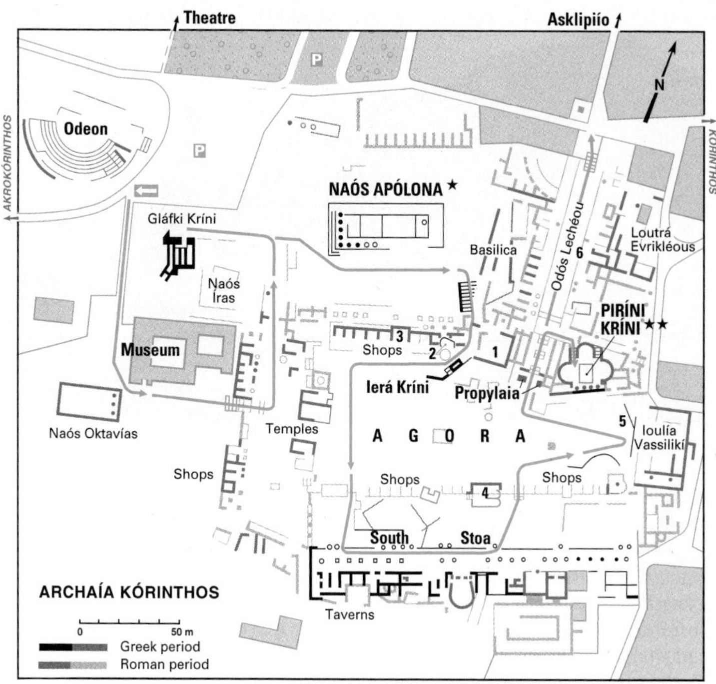

Make for the upper level of the agora and then bear left round **Naós Íras**, an old sanctuary to Hera, to reach the adjoining **Gláfki fountain**.

Naós Apólona (Temple of Apollo)★

The highest point of Ancient Corinth is marked by remains of the Temple of Apollo: seven out of 38 monolithic Doric columns, that were originally covered with stucco. The site affords spectacular views of the Gulf of Corinth and of Acrocorinth.

A grand flight of steps built in the 5C BC leads down to the lower level of the agora. The façade (**1**) of a Roman **basilica**, which stood in the centre of the north side, was adorned with four huge statues (two are displayed in the museum).

Ierá Kríni

The base of the **sacred fountain**, with its rhythmic frieze of triglyphs, is still visible. Steps lead down to the underground spring, which was linked by a secret passage with the **Sanctuary of the Oracle** (**2**). A priest hidden beneath an altar answered the petitioners, who thought they were in direct communication with the god.

Agora

This huge, rectangular open space provides remarkable views up to Acrocorinth. Along the north side, below the terrace supporting the great temple, are the remains of 15 Roman shops; the one in the centre (**3**) is still roofed.

A redoubtable magician

Medea, a charming sorceress, fell in love with Jason during his quest for the Golden Fleece and gave him a magic balm to protect him in his adventures. Upon the Argonauts' triumphant return, Jason married Medea. One day King Creon gave his daughter, Glauce, in marriage to the Argonaut hero, who abandoned Medea. The sorceress gave her rival a poisoned wedding dress, which ignited, causing Jason's bride to throw herself into the fountain.

H Champollion/MICHELIN

Temple of Apollo, Corinth

South Stoa

On the south side of the agora *(upper level)*, stood the South Stoa, an immense building which was used by the Greeks as a guesthouse and converted by the Romans into an administrative centre. At the west end you can still trace the arrangement of each 'compartment' with its courtyard and well.

In front of the stoa stood **Bema** (**4**), a platform from which the governor Gallio passed judgement on **St Paul** (there was a church on the site in the Middle Ages).

To the east lie the remains of the **Julian Basilica** (Ioulía Vassilikí) dating from the Roman era. Excavations in front of it have revealed earlier Greek paving with the starting line of a racetrack (**5**).

Propílea

The base of the monumental entrance *(propylaia)* to the agora remains. In the Roman era it was surmounted by gold chariots for the god Helios and his son Phaeton.

Piríni Kríni★★

Many times remodelled, the **Peirene Fountain** dates from the 6C BC. The original Greek part is at the back of the atrium *(south side)*: six stone arches stand in front of a row of underground reservoirs.

Leave the Ancient city by the **Lechaion Way** (Odós Lehéou), the beginning of a road running from the agora to the harbour at Lechaion. In the Roman period it became a ceremonial way leading to the Propylaia and bordered by porticoes housing the **Baths of Eurykles** (Loutrá Evrikléous) with their public latrines (**6**) which are well preserved.

Odeon

Excavations have revealed a small, semicircular Roman theatre dating from the 1C AD. The banks of seats could accommodate about 3 000 spectators.

Theatre

Begun in the 5C BC it was remodelled several times; the stage was enlarged to accommodate gladiatorial combats and nautical spectacles. It held about 18 000 people.

Asklipío

The plan of the temple dedicated to Asklepios, the god of medicine, can be clearly traced on the ground. Near the entrance *(east)* is an unusual stone offertory. West of the temple is the Fountain of Lerna, for hydrotherapy.

AkroKórinthos★★ (Acrocorinth)

Take the signposted road on the left going uphill (7km/4.5mi there and back) which passes the old potters' district on the right, bears left in front of a Turkish fountain not far from the excavated remains of a temple to Demeter and then climbs in a succession of bends up to the citadel entrance. Open 1 Apr-30 Oct daily 8am-7pm; 1 Nov-31 Mar Tue-Sun 8.30am-3pm. No charge. (27410) 31 266.

Poised between heaven and earth and almost indistinguishable from the rock, the ruins of Acrocorinth are some of the most impressive in the world because of their extent, the desolate grandeur of their elevated site and the immense panorama which they command.

Acrocorinth was first a Greek acropolis, then a Roman citadel and then a Byzantine fortress. Frankish, Turkish, Florentine and Venetian occupiers possessed it in turns, adding to it over the centuries.

The access ramp from the car park to the fortress offers spectacular views of the three lines of defence and the three gates that protect the citadel on the western approach.

Monumental Gateways

The first gateway (14C) is defended by a moat; a tower flanks the second (also 14C). The third is flanked by two powerful rectangular towers: the one on the right is mainly Ancient (4C BC).

A steep path leads up the slope among the ruins (note the fine views of the Gulf of Corinth), through the old Turkish district (remains of mosque – *left*) to the rampart and the northern postern. Return to the decapitated minaret and pass a fine brick-vaulted cistern to reach the medieval keep.

Keep

The keep dominates the remains of the Frankish castle of the De Villehardouins, princes of Morea in the 13C and the 14C. Fine view of the Byzantine ramparts with their rectangular towers, the surrounding heights and the Gulf of Corinth.

From the keep, return along the south ramparts and continue eastwards (view of the mountains of the Peloponnese) to the Peirene Spring, which is to be found near a bend in the wall next to a ruined Turkish barracks.

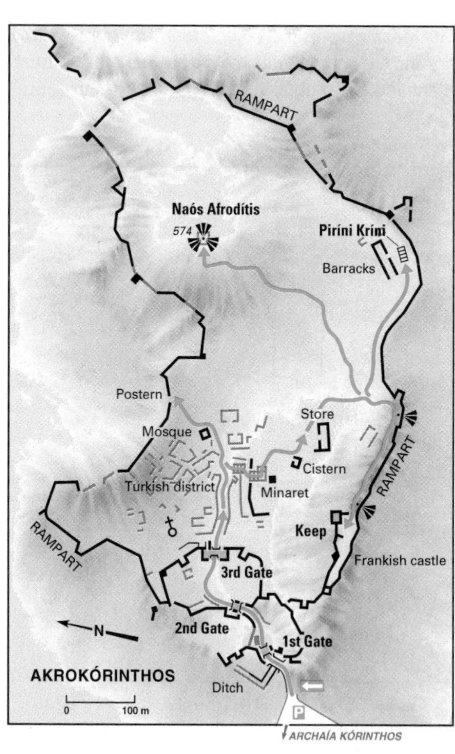

Piríni Kríni (Peirene Spring)

Steps lead down into a Hellenistic underground chamber (Ancient graffiti), thence to another chamber, which has since flooded with water.

According to legend the Spring was created by the winged horse Pegasus stamping its foot; Pegasus was then captured by Bellerophon while drinking at the spring.

Naós Afrodítis (Temple of Aphrodite)

The site of the famous temple is now marked by a column. There is a splendid **panorama★★★** extending beyond the isthmus of Corinth to Mount Parnassos *(north)*, across Attica *(east)* and to the Peloponnese *(south)*. To the southwest, perched on a rocky peak, are the medieval ruins of the Frankish Castle of Montesquiou.

Outskirts

From the canal, turn right to the Possidonía Bridge (2km/1.25mi) at the west end of the canal.

Diolkós

The central section of the bridge sinks onto the canal bed to let boats pass.
Near the bridge on either side of the modern road one can see the *diolkós*, an Ancient portage way paved with stone along which the ships were dragged on chariots or on wooden rollers across the lowest and narrowest part of the isthmus. On the side near the Gulf of Corinth the paving stones are marked with letters of the Corinthian alphabet; on the other side the ruts worn by the chariots can be seen. This stone slipway was probably built in the 6C BC and was still in use in the 12C AD.

Isthmía (Isthmian Sanctuary)

From Athens, exit the expressway at the interchange just after Corinth Canal and proceed as for Ancient Epidauros; on leaving the village of Kirás Vrissi turn right at the junction, then immediately left into the first uphill road; the museum is at the entrance of the site. Open Tue-Sun 8.30am-3pm. No charge (site); 2€ (museum). ☎ (27410) 37 244.
The **museum** presents objects found during the excavations of the Isthmian Sanctuary and the port of Kenchreai. There are some unusual glass mosaics (decorated with plant and bird motifs, human figures and landscapes) found in submerged packing

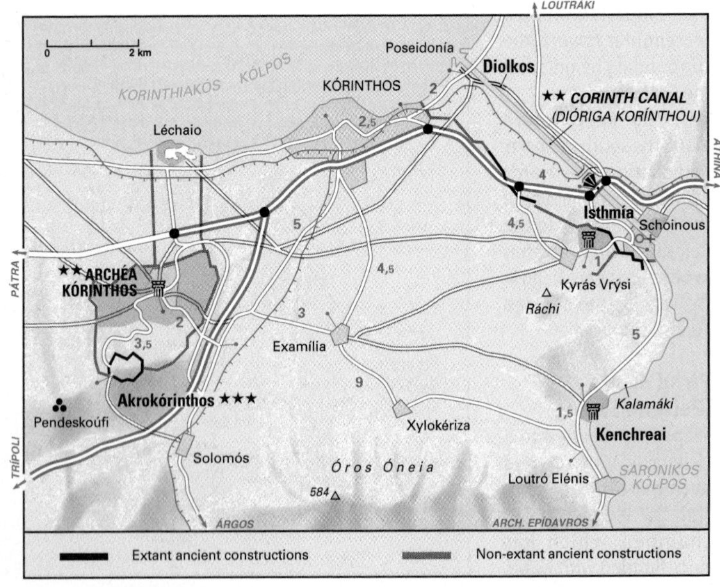

The Corinth Project

A million years ago, the Peloponnese formed part of the mainland, but Greece, and especially the Gulf of Corinth, is subject to a great deal of seismic activity. The movement of tectonic plates pulls the peninsula 1.5cm farther away from the mainland every year and has created the Gulf of Corinth. All this activity has meant the development of a major programme of research: The Corinth Project. The establishment of a permanent observation station will allow information to be gathered which will permit scientists to better understand seismic faults.

cases at Kenchreai; they were probably imported from Egypt. Amphoras, gymnastic apparatus and ceramics are also on view.

The **excavations** have revealed the foundations of a Temple to Poseidon (5C BC) and the stadium that from 582 BC hosted the biannual Isthmian Games; note the 16 grooves made in the stone which diverge near the starting line. Fine mosaics include one depicting a dancing Dionysos surrounded by dolphins; this was originally the floor of a Roman swimming pool. At the southern end of the stadium, traces remain of the Palémonion (1C BC). Beyond are the ruins of a Roman theatre, a defensive wall and the Roman fortress.

Port of Kenchreai

7km/4mi south of Isthmia by the coast road.

In Antiquity, this was the port for Corinth on the Saronic Gulf. Traces of harbour installations extend beneath the water. To the south lie the foundations of a Christian basilica (4C) which replaced a temple to Isis.

St Paul disembarked here in AD 51 to begin his sojourn among the Corinthians.

Loutráki★

Combining the charm of a traditional spa with the modern attractions of a seaside resort, Loutráki lies in the crook of the Bay of Corinth at the foot of the **Mount Gerània** chain. Luxury hotels, a palm-tree walk and a luxuriant public garden bordering a little harbour all add to the visitor's pleasure.

Loutráki is the largest spa in Greece; its radioactive warm water is used to treat various ailments. Bottled Loutráki **mineral water** is sold throughout Greece.

Akrotírio Iréo★★★ (Heraion Headland)

46km/29mi return trip from Loutráki. The corniche road runs north, offering admirable views of the coast and the Bay of Corinth; then it bears right inland by a taverna (view north towards the headland crowned by a lighthouse). On the outskirts of **Perahóra** (small archaeological museum) turn left into a narrow road *(sign 'Limni Heraion')* which passes through olive groves and then skirts **Lake Vouliagméni**. At the junction marked by a chapel bear right

The **Heraion** (a sanctuary dedicated to **Hera**) occupies the rocky slopes of the headland separating the Bay of Corinth from the Gulf. Its remote and wild **site**★ is hidden in the bottom of a narrow valley below an acropolis. From the car park walk down into the valley. Near a house are the ruins of a Hellenistic cistern. Above are the remains of temples to Hera Limenia (6C BC) and Hera Akraia (8C BC).

The path from the car park to the lighthouse *(30min on foot there and back)* provides a splendid **panorama**★★★, particularly at sunset, of the ancient site, the coast and mountains of the Peloponnese *(southwest)*, the Gulf of Corinth stretching northwest, the Halcyonic Gulf *(Kólpos Alkionídon)* on the north side of the headland and on the skyline to the north the Parnassos massif towering over Delphi.

Sikióna

25km/16mi west of Corinth. Follow the coastline; from Kiáto take the small road (sign 'Ancient Sikyon') through the modern village of Sikióna to the Ancient site. Open daily 8.30am-3pm. No charge. (27410) 312 07.

The ruins of Sikyon recall an earlier Ancient city that flourished in the Archaic period. That city stood in the plain, but it was razed in 305 BC, and rebuilt on the plateau. It became famous for its school of painting on wax, which produced among others Pamphilos, the master of Apelles.

The **ruins** date from the Hellenistic and the Roman periods. Beyond the museum, which stands on the site of the old Roman baths, is a large theatre (3C BC) (restored) on the right built against the flank of the former acropolis. Below to the left are the foundations of a huge gymnasium on two levels bordered by porticoes and linked by a central staircase between two fountains that are clearly identifiable. The ground also shows traces of a temple, presumably dedicated to Apollo, and a senate house *(bouleuterion).*

LÁRISSA

Λαρισα

POPULATION 124 786

MICHELIN MAP 737 G 5 – THESSALY.

Situated 151km/94mi southwest of Thessaloníki and around 360km/225mi northwest of Athens, Lárissa is the capital of Thessaly and an important junction on the south bank of the River Piniós. Occupied by Turks for five centuries, it is today a market for produce and a food-processing centre, and the ideal base from which to explore the archaeological and natural attractions of the area.

Odós Epirou 58, (24106) 704 37. Open Mon-Fri 8am-2.30pm.

Visit

In **Odós Venizélou**, the main street in the old part of town, the low houses with awnings and the open-air street stalls recall the Turkish occupation. The ruins of a Hellenistic **theatre** are visible from the corner of Odós Papanastasiou. The street climbs up to the site of an Ancient acropolis where a **medieval castle** stands. Excavations *(in progress at the time of publication)* in front of the castle have revealed an early-Christian **basilica**; the painted tomb may be that of St Achileos. Visit the **Archaeological Museum** *(Odós 31-Avgoustou 2, open Tue-Sun 8.30am-3pm; no charge; (24102)885 15)* to see Hellenistic and Roman sculptures, Neolithic vases, and mosaics, all housed in a 19C mosque.

Locals enjoy strolling in pleasant Alkazar Park.

Outskirts

Kiláda Ton Témbon★

22km/14mi northeast of Lárissa. On the northern border of Thessaly stretches the valley of the River Piniós, once known as the 'Wolf's Mouth' (Likóstomo). It was created by a seismic fracture between Olympos and Óssa that formed a channel through which Lárissa Lake drained into the sea.

In Antiquity this region was sacred to **Apollo**, son of Zeus and Leto. After killing Python at Delphi he came to wash in the waters of the Piniós. There he fell in love with the nymph **Daphne**, who was changed into a laurel tree *(dáphni)* to escape his advances. Disappointed, Apollo gathered a sprig of the laurel and planted it at Delphi near the Kastalian spring.

The Vale of Tempe was much praised in Antiquity for its cool freshness compared with the torrid summer climate of the neighboring plains. It enchanted the **Emperor Hadrian**, who had it recreated in the grounds of his villa at Tivoli near Rome.

Tour the valley by travelling upstream from east to west; most of the sights lie on the north (right) side of the road.

Daphne's Spring

Also known as Apollo's Spring, this shady site is cool and restful.

Agía Paraskevi

This important place of pilgrimage dedicated to the Virgin is on the north bank of the River Piniós at the foot of an impressive cliff of rock. From the footbridge over the river there is a beautiful **view★** of the Vale.

Aphrodite's Spring

This spring is located down by the river beneath the sheltering plane trees.

Ambelákia

This pleasant small town is splendidly situated on the northwest slope of Mount Óssa, at the opening of the gorge in the Vale of Tempe, with an extensive view of the River Piniós basin and the heights of Mount Olympos.

In the 17C and 18C Ambelákia bustled with workshops producing fabrics dyed scarlet with madder from the neighbouring plain. A sales and production cooperative, the first of its type, was founded in 1780; its commercial agents operated throughout Europe for nearly forty years. The richly decorated **residence★** of George Schwarz, head of the cooperative, is a superb example of a typical 18C Thessalian house.

Platamónas Castle★

55km/34mi northeast of Lárissa. Access by a footpath road in Néa Pandeleimónas.

On a hill between the sea and Mount Olympos stands the Frankish castle of Platamónas. Begun in 1204, it occupies a commanding position at the seaward end of the Vale of Tempe. The **fortress★** is an excellent example of medieval military architecture; note especially the entrance to the keep, which could only be reached by ladders.

P Nail/MICHELIN

Platamónas Castle

MÁNI★★

Μανι

POPULATION 23 887

MICHELIN MAP 737 G 12-13 – LAKONÍA – PELOPONNESE.

The southern spur of Mount Taígetos, (1 214m/3 970ft) extends south between the Messenian and Lakonian Gulfs to form a promontory which ends in Cape Matapan (Akrí Ténaro), the southernmost point of continental Greece. This is the Máni peninsula, a barren windswept landscape. Today it is largely depopulated; the villages with their abandoned towers and Byzantine chapels and churches appear frozen in time. *at Gíthio, 20 Odós V Georgiou, ☎(27330) 24 484. Open Mon-Fri 11am-3pm.*

- **Orient Yourself:** 43km/27mi south of Sparta, in a wild and rocky region. Access is easiest by road from Sparta; also from Kalamáta by the coast road.
- **Don't Miss:** The isolated region between Areópoli and Cape Matapan.
- **Organizing Your Time:** Plan three days, alternating between sight visits and beach time.
- Kids **Especially for Kids**: The spectacular Dirós Caves (Spílea Diroú).
- **Also See:** Kíthira, Kalamáta, Monemvassia, Mistrás, Spárti.

A Bit of History

Originally from the north of Lakonia, the defiant Maniot people maintained their autonomy from Greece's many occupiers, particulary the Turks. Introspective and bellicose, the Maniots lived in tribal villages under the rule of the local chiefs, sometimes confronting one another in vendettas. These disputes explain why the houses and even the fields were fortified.

H Champollion/MICHELIN

Maniot shepherd

There are about 800 **Maniot towers**, some dating from the 17C. Made of stone and square in shape, they comprised three or four rooms linked by ladders and trapdoors. Many towers may be found in **Kíta** and **Váthia** in the south. Small **churches** and chapels in this region date from the 11C and the 12C; their interiors are often decorated with charming 12C-13C and 14C frescoes. *The sites of interesting Byzantine churches are underlined in red on the map of Máni.*

Few in number, the Maniots live in their steep villages, preserving the tradition of honour and hospitality. Women still wear the long black dress and veil of mourners in Antiquity and perpetuate their tradition of singing funeral dirges *(mirológia).*

Driving Tour

Starting from Gíthio *160km/100mi*

Plan two days for this driving tour; progress will be slow along the narrow, winding roads. Summer heat is intense, but villages along the way provide opportunites to stop and refresh. Check the Address Book for overnight accommodations enroute.

Gíthio

Situated just west of the mouth of the **River Evrótas** (Eurotas) overlooking the Lakonian Gulf and the island of Kythera, Gíthio is a quiet seaside resort and a port. Dominated by a medieval castle, the harbour area consists of picturesque alleys; the street parallel to the quayside is lined by attractive Turkish houses with balconies. There is a small Ancient theatre next to the barracks northwest of the town. On the island of Marathónissi stands one of the typical towers of Máni. The **Historical and Ethnological Museum** (in the Tzanetáki Tower), traces the history of Maní.

Address Book

For coin categories, see the Legend on the cover flap.

WHERE TO EAT

To Nissi – *Gíthio, islet of Kranai.* One of Gíthio's best and quietest spots: salads and grilled fish, excellent espresso.

O Bárba Pétros – *Areópoli – ☎ (27330) 51 205.* The best place in town, set in a flowered courtyard. Well-prepared Greek dishes, and local wine served chilled.

Theodorákis – *Geroliménas, far end of the harbour.* This taverna serves fresh grilled fish and good traditional Greek cuisine. A warm welcome and mainly Greek clientele.

WHERE TO STAY.

Tsimova – *Areópoli, behind the church – ☎ (27330) 51 301 – 7rm.* A guesthouse in a real Maniot tower. Kitsch decor with war souvenirs of the grandfather, a former resistance fighter.

Kastro Maïnh – *Areópoli – ☎(27330) 512 38, www.kastromaini.gr – 29rm, 3 suites.* 3km from the sea, a charming hotel, beautifully decorated; swimming pool.

Porto Vitilo – *Itylo – ☎ (27330) 592 20 – 33rm.* Luxurious hotel (priced according to the view), elegant furnishings. Excellent breakfast.

Marmari – *Marmári (south, end of the point) – ☎ (27330) 52 111, www.touristorama.com – 24rm.* Overlooking the beach, this is the more attractive of the two hotels here. Simple rooms with fresco decoration ; good restaurant ( ). Magnificent sunset views.

Aktaion – *Gíthio, 39 Odós V. Pávlou – ☎ (27330) 23 500, www.aktaiong@otenet.gr – 20rm and two suites.* On the harbour along a noisy street, this large hotel has rooms with balconies overlooking the port. Prices rise in summer.

Skoutari Beach Resort – *Skoutari – ☎ (27330) 93 684 – 20rm. . Open end May-Oct.* Very good hotel above quiet Skoutari beach. Vehicle a must. Clean rooms, all with kitchenettes.

Akrotiris – *Porto Kagio – ☎ (27330) 52 013.* Large, clean, simple rooms with fridges and balconies overlooking the sea. Peace and quiet, especially out of the August high season.

SHOPPING

Hassanakos Art Gallery – *Githio, facing the port.* Excellent newsstand (maps available) and gallery with old photos of the town, books and paintings.

EVENTS AND FESTIVALS

The **Marathonissia Festival** takes place between 15 July and 15 August in Gíthio and features concerts and theatrical performances.

Take the Areópoli road; 3km/2mi from Gíthio is the village of **Mavrovoúni**.

The road climbs into the mountains through a gorge *(11km/7mi from Gíthio)*, guarded at its northern end by Passavant Castle (**Pasavás**), a Frankish fortress.
Continue on the Areópoli road across the mountain chain; the western approach is guarded by Kelefá Castle *(3km/2mi on)*, a huge Turkish fortress (16C-17C).

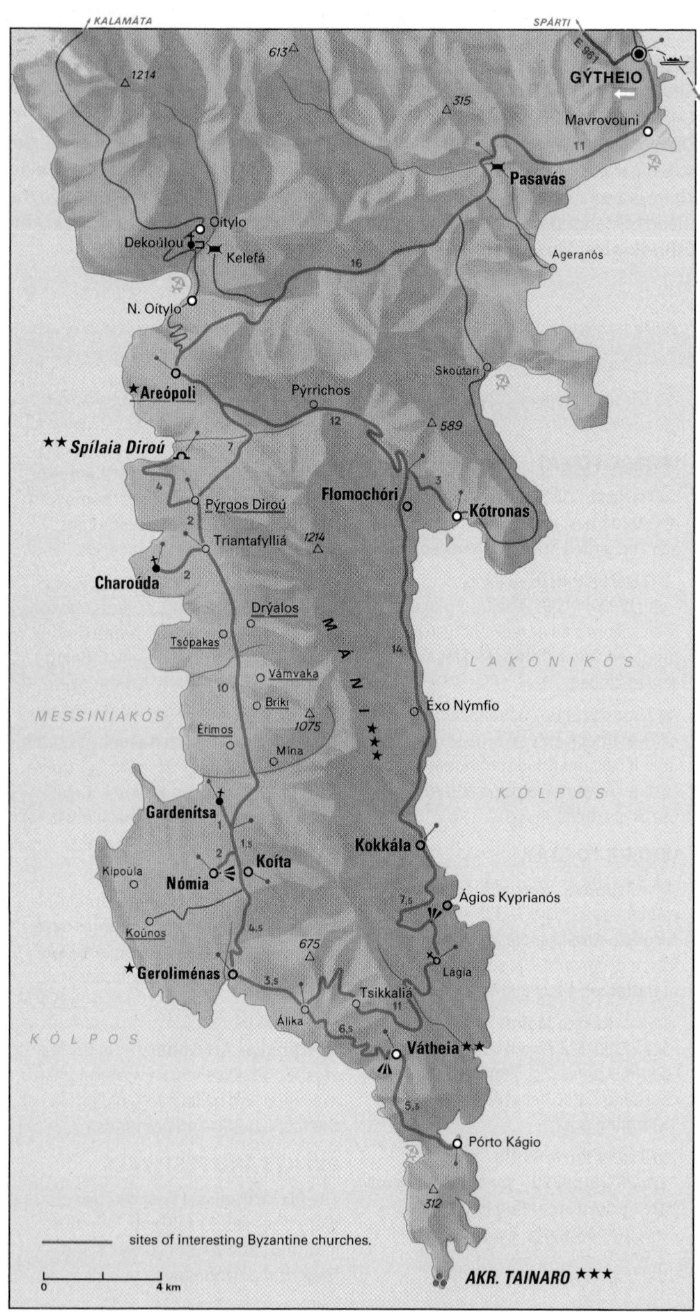

Areópoli★

Capital of the Maní region, this is a large, typically Maniot village with services for tourists. It was here on 17 March 1821 that the Maniots rose up against the Turks. The **Taxiarchs' Church** (18C), is unusual for its sculpted decoration; **St John's Church** (Ágios Ioánis), in a neighbouring street, is decorated with naïve frescoes (18C).

▸ *At the junction with the road to Kótronas (left), bear right to the Dirós Caves.*

Spílea Diroú★★

Kids *Open June-Sept daily 8.30am-5.30pm; Oct-May daily 8.30am-3pm. 12€. ☎ (27330) 522 22.* Part way down the west coast of Máni, are two caves; the largest, Glifáda, is one of the most spectacular natural sights in Europe; the other, Alepótripa, shows traces of prehistoric occupation *(closed to the public).*

Glifáda Cave

The cave consists of chambers and a gallery created by an underground river forcing its way through the limestone of Máni to reach the sea below the actual entrance. Guided boat tours *(about 2km/1.25mi)* explore both arms of the river. All along the route are white or coloured concretions: pillars, curtains, stalactites and stalagmites namd for their appearance (the Dragon's Cave, the Cathedral, the Pavillion).

Moussío (Neolithic Museum)

Open daily 8.30am-3pm. 2€. ☎ (27330) 522 33. Items from the Neolithic period found in Alepótripa Cave are on display: a fine collection of weapons, tools made of stone and bone, earthenware jars and other vessels, utensils and other domestic items (such as needles), as well as human skulls and skeletons. The cave was abandoned when an earthquake blocked the entrance.

Return to the Geroliménas road, which runs along a sort of limestone terrace between the mountain and the sea, dotted with villages of tower houses, such as Drίalos. At the village of **Haroúda**, the Taxiarch's Church (12C) features interesting frescoes.

Gardenítsa

1km/0.5mi west of the road (sign).

St Saviour's Church (Ágios Sotírios), (12C), has a porch and an interesting apse with a sculpted decoration in Kufic script; inside are 13C-14C frescoes.

H Champollion/MICHELIN

Spílea Diroú Caves

Nómia

Nómia lies on the west side of the road with **views★★** of the towers of Kíta. Along the road stands the white Taxiarchs' Church (fine series of frescoes, 13C-14C).

Kíta

The village appears abandoned, despite its many towers. In the hamlet of Tourlotí, St Sergius's Church (12C) is well proportioned.

Northwest of Kipoúla rises a rocky bluff on which the famous **Castle of the Great Maina** (Kástro tis Oriás, *difficult access*) was built in 1248.

Geroliménas★

This is a simple resort and fishing village, tucked into a rocky inlet in remote and wild **surroundings★**.

Váthia★★

Forsaken by almost all its inhabitants, Váthia is the most impressive of the Máni's tower communities. Stony paths wind between the silent towers and empty houses. From Váthia the road continues south to **Pórto Kágio** (Quail Port), situated on the neck of a precipitous peninsula, and ends in **Cape Matapan**.

Cape Matapan★★

Akrotírio Ténaro, the southernmost tip of the Peloponnese, was once crowned by a temple to Poseidon, which was replaced by the **Church ton Assomatón**, of which traces remain.

Return to Álika and bear right into the road to Lágia over the ridge of the Máni. Beyond Lágia (towers) it descends, offering magnificent s **views★★** of the Maniot coast. Beyond **Ágios Kiprianós** it skirts the east coast of the Máni. The corniche road provides spectacular views of the coastline and of the occasional villages and feudal ruins on the mountain slopes. Worth exploring are the villages of **Kokála**, in an attractive sheltered inlet; and **Flomohóri**, with tall towers and cypress trees. A mile beyond the latter, turn right to **Kótronas**, a small seaside resort and fishing port.

METÉORA★★★

Μετεορα

MICHELIN MAP 737 E 5 – THESSALY.

North of Kalambáka in the northwest corner of the Thessalian plain a group of precipitous grey rocks rises up out of the trees in the flat Piniós Valley. Perched on top are the coenobitic monasteries known as the Metéora, sacred sites of orthodox monasticism. The landscape and near-miraculous construction draw many tourists, yet the monasteries maintain their magical, mystical air. *Town Hall Square in Kalambáka, ☎ (24320) 77 900. Open daily 8am-2.30pm in summer.*

- **Orient Yourself:** 125km/78mi east of Ioánina and 85km/53mi west of Lárissa. The town of Kalambáka makes a good base from which to explore the Metéora.
- **Don't Miss:** The driving tour of monasteries but remember, photographing frescoes is not permitted, and visitors must be modestly dressed.
- **Organizing Your Time:** See Megálo Metéoro and Varláam in the morning, the rest in the afternoon. Avoid visiting at Christmas and Easter if possible.
- **Also See:** Ioánina, Lárissa

A Bit of History

These towers of sandstone and tertiary conglomerate stand on the border between the Píndos massif and the Thessalian plain at the lower end of the gorges carved by the Piniós River and its tributaries. There are some 60 of these columns of rock, and they rise up to 300m/984ft high.

In the 11C, hermits sought refuge in the solitary caves of the Metéora. When the Serbs invaded Thessaly in the 14C, the hermits began to establish monasteries. The first was founded by **St Athanasius** from Mount Athos, who founded the Great Meteoron. Others followed, despite the monumental task of transporting the building material to the top of the rock pillars.

During the 15C and 16C the number of monasteries grew to 24 and the buildings were decorated with frescoes and icons by the great artists of the day such as **Theophanes**. Today only five monasteries are inhabited by monks or nuns: St Nicholas, Roussánou, the Great Meteoron, Varlaám and St Stephen's. The Metéora draws many tourists, and some monks have sought isolation at Mount Athos or other monasteries.

Address Book

For coin categories, see the Legend on the cover flap.

WHERE TO EAT

Taverna Gardenia – *Kastráki, below the church.* Fresh, family-style dishes served on the pretty terrace.

Filoxenia Taverna – *Kastráki, road leading to the Metéora.* A pleasant spot to sample brochettes or souvlaki.

Taverna Kosmiki– *Kastráki, main street.* Lovely terrace with views of the Metéora; vegetable specialties.

Panellínion – *Kalambáka, Platía Dimarheíou.* Great for a drink or good, plain Greek food.

WHERE TO STAY

Meteora – *Kalambáka, 13 Odós Ploútarchou – ☎ (24320) 22 367, www.meteorahotels.com – 10rm.* A small simple establishment with quiet rooms that are spotlessly clean.

Odysseion – *Kalambáka, 30 Odós P. Dimitriou – ☎ (24320) 223 20, www.hotelodysseon.gr – 22rm.* Modern hotel with great views; breakfast on the terrace. Charming welcome.

Aeolic Star – *Kalambáka, 4 Odós A. Diákou , up from the Town Hall square – ☎ (24320) 22 325 – 16rm.* Simple accommodation; some rooms with TV and balconies. Generous breakfast.

Hotel Tsikéli – *Kalambáka, from the main road for the Metéora, take the street diagonally left – ☎ (24320) 22 438, – 18rm.* Welcoming place; breakfast served overlooking the garden. Some rooms with view of the Metéora.

Vasilikí & Gregóry Ziógas – *Kastráki, main street – ☎ (24320) 24 037 – 10rm.* Friendly welcome, comfortable rooms with views over the Metéora.

Doupiani House – *Kastráki outskirts, turn left – ☎ (24320) 75 326, doupiani-house@kmp.forthnet.gr – 11rm.* Quiet, secluded hotel with lovely views. Generous breakfast on the terrace. Walking routes and maps provided.

Kastráki – *Kastráki, outskirts of the village in the direction of the Metéora – ☎ (24320) 75 336, fax (24320) 75 335, www.trikala.cc/market/kastraki – 27rm.* A modern, comfortable hotel; some rooms have views of the Metéora.

France – *Kastráki, outskirts – ☎ (24320) 24 186 – 26rm.* A hotel run by a friendly Franco-Greek couple. Faultless rooms, some with views of the Metéora.

EVENTS AND FESTIVALS

Traditional folk dances are held in **Kalambáka** and **Kastráki** on Easter Sunday. In May, dances and sporting events take place in **Tríkala**.

SHOPPING

Korákis Bros, *Platía R. Feréou.* An Ali Baba's cave with wood and copper crafts, plus icons and jewellery.

Originally the only access was by means of very long ladders or by baskets suspended from winch-drawn ropes. Steps have now been cut in the rock face and there is a fine modern road serving the main monasteries.

Driving Tour

The 17km/11mi. Begin at Kalambáka.

Kalambáka

The 14C **Mitrópoli** (cathedral) stands on the foundations of an earlier church. Inside, note the marble pulpit, canopy, and dark 16C frescoes in the Cretan style.

Drive west; after passing Kastráki, park the car and take the path on the left.

Doúpiani

The **Chapel of the Virgin on the "Column"** was part of the Doúpiani hermitage to which, until the 14C, the scattered hermits were attached.

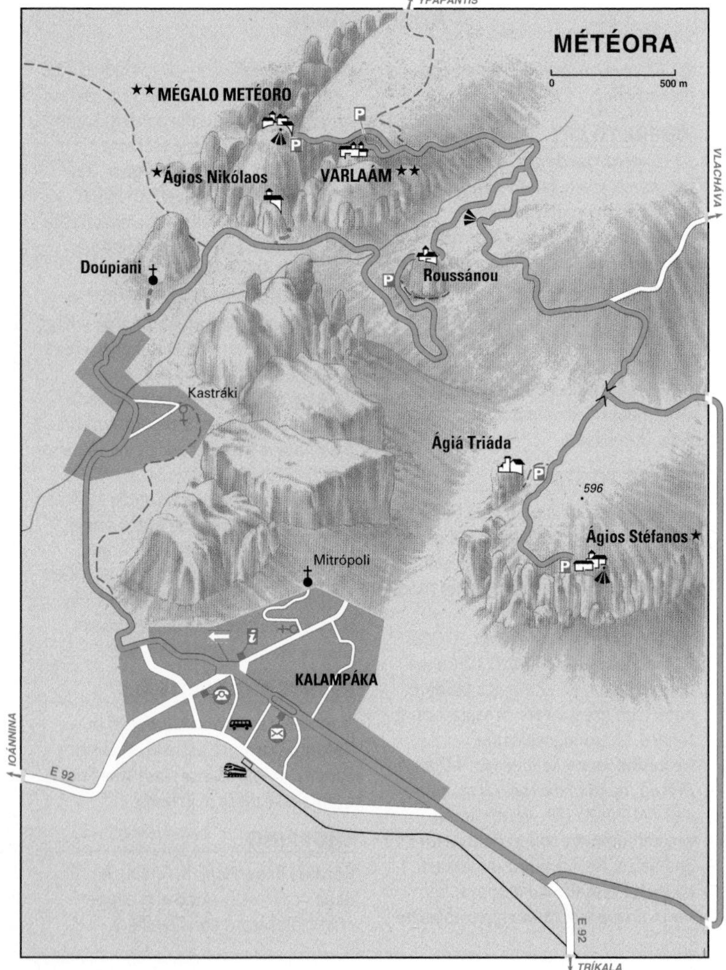

Ágios Nikólaos★

Open Sat-Thu, 9am-3.30pm (1pm in winter). 2€. ☎ (24320) 773 92.

Although the monastery dates from the 14C the church was built in the 16C and was decorated at that time by Theophanes the Cretan with remarkable frescoes. The monastery itself is small; it is composed of ten cells and its *katholicón* is only large enough to accommodate three worshippers. It was abandoned in the late 19C.

Roussánou Monastery

Open Thu-Tu, 9am-6pm (2pm in winter). 2€. ☎ (24320) 225 19.

This monastery is also known as St Barbara; for many years the head of the saint was among the relics venerated here. Note the 16C frescoes in the *katholicón*.
The road skirts the foot of the rock then reaches a T-junction. Bear left past the Varlaám Monastery to reach the Great Meteoron Monastery.

Megálo Metéoro★★

Open Wed-Mon, 9am-6pm (summer); daily except Tue and Thu, 9am-4pm (winter). 2€. Access by steps cut into the rock.

The foremost of the Metéora monasteries was founded in 1356 by St Athanasius and enriched with relics and works of art by his successor St Ioasaph (John Uros).

Church

The apse and the chancel (14C) and are decorated with mid-15C frescoes; the rest of the building was rebuilt in the mid-16C according to the architectural style of Mt. Athos (square-cross plan with lateral apses roofed by domes). St Ioasaph's tomb is in the narthex. The imposing 16C **refectory** now houses the Treasury: manuscripts, icons, liturgical ornaments, reliquaries and a carved cross of St Daniel. From the southeast of the monastery there is an impressive view over the valley.

Varlaám Monastery★★

Open Fri-Wed, 9am-2pm and 3.30-5pm (summer); Sat-Wed 9am-3pm (winter). 2€. ☎ (24320) 753 86.

A footbridge and a stairway lead up to this monastery (1518), in the 16C, visitors and provisions were hoisted up from the winch tower.
All Saints' Church, which incorporates the original 14C chapel dedicated to the Three Hierarchs, was completed in 1544. It has a remarkable collection of frescoes. Note also the 17C frescoes in the **Chapel of the Three Hierarchs,** the carved and gilded iconostasis (16C icon) and the inlaid furnishings.

Holy Trinity Monastery

B Kaufmann/MICHELIN

The Dormition of the Virgin, Varlaám Monastery

Conventual buildings include the refectory housing the Treasury (icon of the Virgin by Emmanuel Tzanés), the infirmary, the storerooms (enormous barrel holding 12 000 l/2 640 gal), the winepress and the tower with its winch.

Return to the junction across the river; bear left: spectacular **view**★★ of the **Roussánou Monastery**. Continue on, turning right at the second T-junction.

Agía Triáda

Open Fri-Wed, 9am-12.30pm and 3-5pm. 2€. ☎ (24320) 753 86.

The Monastery of the Holy Trinity (15-17C) was richly endowed with precious artefacts and manuscripts, but its Treasury was looted in the Second World War. The little chapel of St John the Baptist hewn into the rock face has some fine 17C frescoes, as does the *katholicón*, which dates to the 15C.

Ágios Stéfanos★

Open Tue-Sun, 9am-2pm and 3.30-6pm (summer; 9.30am-1pm, 3-5pm (winter). 2€. ☎ 24320 222 79.

St Stephen's Convent is reached by a bridge spanning the chasm that separates the rock pillar from the mountain mass. It is occupied by nuns, who maintain the traditions of icon painting (examples available to visitors for purchase).

The older one, St Stephen's (15C) is closed to visitors; the more recent church (18C) is contains a reliquary of St Charalambos. The refectory houses fine 16C and 17C icons by Emmanuel Tzanés, 17C illuminated manuscripts and 16C embroidery.

Splendid **views**★★ of the Piniós Valley and Thessaly.

Excursions

Tríkala

22km/14mi south of Kalambáka on the E 92.

Today an agricultural market, Tríkala was famed In Antiquity for its sanctuary to Asklepios, oldest in Greece. It was the Thessalonian capital during Turkish occupation.

Containing the main churches and a picturesque bazaar, the **Old Town** spreads over the lower slopes of Mount Ardáni below Fort Trikkis, a Byzantine restoration of a 4C BC original. Head for the top of the hill, a pleasant spot with a busy café.

South of town enroute to Kardítsa stands a 16C **mosque** with an imposing dome.

Stená Pórtas★ (Pórta Defile)

2km/1.25mi from Tríkala. Take the road to Píli up the south bank of the Portaïkós. Narrow and high, the **bridge**★ (16C) spans the river in one impressive arch at the entrance to the pass.

▶ *Return to Píli, cross the stream and climb up the north bank.*

Sanctuary of Pórta Panagía★

The isolated monastery dates from 1283, and comprises two buildings set in a beautiful landscape. In the eastern church (Latin style) note the dressed stone, the transept, and the nave buttressed by side aisles. The entrance to the chancel is framed by mosaics. The western church (Orthodox), reveals the Greek cross plan beneath a dome (15C); the façade and the stone walls seem to date from the 13C.

MIKÍNES★★★

MYCENAE – Μυκινεσ

MICHELIN MAP 737 G 10 – ARGOLID – PELOPONNESE.

Gateway to the rich Argolid region, Mycenae occupies a wild site★★ on a rocky hillside surrounded by barren mountains. Dating from the second millennium BC, the settlement gave birth to the Mycenean civilisation. The proud ruins are beautiful and rich in archaeological finds.

- **Orient Yourself:** On the old national route, about 40km/26mi southwest of Corinth and about 120km/75mi west of Athens. The road passes through the modern village of Mycenae, before heading up to a car park on the left.
- **Don't Miss:** The treasures in the new museum.
- **Organizing Your Time:** Plan two hours; visit in the cool of the morning.
- **Also See:** Árgos, Kórinthos, Náfplio, Tírinth

Address Book

For coin categories, see the Legend on the cover flap.

WHERE TO EAT

Modern Mycenae is well developed for tourism with a plethora of restaurants and cafés, but most of these close evenings in the off-season. In the center of the village, you'll find a few spots favoured by locals, including:

Spiros – Small family restaurant with modest but excellent grilled dishes (try the lamb).

Mykainos – A local favourite; stop in for a drink or the daily special.

WHERE TO STAY

Belle Hélène – *In the middle of the village on the left as you descend from Mycenae – ☎ (27510) 76 225 – 8rm.* This old hotel (1862) offers plenty of character, antique furniture, etc. Bathrooms at the end of the corridor. Restaurant on ground floor. Open Mar-Nov.

Petite Planète – *Between the village and the archaeological site – ☎ (27510) 76 240 – 30rm.* Modern hotel, comfortable rooms with terraces. The view over the Argolid from the restaurant is magnificent. Rates vary depending on the season.

A Bit of History

According to legend, Mycenae was founded by Perseus, son of Zeus and Danaë, who raised the city walls with the help of the Cyclops, giant builders who had one eye in the middle of their forehead.

After the Perseids came the Atreids, an accursed clan whose members and their exploits of fratricidal vengeance are recounted in the *Iliad* by Homer and other plays by Aeschylus, Sophocles and Euripides. For many years the story was thought to be the stuff of legend, but historians and archaeologists now think that the Atreids did exist. Regardless, from the 16C to the 12C BC, Mycenae was the most powerful state in the Mediterranean world and had close relations with Crete and even Egypt.

Excavations

By the 2C AD Mycenae was reduced to a few overgrown ruins. Enter **Heinrich Schliemann**, a wealthy German businessman with an obsession for the Homeric heroes. This brilliant amateur had discovered the site of Troy on the coast of Asia Minor in 1874 Two years later he began to dig on the site of Mycenae in the hope of finding the Tomb of Agamemnon. Guided by a sentence in Pausanias which said that Agamemnon had been buried within the city walls, Schliemann discovered, just inside the Lion Gate, a circle of royal tombs containing 19 corpses, which he thought to be those of Agamemnon, Cassandra and their companions. Within a month a large collection of jewellery, vases and precious items was recorded. Today they can be seen on display in the Mycenaean Room in the Athens Museum.

Extensive excavations and restoration of the site have continued in this century, including the discovery in 1951 of a second circle of royal tombs near the Tomb of Clytemnestra. Excavations continue today on the site within the western wall.

The tragedy of the Atreids

The Atreids' complicated history is well known thanks to the works of the Greek poets. The best known of this accursed family are:

Atreus, son of Pelops, who killed the sons of his brother Thyestes and served them to him during a banquet.

Menelaus, son of Atreus and King of Sparta, whose wife **Helen** was seduced by Paris, son of Priam, King of Troy, thus provoking the Trojan War.

Agamemnon, Menelaus's brother, King of Mycenae and husband of **Clytemnestra**, Helen's sister; he was the leader of the Achaeans in the expedition against Troy, and ordered the sacrifice of his daughter Iphigenia at Aulis to obtain a favourable wind.

Aigisthos, younger son of Thyestes who killed his uncle Atreus to avenge his father's death and became Clytemnestra's lover; she asked him to get rid of Agamemnon, just returned from Troy, and his captive **Cassandra**, Priam's daughter, known for her gloomy predictions which all refused to believe.

Orestes, son of Agamemnon and Clytemnestra, who was persuaded by his sister **Electra** to kill Clytemnestra and her lover Aigisthos; he was pursued by the **Furies** but acquitted on the Areopagos in Athens by a jury presided over by Athena and then purified by Apollo on the *omphalos* in Delphi before ascending the throne of Mycenae; he gave his sister Electra in marriage to his faithful friend **Pylades**.

Ancient City★★★

Acropolis

Open daily 8am-7pm (summer), 8.30am-3.30pm (winter). Museum: Mon noon-3pm; Tue-Sun 8.30am-3.30pm. 8€. ☎ (27510) 76 585. A flashlight is useful for visiting the tombs and cistern.

The **acropolis** hill is fringed to the north and south by two deep ravines. Triangular in shape and surrounded by ramparts, the acropolis housed the king, the royal family, the nobles and the palace guard. The town lay at the foot of the fortification.

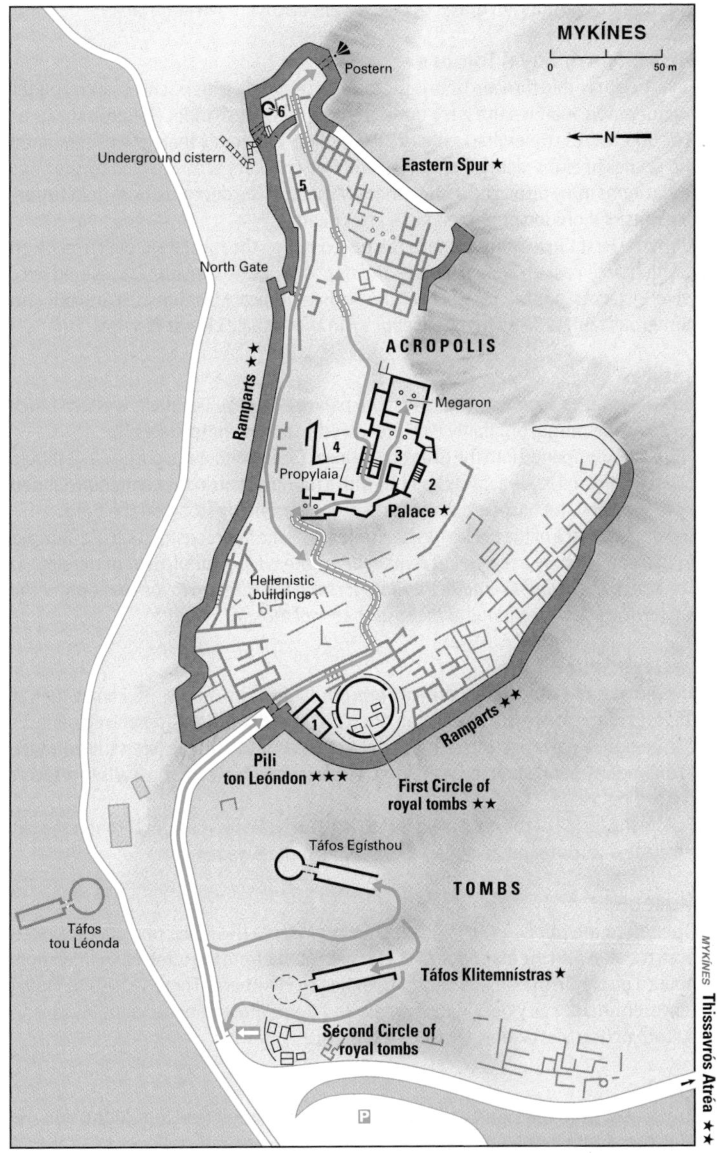

Ramparts★★
Built of stone, the Cyclopean fortifications date mostly from the 14C-13C BC.

Píli ton Leónton★★★ (Lion Gate)
The main entrance to the acropolis takes its name from the two headless wild animals (probably lionesses) sculpted on the huge **monolithic pediment**. A symbol of Mycenaean power, the animals stand on either side of a central column, their front paws resting on a double altar which also supports the pillar and an entablature.
The gateway proper is flanked by two protective walls. Note the enormous stone blocks used in the construction; the lintel weighs over 20 tonnes. The wooden doors were reinforced by a bar, which slotted into holes that are visible in the uprights.
Just over the threshold lay the porter's lodge *(left)* and the remains of a **grain store** (**1**) *(right)* where carbonised grains of cereal were discovered in large jars.

First Circle of Royal Tombs★★
On the right within the Lion Gate is the famous cemetery where Schliemann thought Agamemnon and his suite were buried. It is, in fact, much older (16C BC).
A double row of stones marks the circular outline. Within, six shaft graves contained the bodies of eight men, nine women and two children, accompanied by precious burial items (now displayed in the Athens Museum). The deceased bore gold **funerary masks** moulded onto their faces after death.
From the First Circle of Tombs take the paved ramp, 'the royal way', which leads up to the palace past an area of houses and depositories *(southwest)*. Discovered here were terracotta idols (on display at the Archaeological Museum of Nauplion) and numerous tablets (used for bookkeeping) in the Archaic **Linear B** script.

Palace★
Only foundations are visible of the royal palace (15C BC). The main western block contains the **megaron,** (fairly well preserved), and the **main stairs** (**2**).
The *propylaia* opened into the **great courtyard** (**3**). Beyond was a portico, a vestibule and the *megaron* itself, a royal chamber with a round hearth in the centre surrounded by four pillars (the bases are extant); the throne probably stood on the right.
The upper terrace of the palace has been altered by the later construction of a **Temple to Athena** (**4**); only a few traces remain but there is a beautiful view of the site.
The visit to the acropolis is quite tiring; visitors can either return to the Lion Gate or the more energetic can continue to the eastern spur of the site.

Eastern Spur★
The remains of a later set of **fortifications** (**5**), dating from the 12C BC, can be seen at this end of the fortress, as well as an open **cistern** (**6**) from the Hellenistic period.
On the right a postern *(no access)* opens to the southeast. On the left is the entrance to an underground stairway; its 99 steps bend round beneath the walls to a secret **cistern** below.
Follow the inside of the north rampart to the **North Gate**; walk out through the gat e for a few yards to get an overall view of the impressive ramparts.

Museum★
Opened to the public in 2003, the museum presents the finest objects excavated from the site, with the exception of the funerary items from the tomb of Agamemnon, now on display in the Athens Museum (copies on view here). There's a helpful model representing the city during its heyday, and items illustrating Ancient Mycenean culture of (terracotta idols, frescoes, etc.).

Tombs
As you exit from the Lion Gate, paths lead to the Tomb of the Lions (right) and the Aigisthos Tomb (left).

Táfos Klitemnistras★

This communal royal tomb dates to the 14C BC. The huge round funeral chamber is roofed with a dome 12.96m/42ft 6in above the floor.

Second Circle of Royal Tombs

Dating to the 17C BC, the second circle enclosed 24 graves; excavations have uncovered important archaeological material now on view in the Athens Museum.

Drive down the road to the Treasury of Atreus (right).

Treasury of Atreus or Tomb of Agamemnon★★

This tomb (13C BC) is the largest and the most beautiful of the nine communal beehive tombs which have been discovered near the Acropolis of Mycenae. Partially hewn out of the hillside, it features remarkable stone construction including a majestic **funerary chamber**. A passage leades into a smaller rectangular chamber hollowed out of the rock; some think it was the funeral chamber of the head of the family, others that it was the treasury itself.

MISTRÁS★★★

MYSTRA – Μυστρασ

MICHELIN MAP 737 G 11 – LAKONÍA – PELOPONNESE.

Occupying an exceptional site★★★ on a steep spur of Mount Taígetos overlooking Sparta and the Evrótas Valley, Mystra was known as the 'pearl of Morea' during the Frankish and Byzantine periods. Today the churches, monasteries, ruined palaces and houses are largely deserted, yet retain their architectural grandeur; the churches especially are outstanding examples of Byzantine religious art and architecture. *No local office. For information: ☎ (27310) 262 43/258 98.*

- **Orient Yourself:** 144km/90mi southwest of Corinth and 5km/3mi west of Sparta. The ruins of Ancient Mystra lie above the modern village; there are separate entrances for the Upper and Lower Towns.
- **Parking:** Lots at the entrance of the modern village and near the Lower Town.
- **Organizing Your Time:** Allow a full day; stick to the Lower Town if you're pressed for time.
- **Also See:** Spárti, Kalamáta

A Bit of History

Franco-Byzantine conflicts – The famed fortress of Mystra was built in 1249 when **William de Villehardouin**, Frankish Prince of Morea and Duke of Achaia, began to construct an impregnable stronghold to control the region of Lakonía. The site he chose was a high bluff commanding the Eurotas Valley.
The Franks did not hold Mystra for long. In 1259 de Villehardouin was captured in Macedonia and held prisoner for three years. He regained his freedom only by ceding three fortresses (Monemvassía, the Great Maina and Mystra) to his captor, Michael VIII Palaiologos, Emperor of Byzantium.

Florence of the Orient – In the 14C and 15C Mystra became the capital of the **Despotate of Morea**, a province of the Byzantine empire that covered almost the whole of the Peloponnese and was ruled by the heir (despot) to the emperor.

The despots made Mystra a centre of Hellenic politics and culture, building a palace and arranging for the construction of many churches that combined Eastern and Western influences.
The intellectual life of Mystra flourished under cultivated emperors such as John VI Kantakouzenos and particularly Manuel II Palaiologos. Neo-Platonic philosophy was espoused by **Manuel Chrysolorás**, 'the sage of Byzantium', who had taught in Florence in 1397 where he influenced the architect Brunelleschi.

A long decline – When Mystra was surrendered to Turkey in 1460 its churches were converted into mosques, the despots' palace became the residence of the Pasha, and the town continued to thrive. During the centuries following the Venetian occupation, however, it declined as a result of invasions by Russians, Albanians and the Egyptian troops of Ibrahim Pasha. In the 19C it was abandoned in favour of the new town of Sparta.

WHERE TO EAT AND STAY

O Palaiológos – ☎ *(27310) 83 373*. Convivial atmosphere and traditional dishes; popular with families from nearby Sparta.
Xenia – *Above the village* – ☎ *(27310) 20 500*. Overlooking the Sparta plain. Traditional Greek cuisine and a pleasant rosé wine. Reserve in advance on weekends.
Byzantion – *Village centre* – ☎ *(27310) 833 09, www.byzantion-hotel.gr – 6rm.* P Spacious rooms and bathrooms, swimming pool.

EVENTS AND FESTIVALS

Exhibitions and concerts at the site start in July and run into the autumn.
Local festival – 26-31 August, market and traditional music concerts.

Visit

Open every day in summer 8am-7pm (site closes at 7.30pm); winter 8.30am-3pm. 5€. ☎ (27310) 83 377. Bring water and comfortable shoes; modest dress required to visit the churches.
The road from Sparta presents a lovely **view**★★ of Mystra, a patch of white on the dark bulk of Mount Taígetos. Beyond Néa Mistrás, a pleasant flower-bedecked village, rise the ruins of old Mystra widely scattered on a stulling hillside **site**★★★.
The Ancient city consisted of three distinct sections: the castle *(kástro)* built by the De Villehardouins, the Upper Town for the aristocracy, and the Lower Town where

R Mattes/MICHELIN

Upper Town of Mystra, cultural and spiritual centre of Byzantine Greece.

the citizens lived. There are two entrances: to the Lower Town through the main gate; and to the Upper Town, via the road that skirts the site.

Lower Town★★ 1

The 14C defensive wall enclosed the cathedral, several churches and monasteries, elegant houses and craftsmen's workshops. Enter through the little **fort** that marks the site of the old town gate and turn right towards the cathedral.

Mitrópoli★★

The Metropolitan Orthodox Cathedral of St Demetrios (1270) stands below street level. The narthex was added in 1291 by Nikephoros (named as the founder of the church in an inscription on the wall of the stairway).

In the precinct there is a court with steps descending to the parvis of the cathedral.

The paving continues round the northeast side of the church into an 18C arcaded court overlooking the Evrótas Valley; the Roman sarcophagus decorated with a carving of a Bacchanalian revel and winged sphinxes was used as a basin for the Mármara Fountain.

Church

Built in the late 13C as a basilica with a central nave and two vaulted side aisles, the church was reconstructed (15C) on a cruciform plan with domes: in the nave the join between the 13C and 15C work is clearly visible. The columns in the nave bear engraved inscriptions listing the privileges bestowed on the cathedral by the emperors.

Note on the floor in front of the iconostasis a stone bearing the crowned Byzantine eagle showing the place where Constantine Palaiologos is said to have been consecrated Emperor of Byzantium in 1449. There are a few low-relief sculptures (9C-11C) taken from the ruins of Ancient Sparta. Note also the 13C-14C **frescoes**★ throughout the interior (Last Judgement in the narthex; martyrdom of St Demetrios in the north aisle; Virgin and Child in the central apse).

Museum

Same opening hours as site. Closed Mon.

The collection, founded by Gabriel Millet, is displayed in the old bishops' palace. Among the Byzantine sculptures are an Eagle seizing its Prey (11C) and a Christ in Majesty (15C).

Farther west along the street is the mortuary chapel of the Evangelístria (14C-15C); the well-proportioned cruciform distyle structure stands in a little cemetery not far from the Brontocheion Monastery.

Moní Vrondohíou★★

Within the walls of the Brontocheion Monastery are two great churches.

Ágii Theódori★

St Theodore's Church was built on the cruciform plan late in the 13C; it has been heavily restored. The dome, which rests on a 16-sided tall drum, is the most imposing feature. The angles of the cruciform plan contain four funerary chapels.

Odigítria★★

Dedicated to the Virgin, this church is also known as the *Afendikó* (belonging to the Master) because it was built in the 14C by Pachomios, an important ecclesiastic in the Orthodox Church. Its architecture is a combination of the basilical plan with a nave and side aisles on the ground floor and the cruciform plan topped by domes in the upper storey, according to a design found only in Mystra. The approach provides a spectacular view of the apse with triple windows, blind arches and the different roof levels. Both the church and the belfry have been restored.

The interior is decorated with remarkable **murals**★★ (14C) by several different artists. Those in the narthex reveal flowing composition, harmony of colours and introspective expressions suggesting the hand of a great artist, perhaps the equal of Duccio and Giotto.

The funerary chapel at the far end of the narthex *(left)* contains the tombs of Pachomios, shown offering his church to the Virgin, and Theodore I Palaiologos, shown both as despot and as the monk he became at the end of his life; among the other paintings is a very well-preserved Procession of Martyrs in red raiment.

The walls of a second chapel at the other end of the narthex are covered with inscriptions copied from *chrysobulls*, the imperial decrees granting goods and privileges to the monastery.

The paintings on the ground floor are mostly effigies of saints; in the central apse are the saintly hieratic prelates. The brilliantly coloured paintings in the galleries evoke the Resurrection and the Flight into Egypt; saints are portrayed on the walls *(access through the Chrysobulls Chapel).*

▶ *From the monastery precinct take the path leading uphill towards the Pandánassa Monastery.*

Moní Pandánassas★★

Dedicated in 1428, the **monastery** is today inhabited by a few nuns who do very fine embroidery work. The main entrance leads into a narrow courtyard; on the left are the conventual cells; straight ahead are steps ascending to the church.

Church

The elegant east portico of this beautiful 15C structure is a charming spot to pause and enjoy the magnificent **view**★★ of the Evrótas Valley. The narthex contains the tomb of Manuel Katzikis, who died in 1445 and is shown in effigy on the wall. The church itself is decorated with **paintings**★ from various periods.

Beyond the church, the path descends past the **house of Phrangopoulos** (Ikia Frangópoulou), which dates from the 15C; note the machicolated balcony.

Moní Perivléptou★★

This tiny **monastery** dates from the Frankish period (13C) but was altered in the 14C when the murals were executed.

The entrance to the precinct is an attractive arched gateway; over the arch is a low relief showing a row of fleurs-de-lis surmounted by the lions of Flanders flanking a circle containing the word *'perívleptos'* (which means 'attracting attention from every side') in the form of a cross; this heraldic device and motto indicate the founder of the monas-

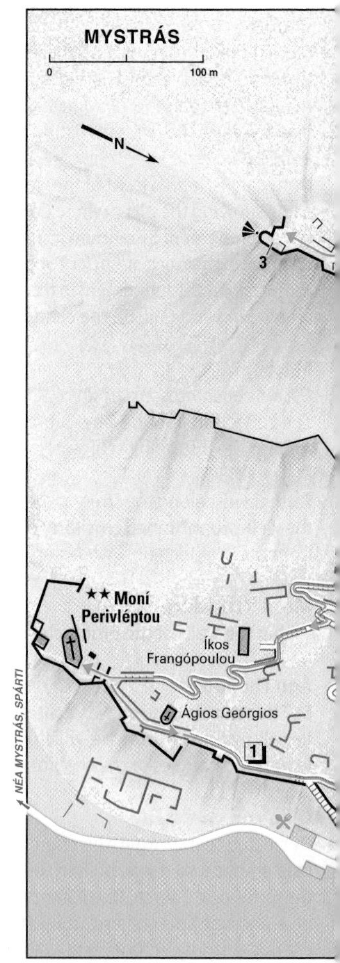

tery, who was one of the first two Latin emperors of Constantinople, Baldwin of Flanders or his brother Henry.

Church

From the gateway there is a picturesque view of the church with its two external funerary chapels beyond which rises a 13C tower. A door to the right of the chevet leads into the interior, which is decorated with an exceptional series of 14C **murals**★★★ illustrating the New Testament and the Life of the Virgin.

The church is linked to the old monolithic **hermitage,** which consists of a single chamber converted into a chapel and to St Catherine's Chapel, an early sanctuary surmounted by a belfry on the clifftop.

On leaving the Perívleptos Monastery take the path which passes **Ágios Geórgios**, a baronial funerary chapel dedicated to St George, the entrance *(right)* to the Kríni **Marmáras**, which takes its name from a marble fountain, and Ágios Hristoóforos *(left)*, a funerary chapel dedicated to St Christopher.

Íkos Láskari

The Lascaris House is a fine example of a 14C patrician house. It is thought to have belonged to the famous Lascaaris family, related to the emperors of Byzantium and

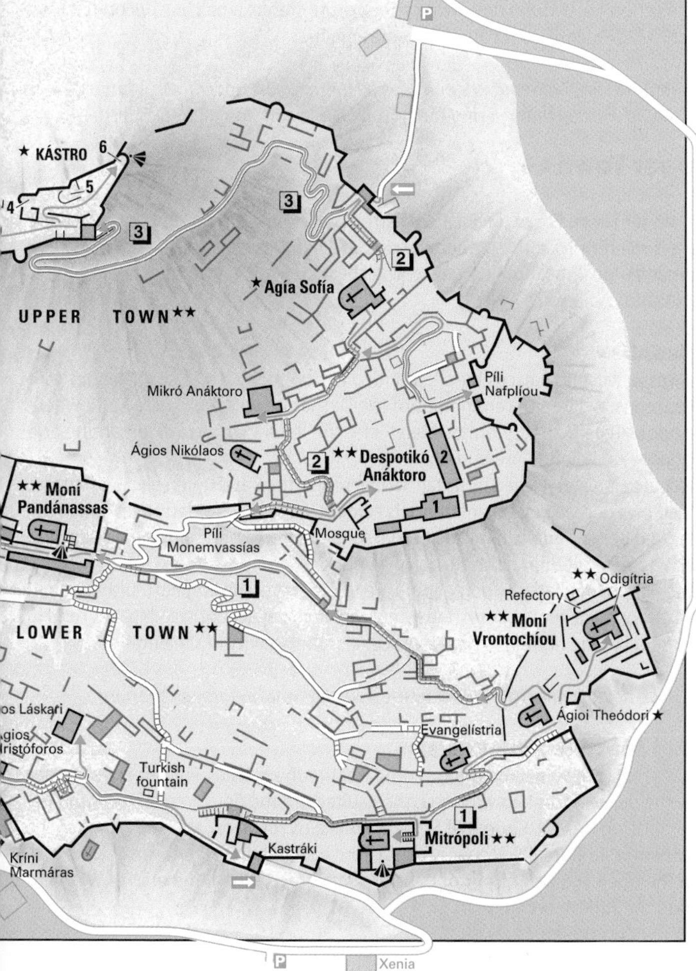

Moní Perivléptou

family of the humanists, Constantine and **John Láscaris** (1445-1534). The vaulted chamber on the ground floor was probably the stable; a balcony decorated with machicolations looks out over the Eurotas plain.

Return to the main entrance and drive up the hill to the Upper Town. Visitors on foot should walk up through the Monemvassía Gate and start at the Despots' Palace.

Upper Town★★ 2

The Upper Town, site of the Castle (Kástro), is enclosed within 13C ramparts; there were two entrances: the Monemvassía Gate *(*Píli Monemvassías – *east)* and the Nauplion Gate (Píli Nafplíou – *west).* Near the modern entrance from the upper car park stands Agía Sofía.

Agía Sofía★

St Sophia was the palace church, founded in the 14C by the Despot Manuel Kantakouzenos, where the ceremonies of the Despotate were conducted and where Theodora Tocchi and Cleophas Malatesta, the Italian wives of Constantine and Theodore Palaiologos, are buried.
The church is distinguished by its tall narrow proportions and by its spacious narthex, roofed by a dome. Western influence is evident in the three-sided apses and in the detached bell tower, Traces of an internal spiral staircase suggest that the tower was used as a minaret during the Turkish occupation.
In the interior beneath the dome there are fragments of the original multi-coloured marble floor. The most interesting murals are in the apse (Christ in Majesty) and in the chapel to the right (fine narrative scene of the Nativity of the Virgin).

Head down to the Little Palace by the path that weaves through the ruins.

Mikró Anáktoro (Little Palace)

This is a huge house incorporating a corner keep with a balcony. For defensive reasons only the upper floors had windows; the vaulted ground floor was lit by loopholes. After passing the 17C Church of St Nicholas (Ágios Nikólaos), the path reaches the **Monemvassía Gate** (Píli Monemvassías). Turn back uphill past the ruins of a mosque into the open square in front of the Despots' Palace, where the market was held during the Turkish occupation.

Despotikó Anáktoro★★

Closed to the public for restoration.

The Despots' Palace consists of two wings: the northeast wing dates from the 13C-14C, the northwest from the 15C. The building at the east end of the **northeast wing** (**1**) dates from the 13C and was probably built either by the Franks or by the first Byzantine governors. Under the despots it was probably used as a guardroom. Next come two smaller buildings; the more northerly contained kitchens.

The last building in this group is a great structure with several storeys (late 14C). It was designed as the residence of the despot Manuel Kantakouzenos. The north façade sports an elegant porch supporting a balcony decorated with machicolations overlooking the Lakonian plain.

The **northwest wing** (**2**) wing consists of an imposing three-storey building constructed by the Palaiologi early in the 15C. The lowest floor, which is partially underground, is faced on the courtyard side by a row of round-headed arches supporting a terrace on the middle floor. The top floor consisted of an immense hall for receptions and entertainment. The throne stood in the centre of the east wall in a shallow alcove.

Turn right at the south end of the wing down to the **Nauplion Gate** (13C) for a fine external view of the ramparts before returning to the modern entrance.

Kástro★ 3

A steep and winding path (steps) leads up from the modern entrance to the Kástro (45min on foot there and back).

Built in the 13C by De Villehardouin, the structure was much altered by the Byzantines, the Venetians and the Turks. William II de Villehardouin and his wife Anna Comnena held court there in grand style, surrounded by knights from Champagne, Burgundy and Flanders.

The fortress consists of two baileys. The entrance to the first is guarded by a vaulted gateway flanked by a stout square tower; the southeast corner of the bailey is marked by an underground cistern and a huge round tower (**3**) which gives impressive **views**★★ of the ravine facing Mount Taígetos.

The inner bailey *(northwest)* contained the baronial apartments (**4**) *(left on entering)*, another cistern and the castle chapel (**5**) of which only traces remain. The ruined tower (**6**) on the highest point provides spectacular **views**★★ down into the many gullies in the wild slopes of Mount Taígetos; in the other direction lie the ruins of Mystra, modern Sparta and the Evrótas plain.

MONEMVASSÍA★★

Μονεμβασια

POPULATION 90

MICHELIN MAP 737 H 12 – LAKONÍA – PELOPONNESE.

Invisible from the coast, this silent, partially ruined medieval fortified town sits in a slight depression on the southern face of a steep rocky peninsula. The peninsula, linked to the mainland by a narrow causeway and a bridge, takes its name from the Greek words móni emvassía meaning 'only entrance'.

- **Orient Yourself:** 350km/217mi from Athens, 202km/126mi south of Nauplion and 110km/69mi southeast of Sparta. Monemvassía is difficult to access by road. It is easily reached by hovercraft from Piraeus (2hr 30min). A dike connects Monemvassía to the town of Gefyra; shuttles operate from there (every 15min).
- **Parking:** Vehicles are banned from the medieval centre.
- **Don't Miss:** The view from the citadel, at dawn and at dusk.
- **Organizing Your Time:** The best light is in the morning.
- **Also See:** Máni, Spárti, Kíthira

A Bit of History

Monemvassía was fortified by the Byzantines against the Slav invasions, but in 1248, after a three-year blockade, it fell into the hands of **William de Villehardouin**. The Franks repaired the castle, but in 1263 William was obliged to return it to Michael VIII Palaiologos as part of his ransom.

Under the Despotate of Morea *(see MISTRÁS)* and during the subsequent Turkish and Venetian occupations, Monemvassia was an active trading port. The town was protected by a fortified bridge, by a castle on the top of the rock and by a circuit wall that enclosed the town on three sides.

In 1909 **Iánnis Rítsos** was born here. The dissident Greek poet was persecuted (and imprisoned) by the authorities for his beliefs.

The city has undergone a major restoration programme and all construction is strictly controlled. Since the 1970s it has become a popular location for holiday homes.

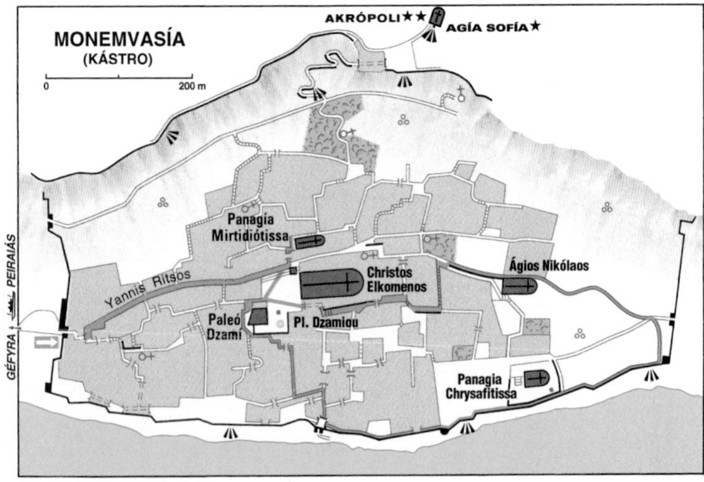

Visit

Kástro★★

This forms the old or lower town. Begin at the causeway and proceed through the West Gate; both it and the walls date from the Despotate.

Walk up the main street between the ancient houses to the main square.

Platía Dzamíou

This charming square extends south into a terrace graced by an 18C cannon and the observation hole of an underground cistern. On the east side stands the **Church of Christ in Chains** (Hrístos Elkomenós), a former cathedral (12C; rebuilt 17C); note the detached Italianate bell tower, and the symbolic peacocks carved in low relief on a piece of Byzantine sculpture that has been re-used in the façade. Inside are some beautiful Byzantine icons, including one of the Crucifixion (14C). In a 16C mosque, there is a fine **archaeological collection** highlighting everyday life in Monemvassia; it's a good introduction to the visit *(open Tue-Sun 8.30am-3pm; no charge)*.

Walk down to the ramparts along the seafront and follow them eastwards.

Address Book

For coin categories, see the Legend on the cover flap.

WHERE TO EAT

Fótis – *Géfira, beginning of the seafront road.* Unpretentious bistro offering souvláki and pita dishes.
Limanáki – *Géfira, just before the bridge.* Traditional taverna where dishes are selected from the kitchen.
Matoúla – *Monemvassía, Kástro, below the main street.* Lovely outdoor location. Fine dishes such as *saganáki* and delicious *arnáki*.
To Kanóni – *Monemvassía, off the main street.* The *pikilía* (appetisers) are especially good.
Le Castellano – *On the dike – ☎ 7320) 199 94 – Breakfast and dinner.* Traditional Greek specialties along with classics of French and Italian cuisine. Excellent wine list.

WHERE TO STAY

Villa Doúka – *Géfira, 3km/2mi north of the town – ☎ (27320) 61 181, fax (27320) 61 751 – 25 studios and apts (4-7 pers.).* Activities include table tennis and basketball; long sandy beach. Good base for families with cars.
Beléssis – *Géfira, to the right of the main road. – ☎ and fax (27320) 61 217 – 10rm and 5 apts.* Traditional old house, close to the road; more modern rooms set back a little off a quiet patio.
Villa Diamantí – *Topalti district, just before Géfira – ☎ (27320) 61 534 – 9rm and 12 bungalows.* Decent rooms and communal kitchen in the hotel. Well-equipped bungalows with terraces.
Malvasia – *Monemvassía, Kástro – ☎ (27320) 61 323, fax (27320) 61 722 – 28rm.* Occupying three historic properties in the town, the magnificent rooms with traditional decor tempt the visitor to stay a little longer in Monemvassía. Below one of these houses (Ritsou) is a permanent bathing platform.

TAKING A BREAK

Traditional cake shop in Géfira below the Minoa Hotel, on the main street. Almond shortbread biscuits, etc.

EVENTS AND FESTIVALS

Local festivals – For five days around 23 July the town celebrates its liberation from the Turks. Traditional singing and dances.

The citadel and lower town of Monemvassía

Southern Rampart

There are extensive views of the sea and the Peloponnese coast south towards Cape Malea. The landing at Portello is an excellent spot for a swim as are nearby **beaches**: Géfyra and, farther north, Xifias *(6km/3.75mi)* and Pori *(4km/2.5mi)*.

Panagía Hrissafítissa

The façade of this 16C church looks very Venetian with its framed doorway surmounted by an oculus; the open space in front was used as a parade ground. Near the ramparts stands a tiny chapel built over the "sacred spring"; it contains an icon from Chrysapha (Hríssafa) near Sparta.

Stroll the sentry walk to the corner bastion; return and descend to visit **St Nicholas'** (Ágios Nikólaos) which has a 16C Venetian doorway. The churches of St Demetrios (Ágios Dimítrios), St Anthony (Ágios Andónios), St Andrew (Ágios Andréas) and St Anne (Agía Anna), a 14C basilica, can also be visited. Nearby are several Venetian houses; note the door and window mouldings, flamboyant recesses and broad-mouthed chimneys.

▸ *Return to Dzamiou square; an alley leads to the Church of Panagía Mirtidiótissa.*

Panagía Mirtidiótissa or Kritikia

Closed for restoration at time of publication.

This little church dates from the Frankish period (13C); It has a beautiful iconostasis carved in wood. It was once a command post belonging to the Templars and then to the Knights of St John of Jerusalem.

Akrópoli★★

Originally the citadel covered a wide area; the ruined fortifications are mostly Venetian (16C). Visitors who cannot climb all the way to the citadel *(15min)* are advised to go halfway up, if possible, for a very fine **view**★★★ of the lower town.

A vaulted passage in the fortified entrance emerges into an open space; take the path leading north up the hill to the Church of St Sophia.

Agía Sofía★

Principal church of the citadel, this large Byzantine church on the cliff's edge offers a vertiginous **view**★★★ of the sea below.

The recently restored building (11C) may have been occupied by Cistercians during the Frankish period; it was refurbished during the 14C-15C. There are some unusual

M Guillochon/MICHELIN

The church of Agía Sofía, built on the edge of a cliff

early-Byzantine capitals in shallow relief, Byzantine marble carvings over the doors in the narthex and traces of murals.
A rough path leads to the **highest point** on the rock overlooking the isthmus and the mountains to the west. From there, return to the main gate and follow the sentry walk westwards to reach the highest point along the circuit wall: splendid **views**★★ of the old town and the coast.

Excursions

Liménas Géraka

16km/10mi north of Monemvassía on the coast road. Hydrofoil landing stage.
A charming fishing village tucked away in an impressive little rocky bay.

Molái

24km/15mi northwest of Monemvassía on the road to Sparta.
A few remains, a palaeo-Christian Byzantine church and the ruins of a medieval fort are visible here; mosaic paving of three 6C BC temples can be seen in Halasmata.

Neápoli

61km/38mi south of Monemvassía.
This small town stands opposite the wonderful little island of Elafónissos. There are only a few remains here, since the Ancient city is now beneath the waves. The bays with their crystal-clear water and golden beaches are perfect for swimming.

NÁFPAKTOS

NAUPAKTOS – Ναυπακτοσ

POPULATION 12 924

MICHELIN MAP 737 F 8 – AKARNANÍA – CENTRAL GREECE.

A charming city 100km/63mi west of Delphi makes for an agreeable alternative to Patras as a base for exploring the surrounding area. It is better known by its medieval name of Lepanto, recalling the naval battle which took place in 1571 off Missolonghi. *At the port, 1 Noti. Botsaris. (26340) 385 33. Open daily.*

Address Book

WHERE TO EAT

⊖ **Spittikó** – A traditional taverna on the beach, popular with locals.
⊖**Tsaras Taverna** – *Odós Ioan. Kanavou* – ☎ *(26340) 278 09.* Tasty traditional dishes, views from the terrace.

WHERE TO STAY

⊖ **Diethnes** – *3 Athinas Nova, near the port* – ☎ *(26340) 27 342.* Pleasant, colorful interior; good value hotel.
⊖ **Akti** – *East of the town, looking out to sea* – ☎ *(26340) 484 64 – akti@otenet.gr – 59rm.* Very near the beach, contemporary decor with all modern comforts. All rooms have balconies.
⊖ **Lepando Beach** – *Odós Gribova* – ☎ *926340) 239 31, lepangoh@otenet.gr – 48rm.* Large, comfortable hotel.

SPORTS AND LEISURE

For information on outdoor sports, (kayaking, hiking, mountain biking), check with **Club Metavasi** ☎ *(26340) 245 56, www.metavasi.com.*

G Gautier/MICHELIN

Visit

Harbour

The entrance to the oval basin is protected by two towers fortified with crenellations and merlons. Views of the town and the citadel from the parapet walk.

Citadel

Access from the west of the town by a narrow road that climbs through the pine trees. The Venetian fortress dates from the Middle Ages; its walls extend downhill to link it with the harbour; other walls built laterally divide the town into compartments, each one forming one forming a keep. Views of the town and the straits from the top.

NÁFPLIO★★

NAUPLION – Ναφπλιο

POPULATION 13 822

MICHELIN MAP 737 G 10 – ARGOLIS – PELOPONNESE.

Nauplion occupies a delightful site on a rocky peninsula jutting into the Argolic Gulf. It is a charming old town dominated by its citadel and the powerful Venetian fort of Palamedes. Nauplion is a pleasant place to stay, having harmoniously integrated the many different styles of its successive invaders. *Odós 25 Martiou.* ☎ *(27520) 24 444.* *Open daily 7.30am-2.30pm, 4-8pm.*

- **Orient Yourself:** 64km/40mi south of Corinth and 132km/85mi southwest of Athens. by the Corinth motorway. From the exit, follow signs to the centre of town.
- **Parking:** Free lot at the port (crowded on weekends!)
- **Don't Miss:** A stroll through the charming old town.

Organizing Your Time: A day won't do it; if time permits, stop here for a sojourn of several days.
Especially for Kids: Kombolóï Museum, Folk Art Museum
Also See: Argolída, Aktí, Arkadías, Arhéa Epídavros, Mikínes, Tírintha

A Bit of History

Legend has it that Nauplios, grandson of the sea god Poseidon, founded the city. Nauplion passed from the Byzantines to the Franks in 1247, then to the Venetians, who fortified the city and Boúrdzi Island. Turkish forces occupied the region in 1540, making Nauplion capital of Morea. In the 17C the town, together with Chios, was one of the main centres of trade with the West.
In 1686, however, Nauplion was recaptured by Venetian troops. For 30 years Nauplion boomed with new construction and an influx of people. This period of prosperity ended in 1715 with the return of the Turks; pillage, massacre and deportations followed. Not until 20 November 1822, when **Staïkópoulos** captured the Palamedes Fort, was Nauplion wrenched from Turkish control.
In 1828 **John Kapodístrias**, the first Governor of Greece, installed his government in Nauplion and the city officially became the capital of Greece in the following

Address Book

For coin categories, see the Legend on the cover flap.

WHERE TO EAT

To Sokáki – *Between Sýndagma Square and the King Otto Hotel.* Excellent full breakfasts, giant crepes, and enormous mixed ice creams.
O Noulis – *22 Odós Moutsourídou, an alley on the right at the bottom of Odós Papanikolaou.* Traditional, popular with locals. The tray with 10 different types of *meze* is a meal in itself.
Ta Fanaria – *Odós Stoikopoulou.* Excellent cooking (the chef has been here for 25 years); and streetside tables.
Nautikos Omilos Náfplio – *Nauplion Sailing Club, seafront road at the foot of the walls.* Fine views over the Gulf of Argolid, traditional cuisine and quality service. Book ahead.

WHERE TO STAY

Pension Dimitri Becas – *Odós Efthimiopoulou – ☎ (27520) 27 549 – 8rm.* This modest guesthouse has some rooms with showers and WCs. Fine views over the town; good value.
Omorphi Poli – *5 Odós Sofróni – ☎ (27520) 21 565 – 7rm (2 suites).* Creatively decorated hotel feels like a traditional Greek house. Breakfast on the ground floor. Good value.
King Otto – *4 Odós Farmakopoúlou – ☎ and fax (27520) 27 595 – 11rm.* Ideally located, this hotel is a refurbished neo-Classical house. Small but comfortable rooms. Copious breakfast.
Marianna – *9 Odós Potamianoú – ☎ (27520) 24 256 – 12rm.* Bright and clean, all the rooms look out onto the harbour and the town. Laundry service and good breakfast.
Nausimedon – *9 Odós Merarhías, near the old railway station – ☎ (27520) 25 060 – 13rm, 3 bungalows.* Magnificent mansion with high-ceilinged rooms and antique furnishings. Cocktails served under the palm trees in the gardens.

TAKING A BREAK

Stathmós – The ideal spot for a train buff; located in the old railway station.
Antica Gelateria di Roma – *Odós Farmakopoúlou, in front of King Otto Hotel.* Serving artisanal ice cream since 1870.

SHOPPING

Don't leave Nauplion without worry beads (*komboloï*); great selection at the **House of Amber** *(12 Odós Konstandinou).* Food of the gods, all honey-based delicacies, can be sampled at **Nectar and Ambrosia** *(Odos Farmakopoulo).*

year. But bitter dissension developed and on 27 September 1831 Kapodístrias was assassinated on the steps of St Spiridon's Church by his political opponents. The Great Powers – England, France and Russia – turned to **Otto of Bavaria**, then 17 years old; his accession to the throne was ratified in 1832 by a National Assembly held in **Prónia**.

Otto's reign was marked by the construction of neo-Classical buildings, their sober lines lend the city its aristocratic character. A colossal carved lion in Prónia commemorates the sacrifice of the Bavarian soldiers who fell in the Greek cause. There are other monuments and inscriptions recalling the days of newly won independence.

Visit

Palamídi★★

Access by Leofóros 25 Martíou and the road leading to the east entrance or by steps (20min climb) from Platía Arvanitiás. Open daily, 8am-6.45pm. 4€. (27520) 28 036.

The **Palamedes Fort** dates from the second Venetian occupation (1686-1715) and is a powerful complex of eight bastions linked by defilades, vaults, corridors and secret passages. St Andrew's Bastion enclosed a courtyard overlooked by the quarters of the Governor of the Fort and by St Andrew's Chapel, near the cell in which Kolokotrónis was detained.

The parapet walk provides magnificent views of Nauplion, the bay, the Argolid plain and the coastline of the Peloponnese.

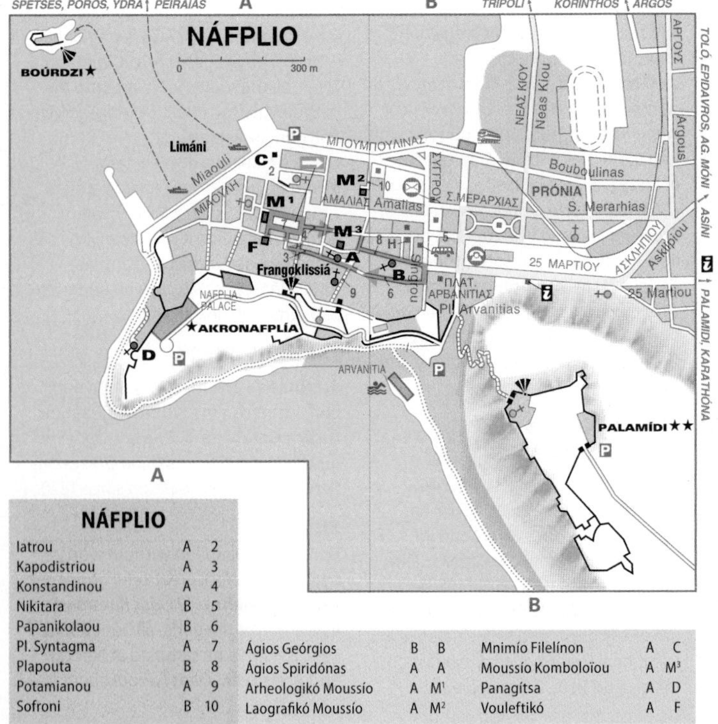

NÁFPLIO

Street		
Iatrou	A	2
Kapodistriou	A	3
Konstandinou	A	4
Nikitara	B	5
Papanikolaou	B	6
Pl. Syntagma	A	7
Plapouta	B	8
Potamianou	A	9
Sofroni	B	10

Sight		
Ágios Geórgios	B	B
Ágios Spiridónas	A	A
Arheologikó Moussío	A	M¹
Laografikó Moussío	A	M²
Mnimío Filelínon	A	C
Moussío Komboloïou	A	M³
Panagítsa	A	D
Vouleftikó	A	F

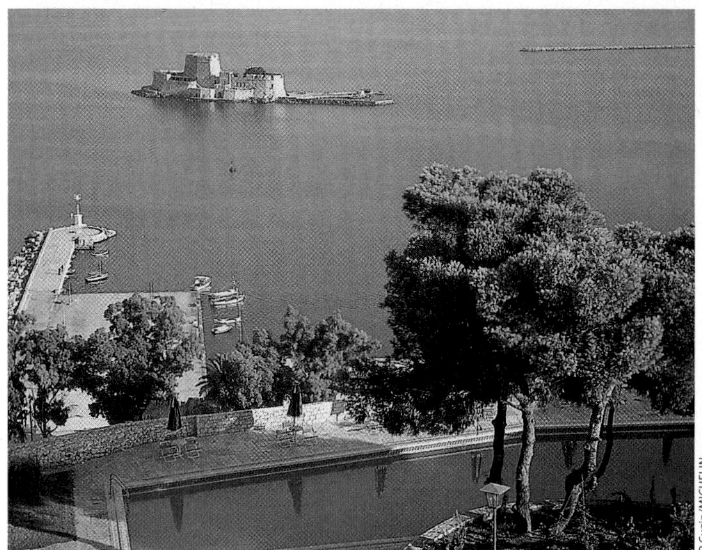

R Cuzin/MICHELIN

View from Palamedes Fort

Old Town★★

Platía Síndagmatos

Centre of Nauplion, the square served as the political forum during the struggle for independence. At the west end of the square stands a naval warehouse (1713) now converted into a museum; the cinema opposite was once a mosque. In the southwest corner of the square, a flight of steps leads to another former mosque, which was the site of the first meeting of the Greek National Assembly in 1822.
The **Archaeological Museum** *(closed for renovation at press time; ☎ (27520) 275 02)* is of interest for its rare Neolithic pottery and a magnificent fresco known as *'The Lady of Mycenae'*, and Archaic art found during excavations in the Argolid.

From the centre of the east side of the square take Odós Konstandínou, a busy shopping street; turn right and then left into Odós Plapoúta.

Ágios Geórgios

St George's Cathedral was built in the 16C in a mixture of Byzantine and Venetian architectural styles. The interior contains the throne of King Otto.

Turn right into Leofóros Singroú and return to the old town by Odós Papanikoláou, a narrow street crossed by steep lanes leading up to the Acronauplia. One of these lanes on the left (Odós Potamianou) leads to the Frankish Church.

Frangoklissiá

A flight of steps and an attractive 13C porch lead up to the **Frankish Church**. It was later converted into a mosque and then reverted to Roman Catholicism.
Inside stands a **Memorial to the Philhellenes** who fell in the Greek War of Independence. Behind the high altar is the Muslim prayer recess *(mihrab)*.

Return down Odós Potamianou to St Spiridon's Church near a Turkish fountain.

The Battle of Lepanto (7 October 1571)

The last and greatest battle to engage oar-propelled vessels took place in the Bay of Patras to the leeward of Oxiá Island, where the Christian fleet from Cephallonia met the Turkish fleet from Lepanto. The fleet of the Holy League was commanded by **Don John of Austria** (1547-78), then 23 years old. The Turkish fleet, led by Ali Pasha, consisted of 200 galleys.

The 12 Venetian galleys—huge ships carrying 750 men, of whom half manned the oars—wrought havoc among the Turkish fleet, most of which was destroyed. It was a severe blow to Turkish sea power.

The battle was the subject of many paintings by celebrated artists such as Titian, Tintoretto and Veronese; it also inspired some well-known works of poetry.

Ágios Spirídonas

St Spiridon's is a tiny Orthodox church built in 1702. Here on the threshold two members of the Mavromichalis family from the Máni assassinated Kapodístrias, who had imprisoned one of them, **Petrobey Mavromihális** (picture inside the church).

Continue along Odós Kapodistríou past another Turkish fountain and turn right on Odós Kokkinou to Odós Staikopoulou, a shopping street.

At no. 25 Odós Staikopoulou, stop in at the intriguing Kids **Kombolóï Museum** (*open Wed-Mon 9.30am-8.30pm, weekends 10am-8pm)* with over 200 *kombolóï* made of amber, stone, glass beads, ivory and shells.

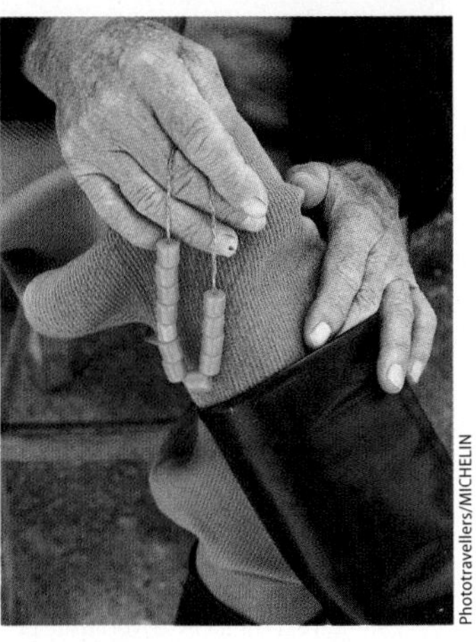
Phototravellers/MICHELIN

Man holding kombolóï

Seafront★★

About 2hr on foot. Starting from Platía Nikitará (northwest corner), take Leofóros Amalías and turn right on Odós Sofroni.

Well worth a stop, the charming Kids **Folk Art Museum** (*open daily 9am-1.30pm, 6-9pm; 4€)* presents daily life of centuries past via a remarkable collection of costumes from the Peloponnese, tools, jewellery and traditional embroidery

Harbour

This extends on both sides of Platía Iatroú, a square containing the Town Hall, St Nicholas' Church for sailors (early 18C) and the French Philhellene Monument. Views of the Isle of Boúrdzi.

The western waterfront (Aktí Miaoúli) continues into a path that skirts the ramparts and the headland, providing fine views of the bay. Just short of the southern tip of the promontory a path *(left)* leads up to the **Chapel of the Little Virgin** (Panagítsa), clinging precariously to the rocky slope.

Follow the coast (magnificent views of the sea and Palamedes Fort) to Arvanitiá, Nauplion's beach; then make for Platía Nikitará.

Isle of Boúrdzi★

Ask at the harbour for the times of the shuttle boats.

The island was first fortified in 1471 by the Venetians to protect the harbour entrance and was reinforced early in the 18C; view of the city and its two citadels.

Akronafplía★★ (Citadel of Acronauplia)

Access on foot by one of the steep lanes leading off Odós Potamianou; by car by the road from Arvanitiá.

First a Greek and then a Frankish fortress were built on Acronauplia. The final structure, which until recently housed a hospital, barracks and prison, consists of several wards with the lion of St Mark over the gates. From the walls there is a fine view down over the city, the harbour and the bay and up to the Palamedes Fort.

Outskirts

Karathóna Bay and Beach★★

3km/2mi south. Access by car by the road marked Palamídi from which a secondary road branches off to the bay.

A gently curving bay protected by an island encloses a huge sandy beach. From the neighbouring heights, views of Palamedes Fort and the Acronauplia.

Kazarma Acropolis

14km/8.75mi east, near the small town of Arkadiko: take the path (signposted) which leads to the top of the mountain (20min walk).

Remains of the fortress built by the Argives (5C BC) can be seen on the hillside.

Lerní

On the northwest shore of the Argolic Gulf near the modern village of **Míli** *lies the site of Ancient Lerna.*

The narrow tract of land between the road and the seashore contains the Hydra Springs and the Lerna Marshes, now much reduced in size but still inhabited by huge eels. The Ancient Greeks thought that the Lerna Marshes were bottomless and an entrance to the Underworld.

House of the Tiles

On leaving Míli going south, bear left after a church into a path leading to the site (200m/220yd). Open every day, 8.30am-2.30pm. 2€.

There is evidence of Neolithic activity here but it was during the Bronze Age that the settlement became prosperous. The **House of the Tiles** takes its name from the great quantities of tiles that were found among the foundations. This Ancient palace (2200 BC) is the best-preserved large building from the early Bronze Age.

Excursions

The Road to Toló

12km/7.5mi southeast. From Nauplion take the Epidauros road; after 1.5km/1mi turn right into a narrow road (sign 'Agía Moní').

Agía Moní

The monastery was founded in 1144 near the Kánathos Spring *(on the right below the convent)* which in mythology was supposed to return Hera to a state of virginity once a year. There is a guided tour by the monks of the 12C Byzantine church.

▶ *Return to the Epidauros road and continue for 2km/1.25mi. Turn right into the road to Toló; before reaching the coast, turn left into the road to Drépano, which passes a chapel near the Assíni acropolis.*

Assíni (Asine)

The acropolis of the Ancient city was mentioned by Homer in the Iliad. The remains of the ramparts are part Mycenaean and Archaic and part Hellenistic. Huge beehive tombs have yielded Mycenaean objects. From the top, fine **views**★★ of Toló.

Toló★

Toló is a popular and pleasant seaside resort sheltered by the Assíni promontory at the end of a long sandy beach with the islands of Rómvi and Platía offshore.

North to Agía Tríada

8km/5mi north. Take the Árgos road; immediately after the site of Tiryns (Tírintha) turn right into a minor road which runs through orange groves in the direction of Midéa.

Agía Triáda

On the left just before the village is the 12C **Church of the Virgin** (Kimisseos tis Theotókou). The village was previously known as Mérbaka after Wilhelm van Moerbeke, a Fleming who was Archbishop of Corinth in 1280.

Dendra

3km/2mi northeast of Agía Triáda.
1km/0.6mi from the village *(signposted)* is the burial chamber where the oldest known cuirass (15C BC) – was found (now in the Archaeological Museum of Nauplion).

Midéa

Follow the road out of Dendra up to the little village of Midéa (signposted). Turn right onto an asphalt road (3km/2mi) which leads up to the top of the mountain.
On a terrace on the mountainside lie the remains of the Cyclopean surrounding wall of a Mycenaean acropolis; Magificent **views**★ of the Plain of Árgos.

NEMÉA★

Νεμεα

MICHELIN MAP 737 G 10 – KORINTHÍA – PELOPONNESE.

The ruins of Neméa, legendary site of Herakles' (Hercules') first 'labour', lie in a peaceful valley between Mount Kilíni to the west and the slopes of the Argolid and Arcadian ranges to the south. It is 35km/22mi southwest of Corinth, and about the same distance northwest of Nauplion, with easy access by the E 65 Corinth-Tripoli motorway.

A Bit of History

Herakles' (Hercules) first labour or task was to kill the ferocious lion that lived in a nearby cave; the mythological hero strangled the beast and wore its skin as a trophy. Lions did, in fact, roam the region in the Mycenaean period (there are lion hunts depicted on items found at Mycenae).

Herakles and the Hydra of Lerna

In this labour Herakles (Hercules) had to confront the multiheaded monster Hydra, daughter of the viper Echidna, whose putrid breath had the power to kill. The Hydra was protected by the Goddess Hera, who hated Herakles (her husband Zeus's illegitimate son). While he was doing battle with the monster, she sent a giant sea creature who attacked Herakles, injuring his heel before being killed by him.

Herakles could not kill the Hydra single-handedly (the heads grew back as soon as they were cut off); his nephew Iolaos came to his aide by setting the nearby woods alight and applying flame to the severed necks of the monster. Thus cauterised, the Hydra was unable to regenerate its heads.

In the Archaic and Classical periods the Nemean Games were one of the four great competitions of the Greek world. Nowadays modern Neméa's reputation rests on its red wine, which is strong and sweet and known locally as 'the blood of Herakles'.

Visit

Ruins★

Open Tue-Sun 8am-7pm; Mon 8am-12pm. 3€ (combined ticket with Stadium 4€).

The largest set of ruins here were part of a huge Doric **temple of Zeus** (4C BC). Three columns are still standing, and other displaced drums lie about. A ramp marks the centre of the façade; in front stood an immense sacrificial altar.

Formerly a grove of sacred cypress trees ringed the sanctuary, which was surrounded by buildings including nine houses *(oikoi)* built for participants in the Nemean Games. To the north were potters' ovens *(now reburied)*. The thermal baths from the same period *(recently laid bare and roofed over for protection)* consisted of two covered underground rooms, reached by stairs lined with columns.

South of the temple are some Ancient remains converted by the Byzantines into a church. To the south of this, one of the cemetery's 200 tombs is reconstructed.

H Champollion/MICHELIN

Remnants of the Temple of Zeus

Museum★

The museum displays engravings, drawings, photographs and visitors' notes relating to the site. Among the objects in the collection are architectural elements and inscriptions unearthed during the excavations, most notably 312 items from the **Mycenaean cemetery of Aidonia**. The treasure comprises many objects of precious stone and metal: rings, seals, ornaments, necklaces and pendants. A scale model depicts the site and the sanctuary as they were in the 4C BC.

Stadium★

Turn left when exiting the ruins, then left again at the next junction; the stadium is 100m/110yd farther, on the right, before a bend. Same opening hours as the ruins.
In the hillside southeast of the Temple of Zeus lie the remnants of the stadium (4C BC) where the Nemean Games took place. It held 40 000 spectators. South of the arena, earthenware pipes supplied the stadium with spring water, purified in a system of basins and stone gutters around the arena. The starting line, marked with stones, is well preserved; it supported the wooden mechanism which gave the starting signal. The competitors, trainers and judges entered the stadium through a building whose interior was decorated with colonnades on three of its sides. It was here, too, that the athletes got ready for the competition, before entering the arena through a vaulted passage. The names of some of the winners and young athletes are clearly legible on the walls.

Excursion

Límni Stimfalía★ (Lake Stymphalos)

30km/19mi west of Neméa. Take the road to Kalianoi; follow signs to Karteri.
The route crosses the coastal plain and then climbs the eastern foothills of Mount Kilíni overlooking the Gulf of Corint. The road then descends into the huge and barren depression at the bottom of which lies Lake Stymphalos. *Park in the car park and take the path up the hill overlooking the lake.*

Lake★

Below the acropolis of the city of Stymphalos extends an immense reed-covered marsh surrounded by a ring of dark peaks. This vast tract of land is inhabited only by herds of cows or flocks of sheep grazing in the custody of herdsmen swathed in thick cloaks and carrying crooks. Stymphalos is on the borders of Arcadia.

The Stymphalian Birds

According to the legend the gloomy waters of Lake Stymphalos were haunted by nauseating birds with huge wings who seized on passers-by, suffocating them and killing them with their beaks before eating them. **Herakles** (Hercules) rid the region of them as the fifth of his Twelve Labours by killing them with his arrows and then offering them to Athena.

Old Abbey of Zaraká

On the east side of the road from Kiáto lie the ruins of a Cistercian monastery (13C). The church was Gothic: the pillars in the nave were formed of engaged columns and the chancel was square, a Cistercian hallmark. The cloisters were on the south side. A single tower marks the entrance to the precinct.

Remains of the city

500m/550yd beyond the town and old abbey, take the path through the fields that leads to the foot of the rock.
Here lie traces of the Temple of Athena Polias, a palaestra, and stairs carved into the rock. Make a detour to the small town of Kartéri *(good tavernas)* and at the church turn left towards Lafka: here, at the entrance to the village, a road on the left leads to the opposite side of the lake.

OLIMBÍA★★★

OLYMPIA – Ολυμπια

MICHELIN MAP 737 E 10 – ELIS – PELOPONNESE.

Here at the heart of the idyllic Alfiós Valley, the ruins of Olympia bear witness to the grandeur of the Ancient Sanctuary of Zeus which, through the Olympic Games, was a symbol of Greek unity. Physical and intellectual prowess, a spirit of concord and peace; such were the aspirations which in Antiquity drew Greeks from all states to the Games at Olympia some 2800 years ago. *in the middle of the main street. ☎ (26240) 23 100. Open daily Jun-Sep 9am-9pm.*

- **Orient Yourself:** The ruins of Olympia lie in the western Peloponnese, 110km/69mi south of Patras, 17km/11mi east of Pírgos and 215km/134mi south-west of Corinth. The modern village extends past the ruins.
- **Don't Miss:** The Ancient ruins and the Archaeological Museum.
- **Organizing Your Time:** Allow 1 day; see the museum in the heat of the day.
- **Also See:** Hlemoútsi, Kalamáta, Pátras

A Bit of History

The site★★ – Below the wooded slopes of Mount Kronion (125m/410ft) the Sanctuary of Zeus shelters in a grove of trees between the Alfiós (Alpheios) and its tributary the Kládeos. Upstream the valley of the Alfiós narrows between the foothills of the mountains of Arcadia; downstream it widens out towards the Elian plain in a fertile basin surrounded by gently rolling hills.

The first primitive cult centre at Olympia seems to have been a sacred grove, the Áltis, which was succeeded by a sanctuary, dedicated to Kronos, the god of Time. The subsequent cult of Kronos' son Zeus drew pilgrimages to Mount Kronion.

The Olympic Games – The Herakles legend aside (the hero is said to have founded the competitions), the institution of the Olympic Games seems to date from the 8C BC when Iphitos, King of Pisa, and Lycurgus of Sparta organised a sporting competition among the Greek people, to occur every four years. While the games were in progress a sacred truce lasting one month was observed. The games reached the height of their popularity in the 5C BC, drawing 150 000 to 200 000 people.

Address Book

For coin categories, see the Legend on the cover flap.

WHERE TO EAT

Bacchus – *Mirakas*. This village taverna serves inventive and enjoyable local dishes. Try the aubergine fritters, sausage *(loukániko)* or the perfectly cooked kebabs.

WHERE TO STAY

Poseidon – *Karamanli – b (26240) 225 67 – 10rm.* Simple, quiet and clean; attractive price.

Krónio – *Odós Kondíli (the main street) – ☎ (26240) 22 188 – 24rm.* Simple hotel, good value; comfortable rooms with balconies and bathrooms.

Europa – *On the hill overlooking Olympia – ☎ (26240) 22 650 – www.bestwestern.com – 78rm.* An excellent hotel situated in the middle of wooded parkland; taverna under the trees, swimming pool.

Antonios – *Near the cemetery – ☎ (26240) 22 348 – 65rm.* A large, modern establishment surrounded by pine trees. Very comfortable rooms.

The festivities, which included cult ceremonies, took place in summer. The athletic contests themselves lasted for only five days and included running, boxing, wrestling, the pancration (combination of wrestling and boxing), the pentathlon (running, jumping, wrestling, discus and the javelin), horse racing and chariot racing.
The victors were crowned with olive wreaths and honored at a banquet. Their native cities often built monuments or treasuries for offerings honouring the gods.

The Roman era – **Nero** supplemented the athletic contests with music and poetry competitions, and in the 2C AD Hadrian and Herodes Atticus carried out repairs to houses, paths, aqueducts and *nymphaea*.
But gradually the Games declined. People no longer attended the religious festival and then Theodosius prohibited the pagan cults; the Games were held for the last time in AD 393. The statue of Zeus was sent to Constantinople where it was destroyed in a fire in AD 475. Dilapidation and destruction assisted by earthquakes, rock falls and the Alfiós floods reduced the site to ruins. Eventually it was plundered, then covered in a thick layer of mud.

Rediscovery and Excavation – The first excavations were conducted by scholars accompanying a 1828 French military expedition to the Morea. They explored the Temple of Zeus in 1829, removing metopes and some mosaics to the Louvre.

Visit

Ruins★★

Open daily, 8am-7.30pm (sunset in winter). 6€ (joint ticket for site and museum: 9€). ☏ (26240) 22 517.
As you enter, note the archaeological traces on the right. The **gymnasium** was built in the Hellenistic era (3C BC) and surrounded by covered porticoes; only the foundations of the eastern and southern porticoes remain.

Palaestra★

The double colonnade of the porticoes makes it possible to envisage the Hellenistic *palaestra*, a sports arena. The athletes trained in the courtyard and bathed or anointed themselves with oil in the surrounding rooms.

H. Champollion/ MICHELIN

Entrance to the stadium

South of the *palaestra* lies the **Hérôon** (6C BC), a single circular room, where there was an altar dedicated to an unknown hero. Adjacent to this is the **Théokoleon**, residence of the priests (Théokoloi) of Olympia, which dates from the 4C BC.

Egastírio Fidía (Pheidias's Studio)

The studio was specially built for the sculptor Pheidias to work on the great statue of Zeus. Farther south are the remains of a Roman villa and a Byzantine church constructed in the ruins of of the studio

Leonidaion

The ground plan of this huge hostelry is reasonably clear. It was built in the 4C BC and consists of four rows of rooms set round an atrium, with a circular pool in the centre. Follow the Roman processional way that skirts the south side of the sacred precinct enclosing the sanctuary. Next come traces of a **bouleuterion** (6C BC), two long chambers where the members of the sanctuary's administrative council met.

Continue into the sanctuary.

Áltis (Sanctuary)

In the Classical period the sanctuary covered an area about 200m/656ft square and was slightly enlarged by the Romans. Temples, altars and votive monuments were added over the centuries. On the right within the entrance stands a triangular pedestal which supported a Victory *(in the museum)* by the sculptor Paionios.

Naós Díos★★

A ramp leads up to the terrace supporting the **Great Temple of Zeus**, which was built in the 5C BC of local shell-limestone, covered with a layer of stucco. An earthquake in the 6C AD turned the temple into a chaotic heap of stones, drums and capitals.
The temple was built in the Doric Order and had a peristyle with six columns at either end and 13 down the sides. It was nearly as large as the Parthenon in Athens. The pediments were decorated with sculptures *(in the museum)*; the friezes at the entrance to the *prónaos* and the *opisthódomos* were composed of 12 sculpted metopes *(in the museum)*. The floor was paved with stone and mosaics, some still visible.
The naos contained the famous **statue of Olympian Zeus**, one of the Seven Wonders of the Ancient World. It was a huge chryselephantine figure, about 13.50m/44ft high, representing the king of the gods in majesty, seated on a throne of ebony and ivory, holding a sceptre surmounted by an eagle in his left hand and a Victory, in his right; his head was crowned with an olive wreath.

The Revival of the Olympic Games

It was a Frenchman, **Pierre Fredy, Baron de Coubertin** (1863-1937), who revived the famous Games of Antiquity, the last of which took place in AD 393. A **monument** to the baron stands outside the ruins, along the road to Tripoli.
Rejecting the military path of his family, Baron de Coubertin devoted all his energy to promoting the importance of physical activity in education. He wrote articles, pestered authorities, undertook missions and set up sporting bodies. In June 1894 a conference was held at the Sorbonne "with the aim of the restoration of the Olympic Games"; by the end, Coubertin's cause was won. The Stadium in Athens was restored and on 5 April 1896, before 60 000 spectators, George I, King of Greece, uttered: "I declare open the first international Olympic Games." Since then they have been held every four years, except in time of war, and seek to promote the universal brotherhood of mankind.
The first Winter Games took place until 1924 in Chamonix, France, with skiing and skating as their main focus. Athens hosted the 2004 Olympic Games.

This statue has almost entirely disappeared except for a few low reliefs (copies) from the throne; the originals are now in the Hermitage Museum in St Petersburg.
A few scattered stones north of the temple mark the site of the **Pelopion**, dedicated to Pelops; nearby were the sacred olive tree and the Great Altar of Zeus.

Bear left towards a spinney which hides the remains of the Philippeion.

Philippeion

You can just discern the outline of this votive monument (4C BC). It was begun by Philip of Macedon and completed by Alexander the Great. A bit farther on lay the **Prytaneion**, administrative centre of the sanctuary, with its perpetual flame.

Naós Íras★ (Heraion)

A few columns have been re-erected among the remains of the imposing foundations of the temple of Hera.
Built about 600 BC in the Archaic Doric Order, the temple had six columns at either end and 16 down the sides; these columns, originally of wood, were soon replaced by others of tufa, short and stout, to support the typical Archaic capitals shaped like round cushions. The footings of the naós were of tufa, the walls of brick.
Inside stood an effigy of Hera (the colossal head has been found), and one of Zeus, as well as many other statues including the famous *Hermes* by Praxiteles.

Exédra of Iródou Atikoú★

This unusual, semicircular Roman monument was built in AD 160 by **Herodes Atticus** as a conduit head supplying drinking water. A basin, architraves and columns are still extant. The *exédra* formed a sort of nymphaeum with niches containing effigies of the Emperor Hadrian and the imperial family and also of Herodes Atticus and his family.

Ándiron Thissavrón (Terrace of the Treasuries)

Steps lead up to the terrace which bore an altar consecrated to Herakles and some dozen treasuries. These small Doric temples were built by the cities of Greek colonies (Mégara in Attica, Gela and Selinus in Sicily, Cyrene in Africa, Byzantium, etc.) to receive offerings made to the gods. At the foot of the terrace is a row of pedestals on which stood the bronze statues of Zeus erected out of the proceeds of the fines which were imposed on those who broke the code of the Olympic Games.
Below the Terrace of the Treasuries was the **Métrôon**, a peripteral temple built in the 4C BC in the Doric Order, and first dedicated to the goddess Rhéa.

Stadium★

In the 3C BC a passage was built beneath the terraces to link the sanctuary to the stadium; a small section of the vaulting remains. The starting and finishing lines are still visible; the distance between them was a *stadion* (about 177m/194yd).

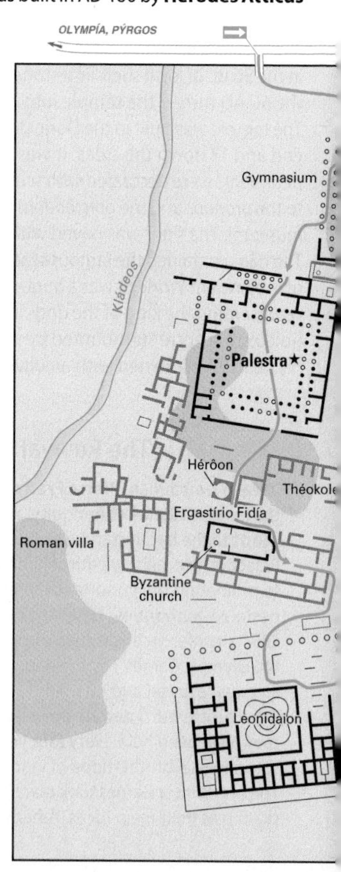

The spectators, men only, occupied removable wooden stands mounted on the bank surrounding the stadium. It was enlarged several times until it could accommodate 20 000 people.
Parallel with the south side of the stadium was the **race course**; it was destroyed in the Alfiós floods.

Eptaéchos (Poikilí)

The Echo Portico, erected in the 4C BC with a façade of 44 Doric columns, separated the stadium from the sanctuary. Its name was due to the resonant acoustic (a voice echoed seven times) and also to the various frescoes decorating the interior walls.

Archaeological Museum★★

Open Tue-Sun, 8am-7.30pm (Mon 12.30-7.30pm). 6€ (joint ticket for site and museum: 9€). ☎ (26240) 22 529; www.culture.gr.
A model of the archaeologcial site is on view in the vestibule. Objects uncovered at Olympia are organised in chronological order around the central hall.
Among the items from the Archaic and Geometric era there is a colossal **head of Hera**★ which was excavated in the temple of the goddess; and bronze armour.
Also on display is a reconstruction of the pediments of the Treasury of Mégara, and of the Treasury of Géla in painted terracotta. Note also the battering ram, a war machine made of bronze (mid-5C BC).
Among the museum's finest exhibits is a remarkable terracotta group showing **Zeus abducting Ganymede**★★ (c 470 BC).

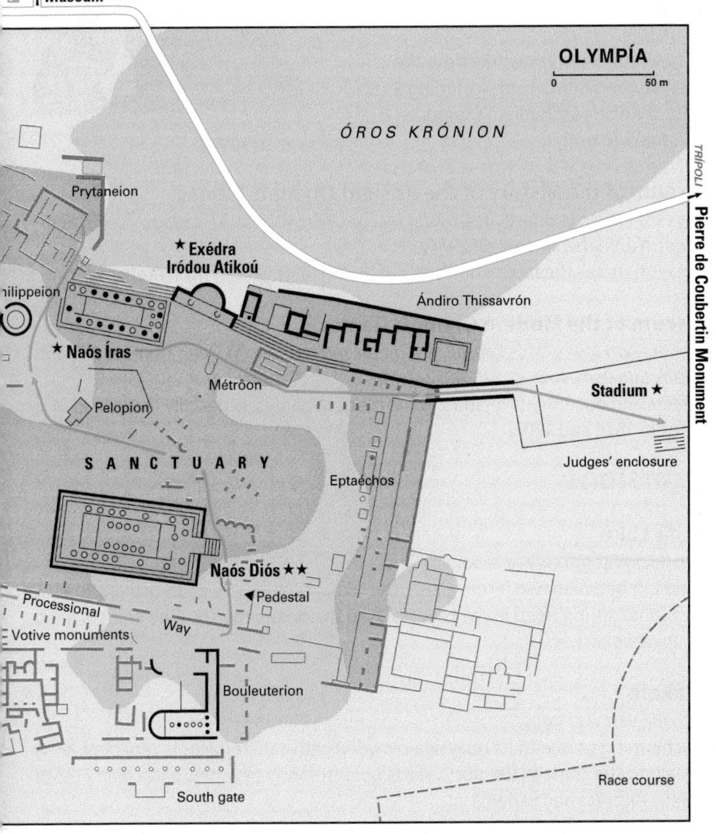

The sculptures of the two **pediments**★★ from the Temple of Zeus have been largely reconstructed with pieces found on the site. The originals were carved in Parian marble (470-456 BC) in a striking and monumental style. The central hall also displays the **metopes**★ from the temple frieze illustrating the Labours of Hercules.
Another item of particular interest is the **Victory**★ (5C BC) by the sculptor Paionios, at the moment of landing on earth to announce the triumph of the Messenians and the Naupaktians over the Spartans. Also on view are the helmet consecrated to Zeus by Miltiades before the Battle of Marathon, ceramic items from the studio of Pheidias (440-430 BC).
Among the exhibits from the late Classical and Hellenistic period is a fine head of Aphrodite attributed to Praxiteles.

Hermes Room

The famous statue of **Hermes by Praxiteles**★★★, a 4C BC masterpiece of Classical art in polished Parian marble, was found in the Temple of Hera near a pedestal bearing an inscription relating to the sculptor Praxiteles (the attribution is disputed).
Hermes, the messenger of the gods, is depicted carrying the infant Dionysos, son of Zeus and Semele, to the care of the nymphs out of reach of Hera's jealousy. The perfection of the modelling and the harmony of the proportions are remarkable.
The last rooms display works from the Hellenistic and Roman eras including a statue of **Antinoús** (Hadrian's favourite) and a **marble bull**★.

B Kaufmann/MICHELIN

Hermes by Praxiteles

Museum of the History of the Ancient Olympic Games

Access via the stairs above the parking lot. Open Mon 12.30-7.30pm, Tue-Fri 8am-7.30pm. No charge. ☎ (26420) 291 07.
Displays here tell the fascinating story of the Ancient games, from prehistory on.

Museum of the Modern Olympic Games★

In the modern town, Odós Kapsali, just off the main street. Open Mon-Sat 8.30am-3.30pm, Sun 9am-4pm. ☎ (26240) 225 44.
Artifacts and documents relating to the modern games, especially those held in Athens in 1896 and 1906.

Excursions

Kaïafa Lake

22km/13.5mi south via Kréstena.
Stretching between two fertile plains, the lake is home to a wealth of waterfowl. A hot sulphur spring deep in the caves is used by the nearby spa. The coast is lined with lovely beaches.

Katákolo

3km/2mi west via Pírgos.
This charming port with its quayside crowded with café terraces is very popular. A walk along the coast to the north skirts golden sandy beaches, particularly those of Ágios Andréas and Skifadiá .

ÓROS ÓLIMBOS★

MOUNT OLYMPOS – Οροσ Ολιμβοσ

MICHELIN MAP 737 G 4 – THESSALY AND MACEDONIA.

To the Ancient Greeks Olympos was a mysterious mountain, usually wreathed in clouds, the godly home of Zeus and the immortals. Today, walkers and hikers enjoy it for its earthly attributes. On the northern flank of the mountain is Dion, the sacred city of Macedonian Antiquity. *16 Odós A. Nikolaou, in front of the Hotel Mirto. ☎ (23520) 83 100. Open 9am-9pm.*

A Bit of History

Olympos is a huge and complex massif of crystalline schist. It is the highest mountain range in Greece, consisting of nine peaks (exceeding 2 600m/8 530ft). The southern section, Lower Olympos, is wooded and fairly easy to climb. Upper Olympos' precipices cleft by deep ravines pose more of a challenge. The first successful ascent of the mountain was achieved in 1913.

Litóhoro is the main town on Olympos and the principal base for walking and climbing in the region. The four major peaks form a rocky cirque including **Mítikas** or **Pantheon** (2 917m/9 580ft) and Zeus's Throne or Crown *(stepháni)* (2 909m/9 547ft). The peaks can be viewed by car: from Litóhoro take the road to the monastery (Moní Ágios Diónissios) and continue along a track *(suitable for motor vehicles)* to the hamlet of Prióna (about 1 000m/3 280ft).

Address Book

For coin categories, see the Legend on the cover flap.

WHERE TO EAT

To Pazari – *Litóhoro, Odós 28 Oktomvríou.* Taverna, grilled meat and fish.

Erato – *Litóhoro, Platía Kentrikí.* Good atmosphere; mountain view.

WHERE TO STAY

Olympos – *Litóhoro, 30 Odós Agías Paraskevis – ☎ (23520) 81 838 – 17rm.* A warm welcome awaits at this guesthouse offering small, clean and simple apartments with balcony.

Papanikolaou – *Litóhoro, Odós Kitrous on the left of the square – ☎ (23520) 81 236 – 16rm.* Rooms with kitchen facilities are split between two pleasant buildings surrounded by flowers and trees. A good place to stay.

Enipéas – *Litóhoro, Platía Kentrikí – ☎ (23520) 84 328 – 25rm.* A small, quiet, well-run establishment with a lovely view of Olympos.

Mirto – *On the right of the main road, just before the main square – ☎ (23520) 81 398 – 31rm.* Pleasant rooms with balconies; one of the best in town.

Villa Pantheon – *From Platía Kentrikí, take the street leading to the Mylos Restaurant, on the right, and follow the coast road – ☎ (23520) 83 931 – 12rm.* A white building visible from the village, this hotel has rooms with balconies, which are spotlessly clean and comfortable.

Refuge A – *Spílios Agapitós – ☎ (23520) 81 800 – 110 beds – May-Oct 6am-10pm.* Mountain refuge.

SPORTS AND LEISURE

Alpine Club – *EOS, 20 Odós Korovagou (from Odós Nikoloáou turn left near the Mirto Hotel) – ☎ (23520) 84 544 – Jun-Sep.* This association runs several refuges and has loads of information on Mount Olympos.

EVENTS AND FESTIVALS

During the Festival of Mount Olympos (July and August), plays and concerts are staged in Dío, Kateríni, and at Platamónas Castle on the coast.

H Champollion/MICHELIN

The ruins of Dion with Mount Olympos in the background

Experienced walkers may park at a junction before the monastery and continue on foot to Petrostrounga *(3hr)* to the right and along the bare Skoúrta Pass to the Muses Plateau (Oropédio Moussón) *(5hr)* to the refuge of the Hellenic Alpine Club of Thessaloníki (2 750m/9 022ft). Engage a guide before venturing to the summit.

Outskirts

Dío★★

16km/10mi south of Kateríni.

At the foot of Mount Olympos in the Pieriá plain lies the sacred town of Ancient Macedon. It was famous in the past for its athletic and dramatic festival known as the **Olympic Games of Dion**, instituted by Archelaos in the 5C BC.

Numerous tombs found on the slopes of Olympos near the town suggest that the area was inhabited in the 10C BC. At the height of its prosperity (the Roman period) the town numbered 15 000 inhabitants, and was served by a river port. The fortifications were built in the reign of Alexander the Great. Dion's demise came in the 4C when it was sacked by the Ostrogoths.

Old town

Open every day, 8am-7pm. 4€.

Access to the site is from the south of the village. Within 4C BC ramparts, the town visible today dates from the Roman period. It had a complete network of streets with administrative buildings, warehouses, houses, baths and public latrines. Fine mosaics have been found in the baths, but the greatest discovery is the villa of Dionysos, which dates to around 200 AD. In the banqueting hall of this house, a mosaic of the **Triumph of Dionysos** depicting the god in his chariot was uncovered in 1987.

Outside the ramparts were numerous sanctuaries, the most important of which was dedicated to the Egyptian divinities Isis, Serapis and Anubis. The Temple of Demeter, the earliest-known Macedonian temple, dates from the 6C BC and remained in use until the 4C AD. Also worthy of note is the Temple of the Olympian Zeus, which Alexander the Great visited before conquering Asia.

Two **theatres**, one Hellenistic, one Roman, two Roman **odeons** and a stadium bear witness to the cultural activities that took place in Dion.

The **museum** (*open Apr-Oct Wed-Thu 8.30am-7pm, Sa-Su 3pm; Mon 12.30-7pm; Nov-Mar Tue-Fri 8.30am-5pm, Sa-Su 3pm, Mon 12.30-5pm; 3€*) displays objects found during excavations at Dion and neighbouring sites: statues, funerary stele, mosaics, etc.

ÓSSIOS LOUKÁS★★★

Οσιοζ Λουκαζ

MICHELIN MAP 737 G 8 – BOEOTIA – CENTRAL GREECE.

Deep in beautiful countryside, this Byzantine monastery ranks among the finest in Greece. Its principal church is decorated with a wealth of 11C mosaics, and is a masterpiece of Byzantine art.

- **Orient Yourself:** 36km/23mi southeast of Delphi, and 24km/15mi from Aráhova, off the main road network; follow the road from Aspra Spitia (19km/12mi).
- **Parking:** There is a large car park at the entrance.
- **Don't Miss:** The church, with its extraordinary decoration and murals.
- **Also See:** Delfí, Aráhova

A Bit of History

The monastery was founded by a hermit, Luke Stiris, who entered a monastery at the age of 14. He lived an ascetic life in Corinth before settling in Phocis. His reputation as a healer led other holy men to join him. A first church, initially dedicated to St Barbara and subsequently to the Virgin, was built. When Luke died in 953, the monastic community became a place of pilgrimage, and a second church was erected in his honour.

Like the abbeys at Daphne and Orchomenos, the convent was occupied in the 13C and the 14C by Cistercians who preferred an isolated site. The monastery was damaged by earthquakes in the 16C and the 17C and restored in the mid-20C; Orthodox monks still reside here.

Visit

Open daily May-Sep 8am-2pm, 4-7pm; winter 8am-5pm. 3€. Modest attire required.

The monastery is set in glorious **countryside**★★ surrounded by mountains. The precinct is shaped like an irregular pentagon with two churches in the centre. The peripheral buildings comprise the monks' cells *(north and west sides)* and a refectory *(south side)*, now housing a museum (small collection of religious artefacts).

Visitors pass through the main entrance under a clock tower into the precinct to arrive in front of the pilgrims' church (Katholikon); set back on the left is the conventual church (Theotókos).

Katholikon★★

The huge pilgrimage church (11C) rises over the tomb of Luke the Hermit. From the **exterior** the building is typically Greek; built on the Greek-cross plan beneath a central dome with an apse, and faced with brick and stone.

The **interior** decor is mostly 11C; the murals, which replaced damaged or lost mosaics, are later (16C-17C). The visitor will marvel at the multicoloured marbles facing the walls and pillars, the jasper and porphyry in the floor, the delicate sculptures decorating the iconostasis and the extraordinary **mosaics**★★ on the ceiling, pediments and pilasters.

To examine the interior decoration start at the main door. The mosaics are set against a gold background, a typical example of the 11C hieratic style, sober and expressive, which was executed by artists from Thessaloníki and Constantinople.

Begin with the fine mosaics in the **narthex (1)**. In the **dome (2)** the original mosaics were replaced by frescoes in the 16C and the 17C. The **iconostasis** is made of white marble and was formerly hung with four great icons (1571), the work of the famous Cretan artist, Mihális Damaskinós, who taught El Greco *(stolen; replaced with copies).*

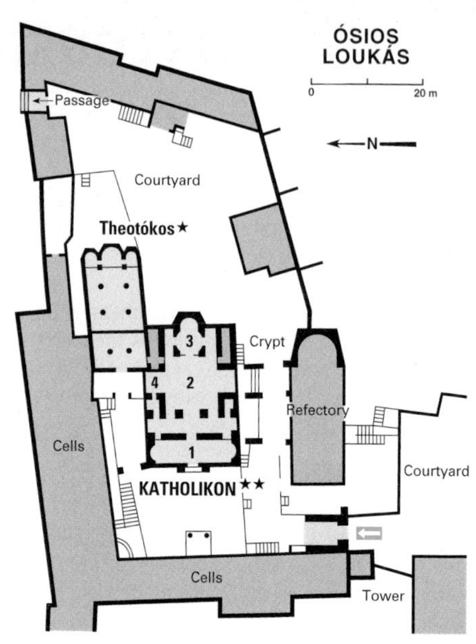

Chancel and Apse (3)
The two mosaics facing one another in the little apse *(right)* are among the most admiredin the churchl: Daniel in the lions' den and Shadrach, Meshach and Abednego in the fiery furnace.

North transept (4)
Fine mosaic of Luke the Hermit.

Crypt
Access from south side outside the church.
The crypt containing the Tomb of Blessed Luke dates from the 10C; murals 11C.

Theotókos★
A doorway beneath a double arch leads into the monastic enclosure and the open court in front of the church.
This church is very different from its neighbour; some experts think it is contemporary with Luke the Hermit, 10C; others think it is 11C. In fact, even if Luke's oratory did stand on this spot, the present church was likely built or rebuilt in the 13C for the Cistercians.
On leaving go round the south side of both churches into the eastern courtyard to compare the east elevations: the Byzantine pilgrims' church is massive and crowned by an imposing round dome; the conventual church soars up to an elegant octagonal lantern. Conventual buildings range the east side of the courtyard.

H Champollion/MICHELIN

Mosaic of Virgin and child

PÁRGA★★

Παργα

POPULATION 2 171

MICHELIN MAP 737 C 6 – PRÉVEZA – EPIROS.

Párga is a charming resort on a particularly attractive site, on the neck of a promontory flanked by two bays, screened from the open sea by rocky islets and a huge sandy beach. Its location on the Epirot coast makes it an ideal base from which to visit sites of cultural interest, with the added benefits of beach and sea.
Platia V. Vassilia, in the town hall. ☎ (26840) 32 107, www.parga.gr

- **Orient Yourself:** 141km/88mi southwest of Ioánina and 78km/49mi northwest of Árta.
- **Don't Miss:** Strolling in the village streets; a tour of the Ionian Coast.
- **Organizing Your Time:** Plan two to three days here.
- **Also See:** Kérkira, Lefkáda, Ioánnina

Address Book

For coin categories, see the Legend on the cover flap.

WHERE TO EAT

Dyonisos – *Párga, on the quayside* Unpretentious taverna serving delicious fresh fish; superb view upstairs.

Ambrosios – *Préveza, Odós Grigoriou, at right angles to the quayside.* This popular taverna, one of the oldest in Préveza, serves good plain food. Try the fish in white wine, under the shade of the trellis: a moment of pure harmony.

Castello – *Párga, in the Hotel Acropol, May-Oct.* A very popular restaurant serving Greek, Italian and French cuisine. Good wine list. Be sure to reserve.

WHERE TO STAY

Paradise – *Párga, Odós Spírou Livadá – ☎ (26840) 31 229, www.paradise-palatino.com – 16rm.* An attractive two-storey hotel offering pleasant rooms with balconies.

San Nectarios – *Párga, 2 Odós Marinas, on the way into town – ☎ (26840) 31 150, www.san-nectarios.gr – 19rm.* A two-storey hotel with simple, decent rooms, excellent value. No breakfast.

Achilleas – *Párga, at the end of Krionéri Beach – ☎ (26840) 31 600, www.hotelachilleas.gr – 33rm. May-Oct.* Comfortable rooms are set around an inner courtyard. The hotel has direct access onto Paleó Krionéri Bay and a pleasant bar at the top of the promontory. Prices vary depending on the view.

Acropol – *4 Platia Agios Apostolon – ☎ (26840) 312 39. zigouriscо@otenet.gr – 10rm.* The oldest hotel in the city, according to the owner. Jacuzzis in every room. Breakfast 5€.

Avra – *Préveza, 9 Odós El. Venizélou – ☎ (26820) 21 230, hotelavra@yahoo.com – 28rm.* A comfortable three-storey hotel opposite the landing stage for ferries to Áktio. Beautiful view over the Bay of Árta. Breakfast 5€.

Minos – *11 odós 28 Oktovriou – ☎ (26820) 284 24, katda@otenet.gr – 23rm.* Simple, clean rooms with small balconies, a good value. Breakfast 6€.

SPORTS AND LEISURE

Shuttles offer service to the **beaches** at Sarakiniko and Lichnos; there are also boat excursions to the islands of **Paxos** and **Antipaxos**. You can also take a boat trip to the cave of Aphrodite.

A Bit of History

From the 15C to 1797 Párga belonged to the Venetians, who called it Le Gominezze, the anchorage. Much against the will of the inhabitants, in 1817 it was sold by the British to Ali Pasha *(see IOÁNINA)* and did not return to the Greeks until 1913.
The **Venetian fortress** (now in ruins) was built late in the 16C. It stood on a now-overgrown rocky peninsula that offers **views**★★ of Párga, the bays and the islands.

Driving Tour

The Ionian Coast

108km/68mi from Párga to Vonitsa. At Párga join the E 55 heading south.

Ephyra Sanctuary★

Near the village of **Messopótamo.** *Open daily, 8am-3pm. 2€. ☎ (26840) 41 206.*
Here stood a sanctuary dedicated to the Oracle of the Dead (Nekromanteion) on the banks of the River Ahérondas (Acheron). The estuary was eventually filled and drained to form the fertile Fanári Plain. In Antiquity the **Acheron** (Ahérondas) emerged from a wild ravine to form a mysterious lagoon, Lake Acheroussia, thought to lead to the mythological underworld realm of **Hades**, king of the dead.

Sanctuary★

A chapel on a hill near the site of the former Lake Acheroussia marks the position of the **Nekromanteion**, a sanctuary dedicated to Hades and his wife Persephone, where seekers came to consult the spirits of the Dead.
The sanctuary existed in the Mycenaean period, but the traces of the building are Hellenistic (3C BC). A series of corridors led to the sanctuary, a huge chamber where priests wreathed in sulphurous vapours pronounced the oracle to the pilgrims, who had previously taken hallucinogenic drugs. The oracle was located in a crypt beneath the central chamber, which was thought to communicate with the abode of Hades.
Items found during the excavations are on display in the Museum in Ioánina.

Continue south along the coast road.

A turning to the left climbs the lower slopes of **Mount Zálongo** and offers glimpses of the colossal sculpted effigies of the 'Souliot Women'. After about 6km/4mi a path, on a bend to the left, leads to the ruins of Kassópi.

Kassópi★

Founded in the 4C BC and later destroyed by the Romans, Kassópi stood on the slopes of Mount Zálongo on a terrace which offers extensive **views**★ south to Leukas and east over the Ambracian Gulf. Excavations have uncovered the agora and the remains of a portico, an odeon and the *prytaneion*, where the city magistrates met.

Continue north from Kassópi for 4km/2.5mi.

Souliot Country

The Acheron flows through a desolate mountainous region, where in the 15C Christians took refuge from the Turks. Albanian in origin, the **Souliots** (named after their major settlement), were brave and indomitable. Protected by the inaccessibility of their mountain fortresses, they long maintained their autonomy.

Zálongo Monastery

In 1803 the **Souliots** fleeing the troops of Ali Pasha hid in this monastery. To escape a worse fate 60 women climbed the bluff above the convent, performed their national dance, and then threw themselves and their children over the precipice. The impressive cement figures recalling the event was sculpted by Zongolopoulos.

Rejoin the E 55 and continue south.

Ruins of Nikopolis★ (Nikópoli)

The Ioánina road crosses the site. Open Tue-Sun 8am-5.30pm; Mon 10.30am-5.30pm (summer), 8am-3pm (winter). (26820) 41 336.

Nikopolis was an important Roman and Byzantine city founded in 30 BC by Octavian Augustus. St Paul is said to have visited the city in AD 64 and it developed into an active centre of Christianity.

The **city** consists of a ruined external wall dating from the time of Augustus and a huge internal Byzantine wall (6C). The main features are the museum *(open daily 8am-3pm; 3€)* (lion, Roman portraits), the remains of Doumetios's basilica (5C, mosaics) and Augustus's Odeon *(restored)*, which from the top gives a good view of the ruined site.

There are impressive traces of the 6C **Basilica of Alkyson** *(on the right of the road going towards the theatre)*: atrium, narthex, nave and four aisles, and mosaics.

The **theatre** dates from 1C BC; note the stage and the rows of seats.

On a hill to the north of the theatre, beyond the village of **Smirtoúla**, are the remains of a monument commemorating the victory of Actium.

Préveza

Founded in the 3C BC by Pyrrhus, King of Epiros, Préveza guards the entrance to the **Ambracian Gulf** (Ambrakikós Kólpos) opposite Cape Áktio (Akteion) where a famous naval engagement, the **Battle of Actium**, took place in 31 BC. Octavian, the future Emperor Augustus, routed the fleet of his rival Antony, who was accompanied by Cleopatra, Queen of Egypt. The town is now a port and pleasant seaside resort.

Continue southeast by the ferry and the gulf coast road

Vónitsa

From Cape Akteion the road leads to Vónitsa. This little old town was once defended by a 17C Venetian **fortress**; glimpses of the coast and the Ambracian Gulf.

H Champollion/MICHELIN

The Basilica of Alkyson

PÁTRA

PATRAS – Πατρα

POPULATION 161 114

MICHELIN MAP 737 E 9 – ACHAIA – PELOPONNESE.

Patras, the modern capital of the Peloponnese and Achaea, lies 133km/83mi northwest of Corinth and 22km/14mi south of Naupaktos, served by the E 65 motorway and by ferries from Italy. It is the third largest city in Greece, a major port, commercial and industrial centre. Its arcaded streets, shady squares and harbour breakwater, where people gather in the evening, provide a pleasant stroll. The local carnival is one of the most spectacular in Greece. *Main office: Othonos Amalias6. Open year-round 8am-10pm. (26104) 61 740-1; www.infocenterpatras.gr. Branch offices also operate from April to September at the entrance to the port and in Trion Simachon Square.*

A Bit of History

Tradition has it that Patras was converted to Christianity during the reign of Nero by **St Andrew**, the Apostle, who was crucified on an X-shaped cross (henceforward known as the St Andrew's cross). In the 4C some of his relics were removed to Constantinople; others were carried off by St Regulus (or Rule) who was shipwrecked off the coast of Fife and founded St Andrews in Scotland. The head remained in Patras, where in 805 a miraculous apparition of the Apostle put to flight the bands of Slavs who were attacking the city. When the city was captured by the Turks, St Andrew's head was removed to Rome where it was kept in St Peter's Basilica until 1964, when it was returned to Patras.

The Turks set fire to the city in 1821; it was rebuilt later under Kapodístrias.

Visit

Akrópoli

Open Tue-Sun 8am-7.30pm.

The Byzantine fortress (9C), on the site of the Ancient acropolis was enlarged and remodelled by the Franks, Venetians and Turks. On the highest point rises the medieval **castle**, defended by towers and a square keep.

The lower ward is reinforced by towers and a round 17C bastion; beautiful **view★** of Patras and the Gulf of Patras as far as Cephallonia and Zakynthos.

Ágios Andréas

The neo-Byzantine **St Andrew's New Church** (1979) receives the great pilgrimage which occurs on St Andrew's Day (30 November). The great icons of St Andrew and of the Virgin, the 'Source of Life', are to be found at the end of the nave. St Andrew's

WHERE TO EAT AND STAY

Mithos – *181 Riga Ferreiou & Trion Navaron* – Charming ambience and a talented chef in this 19C house.

Méditerranée – *Patras, 18 Odós Agíou Nikoláou – (26102) 79 602 – 95rm.* This hotel on several storeys is somewhat noisy and has no character, but is clean and central.

EVENTS AND FESTIVALS

From mid-January to Ash Wednesday, **Karnavali** is one of Greece's most famous festivals.

relics are displayed at the end of the side aisle: a chased gold casket containing the saint's head, which was venerated in St Peter's, Rome from 1462 until 1964, when it was returned to Patras by Pope Paul VI; and a reliquary of St Andrew's cross.

Arheo Odío

Open Tue-Sun 8am-7.30pm. No charge.

The Roman odeon (2C AD) was restored in 1963; today it accommodates 2 500 spectators at the cultural events organised in summer. As part of a programme to renovate the **old warehouses** at the port, the building at no. 6 Odós Athonos Amalias is now a venue for painting, sculpture and photo **exhibitions**.

Museums

The **Archaeological Museum** *(17 Odós Mezonos; open Tue-Sun 8.30am-3pm; no charge)* presents objects excavated locally: ceramic vases, arms, gold ware, sculpture and Roman mosaics. The **Ethnology and History Museum** *(Square King George; open daily Tue-Thu and Sat-Sun, 11am-1pm; no charge)* displays items representing the period from the 1821 revolution up to the Balkan Wars of 1913. In the **Museum of Folk Art** (Moussío Laikís Téhnis; *110 Korytsas and Mavrokordatou; open Mon-Fri 10.30am-1pm; no charge)* you can peruse an interesting collection of costumes, icons, arms, etc.

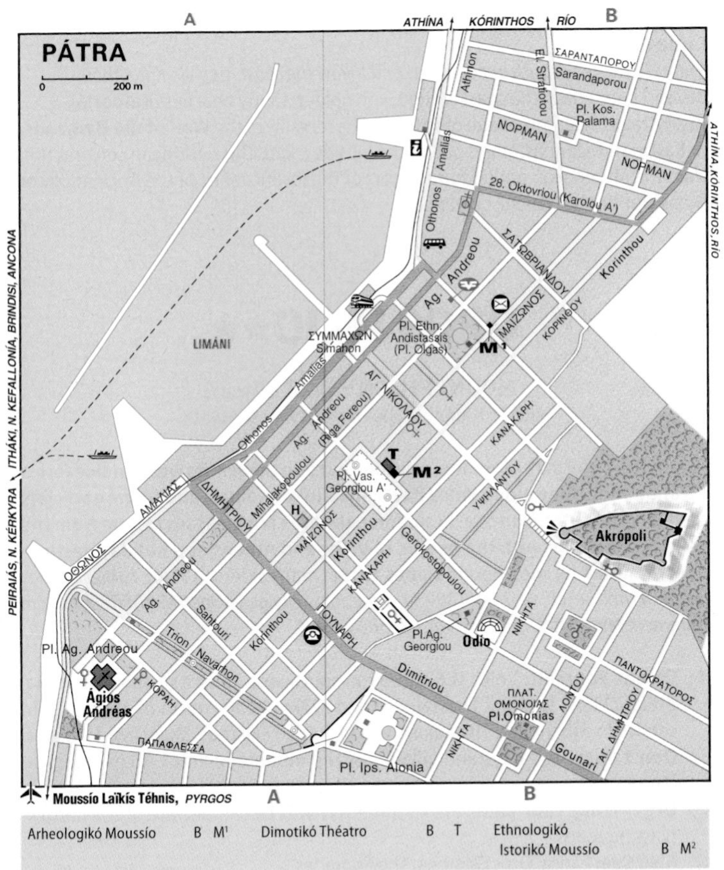

Arheologikó Moussío	B	M¹	Dimotikó Théatro	B	T	Ethnologikó Istorikó Moussío	B	M²

Excursions

Río

7km/4.25mi northeast of Patras. Access via Charilaos Trikoupis, the bridge linking the Gulf of Patras and the Gulf of Corinth (10.50€ to cross). Many beaches nearby.

The **Castle of Morea** (18C; Venetian) commands the narrow passage *(2km/1.25mi)* known as the Little Dardanelles separating the Gulf of Patras from the Gulf of Corinth. Today a prison, the castle is triangular in plan and surrounded by a moat; it has vast casemates and a bastion *(north)*; fine view over the straits.

Achaia Klauss Vineyards in Petroto

8km/5mi southeast of Patras via Mavromandila; Cellars open until 10pm; guided tours every hour 11am-4pm; call ahead (26103) 681 00.

These vineyards were planted by the Bavarian Gustave Klauss and have belonged to the Antonopoulos family since 1920. The beautiful dressed-stone buildings are traditional in style. The guided tour takes in cellars and old warehouses; on display in the 'imperial cellar' are carved wooden barrels containing wine produced in 1873.

Halandrítsa

25km/15mi south of Patras by the road to Agía Triáda then left toward Kalávrita.

Chalandritsa lies deep in the hills above the coastal plain. Reminders of the Frankish period, when it was the seat of a baronly, include a huge square tower and several Gothic churches (St Athanasius's).

Cape Áraxos

45km/28mi. Head south out of Patras and follow the coast road via Kato Ahaïa.

Beyond Kato Ahaïa, the coast is lined with golden sandy beaches (**Kalogriá**). After Áraxos, near the village of Kalogriá, the remains of the **Wall of the Dymeans**, or Kástro tis Kalogrias, stand out on the hillside *(sign)*. This Cyclopean construction from the Mycenaean period formed part of the fortifications of the Ancient city of Dyme during the Hellenistic period.

ÓROS PÍLIO★★

MOUNT PELION – Οροζ Πηλιο

MICHELIN MAP 737 H 6 – MAGNISSÍA – THESSALY.

Mount Pelion forms a promontory jutting out into the sea. Its western side forms a tranquil coastline along Vólos Bay (Pagassitikós Kólpos) and to the east cliffs plunge into the Aegean Sea. In summer, the area is a pleasant respite from the heat, and popular with the people of Vólos and Athens as a holiday destination. In winter, its snowbound slopes attract many skiers. *Vólos, corner of Odós Lambraki and Sekeri, (24210) 309 30, www.volos-city.gr. Open Mon-Fri 8am-10pm (summer), Mon-Sat 8am-8pm, Sun 3.30pm (winter).*

- **Orient Yourself:** Vólos is 62km/39mi southwest of Lárissa and its airport, 216km/135mi south of Thessaloníki and 325km/203mi north of Athens. Train service to Athens and Thessaloniki; ferry links to Skiáthos, Skopelos, Alonissos.
- **Don't Miss:** The bays and villages of the mountain; Volos Archaeological Museum
- **Organizing Your Time:** Plan a three-day visit by car; beware of the narrow, twisting roads.
- **Also See:** Lárisa, Óros Ólimbos, The Sporades.

A Bit of History

The schist mountain range culminates in **Mount Pelion** at 1 551m/5 089ft, extends north towards Mount Óssa (1 978m/6 488ft) and also south, curving west to form the Magnissía peninsula. Mediterranean plants thrive on the lower slopes and mountain types at altitude. The famous Vólos olive is grown here, along with fruit and nuts. Higher up there are forests of beech, oak and chestnut.

Address Book

For coin categories, see the Legend on the cover flap.

WHERE TO EAT

VOLOS

Seafood restaurants abound on the quayside; cafés are grouped at the eastern end of Odós Dimitriados, along the waterfront esplanade.

ON THE MOUNTAIN

Taverna Apaulosi – *Makrinítsa, main street. ☎ (24280) 900 85.* Roast meats, chicken and *spetsofáy* (sausages): all the local delicacies are served here. Try to get a table on the terrace: the view is superb. .

Panthéon – *Makrinítsa, village square – ☎ (24280) 99 143.* Another place to try *spetsofáy* and bean soup. Lovely view.

To Panórama – *Miliés, opposite the museum.* Specialities here include chicken, pork in wine and spinach tart.

Kira Marías – *Miliés, church square.* Simple cuisine (cheese tarts, salads) served in the shade of a plane tree.

To Balconi – *Kalamaki, entrance on the main square.* Excellent cuisine, and magnificent view from the terrace; a great place to eat.

Café Óasis – *Áfissos, near the square on the seafront.* The ideal spot for breakfast or an evening drink. Also has bicycles for hire.

WHERE TO STAY

Admitos – *Vólos, 5 Odós A. Diákou – ☎ (24210) 21 117 – 33rm.* A quiet hotel with simple, spotlessly clean rooms, balconies. Breakfast 6€.

Aegli Pallas – *Vólos, 24-26 Odós Argonaftón – ☎ (24210) 24 471/73, 222.aegli.gr – 75rm.* Recently renovated neo-Classical hotel style has pleasant rooms with views of the port.

Domátia Makrópoulo – *Makrinítsa, above the village – ☎ (24280) 99 016 – 8rm. Jun-Oct.* This small, quiet guesthouse has simple, clean rooms. Terrace overlooks the village.

Domátia Réna – *Áfissos, quayside – ☎ (24230) 33 439 – 10rm.* A pleasant guesthouse offering spacious studio accommodation (a little noisy) with kitchen facilities. Good value for money.

Drosseró Akrogiáli – *Plataniá, on the harbour – ☎ (24230) 71 210 – 30rm.* A long building with comfortable rooms but no sea views. The friendly owner, who speaks only Greek, runs the restaurant of the same name.

Archontikó Repaná – *Makrinítsa, main street – ☎ (24280) 99 067 – 7rm.* Enchanting 19C house with a magnificent view; attractive rooms furnished with antiques.

Parádisos – *Tsangaráda, main street – ☎ (24260) 49 209, www.paradisoshotel.gr – 40rm.* A comfortable, welcoming hotel; good view (but noisier) from the rooms overlooking the street. The hotel organises horse treks.

Maistráli – *Áfissos, near Abovos Beach – ☎ (24230) 33 472, www.maistrali.com.gr – 10rm.* Comfortable, well-presented rooms and balconies with sea views. Management speak English.

SPORTS AND LEISURE

Les Hirondelles – *Vólos, Odós Koumoundourou – ☎ (24210) 32 171, fax (24210) 35 030, info@leshirondelles.gr*

Ágios Ioánnis – *☎ (24260) 31 181, fax (24260) 31 180.* In addition to standard rentals, this agency organises a range of activities (walking, four-wheel drive treks, riding, diving and kayaking), and rents out caiques to allow visitors access to the more isolated beaches.

J Malburet/MICHELIN

Traditional local architecture

Villages here are full of charm. Most feature a shaded central square **(platía)** and traditional-style houses. The local churches diverge from the usual Orthodox style: they are rectangular, wide and low, with detached bell-towers.

Visit

Vólos

Vólos stands at the head of a vast bay. In Ancient timees, this was port from which **Jason and the Argonauts** set sail in search of the Golden Fleece.

Earthquakes are frequent here; the rebuilt city is laid out on a grid pattern, quite modern in appearance. Vólos is an important industrial city and port, transporting goods by ship to the Middle East.

The **Archaeological Museum★★** *(Odós Athanassaki, open Tue-Sun 8.30am-3pm; 2€; (24210) 25285)* displays 300 painted or sculpted Hellenistic funerary stelae, Neolithic objects, Mycenaean vases and jewellery, Hellenistic and Roman ceramics.

Driving Tour

162km/101mi. From Vólos take Odós Venizélou towards Portariá (east).

Anakassiá

Park the car next to the church and walk to Odós Moussíou Theóphilou.

The **Theophilos Museum** *(open Tue-Sun, 8am-3pm, (24210) 473 40)* occupies the House of Kondós, a beautiful building decorated with frescoes by the great primitive painter, **Theophilos** (1873-1934), who spent part of his life in Vólos.

The road continues to climb towards Portariá with a view over Vólos Bay; it passes close to **Episkopí**, a hill crowned with a historic church.

Portariá★

This pleasant resort is cool in summer. The view extends up to Makrinítsa and down over Vólos Bay.

▸ *From Portariá take the road (panoramic view) to Makrinítsa (3km/2mi).*

Makrinítsa★★

Makrinítsa occupies a magnificent **site**★★ on a verdant slope facing Vólos Bay; it is pleasant to stroll through the steep and narrow streets. The main **square**★★ *(platía)* is especially attractive with its fountain and tiny church (18C); beautiful icons inside. Higher up is the former conventual **Church of the Virgin** (18C).

Return to Portariá and continue to climb.

Marvellous **views**★★★ across Vólos Bay to Mount Óthris, northwards into Thessaly and south to Euboia.

Agrioléfkes (Hánia Pass)

Winter sports resort, set in beech and chestnut woods; there is a road from here to the summit of Mount Pelion.
The road descends towards the Aegean through beech and chestnut woods before reaching the level of the orchards. 13km/8mi from the pass bear left to Zagorá.

Zagorá

Zagorá was a centre for hand-woven cloth. The main **square** is at the top of the town near St George's Church (Ágios Geórgios); carved and gilded 18C **iconostasis**★.
From Zagorá a side road plunges downhill to Horeftó, a fishing village with a long beach of fine sand.
Return towards Hánia Pass; take the narrow but picturesque road to Tsangaráda. At **Ágios Ioánis** there is a lovely beach of white sand at the foot of green hills.

Tsangaráda

The peaceful resort village boasts one of the oldest and largest plane trees (15m/49ft circumference) in Greece. Nearby is **Milopótamos**, which has two beaches.
Beyond Xoríhti a splendid sea **view**★★ extends to Skíathos and Skópelos.

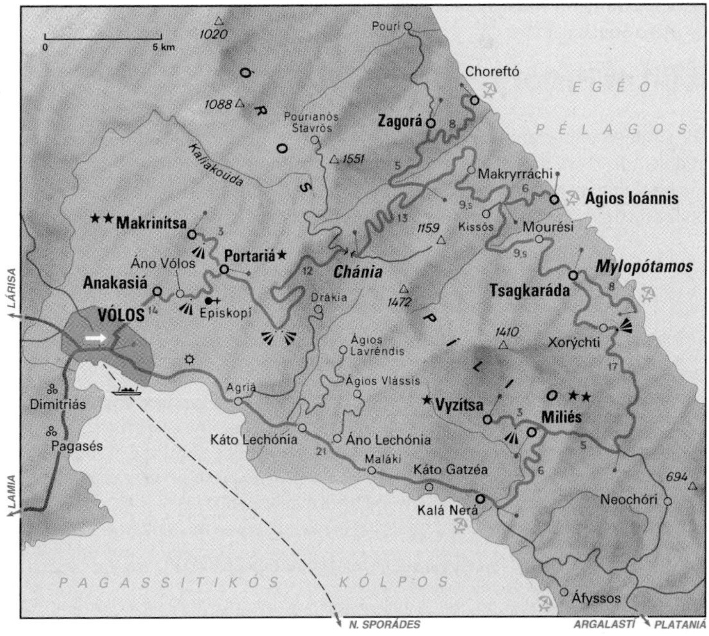

At the next junction, where the road continues south to Argalastí and Plataniá (36km/22mi – beautiful sheltered beach), bear right uphill to Miliés.

Miliés

This attractive village possesses a history **library** containing some 3 000 rare volumes (*open Tue-Sat (closed public holidays), 8am-2pm; (24230) 862 60)*. Nearby lies **Vizítsa**★, with many typical old houses.

The road back to Vólos follows the line once taken by the famous Pelion railway. There are several beaches; stop at **Kalá Nerá**, with a seafront promenade. At the junction, before reaching Kalá Nerá, a road *(left)* branches off to the small resort of Áfissos.

PÍLOS★★

PYLOS

POPULATION 2 104

MICHELIN MAP 737 E 12 – MESSINÍA – PELOPONNESE.

Pylos, better known as Navarino, lies on the southern shore of a majestic bay bounded on the seaward side by the rocky ridge of the island of Sphakteria (Sfaktiría). It is endowed with a good harbour and an excellent anchorage. The town, which boasts a superb beach, was built in 1829 by the French military expedition to Morea and is a good base for making excursions into the southern Peloponnese.

- **Orient Yourself:** 217km/136mi southwest of Corinth and 48km/30mi southwest of Kalamáta, Pylos is located in the southwest Peloponnese on the Ionian Sea.
- **Don't Miss:** Sunset over the bay.
- **Organizing Your Time:** Visit on foot; Pylos is a pleasant small village.
- Kids **Especially for Kids**: Birdwatching at Giálova Lagoon.
- **Also See:** Kalamáta

A Bit of History

The strategic importance of Navarino Bay was recognised both in Antiquity and the Middle Ages from the 6C to 9C. In those days the town lay at the northern end of the bay beneath an acropolis, later a medieval castle (Paliókastro). Later, the Turks built a fortress (Niókastro) to guard the southern approach.

Battle of Navarino

The decisive naval engagement which took place on 20 October 1827 between the allied fleet, made up of English, French and Russians, and the Turks.

The presence of the allied fleet was intended to intimidate **Ibrahim Pasha**, and to force the Porte to agree to an armistice with the Greeks. The allied force, commanded by Admirals Codrington, De Rigny and De Heydden, consisted of 26 ships with a total of 1 270 cannon. The 82 Turkish and Egyptian ships were caught in a trap without room to manoeuvre and were annihilated, despite their superior firepower (2 400 cannon) and the support of the artillery on the Niókastro.

The Battle of Navarino forced the Sultan to negotiate and paved the way for Greek independence.

The focal point of the town is Three Admirals Square (Platía Trion Návarhon), named for the commanders of the victorious fleet at the Battle of Navarino. Stop in at the **Antonopoulos Archaeological Museum** *(Odós Philéllinon, off the square; open Tue-Sun 8.30am-3pm; 2€)* to take in a collection of art, arms, tools and other objects from the Neolithic to the Roman periods.

Sights

Niókastro★

Access from the Methóni road. Open Tue-Sun 8.30am-6pm; 3€. ☎ (27230) 220 10.
This citadel was built by the Turks in the 16C. A large building near the entrance houses a **museum** dedicated to the French philhellene **René Puaux**: lithographs, engravings and objects recalling the struggle for Greek independence. From the southwest redoubt there are remarkable **views**★ over the bay; the tiny islet (south of the Island of Sfaktiría bears a monument to the French who fell in the War of Independence.

Navarino Bay★

In the summer season boats operate from Pylos to Sphakteria and Paliókastro. Information available at the harbour.

Paliókastro★

Accessible by car from Petrohóri taking a bad road that goes to Voidokilia (follow signs for the archaeological site).
On a spur of rock near the northern approach rise the crenellated walls and towers of the **Castle of Port de Junch** (1278). The circuit wall and keep command the lagoon

Address Book

For coin categories, see the Legend on the cover flap.

WHERE TO EAT

O Grigóris – *Pylos, above the main square.* A garden taverna, with several flower-decked terraces, serving good Greek food to the sound of local music.

Klimataria – *Methóni ☎ (27230) 315 44.* Good family-style cooking, vegetarian dishes and live music.

WHERE TO STAY

Zoé – *Giálova, by the beach – ☎ (27230) 22 025 – 32rm (2 ♿) ✕.* A row of native trees separates the beach from this modest, friendly hotel.

Kástello – *Methóni, near the citadel and the sea – ☎ (27230) 31 300, www.castello.gr – 15rm.* This modern hotel with garden has clean, simple rooms. Animals allowed.

Methoni Beach Hotel – *☎ (27230) 287 20, www.methonibeach-hotel.gr – 12rm.* ✕ Recently renovated, contemporary styling, comfortable hotel. Restaurant overlooks the beach.

Karalís – *Pylos, 26 Odós Kalamáta – ☎ (27230) 22 960,www.karalis.room-storent.info– 35rm.* Charming hotel in a historic house on the coast road Small but comfortable rooms with balconies. Generous breakfast.

Karalís Beach – *Pylos, between the fortress and the beach – ☎ (27230) 23 021 – 14rm.* Very well situated among pine trees below the fortress 20m from the sea. Comfortable rooms with large bathrooms; balconies for those overlooking the sea. Pleasant terrace bar.

SHOPPING

Kellari – *facing the harbour enroute to Kalamata.* Family-owned boutique specializing in olive oil above all, but also local products (honey, wine, ouzo, etc.)

EVENTS AND FESTIVALS

On 20 October, Pylos commemorates the Battle of Navarino Bay.

and the Ancient port of Pylos. At the foot of the cliff there is a cave with stalactites, named after King Nestor. There is a beautiful beach farther on, at Voidokilia.

Sfaktiría (Sphakteria)

The uninhabited island of Sphakteria is the site of several monuments commemorating those who died in the cause of Greek independence. On the summit there are traces of an Ancient fortress where 420 Spartans made a heroic stand against the Athenians during the Peloponnesian War (425 BC).

Outskirts

Methóni★★

12km/7.5mi south of Pylos. Methone, the watchtower of the eastern Mediterranean, stands on a pleasant **site**★ overlooking a bay protected by two islands, Sapiéndza and Shíza, which provide good inshore fishing grounds. A beach adjoining the quiet fishing harbour, with several hotels and tavernas, makes it a pleasant place to stay. From the early 13C to the 19C, Methone passed back and forth between Venetian and Turkish control. Ultimately, during the War of Independence, French troops took it from Ibrahim Pasha; the French troops then rebuilt parts of the town.

Citadel★★

Open daily, 8.30am-7pm. No charge.

The citadel was begun in the 13C , but most of the construction occurred during the Venetian period, evidenced by the lions of St Mark and the carved escutcheons. Beyond the counterscarp a bridge spans the moat, which was covered by crossfire from the **Bembo bastion** (15C) *(right)* and the **Loredan bastion** (1714) *(left)*.

An outer gate (early 18C) opens into a passage against the northern rampart (13C); a vaulted approach precedes the **Land Gate** (13C), which has Gothic arches and gives access to the open space once occupied by the medieval town. Follow the eastern rampart (16C-18C); on the left lies the port, on the right the remains of a Turkish bath, some cisterns, a powder magazine and the old Latin cathedral.

The **Sea Gate** on the south side of the citadel gives access to the picturesque **Boúrdzi Tower**★ (16C) on an island of rock linked to the citadel by a bridge; climb to the platform for a splendid **view**★★ of the citadel, the harbour and the islands. The western rampart leads back to the keep; most of its fortifications date from the 15C but it was modernised in the 18C (firing steps for artillery).

M Guillochon/MICHELIN

Boúrdzi Tower, Methóni

Excursion

The Messanian Coast *79km/49mi round trip from Pylos.*

Giálova Lagoon

Kids *3km/1.8mi north of Pylos. ☎ (2108) 279 37. www.ornithologie.gr.*

The peaceful lagoon is an important resting spot for nearly 270 species of migratory birds, 79 of which are endangered, and other wildlife. Best time to visit: May-Sept.

H Champollion/MICHELIN

Tholos near the 'Palace of Nestor'

Anáktora Néstoros★

18km/11mi north of Pylos (bus service 1.8€). Open Jul-Oct daily 8am-5pm; rest of the year daily 8.30am-3pm. 3€. ☎(27630) 314 37.

The buildings comprising the **Palace of Nestor** (destroyed about 12C BC) date from the Mycenaean era. They contained clay tablets bearing inscriptions in **Linear B**, which have contributed to our understanding of the Mycenaeans' language, the earliest known form of Greek.

The ruins reveal that the palace was similar to those in Crete or the Argolid (Mycenae, Tiryns). The entrance *(propylon)* is flanked by two archive rooms where about 1 000 clay tablets were found. On the far side of the courtyard stood the *megaron*, the royal residence; at the centre was a round hearth, the throne was to the right. On the east side of the court are the queen's apartments, which include a bathroom containing a **bath**, the only one known to have survived from this period.

Legendary King

Nestor, youngest son of Neleus and Chloris, attributed his longevity to Apollo's remorse after killing Nestor's siblings. Despite his great age, King Nestor commanded a large fleet of ships at the Siege of Troy; Homer praised him for his wisdom. After Troy fell, he returned to Pylos. Here in his palace Nestor received **Telemachos**, when he came to ask for news of his father Odysseus.

Hóra

This town has an interesting **Archaeological Museum** *(open Jul-Oct daily 8am-5pm; rest of the year Tue-Sun, 8.30am-3pm; 2€; 4€ combined ticket with the Palace of Nestor)* which displays the objects excavated in the palace and the region, especially at Peristéria: fine golden cups and jewellery from the Mycenaean period; fragments of frescoes and mosaics; mouldings of inscribed tablets.

Kiparissía

Kyparissía, the town of cypresses, is set just back from the coastline; in the Middle Ages it was called **Arkadia**, Destroyed in 1825 by Ibrahim Pasha, it is today a modern city, dominated by the ruins of a Frankish castle. From the top there is a fine **view**★ across the Ionian Sea to Zakynthos *(northwest)*. Due west lie the **Strofádes Islands**, Kiparissîa was the legendary home of the **Harpies** (also called the **Furies**), tempestuous divinities represented as birds with women's faces.

Peristéria Tombs

10km/5mi northeast; take the Pírgos road for 5km/3mi; turn right (sign) and continue for 5.5km/3.25mi (very poor road).

Among the green hills looking down into the narrow valley of the Peristéria, excavations have revealed some domed royal tombs dating from the Mycenaean period. A fine collection of jewellery, seals and vases found in one of the tombs is currently on display in Hóra Museum.

SPÁRTI

SPARTA – Σπαρτι

POPULATION 15 828

MICHELIN MAP 737 G 11 – LAKONÍA – PELOPONNESE.

Courage, austerity, physical prowess and patriotism are synonymous with the name of Sparta. Modern Sparta, however, has little in common with the warlike city of Classical times. Today, Sparta is a modern provincial capital and a tourist centre, well placed for visiting the ruins of Mystra and the medieval village of Geráki. Located 61km/38mi east of Kalamáta (airport), 43km/27mi north of Gíthio and 130km/82mi southwest of Corinth, Sparta is served by the E 961. *52 Gortsologiou (4th floor), near the main square; English spoken. (27310) 26 771 Open Mon-Fri 7.30-2.30.*

A Bit of History

An aristocratic and military state – Remains from the Mycenaean period, when Sparta formed part of the kingdom of Menelaeus, have been found at the Menelaion itself **(Geráki road)** and at Amíkles (7km/4.25mi south. Sparta was most influential, however, from the 9C to the 4C BC, in the Peloponnese, and throughout Greece.

The Spartans' oligarchic constitution, was created about 900 BC by the lawgiver **Lycurgus**. The state was led by two kings assisted by a council of 28 elders and five *ephors* who had executive power.

There were three distinct classes: the **Spartiates**, the warrior class, who were also landowners; the **Perioikoi**, who were traders and artisans or farmers; and the **Helots**, or serfs.

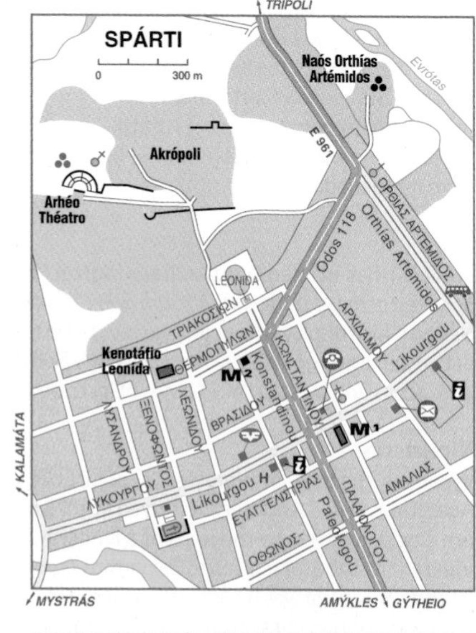

Arheologikó Moussío M1
Ethnikí Pinakothíki Moussío Alexándrou Soútsou M2

Spartan way of life – Forbidden to work, the Spartiates trained continually in combat. They ate communally, living mainly on herbs and wild roots, with a rare feast of black broth (pork stewed in blood). At age seven boys were drafted into youth troops inured to physical exercise. On reaching adulthood (age 20), the young Spartiates faced a series of initiation tests, the *krypteia*; they were flogged, sometimes to death, abandoned in the countryside and instructed to kill any Helots who tarried outdoors after dark. The girls also were given to strenuous exercise, and married women were not expected to be faithful to their husbands.

The Spartiate soldiers gave their lives without hesitation in combat, as did **Leonidas** and his warriors at Thermopylae in 480 BC. The Spartiates' numbers over the centuries, and their defeat in 371 BC at Leuktra began the city's decline. Eventually it was supplanted by Mystra, and Ancient Sparta was abandoned.

B Chabrol/MICHELIN

Visit

Arheologikó Moussío

Open Jul-Oct: daily 8.30am-5pm; rest of the year: Tue-Sat, 8.30am-3pm. 2€. ☎ (27310) 28 575.

The **Archaeological Museum** displays the finds from local excavations, particularly Sparta and Amyklai (Amíkles); sculptures in bronze and marble from the Archaic period; terracotta masks from the Sanctuary of Artemis Orthia; and objects from Mycenaean tombs.

Address Book

For coin categories, see the Legend on the cover flap.

WHERE TO EAT

Elysé – *113 Leofóros K. Paleológou.* Small restaurant serving traditional dishes as well as unusual ones, such as 'petit cochon aux aubergines' and orange-flavored Greek sausages.

Maniatis – *72-76 Leofóros K. Paleológou.* This hotel restaurant has neo-Spartan decor and air-conditioning. The typically Greek menu also includes international dishes. Closed on Sunday.

Menelaion – *91 Leofóros K. Paleológou.* One of Sparta's more elegant establishments,with tables on a cool poolside patio in the hotel of the same name. Greek and French cuisine.

WHERE TO STAY

Cecil – *125 Leofóros K. Paleológou – ☎ (27310) 24 980 – 23rm.* Modest but clean and friendly hotel occupies a pre-war building. Good value.

Maniatis – *72-76 Leofóros K. Paleológou – ☎ (27310) 22 665, www.maniatishotel.gr – 80rm.* A pleasant hotel; some rooms have balconies and views. Good restaurant.

Menelaion – *91 Leofóros K. Paleológou – ☎ (27310) 22 161 – 48rm.* This well-located hotel offers spacious rooms, double-glazed windows and a swimming pool.

SPORTS AND LEISURE

Hiking information and details of refuges may be obtained from the **Sparta Climbing Club**, 97 Odós Górtsoglou, ☎ (27310) 22 574, or from the photographer (member of the climbing club) at 36 Odós Likourgou. There are information offices in the villages of Paleopanagia, Socha, Anavriti and Koumousta.

EVENTS AND FESTIVALS

On 26 November, the city celebrates the feast of its patron saint.

Ancient ruins

No charge.

Most date from the Hellenistic or Roman periods. The **Kenotáfio Leonída** (Leonidas' Tomb) is, in fact, the base of a small Hellenistic temple; Leonidas's tomb was on the Acropolis. The remains of the **Acropolis** buildings are half hidden in an olive grove north of the modern town *(sign: 'Ancient Sparta')*. Go through the Byzantine wall and bear left to reach the theatre (1C BC). Above it are the foundations of a Temple to Athena and a Byzantine monastery (10C AD).

Naós Orthías Artémidos (Sanctuary of Artemis Orthia)

The ruins of a temple (7C-6C) and an amphitheatre mark the site where ritual endurance tests of young Spartans took place: flogging and athletic dances with masks.

Excursions

Tomb of Menelaus (Menelaion)

8km/5mi south by the road to Gíthio, then a narrow road on the left.

After turning, continue on foot up to Prophitis Ilias hill, site of the ruins of a 5C BC sanctuary to Menelaus and Helen. Marvellous **view★** of Mount Taígetos.

Zerbítsa Monastery

12km/7.5mi to the south. Take the Gíthio road, then turn right on the road passing through Xirokámbia and follow the signs.

The monastery has a beautiful 17C Byzantine church with frescoes, and a small museum (**Epitáphios** of 1539, icons, early Christian architectural fragments.)

Geráki★

31km/19mi southeast of Sparta.

The little medieval town of Geráki has no fewer than 30 Byzantine churches decorated with 15C and 16C murals. The ruins of Geráki Castle and of a medieval town *(kastró)* lie on an outlying spur of Mount Parnon, on the northern edge of the Lakonian Plain.

Kastró

Open Tue-Sun 8.30am-3pm. Ask for the keeper in the village (office on the way into the village, next to the post office), then take the road below the village towards Ágios Dimítrios past a school and a cemetery near several Byzantine churches. Turn left after the cemetery towards the kastró and continue for 2.5km/1.5mi to the car park.

The **castle**, built in 1254 in imitation of the one in Mystra, is shaped like an irregular quadrilateral; huge cisterns enabled it to withstand long sieges. The tour includes several Gothic and Byzantine chapels decorated with painted murals, notably **Agía Paraskevi Church** (12C frescoes), and **St George's Church** (13C). Nearby stands the **Zoodóhou Pigi Church**, a basilica decorated with vivid 15C Byzantine frescoes.

The parapet walk offers extensive **views★★** of Mount Parnon *(north)*, the Eurotas Valley running south to the sea and Mount Taígetos *(west)*.

Byzantine churches

Down in the village, by the road to the castle, the early-13C domed church of **Ágios Athanássios,** decorated with frescoes, stands near the cemetery.

A short distance away, a byroad on the other side of the main road leads to the finely proportioned, domed **Ágios Sósson** (12C) and farther down to **Ágios Nikólaos** (13C). The tiny church of Ágii Theodori stands in the middle of a field near the road. Also worth a visit is the **Ágios Ioánnis Chrysostomos Church**, a 12C basilica with early-15C frescoes relating to the Life of Christ and of the Virgin (14C).

Above the cemetery, walk up in the village to the 12C church of the **Evangelístria**; the well-preserved frescoes were probably painted by an artist from Constantinople.

Hríssafa

18km/11mi east of Sparta.

The village boasts several churches, including the 13C Chryssaphiotissa Church (frescoes), the 18C Church of the Dormition and the 13C Church of St John. To visit, contact the priest at the Church of the Dormition (Kimisseos tis Theotokou).

THESSALONÍKI★★

Τηεσσαλονικι

POPULATION 380 000 (1 000 000 METROPOLITAN AREA)

MICHELIN MAP 737 H 3 – MACEDONIA.

Premier port of Greece, Thessaloníki cultivates a reputation as a carefree Mediterranean seaside resort, with its wide avenues plunging toward the sea. It is a city of contrasts, cheerfully blending the trappings of a modern city with 23 centuries of history. *132 Odós Tsimiski, (23102) 52 107.*

- **Orient Yourself:** Thessaloníki lies on a sloping site on the Thermaic Gulf, 530km/331mi north of Athens.
- **Don't Miss:** The Apsída Galeríou, and the Archaeological Museum
- **Organizing Your Time:** Plan on 2 days to visit; be sure to acquire a map.
- Kids **Especially for Kids:** Enjoy an ice cream in Odós Iktinov**.**
- **Also See:** Áigio Óros, Halkidikí, Kavála, Oros Ólimbos.

A Bit of History

Thessaloníki, an imperial city – Founded in 315 BC on the site of the Ancient town of Therme, the city was named for the half-sister of Alexander the Great. Under Roman rule it developed into an important port and staging post.

In 148 BC it became the capital of the Roman province of Macedonia and was an important cultural centre. **St Paul** visited Thessaloníki twice during his journeys, in AD 50 and 56, and addressed several Epistles to the Thessalonian people.

Early in the 4C Thessaloníki became the residence of the Emperor **Galerius,** under whose edict Christians were persecuted; in 306 St Demetrios, was martyred here.

Theodosius the Great (379-95) gave official recognition to the Christian religion.

Under the return to order following the barbarian invasions in 527-65, Thessaloníki became the second city of the Eastern Empire after Byzantium. St Cyril probable inventor of the Cyrillic alphabet, was born here in 827.

After the Fourth Crusade, Thessaloníki was returned to Byzantium and fell prey to anarchy until it was captured by Sultan Mourad II in 1430, who gave it the name Salonika. There followed a period of prosperity, during which some 20,000 Jewish refugees from Spain arrived and formed a community of craftsmen and merchants who traded throughout Europe (by 1910 the Jewish community was 65 000 strong and made up nearly half the population).

Modern era – Under the Turks the city's economy developed in the late 19C; in 1888 it was linked by railway to Central Europe and from 1897 to 1903 a new port was constructed. In 1912 it was returned to Greece and reverted to its original name. During the First World War in 1918 Greek troops joined the Allies in clearing Macedonia of the enemy and advancing into Serbia and Bulgaria; those who fell in the campaign are buried in the Allied military cemetery at Diavatá *(north of Thessaloníki).*

A large part of the city was destroyed by fire in 1917, and rebuilt according to plans by the French architect Hébrard. In 1941 Thessaloníki was occupied by the Germans, who deported some 50 000 Jews; there is a monument at the beginning of Leofóros Langada *(in the direction of Kavála)*. An earthquake in 1978 earthquake grieviously damaged the city.
Thessaloníki stands at the crossroads of the land and sea routes linking Western Europe with the Levant; it has long been a trading centre and since 1926 has organised an International Fair (Diethnís Ékthessi) each September. It is an active industrial centre (zone west of the city), and in 1997 was named the European Capital of Culture under the auspices of the European Union, in acknowledgement of its intellectual and cultural significance.

R Couedel/MICHELIN

Acanthus leaves

Visit

The Lower Town

The lower town is bordered by Odós Olimbiados to the north and by the seafront. Devastated by the 1917 fire, the city centre was completely rebuilt, but has retained numerous important monuments, museums and commercial enterprises.
Under the Ottomans, the lower town was a squalid area confined behind fortifications that were only demolished in 1866.
The main square, **Platía Aristotélous★**, is the termination of the central axis of the city overlooking the sea.

▸ *Turn left (south) along Leofóros Nikis, past restaurants and luxury boutiques. Then turn left again into Odós Agías Sofías and proceed towards the church of the same name, crossing Odós Tsimiki, the main shopping street.*

Agía Sofía★

Open daily, 87am-1pm and 5-7pm.
The **Church of the Holy Wisdom** (8C), is remarkable for its huge dimensions and its unusual design: the standard basilical plan of a nave and two aisles with galleries is combined with the Greek-cross plan beneath a dome. Note the base of a minaret (northwest corner) from the structure's incarnation as a mosque until 1912.
The interior displays unusual **capitals★** with acanthus-leaf decorations probably taken from a 5C building. The **mosaics** (9C-10C) depict the Ascension of Christ and form a particularly harmonious composition.

Panagía Ahiropíitos

56 Odós Agías Sofías. Open daily 7am-noon and 4.30-6.30pm. ☎ (23102) 72 820.
The restored church dates from the 5C. Nearby stands a small baptistery chapel. The church was named after a miraculous icon of the Virgin (Panagía Ahiropíitos, 'not made by human hand') *(to the left of the entrance)*.

Address Book

For coin categories, see the Legend on the cover flap.

WHERE TO EAT

Ouzoumelathron – *21-34 Odós Karipi.* A favourite Sunday afternoon gathering spot, this fun tavern offers inexpensive yet refined traditional food.

Ouzeri Agora – *5 Odós Kapodistriou.* Specialises in excellent local fish dishes.

Life – *1 Odós Filippou.* Calm little brasserie; choose your dish from the line. Popular lunch spot for locals.

Zithos – *5 Odós Katoúni, Ladádika.* Elegant brasserie-style restaurant. Its chic clientèle use it for lunch, dinner, or just a drink.

WHERE TO STAY

Augustos – *4 Odós Svorónou – ☎ (23105) 22 550 – 24rm.* Simple, well-done rooms situated in an alley set back from Odós Egnatía.

Nea Mitropolis – *22 Odós Sigrou – ☎ (23105) 460 97 – 35rm.* In a quiet street, this early-20C is decorated with kitschy flair. Its spacious, high-ceilinged rooms are pleasant, and some have TV and air-conditioning.

Mandrino – *Odós Egnatia and Antigonidon. – 72rms.* Modern hotel downtown, with double-pane windows, minibars, and non-smoking rooms.

Esperia – *58 Odós Olímbou – ☎ (23102) 69 321 – 70rm.* Located in a quiet street, this hotel offers simple, comfortable accommodation. No breakfast or air-conditioning.

Amalia – *33 Odós Ermoú – ☎ (23102) 68 321 – 66rm.* Centrally located by the market, this nine-storey hotel is very comfortable; good value.

Aegeon – *19 Odós Egnatía – ☎ (23105) 22 921 – 59rm.* Recently renovated with small, clean rooms. Those overlooking the courtyard are the quietest.

Tourist Hotel – *21 Odós Mitropóleos – ☎ (23102) 70 501 – 37rm.* Well located and welcoming, this hotel has spotlessly clean high-ceilinged rooms. Very popular and usually full.

ABC Hotel – *41 Odós Angeláki – ☎ (23102) 65 421 – 99rm.* Immaculately clean accommodation; management speaks English.

J Malburet/MICHELIN

Luxembourg – *6 Odós Komninón – ☎ (23102) 52 600, – 36rm.* A very comfortable hotel with pleasant if small rooms. One of the least expensive hotels in its class in this district.

Electra Palace – *9 Platía Aristotélous – ☎ (23102) 94 000 – 135rm.* This hotel offers every imaginable comfort. English-speaking staff. Ask for a room on an upper storey, with a view of the square and the seafront.

TAKING A BREAK

Buzapio – *corner of Odós Ermou and Agia Sofia.* Enjoy a wonderful view of the church, while sampling from the wide selection of pastries or liqueurs.

Kiss Fisch – *on the port, Odós Fokeas Averof.* This large, modern bar is a haven of peace by day, and a techno-music hangout by night.

SHOPPING

For **icons,** peruse the boutiques along Odós Egnatia near the Arch of Galerius. Head for Odós Tsimiski if you're shopping for **clothes** or **home décor**.

EVENTS AND FESTIVALS

The **Thessaloníki International Fair** is held over two weeks in September and ends with a festival of Greek music. This is followed by an international film festival during October and November, which is part of **Demetriosa**, the feast of the city's patron saint.

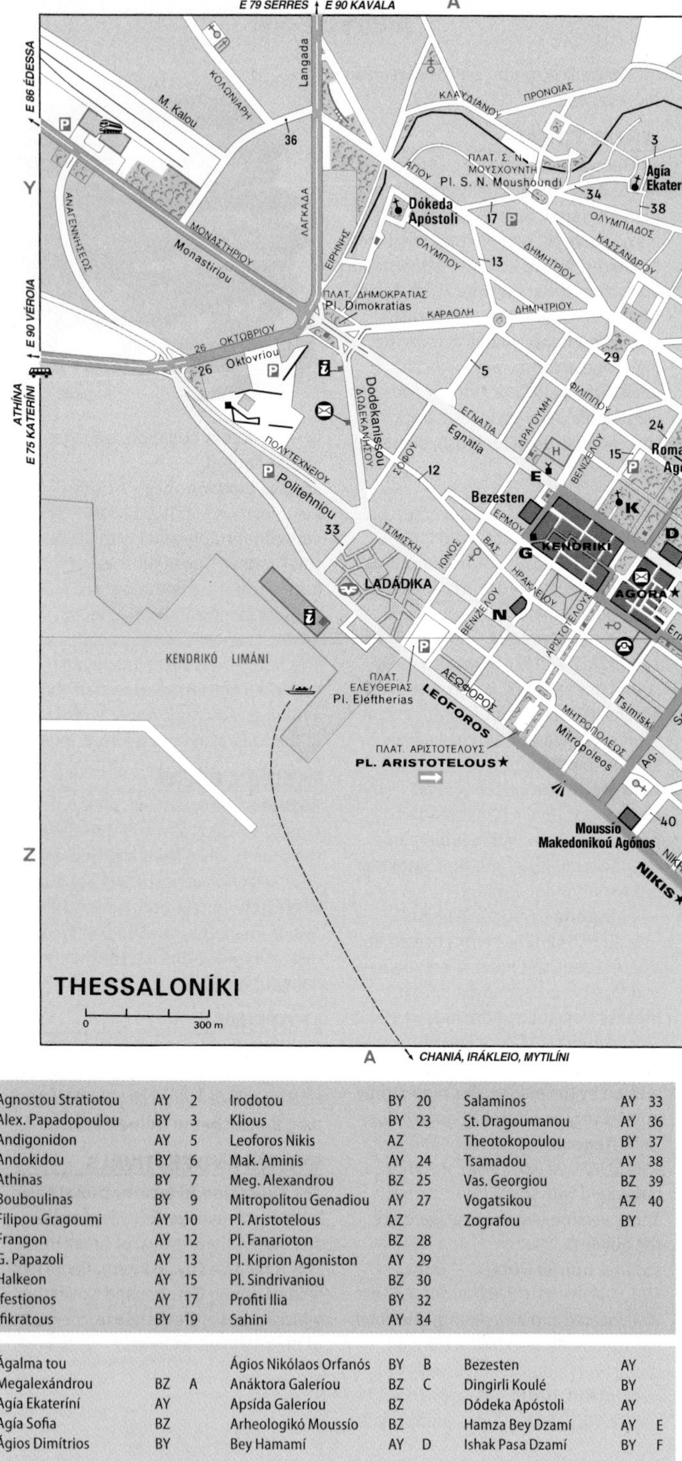

Agnostou Stratiotou	AY	2	Irodotou	BY	20	Salaminos	AY	33
Alex. Papadopoulou	BY	3	Klious	BY	23	St. Dragoumanou	AY	36
Andigonidon	AY	5	Leoforos Nikis	AZ		Theotokopoulou	BY	37
Andokidou	BY	6	Mak. Aminis	AY	24	Tsamadou	AY	38
Athinas	BY	7	Meg. Alexandrou	BZ	25	Vas. Georgiou	BZ	39
Bouboulinas	BY	9	Mitropolitou Genadiou	AY	27	Vogatsikou	AZ	40
Filipou Gragoumi	AY	10	Pl. Aristotelous	AZ		Zografou	BY	
Frangon	AY	12	Pl. Fanarioton	BZ	28			
G. Papazoli	AY	13	Pl. Kiprion Agoniston	AY	29			
Halkeon	AY	15	Pl. Sindrivaniou	BZ	30			
Ifestionos	AY	17	Profiti Ilia	BY	32			
Ifikratous	BY	19	Sahini	AY	34			

Ágalma tou Megalexándrou	BZ	A	Ágios Nikólaos Orfanós	BY	B	Bezesten	AY	
Agía Ekateríní	AY		Anáktora Galeríou	BZ	C	Dingirli Koulé	BY	
Agía Sofia	BZ		Apsída Galeríou	BZ		Dódeka Apóstoli	AY	
Ágios Dimítrios	BY		Arheologikó Moussío	BZ		Hamza Bey Dzamí	AY	E
			Bey Hamamí	AY	D	Ishak Pasa Dzamí	BY	F

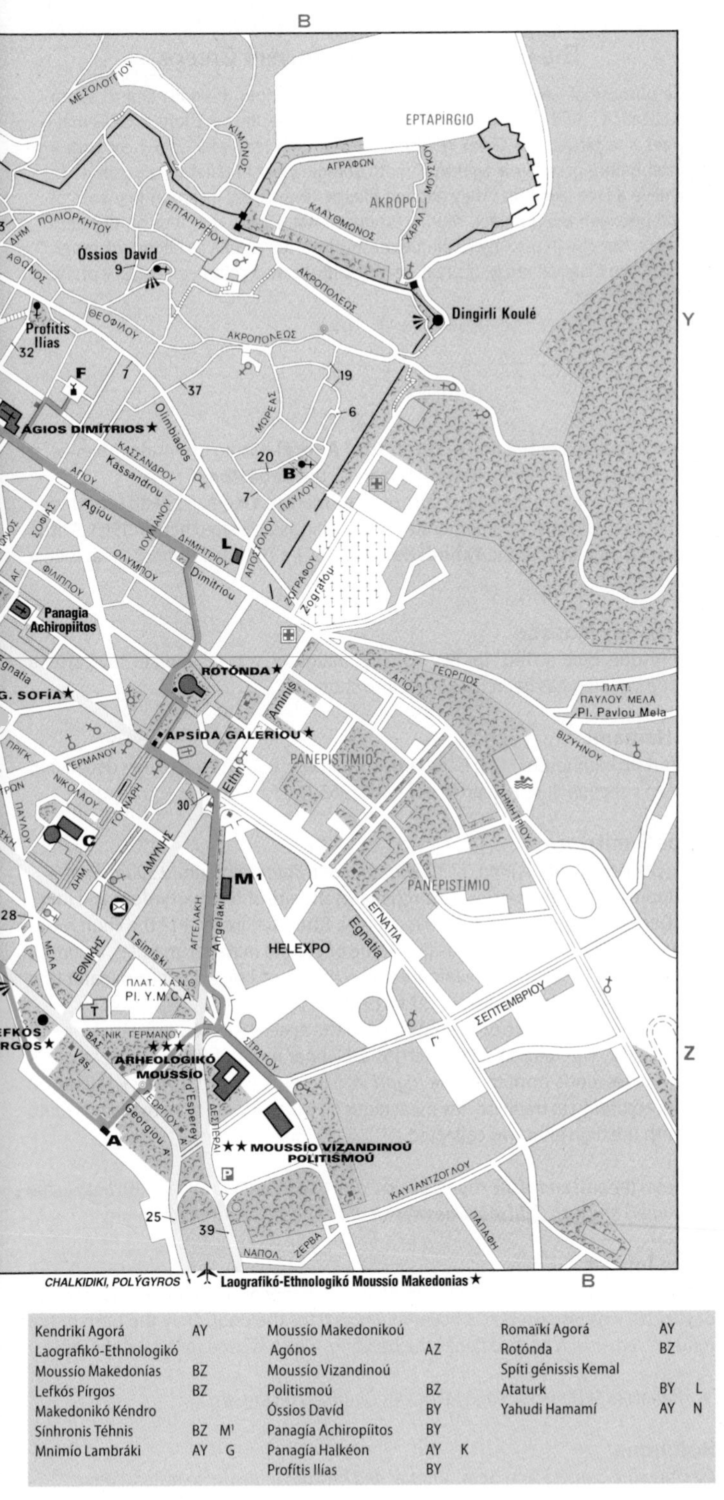

Kendrikí Agorá	AY		Moussío Makedonikoú Agónos	AZ		Romaïkí Agorá	AY	
Laografikó-Ethnologikó Moussío Makedonías	BZ		Moussío Vizandinoú Politismoú	BZ		Rotónda	BZ	
Lefkós Pírgos	BZ		Óssios David	BY		Spíti génissis Kemal Ataturk	BY	L
Makedonikó Kéndro Sínhronis Téhnis	BZ	M^1	Panagía Achiropíitos	BY		Yahudi Hamamí	AY	N
Mnimío Lambráki	AY	G	Panagía Halkéon	AY	K			
			Profítis Ilías	BY				

The Goldsmith's Art in Ancient Greece

The purpose of Greek jewellery was not only to honour the gods and to adorn the dead: it could be given to anyone on certain specific occasions such as marriages and births. The Greek goldsmiths used gold leaf, which they cut with a chisel before pressing it against a motif standing out in relief on a support. To achieve a lace-like effect they applied filigree decoration, inserting tiny balls of gold between the moulded motifs. Produced not only in the cities of mainland Greece, but also in the Greek colonies of southern Italy and Asia Minor, the jewellery of the Classical era is of great beauty and shows a complete mastery of the goldsmith's art.

Market★

Open Mon-Sat.

The picturesque central market **(Kendrikí Agorá)** has an oriental ambience. It extends westwards as the old textiles market, the **Bedesten**.

The monument at the southwest corner of the market, a woman's head surrounded by outstretched arms, commemorates a politician assassinated here in 1963. A little south of the market lies the **Yahudi Hamam** (16C), a Turkish bathhouse that is now a flower market.

Hamza Bey Mosque

The mosque, built in 1467 for Bey Hamza's daughter, was restored in 1620 after a fire. The building has been converted into shops.

Bey Hamami

This Turkish bathhouse (1444) is the largest in Greece; note the stalactities decorating the men's section. It remained in use until 1968.

Ágios Dimítrios★

Crypt opening hours: Mon, 12.30-7pm; Thu-Sat, 8am-8pm; Sun 10.30am-8pm.

The impressive St Demetrios' Church marks the site of the martyrdom and tomb of St Demetrios, patron saint of Thessaloníki. After the fire in 1917 the church was restored to reproduce the 7C basilica; some of the old material (marbles, columns, mosaics) were re-used. To the left are traces of Roman baths and of a minaret (the church became a mosque from 1491 to 1912).

The pillars on either side of the entrance to the apse are decorated with small 7C **mosaics**★★. The relics of St Demetrios are venerated before the iconostasis. A stairway descends from the apse *(right)* into a **crypt** (small **Lapidary Museum**) where, according to tradition, the miraculous oil which flowed from the saint's tomb beneath the high altar was collected.

▶ *From the east end of the church go up Odós Ágios Nikolaou (old Turkish bath in the corner) and turn right into Odós Kassandrou and left into a small square.*

Alaca Imaret

This old mosque built in 1484 by Ishak Pasha, Governor of Thessaloníki under Sultan Bayazid II, was also used as a hospital *(imaret)* for the poor. Only the base of the minaret remains. A portico flanks the building, which is used for art exhibitions.

▶ *Return to St Demetrios and take Odós Dimitriou on the left.*

Rotónda★

Open Tue-Sun, 8.30am-5pm. Minaret and frescoes undergoing restoration.

Generally known as the church of St George, this building was erected in the 4C AD as a circular mausoleum for the Emperor Galerius (he is not buried here). In the following century, the mausoleum was converted into a church, and then under the Turks it became a mosque. The building now houses a **Lapidary Museum**. The interior was decorated with mosaics on a gold ground, of which a few survive, particularly at the base of the dome, where eight saintly martyrs can be seen in prayer.

Apsída Galeríou★

This triumphal arch **(Arch of Galerius)** was part of a monument erected in the 4C AD ; the pillars were faced with stone decorated with low reliefs celebrating Galerius's victories over the armies of Persia, Mesopotamia and Armenia. The south pillar is the best preserved.

Continue towards the seafront along Odós Angeláki to reach the district where most museums are located (see below).

Anáktora Galeriou

Platía Navarínou. It is possible to make out the plan of the imperial Roman palace, built of brick by Galerius, which was arranged round a rectangular courtyard.

Panagía Halkéon (Our Lady of the Coppersmiths): 11C church built on the Greek-cross plan with a central dome and a façade flanked by two towers over the narthex); **Agorá** (remains of 1C forum).

Lefkós Pírgos★

Closed until mid-2007. Icon collection currently on view at the Byzantine Museum.
The **White Tower** was originally incorporated in the ramparts that surrounded the city; it stood in the southeast corner and was the main defensive element in the section fronting the sea. Site of a massacre of rebellious Sultan guards, the building became known as the Bloody Tower, an unwelcome title which the Turks decided to suppress by painting the walls with whitewash and renaming it the White Tower. From the top there is a fine view over the city and the port.
Beyond the White Tower on the seafront stands an equestrian statue of Alexander the Great.

H Champollion/MICHELIN

The White Tower

Arheologikó Moussío★★

6 Odós Andronikou. *Open Mon 1-7.30pm; Tue-Sat 8.30am-7pm. 4€ (6€ combined ticket with the Byzantine museum).* In addition to objects excavated from sites in Macedonia and Thrace, the museum houses an outstanding collection of treasures of Ancient Macedon. Recently discovered in various tombs in northern Greece, the objects bear witness to the splendour of Macedonian society at the time of Philip II and Alexander the Great.

H Champollion/MICHELIN

From prehistory to the Classical era

The ground floor is devoted to prehistoric dwellings in Macedonia from the Neolithic to the Bronze Age. Finds from excavations on the west face of Mount Olympos are also on display, as well as funerary items (9C BC) from the cemetery at Toróni in Chalcidice. Arms, vases and jewellery in copper, gold and silver have been uncovered on the site of Agía Paraskeví southeast of Thessaloníki.

Sculpture, glass and mosaics

Sculptures include a *kouros* and a *kore*, Roman copies of Muses, and Roman portraits, including one of the Emperor Alexander Severus (3C).
The mosaics depicting Ariadne and Dionysios were found in Roman villas in Thessaloníki, and there is a fine Roman glass collection.

Treasures of Ancient Macedon

This stunning collection of precious metal objects, housed in a separate wing, consists of offerings found in tombs dating from the 4C BC and the Hellenistic period. The **Dervéni Treasure** comprises material discovered in 4C BC tombs at Dervéni: golden jewellery, vases and a huge cup in bronze gilt, and reliefs illustrating the life of Dionysos. And the **Treasury of Sindos** groups objects taken from the Sindos cemetery (6C-5C BC) west of Thessaloníki.

Turn right on leaving the museum.

Moussío Vizandinoú Politismoú (Museum of Byzantine Civilisation)

2 Odós Stratou. *Open Tue-Sun, 8am-7pm; Mon, 1-7.30pm. 4€.*
Opened in 1994, the museum houses a collection of early-Christian art and icons formerly in the White Tower. It displays various aspects of Macedonian church decoration and funerary art, and has a fine reconstruction of an ecclesiastical interior. Tthere are many fine icons, as well as embroidery, in particular the famous **Thessaloníki Epitáphios** (14C), used as a corporal cloth.

Macedonian Ethnological Museum★

68 Odós Vassilissis Olgas.
Intriguing displays of the folk art of northern Greece.

Macedonian Centre of Modern Art – Makedonikó Kéndro Sínhronís Téhnis; **Photography Museum**★ – **Contemporary Art Museum**★ – *21 Odós Kolokotroni* (works by Kandinsky, Rodchenko, Malévitch, Rozanova, etc.); **Jewish Museum** – *13 Odós Agiou Mina* (history of the Jewish people in Thessaloniki).

Upper Town

The oriental upper town stretches from Odós Olimdiados to the ramparts; it is a network of paved alleyways leading to the acropolis and the Byzantine citadel.

Dódeka Apóstoli

Open daily, 8.30am-noon and 5-7pm.
This attractive 14C church, dedicated to the Twelve Apostles, features external **brickwork**★ ingeniously arranged to form decorative geometric motifs. The mosaics and frescoes are 14C (note the Dance of Salome).

Óssios David

Open Mon-Sat, 8am-12pm and 6-8pm; Sun, 8-10.30am.
The church (5C) contains a well-preserved **mosaic**★ representing the Vision of Ezekiel. There are also some rare 12C **frescoes**; **view** of the tower from the garden.

Ramparts★

The principal section of the ramparts were built late in the 4C on Hellenistic foundations and were altered in the 14C and again in the 15C.
Following the ramparts entails a 4km walk. There are watchtowers at regular intervals; towards the northeast end is the great **Chain Tower** (Dingirlí Koulé) dating from the 15C. From near the large tower the **view**★ extends over the town and the bay. From this side the ramparts make a fine sight, linking the **towers of Manuel Palaiologos and Andronikos II** (14C).

Church of St Catherine – Agía Ekateríni (13C church with mosaics and frescoes); **Prophet Elijah's Church** – Profítis Ilías (14C building; superb monolithic columns in the transept); **St Nicholas' Church** – Ágios Nikólaos Orfanós – (charming 14C church decorated with frescoes).

THÍVA

THEBES – Θηβα

POPULATION 21 211

MICHELIN MAP 737 H 8 – BOEOTIA – CENTRAL GREECE.

Of the legendary Thebes, home of Oedipus, virtually nothing remains; The Ancient city was razed to the ground by Philip II and devastated by earthquakes; only a few vestiges remain. To get an idea of the past glories of this, the capital of Boeotia, the visitor must spend some time in the Archaeological Museum. Rebuilt in the 19C, Thebes today is a modern commercial centre located 69km/43mi northwest of Athens (84km/53mi by motorway) and 97km/61mi west of Delphi. Thebes is served by the E 75 motorway and the E 962.

A Bit of History

Ill-fated Oedipus – The most famous Theban is legendary **Oedipus**, son of Laios, King of Thebes, and Jocasta. When Laios was told by an oracle that Oedipus would kill his father and marry his mother, he abandoned him on Mount Kitherónas (Kithairon). Some shepherds rescued the boy, however, and he was raised by the King of Corinth in ignorance of his true parentage.

On reaching manhood Oedipus left Corinth; near Thebes he quarrelled with a man and killed him; it was Laios.
At that time the countryside was being terrorised by the **Sphinx**, a winged monster with a lion's body and a woman's head, which devoured passersby who couldn't answer the riddles it posed. Jocasta's brother, **Creon**, offered the throne of Thebes and Jocasta's hand to anyone who would rid the country of the Sphinx. Oedipus accepted the challenge and was asked "What is it that walks on four legs in the morning, on two at noon, on three in the evening?" "Man," answered Oedipus, correctly. In vexation the Sphinx threw herself into an abyss. Oedipus became King of Thebes and married his mother, thus fulfilling the oracle's prediction.
When Oedipus discovered the truth, he destroyed his own eyes and Jocasta hanged herself. Blind, Oedipus left Thebes accompanied by his daughter Antigone to lead a wandering life until his death at Colona (Kolonós) near Athens.

Antigone – After Oedipus's death, Antigone returned to Thebes, ruled by her brothers Polyneices and Eteocles. These two quarrelled, then fought and killed each other. The throne was seized by their uncle, **Creon**, who forbid Antigone to bury Polyneices. Oedipus's daughter defied man-made laws to follow her conscience and buried her brother before suffering her own punishment, which was to be buried alive.
The tragic legends of Oedipus and Antigone inspired the works of **Sophocles**: *Oedipus Rex* and *Antigone.*

Decline and renewal – Thebes' moment of glory came in the 4C BC when the city headed the Boeotian Confederacy and defeated Sparta at Leuktra in 371 BC, initiating a period of Theban hegemony over Greece that lasted 10 years.
After defeat at the Battle of Mantineia in 362 BC, Thebes declined and in 336 BC the city was destroyed by Alexander except for the house of the poet **Pindar**.
Thebes regained importance as a commercial centre in the Byzantine period when the silk industry flourished. It also resumed its political importance in 1205 when the Crusaders occupied the region and became a Frankish possession until the 14C.

Visit

Arheologikó Moussío★

Open Tue-Sun, 8am-7pm; Mon, 12-7pm. 2€. ☎ (22620) 27 913.
The Archaeological Museum stands near a 13C **Frankish tower** at the northern entrance to Thebes. It contains Boeotian Antiquities: in the room on the right of the entrance, Archaic sculptures including *(centre)* a superb 6C BC **kouros**★★; in the third room funerary steles in black stone (5C BC) showing representations of warriors; in the fourth room a series of sarcophagi from the Mycenaean period (13C BC).

Excursion

Glá Fortress

27km/17mi northwest of Thebes by E 75 towards Thessaloníki. In Kástro take the road east to Lárimna; turn right into a stony track which circles the fortress.
The fortress of Glá, which was originally surrounded by the dull waters of Lake Copaïs (Kopaïda), is composed of a rocky plateau enclosed by a perimeter wall built in the 14C-13C BC following the contours of the rock. Enter by the northeast gate, which is flanked by square towers. There are also traces of a Mycenaean-type palace with two *megarons*.

TÍRINTHA★★

TIRYNS – Τιρυνθα

MICHELIN MAP 737 G 10 – ARGOLIS – PELOPONNESE.

Set amid a fertile plain, the Mycenaean fortress of Tiryns is a Cyclopean structure (13C BC), a well-preserved masterpiece of Ancient military architecture. Comparable in size to Mycenae itself, it appears in the epic poems of Homer.

- **Orient Yourself:** 55km/34mi south of Corinth, on the road from Nauplion to Argos.
- **Parking:** Lot on the left, just after the "Tiryntha" sign, 4km/2.5mi north of Nauplion.
- **Organizing Your Time:** Plan 2hrs; the site is a good excursion from Nauplion.
- **Also See:** Árgos, Arhéa Epídavros, Mikínes, Náfplio

A Bit of History

The legend of Herakles – The mythological demigod and hero Herakles was born of the union between Zeus and Alkmene, queen of Tiryns. Brave and strong, Herakles as a baby strangled the serpents sent to kill him by Hera, the jealous wife of Zeus. Later, in a fit of madness, Herakles killed his own children, and the Pythia at Delphi ordered him to enter the service of Eurystheus, King of Árgos, who set him the **Twelve Labours** as a penance: to strangle the Nemean lion, to execute the many-headed hydra of Lerna, to run down the hind of Ceryneia, to capture the Erymanthian boar, to cleanse the Augean stables, to destroy the Stymphalian birds, to tame the Cretan bull, to capture the man-eating horses of King Diomedes, to obtain the girdle of the Amazon queen, to carry off the cattle of Geryon, a three-headed monster, to fetch the golden apples from the Garden of the Hesperides and finally to bring back Cerberus from Hades.

In the Achaean period (13C BC) Tiryns was subject to Mycenae and took part in the Trojan War under Agamemnon. During the Dorian invasion (12C BC) it was an independent kingdom with about 15 000 inhabitants; it was frequently in conflict with its neighbour Árgos. In 468 BC the Argives captured the city and laid it waste.

Visit

Open daily 8am-7pm (summer); 8.30am-3pm (winter). 3€.

H Champollion/MICHELIN

Part of the walls

Acropolis★★

"Wall-girt Tiryns" as Homer described it, stands on a long and narrow rocky limestone bluff; its isolated position and thick walls made it almost impregnable.
The ruins now visible date mostly from the late 13C BC. They comprise the palace on the upper level, and on the lower an elliptical precinct enclosing buildings for military, religious and economic use. Fine views of Árgos and the Argolid, Mycenae, Nauplion and the bay.
Frescoes, ceramics and terracottas from the acropolis may be seen in museums in Athens and Naupliion.

Ramparts★★

Impressive in size and strength, the ramparts were compared by Pausanias to the Ancient pyramids. The ramp (broad enough for a chariot) leads up to the main entrance to the acropolis, leaving would-be attackes exposed from the right. The gateway was reinforced by two flanking towers.
On passing through the gateway, turn left into the passage (**1**) between the outer wall and the palace. It was a real deathtrap; if the attackers managed to force the gate they could easily be annihilated at this point by projectiles hurled from every side.

Palace★

The door to the palace is marked by a stone threshold, and by one of the jambs containing the socket for the wooden bar that held the doors shut. Inside is the forecourt; steps *(left)* lead down to the east casemates.
Built around 1200 BC, the palace replaced an earlier structure. Its layout is typical of Mycenaean architecture.

East Casemates★★

A narrow gallery with a vaulted roof was built in the thickness of the ramparts; it had six casemates which were used as stores or barrack rooms.

Great Propylaia

The monumental main entrance was the forerunner of the Great Propylaia on the Acropolis in Athens, which was designed to the same plan: an inner and an outer porch covering a central passage. The Great Propylaia leads into the great court of the palace from which a staircase descends to the **south casemates**. A bit farther, the **Smaller Propylaia** (**2**) links the great court to the inner or megaron court.

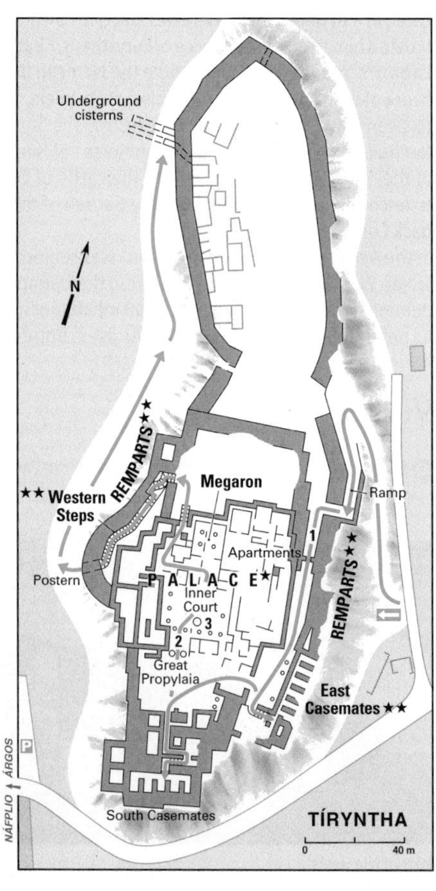

Inner Court

Originally covered with white cement; it was enclosed on three sides by porticoes of which traces remain; at the far end rose the façade of the *megaron*. On the right, within the entrance, stood the royal altar (**3**).

Megaron

As at Mycenae the *megaron* had a porch, a vestibule, and a central hearth; the king's throne stood on the right. In the 7C or 6C the *megaron* was replaced by a Temple to Hera; some of the foundations are visible. The royal apartments were on two floors on the north and east sides of the *megaron*.

Steps and Western Ramparts★★

A flight of steps winds down inside the crescent-shaped wall to a postern gate, an effective defence. If an attacking force succeeded in breaching the gate, it was assailed on all sides by the defenders, and even if some of the attackers managed to climb the steps they fell into a sort of trap at the top. There was, moreover, an additional bastion protecting the heart of the acropolis.

At the foot of the steps at the end of the ramparts are the vaulted **cisterns**.

TRÍPOLI

Τριπολι

POPULATION 25 570

MICHELIN MAP 737 G 10 – ARKADÍA – PELOPONNESE.

Trípoli is the capital of Arcadia (Arkadía) and the central point in the road network of the Peloponnese. The town is built in the centre of a high, flat plain in the limestone massif formed by erosion and surrounded by mountains of up to 2 000m/6 560ft. Because of the altitude, the climate is cool, even in summer. Tripoli is located 85km/53mi southwest of Corinth, 60km/38mi north of Sparta and 87km/54mi northeast of Kalamáta. *Town hall, 43 Ethnikis Andistaseos, ☎(27102) 318 44. Open Mon-Fri 7am-2pm.*

Visit

In the 18C, under the name of **Tripolizza**, the town was the residence of the Pasha of Morea and looked very Turkish according to Chateaubriand. It was destroyed in 1824 by Ibrahim Pasha but rebuilt: the central square is bordered by the metal awnings typical in the mountains, whereas Areos Square is open and planted with gardens; the Bazaar lies to the south on the Kalamáta road.

Archaeological Museum

Take Odós Georgiou right of the church, the n the third street on the right, then immediately left toward Odós Evangistria. Open Tue-Sun 8.30am-3pm. 2€. ☎ (27102) 421 48.

This museum is located in a fine neo-Classical house and contains items from Arkadía dating from the Neolithic and Bronze Age to the Roman period).

Excursion

Tegéa

10km/6.25mi southeast. Follow the road to Sparta for 8km/5mi; in Kerassítsa turn left (sign 'Ancient Tegéa').

Tegéa was the most important city in Arcadia in Antiquity; it came under Spartan domination in the 6C BC, was destroyed by barbarians in the 5C AD, but resurrected later by the Byzantines. Great verbena fairs were held a few miles to the south. Some Ancient vestiges can be seen around the modern **Paléa Episkopi**; nearby is a small warehouse with a mosaic from an early 5C church.

Folk Art Museum (Laografikó Moussio)

In the recreated interior of a traditional house, note the torch that bore the flame of Apollo from Olympia to Berlin for the 1936 Olympic Games.

▶ *Take the tarmac road, which leads to Aléa village.*

Temple of Athena in Aléa

This peripteral Doric sanctuary housed an Archaic ivory statue of the goddess, marble statues of Hygeia (goddess of health) and Asklepios, and the remains of the Calydonian boar. The building was designed and decorated by the great Parian sculptor, Skopas. Several fragments have been found; the most beautiful, of the Calydonian hunt, are displayed in the Athens Museum, others in the little **Archaeological Museum**.

Mandínia (Mantineia)

11km/7mi north on the Olympia and Pírgos road; follow signs up to the crossroads then go straight: after 9km/5.5mi turn right, opposite a church.

In Antiquity Mantineia was a fortified city, rivalling Tegéa for control of the plain. Excavations *(right of the road)* have uncovered traces of the walls and the foundations of several buildings including a theatre, an agora and temples.

On the opposite side of the road stands an extraordinary **church**★ (1978) dedicated to the Virgin, the Muses and Beethoven. It is a fantastic example of surrealism, incorporating multitudinous materials, decorative elements and architectural styles.

Levídi

27km/17mi north of Trípoli by the road to Olympia.

A few remains have been discovered here, notably those of a Doric sanctuary (6C BC). A track leads to the ramparts of the Ancient city, and from here, a path on the right leads to a fairly well-preserved theatre in a beautiful **setting**★.

▶ *Take the road northeast towards Kandíla; after 2km/1.25mi turn right (sign) onto the track leading to the church.*

Kimísseos Theotókou★

This beautiful 17C **Church of the Dormition of the Virgin**, features interior murals, which are interesting both for their picturesque detail and their pleasant colouring: scenes from the Old Testament, Christ's Passion, the Dormition of the Virgin; effigies of oriental saints.

Vitína

45km/28mi northeast by the road to Olympia.

A beautiful, traditional village and a renowned holiday resort, particularly popular in winter. Lovely shops selling natural regional products, good restaurants and attractive hotels. The 16C Church of Agion Apostolon is worth a visit (frescoes), as is the Craft and Folk Art Museum *(open May-Nov Mon-Fri 10am-2pm)*.

TEMPLE OF VASSÉS★★★

TEMPLE OF BASSAE – Βασσες

MICHELIN MAP 737 F 11 – ELIS – PELOPONNESE.

Sitting majestically in an isolated site some 200km/125mi south of Patras and 14km/9mi south of Andrítsena, the Temple of Bassae is thought to be the work of Iktínos, one of the designers of the Parthenon in Athens. The imposing building is the subject of an extensive restoration programme.

Visit

Open daily in summer 8.30am-8.30pm. Taxis serve the temple from the centre of the village of Andritsaina.

The **Temple of Apollo** at Bassae stands alone on a lofty forbidding **site**★★ on the southern face of Mount Paliovlátiza (Kotìlion) surrounded by ravines *(bassai)*; on the distant horizon rise the mountains of Lakonía and Messinía.

Built of greyish limestone in the Doric style, the temple was erected in the mid-5C BC by the inhabitants of Ancient Phigaleia in honour of Apollo Epikourios, a god of war who had preserved them from the plague. The internal frieze and other fragments were acquired by the **British Museum** where they are now displayed. It is one of the best preserved of Greek temples but was in imminent danger of collapse when restoration work began in 1975.

Among other unusual characteristics the building faces north (Greek temples were traditionally oriented east-west). At the southern end of the naos stands a Corinthian column, the first known in this style; the base is extant but the capital, which was decorated with acanthus leaves, is missing; the two flanking columns may also have been Corinthian. The architrave was surmounted by a frieze of sculpted metopes and the walls of the naos were decorated on the inside with another frieze of low reliefs representing the battles between the **Greeks and Amazons** on the one hand and the Centaurs and **Lapiths** on the other. This is the earliest example of a sculptured frieze decorating the interior of a Greek building, and these remarkable works can now be seen in the British Museum in London.

There is an overall view of the site from above the keeper's house.

JP Charbonnier/MICHELIN

The Temple of Apollo

VÉRIA

Βεροια

POPULATION 42 794

MICHELIN MAP 737 F 3 – IMATHÍA – MACEDONIA.

Véria is sited on a spur of Mount Vérmio overlooking the Macedonian plain. Hidden in courtyards and blind alleys among the concrete buildings of the modern town are a few Macedonian houses, Byzantine and post-Byzantine churches and a mosque; nearby are fine Macedonian tombs. Véria is located 73km/46mi southwest of Thessaloníki and 167km/104mi north of Lárissa.

Visit

Hristós

Odós Mitropoléos. *Open Tue-Sat, 8.30am-3pm.*

At the centre of the town in the **Kiriotissa Quarter★★** stands **Christchurch**, a Byzantine brick building (recently restored). Step inside to see the remarkable collection of early-14C frescoes signed by Kaliergis.

Walk a short distance to see two other churches: Ágios Kerikos with 13C frescoes (altered in the 16C); and Ágios Vlassios (Odós Perdika) dating from the 14C, with frescoes of the same date. The **Byzantine Museum** *(Odós Thomaidou)* contains ceramics, mosaics and a fine collection of icons. Also worth a peek is the **Archaeological Museum** *(Odós Mitropoléos)* with a colossal 2C BC head of Medusa.

Excursions

Vergína

15km/9.5mi southeast of Véria on the road to Melíki; after 12km/7.5mi turn right to the modern village of Vergína; at the end of the village turn left (sign 'Royal Tombs').

Address Book

For coin categories, see the Legend on the cover flap.

WHERE TO EAT

Katarrakte – *Édessa, Odós Dimotikós Kípos.* Pleasantly situated in the middle of the waterfall park, this large establishment serves unsurprising cuisine.

Peskaoudritsa – *Veroia. Odós Ioakem, Kiriotissa area.* Small family spot specialising in fish dishes; Good *mezes.*

WHERE TO STAY

Villa Elia - *Veroia, 10 Odós Elias – ☎ (23310) 26 800.* Good breakfast and sizeable rooms at this pleasant spot just steps from the old Kiriotisssa quarter.

Varosi – *Édessa, Paradosiako Ksevodocheio – ☎ (23810) 21 865 – 8rm.* In a traditional house in the old Ottoman quarter, this charming hotel has a warm and friendly atmosphere. Small, but comfortable and attractively decorated rooms. Good breakfast.

Xenia – *Édessa, corner of Odós Filípou and Odós Giannitsón – ☎ (23810) 29 706 – 36rm.* Opened in 1998, this is the most luxurious hotel in town, with a clifftop setting and a fine view over the plain. Extremely comfortable, with a very professional staff.

TAKING A BREAK

Odós Konstantinoupoloeos – *Edessa.* Bordered by a canal, a street of shady terraces invite strollers to take a break.

Erateinon – *Veroia, Odós Ioakem.* Stop for a meal or just a drink in this romantic courtyard, located in the old quarter.

The discovery in 1977 of the spectacular tomb of Philip II positively identified Vergína as the Ancient capital of Macedonia, and site of the royal burial ground. The city was built on the slopes of a hill at the end of a valley separating the Pieran chain from the Vermio massif; the necropolis was down on the plain.

Ancient City

Open Tue-Sun, 8am-7.30pm; Mon, 12-7.30pm. 8€, including museum admission.
The **Palace** (4C BC), of which only the foundations remain, consisted of a large central courtyard accessed via a portico and a tholos. The royal apartments were in the east wing. In the south wing, there are splendid mosaics *(covered for preservation purposes)*. The west wing was composed of a series of huge vestibules, their floors paved in opus sectile. The north wing was an open veranda looking out over the plain and the town.
Just below the palace lie the remains of the theatre where Philip II was assassinated.
Farther down the site is the agora, dominated by the Temple of Eukliea (a Macedonian divinity), where several marble statues, including one thought to depict the mother of Philip II, have been discovered. *To the left of the road.* Dating to the 3C BC, the hypogeum has an Ionic façade. In the funerary chamber, the marble throne has retained some of its original painted decoration.
The route comes to a small plateau from where a path leads to the remains of the little palace, the **Palatítsia**, which dates from the Hellenistic period.

Royal Tombs★★

On the plain below the city. Same opening hours as the Ancient city.
The necropolis is a veritable mass of *tumuli* (300). The royal tumulus has been restored and now houses a superb **museum**★★★. The burial chambers cannot be accessed, but their façades and the stunning finds excavated from them are on display.
The façade of the great central **tomb**, identified as that of Philip II, is closed behind a door with two marble leaves, and is adorned with a magnificent frieze. The interior, which consists of a vestibule and an inner chamber, has yielded a magnificent collection of funerary objects.
A golden coffer *(larnax)* is decorated with a 12-pointed star, the emblem of the Macedonian kings; it contained the bones of a woman and a magnificent gold diadem forming a riot of leaves, twigs and flowers with bees gathering pollen.
A larger and heavier solid **gold coffer**, is decorated with a 16-point star; it contained bones – probably those of Philip II, whose exquisite crown of golden oak leaves is displayed above. Objects thought to have belonged to Philip include a quiver covered in gold leaf embossed with scenes from the sack of Troy, an iron cuirass decorated with bands of gold, an iron sword with gold and ivory hilt and his magnificent bronze shield.
There are also some very expressive, delicately carved portraits made of ivory, probably representing the royal family of Macedon: Philip II with a beard, his wife Olympia and son Alexander.

R Corbel/MICHELIN

Office National Hellénique de Tourisme

Gold coffer

Nearby there is a smaller tomb of the same type, thought to be the tomb of Alexander IV (son of Alexander the Great, assassinated at the age of 15). The frieze in the vestibule depicts a wonderful scene of harnessed horses engaged in a race.
Farther off, a third **tomb** houses marvellous paintings (Persephone being carried off by Pluto), which may have been executed by the great master Nicomachos.

Lefkádia★★

From Véria take the Édessa road to Kopanos, 12km away. From there, follow the signposts. *Open Tue-Sat, 8.30am-3pm; Sun and public holidays, 9am-2pm. The tombs are currently closed for restoration; prior to visiting, telephone: ☎ (23310) 753 33/4.*
The region of **Náoussa**, well known for its fruit and wine production, is also famous for three unusual Macedonian *hypogea* (3C-2C BC), huge temple-like underground tombs located near the little village of Lefkádia on the Véria to Édessa road.

Great Tomb

The tomb, which was excavated in 1954, is built of conchitic limestone. A flight of steps leads down to the two-storey façade; the lower section is Doric, the upper Ionic. It was decorated with paintings; those remaining show a warrior (probably Death), the god Hermes (leader of souls to the Underworld), Aiakos and Rhadamanthos (Judges of Hades) and battle scenes.
The interior comprises a vestibule and a chamber that still contains a sarcophagus.
Walk 150m/492ft beyond the Great Tomb, left of the path, to see majestic steps descending to the superb columned façade of a well-preserved *hypogeum*.

Kinch Tomb

Named after the archaeologist who discovered it in 1880, this tomb is composed of an antechamber and main chamber which still show traces of the original painted decoration.

Lyson-Kalliklés Tomb

This underground tomb (3C or 2C BC) is accessed by a ladder. It is a burial vault for three families furnished with 22 funerary recesses inscribed with the names of the dead; the ornamental paintings are in an excellent state of preservation.

Édessa

Waterfall Park, open daily 10am-8pm ☎ (23310) 41 121.
Built on the edge of a plateau overlooking the Macedonian plain, Édessa was in Antiquity one of the main strongholds in Macedon. The town is known for the waters of the **River Vódas**, which make it an agreeable summer resort. The soothing sound of running water, its mild climate and attractive old Ottoman quarter, make Édessa a pleasant place to stay.

Waterfalls★

East of the town (sign 'Waterfalls' and 'Pros Kataráktes').
A public garden shaded by huge plane trees *(restaurant)* leads down to the point where the various streams flowing through the town meet in an impressive waterfall; the water tumbles down a rock face covered by luxuriant vegetation.

Old town

Below the modern town, north of the Thessaloníki road.
Excavations in the Longos area have revealed the remains of a Macedonian fortress and its surrounding wall built in the 4C BC and restored by the Romans, as well as ruins of early-Christian basilicas.
From here it is possible to continue to the foot of Mount Voras and the spa at Loutra Loutrakiou, where bathers can luxuriate in the warm water (37°C!).

Péla

38km/24mi east of Édessa on the E 86 Thessaloníki road.

The Ancient city of Pella was situated in the heart of the fertile Macedonian plain on the road from Édessa to Thessaloníki. Under Philip II and Alexander the Great it was the capital of Macedon.

Late in the 5C BC King Archelaos abandoned Aigai, (Vergína), and moved to Pella, where he built a splendid palace decorated with paintings by the famous Zeuxis. Here Archelaos maintained a sophisticated court, welcoming artists and men of letters, including **Euripides**, whose play *The Bacchantes* was first performed in the town theatre.

Both **Philip II of Macedon** and **Alexander the Great** were born in Pella. Alexander, who was the son of Philip and Princess Olympia, was educated in literature as well as the military arts; one of his tutors was **Aristotle**, a native of Chalcidice.

Pella grew to be the largest town in Macedon and was linked to the sea by a canal. The Roman Consul Aemilius Paulus laid waste to it in 168 BC , and the city never recovered.

Pella was mentioned or described by the Greek writers Herodotus, Thucydides and Xenophon and by the Roman historian Livy. Excavations begun in 1957 revealed its vast extent and its grid plan, which was recommended by the architect **Hippodamos of Miletus**. Remarkable Hellenistic mosaic pavements (4C-3C BC) have also been excavated.

Ruins

Open Tue-Sun, 8am-7pm; Mon, 12-7pm. €6.

The excavations on the north side of the road have uncovered the foundations of the agora. To the right lay a huge complex of buildings erected round a courtyard and an Ionic peristyle; some of the columns have been re-erected. Certain rooms were paved with mosaics: some geometric *(in situ)*, others figurative *(in the museum)*.

To the left are the foundations of other buildings; the most distant are decorated with fine **mosaic pavements**★★ illustrating the Abduction of Helen and of Deïanira, the Battle of the Amazons and a deer hunt signed by Gnosis.

The **Museum** displays the finds from the excavations, including some superb **mosaic pavements**★ (4C-3C BC): the most beautiful show Dionysos seated on a panther (the god's favourite animal) and a lion hunt in which Krateros, a comrade in arms, is supposed to have saved the life of Alexander the Great.

Among the other Hellenistic figures are a marble dog from a tomb, a head of Alexander, a small bronze statue of Poseidon and some attractive terracotta pieces.

At a distance of 3km/2mi away, on the Pella acropolis, near to the village of Ancient Pella, recent excavations have discovered more ruins, including a royal residence, which could be Philip V's palace. *Excavations in progress at the time of publication.*

Pretty backstreet, Amorgós, the Cyclades
C. Legrand/MICHELIN

DISCOVERING THE ISLANDS

KRÍTI★★★

CRETE

POPULATION 601 131

A visit to Crete offers a unique opportunity to explore some of the most fascinating stories of Antiquity, both mythological and historical. The brilliant Minoan civilization, one of the very first in Europe, flourished here, leaving a legacy of richly decorated palaces. While development has overtaken the north coast, the rest of the island reveals extraordinary gorges, mountainous landscapes and rocky coastal outcrops.

- **Orient Yourself:** Situated 100km/63mi from the Peloponnese coast, Crete is the largest and southernmost of the Greek Islands. Fifth largest island in the Mediterranean, Crete measures 260km/163mi long from east to west. There are three major mountain peaks. It is a distinct administrative region consisting of the districs of Chania, Rethymnon, Herakleion (the capital) and Lassíthi.
- **Don't Miss:** The natural highlights such as the Samariá Gorge, the palm groves of Vaï and Mirambelou Bay; the Minoan palaces of Knossós, Phaistos, Mália, and Zákros.
- **Organizing Your Time:** A three-week stay will allow you to visit all the sights of Crete in a leisurely fashion. If your time is limited (ten days or less), stick to one region—Agios Nikólaos and the East, for example.

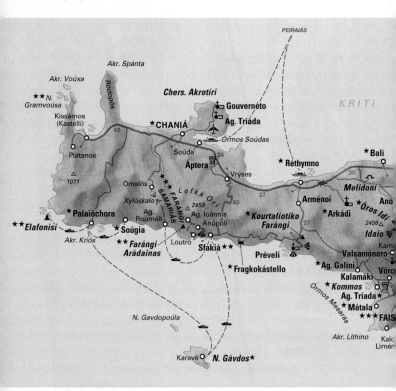

A Bit of History

Minoan civilisation – History and mythology combine in the story of Crete, legendary birthplace of **Minos**, son of the god Zeus and the nymph **Europa**. A wise and powerful king, Minos and his heirs presided over the Minoan civilisation, a sophisticated culture that endured from 2800 BC to 1000 BC. Archaeologists have identified four broad periods:

Pre-Palace period (c 2800-c 2000 BC) marked by domed circular tombs which have yielded jewellery, seals, Cycladic statuettes and pottery.

Old Palace period (c 2000-c 1700 BC) named for the first palaces built round a central courtyard bordered by the public rooms and the private apartments. The pottery, known as Kamáres ware, is decorated with exuberant polychrome patterns. During this period, Crete was the centre of a maritime empire, trading with Egypt and the Middle East. A devastating earthquake about 1700 BC brought an end to this period.

New Palace period (c 1700-c 1400 BC), so-called for the new palaces built at Knossós, Phaistos, Mália and Zákros. The new palaces were larger and incorporated light wells, networks of stairs and piped water. The walls are covered with low-relief sculptures or clean-lined paintings usually depicting ritual scenes. The script current during this period, known as **Linear A**, has not yet been deciphered.

Post-Palace period (c 1400-1100 BC) is marked by the arrival of the Mycenaeans to settle definitively in Crete, where they introduced their less-refined customs, of which traces remain (tombs of warriors buried with their weapons, palaces with a megaron). The Mycenaeans had already been subjected to the influence of Minoan civilisation, but Minoan culture gradually fell to the Mycenaean ways.

The Minoan civilisation extended beyond Crete particularly to Santorini (*see THÍRA*) but in about 1530 BC an earthquake, probably connected with the volcanic

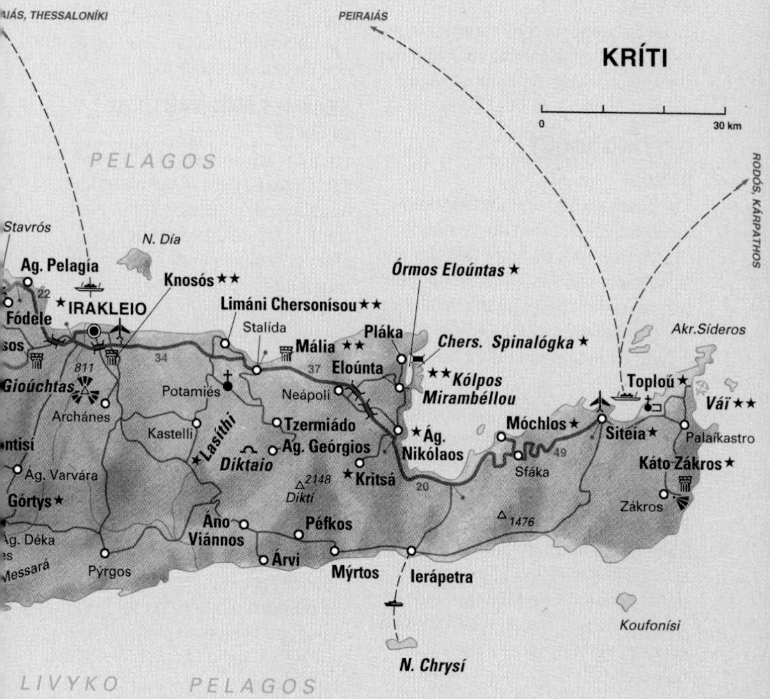

eruption on Santorini, seems to have produced a tidal wave which destroyed most of the (new) palaces. Numerous tablets bearing inscriptions in **Linear B** – a transcription of the Mycenaean dialect considered to be the oldest form of the Greek language – have been found at Knossós.

Rome, Byzantium, Venice – In 67 BC the Romans took over Crete. In AD 59 St Paul landed at Kalí Liménes; his disciple **Titus** was later sent to convert the island to Christianity. From 395 to 1204, except for a brief Arab intervention, Crete was under Byzantine rule.
Following the Fourth Crusade in 1204, Crete was assigned to the Venetians, who retained it for 400 years despite local revolts. The Venetians built many fortresses on Crete and made it their main base, controlling the sea routes for trade with the East. Churches, loggias, houses and fountains in the Venetian style remain today.

The Cretan Renaissance – The fall of Constantinople to the Turks in 1453 brought artists and men of letters to the island. Churches and monasteries were enriched with frescoes and icons by painters of the **Cretan School** in which the traditional Byzantine formality was softened by Italian influence. This school, which migrated to Metéora

Address Book

GETTING THERE

BY AIR

Crete has air links with all the major cities in Europe. The main airports are Herakleion and Hanía. Flights also link Rhodes and Herakleion.

BY BOAT

There are frequent ferry services from Piraeus to the main ports on the island: Herakleion, Hanía, Rethymnon, Ágios Nikólaos (3/wk) and Sitía (3/wk).

GETTING ABOUT

BY BUS

The buses are frequent and the timetables reliable for the two main lines (Herakleion-Sitía via Ágios Nikólaos and Herakleion-Chania via Rethymnon). Be sure to confirm times for the smaller lines to the interior of the island. Service is spotty Sundays and public holidays.

BY BOAT

Boats link certain towns with surrounding beaches and islands, particularly in the southwest: Kastelli, Paleohóra, Sougia, Agia Roumelli, Loutro, Sfakiá.

BY CAR OR TWO WHEELS

Numerous rental car agencies, particularly in Herakleion. Plenty of petrol stations (often closed Sundays and public holidays). The car is best for long journeys; certain places are not accessible by bus.
You can rent bicycles, scooters and motorbikes in all the main towns.

ON FOOT

There is a marked route around the island (yellow and black signs). The route through the Samaria Gorge is the best of the marked routes in Crete. Remember that up in the mountains weather conditions can deteriorate very quickly (storms, snow, fog).

BEACHES AND NAUTICAL SPORTS

Crete has some wonderful beaches. The best lie to the west of the island (around Kastelli) and to the east. Those on the south coast are usually pebbly and often difficult to get to. The beaches on the north coast are the busiest.
There are watersports centres across the island: water-skiing, paragliding, windsurfing, pedalos etc. Head for the south coast for scuba diving.

HANDICRAFTS

Local **crafts** include leather (Chania), rugs, quilts, ceramics, jewellery and embroidery. The island's **gastronomic specialities** include thyme honey, wine (Minos, Lato, Angelo, Gortys, Sitía) and especially the excellent olive oil.
The **markets** usually offer the best choice and the lowest prices. The covered market in Chania is one of the best in Crete.

H Le Gac/MICHELIN

and Mount Athos with Théophane the Cretan in the 16C, reached its apogee with **Damaskinós** and particularly Domenico Theotokópoulos, known as **El Greco** (1541-1614), a painter of icons who emigrated first to Venice, then to Rome and finally to Spain. Later in the 17C other artists such as Emmanuel **Tzanés** settled in the Ionian Islands.

Crete under the Turks – The Turkish occupation of Crete following the capture of Herakleion in 1669 was very harsh, and entailed forced conversions to Islam. Revolts erupted, particularly in 1770 under the leadership of the Sfakiot **Daskaloyánnis**. Works of the Cretan writers, Kazantzákis and Prevelákis, recall this conflict.
Finally in 1878 Crete acquired a certain measure of autonomy under the aegis of the Great Powers and the regency of Prince George of Greece. Crete was finally attached to Greece in 1913.

Battle of Crete (1941) – After occupying mainland Greece the Germans turned their attention to Crete. On 21 May 3 000 parachutists captured Máleme aerodrome to the west of Chania which served the Germans as a base for their penetration along the north coast of the island. The British, Australian and New Zealand troops were obliged to retreat over the White Mountains to embark at Sfakiá. It took the Germans only 10 days to capture the whole island.

ÁGIOS NIKÓLAOS★

Αγιος Νικολαος
POPULATION 10 080
MICHELIN MAP 737 M 16 – LASITHI.

Ágios Nikólaos (St Nicholas) is a lively resort on a small lake linked to the sparkling waters of Mirambélou Bay. On the waterfront, cafés, tavernas and restaurants spill out onto the pavement in typical Mediterranean style, ideal for lingering over a glass of *soumáda*, a refreshing almond drink. Located 70km/44mi east of Herakleion, Ágios Nikólaos makes a good centre from which to explore the eastern end of the island. *North of the canal linking the lake with the sea. ☎ (28410) 22 357. Open daily 8am-8.30pm.*

Visit

Lake Voulisméni★
Steep slopes riddled with caves encircle this pretty lake. The lake was formerly known as 'Artemis' Pool' and believed to be bottomless. In fact it is 64m/210ft deep; the channel to the sea was dug in 1870.

Fishing harbour
Extending behind the quayside, the harbour is a lively spot lined with restaurants. Boats to the island of Spinalónga depart from here. At the end of the quay there is a fine **view**★ taking in island, mountains and bay.

Phototravellers/MICHELIN

The port, Ágios Nikólaos

Kitroplatía Beach

East of the resort, 3 min on foot from the lake.

Bordered by restaurant terraces, this sandy beach is overlooked by mountains. Stroll the north promenade to the port, or along the south **promenade**★ along the parapet; both offer lovely views. Farther to the south are the yachting marina and long, sandy Amnos beach.

Arheologikó Moussío

North of the town, in Odós Konstandínou Paleológou. Open Tue-Sun, 8.30am-3pm. 3€. ☎ (28410) 24 943.

A wealth of objects found at Agía Fotia (near Sitía), the largest Ancient necropolis unearthed on Crete, illustrate the daily life and religious practices of the Early Minoan period. Amongst the museum's showpieces are the Goddess of Mírto, an extraordinary libations vase in the shape of a woman (7C BC) and the head of a young athlete with a laurel crown in gold (1C BC).

Driving Tours

Bay of Elounta★

43km/27mi round trip from Ágios Nikólaos. Allow a day including Spinalónga Island.

From Ágios Nikólaos take Odós Koundoúrou, which turns into a very beautiful corniche road providing frequent **views**★ over Mirambélou Bay.

Elounta

Situated at the end of the bay of the same name, the fishing port of Elounta has become a busy holiday resort known for its luxurious hotels.

Spinalónga Peninsula★

Protected area, access only on foot.

J.-P. Naïl/MICHELIN

Ghostly atmosphere on Spinalónga Island

East of Elounta, the peninsula lies on the far side of the salt pans created by the Venetians.

Oloús, a settlement dating back to Minoan times, rises near two windmills. Most of the ruins now lie underwater but are visible in calm weather. Lovely little bays provide good swimming opportunities, but be careful of the waves. There is a fine **view**★★ of Spinalónga Island and the coast.

Address Book

For coin categories, see the Legend on the Cover Flap.

GETTING THERE

By boat – There is a ferry to **Piraeus** *(5/wk)*, the **Cyclades**, the town of **Sitía** and **Rhodes** *(3/wk)*, **Kárpathos** *(4/wk)*.

WHERE TO EAT

Avil – *12 Odós Príngipa Georgíou, ☎ (28410) 82 479.* Welcoming tables in a gravel courtyard shaded by a huge fig tree. Good food, and very friendly service.

Pelagos – *10 Odós Kateháki, set back from the lake, ☎ (28410) 25 737.* Excellent fish, including swordfish fillets, crayfish, sea-urchin soup and mussels with cheese. The setting is delightful. Booking essential for dinner.

Faros – *on Kitroplatía Beach, ☎ (28410) 83 168.* Enormous barbecue (tended by the owner) beside the pebble beach. Try lamb with cheese or fresh fish grilled over the wood fire.

WHERE TO STAY

Pension Mary – *13 Odós Evans, ☎ (28410) 23 760– 9rm.* Personal service from the charming owner. Visitors have access to a kitchen and a roof terrace. Pleasant and quiet.

Victoria – *34 Aktí Koundoúrou, ☎ (28410) 22 731 – 18rm.* Refined, tasteful decor. Prices are reasonable.

Du Lac – *17 Odós 28-Oktomvriou – ☎(24810) 227 11 – 24rm.* Best location in town; ask for a room with lake view.

Miramara – *Gargadoros – ☎(28410) 229 62/238 75 – 226rm.* South of the town centre, handsome grop of rooms and bungalows overlooking Mirambelou Bay.

Minos Palace – *on the Eloúnda road, running on from Aktí Koundoúrou, ☎ (28410) 23 801/9, minpal@odenet.gr – 148rm.* A huge extravagance! Antique furniture, reception area with flagstone flooring, magnificent terrace shaded by olive trees overlooking the sea. The rooms are also luxurious.

TAKING A BREAK

Café du Lac – *17 Odós 28-Oktomvríou. Open late, every day year-round.* Popular hangout for locals. Quietly trendy atmosphere; subdued lighting. Excellent choice of international music.

Café Candia – *12 Odós Iossif Koundoúrou.* One of the busiest bars in town. Popular for its music and relaxed atmosphere.

Internet café Peripou – *25 Odós 28-Oktomvríou.* Internet access, books and CDs. Lovely terrace overlooking the lake. Opens in the morning for coffee on the terrace and stays open until very late in the evening.

EVENTS AND FESTIVALS

In 1999, the town inaugurated its first **Nationalities Festival**: every day a different European nationality is honoured through its dances and culinary specialities. The festivities, like a sort of village fair, are held at the open-air theatre near the lake in early October. There are also various other musical and theatrical events held over the summer; check with the Tourism Office.

SHOPPING

On Odós 28 Oktomvríou there is a **delicatessen** with a vast and appetising range of island products, including honey, oil, fine spirits and preserves.

SPORTS AND LEISURE

Boat trip to Spinalónga Island: fees and departure times, inquire at the Tourism Office.

Spinalónga Island

Access by boat from Ágios Nikólaos or Elounta. Daily departures 9.30am to 4.30pm.

Off the northern end of the peninsula lies a rocky islet on which the Venetians built a fortress in the 16C. From 1904 to 1958, the island housed a leper colony; today it is uninhabited.

Pláka

The little village is a popular resort with a fishing harbour and pebble beach.

Mirambélou Bay★★

100km/63mi round trip. Head east out of Ágios Nikólaos.

The road follows the magnificent rocky coast of Mirambélou Bay, passing many attractive inlets, some of them suitable for swimming and scuba diving. Fine **views**★★ down over the headlands and islands and up to the inland mountains.

Ruins of Gourniá

20km/12.5mi east of Ágios Nikólaos. Open Tue-Sun, 8.30am-3pm. 2€.

On a hill above Mirambélou Bay lie the ruins of a Minoan city dating from 1500-1450 BC. The town plan is clearly visible; it's easy to make out streets, squares, buildings and houses.

Pahía Ámos

This fishing village flanks a rather windswept beach.

Móhlos★

In Sfakiá the road descends to this little quay which is hidden in an inlet opposite a tiny island where a mass of Minoan material was discovered. Terrace restaurants and cafes make the harbour a pleasant stop.

Wonderful **walks**★★ along the bay departing from Mochlos. *Botanic tours (08430) 947 25.*

Hinterland★

25km/15mi round trip. Head southwest out of Ágios Nikólaos.

Church of Panagía Kerá★

1km/0.5mi from Kritsá. Open Tue-Sun, 8.30am-3pm. 3€. (28410) 51 525.

A clump of cypress trees conceals a charming white church built in the 13C at the beginning of the Venetian occupation. The church contains a remarkable series of 14C and 15C **frescoes**★★, both sophisticated and naïve, in vivid colours.

Kritsá★

This is a picturesque little town: its streets, arches and steps cling to the mountain slope among almond orchards overlooking Mirambélou Bay. In the summer season traditional folklore festivals (enactment of a Cretan wedding) are held.

Return in the direction of Ágios Nikólaos. Take the first left out of Kritsá.

Ruins of Lató★

4km/2.5mi northeast of Kritsá.

This isolated and awesome **site**★★ reveals traces of an Ancient town scattered over the slopes in a sort of suspended amphitheatre.

Lató was founded in the 8C BC on a saddle between two crags, each crowned by an acropolis; the position of the agora is indicated by the rectangular open space at the centre of the site; there are traces of a small shrine and a cistern at its centre.
The steps on the left of the agora led up to a **Prytaneion** (3C BC) where the magistrates met in a small court surrounded by a peristyle. From the northern acropolis there is an extensive view down to Mirambélou Bay.
From the other side a path leads to a polygonal retaining wall below a little **Temple of Apollo** (4C-3C BC). Beyond, a series of steps indicates the site of a theatre.

HANIÁ

CHANIA – Χανια

POPULATION 53 373

MICHELIN MAP 737 J 15 – HANIÁ.

Chania lies at the foot of the peak of Lefká Óri in the northwest region of Crete. Above a fishing port, the old town is criss-crossed with alleyways. Beyond the ramparts of the old Venetian and Ottoman settlement, however, extends a modern industrial area laid out on a grid pattern. *29 Odós Kidonias, (28210) 929 43. Open Mon-Fri, 8am-2.30pm; Sat 9am-2pm.*

A Bit of History

Chania Bay was particularly prosperous during the Minoan period and the palace of Kydonia rivalled Knossós and Gortyn, especially in the 2C BC.

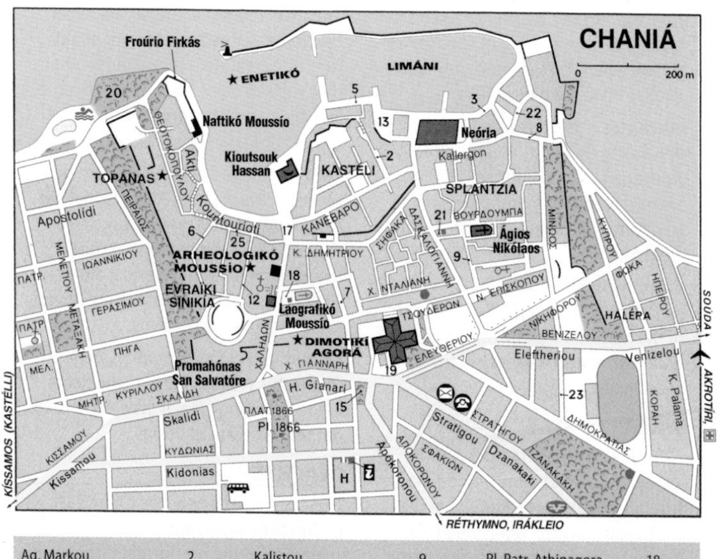

Ag. Markou	2	Kalistou	9	Pl. Patr. Athinagora	18
Akti Enosseos	3	Kondilaki	12	Pl. S. Venizelou	19
Akti Tombazi	5	Pl. 1821	21	Pl. Talo	20
Douka	6	Pl. El. Venizelou	17	Radamanthios	22
Ep. Hrisanthou	7	Pl. Katehaki	13	Trikoupi	23
Epimenidou	8	Pl. Mahis tis Kristis	15	Zambeliou	25

Address Book

For coin categories, see the Legend on the cover flap.

TRANSPORT

GETTING THERE

By air: the airport is 13km/8mi east of the town (bus service to Chania). In summer, there are numerous charter flights from the main cities in Europe. For the rest of the year the main air link (daily flights) is with Athens; also Thessaloniki (2/wk).

By boat: Ferry service between **Piraeus** and the Chania port of Souda, 7km/4mi east of the town (bus links).

WHERE TO EAT

Vassiliko – *Odós Aktí Enósseos, eastern harbour.* A good unpretentious place where locals tackle healthy portions of fish, sea-urchin soup and traditional dishes.

Taverna Dinos – *Odós Aktí Enósseos, after Vassiliko, ☏ (28210) 41 865.* Very good place in the quieter part of the harbour. Stellar service. Aubergine salads, fresh sea urchins and grilled fish.

Taverna Semiramis – *Passageway to the right of Odós Skoufón, as you come from the harbour, ☏ (28210) 98 650.* Live, traditional music, diligent service. Try the succulent Cretan lamb slow-cooked in olive oil and white wine.

Tholos – *36 Odós Agíon Déka, behind the cathedral, ☏ (28210) 46 725.* Housed in an old Venetian mansion. A smart restaurant; menu sagely mixes traditional Cretan dishes with house creations.

Monasteri – *12 Aktí Tombázi, ☏ (28210) 55 527.* In the liveliest part of the harbour. Try 'the nun's mistake', grilled pork with a variety of fried vegetables.

WHERE TO STAY

Stella Rooms – *10 Odós Agélou, ☏ (28210) 73 756 – 8rm.* A good place with affordable rates. Enquire at the craft shop just next door. Very clean medium-sized rooms with new bathrooms. Four rooms have little balconies.

Palazzo Hotel – *54 Odós Theotokopoúlou, ☏ (28210) 93 227. Open Apr-Oct.* Warm welcome at this hotel with its wonderful old façade and antique furnishings. Spacious rooms (safes and fridges) named after Greek gods and goddesses (Athena, Apollo, etc); six have balconies and some have baths. Breakfast on the roof garden with lovely views of town and sea.

Porto del Colombo – *On the corner of Odós Theofánous and Odós Moshón, ☏ (28210) 98 466, columpo@otenet.gr – 10rm.* One of the town's oldest Turkish houses; it may have served as a prison. However, don't be put off: though dark, the rooms are charming.

Casa Delfino Suites – *9 Odós Theofánous, ☏ (28210) 87 400/93 098, casadel@cha.forthnet.gr.* Quite simply magnificent! Enormous, elegant, luxury suites. Immaculate marble bathrooms, large mezzanines preceding the bedrooms and sumptuous floor tiles. Wood and copper details – this old Venetian mansion has been superbly renovated. Booking recommended.

TAKING A BREAK

Konstantinoypolis – *Odós Episkópou Dorothéou, behind the cathedral.* Very effective traditional Greek café decor: two terraces upstairs and a lot of old furniture creating a cosy atmosphere that you can enjoy for hours with a coffee. The parrot that greets you on the ground floor only speaks Greek.

Café Candia – *Aktí Tombázi, 30m before you reach the mosque.* A traditional old café, which is nonetheless quite chic, where Greek couples come at dusk to enjoy the harbour air and a drink. Ouzo served with little snacks of olives, tomatoes, feta and prawns.

Kronos – *23 Odós Mousouron, behind the market.* A smart place in the heart of the shopping area. A little expensive, but the cakes are delicious.

BEACHES

There are several beaches to the east of the town. **Agia Marina**, about 10km/6mi, is the prettiest and the busiest: it can get very crowded in summer.

Phototravellers/MICHELIN

Snow-covered mountains form a backdrop to the town of Chania

Renamed Canea, the city was redesigned in the Italian manner during the Venetian period (1252), but took on some oriental trappings during the Turkish occupation. In 1851, the Turks set up the Cretan headquarters for their Ottoman administration in Canea. The town kept its status as capital of Crete until 1971.

Walking Tour

Venetian harbour★

The old districts of Chania radiate from this superb crescent-shaped quayside, which forms a wide promenade lined with bars and restaurants that attract crowds in the evening. It's charming, and the noble Venetian façades are always a pleasure to look at.

The Topanas District★

Northwest of the Venetian port.

At the end of Koundourioti Quay is the Firkas fort (1629), housing the **Naval Museum of Crete** (Naftiko Moussio). The museum relates the naval history of the island through a fine collection of model ships and other seafaring equipment (*open Apr-Oct daily 10am-4pm; Nov-Mar daily 10am-2pm. 2.50€. ☎ (28210) 91 875.*

Heading back towards the port, the little alleyways are lined with old **Venetian mansions**, their walls a distinctive yellow ochre. Look out for the ornate stone entrances with their coats of arms and carvings. There are also old Ottoman houses, their upper floors made of wood.

The Hevraiki District

South of the Venetian port.

Wedged between the buildings in the heart of the old Jewish quarter is the Venetian Church of Ágios Frangíscos, a majestic 14C basilica. It was later transformed into a mosque by the Turks and now houses a fine **Archaeological Museum**★ displaying stone sarcophagi, Minoan ceramics and Roman mosaics. (*open Tue-Sun, 8.30am-7.30pm; Mon 1-7.30pm; 2€ (including entrance to the Byzantine Collection: 3€). ☎ (28210) 90 334.*

In the Cathedral Square is the old Catholic church which now houses the **Museum of Cretan Folklore** (*open Easter-Oct Mon-Fri 9am-7pm, Sat 9am-1pm; rest of the year 9am-3pm, 5-9pm. 2€. ☎ (28210) 908 16)*, where you can see lovely embroidery work as well as reconstructions of scenes from daily life on Crete.

Around the covered market★

Platia E. Venizélou.

Don't miss a late-morning stop at this bustling market hall purveying all kinds of foodstuffs including fish, seafood, meat, cheese, spices and cakes.

The Kastelli District

East of the Venetian port.
The district lies along the quayside towards the **Janissaries' Mosque** (Kioutsouk Hassan) (17C). Just behind it rises the site of Ancient **Kydonia**.

The Splánzia District

Continue east; the quayside is lined with the impressive arches of the Venetian arsenals (16C). Farther along, in the direction of the new town, take a look at the 14C Church of **Ágios Nikólaos**, flanked by both a campanile and a minaret.

Excursions

Samariá Gorge★★★

South of Chania – 41km/26mi from the car park to Xilóskalo where the walk starts. Open 1 May-15 Oct, daily 7am-3pm. 4€.
The awesome Samariá Gorge pierces the heart of the **White Mountains** (Lefká Óri), where surface water has worn away a huge ravine (18km/11.25mi long) extending from the Omalós Plateau down to the Libyan Sea.

From the trailhead at Xilóskalo, a twisting path makes the steep descent to a platform where there is an impressive **view**★★ of the ravine between sheer rock walls. From there the path descends precipitously to the bottom of the gorge. Farther on sits the village of Samariá, its handful of houses now deserted. Beyond are the **Iron Gates**★★★, where the distance between the vertical walls is not more than 2-3m/7-10ft. Eventually the stream bed widens out and reaches Agía Rouméli (known in Antiquity as Tarrhia) on the edge of the Libyan Sea. From here boats make the trip to Sfakiá.

Walking the Gorge

The simplest way of visiting the gorge, classified as a National Park, is to join an organised all-day excursion starting from Chania; reservations can be made at hotels, a tourist agency or the EOT. Walkers are transported to the top of the gorge by coach. They are collected at the lower end in Agía Rouméli by boat, which docks about 1hr 30min later in Sfakiá (return coach to Chania). The walk through the gorge takes 6-7hrs and makes a 1 250m/4 100ft descent. Be sure to carry water and wear stout shoes and a hat.

Those who do not wish to walk the entire gorge may go down as far as the viewing platform *(1hr 30min round trip)*.

Akrotiri Peninsula

East of Chania.
The arid Akrotiri peninsula separates the Bay of Souda from the Bay of Hani. Although most of it is a military zone (many of the roads are closed to civilians) the island's traditional village and quiet beaches make for a pleasant trip. Worth a stop is the **Tafos Venizelou**★ (Venizelos's Tomb), *at the summit of the Profitis Ilias hills*, tomb of Greek statesman **Elefthérious Venizélos** (1864-1936). There's a grand **view**★★ over Chania, the bay and the White Mountains.

Agia Triada Monastery

17km/11mi east of Chania, near the village of Koumares. Head for the airport; where the runways end take the road for Mouzouras, and then left again. Open Tue-Sun 8am-7pm. 1.50€.

The church (1631) has a beautiful pink façade in the Italian Renaissance style and a campanile with three bells; collection of icons and other liturgical objects.

Gouverneto Monastery

Head north for 4km/2.5mi. Not open to the public.
This enormous, fortresslike monastery looms at the far end of the peninsula. Rebuilt in the 16C by the Venetians, the church shows a strong Italian influence.

Aptera Ruins

17km/11mi east of Chania in the direction of Rethymnon. Take the turning to the right (signposted). No charge. (25410) 51 003.
At the foot of the mountain are the ruins of a town that flourished from the 5C BC to the Byzantine period. Within the fine outer walls are the remains of temples, a Roman theatre and a fine underground Roman cistern with three aisles.
From the fort at the far end of the promontory there is a very fine **view**★★ of the mountain and of **Soúda Bay**, which serves both as the commercial port of Hanía *(ferries to Piraeus)* and as a strategic naval base.

Gonia Monastery

West of Chania by the coast road to Kissamos. Open Tue-Sun 8.30am-12.30pm and 4-8pm, Sat 4-8pm. No charge. (28240) 225 18.
The church and adjacent chapels of this Venetian monastery (1618) house an interesing **icon collection**★. From the rear terrace, there's a lovely view over the bay.

IERÁPETRA

Ιεραπετρα
POPULATION 11 678
MICHELIN MAP 737 M 16 – LASITHI.

Situated on the southeast coast of Crete, Ierápetra is the most southern town in Europe and enjoys a mild winter climate. It is a market for the agricultural products of the coastal plain and also a popular resort with a long sandy beach bordered by a taverna-lined promenade.

Walking Tour

Although devoted to fishing and coastal traffic, the **port** is not unattractive; the entrance is commanded by a 13C fortress with square bastions.
A labyrinth of alleyways and little houses, the **old town** has a tranquil feel. Bearing traces of Turkish occupation, Odós Anagnostaki leads to the **Ottoman fountain** and a minaret. Heading towards the seafront, look out for the house where Napoleon is supposed to have spent the night on his return from Egypt (1799).
The small **Archaeological Museum** *(open Tue-Sun 8.30am-pm; 2€; (28420) 287 21)* features a fantastic Minoan sarcophagus in terracotta.

Excursions

Hrissí Island

Boat trip (allow a day) departs from Ierápetra.
A wild and beautiful island with pretty beaches, clear blue water and cedar forests.

Address Book

WHERE TO EAT

⊖ **Levante** – *Odós Samouíl, heading towards the centre from the Hotel Kástro.* For a good introduction to Cretan cuisine, try the specialty platter.

⊖ **Babi's** – *68 Odós Samouíl, ☎ (28420) 24 048.* Mainly frequented by locals. Go for the fish and seafood specialities: swordfish fillet, cuttlefish in wine, and grilled fish on skewers.

WHERE TO STAY

⊖ **Cretan Villa** – *16 Odós Opiarhigu Lakerda, ☎ (28420) 283 45 – 9rm.* Ierápetra's most charming address. Old stone building with large rooms around a pleasant patio. Warm welcome.

⊖ **Katarina Rooms** – *on the seafront promenade – ☎(28420) 263 45 – 15rm.* Without several regular hotel amenities, this establishment offers very good value for its location and quality.

⊖⊖ **Porto Belissario** – *Ferma, 12km/8mi east of Ierápetra – ☎ (28420) 61 36 – 33 rm.* Modern establishment between the sea and the mountains. Large rooms with balconies and sea views. A pleasant base for a holiday.

TAKING A BREAK

Cafétéria Beterano – *On the corner of Odós M. Kothri and Koundourou.*Popular snack spot, morning and night.

Phototravellers/MICHELIN

West of Ierápetra

The coast has been largely developed for tourism, sometimes to the detriment of aesthetics. After 20km/13mi the road reaches the verdant **Mírtos Valley** (oranges, bananas, vines). Beyond the village of **Péfkos** a track bears left, past an imposing monument dedicated to the victims of German execution squads, down to **Árvi**, a fishing village overlooked by a monastery of unusual construction. Farther along the road is **Áno Viános** (43km/27mi), which stands on a spectacular mountainous site overlooking a great sweep of olive trees.

IRÁKLIO★

HERAKLEION – Ηρακλειο

POPULATION 133 012

MICHELIN MAP 737 L 15 – IRÁKLIO.

Capital of Crete since 1971, Herakleion is a modern town buzzing with life, its grand avenues lined with shops. It is often an obligatory point of reference for many travellers as its airport is the largest on the island. Although the old town has largely been rebuilt since the Second World War, many old buildings have been preserved. There is also a very good museum devoted to the Minoan civilisation. *Odós Xanthoudidi, opposite the Archaeological Museum. ☎ (28102) 46 229.*

▶ **Orient Yourself:** Favourite meeting places include Platía Eleftherías and Platía El Venizélou with their pavement cafés, bookshops and newspaper kiosks; and Odós Dedálou with its souvenir shops, local crafts, restaurants and tavernas.

Don't Miss: The superb archaeological museum at nearby Knossós.

A Bit of History

According to legend, Herakleion takes its name from **Herakles** (Hercules) who landed on Crete to master the Cretan bull that was ravaging the Kingdom of Minos; the task was one of his Twelve Labours (*see Tírintha*).

Known as Candia under the Venetians, the city became a commercial and military centre, the key to the rest of Crete. The Cretans, however, hated the Venetians, who oppressed them with heavy taxes.

Address Book

For coin categories, see the Legend on the cover flap.

TRANSPORT

GETTING THERE

By air: in high season (Jun-Sep), the airport (4km/2.5mi east) is served by daily charter flights from major European cities. Out of season, connecting flights from Athens. Bus shuttle to Odós Eleftherias on the outskirts of town.

By boat: Ferry services between Herakleion and **Piraeus** *(2/day, 12hr)*; **Santorini** *(1/day in season)*; **Thessaloníki** *(2/wk)*; **Páros** *(1/day summer)*; **Náxos** *(1/day summer)* etc.

WHERE TO EAT

Kafeneion – *Odós Minotavrou, ☎ (28102) 27 799.* Pleasant spot near the El Greco Park. Charming frescoes decorate the wall at the back. Excellent Greek dishes. Highly recommended.

Pagopion (Ice Factory) – *Platía Ágios Títos, just behind the town hall.* This ultra-trendy bar-restaurant is perfect for a change from kebabs and moussaka. Copious portions of elaborate international fare.

WHERE TO STAY

Due to the proximity of the airport, planes fly overhead day and night. So choose a room with double glazing and air-conditioning.

Hellas Rent Rooms – *Odós Hándakos 24, ☎ (28102) 88 851 – 13rm.* An attractive, modest little guesthouse. Friendly atmosphere. A delightful terrace on the top floor. Simple, spacious rooms. Very clean shared showers and toilets on the landing.

Hotel Lena – *4 Odós Lahana ☎(28102) 232 80 – 16rm.* Some rooms with en suite facilities, some with shared baths. Warm welcome.

Kastro Hotel – *4 Odós Theotokopoulou – ☎(28102) 850 20 – 38rm.* Modern, tasteful hotel, a good choice in this price range.

Astoria – *Platía Eleftherías, ☎ (28103) 43 080, astoria@her.forthnet.gr – 131rm.* The only luxury international hotel in town. Spacious, impeccable rooms. Roof terrace with a tiny swimming pool and a bar.

TAKING A BREAK

Fix – *Odós Pardiari, on the left coming from Odós Dedálou.* Relaxing atmosphere with gentle jazz in the background. It can get crowded here. Concerts in winter.

Vicenzo – *Corner of Odós Vanou and Pl. Kornarou.* Pleasant refreshment stall where you can take a break with a salad or a sandwich.

SHOPPING

Market – The town's main market has been named after the street in which it is located, Odós 1866. Look out for the olive oil, pistachio nuts (delicious), thyme honey and other Mediterranean specialities.

EVENTS AND FESTIVALS

Herakleion Summer Festival – *Information ☎ (28103) 99 399.* In August the town organises concerts, exhibitions, plays (particularly in Fort Koúles), singing and dancing.

H. Champollion/MICHELIN

The Venetian Fortress commanding the entrance to the port

The year 1648 began the **Great Siege**, a 20-year battle between the Turks and the Venetians for control of Candia (and thereby Crete). The Venetians surrendered in 1669, marking the end of Venetian sway in the eastern Mediterranean.
Under the Turks Candia gradually lost its importance to Chania, which became the capital of Crete until 1971.

Visit

Archaeological Museum★★★

Open Apr-Oct: Tue-Sun, 8am-7.30pm, Mon, 1-7.30pm. Nov-Mar: daily, 8.30am-3pm. 6€ (combined ticket with the site at Knossós: 10€). ☏ (28102) 26 092. Allow 2hr.
The National Archaeological Museum is devoted to the Minoan civilisation discovered at the end of the last century. The exhibits are arranged in chronological order; the most interesting rooms are Room IV and Room VII. Please note that the position of the items may vary.

Room I (5000-1900 BC)

Funerary articles include Vassilikí vases (red decoration on a light ground), golden jewellery from Móhlos Island, and seals used as signets.

Rooms II and III (1900-1700 BC)

Votive offerings and a remarkable series of **Kamáres ware**. Note also the **Phaistos Disk**★★; the hieroglyphs inscribed in a spiral on the clay (not yet deciphered) are suggestive of the labyrinth of the Minotaur.

Room IV (1700-1450 BC)

Masterpieces of Minoan civilisation include the **Snake Goddesses**★★, faience statuettes of barebreasted priestesses found in the central shrine at Knossós; a soapstone **vase**★★ *(rhyton)* in the shape of a bull's head; an extraor-

H. Champollion/MICHELIN

The Phaistos Disk

dinary ivory **acrobat** involved in the ritual bull-leaping and a set of ivory chessmen.

Room V (1450-1300 BC)
Objects of porphyry and alabaster; clay tablets inscribed in Linear A and B. Also funerary objects: the group of sacred dancers and scenes from the cult of the dead in terracotta comes from a *thólos* tomb at Kamilári, southwest of Phaistos.

T.A.P.
The Parisienne

Room VII (1700-1450 BC)
This room is one of the richest in the museum. Note especially the huge bronze double-headed axes; the **Harvester Vase** showing a procession of peasants and musicians; the **Chieftain Cup**; the Boxer Vase, a conical vessel *(rhyton)* decorated with ritual bull-leaping scenes. Note also the curious bronze ingots weighing 40kg/88lb and the **golden pendant**★★ composed of two foraging bees.

Rooms VIII and IX (1700-1450 BC) and room X (1400-1150 BC)
Objects discovered in the palace at Zákros: ritual vases including a rock-crystal *rhyton* with pearl handles, and a splendid green and white stone *amphora*. Also note the *amphora* decorated with an octopus from Palékástro and large female figures with headdresses of birds, horns and poppies.

Rooms XI(1150-800 BC)
Interpenetration of the Minoan, Greek and Oriental styles is evidenced by female idols and a curious chariot drawn by bulls; cinerary urns with lids and bronze objects found in a cave on Mount Ida. A jug *(oinochoë)* depicts the lovers Theseus and Ariadne.

Room XII
Pieces depicting Cretan athletes from the Minoan civilisation to the time of the Panhellenic Games. Note especially the extraordinary **ivory acrobat**.

Room XIII
Minoan sarcophagi from the Post-Palace period (c 1400-1100 BC) often look like baths or chests.

Rooms XIV, XV and XVI
Two rooms are devoted to Minoan **frescoes** from the New Palace period, which show similarities with frescoes from the Palace of Mari (Sumerian civilisation). They have been reconstructed from fragments – some parts are in relief – and show the high quality of mural painting in the palaces of this period.
One of the chief exhibits in the museum is the **Agía Triáda sarcophagus**★★. On the walls are the **Prince of the Lilies**, a bull's head and an acrobat, all from Knossós. **Room XV** contains the famous **Parisienne**★★, found at Knossós; the small-scale but well-preserved figure represents a priestess. Other well-known frescoes: the *Monkey Collecting Saffron*, a *Dancer* and *An Officer of the Black Guard of the Sacred Knots*, and two remarkable frescoes, called *The Olive Tree*, from the Palace at Knossós.

Room XVIII
Objects in gold dating from 2000 BC.

Rooms XIX and XX
The last rooms house Greek and Greco-Roman sculptures, including a marble Aphrodite (1C).

Historical and Ethnographical Museum – (Istoriko Moussio)
Open Mon-Sat 9am5pm. 3€. ☎(28102) 832 19.
in an elegant neo-Classical building, insight into the history and traditions of Crete from the Byzantine period to today; El Greco painting.

Walking Tour

Platiá Eleftherias
Futuristic sculptures and fashionable cafes lend this large, bright square an air of modernity. Stroll south beyond the public gardens to begin a walking tour, starting with the Venetian fortifications.

Market★ (Odós 1866)
In the morning the street is the scene of a lively **market** for local products: yoghurt and honey, herbs, ornamental bread, fruits, cheeses, fish and meat. At the end of the street, in **Odós Kornarou**, note the Bembo Fountain, erected by the Venetians in 1588, and a Turkish fountain converted into a street stall.

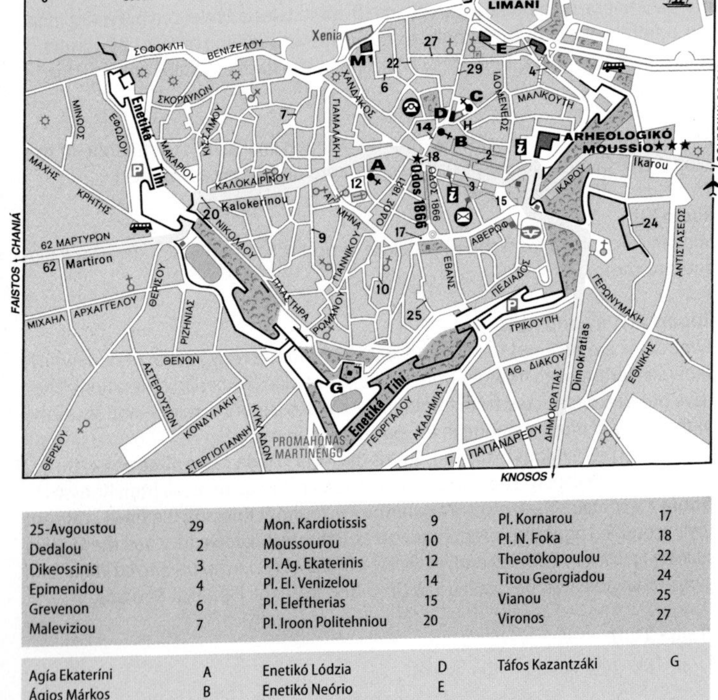

25-Avgoustou	29	Mon. Kardiotissis	9	Pl. Kornarou	17
Dedalou	2	Moussourou	10	Pl. N. Foka	18
Dikeossinis	3	Pl. Ag. Ekaterinis	12	Theotokopoulou	22
Epimenidou	4	Pl. El. Venizelou	14	Titou Georgiadou	24
Grevenon	6	Pl. Eleftherias	15	Vianou	25
Maleviziou	7	Pl. Iroon Politehniou	20	Vironos	27

Agía Ekateríni	A	Enetikó Lódzia	D	Táfos Kazantzáki	G
Ágios Márkos	B	Enetikó Neório	E		
Ágios Títos	C	Istorikó Moussío	M¹		

Agía Ekateríni
The little church, with two centres of worship, which was built in 1555 by the Venetians, contains six remarkable **icons**★ by **Mihális Damaskinós**.

Platía El. Venizélou
Pleasant pedestrian square; note the basin of the 17C **Morosini Fountain**, decorated with sea creatures. Odós Dedálou, leading out of the southeast corner of the square, is a pleasant shopping street lined with boutiques and tavernas.

Ágios Márkos
Italianate **St Mark's Church** (14C) was the cathedral of Candia during the Venetian occupation. The building is now used for exhibitions and concerts.

Venetian Loggia
The reconstruction has been carried out in the style of the 17C original, which was inspired by the Venetian architect Palladio. It was here that the money changers set up their stalls and the merchants met to discuss business. Nearby is the El Greco Park.

Ágios Títos
St Titus's Church was built by the Venetians in the 16C; the Turks transformed it into a mosque; it is now the Metropolitan (cathedral) Church.
The little streets (pedestrians only) around here come alive at night.

Old port
Flanked by a busy highway, **Paleo Limani** (the old Venetian port) now berths fishing boats. At the far end you can see parts of the Venetian Arsenal.
The entrance to the harbour is commanded by the Koúles, the16C **Venetian Fortress**★ still bearing the lion of St Mark. From the terrace (now an open-air theatre) there is a fine **panorama**★ over the port and town. Be careful, as there is no parapet around the tower. *(open Tue-Sun 9am-3pm, Mon, 9am-noon. 4€).*

Venetian walls (Enetiká Tíhi)
The **Venetian town walls** (5km/3mi long) were the work of **Michele Sanmicheli** (1484-1559), architect of the fortifications of Padua and Verona. The road running along under the walls leads to the Martinengo Bastion (Promahónas Martinéngo); on the top is the tomb of the great Cretan writer **Nikos Kazantzákis** (1883-1957).

Excursions

Knossós★★

5km/3mi southeast of Herakleion. Open Apr-Oct: daily 8am-7pm. Nov-Mar: daily 8.30am-7.30pm. 6€ (combined ticket with the Archaeological Museum: 10€). ☎ (28102) 31 940. During ongoing renovations, the Royal Apartments are visible from the outside only.
One of Crete's most important sights, the Palace of Knossós was the first and oldest of the Minoan palaces to be discovered. According to legend, the palace and its **Labyrinth** were designed by the cunning **Daidalos** to confine the **Minotaur**, a monster with a man's body and a bull's head.
The site of Knossós was already inhabited in the Neolithic period; in about 2000 BC a palace was built which was destroyed in 1700 BC. It was replaced by a new palace, of which traces can be seen today. At this point Knossós was one of the greatest cities in the whole of the Mediterranean, with some 50,000 inhabitants.
In c 1530 BC (possibly 1630 BC) an earthquake and a tidal wave, provoked, it seems, by the eruption of the volcano on Thíra (Santorini), laid waste the new palace. Later

The Legend of Daidalos and Theseus

Every nine years the Athenians, in retribution for the death of King Minos's son at the hands of their King Aegeus, had to deliver a human sacrifice of seven youths and seven maidens to be fed to the **Minotaur**. It was as part of this tribute that **Theseus** arrived from Athens and seduced **Ariadne**, King Minos's daughter. The princess gave her lover a thread which Theseus unwound as he penetrated the **Labyrinth**. He was thus able to find his way out after killing the Minotaur, and escaped with Ariadne.

To punish Daidalos for revealing the secret of the Labyrinth, Minos had him imprisoned within the palace, but Daidalos constructed wings using birds' feathers and wax and escaped from the palace with his son **Icarus**. Alas, Icarus flew too close to the sun, which melted the wax, and the unfortunate young man fell into the sea near to the present island of Icarus (Ikaría, west of Sámos in the Aegean).

it was sacked and occupied by the Mycenaeans. It was finally destroyed by fire between 1375 and 1250 BC.

Palace ruins★★

Beyond the entrance gate pass through the trees into the West Court, which was probably an agora. On the left are three disposal pits. Behind the base of an **altar** (**1**) lie the foundations of the palace. Pass the West Entrance and follow the **Corridor of the Procession** (**2**); the walls were decorated with frescoes (Herakleion Museum). Then turn left to reach the partly-reconstructed *propylaia* (**3**), a pillared porch at the foot of the grand staircase.

The upper floor comprised a number of pillared rooms, some of which have been restored and decorated with copies of frescoes; the famous *Parisienne* (Herakleion Museum) may have formed part of the decoration. To the west runs a long corridor serving a series of storerooms, some with provision jars *(pithoi)* still in place.

To the east another staircase leads down into the **central courtyard**. It (or the theatre) was probably the site of the perilous, acrobatic, ritual bull-leaping. Down the west side of the courtyard lie the rooms of the **sanctuary**★.

On the right a **vestibule** (**4**) leads into the **Throne Room** (**5**), which contains a bench and the alabaster throne on which the High Priestess of the Labyrinth may have sat; the Griffin Frescoes are reconstructions.

On the left another vestibule (**6**) leads into the two **pillar crypts** (**7**), site of ritual ceremonies (double axe heads carved on the pillars) and into the **Treasury** (**8**) *(right)* the famous *Snake Goddesses* (Herakleion Museum) were found here.

On the east side of the courtyard, accessed by a flight of steps (**9**) are the **royal apartments**★★★, occupying four floors of rooms built into the slope of the hill above the river. Here, as in other parts of the palace, there are shafts (light wells) providing light and ventilation.

The first rooms are the **Hall of the Double Axes** (**10**), which may have been the Guard Room, and the **King's Room** (**11**), which contained a wooden throne.

The **Queen's Chamber** (**12**) is decorated with a copy of the Dolphin Fresco; adjoining is a tiny bathroom (**13**).

From the royal apartments a covered portico *(views)*, leads to the **outbuildings**★; there were workshops for craftsmen, stone polishers, potters (**14**) (remains of kilns), tailors, gold and silversmiths, and storerooms. The **store** containing the *pithoi* dates from the first palace.

Return to the central courtyard and bear right down a passage.

This lane is lined by a portico leading to the "Customs House" (15); its square pillars are thought to have supported a banqueting hall on the floor above. On the left is the north entrance to the palace; outside it *(left)* is a lustral basin.

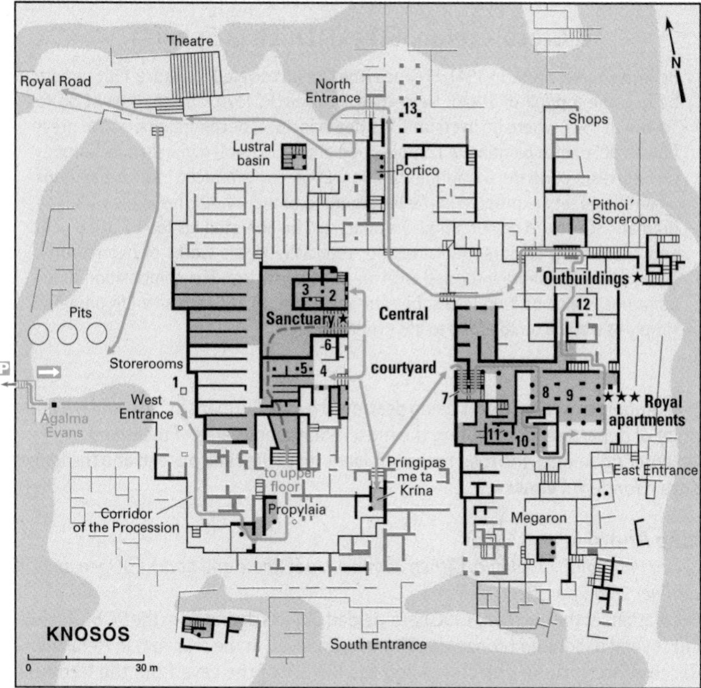

The **Royal Road** probably led to Katsámbas and Amnisós, the harbours to the east of Herakleion. On the right of the road stands a set of terraces, which are thought to belong to a sort of theatre, mentioned by Homer as the setting for ritual dances.

Mount Gioúthas★

15km/9mi south of Herakleion.

It is in this mountain (811m/2 661ft) that the god Zeus is supposed to be entombed. The mountain's silhouette can indeed be said to resemble the profile of a man asleep, which popular belief claims to be Zeus himself. From the pilgrimage church at the top on the edge of a steep cliff there is a vast **panorama**★ over Herakleion and the sea (north), Mount Díkti (east) and Mount Ídi (west), the highest peak on Crete.

Driving Tours

Idaian Massif★

110km/69mi round trip to the southwest. Head west out of Herakleion.

Tylisos ruins

Open daily, 8.30am-3pm. 2€. ☎ (28108) 31 372. Bear left on entering the village.
On the top of the hill are traces of three Minoan villas which are contemporary to those of the palace at Knossós (c 1800 BC).

Anógia

This mountain town occupies a majestic site at the foot of Mount Ida *(Óros Ídi)*, also known as Mount Psiloritis; the summit (2 456m/8 058ft) is snow-capped almost all

El Greco: Cretan, Greek, Italian or Spanish?

Born in Fódele, Crete, in 1541, El Greco (the Greek) traveled to Venice 1566, where he became a pupil of Titian. He settled in Rome in 1570, and then went on to Toledo in 1577 where he lived until his death in 1614, becoming one of the great figures of Spanish painting. A complex personality, schooled in Italian techniques but still respecting the Byzantine tradition, El Greco introduced into his paintings a hieratic quality expressed in the lengthening of the silhouettes in his strikingly dramatic scenes. In developing a visionary art, he liberated his forms, using cold and contrasting colours, thus creating, especially in the works of his maturity, an unreal atmosphere informed with an air of mysticism. The composition of his paintings is also on two levels, heaven and earth, as El Greco saw life on earth simply as a stage on the road to life everlasting.

year. Anógia was rebuilt after being destroyed by the Germans in 1944 and is a good point of departure for exploring the most mountainous area of the island.
On entering Anógia, the road to the left leads up to the Nída plateau and the Idaian Cave. Wonderful **views**★.

Idéo Ándro (Idaian Cave)

22km/14mi south of Anógia, then 30min on foot (there and back). Open daily in summer 9am-2pm, 3€.
Excavations at the end of the 19C here yielded objects dating from the 9C BC, including several decorated bronze shields now displayed in the museum in Herakleion. Recent finds include objects tracing the history of the cave from the Neolithic period to the 5C BC: objects made of gold, silver, pottery and rock crystal as well as small ivory pieces fashioned with skill (probably from Syria). The cave undoubtedly attracted pilgrims from all over the Greek world.

North Coast towards Rethymnon

Rethymnon is 71km/44mi west of Herakleion.
At the end of the bay the road passes Paleókástro, a Venetian fortress.

Agía Pelagía

This fishing village flanks a pleasant beach which is popular with tourists.

Fódele★

This village nestles in a hillside recess, the surrounding slopes covered with olive and carob trees; the well-irrigated valley bottom is carpeted with orange and lemon groves. It is thought to be the birthplace of the painter Domenico Theotokópoulos, known as **El Greco** (1541-1614). Wonderful beach.

Balí★

The village *(tavernas)* in a little creek offers good fishing and walking along the spectacular and rugged rocky **coast**★; small isolated beaches, accessible mostly by boat or on foot.

LIMÁNI HERSONÍSSOU★★

Λιμανι Χερσονησου

POPULATION 2 981

MICHELIN MAP 737 M 16 – IRÁKLIO.

A sizeable resort and fishing village, Limáni Hersoníssou is situated around a little bay. In Antiquity it was a port and the Ancient city retained its importance into the beginning of the Christian era.

- **Orient Yourself:** Situated on the north coast, the town is 30km/19mi east of Herakleion by the old road after Goúmes.
- **Don't Miss:** The superb Minoan palace of Mália.
- **Also See:** Ágios Nikólaos, Iráklio

Visit

Palaeo-Christian Basilica

On the rocky peninsula that shelters the bay to the north, on a fine site overlooking the port, are the foundations of a Christian basilica (6C). The ground plan can be deduced from the remains of the floor, partially decorated with wavy mosaics. Beyond and below the church at the end of the promontory are Roman fish tanks cut into the rock at sea level.

Before departing stop in at the Open-air Museum of Cretan Traditional Life.

Outskirts

Mália Ruins★★

12km/8mi to the east. *Open Tue-Sun, 8.30am-3pm. 4€.* Extending east of the village of the same name, the ruins of Mália are of particular interest since the site ceased to be inhabited at the end of the second millennium BC and is not therefore compounded with later construction. Most of the finds made here are displayed in the archaeological museum at Herakleion.

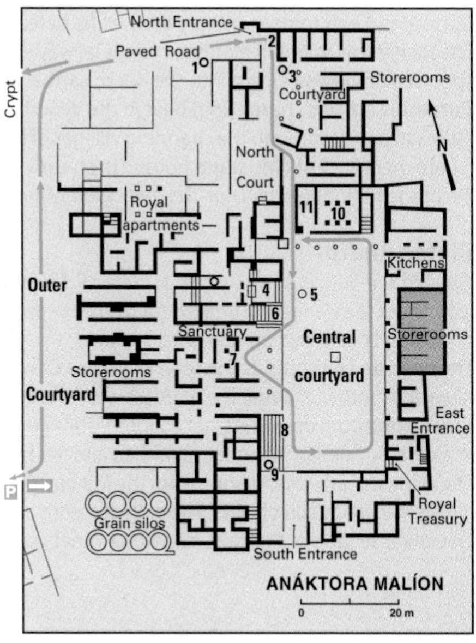

Anáktora Malíon★★

This Minoan **palace**, which was destroyed in c 1500 BC, was smaller and less luxurious than Knossós.

The paved **outer courtyard** is bordered on the east by the foundations of the palace. Walk up the east side of the court towards the sea as far as the Minoan paved road, which leads to the north entrance to the palace; the enormous terracotta vessel *(pithos)* (**1**) could hold over 1 000 litres/220 gallons of oil or wine.

North entrance

Pass through the vestibule (**2**) then a portico. On the left near a row of storerooms was another *pithos* (**3**).

Buildings west of the **central courtyard** were used, as at Knossós, for religious and official activities. At the centre of the courtyard is a shallow pit for sacrifices.

The sanctuary was in the northwest corner. The royal lodge or **throne room** (**4**) is marked by a terrace and a Byzantine cannonball (**5**). Next are the steps of a staircase (**6**), and then a cult room (**7**).

Beyond the four monumental steps (**8**) in the southwest corner is a circular stone table *(kérnos)* (**9**) thought to be either an offering site or a gaming table.

The buildings east of the courtyard comprise the **royal Treasury** followed by a range of storerooms *(not open)* and the kitchens.

The north side of the court is taken up with a hall (**10**) flanked by a vestibule (**11**).

▸ *From the precinct drive northeast.*

The town★

Follow the Minoan paved track, heading west.

This leads to the Hypostyle Crypt. The steps at the end led to meeting rooms, still partially furnished with benches, which were probably part of the Prytaneion.

Other buildings have been discovered on the outskirts of the town.

The **Krysólakos** (gold pit) necropolis on the north side near the sea was a royal graveyard; it contained the famous bee pendant now in the Herakleion Museum. Nearby is one of the loveliest beaches on the coast.

Lassíthi Plateau★

30km/19mi southeast of Limáni Hersoníssou.

Lying in the **Díkti Mountains**, the Lassíthi Plateau is an enormous hanging basin of rich alluvial soil, perfect for the cultivation of crops. Artisans producing honey, pottery and embroidery also ply their crafts here.

The road from Limáni Hersoníssou winds its way up through hairpin bends offering spectacular **views**★ down into the deep, narrow Avdoú Valley. At the entrance to **Potamiés** is a tiny church *(left)* built in the Venetian Gothic style (14C frescoes).

The road passes through the charming villages of **Dzermiádo** and **Ágios Geórgios** where there is a **Folk Museum** housed in an early-19C farm which reconstructs the life of the period*(◷open Apr-Oct daily 10am-4pm. 2€.*

Diktéo Ándro

◷Open Tue-Sun, 8.30am-7pm in summer; 8.30am-3pm in winter. 4€. A small track leads from the village of Psihró as far as the car park (charge). Then proceed on foot down a steep and sometimes slippery slope.

The deep and mysterious **Diktean** or **Psihró Cave** was the mythological refuge of Rhea, the mother of **Zeus**. The goddess was forced to hide from her husband Kronos, to keep him from devouring her children. Thus Zeus, the king of the gods, was born in a cave, suckled by the goat Amalthea and fed by the bee Melissa.

The Diktean Cave was a shrine from the Minoan period to the Archaic period and it has yielded many cult objects. The path descends past enormous rocks to a little lake. The lower section of the cave contains a variety of stalagmites and stalactites.

MÁTALA★

Ματαλα
POPULATION 100
MICHELIN MAP 737 K 16 – IRÁKLIO.

This little fishing village and holiday resort lies in a peaceful bay of the Libya Sea, some 70km/44mi south of Herakleion. According to the myth, it was here that Zeus swam ashore in the shape of a bull, bearing Europa on his back. These days Mátala is better known for its white sandy beach and its caves, which are to be found in the parallel strata of tufa on the north side of the beach.

Driving Tour

Beaches★

North of Mátala.

The ruins of the Minoan city of **Kommos**★ *(3km/1.9mi)*, probably one of the two ports of Phaistos, rise above the sea. Great stone buildings lining a wide paved street are visible from the fence enclosing the area (*not open to the public*). Farther down is a magnificent, undeveloped **beach**★, very popular in summer.

Kalamaki *(7km/4mi north of Mátala)*, a small seaside resort with an excellent **beach**★ sits on the wide bay of Messarás. Another good possibility is **Agía Galíni**★ *(28km/17mi north of Mátala)*, a charming and very popular resort, with a picturesque harbour and many tavernas serving fish. There are boat trips to the sea caves along the coast.

Visit

Ruins of Phaistos★★★

11km/7mi east of Mátala. Open Apr-Oct: daily 7.30am-7pm; Nov-Mar: daily 10am-5pm. 4€ (ticket for Phaistos and Agia Triada: 6€).

On a spur of Mount Ida – a magnificent **site**★★ with a view of the Messará Plain – stand the ruins of the Minoan palace of Phaistos. For 17 centuries this extraordinary city was a powerful force in Crete.

Start in the North Court (traces of Hellenistic and Roman structures) (**1**); then go down the steps (**2**) which lead to the base of the Propylaia and the theatre.

The **theatre** is composed, like the one at Knossós, of straight terraces facing the West Court. There was a little shrine (**3**) in the northeast corner.

Address Book

For coin categories, see the Legend on the cover flap.

WHERE TO EAT

Giannis – *Beyond the market, end of the main street, on the right*. Good classic local fare at affordable prices.

WHERE TO STAY

Nikos – *In the street left of the Hotel Zafiria, entrance of the village, ☎ (28920) 453 75 – 20rm.* An attractive low building with terraces and small gardens. Tropical plants, natural colours, baked clay flooring ... altogether very effective. The welcome is just as good, and the clean spacious rooms all have big showers. Excellent breakfast with freshly squeezed fruit juice.

Pension Antonios – *Same street as Nikos – ☎ (28920) 45 123, info@bodikos-matala.com – 10rm.* Clean spacious rooms all have big showers. Cheaper rates for longer stays.

A flight of steps leads up to the Propylaia (**4**). Beyond and to the left is a huge peristyle (**5**) surrounded by the royal apartment. East of these extend domestic buildings where the famous 'Phaistos Disk' (now in the Archaeological Museum in Herakleion) was discovered. On the north side lies the **King's Megaron** consisting of a reception room (**6**) and a 'lustral bath' (**7**) for ritual purification. On the south side is the **Queen's Megaron** (**8**) connecting with a small court (**9**) and a corridor (**10**) which lead into the central court.

The vast open rectangle of the **central court** was partially flanked by pillared porticoes; it was probably used for bull-leaping. Well (**11**) in the southwest corner.

On the left are traces of a crypt with two pillars (**12**) and a room surrounded by benches (**13**), both part of a **sanctuary**. Farther along is the 'Pillared Hall' (**14**), lined with alabaster.

The rows of **storerooms** contained enormous terracotta jars *(pithoi)*; in the last storeroom on the right (**15**) was a device for collecting the oil from the receptacles.

Return to the West Court. To the left lie the ruins of the first palace.

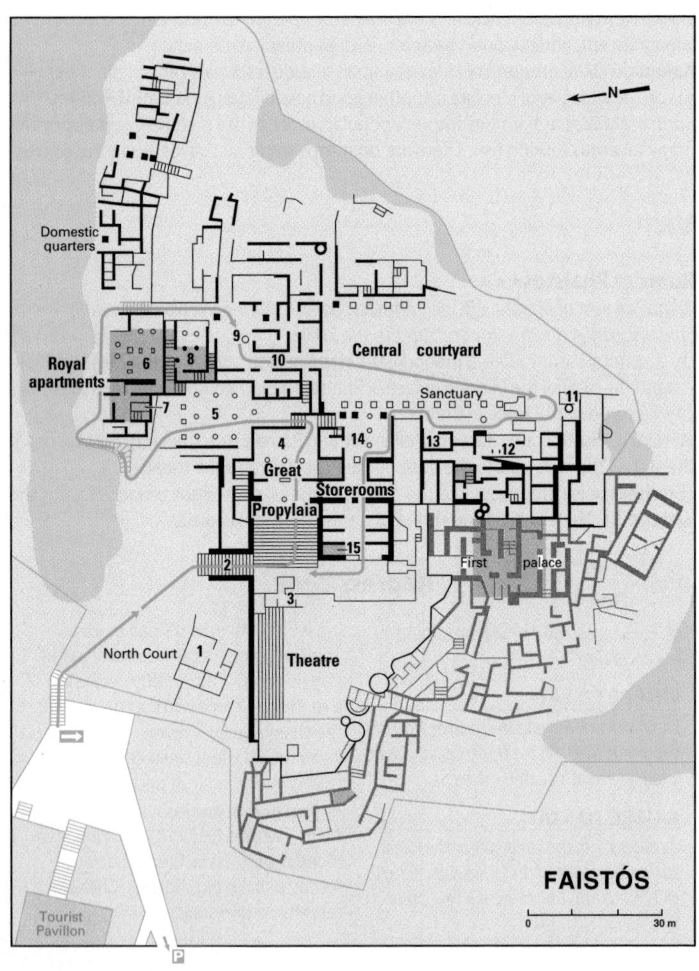

Agia Triada★

14km/9mi north of Mátala, and 3km/1.6mi west of Phaistos. Open Apr-Oct: daily 7.30am-7pm; Nov-Mar: daily 10am-5pm. 4€ (ticket for Phaistos and Agia Triada: 6€). (28920) 91 360.

Minoan ruins here (their Ancient name is unknown) occupy a fine **site**★★ overlooking the Messarás Plain and Bay.

In the **palace,** pass the grand staircase *(left)* leading up to the Altar Court and follow the paved ramp past the north front of the palace; the redans are typical of Minoan architecture. This group of buildings comprised a central block containing the reception rooms, storerooms and the royal *megaron* (alabaster cladding). The west wing comprised living accommodations.

Farther on stands **Ágios Georgios** (St George's Church), a small 14C building decorated with delicate Byzantine sculptures.

Mycenaean Village

The village was built later (1375-1100 BC) on the north side of the palace. The east side of the agora was bordered by a portico with shops. A large number of artifacts have been unearthed at the necropolis on the hillside, including a famed painted sarcophagus, now in the Archaeological Museum in Herakleion.

Ancient city of Gortyn★

28km/18mi northeast of Mátala. Open Apr-Oct: daily 7.30am-7pm; Nov-Mar daily 10am-5pm. 4€. (28920) 31 144.

The impressive ruins straggling beneath the olive trees evoke the past glory of Gortyn, capital of a Roman province and seat of the first Christian Bishop of Crete.

Ágios Titos★

This important building (7C) was erected on the site of Titus's martyrdom. The chevet formed of three parallel apses is still standing; a few fragments of the carved decoration are on display in the Herakleion Museum.

Odeon★

The little theatre (restored) was built early in the 2C AD on the site of – and with materials taken from – an earlier rotunda *(thólos)*. Here and there lie damaged statues.

At the rear of the Odeon under the vaulting of the outer corridor are several blocks of stone bearing the text of the **Twelve Tables of Gortyn**. The Dorian letters, were inscribed in about 480 BC and the lines are written alternately from left to right and right to left; the text deals with individual liberty, property, inheritance, adultery, violence etc.

Retrace your steps, taking the Herakleion road for around 300m/330yd and the path off to the right.

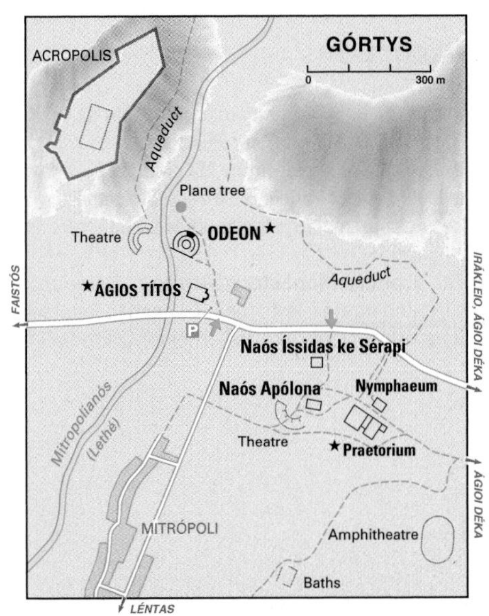

H. Champollion/MICHELIN

Valsamonero Monastery

Naós Íssidas ke Sérapi (Temple of Isis and Serapis)

The remains of a cella and a purification basin mark the site of the **Temple of Isis and Serapis** (1C-2C), which was dedicated to two Egyptian gods whose worship was widespread in the Roman world.

There are also traces of the **Temple of Pythian Apollo** which dates from the Archaic period (7C BC) but was rebuilt later.

Excavations have uncovered the impressive ruins of the enormous **praetorium**★; first built of brick in the 2C, it was reconstructed in the 4C following an earthquake. It is possible to identify a vast chamber (basilica), the baths and the courtyard of a temple.

Opposite the praetorium is a **nymphaeum**, which was built in the 2C as a grotto dedicated to the nymphs and converted into a fountain in the Byzantine era.

Excursions

In the village of Vóroi *(8km east of Mátala)*, the **Cretan Museum of Ethnology**★ *(open daily 10am-6pm; 3€)* displays its very fine collection of objects recalling everyday life in Crete in the 18C and 19C.

In the village of Vorizia *(3.5km east of Kamáres)*, visit the **Valsamonero Monastery**; its fine church boasts Italian-style architecture and wonderful **frescoes**★ from the 14C and 15C.

The **Vrondisi Monastery** *(4km east of Vorizia)* offers a magnificent **view**★ of the surrounding area. Note the 15C Venetian fountain, and, in the double-aisled church (one aisle for Catholics, the other for Orthodox), fine frescoes and icons.

PALEOHÓRA★

Παλαιοχωορα
POPULATION 1 830
MICHELIN MAP 737 I 16 – HANIÁ.

This charming fishing village lies 70km/44mi from Chania, on the Bay of Libya. Such are its many attractions – beautiful beach of white sand, white houses with flowering terraces, little winding streets and alleyways – that it has developed as a holiday resort. *Odós Eleftheriou Venizelou; info@paleochora-holidays.gr – ☎ (28230) 41 507.*

Visit

Village★★

From the seafront there is a wonderful **view**★ of the sea and the mountains. In the evening the main street becomes a pedestrianised area brimming with life. A litte farther to the south is a Venetian **citadel** (13C) up on the rocks.
Paleohóra's excellent **beach**★ is one of the largest on the island, and boasts white sand and turquoise water.

Outskirts

Island of Elafonisos★★

Allow one day. Boat departs at 10am in summer. Reserve the evening before at the agencies in the village.
This lovely little island to the southwest is edged with magnificent pink sandy **beaches**★★. Whales and dolphins sometimes appear alongside the boat enroute.

Address Book

For coin categories, see the Legend on the cover flap.

WHERE TO EAT

Every evening, the main street is transformed into a terrace, with tables and chairs spilling out onto the pavements.

Acropolis – *End of the main street, just before the taxi stand.* Good, fresh and generous portions. Go straight inside and see what's fresh: fish, marinated peppers, grilled octopus. Cheerful atmosphere guaranteed.

Polytia – *On the beach side of the street parallel to the main street, ☎ (28230) 41 288.* The restaurant is laid out among ruins open to the sky and has a rather magical atmosphere. Excellent traditional Cretan dishes.

WHERE TO STAY

There are numerous guesthouses in the village but be aware that in high season it'll be hard to find a room without a reservation.

Rea – *In a street at right angles to the main street, heading towards the beach, ☎ (28230) 41 307, apap@cha.forthnet.gr – 14rm.* Attractive little hotel, hidden behind a wall of greenery. Warm welcome from the kindly owner. The quiet rooms have attractive, simple decor. Breakfast served on the terrace.

TAKING A BREAK

Cretan Traditional Sweet Café – *In the main street, not far from OTE.* A modest establishment with two or three tables on the pavement. Delicious pastries.

SHOPPING

Jewellery Opal – *On the corner of the street which leads to the beach and the road that runs parallel to the main street – ☎ (28230) 41 522.* The shop sells the work of a Greek silversmith – very creative jewellery – hence the prices.

Sougia★

Boat trip – allow one day. Departure at 9.30am in summer. Bookable the evening before at the agencies in the village.

East of Paleohóra is the delightful village of Sougia. A boat trip is a great way to see the mountainous coastline in the south of Crete.

The village is also accessible by a beautiful hiking **trail**★★ from Paleohóra *(5hr; difficult)*.

Island of Gavdos

Boat trip – allow one day. The island is also accessible from Sfakiá.

50km/31mi from the coast, this island of 70 inhabitants is an amazing place but difficult to get to. The coastline is a mass of magnificent rocky outcrops. It is the southernmost point in Europe, just 300km from Tobrouk (Libya) and the Gulf of Soloum (Egypt), at the same latitude as Biskra (Algeria) and Sfax (Tunisia).

RÉTHIMNO★

RETHYMNON – Ρεθυμνο

POPULATION 27 868

MICHELIN MAP 737 K 15 – RETHYMNON.

Located on the north coast of Crete between Chania and Herakleion, Rethymnon offers a variety of attractions including fine beaches, charming squares, and a magnificent fort overlooking the sea. Despite its sprawling suburbs, it preserves the oriental charm characteristic of many Cretan towns. *Odós Eleftheriou Venizelou. Open Mon-Fri, 9am-2pm. (28310) 56 530.*

A Bit of History

A modest Minoan town, Rethymnon experienced its first golden age under the Mycenaeans. During the Venetian period it was the third largest administrative centre on Crete, and became a gem of Italian architecture.

After a late 16C attack by the pirate Barbarossa, the Venetians strengthened the city's protective system by building ramparts and a fortress. Nevertheless, Rithymnon

Phototravellers/MICHELIN

Man with donkeys, Rethymnon

fell to the Turks in 1645. The Ottoman occupation left the interesting examples of oriental architecture visible today.

Walking Tour

A stroll through the pedestrianised streets is a great way to explore the old part of town, where there are numerous working artisans.

Venetian Harbour★★

Framing the semicircular port are pastel-coloured houses converted into cafés and tavernas. Colourful fishing boats and coasters bob in the peaceful water. Just south of the port rises a Venetian **loggia** (17C) that was converted into a mosque. It now houses a a purveyor of reproductions of artworks displayed in local museums.

Arimondi Fountain

Three Corinthian columns mark this monumental fountain (1629). Nearby, along **Odós Thessaloníki**, several 16C-17C Venetian houses with elegant doorways decorated with coats of arms stand next to 18C-19C Turkish houses with balconies and wooden projections. From here look left to see a slim **minaret**★ set back from the street marking the position of the **Nerandzé Mosque**, which replaced a 17C Venetian convent.

Fortétza (or Froúrio)★★

Northwest of the old town. Open Tue-Sun, 8am-6pm. 3€.

Address Book

For coin categories, see the Legend on the cover flap.

WHERE TO EAT

Old Town – *31 Odós Vernádou, (28310) 26 436.* Very touristy, but one of the best in the old town. Good food.

Veneto – *4 Odós Epimenídou, (28310) 56 634.* Magnificent setting in a courtyard garden. Excellent Cretan fare, and superior service.

Avli – *Odós Arkadíou.* Superb decor, excellent service and refined, varied dishes: the best spot in town.

WHERE TO STAY

Olga's Pension – *57 Odós Soulíou, (28310) 28 665 – 17rm.* Pleasant and charming, for small budgets. Sometimes small but very comfortable, rooms have attractive tiled bathrooms.

Castello Pension – *10 Pl. Karaolí Dimitríou, near the Cathedral, (28310) 23 570 – 8rm.* An extraordinary calm reigns in this restored old house. Simple decor, all in white. Lovely cool garden with a little fountain. Quiet, spotlessly clean rooms.

Vecchio – *4 Odós Daliani, (28310) 54 985, vecchio@otenet.gr – – 27rm.* Attractive hotel verging on the luxurious, but at an affordable price. Large rooms decorated in pastels.

Mythos Suites – *12 Platía Karaolí, on the Cathedral square (28310) 53 917, mythoscr@hotelnet.gr – – 14rm.* Suites and cottages of all sizes on the grounds of a 16C manor house. Rooms combine modern comfort with old-world charm.

SHOPPING

Market – beside the public gardens. A big open-air food market is held on Thursday mornings.

Art reproductions are sold in the Venetian loggia *(Odós Paleologou).*

SPORTS AND LEISURE

Scuba diving – **Paradise Dive Center** – *Odós Eleftheríou Venizélou, (28310) 26 317.* The club takes people to the south of the island, near Lefkogia.

The impressive **Venetian 'Fortress'** (1582) is reinforced with seven curious bastions that have an orillion (rounded projection) on one side. On entering follow the ramparts round to the left to take in **views★** of the town and the harbour. There is a small **Archaeological Museum** in the former prison within the walls.

Public Garden★

Located south of the old town, this is a cool haven of peace and tranquillity, complete with refreshment stall and fountains. The central point, in the shape of a star, leads off in eight directions. Look out for the emu enclosure.

Beaches★

Two popular **beaches★** extend east of the old town. The first, with tall breakwaters, is very safe; the second (choppy waters, tidal currents) is dangerous for swimming.

Excursions

Monastery of Arkadi★

24km/15mi southeast of Rethymnon. Follow the coast in the direction of Herakleion, and take the road for Platanès. Open daily, 8.30am-1pm and 3.30-8pm. Museum: 2€.
In 1866 some 1 000 Cretans, including many women and children, took refuge here against an army of 12 000 Turkish solders. After holding out for two days, they blew themselves up with the powder magazine rather than yield to the invaders.
The monastery (11C) enjoys a glorious **site★** on the edge of a plateau overlooking a wild gorge. A few monks still live here.
The church **façade★** (1587) is built of golden stone The Corinthian columns, the arcading and the Italian-style *oculi* give it a Renaissance look; the curves and counter-curves of the pediments add a touch of the Baroque.
The convent buildings (17C) comprise cellars, the kitchen, the huge refectory, the powder magazine and a small **museum** dedicated to the tragic struggle of 1866.
From the monastery, continue to the **Melidoni Cave** *(after Arkadi, access by one of the mountain roads to Margarites, and then Melidoni; open daily 8am-8pm; no charge)*, scene of another massacre of Cretans by the Turcs. There are lovely **views★** of Mount Ida.

Necropolis of Armeni

South of Rethymnon. Open Mon-Fri 8.30am-3pm. No charge.
Next the the road, in a forest of oaks, lie nearly 200 Minoan tombs; it is the most important such site of the period.

Préveli Monastery

To the south.
Situated on the far side of the impressive **Kourtaliotiko Gorge★**, the beautiful Préveli Monastery maintains a revered place in the long and heroic Cretan resistance against the Turkish and German invaders. Built in the late 16C and destroyed several times, the current monastery comprises two complexes 3km/1.6mi apart.
The first one, Káto Monastíri *(entrance prohibited)* was abandoned after the First World War. The second one, **Písso Monastíri**, is still inhabited. The religious festival of the True Cross (named for the monastery's precious relic, reputed to have miraculous powers) takes place on 14 September and is celebrated by pilgrims who come from all corners of Crete. The monastery's small **museum** *(open Jun-Oct: 8am-1.30pm, 3.30pm-8pm; Apr-May :8am-7pm. €3)* houses a collection including beautiful icons dating from the 13-19C.
There is a superb **view★★** of the Libyan Sea from the vast shaded terrace, where one can contemplate the site. A small trail cuts through the wild and rocky pass leading to a lovely **beach★** with palm trees *(30min walk)*.

SFAKIÁ★★

Σφακια

POPULATION 278

MICHELIN MAP 737 J 16 – HANIÁ.

Home to the Sfakiots, as the local sheep farmers are called, this peaceful seaside resort ranges around a little bay. Tavernas and cafes often bustle with hikers from the Samariá Gorge.

- **Orient Yourself:** Sfakiá is situated on the Cretan south coast, 70km/44mi from Chania. Boats carrying hikers from the Samaria gorge disembark here.
- **Don't Miss:** The Samaria and Arédena gorges
- **Also See:** Haniá, Paleohóra, Réthimnon

Samariá Gorge★★★

Allow one day, leaving early in the morning.

Several times a day, the boats make the journey between Sfakiá and Agia Roumeli, the little port at the foot of the gorge. Usually the visitors descend the gorge from Chania (*see HANIÁ*) but those in search of a challenge can climb it, departing from Agia Roumeli. The **boat trip**★★ between Sfakiá and Agia Roumeli, with a stop off at Loutro, is a joy in itself.

From Sfakiá to Ágios Ioannis★★

20km/13mi. West of Sfakiá, via Anopoli.

Near the abandoned village of Arádena *(after 4km/2.5mi)* just before the metal bridge which crosses the Arádena Gorge, there is a particularly **stunning view**★★.

Arádena Gorge★★

Allow a day; take water, a hat and sturdy shoes.

Part of this spectacular gorge can be undertaken by any experienced walker, but the complete descent is only for the more adventurous: it includes negotiating a sheer rock face with steps and a rope. Allow 6hr to get to **Loutro**. From here, take a boat back to Sfakiá, or take the path along the beach *(2hr 30min)*.

From Sfakiá to Vryses★★

40km/25mi to the north.

The road climbs through some of the highest mountains on the island. There are spectacular **views**★★ of the wild and scarcely inhabited south coast.

Vryses is a pleasant well-shaded village by a stream.

From Sfakiá to Frangokástelo

15km/9mi east of Sfakiá.

GETTING ABOUT

By boat: to Loutro and Agia Roumeli, four boats a day, at 10.30am, 12.30pm, 4.45pm and 7.30pm, plus one more boat to Loutro at 7pm.

WHERE TO EAT

Samaria – Delightful view over the bay. The food is also good, with generous portions. Warm welcome.

WHERE TO STAY

Xenia – *At the end of the seafront* ☎ *(28250) 91 202 – 11rm.* A very attractive place. Spacious reception area with pleasant decor. Large cool rooms with blue doors and marble-effect flooring.

H. Champollion/MICHELIN

H. Champollion/MICHELIN

View of the coast near Sfakiá

The coast road cuts between the mountains and the sea, leading to the ruins of the **Frangokástelo citadel**★ (1371). It is rectangular in plan with crenellated walls and a square tower at each corner. Over the sea gate, the lion of St Mark looks down on the remains of a deserted harbour next to a fine sandy **beach**★.

SITÍA★

Σητεια

POPULATION 8 238

MICHELIN MAP 737 N 16 – LASITHI.

The charming town of Sitía nestles deep in a bay at the far east of Crete, 70km/44mi east of Ágios Nikólaos. Its white and ochre houses give it a slightly African appearance. The Sitía white wine is some of the best in Crete. *Odós Konstandinou Karamanli, near the port. ☎ (28430) 24 955.*

Visit

The town has been subjected to destructive earthquakes (1508), pirates (1538) and even the Venetians (c 1650), who destroyed their own fortress so that it would not fall into the hands of the Ottomans. It is pleasant to stroll about the **port**★ and under the shade of the enormous tamarisk trees where the promenade has been pedetrianised. Cafés and tavernas along the quayside serve Cretan specialities al fresco. For a look to the past, stop in at the **Archaeological museum** *(Odós Eleftheriou Venizeliou; open Tue-Sun 8.30am-3pm; 2€)*, which holds a good collection of Minoan finds from the area.

Venetian Fort

Open Tue-Sun, 8.30am-2pm. No charge.

The hillside leading up to the fort is crossed by alleyways and flights of steps flanked with little houses. The pace of life is very relaxed here, far from the crowds in the holiday resorts. Nowadays the fortress houses an open-air theatre. From the keep there is a splendid view of the fort.

Beaches and palm groves of Vaï★★

28km/18mi east of Sitía. Bus service from Siteía (5/day; 1hr).

Situated to the far west of Crete, at the edge of a desert-like landscape, the beaches of Vaï are renowned for their natural palm grove – the only one in Europe. There is no development on this part of the coast – a rare thing indeed.

Now a protected area, the **palm grove**★★ is closed to the public but there are two observation points. One of them *(north of the beach)* is set back from the coast. The other *(to the south, above the restaurant)* offers spectacular **view**★★, over the thousands of palm trees, the coast and out to sea.

Beaches★★

In summer, sunworshippers and their paraphernalia all but cover the large beach. There is a watersports centre where you can hire pedalos.

If it is solitude you seek, head farther south to the bay nestling behind the hill. It takes about 15min (follow the red markers) to a very quiet stretch of beach at the foot of some cliffs. Another beach lies to the north and is only accessible by boat.

Kato Zakros Ruins★

45km/28mi east of Sitía via Palaiokástro. Open Tue-Sun 8am-3pm, €3.

In an isolated **setting**★★, deep in the little bay *(beach)*, excavations have unearthed vestiges of a fourth Minoan palace which rivals those at Knossós, Phaistos and Malia.

Address Book

For coin categories, see the Legend on the cover flap.

GETTING THERE

BY AIR

The town has a small airport, 11km/7mi to the north, which offers flights *(2/wk)* to Athens. No bus service to the airport.

BY BOAT

Ferry service from **Piraeus** *(5/wk)*; also service to Rhodes via Kárpathos *(3/wk)*.

WHERE TO EAT

Sitía Tavern – *161 Odós Eleftheríou Venizélou, ☎ (28430) 28 758.* One of the many tourist restaurants in the harbour area; fish specialties. Warm welcome.

Kretan House – *Odós Karamanlí, 30m from the Hotel Élysée.* Try some authentic island specialities: *omatiés* (little sausages made with rice, liver, onions and almonds), *kochlis boumbouristi* (fried snails with olive oil, vinegar and tomatoes). Friendly service.

The Balcony – *On the corner of Odós Kazantzáki and Odós Foudalikdi, ☎ (28430) 25 084.* This rather chic restaurant on the top floor of an old house prides itself on its creative Cretan cooking. Vegetarian moussaka for a change, or *kléftiko* (a lamb dish with potatoes, cheese and herbs).

WHERE TO STAY

Archondiko – *16 Odós Kondilaki, ☎ (28430) 28 172 – 9 rm.* Delightful guesthouse in a great location. Friendly welcome. The rooms are spacious and comfortable (with and without bathrooms). Remember to book.

El Greco – *13 Odós Arkadíou, ☎ (28430) 23 133 – 20rm.* A simple, friendly little hotel. Traditional decor, warm welcome, and clean comfortable rooms with enormous private balconies.

Itanos – *4 Odós Karamanli, ☎ (28430) 22 900, – itanoshotel@yahoo.com – 72rm.* Marble in the bathrooms, very pleasant roof terrace. Every modern comfort and the decor of an international hotel.

TAKING A BREAK

Drosoulites Platia Brasserie – *Platía Iróon Politehníou.* This large central café, the oldest in town, is an institution. Great for people-watching, with ouzo and pistachios in the evening, when the birds gather in the enormous palm tree that dominates the square.

J.-P. Nail/MICHELIN

The bay to the south of Vaï

The oldest palace was built around 1900 BC. It was replaced around 1600 BC, but the buildings were destroyed around 1450 BC by earthquakes following the eruption of the volcano on Santorini.

Like the other Minoan palaces the buildings are arranged around a central courtyard. To the north is the large kitchen, the only one of its kind that can be identified as such; to the west are the reception rooms and places of worship; to the east, the royal apartments feature a round basin, probably used as a cistern; to the south are the workshops and warehouses near which is the well.

There is a lovely **walk**★★ between the village of Zakros and Kato Zakros *(2hr round trip)* through the Valley of Death.

Monastery of Toploú★

15km/9mi to the east. Open 9am-1pm, 2pm-6pm. 3€. Modest dress required.

The **road**★ follows the coast at the foot of the arid hills. After a large holiday village which resembles an oriental town, turn left. The road then climbs to a barren plateau.

The fortresslike monastery was founded in the 14C as Our Lady of the Cape. The present buildings largely date to the 17C and the 18C.

A handsome Gothic door opens into the entrance court, which leads into an inner court surrounded by arcades and the stairs up to the cells. The Venetian-style church contains two very rich **icons**★ by an 18C Creto-Venetian master, Ioánnis Kornáros (Cornaro)

The **museum** features a collection of icons from the 15C to the 19C, as well as precious ecclesiastical items, rare documents, Ancient editions of the gospels and parchment manuscripts. A permanent exhibition traces the history of Orthodox Christianity, with particular reference to Mount Athos and Toploú Monastery.

THE CYCLADES★★★

POPULATION 112 615

Situated at the heart of the southern Aegean Sea, the Cyclades present a strikingly beautiful landscape of volcanic peaks, barren plains and spectacular beaches bathed in bright sunshine. Historically very poor, the islands have become a major tourist destination in the last three decades.

- **Orient Yourself:** Many of the capital towns on the islands carry the name of the island itself but are referred to locally as "Hóra" (meaning "main city").
- **Don't Miss:** Santorini boasts the archipelago's most impressive landscape; Mykonos and Folegandros have the loveliest villages.
- **Organizing Your Time:** If you have only a few days, stick to the islands nearest the mainland (Andros, Kea, Kythnos). Stay a full week to visit the can't-miss islands: Mykonos, Delos or Naxos, then Santorini. A visit of 10 days can include Ios and Folegandros.
- Kids **Especially for Kids:** Naxos' safe beaches are perfect for families with young children. Sports-loving teenagers will love the horseback-riding and sailboarding opportunities on Naxos, as well as scuba and kayaking on Milos.

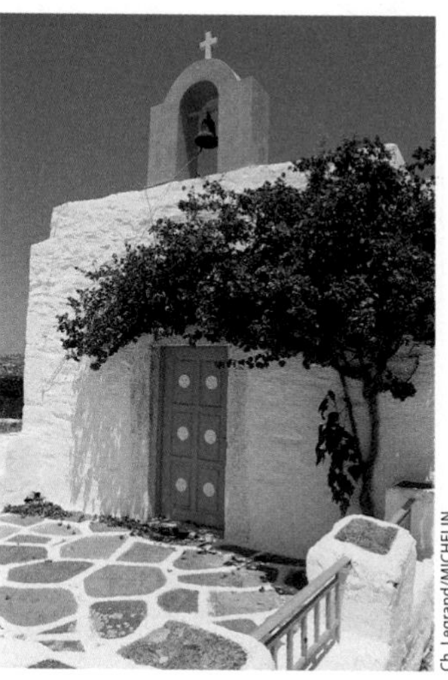

Ch. Legrand/MICHELIN

Bougainvillea-covered chapel, Páros

Address Book

VISITING

WHEN TO GO

During high season (15 Jun-15 Sep), tourists swarm the islands and prices rise into the stratosphere. Try to visit in May or June if possible. In July and August, there is a refreshing north wind *(meltémi)*.

HOW TO GET THERE

Ferries link the Cyclades to Piraeus (Syros, Tenos, Mykonos, Páros, Náxos, Íos and Santorini), Rafína (Andros, Tenos and Syros) and Lávrio (Kéa). Local boat links access the other islands.
Hydrofoils offer faster, but pricier and less scenic service to the islands. It's always a good idea to consult a timetable before travelling, since itineraries can change.
Flights from Athens or Thessaloníki operate every day in summer to Melos, Mykonos, Náxos, Páros, Santorini and Syros. *www.olympicairlines.com*

WHERE TO STAY

See the Address Book sections of each island's entry. Always book accommodation in advance, especially from 15 June-15 September, and during Easter. Prices can rise to extremes in-season; try booking throught the internet for discounts. Ask to be met at the ferry; most hotel operators are happy to do this.

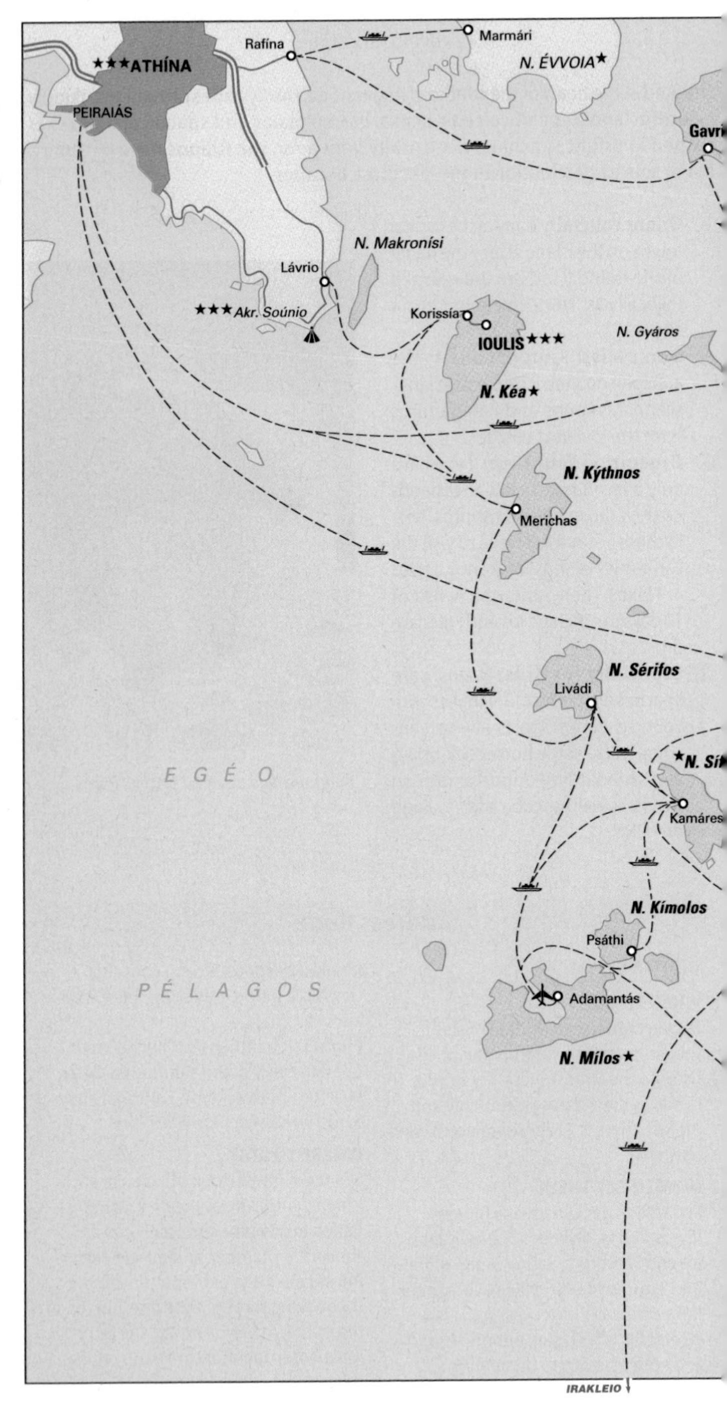

Rafína
Marmári
★★★ATHÍNA
N. ÉVVOIA★
PEIRAIÁS
N. Makronísi
Lávrio
★★★Akr. Soúnio
Korissía
IOULIS★★★
N. Gyáros
N. Kéa★
N. Kýthnos
Merichas
N. Sérifos
Livádi
E G É O
Kamáres
N. Kímolos
Psáthi
P É L A G O S
Adamantás
N. Mílos★
IRAKLEIO

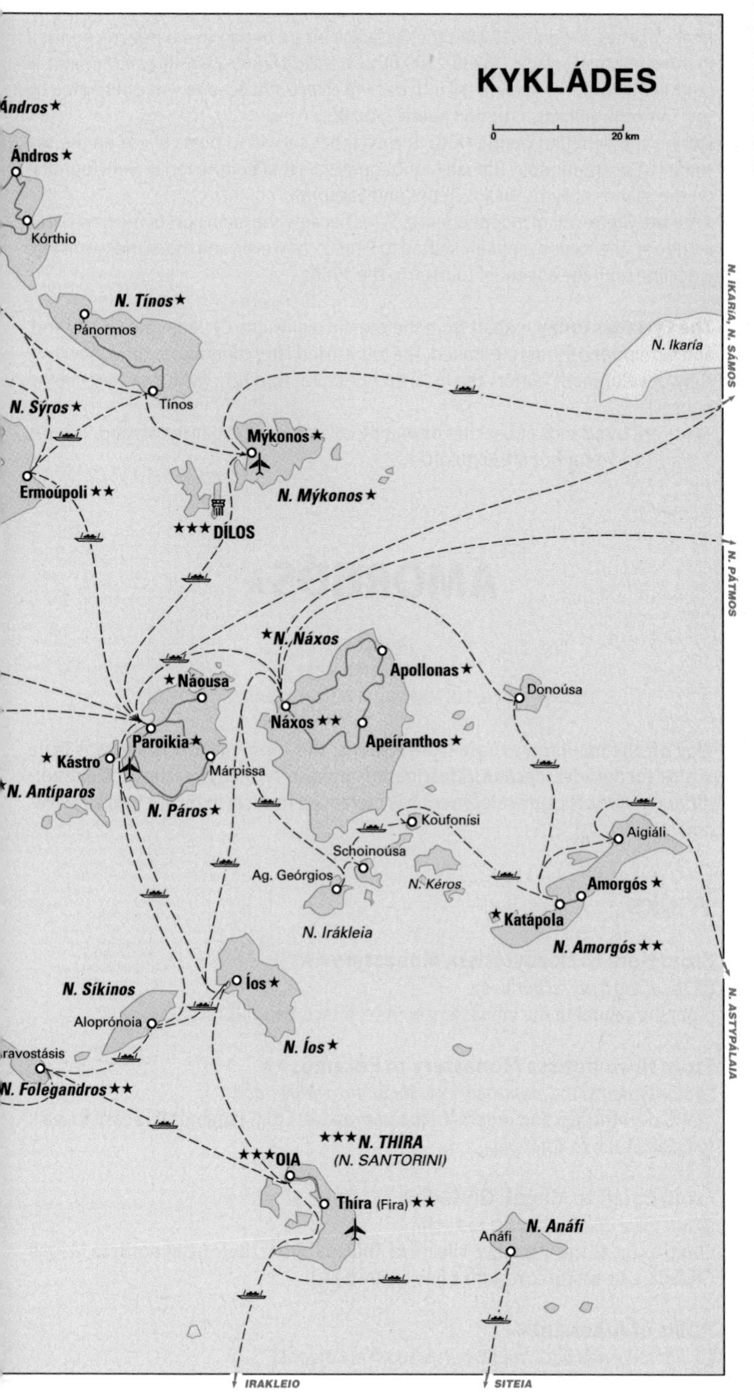
KYKLÁDES
0
20 km
Ándros ★
Ándros ★
Kórthio
N. Tínos ★
Pánormos
Tínos
N. Sýros ★
Ermoúpoli ★★
Mýkonos ★
N. Mýkonos ★
★★★ DÍLOS
N. Ikaría
N. IKARÍA, N. SÁMOS
N. PÁTMOS
★ N. Náxos
Apollonas ★
Donoúsa
★ Náousa
Náxos ★★
Apeíranthos ★
Paroikia ★
★ Kástro
Márpissa
N. Antíparos
N. Páros ★
Koufonísi
Aigiáli
Schoinoúsa
Ag. Geórgios
N. Kéros
Amorgós ★
★ Katápola
N. Irákleia
N. Amorgós ★★
N. ASTYPÁLAIA
N. Síkinos
Íos ★
Alopróniа
N. Íos ★
ravostásis
N. Folegandros ★★
★★★ N. THIRA
(N. SANTORINI)
★★★ OIA
Thíra (Fira) ★★
N. Anáfi
Anáfi
IRAKLEIO
SITEIA

A Bit of History

Cycladic art and civilisation – Some of the Cycladic Islands were inhabited in prehistoric times. Around 3200 BC, the Cycladic culture began to emerge, recognized in three phases; Cycladic I (3200-2800 BC), Cycladic II (2800-2300 BC) and Cycladic III (2300-2000 BC). The culture fell into decline after 2300 BC, and was obliterated by the Santorini volcanic eruption about 1500 BC.

During the Venetian period (13C), the Cyclades served as ports of call on the sea route to Constantinople. Roman Catholic parishes that endure today were founded on the islands of Syros, Náxos, Tenos and Santorini.

After the Greek War of Independence, Syros became the main port of the new Greek kingdom. The focus eventually shifted to Piraeus, however, and the islands went into a decline until the advent of tourism in the 1960s.

The Cyclades today – Apart from the coastal plains, the Cyclades are largely arid, and farming and fishing are limited. The tourism industry continues to grow, however. New development honors the local architectural tradition (whitewashed cuboid houses).

There are thousands of beaches, from tiny coves to vast expanses of sand. The sea is warm and clear but often rough.

AMORGÓS★

Αμοργοζ

POPULATION 1 859

121KM2 – MICHELIN MAP 737 M-N 12 – CYCLADES – AEGEAN.

Way off the main ferry route from Piraeus, this long, narrow island was little visited for decades, despite its fascinating monastery, many beaches and extraordinary beauty. New development has increased tourism in recent years. *www.amorgos.net*

Walks

From Hóra to Hozoviótissa Monastery★★

1hr along a raised pathway.

From the capital to the monastery on its cliff face; beautiful scenery.

From Hozoviótissa Monastery to Potamós★★

Signposted at the monastery exit. 5hr along a ridge track.

Views over the sea and mountain are impressive. From Potamós it is easy to walk to Egiáli *(buses to Katápola).*

From Egiáli to Megali Glyfada★

3hr there and back by a good path.

Climb as far as the attractive village of Tholária. From there head north to Megali Glyfada, a beautiful cove with a fine sandy beach.

Ruins of Arkessíni★

2hr there and back from Vroútsis, south of Katápola.

A paved track, then a path, lead down to the sea, through an arid and desolate, yet magnificent, landscape. A rocky outcrop is the site of a city founded in the 4C BC. There are the ruins of an acropolis, Ancient tombs and a defensive tower.
The return journey may be made via the northern coast road *(allow 1hr extra)*.

Visit

Hozoviótissa Monastery★★★

Open daily, 8am-1pm and 5-7pm. No charge. Visitors must be attired so that arms and legs are covered; if dressed in pants, women must also wear a pareo. For those without a car, access the monastery either on foot from Hóra (mountainous path, allow at least 1hr); or by bus from Hóra or Katápola, which drops off at the parking area below the monastery, from where it is a 15min walk (arrive early to avoid the heat of the day).

This monastery (9C) occupies an extraordinary **site**★★★, perched halfway up a 500m/1 640ft high vertical cliff. Occupied virtually without interruption for over a thousand years, the monastery is one of the great sacred sites of the Aegean.
Visiting this holy place is an entrancing experience. Past the entrance gate, a staircase leads up through a tunnel in the mountain to the reception hall. The church features some fine icons and the library has a collection of embroidered vestments, liturgical objects and important **manuscripts**★ (10C-18C). In keeping with the Orthodox tradition of hospitality, the monks offer visitors tea, lemon liqueur and Turkish Delight.
Below the monastery at the foot of the cliff lies the beach of **Agía Ánna**★.

Chabrol B./MICHELIN
Hozoviótissa Monastery

Katápola★

This appealing town incorporates three villages strung out along the coast of a deep bay: **Katápola**, with its harbour for ferries and pleasure craft; **Rahídi**, still undeveloped; and **Xilokeratídi**, an attractive fishermen's quarter.
Some of the churches, like **Panagía Katapolianí** *(centre of Katápola)* are constructed of stone taken from the site at Mínoa. Attractive beaches nearby.

Ruins of Mínoa

Accessible on foot or by car (2.5km/1.25mi south of Katápola). On foot: take the road that heads from the harbour up the hill overlooking the bay (45min walk). By car: take the Hóra road, then the first right-hand turn. The site, currently closed because of ongoing excavations, can be observed from the perimeter.

The settlement was inhabited from the 10C BC until the 4C AD. Archaeologists have excavated defensive walls, the walls of a gymnasium (4C BC) and the foundations of a Hellenistic temple dedicated to Dionysos. There are fine **views**★ over the bay and mountains.

Hóra

5.5km/4mi east of Katápola. Buses from Katápola (every hour) and Egiáli (3-5 a day).
The **site**★ of this typical Cycladic village, dominated by a rocky outcrop, is extraordinary. It's best explored by wandering through its alleys and little squares.

The small **Archaeological Museum** displays statues, capitals, stelae and, in a wood-ceilinged room, a selection of ceramics. *Open daily except Mon and public holidays, 9am-1pm and 6-8.30pm. No charge.*

The tiny **cathedral** (17C) is in an elegant square. A passageway leads to the citadel (1290), from where there is a **view**★ over the village.

Address Book

For coin categories, see the Legend on the cover flap.

GETTING ABOUT

By Boat – There are one or two services a day from Piraeus *(5-8hrs depending on the vessel)*.

From here there are links to **Náxos** *(daily)*, **Páros** *(daily)*, **Santorini** *(3/wk)*, **Folégandros** *(2/wk)*, and **Syros** *(2/wk)*. In spring, there is a local ferry link from Amorgos to the islands of Náxos, Páros and the lesser Cyclades (Iráklia, Schinoússa, Koufoníssi, Donoússa).

WHERE TO EAT

Liotriví – *Hóra, in a narrow street to the right of the bus station.* Traditional dishes (moussaka) or more original cuisine (rabbit casserole). Arrive early.

Mouráyo – *Katápola, opposite the landing stage.* Superb fish and seafood taverna which is deservedly popular. Try the fried squid and the aubergines.

Níkos – *Langada, lower end of the village, below the Hotel Pagali.* A great place to eat with terraces and arbour, overlooking the boules players. Considered one of the best restaurants on the island; don't miss the 'Nikos Special' eggplant and the zucchini fritters.

Panorama – *Tholaria, middle of the village* – One of the most sought-after dining spots on Amorgos. Delicious *kokoretsi* (meat skewers) and goat-cheese dishes. In summer, local musicians perform traditional tunes; arrive before 9pm.

WHERE TO STAY

In August it is essential to reserve accommodation in advance.

Voula Beach – *Katápola, at the end of an alley running off from the landing stage* – *(22850) 74 052 – 15rm and studios.* Very clean rooms of all sizes off a planted courtyard. Very friendly welcome. No breakfast.

Villa Katapoliani – *Katápola, ask at the delicatessen in the port* – *(22850) 71 054 – 13rm and studios.* A charming establishment centred around a planted courtyard near the harbour. Modest rooms, with balconies, fridges, safes and hairdryers; no breakfast, but communal kitchen facilities.

Pagali – *Langáda, down from the main road* – *(22850) 73 310, www.pagalihotel-amorgos.com – 19rm and studios.* Above the Níkos bar; pleasant, quiet rooms, some with kitchenettes. Bus stop nearby. Management will come to meet guests from the ferries. Breakfast 6.50€.

Aigialis – *(22850) 73 393, www.amorgos-aegialis.com – 50rm.* 1km from the port but served by buses, this is the most comfortable hotel in Egiáli. The rooms overlook the bay. Swimming pool (open to the public), billiards room and nightclub. Transportation to ports available (fee).

TAKING A BREAK

Frou-Frou – *Egiáli, in the alley leading to the harbour.* A good cake shop with a sea view. Breakfast, cakes, crepes and ice cream round the clock.

EVENTS AND FESTIVALS

Church of Panagía Epanohorianí – *North of Langáda.* On 14 and 15 August there are church services followed by a banquet, vegetables only on the 14th and goat on the 15th. This is free to all comers, but it is customary to leave a donation in the church collection box. The evenings see traditional dancing in all Langáda's tavernas.

Feast of the Presentation of the Virgin – *Hozoviótissa Monastery.* On 21 November; this is the only opportunity to dine with the locals in the monastery's refectory.

Tour

The North of The Island★

Narrow and steep, Mount Kríkelos (827m/2 710ft) is accessed by the road linking Egiáli to Katápola; the route threads between the sea and the arid peaks where herds of goats graze. The islet of **Nikoúria** *(fine beaches)* is accessible by boat from the beach of Ágios Pávlos, 2km/1.25mi southwest of Egiáli, below a ruined Hellenistic tower.

Egiáli

Having evolved into a resort, this village is increasingly popular with visitors who enjoy its fine sandy beaches (accessible by boat).

Mountain villages★

Three whitewashed villages built on the mountainside dominate the bay of Egiáli. **Potamós**, standing among thousands of boulders, stands balcony-like overlooking the Aegean. **Tholária** has a pleasant square with a church and café, where visitors can try the local specialities: *rakomelo* (honey *raki*, a strong alcoholic spirit with cloves) and *psimeni raki* (honey *raki* with cinnamon). **Langáda**★, a maze of steep alleys, is the most charming of the three.

Phototravellers/MICHELIN

Tholária

The South of the Island★

The villages of the south (Kato Méria) are reached by a single road which crosses tha island's agricultural region. From Katápola, climb towards Hóra and then head down towards the sea; take the first turn to the right. A little farther along, on the right-hand side *(not signposted)* is the monastery of **Ágios Geórgios Valsamítis** (16C), a stark white group of buildings in a terraced valley. The monastery has 17C frescoes and is renowned for its miraculous spring.

Beaches

Not far from the village of Vroútsis, **Moúros** is located in a wide bay. Farther south lie three popular beaches: **Kalotarítissa**, **Paradísia** and **Gramvoússa**★ (on an islet, access by boat from Paradísia Beach), a stopover for migratory birds.

Excursions

The Lesser Cyclades

Daily (usually) ferry services from Amorgós and Náxos; boats leave from Katápola. This tiny archipelago is made up of four small islands (Iráklia, Schinoússa, Koufoníssi and Donoússa) and hundreds of islets popular for their magnificent beaches.

ÁNDROS★

Ανδροζ

POPULATION 10 009

374KM2/150SQ MI – MICHELIN MAP 737 K-L 9-10 – CYCLADES – AEGEAN.

The northernmost Cycladic island, Ándros is lush and wooded. Its many beaches are rarely busy, except in August, and its mountain paths are ideal for walkers.
Tourist office (Jun-Sep) near the landing stage in Gávrio. www.androsgreece.gr.

Tour

Beaches around Gávrio★

West coast

The beaches at **Vitáli** and **Gídes** are at the end of a 4km/2.5mi track, and are pleasant as long as the wind is not blowing strongly; the former has a taverna.

Address Book

For coin categories, see the Legend on the cover flap.

GETTING ABOUT

By boat – Ferries to Ándros mainly leave from Rafína *(daily, 2hr)*. On Ándros, Gávrio is the only ferry port; from here, there are also boats to Mykonos *(daily)*, Tenos *(daily)*, Syros *(3/wk)*, Páros *(6/wk)*, Náxos *(2/wk)*, Kythnos *(1/wk)* and Kéa *(1/wk)*.
Jeeps are the best way to tour the island; agencies will deliver vehicles to your hotel. Try **Anna Vrettou - Euro Car** ☎ *(2280) 724 40, www.retnacareuro.com.*
Mopeds may be rented from **George Rentabike** *(Gávrio, at the port)*, **Dinos** *(Batsi)*, and **Aris** *(Hóra ☎ (22820) 243 81)*.

WHERE TO EAT

⊖ **Veggera –** *Gávrio, on a shaded square in the village, up from the port.* A terrace establishment serving roast meats and other local specialities.
⊖ **Giakoumissi** – *Gavrio, at the port.* Select your fish, then enjoy it while taking in the sea view. Generous portions.
⊖ **Cavo del mar** – *Hóra, near the beach.* Traditional specialties and fish dishes.

WHERE TO STAY

⊖ **Meltemi** – *Batsi, above the Agios Philippos church – ☎ (22820) 41 016 – 11 studios.* Large studios with balconies in a lovely house covered with bougainvillea.
⊖ **Villa Nora –** *Batsi, end of the coast road – ☎ (22820) 41 252 – 13 studios, 1 apt.* Ravishing studios; large garden with beach view. No breakfast.
⊖ **Riva –** *Hóra, on the beach – ☎ (22820) 244 12 – www.androsrooms.gr – 5rom, 3 apt.* Well-equipped, one of Andros' best lodgings. Scooter rental, touring information warmly offered.
⊖⊖⊖ **Pighi Sariza –** *Apikia – ☎ (22820) 237 99 – 42rm.* A very comfortable large hotel near the Sarizia spring, known for its healing waters.

SPORTS AND LEISURE

Opportunities abound for lovers of the open air; check with **Andrina Tours** *(Batsi, ☎ (22820) 410 64, www.androscyclades.com)* for organized excursions and other information.

SHOPPING

Ándros is an island of beekeepers; take home some delicious thyme honey (boutique near the post office in Gávrio).

Ágios Kiprianos, **Psilí Ámos** and **Kiprí** *(just south of Gávrio)* are attractive, if busy beaches. **Batsí** *(27km/17mi west of Hóra)* is the island's principal resort; the alleys of the village retain their Cycladic charm. Many fine beaches lie to the southeast

Northeast coast

Limanáki, an isolated beach at the end of a track, will appeal to lovers of solitude (except in high season). Magnificent scenery. **Felós**, to the north of Gávrio, has a small and peaceful resort nearby. .

Beaches around Hóra

North of Hóra

Paraporti, Nimborió and **Giália** both offer fine views of the island's capital.

South of Hóra

Located in a narrow inlet, **Sinetí** is an attractive beach readily accessible from the village of the same name. **Órmos** *(10km/6mi south of Hóra)* is a rather charmless resort beyond the lighthouse to the north and Griás Pídima Beach.

Visit

Gávrio and its Environs★

Gávrio

In a narrow-mouthed bay, the harbour of Gávrio is lined by tavernas, cafés, hotels and guesthouses. It's a good base for exploring the north and west of the island.

Amólohos

6km/4mi north of Gávrio.

The village sits in an arid landscape divided up by low walls. There is a pleasant fountain at the entrance to the village and, lower down the valley, three watermills.

Tower of Ágios Pétros

3km/1.9mi northwest of Gávrio, on the Kalokeriní road.

The winding road heads upwards; in an olive grove to the right stands a round tower (Hellenistic; 4C-3C BC) and the white Chapel of Ágios Pétros. The tower has served as a forge as well as a signal and watchtower.

J.-P. Nail/MICHELIN

One of the beaches of Ándros

Monastery of Zoodóhos Pigí

10km/6mi east of Gávrio, on the coast road. Open mornings only.
A track leads up to this monastery, first recorded around 1400, which has a collection of icons (14C-16C), fresco fragments and manuscripts.

Paleópoli★

12km/8mi southeast of Gávrio, on the coast road.
Paleópoli (the name means 'Old City') was the island's capital in Classical times, but was destroyed by an earthquake in the 4C BC. Today it is a modest mountain village; the archaeological site lies on the coast.

Hóra★

Situated on the east coast and seat of shipbuilding and nautical families, Hóra has remained off the main tourist trail. The town retains an atypical charm.

The Medieval District★

Beyond Platía Théofilos Kairis, a vaulted archway (the old town gate) leads into the alleyways lined with pastel-coloured houses, some graced with loggias, which bear witness to the Venetian presence here from the 13C to the mid-16C.
Overlooking Paraporti Beach, the **Church of Ágios Geórgios** (17C) is on a little shaded square. Opposite, on an islet, lie the ruins of a Venetian fortress.

Archaeological Museum (Hermes of Ándros★), *Platía Théofilos Kairis*; Museum of Modern Art, *Platía Théofilos Kairis*; Maritime Museum.

The Messariá Valley and Surrounding Area★

Messariá

The village has a fine example of 12C Byzantine architecture, the **Church of Taxiárhis**★, decorated with marble sculpture and frescoes (18C). The Church of **Ágios Nikólaos** (1734), with its blue cupola, has an interesting iconostasis in carved wood *(under restoration 2006)*. The huge **Monastery of Panahrándou** *(3km/1.9mi south of Messariá, beyond the village of Fálika; opening hours vary)* monastery, dating from the 10C and still active, resembles a white fortress clinging to the mountainside.

Ménites★

West of Messariá.
The village is renowned for its springs, which gush from marble lions' heads. From the terrace outside the church there is a fine view of the village.

Strapouríes

North of Ménites.
In this village are several *archontika*, grand mansions testifying to the wealth of the early shipowners, and a fine church.

Bisti Movella Tower

2km/1.25mi north of Hóra.
One of the fortified houses which are a feature of Ándros. From its terrace there is a view of Hóra and the surrounding hillsides. Dovecots may be seen beside houses.

Steniés

2km/1.25mi north of Hóra.
Hill village of white houses perched on the slopes overlooking the sea. Some of its fine neo-Classical houses have been restored.

J.-P. Nail/MICHELIN

Dovecote

Apikia

Charming village;, the local Sáriza spring water gushes from a marble lion's head.

Ágios Nikólaos

This 16C monastery is perched above a gorge of cultivated terraces. In the courtyard behind the defensive wall, there is a colourful church.

The South of the Island

South of Hóra, take the winding Sinetí road.
South of the resort of Órmos Kórthi, built on a hillside in a sheltered bay, is Kórthi, with many old houses. Farther still are three of the island's most characteristic villages: **Aidonia, Moussiónas** and, **Amonakliós**★, where the traditional architecture blends into a beautiful mountain landscape.

DÍLOS★★★

DELOS – Δηλοζ

3.6KM2/1.4SQ MI – MICHELIN MAP 737 L 11 – CYCLADES – AEGEAN.

Today windswept and desolate, Delos was home to one of the most important sanctuaries in the Greek world and site of the greatest city in the Aegean during the Classical period. In Antiquity it played a leading role both commercially and in religious terms, and the Greek world was in awe of its riches.

- **Orient Yourself:** *Open Tue-Sun, 8.30am-3pm.* Delos is accessible year-round by boat from Mykonos *(30min; 10€ round trip)*; several companies operate guided trips *(approx. 32€ including boat and entrance fees)*.
- **Don't Miss:** The Terrace of the Lions; the Theatre District.
- **Organizing Your Time:** Timetables are displayed at the port and are subject to change. There is no accommodation on the island, and it's best to arrive early in the day. Bring sturdy shoes, water and a snack; there is a small cafe. Boats from other islands stop here, but may not leave much time for sightseeing.

Kids **Especially for Kids:** Delos is an unforgettable visit for young fans of archaeology and mythology.

A Bit of History

Apollo's sacred island – Delos was the mythological birthplace of Apollo, god of light, and by the end of the 8C BC the sanctuary here was one of the most important in the Greek world. In 478 BC Athens formed the confederation known as the **League of Delos**; its treasury was first kept in the Apollo Sanctuary before being transferred in 454 to Athens. In 422, the Athenians built a new temple to Apollo and organised the Delian Festival, which took place every four years in May until the 1C AD. Thanks to its central location, Delos gradually became the main port in the Aegean Sea. Its sacred standing preserved it from attack, and the island flourished. Early

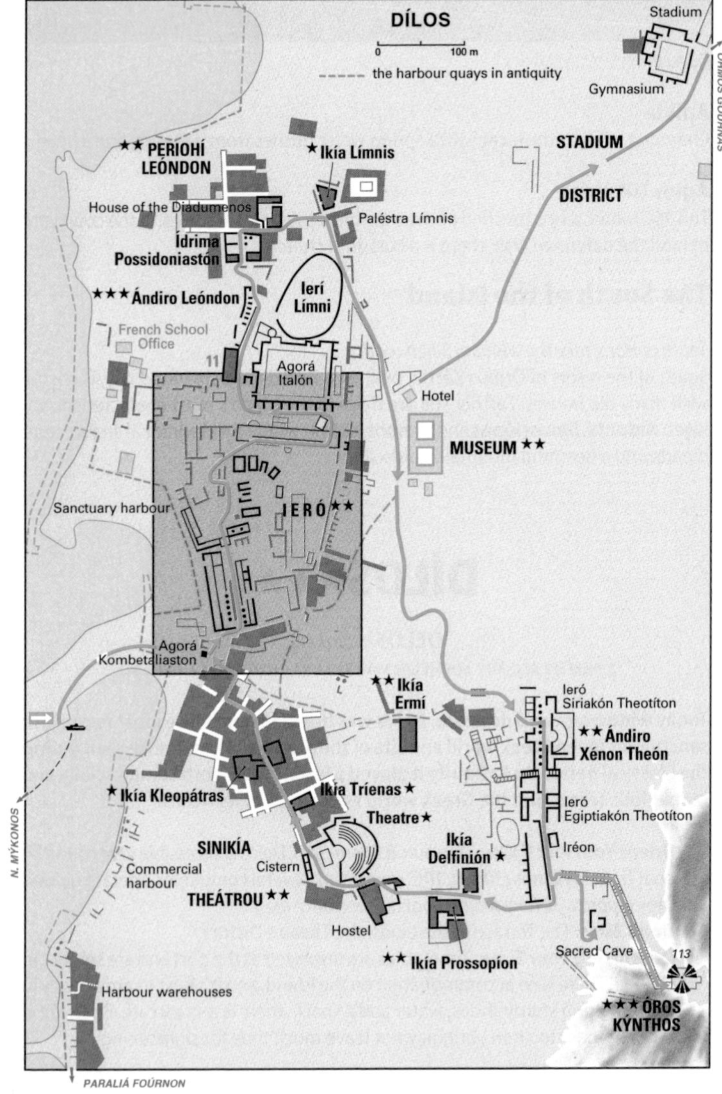

At the Centre of the Greek World

According to legend, **Leto**, whom Zeus had seduced and then abandoned, wandered about the world pursued by the anger of Hera, who had forbidden anyone to receive the pregnant goddess. Leto eventually found a haven on the floating island of **Ortygia** (Quail Land) where after nine days and nights in labour she gave birth to twins, Apollo and Artemis, and the island, now anchored to the seabed by four pillars, became known as Delos (illustrious) in honour of the god of light.

in the 1C BC the prosperity of Delos reached its zenith and the town numbered 25 000 inhabitants.

The decline of Delos began in 88 BC when it was sacked by Mithridates, King of Pontus. Pilgrimages became less popular, depradations by pirates grew and the main shipping routes moved elsewhere. The island was finally abandoned in the 6C-7C.

Visit

Ieró★★ (Sanctuary of Apollo)

Agora Kombetialistón

Entry is through a paved open space called the Agora of the Competialists in honor of the Roman gods of the crossroads. Note the remains of a monumental altar (**1**).

Sacred Way★

This processional road was lined by votive monuments; some of the bases are still visible. On either side stretched two porticoes; the portico on the left, Stoá Fílipou, was built by Philip of Macedon in the 3C BC; the one on the right, Stoá Pergámou, was built in the same period by the kings of Pergamon, a city in Asia Minor.

Propílea

Little is left of this monumental entrance *(propylaia)*, but the numbers of pilgrims who crossed the threshold in Antiquity can be judged by how much the three steps are worn away. On the right stands a marble statue of a bearded Hermes (4C BC) (**2**).

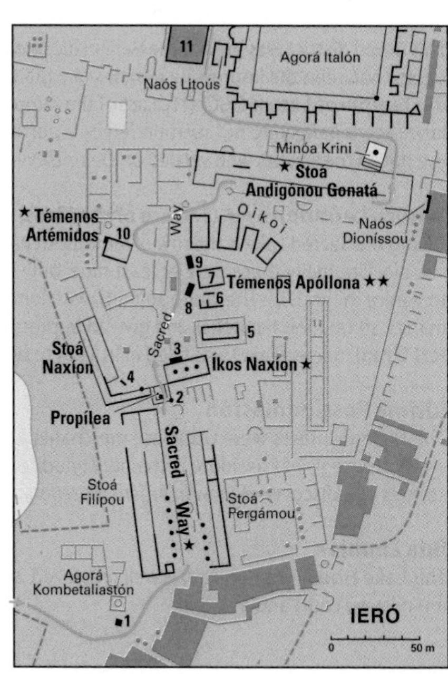

Íkos Naxíon (House of the Naxiots)

On the right beyond the Propylaia lie the foundations of a rectangular building from the Archaic period. Against the north wall stands an enormous block of marble (**3**), that was the base of a Statue of Apollo (6C BC), a colossal votive offering erected by the Naxiots; some parts of it can be seen near the Sanctuary of Artemis.

Stoá Naxíon★ (Stoa of the Naxiots)

On the left beyond the Propylaia are traces of this 6C BC portico; look for the circular granite base (**4**) on which stood a colossal bronze palm tree representing the tree beneath which Leto gave birth to Apollo and Artemis.

Témenos Apólon★★

Lying south to north in the precinct are traces of three successive Temples of Apollo.

The **Temple of Delian Apollo** (**5**), a Doric building begun in the 5C BC. The **Athenian Temple** (c 420 BC) was also Doric (**6**); the naos contained seven statues. The smallest and oldest was the **Porinos Temple** (**7**), built of hard limestone tufa, which contained an Archaic statue of Apollo and the treasure of the Delian League.

Near the Porinos Temple stand two pedestals; one (**8**) is decorated with a Doric frieze of alternating roses and bucranes (ox heads) and the other (**9**) in blue marble is inscribed in honour of Philetairos, first King of Pergamon.

Témenos Artémidos★ (Artemision)

Set back from the Sacred Way, on the site of an Ancient Mycenaean palace, are the truncated columns of the façade of the Temple of Artemis, an Ionic building (2C BC) that succeeded two others.

Behind the Temple of Artemis lie the torso and the pelvis pieces of the colossal **Statue of Apollo**★★ (**10**) which was hauled this far by the Venetians in 1422.

Stoá Andigónou Gonatá★

Bordering the sanctuary on the north side, the stoa was built in the 3C BC. Two rows of statues lined the façade; their bases still exist. Behind the eastern end of the portico stands the Minoë Fountain *(Minóa Kríni)* which dates from the 6C BC. Nearby are the remains of the precinct wall and of a Temple to Dionysos.

There is also evidence of subterranean corridors in the theatre (3C BC), which allowed the actors to pass from the front of the stage to the orchestra.

Periohí Leóndon★★ (Lion District)

This urban district was built in the Hellenistic period. The path out of the sanctuary passes between the impressive remains of a granite building *(left)* and the walls of the **Temple of Leto** (6C BC) (11). East of the temple extends the Agora of the Italians *(Agorá Italón)* (2C BC) surrounded by a portico into which opened the cells of the Italian merchants who settled on Delos (several mosaics).

Ándiro Leóndon★★★ (Terrace of the Lions)

Facing the Sacred Lake is the row of famous Archaic lions sculpted in grainy Naxian marble. Originally there were at least nine; only five remain (a sixth was removed to Venice in the 17C). The stone animals, with long bodies and scarcely perceptible manes, sit on their haunches and give an impression of restrained power.

Ierí Límni (Sacred Lake) was filled in in 1924 to prevent malarial mosquitoes.

Ídrima Possidoniastón

The Poseidoniasts were Lebanese merchants and ship owners who worshipped under the aegis of Poseidon. In the peristyled court a group of Aphrodite and Pan statues was discovered *(now in Athens Museum)*.

Ikía Límnis★

This Lake House (Hellenistic) is well preserved (stucco and mosaics) with a charming pillared court and a cistern.

Stadium District

Beyond the ruins of the Sanctuary of Archegetes, are the remains of the gymnasium (3C BC) and of the stadium with its track and starting line.

Museum★★

Among the most interesting items are the votive statues of the *kouros* and *kore* type, mostly from the Temple of Artemis; the marble statue of Apollo attributed to Praxiteles; the bronze mask of Dionysos; the ivory plaques; and Mycenaean jewellery.

Óros Kínthos★★★ (Mount Kynthos)

Ikía Ermi★★
The two-storey **House of Hermes** (2C BC) is named after a fine head of Hermes *(in the museum)* found there. The ground floor includes a vestibule, an inner courtyard bordered on three sides by a portico and a *nymphaeum*.

Ándiro Xénon Theón★★
The **Terrace of the Foreign Gods** was built in the 2C BC for shrines to the non-Greek divinities worshipped by Delos' many immigrants. On either side of the path lie traces of semicircular shrines and rooms; one of the porticoes enclosed a theatre where orgiastic mysteries were celebrated in honour of Atargatis, the Syrian Aphrodite.
The **Shrine of the Egyptian gods** contains the remains of a temple to Serapis and a temple to Isis; its naos sheltered a **statue** of the goddess. Nearby, foundations mark the site of a little Doric temple built of marble and dedicated to Hera (6C BC).

Ascent of Mount Kínthos★★★
(45min on foot there and back). The Sacred Cave in the rock was covered with enormous slabs of granite in the Hellenistic era to form a shrine to Herakles.
The **summit** (113m/370ft) has traces of a sanctuary to Zeus and Athena (3C BC) and a magnificent **panorama**★★★ over Delos and the Cyclades.

Siniká Theátrou★★★ (Theatre District)

The Theatre District was built from the 2C BC onwards to house the many foreigners who came to live on Delos. It comprised many luxurious houses built round courtyards and decorated with superb mosaic floors in lively colours.

Ikía Delfinión★
The central courtyard of the **House of the Dolphins** is paved with a mosaic signed by Asklepiades of Arados.

Ikía Prossopíon★★
The **House of the Masks** is a huge two-storey house, with a central courtyard surrounded with a peristyle. The rooms giving onto the courtyard are decorated with magnificent mosaics showing figures wearing theatre masks.

Theatre★
Dating from the Hellenistic era, this majestic construction is fairly well preserved, with marble walls and 43 rows of seats for 5 000 spectators.

Ikía Tríenas★
The **House of the Trident** has mosaics decorated with a trident, a dolphin entwined round an anchor and geometric motifs.

Ikía Dionίssou★

The central motif of the mosaic in the peristyled courtyard of the **House of Dionysos** shows Dionysos on a panther; the panther's head is remarkable.

Ikía Kleopátras★

In the 2C BC the house was inhabited by a woman named Cleopatra and her husband Dioskourides, whose damaged effigies can be seen on the north side of the peristyled courtyard. The well still provides excellent drinking water.

H. Champollion/MICHELIN

Dionysos mosaic, Delos

FOLÉGANDROS★★

Φολεγανδροζ

POPULATION 667

32KM²/13SQ MI – MICHELIN MAP 737 K-L 12 – CYCLADES – AEGEAN.

Despite its popularity, Folégandros remains a haven of tranquillity. It is typically Cycladic in character, with whitewashed houses, mountain churches, terraces planted with olive trees, and a little fishing port. Lapped by clear blue water, the beaches are particularly fine. *Northern outskirts of Hóra, ☎ (22860) 41 158.*

- **Orient Yourself:** Of volcanic origin, this small island is between Melos and Síkinos. Folégandros is linked to Piraeus along two routes.
- **Don't Miss:** The town of Hora, a swim at Katergo Beach.
- **Organizing Your Time:** Plan a three-day visit; the boat trip round the island will take an entire day.
- **Also See:** Mílos, Thíra

Ch. Legrand/MICHELIN

Mountain village, Folégandros

Visit

Karavostássis

The island's port is clustered around the Church of Ágios Artémios and along a pebble beach bordered by fish restaurants. The best beach is at Várdia to the north, accessible by a long flight of steps *(10min walk)*. To the south there are narrow beaches.

Kátergo Beach★★

The island's best beach can be reached by boat or on foot *(2hr there and back)* by a track which leads behind the campsite at Livádi, south of Karavostássis.

Hóra★★★

3.3km/2mi northwest of Karavostássis.

The island's capital is on a fine **site**★★ at the top of a cliff some 200m/650ft above the sea. Built around its citadel, it is a charming maze of alleys and squares. From the end of Platía Pounda there is an impressive **view**★★ of the cliff.

Built in 1204, the **kástro**★★ (citadel) has houses making up its ramparts, transforming the citadel into a pleasant residential quarter that is often deserted.

The Church of **Panagía Pantánassa** (17C) is built on the cliff edge; fine icons.

The rest of the town is composed of paved alleys centred around shaded squares, each with a little white church. The oldest is Platía Piátsa. Bar and restaurant tables are laid out all over the place, creating a festive feel.

On the outskirts of town, lie three attractive chapels: Ágios Vassílios, Ágios Sávas (west of town) and Panagía Plakianí (to the northwest, beyond the citadel wall).

Address Book

GETTING ABOUT

By boat – There are daily ferries from Piraeus *(6-10hr)* and Santorini plus service from Íos *(5/wk)*, Náxos *(5/wk)*, Páros *(5/wk)*, Melos *(4/wk)*, Sifnos *(4/wk)*, Kythnos *(3/wk)*, Amorgos *(2/wk)* and Sérifos *(2/wk)*.

Buses meet all ferries, and depart from Hora 1hr before ferry departures. Buses link Hora-Pano Meria, and Hora-Karavostasis; see schedules posted at stops.

WHERE TO EAT

Local specialities – *Mátsata* (fresh pasta served in a rabbit and tomato sauce), *liókafta* (dried fish) and *kalasouna* (pastry with cheese).

⊖ **Pounta** – *Hóra*. Excellent local specialities and breakfasts.

⊖ **Kritikós** – *Hóra, Platía Piátsa*. Specialising in grilled local meats.

⊖ **Chic** – *Hóra*. Spinach balls, *mezes*, carrot soup...delicious.

⊖ **Mimis** – *Pano Meriá, near the museum*. Excellent *mátsata* and meats.

WHERE TO STAY

⊖ **Imerovigli** – *Pano Meriá – ☎ 69 34 090 349 – 3rm*. Restful farm atmosphere in the country. Breakfast 5€.

⊖⊖ **Kástro** – *Hóra – ☎ (22860) 41 230, www.hotel-castro.com – 12rm*. Impressive vaulted ceilings on the ground floor, roof terrace with sea views and nice rooms. Breakfast 11€.

⊖⊖⊖ **Kallisti** – *Hóra – ☎ (22860) 41 555, www.kallisti.net.gr – 14rm*. Lovely Cycladic building; pool. Breakfast 8€.

⊖⊖⊖ **Ampelos** – *Hóra – ☎ (22860) 41 544, www.ampelosresort.com – 10rm*. Traditional decor and style in this handsome structure. Classes offered in watercolor painting and cooking.

TAKING A BREAK

Astárti for Greek music, **Patitiri** for ambiance or, for a more lively atmosphere, the **Greco Bar** with rock music.

EVENTS AND FESTIVALS

Late July, excellent world music **concerts** at Hóra. *www.mediadellarte.gr*

Church of Panagía Kímissis★★

1hr there and back. Reached by a path which zigzags up from Hóra, this large church is built at the top of a cliff. From the top of the path, the views down over Hóra, the cultivated terraces, the coast and its cliffs are remarkable.

Monastery of Ágios Nikólaos

1hr south of Hóra, not far from the heliport. This beautiful, partially ruined monastery in an austere landscape will appeal to lovers of solitude.

The north of the island★★

Head west on the Pano Meriá road. After 1.5km/0.9mi, a left turn leads to the sea. Magnificent desolate landscape; after 30min the track reaches Firá Beach, in a broad bay not far from Angáli (to the north), with numerous tavernas.

Pano Meriá

This strange village is a scattered settlement of hamlets and outlying farms.

Before the village of **Merovigli** (the last settlement on this road) is the Church of Ágios Ioánnis Pródromos, one of the island's oldest. Beyond the village, a track (20min) leads to the Church of Ágios Pandeleímon, sitting in a beautiful landscape.

Beaches of the north coast★

Accessible by tracks from Merovigli, the best beaches are **Livadáki, Ambéli** (surrounded by greenery) and **Serfiótiko** (views of the seabed, tamarisks).

Boat trip around the island★★

Daylong excursion. Book at the tourist office. 20€, including lunch 25€.
This delightful trip follows the rocky coastline, passing below Hóra before making its way around the bays.

Κεα

POPULATION 2 417

131KM²/52SQ MI – MICHELIN MAP 737 J 10 – CYCLADES – AEGEAN.

The westernmost of the Cyclades and the closest to Attica, Kéa has many villas and hotels on its west coast. The mountainous and fertile island is popular with Athenian families and yachting types. Remains of numerous settlements bear witness to Kéa's long history. *Opposite the landing stage. 22880 215 00. www.kea.gr*

Touring

Around Korissía

Gialiskári is the better of the two beaches near the port. Just 7km/4mi to the south is the attractive and little frequented beach at Xíla. To the northeast is Kéfala Beach, at the far end of the Kóka Peninsula. There is another huge beach in Otziás Bay.

East coast★

Accessible by little paths, the island's best beaches are usually deserted. Spathí, Kalidoníhi, Psili Ámos, Sikamniá, Psathí and Orkós are all fine beaches to the north; the south has Ágios Fílipos, Órmos Póles (near the ruins at Karthéa) and Kaliskiá.

West coast
Among the best beaches are Písses (near the village of the same name), Koúndouros (near one of the island's biggest resorts), Ágios Emilianós, Kambí and Liparós.

Visit

The Northwest of the Island★

Korissía
The island's main port is situated at the foot of a hill; at the top lie the ruins of a Temple of Apollo, all that remains of a Classical city. The walk is worth it for the fine **view**★ over the bay and the port.

Agía Iríni
Open Tue, Thu-Sun, 9am-2pm. 2€. ☎ (22880) 212 64.
North of Korissía, this promontory was inhabited from the late Neolithic period until around 1500 BC; the maze of ruins makes an interesting visit.

Hóra and its Environs★★

Hóra★★★
Kéa's capital is one of the most beautiful towns in Greece. Along its winding alleyways, houses with tiled roofs sit cheek by jowl with typically Cycladic cuboid buildings. From the Rokoménos Fountain, climb up to the pleasant square and continue through the vaulted passageway. Odós Harálambos leads to the site of the Ancient acropolis,where the Venetians built their **kástro** (13C). Fine **views**★.
In the lower town, the main square, dominated by the **Town Hall** (1902), has shops and restaurants. Above the main street, Odós Ieromnímonos has some fine houses. The small **Archaeological Museum** (*open Tue-Sun 8.30am-3pm; no charge; ☎(22880) 220 79*) displays objects from the temple of Athena at Karthéa.

Address Book

For coin categories, see the Legend on the cover flap.

GETTING ABOUT
By boat – Ferry service *(daily in summer, 1h15mn)* from Lávrio in Attica. From there, service to Kythnos *(3/wk)*, Syros *(3/wk)*, Andros *(1/wk)*, and Páros *(1/wk)*.
Buses link Hóra, Korissia, Vourkari and Otzias.
Mopeds are a great way to explore. Rentals available in Hóra and Korissia.

WHERE TO EAT
Strofí tou Mími – *Vourkári, beginning of the Otziás road.* Fish and grilled dishes served in this attractive building with terrace on the waterfront.
Cyclades – *Otziás, right-hand side on entering the village.* The best place for home cooking.

WHERE TO STAY
Corali – *Korissía, on the Vourkári road – ☎ (22880) 21 422 – 8 studios.* Pleasant, well-equipped studios in a large house. Warm welcome; no breakfast.
Ágios Geórgios – *Koúndourous – ☎ (22880) 31 277 – 20rm, open Apr-Oct.* Pleasant rooms with terrace in a typical Cycladic-style building. The restaurant has a fine view over the bay and a good reputation for its cuisine.

SHOPPING
Kéa's **honey**, subtly flavoured with thyme, is an ingredient in **pastéli** (nougat with sesame seeds). The island also produces large quantities of almonds. Also worth a try is **mávro**, the wine made here.

The lion's enigmatic smile

According to the myth, Kéa, with its springs and oak woods, was inhabited by nymphs as well as people when the gods ruled the world. One day a lion came down from the mountains, terrifying the nymphs who fled to Euboia. A drought occurred, and the people asked Kéos – Aristee, son of Apollo and the nymph Cyrene, to help them. He settled on the island and erected a temple dedicated to Zeus, who sent a cooling breeze and rain to save Kéa from catastrophe. The inhabitants carved an image of the lion out of the rock on the top of a hill; this strange sculpture (6C BC) has a strikingly enigmatic smile.

The Lion

1.5km/1mi northeast of the town centre.

Near Ágios Spirídon is the famous Lion of Kéa, monumental hillside sculpture.

Messariá

Head southeast towards Kastaniés and Orkós.

Among the ruins of the **Monastery of Panagía Episcopí** is a fine white church. From Mount Profítis Iliás (560m/1 835ft), the **view**★ is breathtaking.

Péra Meriá

The few inhabitants of this area live in fine traditional houses called *katikíes.*

Spathí Valley★

Northeast of Hóra; the valley is accessible by a stony track.

The Chapel of Ágios Dimítrios marks the beginning of this valley which runs to the sea. Down on the coast *(8km/5mi from Hóra)*, the **Monastery of Panagía Kastrianí** is a veritable eyrie; there is a splendid view over the island and the Aegean. The original church (1708), built on the site of the miraculous discovery of an icon of the Virgin by shepherds (feast day 15 August), is enclosed within a later structure.

S. Sauvignier/MICHELIN

Outskirts of Hóra: **Monastery of Agía Marína**★, *6km/4mi to the southwest* – **Ruins of Karthéa**★ (partially submerged Classical remains), *19km/12mi to the southeast (accessible by a 2km/1.25 path from Stavroudáki).*

KÍTHNOS

KYTHNOS – Κυθνοζ

POPULATION 1 608

99KM² – MICHELIN MAP 737 J-K 11 – CYCLADES – AEGEAN.

Though flat and arid with little habitation, peaceful Kythnos has a certain charm. Its many beaches are usually deserted (except in August), its coastal paths feature lovely views, and its quiet villages and hot-spring spas offer rest and retreat.
On the landing stage at the port. www.kythnos-island.gr.

Touring

Beaches of the West Coast

Martinákia

5min from the landing stage at Mérihas, by the steps to the left.
In summer, this is the only beach on the island that gets crowded.

Address Book

For coin categories, see the Legend on the cover flap.

GETTING ABOUT

By boat – Mainland ferry service to Piraeus *(daily, 1-3hr)* and Lávrio *(6/wk, 2h)*. Also links to Sérifos *(daily)*, Sifnos *(daily)*, Melos *(daily)*, Kéa *(3/wk)*, Folégandros *(3/wk)* and Santorini *(2/wk)*.
Buses meet all ferries. Service to Hóra and Louitrá nearly every day.
Scooters and **car rentals** are available at **Adonis** ☎ *(22810) 32 104*

WHERE TO EAT

Ostria – *Mérihas, near the landing stage.* The varied menu offers grilled meats and home cooking. Don't miss the *astakomakaronádha* (spaghetti with lobster), a house speciality.
Kantouni – *Mérihas, other end of the beach from the landing stage.* Dine on the terrace or on the beach; grilled meat specialists, including *kontosoúvli* (kebabs), *kokorétsi* (tripe), *paidhakia* (lamb chops), all accompanied by the island speciality *sfougáto* (little balls of cheese).

WHERE TO STAY

Panorama – *Mérihas, up the steps behind the port* – ☎ *(22810) 32 184 – 7 studios.* Overlooking the whole bay, this white building in the Cycladic style has rooms opening onto a terrace shaded by a blue wooden pergola. The studios have the bare necessities, but at a competitive price.
Paradeisos – *Mérihas, next to Panorama* – ☎ *(22810) 32 206 – 6 studios.* Same level of comfort as Panorama, with the same wonderful view.
Porto Klaras – *Loutrá, near the pier* – ☎ *(22810) 31 276, www.porto-klaras.gr –11rm.* This pleasant two-storey construction in the Cycladic style is the smartest place in town. Fine views from the balconies.

SPORTS AND LEISURE

Undersea adventures await off the coast of Loutrá. For information and equipment rental, **AquaTeam** *(22810) 322 42, www.aquakythnos.gr*

EVENTS AND FESTIVALS

An enormous meal, music and dancing usually make up the island's village festivals. The biggest diary dates are Panagía Kanála (15 August and 8 September), Panagía tou Nikoús (15 August), Panagía tis Flambourias (24 August), Agía Triáda at Hóra (end of June) and Ai Lia (in the mountains, 20 July).

Episkopí

2km/1.25mi north of Mérihas.

Between two hills, this west-facing beach is fringed by tamarisks.

Fikiáda★ and Kolóna★

Access by the path north from Apókrissi (30min) or by boat from Mérihas (summer).

These two beaches, separated by a ribbon of sand leading to the Ágios Loukás peninsula, are the finest on the island.

Loutrá and its Beaches

4.5km/3mi north of Hóra.

Loutrá has two hot springs (38°C and 52°C respectively), rich in iron and mineral salts, which are supposed to help treat eczema and rheumatism.

To the north are the beaches of **Maroulá, Kavourohéri** (popular with naturists) and **Potámia**, all within easy walking distance.

Beaches of the Southeast Coast

Beaches along the coastline here are little visited. From south to north: **Ágios Dimítrios** *(southern tip of the island)*, **Skílou** *(4km/2.5mi south of Driopída, access by road)*, **Megáli Ámos** and **Antonidés** *(near Panagía Kanála)*, Zogáki, Kourí and Náoussa *(north of Léfkes)* and Ágios Stéfanos *(east of Hóra, access by a stony path).*

Visit

Mérihas

Kythnos's main port is on the west coast. The old fishing village has grown a great deal since 1974 harbour development. Good tavernas along the waterfront.

Hóra★

7.5km/5mi northeast of Mérihas.

Built atop a hill, Hóra is a charming town with quiet alleys and fine churches. Note the decorated paving of its streets. The Church of **Ágios Sávas** (1613) was designed to accommodate both Orthodox *(to the right)* and Catholic *(to the left)* traditions. The Basilica of **Agía Triáda** is constructed of elements from earlier buildings.

Eolikó

2km/1.25mi east of Hóra.

A wind farm and solar-energy park here allow Kythnos to generate much of its electricity. South of Eolikó are two immaculately white religious foundations, the Church of **Panagía tou Nikoús** (Our Lady of Victories) and the **Monastery of Pródromou** (with a fine wooden iconostasis, 16C).

Ruins of Vriókastro

North of Mérihas, at the far end of the bay – allow 30min heading south.

From Apókrissi, a path leads to the remains of the island's former capital. It spread over an immense area. Three cisterns, the foundations of a tower and the remains of a wall are visible. The partially submerged site is accessible by boat from Mérihas.

Ruins of Kefalókástro

2hr there and back on foot by mule track from Loutrá.

Not far from the coast at the northern end of the island, Kefalókástro was the capital during the Byzantine and Frankish periods. Ruins include the remains of the defensive wall, houses and two churches. The **view**★ of the sea and the coast is exceptional.

Driopída★

5km/3mi east of Mérihas.

Small houses with tile roofs mark the island's most beautiful village. The main church, **Agía Ánna**, has a blue dome and twin bell towers. The adjacent **Byzantine Museum** (*no fixed opening hours; key available from the parish priest)* houses some of the finest icons on the island while **Ágios Minas**, features a carvediconostasis and a bishop's throne. **Views**★ of the island extend from the terrace of Ágios Nektários.

Léfkes

East coast, 2km/1.25mi from Driopída.

Barely 30 house comprise this agreable village next to a tamarisk-fringed beach.

Panagía Kanála

7km/4mi from Driopída.

The village is named for the 19C basilica which stands among nearby pine trees. Dedicated to the Virgin Mary, the church has an icon said to have been found in the sea. This is the focus for an important pilgrimage every 15 August. Fine sandy beach.

MÍLOS★

MELOS – Μηλοζ

POPULATION 4 771

151KM²/60SQ MI – MICHELIN MAP 737 J-K 12 – CYCLADES – AEGEAN.

The world-renowned Venus de Milo statue was discovered on Melos in the 19C. The island's picturesque landscape features sea caves, rocky outcrops, cliffs of extraordinary colours, ribbons of sand, boulder-strewn mountainsides, green valleys and bright, white villages. *In the port.* ☎ *(22870) 22 445.*

A Bit of History

The Melos Aphrodite – Widely known as the Venus de Milo, this world-famous statue of Aphrodite, goddess of love, dates from the 2C BC and is considered one of the finest examples of Classical art.

The broken sections of the statue were discovered on Melos near an Ancient acropolis around 1820 by a peasant farmer, who hid the pieces for a time. Eventually they were confiscated by Turkish officials, who planned to present the statue to the Turkish governor of the Cyclades. Before they could deliver it the French ambassador to Turkey, alerted to the statue's artistic significance, arranged to purchase it. It was quickly shipped to France, presented to Louis XVIII and put on display in the Louvre.

Touring

The Beaches of Melos Bay

A road along the bay provides access to a number of sheltered beaches. The long beach at **Chivadolimni** is good for water sports.Northwest of Pláka at the mouth of the bay is **Plathienά**, one of the island's most attractive beaches.

The Beaches of the North Coast

Near the village of Kápros is the delightful Bay of **Papafrága**★★, a narrow inlet divided from the open sea by a stone arch *(access by steps carved into the rock)*. To the east of Polónia are some fine sandy beaches, such as **Písso Thálassa**.

The Beaches of the South Coast★

In a wide bay, **Paliohóri**★ is a huge pebble beach, arguably the finest on the island. It is surrounded by multicoloured cliffs.

Agía Kiriakí★

Beautiful beach of volcanic origin.

Gérontas★ and **Kléftiko**★★★ may be reached by boat from Kípos. Kléftiko is at the foot of imposing white cliffs.

Address Book

For coin categories, see the Legend on the cover flap.

GETTING ABOUT

By Boat – Several ferries a day from Piraeus via **Le Pirée** *(3-7hr)*; also super-jet service *(5hr, daily Jul-Aug, weekends offseason)*. **Lane Lines** offers service to Piraeus *(2/wk, 5hr), www.lane.gr.*
Also daily links to Sifnos, Sérifos, and Kythnos; and links to Santorini *(4/wk)*, Folégandros *(4/wk)*, Ios *(4/wk)*, Páros *(3/wk)*, Náxos *(1/wk)*, Siros *(1/wk)* and Lavrio *(1/wk)*.
By Air – Olympic Airways, Adámas, ☎ (22870) 22 380. At least 1 flight/day to Athens.

WHERE TO EAT

Barco – *Adámas, main street.* Tasty, fresh dishes; try the *pitaraki*.
Archondoula– *Plaka, main passage of the upper town.* Attractive tavern in a historic building.
Armenaki – *Polónia, on the main street upon entering the village.* Popular for its delicious lobster pasta. Delicious cold dishes as well; attentive service.
Sirocco – *Paleochori, on the beach.* The house specialty: fish cooked on the beach.

WHERE TO STAY

Delfini – *Adámas, west of the landing stage and up from Lagáda Beach* – ☎ *(22870) 22 001 – 22rm*. This peaceful hotel is near the beach. Clean rooms; breakfast served on the terrace.
Villa Hélios –*Adámas, above the port* – ☎ *(22870) 22 258 – 15rm.* Quiet, charming, with a lovely terrace.
Portiani –*Adámas, at the port* – ☎ *(22870) 22 940 – 23rm*. Large hotel with views over the bay. Comfortable rooms, lavish breakfast.
Apollon – *Polónia, in the residential district* – ☎ *(22870) 41 347 – 11rm.* Clean and comfortable rooms, a family atmosphere and an attractive setting by the water's edge. Breakfast 6€.

TAKING A BREAK

Utopia – *Pláka, in the centre of the village,* ☎ *(22870) 23 678*. The ideal spot from which to watch the sun go down while having a drink.

SPORTS AND LEISURE

Scuba diving – *Diving Center Milos, Polónia,* ☎ *(22870) 41 296; info@milos-diving.gr.* Equipment hire, organised dives and disabled facilities.
Sea kayaking – *Brau Kat,* ☎ *2280 235 97, www.seakayakgreece.com*. The ideal way to discover Melos' rock formations.

J. Souty/MICHELIN

Ch. Legrand/MICHELIN

The beautiful Melos coastline

Visit

Adámas

On the Bay of Melos, Adámas is the island's main port and the ferry terminal. It was founded in the early 19C by Cretan refugees. Perched on top of the hill, the Cathedral of **Ágios Harálambos** offers good views of the surrounding area.

Agía Tríada★

Open daily except Mon, 9.15a-1.15p and 6.15-10.15pm. No charge.
The church (13C) has an **Ecclesiastical Museum** with a fine icon of John the Baptist (1639), and an ornate iconostasis. Interesting temporary exhibitions of sacred art.

Mining Museum *near Papikinou beach* (minerals, rock formations of Melos).

Pláka★★

4.5km/3mi northwest of Adámas.
The island's capital is a charming hill town of narrow alleys winding among bright white houses bedecked with flowers. From the **kástro**★★ at the top of the hill, the views over the bay and the hillside villages are impressive. On the way down, note the attractive Church of **Ipapánti**★ (Thalassitra) which has some fine 17C icons.

Museum of Folk Art; Archaeological Museum (Cycladic statuary, the Lady of Filakopí).

Klíma

2km/1.25mi south of Pláka.
The Ancient capital of Melos is now a fishing village with colourful boathouses (*sirmata*) between the cliff face and the water's edge. The remains of the Ancient city include a **Roman theatre**, its marble seating terraces looking out to sea. (*Open Tue-Sun, 8.30am-3pm; no charge).*

Mantrákia★

Northeast of Pláka.
This little harbour also has colourful *sirmata* boathouses. Dwellings carved out of the rock are still used as holiday homes in summer.

Sarakinikó★★

East of Pláka.

An impressive natural site; the volcanic tufa is bright white, sculpted by the winds into cones, domes and terraces by the sea. Swimming is possible in calm weather.

Mítakas

Farther east is this village with painted sirmata dug into the rock. Beyond, at the hamlet of **Ágios Konstandínos**, you'll see pozzolana stacks and solidified lava flows.

Filakopí

North coast. Open Tue-Sun, 8.30am-3pm.

Excavations in this cove have uncovered traces of three superimposed cities dating from the Bronze Age, the Minoan period (c 1600 BC) and the Mycenaean (1200 BC). Their stone houses are the first indications of urbanism in the Cyclades and were decorated with frescoes (now in the National Archaeological Museum).

Tripití catacombs (paleo-Christian catacombs, 2C), *1.5km/mi south of Pláka* – **Firopótamos** (attractive port), *north of Pláka* – **Polónia** (popular resort), *facing the island of Kímolos.*

Excursion

Boat trip around the island★★

Departures from Adámas (1 day with stops and lunch break) 9am. Approx. 25€.

This trip shows the island's amazing geological phenomena and delightful seascapes. The volcanic islet of **Glaronissa**★★ has imposing basalt cliffs. In the **Sikía Cave**★★ the light shining through the collapsed vault turns the water lovely colours. To the southeast are the tall white cliffs of **Kléftiko**★★★.

Excursion

Kímolos

Separated from Melos by a narrow channel, this is one of the smallest islands in the Cyclades. Kímolos is renowned for its volcanic rocks of extraordinary colours, its jagged coastline and its white beaches.

Psáthi

The ferries arrive at this fishing port, which has an easily accessible beach nearby.

Hóra★

2km/1.25mi north of Psáthi.

The fortifications and three gateways of the kástro (16C) are still in excellent condition. The Archaeological Museum at the entrance to the village displays items from the Cycladic period. *Open Tue-Sat, 8am-12.30pm. €3.*

A Bit of Advice

Getting around: Kímolos is served by ferries from Piraeus and neighbouring islands; there is a link with Melos (Polónia) four times a day.

Ch. Legrand/MICHELIN

The harbour, Mantrákia

Prassá

5km/3mi northeast of Hóra.
The Church of the Evanghelístria dates from the 17C.

Ágios Andréas

To the southwest of Hóra, 2hr on foot there and back.
Just offshore from Elliniká, this small island has the remains of a submerged city dating from around 1000 BC.

Beaches★

The finest are at **Aliki**, **Bonatsa**, **Klima**, **Limni** and **Prassá**. Some may be reached by boat from Psáthi. Ask the fishermen in the port; some will be able to show you magnificent sea caves and take you to the most isolated beaches.

MÍKONOS★★

MYKONOS – Μυκονος

POPULATION 9 306

86KM²/34SQ MI – MICHELIN MAP 737 L-M 10-11 – CYCLADES – AEGEAN.

The granite island of Mykonos attracts tourists from all over during the summer to its beaches and nightlife. In autumn and winter the island regains its traditional appeal. *At the old ferry port. www.mykonos.gr, www.mykonosgreece.com.*

- **Orient Yourself:** Hóra, the main city, is the heart of the island. Seaside resorts dot the southern coast, while the northern coast is less developed. There are three ports:
- **Don't Miss:** Sunset from "Little Venice"
- **Organizing Your Time:** You'll need three days to enjoy Míkonos.
- **Also See:** Dílos, Náxos, Páros, Tínos, Síros

A Bit of History

Venetians ruled Mykonos until the early 18C , building warehouses where the merchants of Venice and Marseilles came for supplies. Later it was a haven for pirates. The renown of Mykonos' gorgeous beaches has grown so that Hóra, once a fishing village, has become a destination for the Greek and international jet set. It is currently known as a gay resort, but trends change quickly here and Mykonos is not easily categorised. Nevertheless, its reputation as a pleasure island remains strong.

Touring

Beaches★★

Most of the beaches are accessible by boat from Hóra's fishing port (departing in the morning and returning in the evening).

Psaroú, Platís Gialós

In an enclosed rocky bay; the island's main resort is also located here.

Paránga★, Paradise★, Super Paradise, Agrari★
The granite hills behind these beaches are rapidly disappearing under development. Paradise (naturist) is bordered by a campsite and has a loud open-air disco. Super Paradise (accessible by boat from Paradise, Platís Gialós or Psaroú), long popular with naturists, today has speakers blaring techno music, making it the island's liveliest gay beach. Agrari is a bit quieter.

Agía Ána, Kalafáti★, Liá★
These three pleasant beaches are near a fishing village built on a promontory.

Address Book

For coin categories, see the Legend on the cover flap.

GETTING ABOUT

By Air – Several Olympic Airways flights a day from Athens. Also at least one flight a day from Thessaloníki, 2 a week from Rhodes, and Santorini and Herakleion flights in season.
By Boat – Several daily ferries from Piraeus *(3h20-6h40)*, Rafína *(2h10-5h40)* and Lavrio *(3h)*; Also daily links to Andros, Tenos, Siros, Páros, Náxos, Ios and Delos.
By Car – Rentals available near the port from **Avis** ☎ *(22890) 229 60;* **Europcar** ☎ *(22890) 271 11;* **Hertz** ☎ *(22890) 237 91;* **Kosmos** ☎ *(22890) 240 13.*

WHERE TO EAT

O Níkos – *Hóra, behind the town hall.* Good traditional Greek cuisine, fresh fish and very reasonable prices.
Chez Maria – *Hóra,Odos Kalogera.* Excellent-quality traditional dishes served in a lovely atmosphere (flowered garden in summer).
Mathios – *Tourlos.* Sample a wide variety of appetising Greek dishes while drinking in the bay views.
Vangelis – *Ano Mera, main square.* One of the best restaurants on Mikonos; Freshly prepared authentic dishes such as grilled octopus or skewered meats.

WHERE TO STAY

Karboni – *Hóra, Odos Matogiani, in the old town* – ☎ *(22890) 22 217 – 40rm.* Well-located and comfortable, an aging yet charming hostelry. The best rooms have balconies.
Matina – *Hóra, 3 Odós Fournákia, centre of town* – ☎ *(22890) 26 433, www.hotelmatina-mykonos.com – 19rm.* Balconied rooms overlooking a green garden. Breakfast 10€.
Hotel Carbonaki – *Hóra, 23 Odos Panachrantou, centre of town*– ☎ *(22890) 241 24, www.carbonaki.gr – 21rm.* Attractive, comfortable Cycladic-style hotel, with a small but refreshing pool. Breakfast 8€.
Rochari – *Hóra, Odós Matogiannis* – ☎ *(22890) 23 107 – www.rochari.com – 60rm.* Views over the sea or the garden. Comfortable hotel overlooking the town.

TAKING A BREAK

In the evenings, Hóra becomes one big nightclub. Start by having a drink in the Little Venice district (**Caprice** for sunsets, or **Kastro Bar** for classical music). After dinner, choose from a multitude of bars, bearing in mind that things don't heat up until 11pm or later.
Montparnasse – Little Venice. Trendy bar for blues lovers.
Notte – Near the port. Greek music.
Astra Club – Odós Matogiannis. Popular with the 35-45 age group.
Pierro's or **Manto** - popular with gay clientele and open all night.

SPORTS AND LEISURE

Paradise Scuba Diving Club – *Paradise Beach* – ☎ *(22890) 26 539, www.diveadventures.gr*
Psarou Mykonos Diving Center – ☎ *(22890) 248 08, www.dive.gr*

Visit

Hóra★★★

The best way to discover Hóra is to leave the main shopping streets and meander the alleys, winding past vaulted passageways, chapels, tiny squares and walls topped by hibiscus and bougainvillea.
From the **Bóni Windmill** (16C) to the east, there is a fine **view**★ of the village.

Limáni (fishing port)

The terraces of cafés and restaurants line the quayside; it's very lively in the evenings. Nearby is the arcaded 18C town hall, and a little chapel dedicated to St Nicholas, patron saint of navigators.
At the beginning of **Odós Andrónikou**, lined with jewellers and souvenir shops, is the Church of Agía Kiriakí, which has some fine icons.
Next comes the **Platia Tría Pigádia**, bordered by arcades.
Head right towards the **Mitrópoli** (cathedral), an imposing edifice an elaborately decorated interior. Behind this is the **Catholic Church**, with a blue cupola.
To the left, the **five windmills**★ (Káto Míli) stand in a row on a low hill above the harbour; one of them still works. Head back towards the Catholic Church and the water.

Alefkándra★★★

A number of the houses here have colourful loggias, giving the district the nickname **Little Venice**. Several waterfront cafés offer sunset views.

Kástro★

The oldest part of the town began as a fortified stronghold. The Church of **Panagía Paraportianí**★★ stands between the sea and the citadel gate.

Ag. Anargiron	2
Ag. Gerassimou	3
Ag. Stefanou	5
D. Mavrogenous	7
Drakopoulou	8
Enoplon Dinameon	9
Kalogera	10
Kambani	12
Leondiou Boni	13
Mandos Mavrogenous	14
Mitropoleos	15
Panahrandou	16
Paraportianis	18
Polikandrioti	19
Skardana	20
Zani Pitaraki	22

Agía Kiriakí	A
Ágios Nikólaos	B
Arheologikó Moussío	M[1]
Arhondikó	D
Dimarhio	H
Katholikí eklissía	E
Laografikó Moussío	M[2]
Mitrópoli	F
Mnimío Mandó Mavrogénous	G
Naftikó Moussío Egéou	M[3]
Paraportianí	K
Platía Trión Pigadión	L

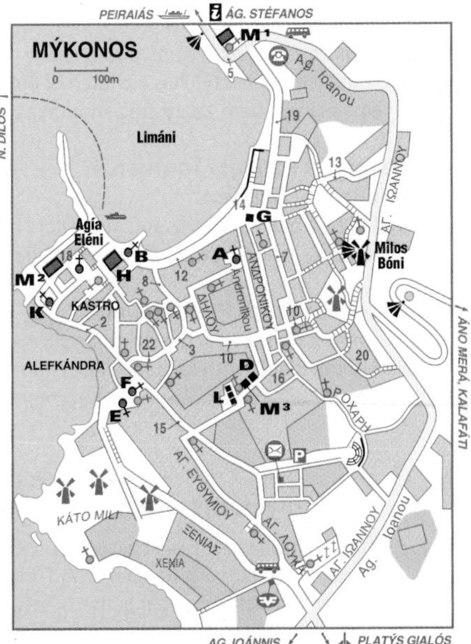

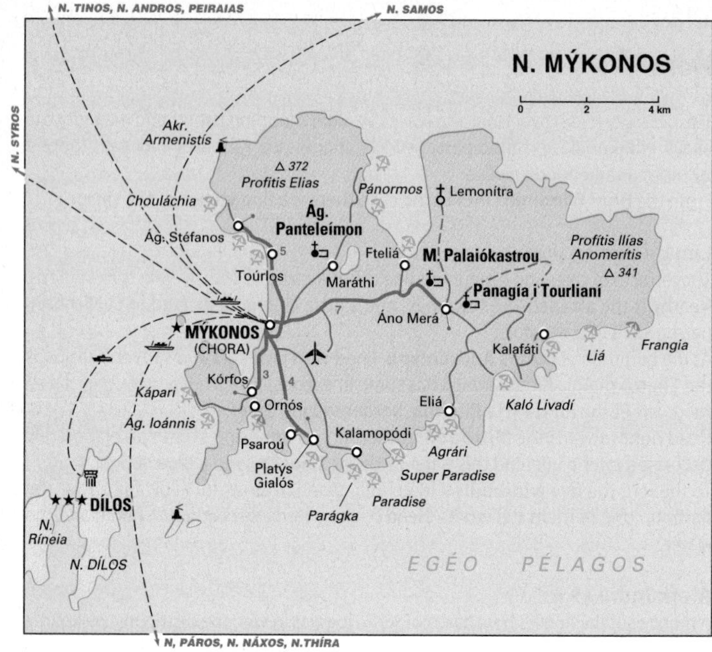

Aegean Maritime Museum – *Naftikó Moussío Egéou*; **Museum of Folk Art; Archaeological Museum** (7C BC amphora, statue of Herakles, items from the site on the island of Rínia).

Monasteries

Monastery of Paleókástro

10km/6.25mi east of Hóra, toward Ano Meraá

The 18C monastery on a hill has a church of beautifully pure lines. The walls of a kástro remain. From here, there are panoramic views of the island and sea.

Monastery of Panagía Tourlianí★

1km/0.6mi east of Áno Merá.

Dominated by a bell tower, this 16C monastery has a carved-wood iconostasis and some fine icons, including that of the island's patron saint.

Monastery of Ágios Pandeleímon

4.5km/2.8mi from Hóra. Near the charming village of Maráthi, this group of buildings is typical of the island, with its stark white church.

How many chapels does Mykonos have?

For centuries chapels have been built on the island. Why? In stormy weather, many sailors (and pirates too) vowed to erect one if God returned them safely home. Given the Aegean's volatile weather patterns, there are many chapels on Mykonos. Indeed, they are almost as numerous as the island's surviving historic houses.

NÁXOS★★

Ναξοζ

POPULATION 12 089

430KM²/168SQ MI – MICHELIN MAP 737 L-M 10-11 – CYCLADES – AEGEAN.

The largest of the Cyclades remains relatively unknown despite its magnificent beaches, dramatic coastline, fragrant valleys and imposing mountains. Hóra is renowned for its Ancient citadel; perched atop a hill, its alleys and ramparts have changed little since the Middle Ages. *At the port, to the right of the landing stage. ☏ (22890) 22 490. www.naxosnet.com.*

- **Orient Yourself:** Naxos is a fertile island among its arid neighbors. The capital city Hóra has links to Piraeus and the main islands in the region.
- **Don't Miss:** The Kastro of Hora, the climb up Mount Zeus.
- **Organizing Your Time:** The island merits a stay of at least four days.
- **Also See:** Amorgós, Páros

Address Book

For coin categories, see the Legend on the cover flap.

GETTING ABOUT

By Air – Daily Olympic Airways flights from Athens.

By Boat – Several daily ferries link Náxos to Piraeus *(5h30-7h30)*, Rafina *(3h30mn-6h)* and Lavrio *(2h40mn-3h)* on the mainland. Ferries run daily from Náxos to Amorgos, Ios, Páros, Mykonos, Santorini, Siros and Tinos; also Andros (2/wk), Folegandros and Milos.

Vehicle Rentals – Car and scooter rental agencies near the port.

WHERE TO EAT

To Iriniss – *Hóra, at the harbour.* Good traditional Greek cuisine; try the feta-stuffed peppers.

Metaxu Mas – *Hóra, in the kastro.* A tiny, smoky *ouzerie* serving tasty *mezes* and excellent *tarama*.

Gorgóna – *Agía Ánna, on the beach.* A large cafeteria; place your order at the counter. Very popular with the locals.

WHERE TO STAY

Ánixis – *Hóra, north of the kástro – ☏ (22850) 22 932, www.hotel-anixis.gr – 19rm.* A bright, charming hotel with a flowery garden terrace. Breakfast 5€.

Chateau Zevgoli – *Hóra, foot of the kástro (follow signs) – ☏ (22850) 22 993 – 19rm.* Each room is unique; tester bed in n° 8, romantic balcony with n° 12 and harbour view from n° 10.

Hotel Elizabeth –*Agios Georgios, along a lane paralleling the beach – ☏ (22850) 23 505, www.hotel-elizabeth.com– 9m, 3 studios.* Clean, quiet rooms with balconies; near the beach. Breakfast 4€.

Hotel Spiros – *Agios Georgios, 15mn walk from the port – ☏ (22850) 24 854 – 40 studios.* Modern, quiet, comfortable and well-run; rooms with balcony or terrace.

TAKING A BREAK

Elli bar – *Hóra, street to the left of the tourist office.* Live *rembétiko* concerts.

Lefteris– *Aprianthos, main street.* A charming tearoom on a pretty terrace.

SHOPPING

Local specialities – Lemon liqueur *(kitro)*, wines (rosé) and cheeses (try *xenotiri* and *graviera*).

EVENTS AND FESTIVALS

On **14 July** Hóra celebrates the Feast of St Nicodemus, patron saint of the town. On **15 August** the Assumption is celebrated with processions in Sangrí, Apíranthos and Filóti.

SPORTS AND LEISURE

Wind and **water sports** abound; for information: *www.flisvos-sportclub.com*, or *www.naxos-windsurf.com*.

For **horseback riding** (a superb means of seeing Náxos), write to: *info@naxos-horseriding.com* (beginners welcome).

A Bit of History

Naxos was the mythological childhood home of the god Dionysus, who discovered his love Ariadne on the beach here after she was abandoned by Theseus, son of Aegeus. The island today retains the appearance given it during its long occupation by Venetian families.

Touring

Beaches

Ágios Geórgios

South of Hóra.

This large beach, popular with surfers is in a shallow bay. From the far end of the beach there are are good **views**★ of Hóra, dominated by its kástro.

Western beaches★

Beyond Ágios Prokópios Beach is **Agía Ánna** with its charming fishing port, and farther on is the vast expanse of sand at **Pláka**★. There are quieter beaches to the south: Alikó, Pirgáki and Agiassós, its sand a shimmering white.

Walk

Mount Zeus

Walkers will enjoy climbing this island giant (1 001m/3 284ft) with mythological associations, the highest peak in the Cyclades.

The walk (*1hr*) starts at the chapel of Agía Marína on the Danakos road. Descend along a steeper route to see the Grotto of Zeus (the god's mythological birthplace).

Visit

Hóra★★★

Centred around its citadel, the island's capital is built on the site of an ancient city which was at its peak during the Archaic period.

J.-P. Naïl/MICHELIN

Kástro★★★

Take the alley to the right of the Old Captain's café.
This Venetian citadel (13C) is one of the finest in the Cyclades. To the right of the entrance gateway is a Venetian metre measurement used as an aid by merchants. Wander about this a peaceful quarter to discover its alleys, vaulted passageways, flights of steps and hidden gardens.
The Catholic **cathedral** (13C) features a main altar with an icon of the Virgin and Child with St John the Baptist; there are some fine funerary monuments.
To the rear is the Jesuit College built in the 17C; this houses the **Archaeological Museum**★, renowned for its collection of Cycladic idols (3200-2300 BC) found on Náxos and neighbouring islands. The ceramics collection, including items from the Mycenaean (late second millennium BC) and Geometric (9-8C BC) periods, is remarkable. *Open Tue-Sun, 8.30am-3pm. 3€. ☎ (22850) 22 725.*

Port

The **promenade**★, closed to vehicles in the evenings, is bordered by shops, cafés and restaurants. The area is very busy late into the night.
In the Burgos quarter to the northeast of the port is the **Mitrópolis Museum** on the Orthodox Cathedral square, which allows visitors to examine the stratified archaeological layers beneath the town (*open Tue-Sun, 8am-3pm. No charge. ☎ (22850) 24 151).*

Islet of Palátia

Northern end of the port; access by a paved causeway.
Visible from some distance, the door of the Temple of Apollo is all that remains of an never-completed Archaic sanctuary (6C BC). The door gives an idea of the monumental scale of the project. From here there are beautiful **views**★.

Flerio Koúros★

12km/7.5mi east of Hóra. Take the Halkí road; turn left after 3km/1.9mi. Continue for 1km/0.6mi; turn right to join the Míli road. Beyond this village, follow the road along the Mélanes Valley. A track descends to a stream; leave the car here and continue on foot.
Unfinished and abandoned, this work of sculpture dates from the 6C BC.

Driving Tour

The Tragéa Valley★★

80km/50mi. Allow 1 day. Head southeast from Hóra towards Halkí. Turn right 6km/3.5mi after Galanádo.

Belónia

This tower is a good example of the Venetian fortified houses built to repel pirate attacks. Nearby is the double Church of Ágios Ioannis (13C), accommodating the Catholic rite (on the left) and the Orthodox rite (on the right).

Potamiá Valley★

Continuing towards Halkí the itinerary reaches a valley planted vineyards and orchards. Below the road is the Church of **Ágios Mánas**, seat of an Orthodox bishopric in Byzantine times *(reached by a path on the left 8km/5mi from Náxos)*. On the other side of the valley lie the ruins of Apáno Kástro, a 13C Venetian fortress.

Temple of Demeter

Head right towards Áno Sangrí.
This simple Doric building in the fields honors the island's protector-goddess.

Return to Áno Sangrí.

Halkí

The old capital of the island is at the foot of a mountain; its Byzantine Church of **Panagía Protothrónos** dates from the 9C-12C and is decorated with frescoes. The **Barozzi Tower** has a marble doorway adorned with a coat of arms.

Turn left just before Akádimi.

Panagía Drossianí

The simple church (9C) of this fine monastery has some impressive frescoes.

Filóti

One of the principal settlements in the Tragéa Valley; the road to the village climbs the slopes of Mount Zeus; good **views**★ of the west of the island.

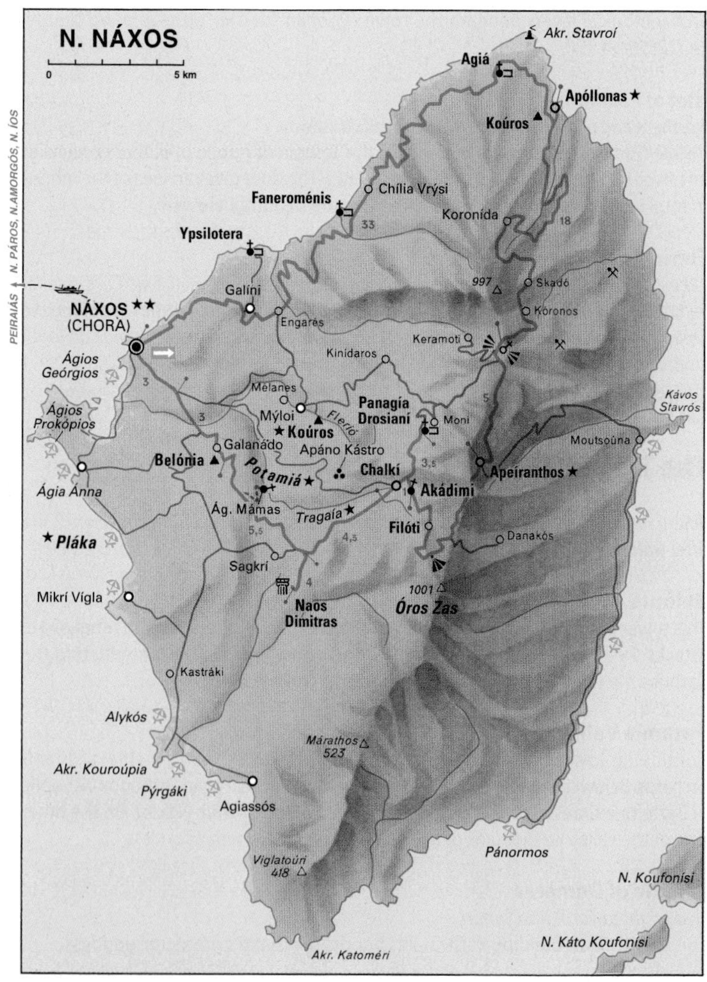

Apíranthos★★
This mountain village has two Venetian towers. The white-marble paved main street has alleys and covered passageways running off it, watchtowers and a church. There are several small museums *(Natural History, Geology and Folklore; opening hours vary; 1.50€ for all three).*
The **Archaeological Museum** *(open Tue-Sun 8am-2pm; no charge)* displays items found on the island, including engraved marble plaques from the 3C BC.

Apólonas★
This fishing village has become a popular resort. Close to the coast road on the way back to Hóra is an immense 7C BC marble **kouros** (10m/33ft long), which was abandoned before completion.

Agía
Below the ruined Venetian watchtower constructed to protect the northwest coast is an Orthodox monastery nestling among the greenery.

Faneroménis
This fortified 17C monastery has a chapel with an iconostasis and a library.

Ipsilotéra
Another fortified 17C monastery with loopholes, machicolations and crenelles.

Return to Hóra by the coast road.

Excursion

Íos

This little island has wild coves, rocky peaks and isolated coasts. Renowned for its nightlife, Íos draws many young tourists from all over Europe.

Port
The sheltered port lies in a **rocky bay**★. Near the waterfront, at its western end, stands the white silhouette of the Church of Agía Iríni. The town has many hotels, shops and restaurants; the adjacent Gialós Beach is fringed by tamarisks.

Hóra★
Standing on a hill, the island's capital is a beautiful town with white houses, churches with blue cupolas, narrow alleys, windmills and chapels perched near the summit.
The **Archaeological Museum** *(open Tue-Sun 9am-1pm; 2€)* displays Cycladic artifacts discovered near Stavros; interesting bas-reliefs.
Near the windmills, a walkway offers fine views over the town. Nearby is a modern open-air theatre. A little higher up, the Church of Panagía Gremiotissa has a miraculous icon of the Virgin. The lower town becomes very lively later in the evening, with crowds of clubbers here to drink and dance the night away.

Beaches★★
There are excellent beaches on the island, many of which are rather inaccessible.

South of Hóra – Against an impressive backdrop of barren mountains, **Milopótas**★ Beach is a long ribbon of fine sand facing due west.

2km/1.25mi east of Páno Kámbos.

Íos Address Book

GETTING ABOUT

By boat – Mainland ferry service to Piraeus *(3-9hrs, depending on the vessel)*. Daily ferry service to Náxos, Páros, Santorini, and Mykonos. Ferries also run to Folégandros *(5/wk)*, Siros *(4/wk)*, Melos *(4/wk)*, Sifnos *(2/wk)* and Sérifos *(2/wk)*.
Bus - Frequent daily service between Milopotas, the port and Koumbara.
Vehicle Rental – Several agencies; try **Trohokinisi** *(Hóra), www.trohokinisi.com* or **Vangelis** *(Hóra)* for mopeds.

WHERE TO EAT

The Nest – *Gialós 2nd lane after the main square.* Fast service, varied menu, good prices in a smallish dining room. Try the *kieftiko* (lamb with 4 cheeses).
Aphrodites – *Gialós, at the harbour.* Simple, well-run, with good fresh fish dishes. Reasonable prices.
Polydoros Pouseos – *Koumbára, on the beach to the right.* ☎ *(22860) 911 2.* Best to reserve; this is Ios' best restaurant. Fish, barbecued meats, salads and a good wine list. The place to try specialities like the local cheeses.

WHERE TO STAY

Galíni – *Gialós, centre of the beach* – ☎ *(22860) 91 115 – 18rm.* Comfortable guesthouse, in a peaceful spot with a shady planted terrace.
Hermes – *Between Hóra and Milopótas, near the bus stop* – ☎ *(22860) 91 471, hermesio@otenet.gr – 18rm.* A comfortable hotel with a nice pool and impressive view. Good value.
Far Out – *Above Milopótas Beach* – ☎ *(22860) 91 446, www.farout-club.com – 90rm.* A smart hotel with a main building peacefully located just steps from the beach, and more modern bungalows in a livelier spot closer to the water. Nice pools, good value.

TAKING A BREAK

Phots – *Milpotas.* Large seaside terrace; live music, pleasant decor; a bit pricey.
Anaïs – *Hóra, near the church.* Vast selection of pastries made with almonds and other nuts.

The beach at **Agía Theódoti** is dominated by a 16C church and the ruins of the Byzantine fortress of Paleókastro. It is accessed by a path to the right of the beach (2km/1.25mi).
Turtles visit the beach at Psáthi (east coast) to lay their eggs.

Southern end of the island – Bordered by bars and tavernas, the beaches at **Manganári**★★ are situated in a calm, deep bay where many yachts drop anchor.

PÁROS★

Παροζ

POPULATION 12 853

196KM²/77SQ MI – MICHELIN MAP 737 L 11-12 – CYCLADES – AEGEAN.

Famed since Classical times for its finely grained white marble, Páros is a large island rich in both natural beauty and monuments. It has excellent natural harbours, and its summer breezes make it a popular destination for windsurfers.
On the quayside at the ferry port.

Touring

All over the island there is evidence of the expanding tourist industry: holiday homes, hotels, guesthouses and restaurants. Náoussa has become one of the liveliest resorts in the Cyclades, with nightclubs, trendy bars and shops.

Náoussa beaches

To the northwest is **Kolibíthres**, lying below chaotic rock formations. Busy **Monastíri** (accessed by boat from the harbour) lies at the north of the bay. Just to its east (10min walk) is a virtually deserted beach, with white sand and clear water.

Beaches of the east coast

Mólos, lying in a bay, is quite pleasant. The strip of coast between Písso Livádi and Dríos is a developed tourist area and includes **Hrissí Aktí** (Golden Beach), one of Paros' largest beaches, which hosts windsurfing competitions.

Beaches of the west coast

Fáranga is an isolated beach, set against a backdrop of arid hills. Near the village of Alikí is a quiet beach; farther north is exotic Agía Iríni, fringed by palm trees.

Visit

Parikía★★ (Páros Town)

The capital of the island has a busy port which teems day and night with ferries from all over the Aegean. Traffic, pedestrians and bars pumping out music add to the

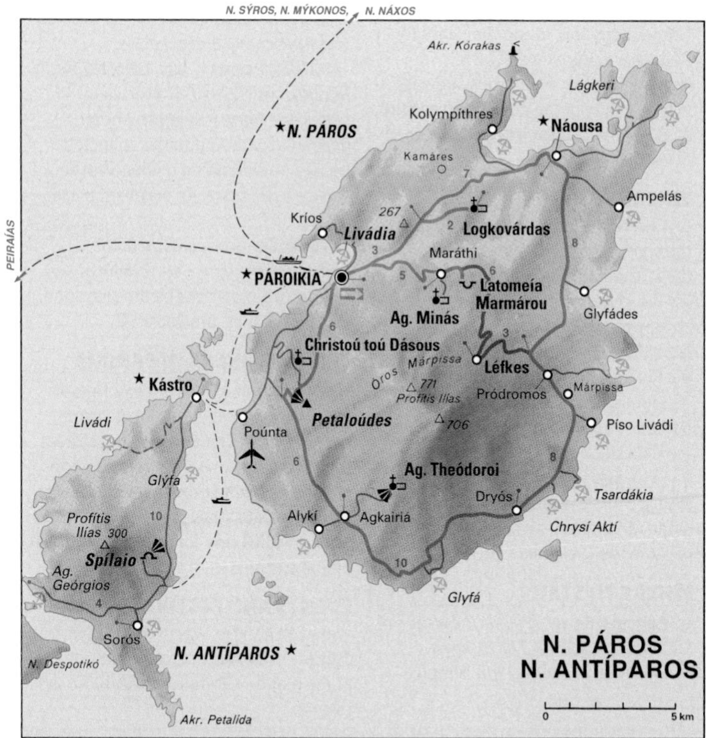

chaos. A short distance from the port, however, lie quiet white alleyways. The long, wide promenade at the foot of the kástro hill is pleasant in the evenings.
Built on the site of an Ancient city, Parikía is composed of two distinct districts: to the north lies the modern quarter of Livádia (hotels and restaurants) bordered by beaches; to the south is the old town, dominated by a small Venetian fortress.

Old Town★
This lower part of Parikía has long alleys, shaded squares, fountains, vaulted passageways and chapels. In its blue-domed churches are some fine iconostases and, at the top of the hill where the acropolis once stood are the ruins of a 13C Venetian fortress (kástro). Foundations of a temple can be seen near the Church of Ágios Konstandínos. Here there is also a terrace with fine views of the Gulf of Páros.

Address Book

For coin categories, see the Legend on the cover flap.

GETTING ABOUT

By Boat – Mainland ferry service daily to Piraeus *(3h15mn-4h15mn)*, Rafina *(3h-5h30mn)* and Lávrio *(2h30mn)*. Also daily ferries to Amorgos, Náxos, Ios, Mykonos, Santorini, Siros and Tenos. Also service to Andros *(6/wk)*, Folégandros *(5/wk)*, Melos *(3/wk)*, Sifnos *(2/wk)* and Kéa *(1/wk)*.
By Air – There are two flights a day from Athens and, in summer, links to Rhodes and Herakleion (Crete).
Vehicle Rental - Numerous agencies in the vicinity of the port. For cars, **Sixt** *☎ (22840) 510 37)* or **Iria Rent a Car** *☎ (22840) 212 32.*

WHERE TO EAT

Christos – *Parikia, along the quay to the right of the port.* A tiny room open to the kitchen; simple, copious and good. Try the *imam* (stuffed eggplant).
Happy Green Cows – *Parikia, behind the National Bank.* Generous portions of inventive vegetarian cuisine.
Sigi Inthios – *Náoussa, by the small harbour.* Tasty Greek food with a modern flair; sit on the terrace in summer.
Le Sud – *Náoussa, in an alley by the big church.* A sophisticated menu along Mediterranean lines, one of the finest in the Cyclades.

WHERE TO STAY

Pension Rena – *Parikia, near the landing – ☎ (22840) 222 20, www.cycladeesnet.gr/rena – 12rm.* Simple yet charming, excellent vallue. No breakfast.
Stergía – *Parikía, left of the landing, on the lane running up from Restaurant Katerina – ☎ (22840) 21 745 – 15rm.* An attractive hotel with plenty of flowers; comfortable rooms and a warm welcome.
Argonauta Hotel – *Parikia, behind the market to the right of the landing – ☎ (22840) 214 40, www.argonauta.gr – 15rm.* Tastefully renovated rooms with balconies. Great service and warm welcome. Breakfast 5€.
Petres – *3km/1.9mi before Náoussa – ☎ (22840) 52 467, www.petres.gr – 16rm.* A delightful hotel decorated with Antiquities collected by Cléa, the charming owner. Shuttle service to Náoussa. An excellent place to stay.
Ártemis – *Andíparos, near the harbour on the right – ☎ (22840) 61 460, – 30rm.* Set in gardens by the sea; good value for money. Breakfast 5€.

TAKING A BREAK IN PARIKIA

The **Pirate Bar** *Market Street)* offers a welcoming jazz-blues ambience and decor. Nearby, **The Balcony** has a great terrace overlooking the street. Or stop at Micro Café, Old Greece revisited with low tables and straw chairs.
Stop at **Sulla Luna** for a refreshing dose of fine artisanal ice cream.

EVENTS AND FESTIVALS

Wine and Fish Festival in Naoussa on **July 6.** On **23 August**, commemoration of the island's resistance to Barbarossa's raiders.

Panagía Ekatondapilianí★★★
Open daily, 8am-1pm and 4-9pm; 7am-10pm in summer.
In a square to the east of the port, this church was founded by St Helen, mother of the Emperor Constantine (280-337). Also called the Church of the Hundred Doors, the existing structure dates from the 10C. Inside, the bright church combines a basilica layout with a Greek-cross plan. Note the fine icon of the Virgin (17C).
A chapel on the right dedicated to St Nicholas has 6C **fonts**★ carved into the floor for total-immersion baptism. A small **Byzantine Museum** *(to the left on exiting the church; open daily, 9.30am-1pm and 5-9pm, 9am-10pm in summer. 3€)* has some fine icons and relics.

Archaeological Museum (fragment from the 3C BC *Parian Chronicle*).

J.-P. Nail/MICHELIN
Typical Cycladic chapel on Páros

Tours

The Centre of the Island

This fairly mountainous area has numerous traditional villages.

Léfkes★
Perched on the mountainside and surrounded by trees is the ancient capital of the island. Its steep alleys have seats, arcades and wells made from the famous local marble which is quarried nearby.
The Church of **Agía Tríada** (19C) has two fine marble bell towers. Inside, the pulpit, bishop's throne and iconostasis are also marble. There is a small museum of local crafts in the Hotel Léfkes Village.

Marble quarries
East of Maráthi, a rough track leads to the now-defunct marble quarries. The approach is marked by abandoned buildings; walk 100m/110yd beyond a chapel before climbing over the low wall and following the track to the site. There are three pits, their steep galleries extending down quite deep to reach the best-quality marble. An Ancient bas-relief stands at the entrance to one of them.
Beyond the quarries lies the **monastery of Ágios Minás**, fortified in the 17C.

Tour of the Island★

Allow 1 day. Head northeast on the Náoussa road.

Monastery of Longovárdas
Down a small road on the right, halfway between Parikía and Náoussa. Open daily, 9.30am-noon. Women not admitted; men must wear long pants.
The shaded courtyard is surrounded by buildings where the monks live and pray. Visitors can view cells, communal areas, an icon workshop and the interesting library. The church's façade is typically Cycladic in style; good **view** of the coast.

Náoussa★

This charming little fishing port lies in a bay, its white houses huddled around the imposing parish church. The newly opened **Archaeological Museum** *(by the post office; daily 10am-1pm, 6-8pm. 2€)* displays finds from the area, including artefacts from **Koukounariés**, a Mycenaean and Archaic site to the southwest.

Náoussa's narrow alleys throb with music from trendy nightclubs and discos. Things are quieter down by the port. Enjoy a meal on the shady terraces by the waterfront, looking up at the ruins of the fortress. Two big annual festivals attract thousands of visitors: July 6 sees the **Festival of Wine and Fish;** on August 23 the bay fills with illuminated ships and folk groups dance on the quayside in commemoration of their forebears' heroic resistance against raiders in 1537.

From Náoussa, head down the east coast, which faces the island of Náxos and has numerous beaches and resorts.

Petaloúdes

At the junction where Poúnda is to the left, turn right along a minor road to the **Valley of the Butterflies** where cypresses, plane trees, laurels and carob trees provide ideal habitat for breeding butterflies. *Open daily in summer, 9am-8pm. 1.50€.*

Convent of Hristoú Dássous

North of Petaloúdes. Women only admitted to convent areas.

Dedicated to 'Christ of the Forest', this convent stands on top of a hill (fine views) and houses the tomb of St Arsénios, the island's patron saint.

Musee Scorpios★★

Enroute to the main road, toward the airport. Open daily 10am-12pm, 5-6pm; 2€.

Astonishing scale model representations of scenes from Cycladic history.

Monastery of Ágii Theódori (fine **view**★), at Angeriá in the southwest; take a minor road to the right.

Excursion

Andíparos★

Accessible by boat from Parikía (6/day, 30min, 2€ round-trip) or by car ferry from Poúnda (every 15min; 10€ round-trip for cars, 1.50€ for pedestrians).

Once a stronghold of French and Maltese pirates, this peaceful island is a haven of tranquillity. The **boat trip**★ from Parikía is very pleasant; the vessel follows the rocky coast of Páros before picking its way between several islets. The arrival in the colorful, boat-filled port of **Kástro**★ is delightful. Restaurant terraces line the quayside.

Grotto of Stalactites

6km/3.75mi south of Kástro. Open daily 10 May-10 Sep. Open 10am-3pm. 3€.

Four hundred steps lead to a huge cave with a wealth of stalactites and stalagmites.

Beaches

The best beach, **Livádi**★, lies to the west and is only accessible on foot. South of Kástro, an attractive coastal path leads past narrow beaches fringed by tamarisks.

SÉRIFOS

Σεριφοζ

POPULATION 1 414

75KM²/30SQ MI – MICHELIN MAP 737 K 11 – CYCLADES – AEGEAN.

Although relatively close to Piraeus, Sérifos is little visited, thanks to its industrial mining past. Its mining deposits petered out between the wars, and it is only recently that Sérifos has opened up to tourism. Its strikingly white main town is one of the most attractive in the Cyclades. *Opposite the landing stage.*

Touring

Beaches★

East coast

From Livádi it is a 30min walk to **Lia**★ Beach, then to Ágios Sóstis Bay, where the most popular beach is **Psilí Ámos**★. Beyond it is the quieter Ágios Ioánnis Beach.

South coast★

Sheltered from the winds, Ambeli Bay is reached by taking the first path on the left after Rámos. In **Koutalás Bay**★ there are three large beaches accessed by a track.

North coast★

Near the village of Panagía, a path leads to the pleasant Bay of **Sikamiás**★ and a fine sandy beach. North of the monastery of Taxiárhes lies attractive Platís Gialós Beach.

Address Book

For coin categories, see the Legend on the cover flap.

GETTING ABOUT

By boat – Daily ferry service to Piraeus (2h20mn-5h10mn) *on the mainland;* also to Kythnos, Sifnos and Melos. less frequent service to Siros *(3/wk)*, Folégandros *(2/wk)* Ios *(2/wk)*, Santorini *(2/wk)* and Tenos *(1/wk)*.

By Bus – Frequent runs between Livadi and Hora.

Vehicle Rental – **Krinas Travel** ☎ *(22810) 514 88* or **Blue Bird** ☎ *(22810) 515 11.*

WHERE TO EAT

Margarítta – *Livádi, end of the road along the beach, along the dirt track to the left.* A traditional restaurant offering good food and authentic ambience.

Takis – *Livadi, by the port.* Typical but quality Greek food. Good *moussaka.*

Zorbas – *Hóra, on the town hall square.* Check out the interior decoration, handiwork of the proud owner. A good place to sample *mezes.*

WHERE TO STAY

Maistrali – *Livadi, end of the harbour on the right.* ☎ *(22810) 512 20 – 20rm.* Peaceful rooms, a bit away from the nightlife noise; lovely sea views. Breakfast 5€.

Aretí – *Livádi, up the steps from the landing stage* – ☎ *(22810) 51 479 – 13rm, 5 studios.* A well renovated hotel above the harbour. Comfortable rooms with balcony or terrace overlooking a garden. Breakfast 5€.

TAKING A BREAK

There is plenty of choice along Livádi Beach. **Alter Ego** and **Captain Hook** will appeal to those who like Greek music.

Alternatively **Bar Karnágio** has rock music and tables on the beach. There's a disco on the left, **Edem Club**, heading toward Hóra.

EVENTS AND FESTIVALS

Numerous processions on saints' days; in Koutalás on 5 May, in Panagía on 6 August and in Livádi on 7 September.

Visit

Livádi

Located in a sheltered bay on the east coast, Livádi is the island's port, and a resort which extends from Pounti (where the ferries dock) to Avlomónas Beach. Modern architecture here respects the Cycladic style.

J.-P. Nail/MICHELIN

White houses, Sérifos

Hóra★★

Accessed by bus from the port or on foot up a wide flight of steps.

Occupying a spectacular **site**★, the island's main town is typically Cycladic in style, its single-storey white houses clinging to the hillside. It is a town of steep alleys, flights of steps and little squares which invite the visitor to wander.

Town Hall

Its late-19C neo-Classical façade looks onto a pretty square with tavernas.

Ágios Athanássios

Near the town hall, this 18C church sparkles in the bright sunshine.

Kástro

At the top of the hill, little remains of the citadel. On the site stands the Church of Ágios Constantínos and Heléni; fine **view**★ of the bay and the island of Sífnos.

Museum of Folk Art; Archaeological Museum.

Panagía

4km/2.5mi north of Hóra.

This pretty Cycladic village stands on the slopes of Óros Troúlos (fine views over the island). The **church of Panagía**★ is the oldest on the island (10-11C) and has some fine 13C frescoes.

Monastery of the Taxiarchs★

8km/5mi north of Hóra. Beyond the hamlet of Galaní, follow the path to the left for 2km/1.25mi.

Built on a seacliff, the island's largest structure (1600) looks like a white fortress. Fine iconostatis In the church.

Kéndarhos

10km/6.25mi north of Hóra.

The village is sited on a hill overlooking a little agricultural valley .

Megálo Livádi

13km/8mi southwest of Hóra.

Situated in a narrow-mouthed bay, this port was used for shipping bauxite from around 1880 and was the headquarters of the mining company.

SÍFNOS★

SIPHNOS – Σιφνοζ

POPULATION 2 442

74KM²/29SQ MI – MICHELIN MAP 737 K 12 – CYCLADES – AEGEAN.

Formerly an active mining area, Sifnos is today an attractive island sporting fine sandy beaches, cultivated hillsides and Ancient olive groves. The white cuboid houses, windmills, dovecots, chapels and monasteries all add to its air of authenticity. *At Kamares, opposite the landing stage ☎ (22840) 31 997. info@sifnos.gr.*

Touring

Herónissos Beach

15km/9.5mi north of Apolonía.

This tiny fishing port is hidden in a rocky cove. The sandy beach, tavernas, quays, fishing nets and boats make an attractive scene.

Vathí Beach★★

Southwest coast, 9km/5.6mi from Apolonía.

The pleasant, sheltered beach and its little fishing port lie in a pretty bay. The twin-domed Monastery of Taxiárhis (16C) stands on a mole along the shoreline.

Platís Gialós Beach

South coast, 6km/3.75mi from Apolonía.

Address Book

For coin categories, see the Legend on the cover flap.

GETTING ABOUT

By boat – Daily ferry service from the Piraeus *(2h40mn-6h20mn)*, as well as Kythnos, Sérifos, and Melos. Also links to Folégandros *(4/wk)*, Siros *(3/wk)*, Páros *(2/wk)*, Ios *(2/wk)*, Santorini *(2/wk)*and Tenos *(1/wk)*.

WHERE TO EAT

Liotrivi – *Livádi, in front of the church*. Small wooden tables in a charming setting; local cuisine (try the chickpea soup).

The Star – *Kastro, main street*. Sample the tasty dishes including *moussaka* and chickpea patties; lovely terrace.

WHERE TO STAY

Pétali – *Livadi, on the pedestrian street leading between Apolonia and Artemónas – ☎ (22840) 33 024, www.hotelpetali.gr – 23rm*. Magnificent view, pleasant swimming pool and efficient service. Tasteful decoration.

Villa Maria – *Faros, near the beach. ☎ (22840) 714 21, www.sifnovillamaria.gr – 5 studios, 2 apts*. Very well-kept rooms around a flowered garden.

Kalypso – *Vathi, by the sea. ☎ (22840) 711 27 – 5rm*. Idyllic location, perfect for a morning dip in the sea.

TAKING A BREAK IN APOLONIA

Nightlife concentrates along Odos Stilianou Prokou. Greek music at **Aloni**, and **Argo** offers cocktails and dancing. **Gerontopoulos** serves Greek pastries, plus housemade ice cream

SHOPPING

Ceramics and **jewelry** are the specialities on Sifnos.

EVENTS AND FESTIVALS

Feast of Hrissopigí (40 days after the Orthodox Easter), Church of Taxiárhis in Vathí (12 June), Monastery of Profítis Ilías (19 July), Church of Panagía ta Ghournia (15 August), and Monastery of Ágios Simeon (31 August).

This fine sandy beach is Sífnos' main resort. To the north, overlooking the beach, is the white Monastery of Panagía Vounoú (1813) with an impressive view.

Fáros

Southeast coast, 7km/4.4mi from Apolonía.
Fishing boast still dock here at the island's former port. Along the path to the lighthouse is the little beach of Fassolou. To the left is the sandy Apokofto Beach.

Visit

Kamáres

This port and family resort in the rocky Bay of Kamáres boasts a pleasant long beach. Tavernas, cafés and bars border the harbour and alleyways. On the other side of the bay is Agía Marína, which has two potteries still in operation.

Apolonía

Centre of the island.
Nestling in a natural bowl surrounded by terraced hillsides, Apolonía converges with several other villages to form a broad settlement.

Platía Iróon

The main square has a small **Folk Museum** (*open daily except Sun morning, 15 Jun-15 Oct, 10am-2pm and 7pm-11pm. 1€)* displaying tools, textiles, ceramics etc.

Stilianoú Prokou

This little alley of cafés, tavernas and shops leads to the Cathedral of Ágios Spirídonos (Hrissopigí icon) with its museum.

Ágios Athanássios

This church has fine frescoes and an impressive wooden iconostasis.

Panagía Ouranofóra★

In the upper town, towards Páno Petáli, reigns Apolonía's finest church (18C); don't miss its fine iconostasis.

J.-P. Naïl/MICHELIN

Kástro cemetery

Páno Petáli★
Stop here to visit the Italianate church of Ágios Ioánnis and the church of Panagía ta Gournía, decorated with frescoes and a fine wooden iconostasis.

Artemónas★
Once home to Sifnos' elite, this village was named for Artemis; a temple to the goddess once stood on the site now occupied by the Church of Kohis. Grand homes from the 18C and 19C rub shoulders with traditional village houses.
In the centre, the Church of **Panagía tis Ámou** has a fine giltwood iconostasis. The Church of **Ágios Konstandínos** (1462) is a magnificent example of Cycladic architecture. Above the church of Ágios Merkoúrios, there is a splendid **view**★.

Kástro★★
Northeast of Apolonía. Accessible on foot (45min) or by bus.
Former capital of the island, Kástro is an attractive example of a fortified town. As at Folégandros, the ramparts are formed by houses. Today the town has many cafes, restaurants and artists' studios punctuated by flights of steps and narrow alleys.
The **Archaeological Museum** (*open Tue-Sun, 8.30pm-3pm; no charge)* displays Archaic and Classical statuary, Antique and Byzantine ceramics.

Monasteries and Churches

Profítis Ilías★
West of Apolonía, at the island's highest point. The path begins 3km/1.9mi from Apolonía, to the right of the Vathí road. Walk of 2hr there and back.
Sifnos' most important Byzantine building looks like an imposing fortress. Parts of the structure date from the 12C. Areas of the monastery, including the cells, may be visited. On a clear day, the **view**★★ over the Cyclades is breathtaking, taking in Sérifos, Syros, Andíparos, Íos, Síkonos, Folégandros, Políegos and Kímolos.

Panagía Pouláti
North of Kástro. This abandoned monastery (1871) occupies a dramatic **site**★.

Panagía Vríssis
Behind its fortified walls, this monastery, dating from 1600, has a courtyard in the centre of which stands its catholicon (Byzantine Museum).

Panagía Hrissopigí★★
Dedicated to the island's patron saint since 1650, this church stands on a rocky promontory. It is the symbol of Siphnos and a popular place of pilgrimage.

J.-P. Nail/MICHELIN

Panagía Pouláti

SÍROS★

SYROS – Συροζ

POPULATION 19 782

86KM²/34SQ MI – MICHELIN MAP 737 K-L 10-11 – CYCLADES – AEGEAN.

A truly Greek island that remains largely undiscovered by foreign tourists, Syros is a charming haven of tranquillity for those who prefer to avoid the busier islands in the Cyclades. *Tourist office on the ferry-port quayside.*

A Bit of History

In the 13C Venetian and Genoese settlers founded Ano Syra (Áno Syros) here and introduced Catholicism. It remains a staunchly Catholic outpost.

Always an important shipping destination, Syros welcomed thousands of Greek refugees in the early 19C. At one point the town of Ermoupoli nearly became the capital of the newly established Greek kingdom. After the opening of the Corinth canal in 1828, however, Ermoúpoli was eclipsed by Piraeus.

Address Book

For coin categories, see the Legend on the cover flap.

GETTING ABOUT

By Boat – Daily mainland ferries to Piraeus *(2h30mn-5h)* and Lavrío *(2h30mn-5h20mn)*. Daily service to Tenos, Mykonos, Páros and Náxos. Service to Santorini, Ios *(4/wk)*, Andros *(3/wk)*, Sérifos *(3/wk)*, Sifnos *(3/wk)*, Kéa *(3/wk)*, Amorgos *(2/wk)* and Melos *(1/wk)*.

By Air – 4 flights/day between Athens and Siros.

Vehicle Rentals – Several agencies near the port. **Siros rent a car** *(22810) 837 77, www.syrosrentacar.com.*

WHERE TO EAT

Nisiotopoula – *Ermoúpoli, street parallel the port.* Delicious Greek cuisine includes tomatoes, zucchini, and honey yoghurt.

Ioánnina – *Ermoúpoli, on the harbour to the left of the Hermes Hotel.* A traditional spot with seafront terrace; grilled lamb a speciality. Good value.

WHERE TO STAY

Espérance – *Ermoúpoli, Odos Folégandrou and Akti Papagou – (22810) 816 71, www.esperance.gr – 32rm.* Tastefully done rooms in three neo-Classical houses. No breakfast.

Hermès – *Ermoúpoli, Place Kanari, end of the quay. – (22810) 830 11, info@hermes-syros.com – 71rm.* The "grand hotel" of Ermoúpoli, with balconied rooms overlooking the sea or a garden. Fitness centre. Open all year.

Syrou Melathron – *Ermoúpoli, 5 Odos Babagiotou, (22810) 859 63, www.syroumelathron.gr – 21rm.* Elegant historic structure (1850) in old Sirous. Internet access, terrace.

Hotel Alkyon – *Mega Gialos. (22810) 617 61), www.alkyonsyros.gr – 25rm.* Tennis, swimming pool and garden available at this comfortable modern hotel.

TAKING A BREAK IN ERMOÚPOLI

For teatime, stop in at lovely **Megaron**, just behind the port. Or grab a coffee in the café at the **Plastigga** bookshop. The Greek pastries at **Kanakari** are well worth sampling.

Siros Casino – *Ermoúpoli, on the waterfront.* Roulette, blackjack and slots, plus a large restaurant and nightclub.

EVENTS AND FESTIVALS

The biggest events take place on Good Friday. From mid-July to mid-August the Ermoupólia includes concerts, plays and exhibitions.

Ermoúpoli

Visit

Ermoúpoli★★

Capital of the archipelago, Ermoúpoli is a charming town of medieval alleyways, monumental squares and neo-Classical buildings. The visitor arriving by boat gets an arresting view of the town's **site**★★. The 19C administrative and commercial centre occupies the waterfront area. Above it rise Áno Syros *(left)*, the old Roman Catholic town dating from the 13C, and Vrondádo *(right)*, the Orthodox district.

Fishing Port

This is one of the busiest parts of town, cluttered with banks, travel agents and shops. Café and restaurant terraces curve around the edge of the old port. Beyond the elegant marble façade of the customs house (1861) is a jetty marking the limit of the port, from here extends a good **view**★ of the town.

The Neo-Classical Town★★

This is centred on marbled **Platía Miaoúli**★, a pleasant square of palm trees, cafés and arcades. The monumental **town hall**★ resembles the Athens Parliament building; its main chamber houses a collection of historical fire fighting equipment. Adjacent neo-Classical houses contain the Cyclades' archives and the Hellas cultural centre.
Behind the town hall, the **Archaeological Museum** (1834) displays funerary steles, Cycladic idols, marble sculpture, an Egyptian black-granite statuette (8C BC) and ceramics from the third millennium BC (*open Tue-Sun, 8.30am-3pm; no charge)*.
Not far away, the precinct of the **Church of the Metamórfossis** (1824) is paved with stone from Rhodes and inside there are many fine icons donated by local guilds.
Below the Orthodox quarter are the fine **Apollo Theatre**★ (1864) and a scaled-down model of Milan's La Scala. Some of Europe's greatest theatre companies performed here for the local aristocracy (*open daily 10.30am-1pm and 6-8pm; 2€)*.
The administrative district, **Nomarhía**★, *(around Odós Apólonos, climbing toward the Orthodox Cathedral)* is a peaceful area of neo-Classical buildings. Above is the Cathedral of Ágios Nikólaos (1870); inside is an iconostasis of Páros marble. Farther up is Vapória, an elegant residential district. Head down to the landing stage; the **view**★ of the town, Orthodox Cathedral, port, sea and islands is unforgettable.
As you head toward the port area, turn right on Odós Kitinou and enter the Church of **Kimissis**★. It contains an **icon**★ representing the Dormition of the Virgin by the

famed painter Domenikos Theotokopoulos, also known as **El Greco** (*open Apr-Aug 7.30am-noon, 5.30-6.30pm; Sep-Mar 7.30am-noon, 4.30-5.30pm).*

Siros Industrial Museum
Odos Papandrou. Open daily except Tue, 10am-2pm, Sun and Mon 10am-2pm and 6-9pm. 2.50€, Wed no charge.
Aspects of the town's economic expansion at the dawn of industrialization.

Vrondádo★

This lively quarter stretches from the neo-Classical section up to the Byzantine Church of Anástasi. The immense **flight of steps**★ to the church is a tiring climb up tall, irregular steps. From the top there are views of the sea, the port, the dockyards, the neo-Classical town and the Áno Syros quarter.

Áno Síros★★ (Áno Syros)
The old Catholic district dates from the 13C; typically Cycladic in feel, it is criss-crossed by steep and winding streets lined by chapels and convents. Side by side at the top of the hill are the bishop's palace and St George's Cathedral, built in 1843. From the terrace there is a **view**★ down the valley to Ermoúpoli and the harbour.

Tour

Áno Meriá★

This mountainous area north of the capital has beaches that are only accessible on foot *(bring strong footwear and plenty of drinking water).*

Ferikídi grotto

Turn right along a track after Mítikas.
This rocky cave is said to have been occupied at one time by Pherecydes, one of Pythagoras' teachers.

Site of Halandrianí

Accessible by car, on a poor road which is signposted.
In a rocky landscape are the remains of an imposing Cycladic construction and a necropolis built in the third millennium BC. The **view**★ of the surrounding hillsides and out to the islands is impressive.

Northern beaches★

The two beaches *(Lía – 30min, Mármara – 1hr)* are accessibly by paths from Kámbos, the village where the road peters out. It is also possible to take a boat from Kíni.

The South★

Head west from Ermoúpoli up a hill crowned by a windmill. From here the view takes in both sides of the island. Head downhill; to the left is the Orthodox Convent of Agía Varvára, from where examples of the nuns' weaving may be purchased.

Kínia

This tiny fishing port on the west coast has a beach shaded by tamarisks. Above the quay, a coastal path leads to Delfíni Beach, popular with naturists *(30min; also accessible by car).* North of the beach, the narrowing path leads across a promontory to an isolated bay. In the distance is the uninhabited island of Giaros.

Galissás

This is situated in a **bay**★ formed by a rocky peninsula. To the south a promontory is the site of a chapel, from where the **view**★ in all directions is breathtaking *(access by steps to the left of the sea wall and then a path which requires caution in places)*. To the north is a beach with clear waters, which is popular with naturists.

Beaches and resorts of the south

Fínikas is well known for its marina, **Possidonía**★ for its grand villas hidden among conifers, and **Angathopés** as the destination for a fashionable crowd. Farther east are the less exclusive resorts of Ahládi and Azólimnos.

THÍRA★★★

SANTORINI – Θηρα

POPULATION 13 670

83KM²/33SQ MI – MICHELIN MAP 737 L 11-12 – CYCLADES – AEGEAN.

Santorini is the most spectacular island in the archipelago. The ancient volcanic crater or caldera, which for millennia has been submerged by the sea, is surrounded by giant, strangely-coloured cliffs. The huge caldera forms a large bay dotted with volcanic cones, reminders of the seismic catastrophe that engulfed the island in Minoan times. *www.santorini.gr.*

- **Orient Yourself:** The island is well served by ferries and by flights. The ferry port at Athinios is several miles south of the capital (bus and taxi services).
- **Don't Miss:** A boat trip in the Caldera.
- **Organizing Your Time:** You'll need four days to visit Santorini
- **Also See:** Folégandros, Náxos

A Bit of History

Around 2000 BC a sophisticated civilisation, comparable to the Minoans of Crete, developed on Santorini. Around 1500 BC a huge volcanic explosion devastated the island (*see below*) and in the 3C BC renewed seismic activity split the north part of the island in two. Since the 16C seismic events have continued to

Ch. Legrand/MICHELIN

View of Ía

transform the Santorini landscape, most recently in 1956 when a huge earthquake destroyed many structures and killed around 50 people.

Archaeological explorations here have sought to prove that Minoan Crete and Santorini were once part of the continent of Atlantis, where according to Plato an advanced and highly civilised people was engulfed suddenly by fire and water. The discoveries, however, were insufficient to prove the Atlantis myth.

After the great eruption, several generations of Phoenicians, then Spartans occupied the island. The latter named it Thera, after their leader. Venetian occupiers in the 13C called the island Santorini after a shrine to St. Irene. After gaining independence in the modern Greek State, the island officially resumed its ancient name of Thera (Thíra) but the majority of Greeks continue to call it Santorini.

Address Book

For coin categories, see the Legend on the cover flap.

GETTING ABOUT

By Boat – Several daily ferries to Piraeus on the mainland *(3h30mn-13h20mn depending on the vessel)*, Ios, Melos, Néaxos, Páros and Mykonos. Also service to Siros *(5/wk)*, Amorgos *(3/wk)*, Folégandros *(2/wk)*, Kythnos *(2/wk)*, Sérifos *(2/wk)*, Sifnos *(2/wk)*, and Lavrio *(1/wk)*.

By Air – Flights daily to and from Athens and European cities; intermittent air service to Mykonos, Rhodes and Herakleion. Shuttle bus to Fíra from the airport.

Vehicle Rentals – Numerous agencies; it's best to use one in the same village where you're staying. Scooter-riders should always wear a helmet.

WHERE TO EAT

The island's cuisine has its own identity; look out for *kounéli tirávgoulo* (rabbit with onion and cheese), *fáva* (puréed broad beans), *domatokeftédes* and *pseftokeftédes* (vegetable fritters), *skordomakaronáda* (little garlic pastries) and *moshári tis panegíris* (literally festive beef, a stew cooked in wine).

Archipelagos – *Firá, www.archipelagos-santorini.com*. Excellent fresh fish and giant salads.

Selene – *Firá, outskirts, near the Atlantis hotel, www.selene.gr. on its own to the south of the Orthodox Cathedral.* Creative interpretations of Greek cuisine: Cyclades ham, *fáva* puree, rabbit and seafood. Varied wine list is varied.

Thomas Grill – *Ía, on the street between the bus stop and the church.* Unpretentious taverna popular with locals. Tasty, simple cuisine.

Papagalos –*Ía, along the cliff, www.papagalosrestaurant.com*. Sober chic decor in grey; nouveau Greek cuisine focusing on organic local produce and Mediterranean seafood.

WHERE TO STAY

Santorini is among the most expensive islands in the Cyclades. The caldera side of the island features great views and nightlife, but is a good 30min trip to the beach. Some hotels have pools, but are priced accordingly. Prices are lower on the east side. If proximity to the sea is important, opt for Kamari or Perissa, which are linked by bus to Firá and Ía. In Firá, seek accommodations in Firostefani, along the hillsides, or south of the Orthodox cathedral.

Pension Galíni Ía – *Ía, on the right-hand side on entering the village – ☎ (22860) 71 396, www.galini-ia.gr – 17rm.* A charming traditional establishment, simple and comfortable. View over vineyards and sea; friendly welcome.

Hotel Keti – *Firá, near the Orthodox cathedral – ☎ (22860) 223 24, www.hotelketi.gr – 7rm.* Small, peaceful rooms with view of the caldera.

Hotel Galini – *Firostefani, – ☎ (22860) 220 95, www.hotelgalini.gr – 13rm.* Nice rooms overlooking the caldera. Pleasant bar, warm welcome. Breakfast 7€.

TAKING A BREAK

Kastro – *Firá*. Large bar on two levels, with superb views of the caldera.

Jazz Bar – *Firá, main street*. Good music and relaxing atmosphere.

Fanari Bar – *Ía, end of the village facing Thirassia*. Lounge atmosphere, great views.

Touring

The Santorini coastline is unlike any other in the Cyclades; the sea becomes deep very quickly (except at Monólithos) and the currents can be very strong.
The finest beaches are to the south and east: Monólithos, Kamári (the island's main resort), Períssa, Vlihàda (known for its forbidding rocks), Kókini, Lefkí Pigádia and Méssa Pigádia.

Firá★★

Occupying an extraordinary **site**★★★, the island's capital perches atop a precipitous cliff. Rebuilt after the 1956 earthquake, it lacks authentic charm, but there are magnificent views of the caldera, the volcanic cliffs, the lava islets and the vast sea.

Upper Town

This modern district of tavernas, shops and bars is dominated by the enormous white profile of the Orthodox Cathedral (1970). The area around Platía Theotokopoúlou, near the bus terminal, is always lively and noisy.

Prehistoric Museum★★

Open Tue-Sun. 8.30am-7.30pm. 3€ (combined with Archaeological Museum). (22860)232 17.
Famed 4 000-year-old frescoes, plus displays of the islands since neolithic times.

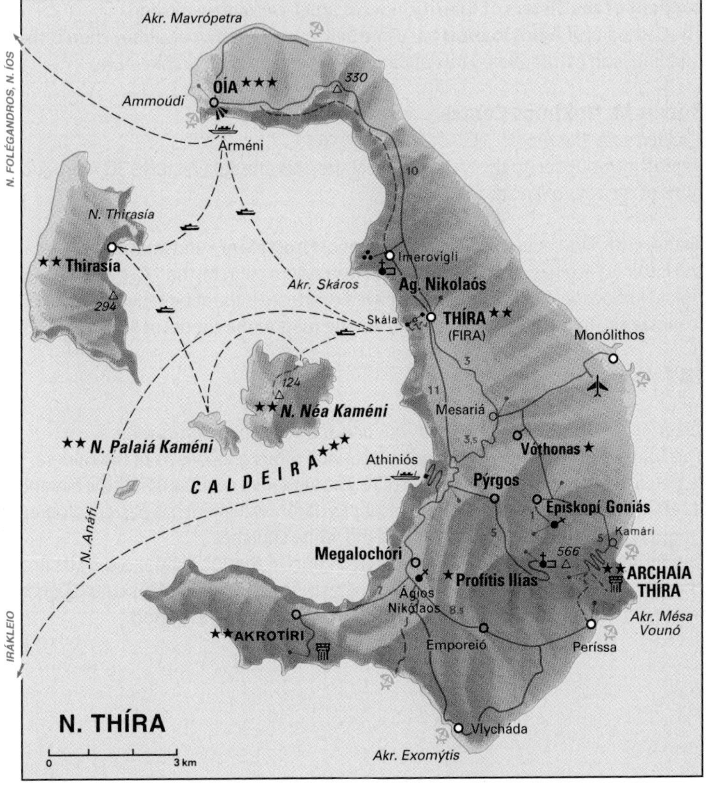

The White Wines of Santorini

The island's volcanic soil is particularly suitable for viticulture. Santorini produces a white wine with an unmistakable bouquet which is among the best in Greece. The **assirtiko** vine produces a fairly fruity, medium-dry white wine, **vinsando** (made by leaving the grapes to supermaturation), **aidani** (known for its jasmine bouquet) and the rarer **nyhtari** are sweet fragrant wines. Surprisingly, the vines are grown in a spiral which makes them more resilient in the strong winds. Some tavernas and winemakers offer tastings, notably in Messariá and Megalohóri.

Lower Town

Known as Káto Firá, the district is a maze of alleys. Among its houses are two white-washed churches, Ágios Ioánnis and Ágios Minás, crowned by a lantern.

Archaeological Museum

Open Tue-Sun 8.30am-3pm. 3€ (combined with Prehistoric Museum). ☎(22860)22 217.
Ancient Cycladic idols and vases (3 000 BC), plus ceramics, statues and fragments.

Catholic Quarter★

On the north side of the town, this is the best preserved part of Firá. Follow Odós Agíou Miná along the precipice before wandering the alles lined with ochre houses.
The **Guizi Palace** (1700) commemorates life before the 1956 earthquake in photographs, prints, books, manuscripts, traditional costumes and objects *(open Mon-Sat, 10.30am-1.30pm and 5-8pm, and Sun, 10.30am-4pm. 3€)*. Nearby is the former **convent of the Sisters of Charity**, now a carpet-weaving workshop.
The Cathedral of **Ágios Ioánnis** has a fine bell tower. Nearby is an abbey church; the building is an extraordinary mix of Baroque art and Cycladic architecture.

Petros M. Nokimos Centre

Open daily 10am-6pm. 3€. ☎(22860) 230 16 19.
A good introduction to the archaeological site, this museum features 3D reproductions of frescoes of ancient Thira.

To the north, Firá converges with the villages of **Firostefáni**★ and **Imerovígli**★. Near the latter (which has a fine iconostasis in its modern church), the 17C Monastery of Ágios Nikólaos lies in a dip. Around its paved courtyard is the abbey church (beautiful iconostasis). To the west of the village are the ruins of the citadel of **Skáros**.

Ía★★★

10km/6.25mi north of Firá. Access by bus or a 3hr walk along clifftop path.
The coast road can be vertiginous in places and offers good views of the caldera. Ía, perched on the cliffs, is quieter than Firá. The **view**★★★ over the island, the bay and its many islets is magnificent. This typically Cycladic settlement has pastel-coloured troglodyte dwellings, patrician houses and white churches.
The Ammoudi district of Ía was a prosperous port in the 19C, evidenced by its fine churches, opulent houses and marbled squares. A small **Maritime Museum** *(open Wed-Mon, 10am-2pm and 5-8pm. 3€)* displays items from this period.

Akrotíri

Visit

Site of Akrotíri★★

Southwest of the island. Open Tue-Sun, 8.30am-3pm. 5€ (under restoration at press time) (22860) 81 366.

This Bronze-Age (second millennium BC) city predates the great eruption. Like Pompeii, it was buried in ash until discovered in 1967. Miraculously preserved, Akrotíri retains its streets, paved squares and houses. The huge jars *(pithoi)* in which stores were kept have been left where they were found. It seems the city must have been evacuated before the catastrophe because no human remains have been found.

Arhéa Thíra★★★ (Ancient Thera)

East coast. Access from Perissa by a winding road; park the car at the top and take the path leading up to the ruins. Open Tue-Sun 8.30am-2.30pm. No charge.

Ancient Thera occupies a magnificent **site**★★★ above the Aegean Sea. Founded in the 9C BC, it thrived in Hellenistic times but was abandoned in the 13C. In the sacred entry enclosure there are unusual sculptures representing Artemidoros, the lion of Apollo, the eagle of Zeus and the dolphin of Poseidon. The agora was divided into two parts: the first was overlooked by a Temple to Dionysos and the second by the Royal Portico. Beyond the agora is the theatre *(left)*; the Sacred Way leads to the Temple of Apollo, which was preceded by a court *(right)* flanked by two chambers.

On the way back, take the street by the theatre which climbs towards the Sanctuary of the Egyptian Gods, Isis, Serapis and Anubis.

Excursions

Boat Trip in the Caldera★★★

Departure from the old port (Skála) below Firá; trips also leave from Ía. A staircase leads down from Firá to Skála (20min). Those not wishing to walk can make the journey by donkey or by cable car. Take sturdy shoes, water, a hat and a swimsuit. The trip described here takes about 3hr. Tickets can be purchased at travel agents; around 15€ for the boat trip; 20€ including climb to Thriassia; add 2€ to walk on the volcano.

The view of the towering cliffs of the crater, the precariously sited villages, the bay and the volcanic outcrops is most impressive from the deck of a small boat.

A Natural Disaster

Around the year 1500 BC, the inhabitants of Santorini experienced powerful earthquakes over the course of several months. The volcano began to rumble and the population fled. Eventually the pressure in the mountain discharged with a huge eruption, destroying the centre of the island and sending an enormous column of ash and dust several miles into the sky. A tidal wave some 200m/650ft high devastated coastlines as far away as Crete. At the centre of the island the new crater was flooded by the sea. This eruption was one of the most violent ever experienced by mankind; archaeologists believe that it brought the brilliant Minoan civilisation to its end (see CRETE).

Néa Kaméni★★

This cone of solidified lava is only a few centuries old. The climb to the summit takes about 30min. Here and there, puffs of smoke burst from the sulphur crust.

Paleá Kaméni★★

The boat halts at the mouth of a cove; as you swim to the shore the water grows warmer and is coloured red by volcanic mud; gas bubbles erupt on the surface.

Thirassía★

Also accessible direct from Ía.

At the top of the cliff there is a little village. The boat returns to Firá via the Skála of Ía (see below), skirting the forbidding and precipitous cliffs of the crater.

The Centre of the Island★

From Firá, go southeast; take the minor road to the right beyond Messariá.

Vóthonas★

The village lies in a fold in the layer of pozzolana. All that can be seen above the surrounding countryside are a few domes and a church's bell tower.

Episkopí Goniás★

Southeast of Vóthonas, near Méssa Goniá, a path *(right)* runs south to the Church of Panagía Episkopís, one of the most beautiful on the island (11C). The frescoes date from about 1100; note the re-use of Ancient columns.

Pírgos

The highest village on the island is composed of concentric streets; there are several handsome neo-Classical houses and traces of a Venetian castle.

Prophet Elijah Monastery★ (Profítis Ilías)

From this 18C structure, there is a fine **view**★★ over the caldera and the island. The library and cellars house a museum of religious art and popular traditions.

Return to Pírgos and head towards the caldera.

Megalohóri

Near this village stands St Nicholas' Chapel, a small white marble structure; it is an Ancient funerary temple (3C BC), perfectly preserved. Just outside **Emborío** lie the remains of a Venetian fortress (15C Church of the Virgin).

TÍNOS★

TENOS – Τηνοζ

POPULATION 7 747

195KM²/77SQ MI – MICHELIN MAP 737 L 10 – CYCLADES – AEGEAN.

Tenos is an important centre of Christian pilgrimage, particularly during the feast of the Assumption, when a long procession follows a miraculous icon of the Virgin as it is borne aloft by sailors. With its mountains, beaches and unspoilt coastlines, Tenos presents a landscape of great beauty. *Kalypso tourist office, Odos Taxiarchon, ☎(2830) 254 07. www.tinos.biz.*

Touring

Beaches

Ágios Márkos and **Ágios Fokás** are the island's busiest beaches; for quiet, head to **Kiónia**★, west of the port. The rocky cove of Stavrós (halfway between Ágios Márkos and Hóra) is sheltered enough to swim in safety even when windy.

Address Book

For coin categories, see the Legend on the cover flap.

GETTING ABOUT

By boat –Mainland ferry service daily to Piraeus *(3h-5h30mn)*, Lavrio *(2h20mn)* and Rafina *(2h-3h40)*; daily service to Andros, Mykonos, Siros, Máxos, and Páros. Also service to Sérifos *(1/wk)* and Sifnos *(1/wk)*.

WHERE TO EAT

Among the island's specialities, the veal *(moshári)* is the best in Greece. Also look out for rabbit *(kounéli)*, lamb *(arnáki)*, goat (*katsíki*, either cooked in a lemon or tomato sauce or simply roasted), and potato and pork omelette *(froutaliá)*.

⊖ **Arkyra** – *Hóra, near the port.* Small family-run ouzerie serving very good fried fish and excellent local cheese.

⊖ **Kapilio** – *Hóra, Odos Aristidou Kodogiorgi.* Come for live Greek music on Saturday evenings, and to sample the tasty pork in mustard sauce and the tzatziki.

⊖⊖ **To Thalassaki** – *Isternia, turn left toward the beach.* An excellent spot for sampling fine local cuisine while dangling your feet in the water! Excellent fresh *mezes*, impeccable grilled fish, and sublime halvah with honey and pistachios.

WHERE TO STAY

⊖ **Eleana** – *Hóra, 1 Odos Agio Ioannou, ☎ (22830) 225 61 – 17rm.* Tucked between two charming churches, this large hotel has impeccably kept rooms.

⊖⊖⊖ **Tinion** – *Hóra, east of the port – ☎ (22830) 22 261, www.tinionhotel.gr – 18rm.* An almost colonial feel to this white-painted historic residence.

⊖⊖ **Boreádhes** – *Hóra, after the church of Ágios Antónios – ☎ (22830) 23 845, www.voreades.gr – 12rm and one apt.* An attractive building in the traditional style which is tastefully decorated (tester beds).

⊖⊖⊖ **Golden Beach** – *Agios Folkas, on the beach. ☎ (22830) 225 79, www.goldenbeachtinos.gr – 19 studios.* An attractive group of buildings situated in a large garden; nice tavern adjacent.

TAKING A BREAK IN HÓRA

For cocktails try **Sympossio** for its lounge atmosphere, **Mycro Café** for a more upbeat experience.

EVENTS AND FESTIVALS

Tenos has no shortage of events, ranging from saints' days to raki festivals. Among such festivals are Kardianí (mid-June, 50 days after Easter), Agía Paraskeví in Istérnia (26 July), Agía Marína in Pírgos (17 July), and Ágios Ioánnis in Kómi.

Chabrol B./MICHELIN

Dovecot, Tenos

Southeast coast
The strip of coastline facing Mykonos has two fine beaches: sandy Ágios Ioánnis Porto and the superb crescent beach of **Pahiá Ámosa**★, *(access by footpath).*

Visit

Hóra★
The whitewashed capital of Tenos is a pleasant town and a busy port.

Church of Panagía Evangelístria★★
Open daily 9am-12pm. No charge.
A broad steeply sloping street, which some pilgrims climb on their knees, leads up to the imposing white marble church (1823). The church was built after the discovery of a miraculous icon of the Virgin, object of pilgrimages by the sick and the faithful.
A ceremonial flight of steps approaches the church. In the nave is the holy icon, encrusted in jewels and hung with votive offerings.
On the left below the church are the 'caves' where the icon was discovered; a neighbouring building contains a little Museum of Religious Art (icons) and an art gallery which displays works by well known local artists.

Archaeological Museum (colossal provisions vase from the 7C BC).

Kehrovouníou Convent ★
6km/3.75mi northeast of Hóra. Open daily, 7-11.30am and 2.20-7pm; pants or long skirts required.
The convent (11C) features fine frescoes and an iconostasis in its Church of Kímissis tis Theotókou. Visitors may see the cell of St Pelagía, 18C and 19C icons and devotional objects. Items made by the nuns (candles, honey, icons) are available for sale.

Exómvourgo
9km/5.5mi north of Hóra, plus 1hr on foot there and back.
This little mountain crowned by a white cross has at its summit the ruins of a Venetian citadel built on the site of an Ancient acropolis. Lovely **view**★ from the top.

Driving Tours

The Inland Villages★

Allow a whole day.

There are many villages on Tenos, all packed close together. Their narrow alleyways and vaulted passages provided protection against the sun and wind, and against pirates.

L. Campion/MICHELIN

One of the pretty villages to be found on Tenos

Agápi
A good example of the classic medieval plan used in all the inland fortified villages; where peripheral houses formed the ramparts.

Arnádos
Close to the parish church, a **Religious Museum** displays icons and other objects.

Dío Horiá
Spend a little time in this pretty village (note the communal fountain), wandering the alleyways around the Church of Kímissis tis Theotókou (Dormition of the Virgin).

Koumáros
Traditional village on the slopes of Exómvourgo; lovely views of the island.

Loutrá
The imposing old college (17C) was a Jesuit seminary. Inside is a small Folk Museum; some of the original items of furniture remain *in situ*.

Méssi
Extraordinary church resembling ecclesiastical architecture of central America.

Moundádos
This abandoned village is a network of paved whitewashed alleys; good views from the roof of the Church of Ágios Ioánnis tou Prodrómou *(flight of steps)*.

Skaládos
The church bell tower is a good example of the local architecture. On the outskirts of the village is a café-grocery with a terrace that has a fine **view**★ over the valley down to the gulf of Kolimbíthra.

Sklavohóri
The village has a remarkable communal washhouse dating from the early 19C.

Triandáros
In a verdant location, this village has a church (Ágii Apostóli, built in 1887) with an impressive gabled façade. From here, a track leads to the pebble beach at Lihnáftia 4.5km/2.8mi away.

Tripótamos

Follow the quiet alleyways to the Church of Isodion tis Theotoku (Presentation of the Virgin), which has rich marble decoration; lovely view over the valley and the sea.

Vólax

A right turn leads to this village lost in the meadows. Here and there, among its houses, are large boulders of volcanic origin.

Xinára

The seat of the Catholic see of Tenos; its cathedral is dedicated to the Virgin.

Éxo Meriá★

Allow one day. 70km/44mi round trip. From Hóra, head northwest to Pánormos.

Tarabádos dovecots★★

Down in the valley (from Kámbos, head to the nearby hamlet of Tarabádos) are the finest dovecots on Tenos, some of them dating from the Venetian period.

Kardianí★

Amid the treese, the white houses of Kardianí look down over the sea. The village boasts two fine churches, Genéthliou tis Theotókou and Agía Triáda.

Istérnia

The large church sports ceramic tiled domes. The **Museum of Artists** displays the work of local painters and sculptors *(open Tue-Sun 8.30am-3pm; no charge).*
The road follows the contours of a col before heading down to the dry and rocky landscape on the other side of the island.

Pírgos★

Below the town, Pírgos has several active sculpture workshops.

Pánornmos

At the end of the road, this pretty little port sits in a sheltered rocky bay.

THE DODECANESE★★

Dotting the southern Aegean Sea just a few kilometres off the Turkish coast, this archipelago is composed (as the name suggests) of 12 main islands and roughly 200 smaller islets. Mountainous and picturesque , the Dodecanese islands played an important role in Antiquity and during the Middle Ages, when they were the front line of the Christian world as it faced the threat of invasion by Turkey (the islands finally succumbed in the 16C). The islands were occupied by Italy in 1912 and joined the Greek State in 1947-48.

The administrative capital is at Rhodes Town, and the 12 main islands are Rhodes, Pátmos, Kos, Léros, Kálimnos, Nissiros, Tílos, Sími, Astipálea, Kastelório, **Kárpathos** and **Kássos**. To these are added numerous smaller islands such as Hálki near Rhodes, Lipsí and Arkí near Pátmos, and Télendos and Pserimos near Kálimnos.

GETTING THERE

Flights link Kárpathos, Kos, Léros and Rhodes to Athens and Thessaloníki. Kos and Rhodes are also linked to many European airports.

Boats serve the Dodecanese from Piraeus and Thessaloníki via the Cyclades but the journey is a long one. The ferries stop at Astipálea, Kálimnos, Léros, Pátmos, Kos, Níssiros, Tílos and Sími and Rhodes; and some go on to Kárpathos. Another service links Sitía (Crete) to Rhodes.

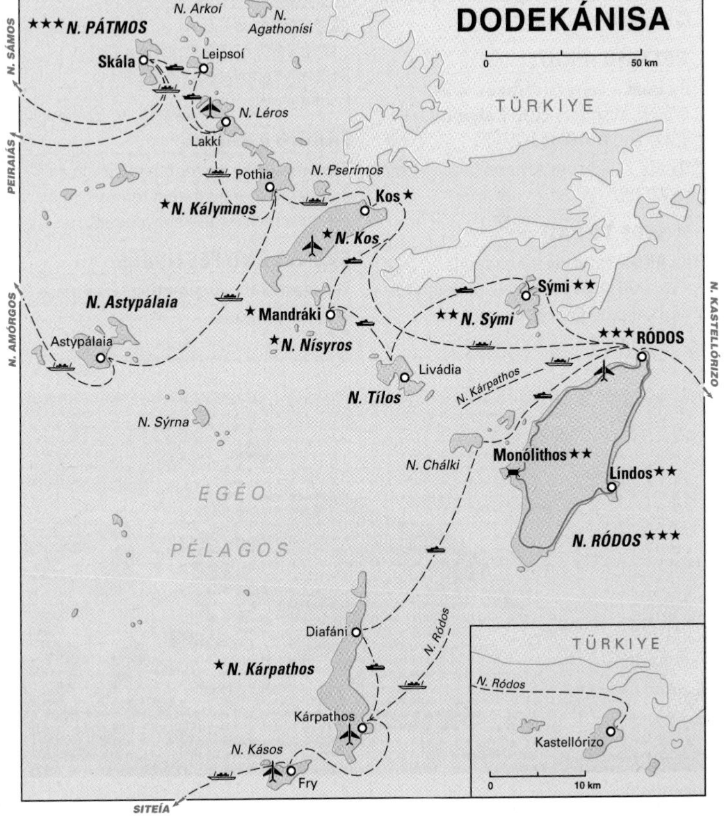

ASTIPÁLEA

Αστυπαλαια

POPULATION 1 036

96KM²/38SQ MI – MICHELIN MAP 737 N-O 12-13 – DODECANESE – AEGEAN.

Close to the Cyclades (45km/28mi from Amorgós), Astipálea is mountainous, yet relatively fertile. The capital is a pretty village of white houses scattered around a Venetian fortress. Because of its isolated location, the island is little visited, even in high season. *At Hóra, ☎ (22430) 61 412 – www.astypalaia.com*

Astipálea Town (Hóra)

This attractive coastal village has many old houses dating to the Venetian period. Below is the Convent of Panagia Portaitissa. The **Archaeological Museum** includes objects from the Mycenaean tombs at Armenochori and Syngairo, as well as many architectural fragments from the Classical and Hellenistic periods *(open Jul-Oct Tue-Sun 11am-1pm, 5-10.30pm; Nov-Jun 9am-2.30pm; no charge; ☎ (22430) 61 500)*. Pleasant excursions from Hóra include **Analipsi (Maltezana)** *(9km/6mi)*, with fine sea caves in its sheltered bay; **Vathy** *(20km/12mi east)* with intriguing sea caves; and **Livadi** *(1km/0.6mi south)*, a seaside resort with a fine beach.

Address Book

For coin categories, see the Legend on the cover flap.

GETTING ABOUT

By boat – Ferry to **Piraeus** *(4/wk; 8-13hr)*. Also service to **Kalymnos** *(3-4/wk)* and **Amorgós** *(2/wk)*.

By air – Flights to **Athens** (*several each week; 1hr*).

WHERE TO EAT

Akti – *Hóra, on the quayside – ☎ (22430) 61 114*. Small, pleasant terraces; typical Greek cuisine.

WHERE TO STAY

Paradissos – *Hóra, on the quayside – ☎ (22430) 61 224. Open Apr-Oct.* Recently renovated, clean rooms. Friendly welcome.

TAKING A BREAK

Toxotis – *Hóra, on the quayside* – In an agreeable spot (with roof terrace), this establishment is also a restaurant.

EVENTS AND FESTIVALS

The feast of the Assumption takes place around 15 August.

Phototravellers/MICHELIN

View of Hóra, Astipálea

KÁRPATHOS★

Καρπαθοζ

POPULATION 2 077

300KM²/117SQ MI – MICHELIN MAP 737 P 14-15 – DODECANESE – AEGEAN.

Located between Crete and Rhodes, Kárpathos stretches from north to south like a huge sea serpent at the frontier between east and west.

Visit

Kárpathos (Pigádia)

Located in the southeast of Kárpathos, the capital and port is an attractive town. Numerous hotels have been built by returning expats, and fish restauraunts welcome visitors and local clientele. Amopi Beach lies 6km/4mi to the south.

The East Coast and North of the Island★★

Heading north from Pigádia, a road to the right leads 3km/2mi to the beautiful **Aháta Beach**, bordered by arid cliffs.

Address Book

GETTING ABOUT

By air – The airport is at the southern end of the island, 18km from Pigádia. Service to **Rhodes** *(4/day)* and **Athens** *(5/wk; 3/wk in winter)*.

By boat – Ferry service to **Piraeus** via Crete, Santorini and Milos *(2/wk)* and **Rhodes** via Diafani *(3/wk)*.

WHERE TO EAT

⊖ **To Ellinikon** – *Pigádia, Odós Apodimon Karpathion* – ☎ *(22450) 239 32*. In the kitchen, choose a variety plate of fresh vegetables, or the *makarones* pasta with goat cheese.

⊖ **The Milos** – *Ólimbos, end of the village near the windmills* – ☎ *(22450) 513 33*. *May-Sept*. Choose a sea or mountain view. Wide variety of dishes (some cooked in view of the tables in the traditional oven).

⊖ **Ánixis** – *Diafáni, near the church* – ☎ *(22450) 52 26*. *May-Oct*. Simple, authentic and tasty dishes that depend on the day's catch. Specialities include *dolmades* made with hibiscus leaves and delicious *loukoumádes*.

WHERE TO STAY

⊖ **Hotel Dolphin** – *Above the port* – ☎ *(22450) 226 65/69761 316 32, www.dolphinstudios.gr – 6rm, 4 apts*. Light, spacious rooms in a charming lane leading to two isolated chapels at the end of the bay. No breakfast.

⊖ **Pine Tree** – *Adia Beach* – ☎ *(22450) 290 65, www.pinetreerestaurantkarpathos.cjb.net – 9rm, 3apts*. *May-Oct*. Isolated in Adia Bay on the pine-covered slpes of Kali Limni. Fresh, local fruit served at breakfast.

⊖ **Hotel Aphrodite** – *Olimbos, top of the village* – ☎ *(22450) 513 07 – 8rm*. Pleasant small rooms in a good location.

⊖⊖ **Krínos** – *Lefkós* – ☎ *(22450) 71 410, www.krinos-hotel.com – 42rm*. *Apr-Oct*. Very comfortable hotel overlooking the sea; all rooms have balconies with views. Greek dancing.

EVENTS AND FESTIVALS

Local feasts – On Kárpathos, Easter is celebrated with fervour. On the Tuesday of Holy Week the men go on an icon procession through the villages. Lamb feast on Easter Monday with music (*tsaboúna*, bagpipes, and *láouto*, lute).

BEACHES

Some beaches are accessibly only by footpath or by water-taxi. Some of the best are on the east coast: Kira Panagia, Agios Nikolaos (Spoa) and **Apela**.

The **Apéri-Spóa**★★ stretch of road requires a four-wheel drive vehicle or can be walked. It offers fine panoramic views over the island. Kirá Panagía, Apéla and Ágios Nikólaos are the finest beaches on the island.

Between Spóa and Ólimbos, another road leads to the north of the island. To the right are the superb, deserted beaches of Ágios Minás and Forókli.

Ólimbos★

This high, fortified village overlooked by windmills is little changed since the 15C. Elderly women still wear the traditional garb of long black dress and scarf, with the neck and cuffs embroidered in coloured patterns; the very ancient local dialect is still in regular use. A **traditional house** is open to the public; its sole room is centred around a pillar, with folding beds, icons, photos and personal effects.

Diafáni

This pleasant town sits at the northeast end of Kárpathos.

The West Coast★

From the well-maintained coast road there are fine **views**★ of the mountains, the sea and the island of Kássos. Near the pleasant village of Arkássa and the beach of Ágios Nikólaos is the **Agía Sofía Basilica**, some 15 centuries old. Inside are mosaics and artefacts dating from the paleo-Christian era.

Phototravellers/MICHELIN

Windmills, Kárpathos

The Mountain Villages★

The mountain villages, with whitewashed houses, seem unchanged by time. Worth a stop is **Othos**, a busy community with grand houses, a modest market and numerous tavernas. Local artist Saunis Hapsis holds the keys of the **Ethnographic Museum**.

Excursion

Island of Kássos

Accessible by ferry from Kárpathos or by plane; two hotels at the harbour in Fri.

This island is very close to Kárpathos but little visited. The capital, Fri, is a small port with numerous waterside restaurants; excursions depart from here to the Island of **Armathia**, which has magnificent beaches. Near Fri are four charming villages, and many inlets; the most striking of these is **Kelatros** *(15km/9mi from Fri).*

KOS★

Κωζ

POPULATION 26 379

290KM²/113SQ MI – MICHELIN MAP 737 P 12 – DODECANESE – AEGEAN.

Close to the shores of Turkey, Kos is a mountainous island rich in agricultural resources. The resorts at Kos Town and Kardámena are among largest in Greece.
Vasileos Georgiou, by the hydrofoil terminal. ☎ (22420) 24 460. Open Mon-Fri 8am-8pm (2.30pm off-season). www.hippocrates.gr

Touring Kos

Beaches and Resorts

Away from Kos Town and its renowned nightlife, the island has many popular resorts and some of the finest **beaches**★ in Greece.

Kardámena

This large resort teems with people in summer and virtually deserted in winter. At night, the music from the bars, pubs and discos is deafening. From the port, there are excursions to Níssiros, renowned for its volcano.

Kéfalos Bay (Kólpos Kéfalou)

Enclosed by Mount Látra, this submerged section of a volcanic crater is bordered by fine sandy beaches, notably **Parádissos**★ (Paradise Beach) and **Camel**★. Near the beach at Kamári is a rock terrace above the Club Med beach; here lie the ruins of a palaeo-Christian basilica, **Ágios Stéfanos** (5C).
To the west of Kos Town lie dune-fringed resorts of Mastihári, Marmári and Tingáki.

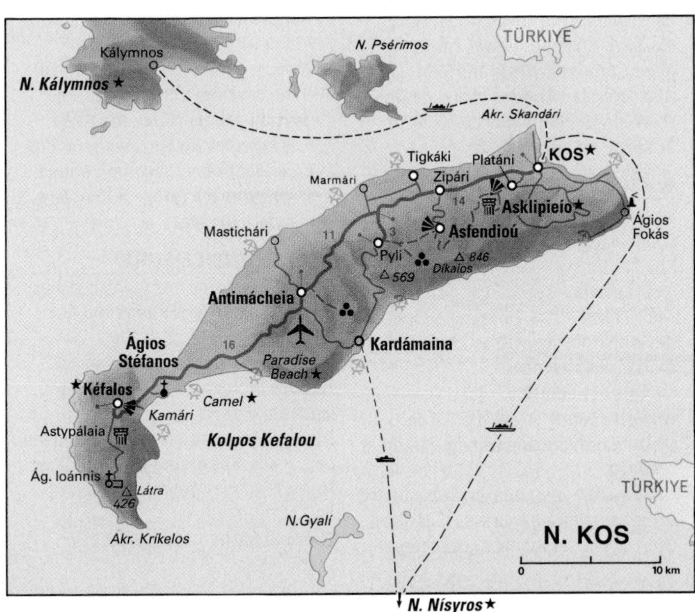

Visit

Kos Town★

R. Mattes/MICHELIN

Capital of the island and its main resort, charming Kos Town offers terraced cafés, palm-lined walks and gardens of flowering hibiscus. There are some **Ancient ruins** in the port quarter, including foundations and columns of a temple to Aphrodite. The vast **Archaeological Site** *(Odós Grigoriou, south of the town; free of charge)* includes traces of a Temple of Dionysos, a colonnaded *palaestra*, baths, houses decorated with **mosaics**★ and frescoes. At the **Archaeological Museum** *(Platia Eleftherías; open Tue-Sun 8am-3pm; 3€)* you'll see an interesting collection of Hellenistic and Roman sculptures.

Plane Tree Square★ (Platía tou Platánou)

The centre of the town takes its name from the enormous plane tree beneath which Hippocrates, the famous doctor, is said to have taught. Next to the tree stands a

Address Book

For coin categories, see the Legend on the cover flap.

GETTING ABOUT

By air – Service to Athens *(daily)* and Rhodes **(2-3/wk)**. The airport is 25km/17mi southwest of Kos Town; *(22420) 51 225.*

By boat – Ferry service (Kountouriotou dock, behind the Kastro) to **Piraeus** *(daily)* via Kalimnos *(6/wk)*, Patmos (6/wk), Amorgos *(1/wk)* and Siros *(2/wk)*. Also service to **Rhodes** *(daily)* via Simi *(1-3/wk)*. For information, (22420) 285 07.

WHERE TO EAT

Mummy's Cooking– *Kos, 27 Odós Bouboulinas – (22420) 85 25.* Popular spot, with Greek music.

Stamatia – *Kefalos Bay, on the beach – (22420) 712 45.* Housemade specialties with fruit, vegetables, chicken. Glorious bay window.

Agios Theologos – *Agios Theologos, above the beach – 697455 035 56.* Tasty dishes made with fresh farm products.

Seaside – *Mastihári, at the beginning of the beach facing west – (22420) 59 284.* Dine in the cool of a sea breeze. Friendly welcome; open all year for lunch and dinner.

WHERE TO STAY

Hotel Maritina – *Kos, 19 Odós Vironas – (22420) 235 11, www.maritina.gr – 82rm.* Fine establishment with very comfortable rooms facing the Temple of Dionysos.

Panorama – *Kefalos Bay – (22420) 719 24, www.panorama-kefalos.gr – 17apts.* *May-Oct.* Gorgeous views over the bay from this isolated spot.

Syrtaki – *Kefalos Bay – (22420) 721 39, www.kefalos.biz – 6apts.* *May Oct.* Excellent value, and open-armed welcome from the owner. Rooms and studios face the sea.

SPORTS AND LEISURE

Beaches – Several fine sandy beaches; among the best are Empros and Agios Theologos.

Boat trips – To other islands and Turkey. *Departures between 8.30-9.30am; inquire at the port.*

Diving – Several boats depart from the port at Kos. **Kos diving center**, *5 Odós Mitrop Nathanail (south of the agora), (22420) 202 69.*

Thermal baths – At **Empros**, 12km south of Kos.

covered Turkish fountain composed of Ancient materials; note the sarcophagus converted into a basin. The Mosque of the Loggia (18C) has a tall minaret.

Kástro★ (Knights' Castle)

Access: Over a bridge from Platía tou Platánou. Open Tue-Sun, 8.30am-2.30pm. 3€.

The castle's two concentric sets of walls, (1450–1514) are constructed with pieces taken from Ancient buildings: note the Hellenistic frieze over the entrance door. The parapet walk gives a succession of picturesque views of the town, the harbour, the sea and the Turkish coast.

Driving Tour

Across the island★

86km/54mi round trip. Follow a scenic road that runs the length of Kos.

Asklipiío★

4km/2.5mi southwest of Kos Town. Open Tue-Sun, 8am-7pm (3pm in winter).

This important sanctuary (4C-BC) commemorating the skills of Hippocrates occupies a magnificent **site**★★ overlooking the Kos Plain. Replete with healing sulphurous waters, it served as both a place of worship and a treatment centre.

Climb up the successive terraces past the monumental entrance *(propylaia)*, altars and temples to the top terrace, where stood the great Temple of Asklepios. From here, there are magnificent **views**★★ down over the sanctuary and the surrounding woods to the town of Kos and over the sea to the Turkish coast.

From the village of **Asfendioú** *(8.5km/5mi from Kos Town, turn left onto a little mountain road)* there is a good view over the island and out towards Kálimnos.

Andimáhia

22km/14mi from Kos Town.

This village is adjacent to a Hospitallers' fortress (take the path to the left before the village), with ruins of churches, houses and cisterns.

Kéfalos★

The old village of Kéfalos lies above the ruins of its castle. From the foot of the wall there is a splendid **view**★★ over the vast Bay of Kéfalos to the east and beyond.

Excursions

Kálimnos★

Island northwest of Kos. For access, see Address Book.

The influx of visitors has made the island prosperous, but it retains its wild grandeur: striking rock faces, attractive beaches, and paths bordered by fragrant flora.

Kalimnos (Póthia)

Along the quayside and scaling the hillside rise tall houses, often painted in the national colours of white and blue and built in the neo-Classical style. To the north-east, the **Vathis Valley**★ is an oasis of coolness. Rina is an attractive village, and the port of Vathís nestles in the curve of a bay as steep-sided as a fjord.

Péra

Northeast of Horió. Open every day, 8.30am-3pm. No charge.

The steep climb to Péra castle is worthwhile for the superb **view**★. There are fine beaches on the west coast: Kandoúni, Linária and Platís Gialós.

Kálimnos Address Book

For coin categories, see the Legend on the cover flap.

GETTING ABOUT

By boat – From Póthia, ferry service to **Piraeus** *(daily; 14hr)*, to Kos *(2/day)*, and to Rhodes *(2/day)*. Also ferry or hydrofoil service to Pátmos *(9/wk)*, Léros *(6/wk)*, Kárpathos and Lipsí *(2/wk)* and Mykonos, Amorgós, Astipálea and Kastelórizo *(1/wk)*.

WHERE TO EAT

Xeftéries – *Póthia, in the street to the right of the cathedral – ☎ (22430) 28 642*. Simple but appetising food in generous portions. Pleasant open-air dining in the shade. Greek specialities, but no fish. Good value.

The Harbour Taverna – *Vathís, on the quayside to the right – ☎ (22430) 31 206.* Good atmosphere and friendly welcome. Fresh fish depending on the catch, and traditional Greek fare served in a typical ambience.

WHERE TO STAY

Panorama – *Póthia, on the left heading up from the port – ☎ and fax (22430) 23 138, smiksis2003@yahoo.gr – 13rm.* In an elevated location overlooking the port (good view of the bay), this tranquil establishment has clean, comfortable rooms, and offers friendly, welcoming service.

Villa Themelina – *Póthia, northeast part of the town – ☎ (22430) 22 682, – 23rm.* All the charm of a 19C mansion, conveniently yet quietly located in town. Pleasant garden.

EVENTS AND FESTIVALS

Easter Sunday sees traditional celebrations in Póthia's main square.

The Northern Tip★

North of Mirtiés, Emporiós is a charming coastal village.

Níssiros★

This island south of Kos is a partially active volcano. The village of **Mandraki**★, is one of the most beautiful places in the Dodecanese, dominated by an Ancient defensive wall and a medieval castle; inside is the Monastery of Panagía Spilianí and its rock church. Also worth a visit is the **Folk Museum**. Nissiros' **beaches** are of black sand; the finest are to be found at the northern end of the island

Volcano★

Wear strong shoes. Bus from Mandráki.

Above the coastal villages of **Loutrá** and **Páli** (curative hot springs) lies the Láki plateau. It is possible to descend into the smoky, sulphurous Stéfanos crater.

Níssiros Address Book

For coin categories, see the Legend on the cover flap.

GETTING THERE

By boat – Ferry services from Kos *(daily)*, Rhodes *(2-3/wk)*, Tilos *(1/wk)* and **Piraeus** *(1/wk)*.

WHERE TO EAT

Níssiros Taverna – *Mandráki*. A good menu offering local specialities; excellent value.

WHERE TO STAY

Pofyris – *Mandráki, centre of the village – ☎ and fax (22420) 31 376.* Modern rooms; salt-water swimming pool.

PÁTMOS★★★

Πατμοζ

The tiny, arid island of Pátmos derives its extraordinary renown from its association with St John the Divine, the disciple who wrote the Book of Revelation in the Bible, and from its 11C monastery, an important shrine of the Orthodox Church. The houses surrounding the monastery form the finest architectural group in the Aegean. *EOT; white building facing the ferry landing. (22470) 316 66. www.patmos-island.com*

- **Orient Yourself:** The northernmost of the Dodecanese, Pátmos is also one of the smallest islands in the Aegean Sea.
- **Don't Miss:** The monaster of St. John; Holy Week activities.
- **Organizing Your Time:** Plan a two-day visit.
- **Also See:** Sámos, Léros

A Bit of History

The author of the Apocalypse, by tradition identified as St John the Divine, was said to have been banished to Pátmos in AD 95 for preaching the Gospel at Ephesus. At the end of the 11C, the Emperor **Alexis I Comnenos** ceded the island to the monk **Christódoulos** for him to found a monastery dedicated to the saint.

Address Book

For coin categories, see the Legend on the cover flap.

GETTING ABOUT

By boat – Ferry services to **Piraeus** *(6/wk)* via Náxos *(3/wk)* and Páros *(2/wk)*. Links to **Rhodes** *(6/wk)* via Kálimnos *(5/wk)*, Kos *(6/wk)* and Simi *(1-3/wk)*. Links to Límnos via Sámos, Chíos and L'svos *(1/wk)*. During the summer months, the Dodecanese are well served by hydrofoil services.

WHERE TO EAT

Khilimodi – *Skála, second alley to the left of the road to Hóra – (22470) 34 080. Open all year, evenings only.* In a narrow street next to a small garden, this traditional little taverna is modest yet pleasant. Simple but tasty dishes and a warm welcome.

Tzibaeri – *Skala, front of the passenger harbo – (22470) 32 405.* Excellent traditional cuisine; shaded terrace.

Loza – *Hóra, lane leading to the town hall square – (22470) 32 405.* Prettiest terrace in Hora, overlooking the north of the island. Creative, tasty dishes.

Lampi– *Lampi, on the beach– (22470) 31 490. Open Easter-early Oct.* Tables and chairs on the beach! Lobster, mackerel and cod on the menu.

WHERE TO STAY

Sydney – *Skála, yacht harbor, head up the alley to the left behind and above the Australis Hotel – (22470) 31 689 – 11rm. Apr-Oct.* Inexpensive guesthouse; warm welcome; comfortable rooms with fridges.

Australis – *Skála, after the first yacht moorings head up the alley to the left – (22470) 31 576 – 20rm, 4 apts. Apr-Oct.* Set in a magnificent garden, this hotel has comfortable, well-equipped rooms. Apartments for up to six people with kitchens.

EVENTS AND FESTIVALS

Holy Week is marked by fasting across the island.

In **Kámbos** there are major festivals on 6 August (the Transfiguration) and 15 August.

H. Champollion/MICHELIN

View of Gríkou Bay

Beginning in 1089 Christódoulos and his companions built massive walls to protect the monastery from pirate and Turkish raids, but shortly thereafter were forced into exile. Nonetheless, the community received extraordinary support: Christodoulos' relics were eventually returned to Pátmos, pilgrims soon thronged the monastery, and emperors and patriarchs donated the profits of arable land toward the monastery. The library founded by Christodoulos enriched its collections and the monastic community produced many scholars.

At the end of the 13C the lay population resettled for protection at the base of the monastery's wall and founded the capital Hóra. In 1948, after centuries under Norman, Turkish and Italian rule, Pátmos was finally united in Greece.

The development of tourism in Pátmos in recent years has not affected the great moral and spiritual influence of the Monastery of St John, and religious festivals continue to be of great relevance in the lives of the inhabitants. A text recounting his voyages and miracles is illustrated on the walls of the monastery and of many other shrines; several places on the island are associated with the saint.

Touring Pátmos

From Skála, boats offer service to many Pátmos beaches. **Psiliámo Beach**★ (south of Hóra) may be the most beautiful on the island, and is often deserted.

Gríkou Bay★

By bus or 45min on foot from Hóra.

Traonissí Islet rises at the far end of the curving bay; just to the south is Pétra Beach, a sandy crescent fringed by marshland. Close by is Kalíkastrou rock, honeycombed with caves, and beyond is a tiny fishing port.

Kámbos and Lámbi

By boat or by bus to Kámbos and its beach, then about 35min on foot to Lámbi.

Kámbos is a large village overlooking a fertile valley. The vast and shady **Kámbos Beach** *(sand and pebbles)* is very popular in summer. The windswept **Lámbi Bay** *(2km/1mi north)* is famous for its coloured pebbles.

Skála

The biggest town on the island, Skála is an attractive port with white cube houses; most of Pátmos' hotels, guesthouses and restaurants are located here.

Kastéli Hill★★

20min on foot, west of Skála.
There are traces of a Hellenistic wall and a small chapel, with a magnificent view of Skála harbour, Hóra, St John's Monastery and the neighbouring islands.

Ágios Ioánnis Theólogos★★★

Between Skála and Hóra (just outside the latter). Access by bus or taxi, or on foot (about 30min) by an old mule track from Skála. Open daily 8am-1.30pm (Sun, Tue, Thu also 4-6pm). No charge.

Exterior walls★★

Brooding over the white houses below, the circuit wall was built on a polygonal plan in the 11C-12C by the Blessed Christódoulos; its massive canted buttresses were added in the 17C. The terrace at the entrance affords a good **view**★ of Skála Harbour.

Central courtyard

Beyond a dark zigzag passageway, the monastery's fortress-like appearance gives way to a maze of courtyards, stairs and domed white buildings with stone arcading. At the far end on the left is a huge jar in a round cistern, previously used to store the monastery's wine.

Main church★ (Katholikón)

The 17C outer narthex (frescoes of the life of St John) leads to the 12C inner narthex. The **Chapel of the Blessed Christódoulos** was constructed in the 16C as the final resting place of the monk's relics, contained in an 18C wooden reliquary.
The main church is the oldest part of the monastery. Note its grey-and-white marble floor and heavy gilt-clad wood iconostasis (1820). Most of the frescoes on view were painted in the 19C on top of 17C murals.

Chapel of the Virgin

Access from the main church.
The chapel of the Virgin has admirable late-12C **frescoes**★ that were uncovered during restoration work, and portray biblical scenes. The remaining murals depict,

Office National Hellénique de Tourisme

St John's Monastery, Pátmos

in the main, oriental saints and patriarchs. The chapel also contains a fine Cretan iconostasis in painted wood (1607) with an Antique threshold step.

Old Refectory★

It contains two long stone tables faced with marble with niches in the bottom for the monks' cutlery. The floor comprises fragments from the Ancient foundation and the early-Christian basilica. The style of the late 12C-13C **frescoes**★ on the upper west wall is more expressive than the 18C murals from the Chapel of the Virgin on the east wall *(opposite the entrance)*. The earliest murals appear on the tympanum of the north arch *(left of the entrance)*.

▶ *Return to the main courtyard by the vaulted passage.*

The old storerooms with the monks' cells *(not open)* behind are on the left on the south side; the museum and shop are on the west side of the courtyard.

Museum★

Same opening hours as the monastery; 3€. Some objects may not be on display because of exhibitions and religious ceremonies.
The museum displays the most precious articles from the monastery's library, archives and treasury. The icon collection includes a rare 11C icon in mosaic of St Nicholas, probably from Asia Minor.
The treasury dates mostly from the 17C and is made up of donations from priests and patriarchs who were born or who studied in Pátmos, including a cross and medals given by Catherine II of Russia. The cloth squares *(epigonátia)* placed at knee level on the liturgical vestments are used in rotation by the superior on Maundy Thursday each year for the ceremony of the washing of the feet *(niptíras)*, which is held in a square in Hóra. Among the votive offerings are delicate sailing ships in silver gilt and enamel set with precious stones.

Library

Closed to the public. One of the oldest libraries of the Byzantine world, it includes over 4 000 works; manuscripts, rare early books and archive material, mainly in Greek, but also some in Latin, Aramaic, and certain Slavic languages. Each year a team of restorers visits the library to undertake preservation work. Much of the material stored here has been computerised to allow access to scholars from around the world.

Terraces

Access from the first floor in the museum or from the courtyard.
The lower terrace, where the Chapel of the Holy Cross stands, provides an interesting bird's eye view of the main courtyard and part of the island. *At present the upper terraces are not accessible to visitors.*

Hóra★★

The white houses of Hóra (the name means 'principal town'), which is also called Pátmos Town, form a sparkling necklace around the dark fortress. The houses (the oldest probably dates back to the 16C) line a maze of steps and lanes; traces of the walls of the fortified town are visible in the town centre.
The corbelled houses built by refugees from Constantinople stand in the Alótina district west of the monastery. In the 17C Cretans settled in Kritiká to the east; in the 17C and the 18C prosperous families built their mansions on the hillside to the north. High walls screen the courtyards and façades, but the neo-Classical doorways decorated with carvings and mouldings, pedimented windows and, more rarely, balconies, can be seen from the street.

The town hall, a fine neo-Classical building, stands in **Lozia Square** *(Platía Lozia)*; from here there is a beautiful **view**★★ of the Convent of the Apocalypse on the north face of the hill and of Skála Harbour.

Convent of the Source of Life (Zoodóhos Pigí)

To the west of the town.
Frescoes from the 17C decorate this church dating from 1607, which is surrounded by courtyards bright with flowers.

Panorama★★★

From Pátmos Town head east to the three windmills overlooking the Gríkos road.
The area around the windmills provides admirable views of the island and the archipelago: west, Hóra and the monastery walls; Skála Harbour and Mérika Bay beyond the isthmus; on the horizon *(left to right from Hóra)* the elongated shape of Icarus and the islands of Foúrni; north, Kerketéas the tallest peak on Sámos; between the mainland and the northeast tip of Pátmos, the islands of Arkí, Lipsí and Léros.

Grotto of the Apocalypse★

15min on foot by a mule track going down from Hóra or up from Skála. There is a request bus stop near the convent. Open daily 8am-1.30m (Sun, Tue, Thu also 4-6pm). No charge.
17C chapels and monks' cells line charming courts bedecked with flowers on the way down to St Anne's Chapel, which was founded in 1090 and rebuilt in the early 18C. According to a very ancient local tradition, it is in this grotto that St John, the "disciple Jesus loved" had his vision of the Apocalypse and heard the voice of God. The guide points to the three cracks in the rock vault made by the voice of God, to the place where John laid his head to rest and to the rock which served as a desk where he wrote the Apocalypse, the last book of the New Testament. It comprises 22 chapters written in Greek in the year 96 and relates prophetic visions of the end of the world, told in symbolic terms.

Excursions

Lipsí

Lying to the east of Pátmos, this little island is unspectacular, but its beaches are peaceful, its paths attractive and its villages charming. The quayside tavernas serve the squid and fish caught by local fishermen each morning.

Lipsí Address Book

GETTING THERE

By boat – Hydrofoil services depart from Pátmos and Léros *(20min)*. From **Piraeus**, ferry service several times a week *(11 to 17h)*

WHERE TO EAT

Café du Moulin – *Lientou, on the church square.* Local specialities.

WHERE TO STAY

Hotel Aphrodite – *Lientou, near the landing stage – ☎ and fax (22470) 41 000.* Attractive modern studio accommodation looking onto the beach.

EVENTS AND FESTIVALS

23 to 26 August: **pilgrimage** to Lientou Church and village festival.
Around 10 August: **wine festival**.

Lientou

Nestled in a small bay near a popular beach, this attractive little port is Lipsi's capital. In the Church of **Panagia tou Charou** is a fine icon representing the Virgin bearing the crucified Christ.
From the port, boats serve neighboring islands and the **beaches**★ of Lipsi: **Platis Gialos** (north) and **Monodendri** (east); there are excellent **walks**★★.

Paths

A network of undemanding paths *(maps available in the village)* allows visitors to explore the island's peaceful landscape.

Léros

Made up of three peninsulas, this island lying to the southeast of Pátmos has seven deep bays with beaches sheltered from the wind and the waves. Traditionally Léros has been an island of exile, and its bleak reputation, coupled with the existence of a huge psychiatric hospital, has not helped tourism to develop. It is, however, an attractive place popular with many Greek visitors, who appreciate its seascapes and hillsides planted with tobacco, fruit trees, olive groves and vineyards.

Platanos

Bordered by the neighbouring villages of Pandeli and Agia Marina, Platanos is the capital of the island. A large Byzantine fortress which serves as a military observatory dominates the town. Agia Marina is the point of arrival for many tourist boats and merchant vessels. To the south of Pandeli, Vromolithos Beach is lined with hotels and restaurants.

Blefouti Beach★

East of the airport (9km/6mi north of Platanos), this is the finest beach on the island.

Alinda

To the north of Platanos; made up of modern buildings along the beachfront, this is the island's main resort.

Ágios Isidoros

To the west of Platanos. This church, the symbol of Léros, sits on a rocky outcrop linked to the rest of the island by a narrow isthmus.

Lakki

Situated in a bay, this was the site of an Italian naval base in the Second World War. Its imposing buildings are mostly deserted. To the west of Lakki are the two fine beaches of **Koulouki** and **Merikia**.

Léros Address Book

GETTING ABOUT

By boat – Daily services from Kos, Kálimnos, Rhodes, Sámos, and Lipsí. From **Piraeus**, ferry service daily in summer *(11hr)*.
By Air – Daily flight from **Athens** (1hr). The airport at Partheni is around 10km/6mi from the capital, and is linked by taxi and bus services.

WHERE TO EAT AND STAY

O Neromilos – *Agia Marina, on the Alinda road*. Fine regional cuisine in an exceptional setting.
Margarita – *Vromolithos* – ☎ *(22470) 22 889*. Simple and friendly family guesthouse.

TAKING A BREAK

Bar Le Faros – *Agia Marina*. Underground bar with music.

RÓDOS★★★

RHODES – Ροδοζ

POPULATION 98 357

1 400 KM²/540 SQ MI – MICHELIN MAP 737 Q-R 13-14 – DODECANESE – AEGEAN.

Close to the shores of Turkey, the island of Rhodes is popular with visitors all year round. The landscape is varied and often mountainous (Mount Atáviros reaches a height of 1 215m/3 986ft). Renowned for its plant life, the 'island of roses' is covered with conifers, semi-tropical shrubs, red hibiscus, mauve bougainvilleas and white scented jasmine. *EOT: Corner of Odós Arhiepiskopou Makariou and Odós Papagou, ☎ (22410) 443 35/443 36. Open Mon-Fri 8am-3pm. Municipal office: Platia Rimini, ☎ (22410) 205 55. Open Jun-Oct 9am-8pm. www.ando.gr/eot*

- **Orient Yourself:** Situated near Turkey, Rhodes is the fourth-largest Greek island.
- **Don't Miss:** The splendid citadel of Rhodes Town; Monolithos Castle; Lindos.
- **Organizing Your Time:** Plan a five-day stay on the island; you'll need three of those days to see all of Rhodes Town.

A Bit of History

The island of Helios – According to Greek myth, Rhodes was given to **Helios** the sun god, and his descendants founded Ialyssos (near Filérimos), Líndos and Kámiros. In the 7C BC these three cities were already trading throughout the Middle East as far as Egypt and founding colonies elsewhere. In 408 BC the three cities jointly founded the city of Rhodes, which rapidly eclipsed them.
During the 3C and the 2C BC, the island became the main maritime power in the eastern Mediterranean because of its fleet and its wealth. The arts flourished, particularly a school of sculpture, as immortalised by the famous **Colossos**.

Front line of Christianity – From 1306 until 1522 the island was a Christian bastion under the very noses of the Turks, and the Knights of St John of Jerusalem who served here constructed many buildings with French influences. In 1523, the knights fell to Suleiman the Magnificent; the Turks were to stay for nearly four centuries.

R. Mattes/MICHELIN

Palace of the Grand Masters, Rhodes Town

Address Book

For coin categories, see the Legend on the cover flap.

GETTING ABOUT

By air – During the summer there are many flights to Rhodes from most European capitals. Several flights a day from Athens (1hr). The airport is near Paradisi on the northwest coast, 16km/10mi from Rhodes Town; regular bus service.

By boat – Rhodes is an important hub of maritime traffic. Service from **Piraeus** *(22/wk)*, **Kos** *(29/wk)*, **Kálimnos** *(28/wk)*, **Pátmos** *(11/wk)*, etc. **Dodecanese Hydrofoil Company**, *6 Platía Neoriou, ☎ (22410) 70 590;* **ANES**, *88 Odós Amerikis, ☎22410) 377 69;* **Blue Star Ferries**, *111 Odós Amerikis, ☎(22410) 224 61;* **Dodekanisos Seaways**, *3 Odós Australias, ☎(22410) 705 90;* **Flying Dolphins**, *Odós Sahtouri.* Travel agencies sell tickets for most companies; The **EOT**, local tourist office and harbourmaster's office all have timetables.

WHERE TO EAT

Sea Star – *Rhodes, Old Town, 24 Odós Sofokléous – ☎ (22410) 22 117 .* Reputed to be the best fish restaurant in town. Simple decor; ask to choose from the cold table.

L'Auberge – *Rhodes, Old Town, 21 Odós Praxitélous – ☎ (22410) 34 292.* Slightly off the beaten track in the north of the Old Town. Excellent cuisine and a fine choice of French and Greek wines, impeccable service and a friendly welcome.

Baki Brothers – *Émbonas, upper village – ☎ (22460) 41 247.* Traditional dishes; meats are the specialty. Try the lamb cutlets, veal souvlaki or the steak.

Mezedákia – *Genádi, 500m out of town on the Rhodes Town road – ☎ and fax (22440) 43 627.* A fish restaurant, very popular with locals on Sundays. Very good food and friendly welcome.

Broccolino – *Lindos, east of town – ☎(22440) 316 88.* Italian-American proprietors at the helm of this charming, artistic restaurant. Housemade pastas, excellent cheeses.

Chalki – *30 Odós Kathopouli – ☎(222410) 312 35. May-Oct.* Traditional tavern with icons, old photos; excellent dishes, including marinated tuna, eggplant stuffed with tomato.

Old Story – *Rhodes, Modern Town, 108 Odós Mitropóleos – ☎ (22410) 32 421.* Very popular with locals; pleasant setting, original decor, and attentive service. A good wine list accompanies the carefully prepared, modern Greek cuisine. Reservations essential.

WHERE TO STAY

Mike's Pension – *Rhodes, Old Town, 28 Odós Menekleous – ☎ (22410) 253 59 – 10rm.* Youth hostel open to all; double rooms 25€.

Pension Minos – *Rhodes, Old Town, 5 Odós Omírou – ☎ (22410) 31 813, www.minospension.com – 20rm.* Clean, renovated guesthouse with spacious rooms; roof garden offering panoramic views over the Old Town.

Pink Elephant – *Rhodes, Old Town, 9 Odós Timakida – ☎ (22410) 22 469, www.pinkelephantpension.com – 10rm. Apr-Oct.* Near the walls in the southern part of the town, in a quiet area. Attractive and well-kept, with pretty faience decor.

Thomás Hotel – *Monólithos – ☎ (22460) 61 291 – 10rm.* Quiet, modern hotel with clean, comfortable, spacious, rooms with terraces and good views. Ideal base for excursions.

Tsampika – *38 Odós Kathopouli – ☎(22410) 268 40 – 7 apts.* Plant-filled passageway invites to simple studios; duplex for groups.

Hotel Via Via – *Rhodes, Old Town, 45 Odós Pithagóra – ☎ (22410) 77 027/69485 220 81, www.hotel-via-via.com – 9rm.* Designer decor in glorious colors; attractive rooms. Rooftop terrace with views of Old Town and the harbour. A charming address.

Marco Polo Mansion – *Rhodes, Old Town, 40-42 Odós Agíou Fanouríou – ☎ and fax (22410) 25 562, www.marcopolomansion.web.com – 7rm. Apr-Oct.* The most charming hotel in the Old Town. Occupying an old Turkish house with its own *hammam* (Turkish bath).

TAKING A BREAK

Marco Polo Café– *Rhodes, Old Town, 40-42 Odós Agíou Fanouríou – ☎ (22410)*

37 889. Steps lead to a quiet garden in a courtyard where good cocktails are served.
Lov'a Lounge – *Platia Arionos.* Relaxed ambience in the lounge; lively concerts in the room at the back.
Haraki Dreams – *Haraki, waterfront.* Internet café, perfect for an afternoon break to drink in views of bay and kastro.

SPORTS AND LEISURE

Watersports – The island of Rhodes offers excellent watersports; there are several diving clubs based in Rhodes Town (Mandráki Harbour).
Golf – 18-hole course at Afanou, *☎(22410) 855 13.*
Turkish Baths – *On Platía Aríonos in the Old Town.* Separate baths for men and women. Tue and Thu, 1-6pm; Wed and Fri, 11am-6pm; Sat, 8am-6pm; closed Sun and Mon. Modestly priced; bring flip-flops or sandals.
Sound and Light Show – Every evening in the municpal garden; information at the tourist office.

G. Gautier/MICHELIN

Shows of folkdancing and folksongs in traditional costume. *Odós Androiko, May-Oct Mon, Wed, Fri evenings.*

SHOPPING

Local arts and crafts – Jewellery (gold and silver), goldware, leather and ceramics – is of good quality. There are plenty of shops around **Platía Kíprou** and **Odós Griva** in the modern town. Look for Oriental rugs at Afántou, embroideries at Líndos, leather boots at Archángelos.

Ruled in the 20C by Italians, Germans and lastly the British, Rhodes became part of the Greek State on 7 March 1948.

Visit

Ródos (Rhodes Town) ★★★

The city is situated at the northeastern end of the island, facing the Turkish coast. The superb medieval 'Old Town' was restored by Italian architects early in the 20C, and the modern town attracts visitors to its beaches, hotels, nightclubs and countless boutiques. This is a resort of international repute, popular in both summer and winter.

The Old Town★★★

Citadel★★

Despite its troubled history and restoration works of varying success, the citadel remains an imposing sight. The knights and their attendants lived in this part of the city, which was fortified on all four sides and called **Collachium**.

▶ *Enter the fortress by the Amboise Gate.*

Píli Amboise (Amboise Gate)

An arched bridge over a moat stood at the approach to the gate (1512). A passage leads to St Antony's Gate which opens into the Palace Square.

One of The Seven Wonders of the Ancient World

Nothing remains of the Colossos of Rhodes, the huge bronze statue of the sun god Helios that came to embody the island's power. Created by Chares of Líndos around 300 BC, it ranked among the Seven Wonders of the Ancient World. Believed to have been 30m/98ft high (the Statue of Liberty measures 46m/150ft), the statue was destroyed by an earthquake in 225 BC. It lay in ruins for 800 years before being removed by a Syrian merchant who needed 900 camels to carry away all the pieces. Its exact location is a topic of debate: was it at the harbour mouth, on the shoreline, or in the town itself?

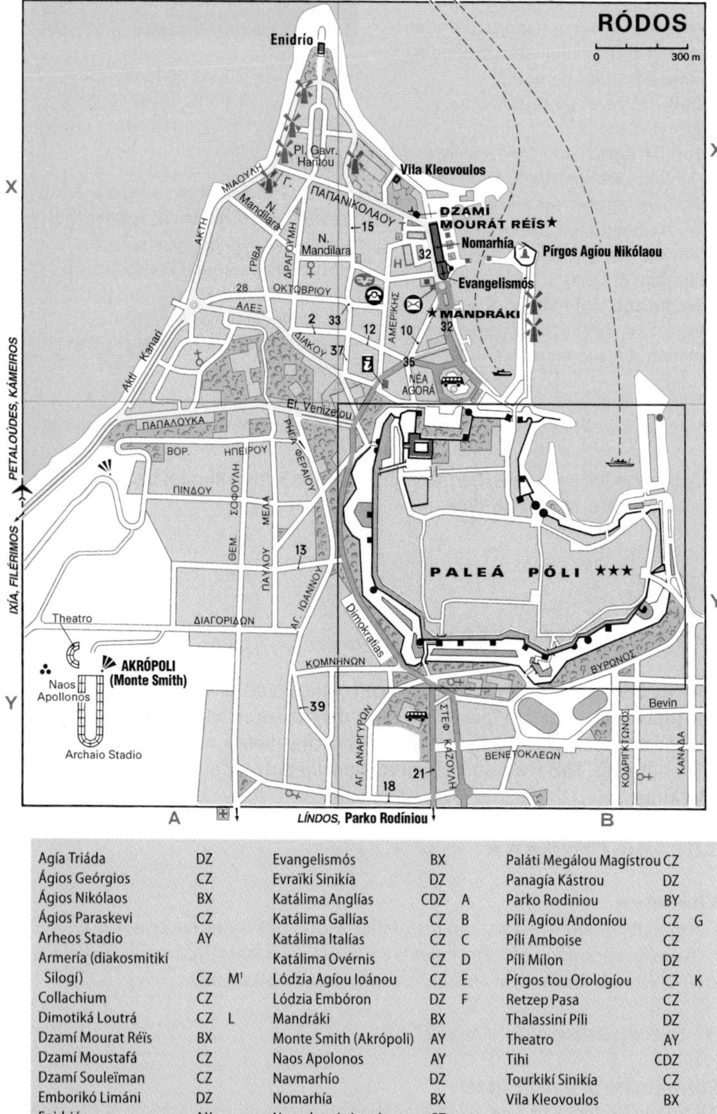

Agía Triáda	DZ		Evangelismós	BX		Paláti Megálou Magístrou	CZ	
Ágios Geórgios	CZ		Evraïki Sinikía	DZ		Panagía Kástrou	DZ	
Ágios Nikólaos	BX		Katálima Anglías	CDZ	A	Parko Rodiniou	BY	
Ágios Paraskevi	CZ		Katálima Gallías	CZ	B	Píli Agíou Andoníou	CZ	G
Arheos Stadio	AY		Katálima Italías	CZ	C	Píli Amboise	CZ	
Armería (diakosmitikí Silogí)	CZ	M[1]	Katálima Ovérnis	CZ	D	Píli Mílon	DZ	
Collachium	CZ		Lódzia Agíou Ioánou	CZ	E	Pírgos tou Orologíou	CZ	K
Dimotiká Loutrá	CZ	L	Lódzia Embóron	DZ	F	Retzep Pasa	CZ	
Dzamí Mourat Rëís	BX		Mandráki	BX		Thalassiní Píli	DZ	
Dzamí Moustafá	CZ		Monte Smith (Akrópoli)	AY		Theatro	AY	
Dzamí Souleïman	CZ		Naos Apolonos	AY		Tihi	CDZ	
Emborikó Limáni	DZ		Navmarhío	DZ		Tourkikí Sinikía	CZ	
Enidrió	AX		Nomarhía	BX		Vila Kleovoulos	BX	
			Nossokomío Ipotón	CZ				

Paláti Megálon Magístron★ (Palace of the Grand Masters)

Open Tue-Sun 8.30am-7.30pm, offseason 8.30am-2.30pm. 6€ (combined ticket for the palace, and the Byzantine, Archaeological and Decorative Arts museums: 10€).
The Grand Masters' residence (14C) more closely resembles a fortress than a palace. It was protected by a moat, crenellated walls and towers, and a keep, and had three underground floors of storerooms to hold victuals and munitions.

Odós Ipotón★★ (Knights' Street)

This medieval cobbled street is lined with **Inns**, the 15C and 16C Gothic buildings in which the knights lived according to their nationality.

Panagía Kástrou

Open Tue-Sun, 8.30am-2.30pm. 2€.
St Mary's Church (12C) was transformed into a Latin cathedral by the knights, who incorporated it into the ramparts. Later the Turks turned it into a mosque; today it houses the Byzantine Museum (frescoes, mosaics).

Katálima Anglías

The **English Inn** was built in 1483 but later demolished; it was rebuilt in 1919.

Nossokomío Ipotón★

Open Tue-Sun, 8.30am-2.30pm. 3€. ☎ (22410) 31 048.

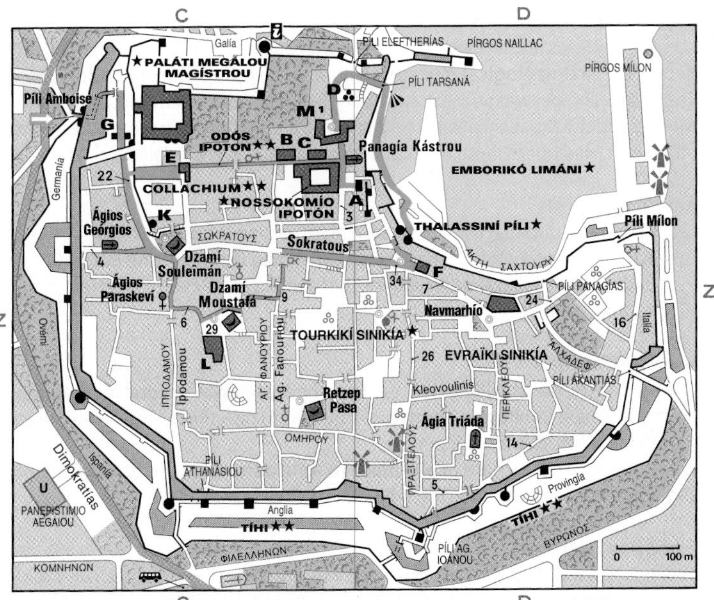

RÓDOS

Street	Grid	No.
Amohostou	AX	2
Apelou	CZ	3
Apolonion	CS	4
Arh. Efthimiou	DZ	5
Arhelaou	CZ	6
Aristotelous	DZ	7
Ergiou	CZ	9
Ethn. Makariou	BX	10
Gr. Lambraki	BX	12
Himaras	AY	13
Ipotón	CZ	
Irinis	DZ	14
Iroon Politehniou	BX	15
Kisthiniou	DZ	16
Konst. Paleologou	BY	18
Meg. Konstandinou	BY	21
Odós Ipotón	CZ	
Orfeos	CZ	22
Pindarou	DZ	24
Pithagora	DZ	26
Pl. Arionos	CZ	29
Pl. Eleftherias	BX	32
Pl. I. Zigdi	BX	33
Pl. Ipokratous	DZ	34
Pl. Kiprou	BX	35
Sof. Venizelou	BX	37
Sokratous	CDZ	
Vas. Irakliou	AY	39

Knights of Rhodes

Founded in the 11C to protect pilgrims in the Holy Land, the Order of the **Hospitallers of St John of Jerusalem**, was both a religious and a military body. In 1291, the Knights of St John had to leave the Holy Land; they moved first to Cyprus then to Rhodes, a Genoese possession, which became their main base in their struggle against the Turks in the eastern Mediterranean.

The knights were divided along national lines – France, Provence, Auvergne, Aragon, Castille, Italy and England. The Order was ruled by the Grand Master; French and Latin were the official languages. The knights took vows of poverty and chastity and were assisted by squires.

When the Knights Templar were suppressed in 1312 and their possessions and duties passed to the Hospitallers, the latter built a fleet which took part in the papal crusades. In 1331 the Hospitallers signed a treaty with the French, the Italians and the Byzantine Emperor against the Turks.

In 1444 and again in 1480 Rhodes was besieged by the Turks but without success. A third siege in 1522 was to signal the end for the knights on Rhodes. For a good six months, 650 knights and about 1 000 auxiliaries held out against an army of 100 000 Turks led by **Suleiman the Magnificent** before surrendering. On 1 January 1523, the Grand Master, **Villiers de l'Isle-Adam** (1464-1534) and the 180 knights who had survived left Rhodes for Malta.

The impressive Knights' Hospital was completed in 1505. Beyond the door a vaulted passageway leads into an inner court; there were shops on the ground floor. Today it houses the **Archaeological Museum**, featuring the **Aphrodite of Rhodes★.**
The hospital proper was on the upper floor. The Great Ward of the Sick could accommodate about 100 patients. Note the chapel entrance, which is carved with festoons, and the alcoves where those with contagious diseases were isolated.

Katálima Ovérnis

Leave Hospital Square by the northwest corner, passing in front of St Mary's Church to reach Platía Alexándrou, a small square containing the **Auvergne Inn** (14C).
Pass under the arch into another square; the fountain at the centre was created out of Byzantine baptismal fonts.

Arméria (Arsenal)

One wing of the main building (14C) contains the **Museum of Decorative Arts** (Diakosmitikí Silogí): furniture, costume and a beautiful collection of Rhodian ceramics *(Open Tue-Sun, 8.30am-2.30pm. 2€).*
Continue north to the ruins of a **Temple to Aphrodite** and then turn right *(east)* through the Arsenal Gate (Píli Navarhíou) onto the harbour quay.

Embório★ (Harbour)

In the days of the Hospitallers the entrance was closed by an enormous chain strung between the square Naillac Tower (Pírgos Naillac), and the Mill Tower (Pírgos Mílon). From the waterfront on the seaward side of the Arsenal Gate there is a fine perspective *(south)* of the ramparts, and the minarets of the Turkish district.

Píli Agías Ekaterínis★

Impressive **St Catherine's** (or **Marine**) **Gate** (1478) has four machicolated towers.

Town★
Bear left through the gate into **Platía Ipokrátous** with its Turkish fountain; on the far side stands the **Lódzia Embóron** (Merchants' Loggia); behind it *(southeast)* lay the Jewish district.

- *Turn west along Odós Sokrátous which marks the northern limit of the Turkish district.*

Turkish district★
After the Aga Mosque turn left on Odós Fanouríou, one of the oldest and most picturesque streets; take the second turn on the right which leads to Platía Aríonos to see the 18C **Mustapha Mosque** (Dzamí Moustafá) and the **Turkish Baths** (16C). Take Odós Arheláou and Odós Ipodámou *(northwest)* past the 15C Church of **Agía Paraskeví** *(left)* to reach the **Suleiman Mosque** (Dzamí Souleimán). Turn off into Odós Apolonion to visit **St George's Church** (Ágios Geórgios) *(nº 18)*.

- *Return along Odós Apolonion and turn left into Odós Orféos passing beneath the Clock Tower or belfry to return to St Anthony's Gate and Amboise Gate.*

Ramparts★★
The rampart walk *(open Tue, Sat 2.45pm; 6€)* covers four sections called boulevards, and assigned respectively to Germany, the Auvergne, Spain and England; the next two boulevards running east to the shore were assigned to Provence and Italy.

Mandráki★
On either side of the entrance to this protected harbour, the Italians erected a column supporting two bronze deer (a buck and a doe), the symbolic animals of Rhodes. According to tradition this was originally the site of the Colossos of Rhodes.
The east mole (three windmills), ends in St Nicholas' Tower (Ágios Nikólaos).

Modern Town
The northern part of the town west of Mandráki was built during the Italian period (1912–1943). Liberty Square (Platía Eleftherías), a lively stretch of waterfront with pleasant gardens, is closed at the southern end by New Market (Néa Agora), and on the north by St John's Church **(Ágios Ioánis)**. Platía Vassilíou Georgíou, the administrative centre, is bordered by the **Governor's Residence** *(Nomarhía)*, the Town Hall *(Dimarhío)* and the theatre. Farther north, the charming **Murad Reis Mosque**★ (Dzamí Mourát Réïs) is surrounded by Muslim tombstones; the graves of the men are distinguished by a turban *(open daily 1-2pm; no charge)*. To the west are a number of pedestrianised streets with hotels and restaurants.

Akrópoli (Mount Smith)
4km/2.5mi or 1hr 30min on foot there and back; nº 5 bus from the New Market.
Several elements of the Ancient city (5C BC) still exist; the theatre (2C BC) – only the lower terrace is authentic – the stadium (2C BC) and the Temple to Pythian Apollo. From the top of Mount Smith there are superb **views**★★, particularly at sunset.

Rodíni Park
2km/1.3mi south: access by nº 3 bus near New Market.
This large, pleasant park is perfect for strolling; there is a small zoo.

Phototravellers/MICHELIN

Kalithéa Spa

Tour

Tour of the Island★★

Around 200km/125mi round trip from Rhodes Town. Allow two days; good hotels in Líndos and Monolithos. The best beaches are marked on the map.

Kalithéa Spa★

15km/9mi along the coast road.

The waters here were recommended by Hippocrates. In 1929 the Italians built a little spa with white pavilions (no longer in use). There is a charming sandy beach.

Beach and Monastery of Tsambíka

Views extend along the coast from the monastery overlooking the sandy beach.

Feraklós Castle

37km/23mi. Drive through the hamlet of Haráki and park the car at the foot of the hill; 45min on foot there and back.

Only a few ruined walls remain of one of the largest castles built by the Knights of St John, but there is a fine **view**★★ of the bays on either side of the promontory.

Líndos★★

49km/31mi. Leave vehicle at the upper parking area, to the right on arrival.

Líndos is a spectacular **site**★★★ bearing the mark of three civilisations – Ancient, Byzantine and medieval Greek. There is also a fine **beach**★ here.

With its two natural harbours and its easily defended hill, Líndos has been inhabited since the prehistoric era. After the Byzantines and the Genoese, came the Knights Hospitaller who built an imposing **fortress** (1503).

Acropolis and citadel★★

Access by a path and steps (1hr on foot or by donkey there and back). Open daily 8am-7pm; off season Tue-Sun 8.30am-2.30pm. 6€.

A long flight of steps and a vaulted passage emerge near St John's Chapel. Take a second vaulted passage under the Governor's palace on the left which emerges below the **acropolis** excavated in the early 20C. About 20 columns mark the position of the great Doric portico (*stoa*) which was preceded by a great staircase leading up to the entrance *(propylaia)* to the Ancient **Sanctuary to Athena Lindia** (4C BC).

From the hilltop there are splendid **views**★★★ of the headland and the coast.

Town★

Souvenir shops and white houses line the narrow streets of the town; the most beautiful houses were built for wealthy ship owners or sea captains in the 16C and the 17C. Some of the internal courtyards have a black and white pebble pattern. The **Church of the Virgin** (Panagía) in the town centre has 17C and 18C frescoes.

Asklipiío

65km/40mi, 4km/2.5mi inland.

Interesting village because of its site, its old houses and its fortress. The church (1060), is decorated with fine frescoes *(for access, inquire at the museum).*

The itinerary continues across a wilder landscape. If time permits, head south of Kattavia; the beach at **Prassonissi** is popular with windsurfers.

Monastery of Skiádi

104km/65mi, 3km/2mi inland.

This restored monastery is of Byzantine origin, but the church is largely modern.

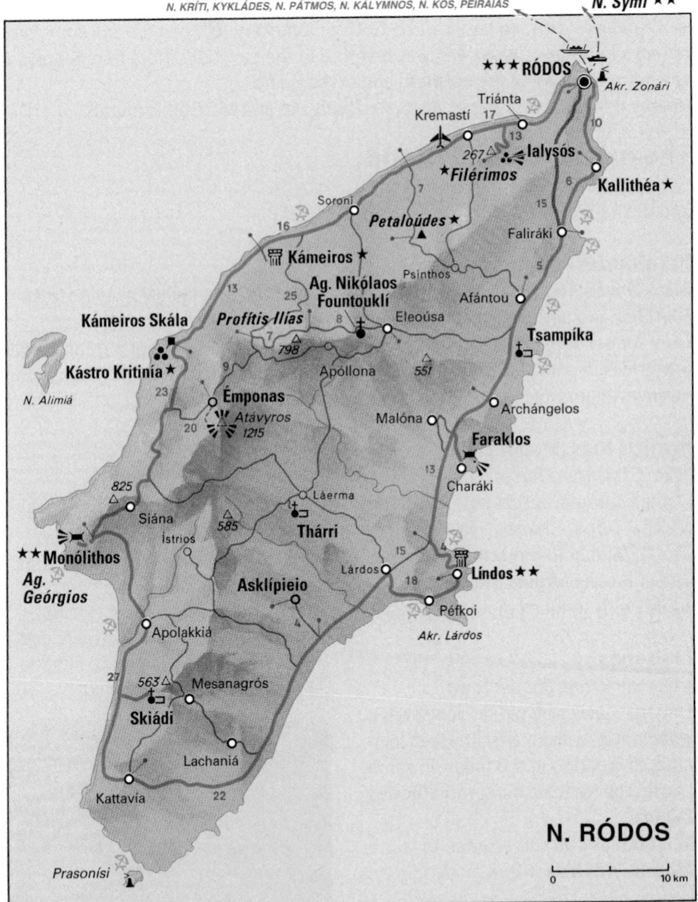

Monólithos Castle★★

121km/76mi. Access by a narrow turning north of Monólithos village.
The Knights of Rhodes built Monólithos Castle on a spectacular **site**★★ at the top of a rocky escarpment. A path leads up to the fortress; the **view** extends across the sea to Hálki Island. Nearby is the attractive beach of **Ágios Georgios**.

Ruins of Kritinía Castle★

144km/90mi. Access by road for 1.2km/0.75mi, then a quarter of an hour on foot.
On a spur over the sea are the ruins of Kritinía Castle; **views**★ from the site.

Ancient Ruins of Kámiros★

157km/98mi. Open Tue-Sun 8am-7.30pm (offseason 8.30am-2.30pm). 4€.
In Antiquity, Kámiros was one of the three great cities of Rhodes. Excavations have brought to light traces of a 3C BC sanctuary consisting of a Doric temple; lower down there is a semicircular seat (exedra), and an area for sacrificial altars; Hellenistic houses, several with peristyles; an agora lined by a long 3C AD portico (stoa), and a temple dedicated to Athena Kamíria, dating from the 5C BC.

Iálissos and Mount Filérimos★

190km/119mi inland.
Founded by the Phoenicians, the Ancient city of **Iálissos** stands on Mount Filérimos, overlooking the coastal plain. On the acropolis are the foundations of a 4C BC temple and a palaeo-Christian basilica. The Gothic monastery *(open Tue-Sun 8am-7pm; offseason 8.30am-2.30pm; 4€)* was restored in the early 20C; from here there is a vast **panorama**★★ of the northern end of the island.
Nearby is St George's Chapel, decorated with 14C and 15C Gothic murals.

The Interior of the Island

Allow at least one day.

Petaloúdes★ (Butterfly Valley)

24km/15mi from Rhodes Town. Open Apr (no charge) & Oct: 8am-4pm; May-Jun & Sep 8am-6pm (3€); Jul-Aug 8am-7pm (5€). Closed offseason. Parking a little out of the way.
From June to September this shady rock-strewn valley is filled with orange and black butterflies. A path climbs up the valley and is carried on wooden bridges over the narrow stream which tumbles in cascades and waterfalls.

Profítis Ilías (Mount Elijah)

49km/31mi from Rhodes Town.
A small summer resort has been built on the upper slopes. To the east, 2km/1.25mi before reaching Eleoússa, is the Church of **Ágios Nikólaos Fountoukli** with some medieval frescoes.

Émbonas

62km/39mi from Rhodes Town.
Émbonas has kept its old-fashioned ways: women in local dress can still be seen spinning, or working in the fields. In some houses the walls are hung with **Rhodes faience**.
In Émbonas you can arrange to climb **Mount Atáviros** with a guide *(6hr on*

Choklakia

On many of the islands of the Dodecanese you will notice decorative mosaic floors made up of black, white and sometimes red tiles. The oldest have geometric motifs; later examples depict flowers or boats. On Hálki, and also on Sími and at Líndos on Rhodes, are some fine floors of this type.

Phototravellers/MICHELIN

foot there and back); from the top, where a Sanctuary to Zeus once stood, there is a fine **view**★.

Monastery of Thári

70km/44mi from Rhodes Town. No charge; appropriate clothing available.
The church has medieval frescoes; fine liturgical chants may often be heard here.

Excursions

Hálki

Lying to the west of Rhodes, this little island has become prosperous as emigrants return, bringing the results of their financial success with them. The restored **harbour** is largely neo-Classical in style. The walk to the abandoned **Monastery of Ágios Ioannis** (*6hr there and back on foot by a road which becomes a track and then a path; take plenty of water and a hat)* is delightful.
From Hálki, you can take a boat to the untouched island of **Alimia**.

Hálki Address Book

GETTING ABOUT

By boat – From **Skála Kámírou**, southwest of **Rhodes Town** *(daily)* and Rhodes Town *(3/wk)*. Also from **Piraeus** *(2/wk summer; 1/wk winter)*.

WHERE TO EAT AND STAY

There are private rooms available and only one hotel; booking in advance is essential.

Maria – *At the harbour.* Good taverna offering local specialities.

Hálki – *At the harbour – ☎ (22460) 45 390 – 29rm.* Balconies with fine views and direct access to the seashore.

TAKING A BREAK

Café Theodosia – *On the harbour.* Ice cream and cakes.

EVENTS AND FESTIVALS

On 29 August, the island celebrates its feast day at the monastery of Ágios Ioannis Alargas.

Kastelórizo (Megísti)

This most eastern of the Greek islands is just a kilometre from the Turkish coast. The island is striking for its attractive beaches and sea caves. The fortified **harbour**, a charming settlement of around 50 neo-Classical houses is dominated by a citadel built by the Knights of Rhodes, and the nearby Megisti Museum displays Byzantine and folk art. *Open Tue-Sun, 8.30am-2.30pm. No charge. ☎ (22410) 49 283.*

Kastelórizo Address Book

GETTING ABOUT

By boat – Ferry service from **Rhodes** *(4/wk in summer)*..
By air – Service from **Rhodes** *(37-seat aircraft; 5/wk)*.

WHERE TO EAT AND STAY

Lazarakis – *At the harbour.* Attractive location. Seafood and fish.

Megisti – *At the harbour – ☎ (22460) 49 272, www.megistihotel.gr.* The only hotel on the island (the other accommodations are guesthouses) and very well maintained. Good view of the Turkish coast from some rooms. Sundeck runs along the shoreline providing direct access to the sea.

The Blue Grotto★

Accessible by boat from the harbour. This magnificent sea cave has a phosphorescent blue tinge. At dusk the stalactites take on a magical hue.

SÍMI★★

Σνμη

POPULATION 2 427

57KM²/22SQ MI – MICHELIN MAP 737 Q 12 – DODECANESE – AEGEAN.

Less than 5km/3mi from the Turkish coast, Sími is a charming, peaceful island. Its rocky mountains rise dramatically from the sea and give it a wild appearance. The island has attractive bays that encourage the visitor to linger and many fine neo-Classical houses. *www.simivisitor.com.*

- **Orient Yourself:** Simi lies 20km northwest of Rhodes. Most beaches are accessible only by boat.
- **Don't Miss:** Simi Town; a swim in a deserted bay or beach.
- **Organizing Your Time:** Plan a two-day stay.

Address Book

For coin categories, see the Legend on the cover flap.

GETTING ABOUT

By boat – Frequent ferry service to **Rhodes** and Kos, in addition to catamarans (all year) and hydrofoils (summer). Also ferry links to **Piraeus** via Kos, Kálimnos and Pátmos.

WHERE TO EAT

Mythos – *On the harbour (Gialós), east quay* – *(22460) 71 488.* One of the best restaurants on the harbour. Fairly windy, but peaceful in the evenings. Fresh fish, carefully prepared dishes.

Mylopetre – *To the left of the square, behind the little bridge – (22460) 72 333.* A peaceful and attractive establishment occupying an old mill. Traditional and modern Mediterranean cuisine. Open evenings only.

WHERE TO STAY

Marika – *Gialós, west quay – (22460)72750/69445 449 81 – 5rm. May-Oct.* Small house just steps from the quay, near the clocktower. No breakfast.

Catherminettes – *Gialós, west quay – (22460) 716 71, marina-epe@rho.forthnet.gr – 6rm.* Elegant, patrician residence (the document declaring the Dodecanese part of Greece wa signed here in 1948). Painted ceilings, balconies offering one of Sími's best views.

Hotel Albatros – *Gialós, alley at centre of the harbour – (22460) 71 829/71 707, www.albatrosymi.gr – 5rm. Apr-Oct.* Recently renovated, this small hotel is spotlessly clean. Helpful management.

Hotel Fiona – *Horió, on the left up the large staircase – and fax (22460) 72 088, symi-vis@otenet.gr – 11rm.* This quiet, clean hotel is in a pleasant location overlooking the sea.

Villa Thalassa – *Gialós, eastern quayside; inquire at the Hotel Albatros – (22460) 71 829/71 707 – 5 apts.* Restored neo-Classical villa, split into a number of apartments (accommodating from two to five persons).

Visit

Sími Town★★

Phototravellers/MICHELIN

The port, Sími

The island's little capital is a triumph of harmony and beauty. Protected by the archaeological authorities, it is composed of two districts: the lively and colourful harbour area, and the upper town with its fine pastel-coloured houses.

Harbour (Gialós)★★

The focus for tourist visitors with many shops, restaurants and hotels. Behind the harbour front is a small **Maritime Museum** with some fine model ships. *Open daily, 11am-2.30pm. 2€.*

Upper Town (Horió)★★

A stairway of 400 steps leads up to this cluster of 18 and 19C neo-Classical houses. The **Simi Museum** (*open Tue-Sun, 10am-2.30pm; 2€*) displays palaeo-Christian statuary, 12C and 13C Byzantine pottery, fine icons and traditional costumes.

Castle

At the top of the hill, this fortress with its church was built by the Knights of Rhodes. From here, there are fine **views**★★ of the sea and the town.

Outskirts of Sími★

The lovely **bay** and **village of Emboriósa**★ *(4km/2.5mi west of Sími Town, 1hr 30min there and back on foot, or by water taxi 10am-2pm, 4-6pm)* offer pleasant walks, and swimming directly off the quay. Also worth a stop is **Pédi**★ *(2km/1.25mi east of Sími Town)* with its charming fishing port and beach.

From Gialós, boats serve the **beaches**★ of Pédi, Georgios Dissalonas, Nano, Marathounda, Agios Vassilios, and Sesklio. Good **walks**★★ along the rocky coast.

Monasteries

The island is richly endowed with monasteries. Some are huge, others tiny. There are some remarkable frescoes to be seen; in the 18C Sími was the centre of a renowned school of religious painting. There are also around 60 chapels.

St Michael Roukouniótis (Ágios Mikhaíl Roukouniótis)

1h on foot from Sími Town, or by vehicle. ☎69777 093 27.

This small monastery has some great treasures; its 14C church (rebuilt in the 16C) houses a fine iconostasis of St Michael made of solid gold and silver.

St Michael of Panormítis (Moní Taxiárhou Mihaíl)

South end of the island. Access by boat (1h) from Sími Town, departing between 10am and 12 pm, returning around 4-5pm. Access by road is difficult.

This huge monastery dedicated to St Michael, patron saint of Sími, is a pilgrimage site which receives very high numbers of visitors during the main religious festivals (Pentecost and 8 November). It is possible to stay here.

The 18C monastery is now surrounded by modern buildings. The church has a fine wooden iconostasis and a **Museum of Religious Art** *(opens to coincide with the boat trips, 1.50€)*, located in a corner of the inner courtyard.

TÍLOS

Τηλοζ

POPULATION 533

63KM²/25SQ MI – MICHELIN MAP 737 P 13 – DODECANESE – AEGEAN.

Lying to the northwest of Rhodes, Tílos is virtually deserted and largely overlooked by tourists. Fairly mountainous, the island has two villages, some Byzantine churches, and sand and shingle beaches. The traditions of religious festivals and folk dances are very much alive here.

Visit

Livadia

This little village has a shingle beach. A tiny harbour is used by fishing boats and the occasional ferry.

Mikrohorio

2km from Livadia by the island's only road.

The abandoned houses of this eerie village were occupied until the 1950s. The village used to have around 1 000 inhabitants.

Megalo Horio

5km from Livadia.

On a hill, the old 'capital' of Tílos was built here for strategic reasons, safe from marauding pirates. It is dominated by a ruined fortress. A small museum *(opening hours vary)* includes dwarf-elephant tusks discovered in the nearby Harkadio cave *(closed to the public)*. Below the village is the little harbour of **Ágios Antonios**.

Beaches

In addition to the one at Livadia, there are two other pleasant beaches. Plaka runs to the west of Ágios Antonios. Eristos, to the south of Megalo Horio, is the largest beach on the island. There are two inlets south of Livadia, at the head of deep bays.

Address Book

GETTING ABOUT

By boat – Ferry service from **Rhodes** *(3-7wk)*; Kos and Kalymnos *(2/wk)*. Also service from **Piraeus** *(1/wk)*.

WHERE TO EAT AND STAY

Blue Sky – *Livadia, on the harbour.* Good quality local cuisine. Inside are some huge wine barrels.

Hotel Irini – *Livadia, set back from the harbour. 41044238. Apr-Oct.* This simple, clean hotel has an attractive garden with swimming pool.

EVENTS AND FESTIVALS

25 to 27 July: **religious festival** at the Monastery of Ágios Pandeleimonas, to the west of Plaka beach.

THE IONIAN ISLANDS★★

POPULATION 197 456
2307KM²/923SQ MI

The landscape of these seven fairly mountainous islands is reminiscent of Italy, with cypresses, vineyards, olive groves and fragrant citrus trees. They lie to the south of the Otranto Channel separating the Adriatic from the Ionian Sea. Well placed for access from the rest of Europe, the Ionians attract visitors year round to their spectacular coastlines, luxuriant flora, white-sand beaches, warm sea temperatures and pleasant climate. Cruising in the Ionian Sea is a great way to discover this region, one of the most beautiful which Greece has to offer.

A Bit of History

The Ionian Islands are the territory of Odysseus, born at Ithaca, and are a key area in the emergence of modern Greece. Their location at the crossroads between the coasts of Greece, Albania and Italy explains much of their troubled history. Cephallonia, Corfu, Leukas, Paxós, Zakynthos and numerous small islets make up the Ionian adminstrative region. The capital is Corfu Town.

Address Book

GETTING ABOUT

BY BOAT

The archipelago is accessible from various Greek ports: Igoumenítsa for Corfu and Paxós, Astakós for Ithaca, Kilíni for Cephallonia and Zakynthos, Patras for the majority of the islands, Gíthio and Nauplion for Kythera. Hopping from island to island can be awkward though. There are numerous services each week from Italy (Ancona, Brindisi, Venice) to Corfu, and you can travel from Kythera to Crete (Kastéli). Leukas is linked to the mainland by a bridge.

BY AIR

The airports on Corfu, Cephallonia and Zakynthos have flights from Athens and Préveza; Corfu's airport has many international flights to Europe.

WHERE TO STAY

See Address Book section for each island. It is wise to book accommodation in advance. Ask to be met at the ferry; most Greeks are happy to do this.

Chabrol B./MICHELIN

Dramatic Cephallonian coastline

KEFALONÍA★★

CEPHALLONIA – Κεφαλλονια

POPULATION 29 400

737KM²/295SQ MI – MICHELIN MAP 737 C 8-9 – IONIAN ISLANDS.

The largest of the Ionian Islands, Cephallonia is formed of jagged hilly limestone. Its landscape is varied: peninsulas, rocky headlands, deep gulfs and sandy beaches. The landscape also includes fertile terraces by the sea and busy beaches along the south coast. The dark peak of Mount Énos (Ainos), one of the highest points in Greece, is covered by a type of spruce tree peculiar to the island. *On the quayside in Argostóli, ☎ (26710) 24 466. www.ionion.com.*

- **Orient Yourself:** Cephallonia is served by ferries from Patras and there are numerous links with neighbouring islands, notably Ithaca and Leukas. Note that there is more than one port. It's best to rent a car to explore the island.
- **Don't Miss:** A swim at Mirtós or Pétani; a climb up Mt. Énos
- **Organizing Your Time:** Count on a four-day stay.
- **Also See:** Hlemoútsi, Párga, Itháki, Lefkáda, Zákinthos

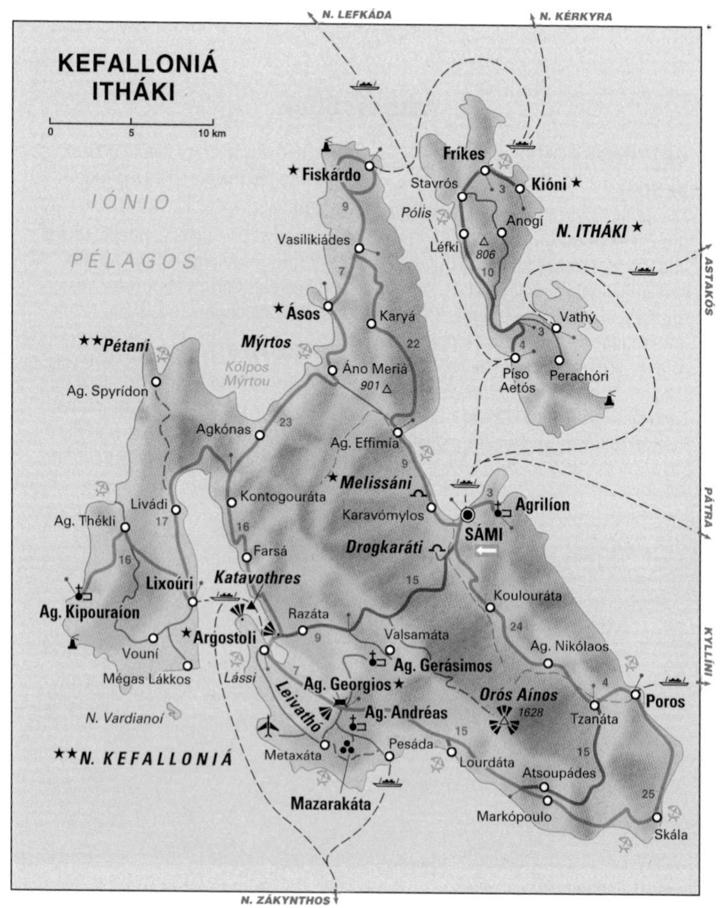

Address Book

For coin categories, see the Legend on the cover flap.

GETTING ABOUT

BY BOAT

Ferry service to Patras (*2/day summer 1/day winter*), to Kilini (*2/day*). There is no direct link to Corfu; to get there it is necessary to return to Patras on the mainland (via Kílini). Boats for Zakynthos leave from Pessáda (*2/day summer, 1/week winter*). For Ithaca (departing from Sámi): links with Pisso Aetós and Vathí. From Sámi, a large ferry crosses to Patras (*2/day summer, 1/day winter*). There is one boat a day from Fiskárdo to Vassilikí on Leukas. Timetables vary over the course of the year; information is available from travel agents.

BY AIR

(27610) 42000. There is a flight (*not every day*) from Athens via Zakynthos. Book well in advance. Taxi service between the airport and Argostóli.

WHERE TO EAT

Zorbas – *Lixoúri, corner of Odós Grigoríou and Odós 25 Martíou.* This establishment benefits from a large, shady courtyard. Attentive service. Greek cuisine including fried fish, *skordaliá, saganáki* and other specialities.

To Arkotikon - *5 Odós Pizospatou* - *(2710) 272 13*. On Platía Valianou, this pretty restaurant serves up fresh, tasty dishes. Swift service, and a large selection of Greek wines.

Fótis – *Póros, in a corner of the seafront square. (27640) 729 72. Open May-Oct.* A delightful two-storey terrace, looking directly onto the beach and the square. Good home cooking and friendly welcome. Rooms also available to let at the other end of the beach.

Tselendí – *Fiskárdo, set back from the harbour in a pleasant little square.* Occupying one of the finest houses in the village; magnificent dining room with an excellent bar. A good place for breakfast too.

WHERE TO STAY

Hotel Olga – *Argostóli, 82 Odós Antoni Tritsi* – *(26710) 24 981 to 984 – 43rm* – . A blue-shuttered façade, well situated behind the palm trees that line the promenade. Friendly welcome; spotless and spacious rooms with pleasant little balconies. Buffet breakfast. Bar. Good value.

Hotel Mirabel – *Argostóli, Platía Valiánou* – *(26710) 25 381 to 383, mirabel@compulink.gr – 33rm.* A well-located hotel with clean, spacious and pleasantly furnished rooms each with a terrace (some overlook the square and can be noisy). Friendly welcome from the proprietor; open year-round.

Hotel Oceanis – *Póros* – *(26740) 72 581/582, www.hoteloceanis.gr – 24rm.* Perched on the rocky promontory beyond the ferry port, this hotel has superb views. Friendly management; spacious and bright rooms with balconies and fridges.

Hotel Sámi Beach – *Karavómilos, to the west of Sámi, at the far end of the large beach* – *(26740) 22 802/824, fax (26740) 22 846, info@samibeachhotel.gr – 94rm.* A lovely place to stay; family atmosphere, despite the size and luxury of the place. The bright, pleasantly furnished rooms are well presented and comfortable, with good bathrooms. Large swimming pool, bar and table-tennis; games for kids.

Kanakis Apartments – *Assos* – *(27640) 51631 – 6rm.* Spacious apartments for 2-4 guests; tastefully decorated. Terrace with splendid views of the sea and the fort. Swimming pool.

TAKING A BREAK

In Argostóli, the **Rock Café** (on the quayside just before the promenade lined with palm trees) has modern decor. More authentic cafés are to be found in the pedestrian precinct (Lithóstrotos) including **Café K**, the **Metropolis** and the **Antika**, or in Platía Valiánou, which is very lively at night.

SHOPPING

Market – Lively open-air market takes place daily in summer near the quayside.

A Bit of History

Archaeological evidence speaks to habitation here 50 000 years ago; in the 5C BC, Thucydides records four large cities here. From the Middle Ages to the mid-19C dominance of Cephallonia passed among French, Turkish and Italian occupiers. In 1864 the island became part of the Greek State.

Chabrol B./MICHELIN

Louis de Bernieres's popular novel, *Captain Corelli's Mandolin* (film by John Madden), records the World War II history of Cephallonia.

In 1953 an earthquake caused severe damage throughout the island; only the village of Fiskárdo was left with its traditional Venetian architecture intact. Afterwards, a large number of inhabitants moved to the mainland to escape further disasters.

Driving Tour

Around the Island★★

Allow two days to include visiting sites and beaches. Around 200km/125mi.

Sámi

On the east coast, the port of Sámi has connections with Corfu, Paxós, Leukas and Patras. Destroyed in the 1953 earthquake, it was subsequently rebuilt, and nestles in a gently curving bay.

There is a fine view of the narrow entry to the bay and of the stark coast of Ithaca.

Drogaráti Cave

2km/1.25mi southwest of Sámi; take the road to Argostóli and after 2km/1.25mi turn right into a track. Open daily May to Oct, 9am-7pm. 3.50€.

A flight of 166 steps leads down into this cave, which is easy to explore. Among the beautiful concretions are some enormous stalagmites.

Head towards the northeast coast.

Melissáni Cave★

Open daily May to Oct, 9am-7pm: winter, weekends, 10am-4pm. 5€. (26740) 229 97.

This underground lake, which receives its water via subterranean passages from the swallow-holes near Argostóli (*see below*), is explored by boat. The intensity and variety of the colours of the water, and the resonance and echo make for a surreal effect.

Just before reaching Fiskárdo, the route from Sami offers a magnificent **view**★★ over the sea and of Ithaca and Leukas.

Fiskárdo★

This charming sheltered port at the extreme north of the island was largely spared by the earthquake in 1953 and has therefore kept its character.

Heading south, the road as far as Ássos has remarkable views, taking in both the sea and the mountains.

Ássos★

This fishing village on the west coast, in an enchanting **site★★**, lies at the neck of a hilly peninsula crowned with a Venetian fortress (16C). The little port and its square surrounded by flower-bedecked houses, all backdropped by a mountain, make Ássos one of the most charming places in Cephallonia.
Farther on, the winding corniche road has fine **views★★** of the Ássos Peninsula, the Gulf of Mirtós and the Ionian Sea.

Mirtós Beach

Probably the best on the island *(very busy in summer)*. with turquoise waters set against majestic white cliffs.

3km after Angónas, turn right towards the Paliki Peninsula.

Known as the Garden of Cephallonia, this is a landscape of vineyards, olive groves and fruit trees.

Lixoúri

The island's second town, with a busy port dating from the 1960s. Behind its modern seafront, the streets are lined with restaurants and shops.

Pétani Beach★★

To the northwest of Lixoúri, this attractive bay is tucked between tall white cliffs.

Monastery of Ágios Kipouríon

Occupying a magnificent site on the edge of a precipice, this little monastery is surrounded by vineyards and olive groves.

Argostóli★

The capital of the island is located on a promontory in a fjord-like bay. The main approach is over a bridge *(closed to traffic)* which crosses the Koútavos Lagoon.
After the earthquake in 1953 Argostóli lost its Greco-Venetian atmosphere. It features an attractive seafront and a large pedestrian area. The **Church of Ágios Spirídon** has a fine iconostasis in carved wood. A small **Archaeological Museum** displays local finds *(open Tue-Sun, 8.30am-3pm, ☎ (26710) 28 300. 3€)*.
A **museum of history and traditions★** houses costumes, documents, decorative arts and artists' workshops *(open Tue-Sun and public holidays 9am-2pm; ☎ (26710) 288 35; 3€)*.

Swallow-holes (katavóthres)

Near the end of the promontory the sea flows into a fissure, reappearing on the other side of the island in the Melissáni Cave. The hydraulic power thus created was harnessed to power mills; one of these, with paddle wheel, is on view.

The Livathó Plain

Ancient olive groves cover this area of innumerable small villages lying to the south of Argostóli. Along the coast are a number of busy beaches.

Ágios Geórgios★

Undergoing restoration; visit not always possible.
Until 1757 St George's Castle was the capital of the island; among the ruins are traces of St George's collegiate church.

A Bit of Advice

To whet the appetite: The local specialities include delicious **robola wine**, the bottles wrapped in jute sacking, and little meat delicacies made with rice and thyme-flavoured honey.

From the castle there are fine **views★** of the Livathó Plain, the Lixoúri Peninsula and Zakynthos.

Monastery of Ágios Andréas

Open daily, 9am-1.30pm and 5-8pm. No charge.

South of Peratáta, this monastery (also called Moní Milapidion) has a remarkable church with frescoes, a fine iconostasis and icons painted on wood and metal.

Ruins of Mazarakáta

Close to the monastery of Ágios Andréas, this is the only Ancient site of significance on the island. This Mycenaean necropolis has many tombs hewn out of the rock.
The southeast of the island has some fine beaches: Káto Kateliós, Kamínia Potamákia and most importantly Skála, bordered by dense pine woods.

Póros

This resort town with a small ferry port is located in a rocky bay.

The Mountain★★

A 40km/25mi round trip from Sámi.

▸ *Take the Argostóli road which heads over the mountain. After about 10km/6mi turn left towards Mount Énos.*

Mount Énos

2h there and back on foot from the TV masts.

Hikers and lovers of scenery will enjoy ascending this mountain, one of the highest in Greece (1 628m/5 941ft). The area is Greece's smallest national park.
The route passes an observatory, then leads up to the gates of the nature reserve *(allow 35min of gentle climbing)*. Leave vehicles at the bend opposite the transmission masts and take the path to thesouth (left). At the next signpost on the right, a well marked footpath (yellow and green) makes its way up. From the summit (marked by a cairn) the **view★** of the island is breathtaking.

Ágios Gerássimos

Between Valsamáta and Mikhata, to the south of Mount Énos. Variable opening hours, 8am-1pm, 4-8pm.

This restored 16C monastery occupies an impressive site on the mountainside. The modern church, built in the Byzantine style, is decorated with frescoes.

KÉRKIRA★★★

CORFU – Κερκυρα

POPULATION 109 537

593KM²/237SQ MI – MICHELIN MAP 737 K 9 – IONIAN ISLANDS.

Corfu, which lies between the Italian Peninsula and the Greek world, is the jewel of the Ionian Islands: luxuriant gardens, rocky bays, large sandy beaches, and a mild climate make it a popular year-round destination. Fashionable in the 19C with the European aristocracy (most notably the Empress Sisi), it has retained its cosmopolitan character. *Platia San Rocco. ☎ (26610) 207 73. www.corfuhomepage.com*

- **Orient Yourself:** Corfu lies at the northern end of the archipelago near Albania. There are ferries from Patras, Igoumenítsa and numerous Italian ports (Otranto, Brindisi, Venice).
- **Don't Miss:** The old town of Corfu, the Achilleion (Ahílio)
- **Organizing Your Time:** Plan a good four days to visit and soak in the Italian ambience.
- **Also See:** Párga

A Bit of History

In the *Odyssey* Homer tells how Odysseus, marooned on Corfu, was feted before his return to Ithaca. In the 8C BC the Corinthians founded a colony on the island, which became known as Corcyra. It came under Venetian control in the 14C.
For some three centuries the Venetians imposed their rule on Corfu, beating back several incursions by the Turks. Italian became the official language, Roman Catholicism held a privileged position, and many of the monuments visible today were erected.

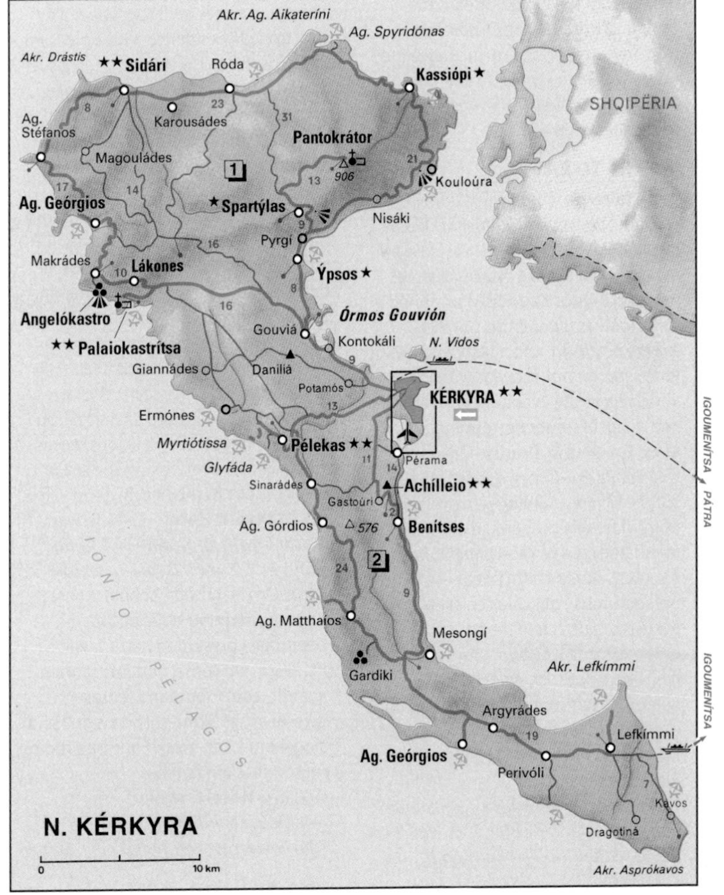

Address Book

For coin categories, see the Legend on the cover flap.

GETTING ABOUT

BY BOAT

The ferry port is to the north of the Old Town. Ferries serve Igoumenítsa (hourly), Patra (1/day) and Paxos (1/day summer); hydrofoil service to Paxos (3/day summer/ 1/day winter). Numerous ferry links exist with Italy: Venice (4/week), Ancona and Brindisi (1/day) and Bari (3/week). Tickets can either be purchased at the port, or from travel agencies in town.

BY AIR

The international airport is just to the south of Corfu Town. ☎ *(26610) 30 180.* There are several Athens flights each day (50min), and many direct charter flights from the big European cities. Taxis and buses to the airport leave from various parts of town. Airsealines offers seaplane service to Ioannina and Paxos ☎ *(26610) 498 00, www.airsealines.com.*

WHERE TO EAT

Taverna Ninos – *Corfu Town, 46 Odós Sebastianoú (corner of Odós M Theotóki).* ☎*(26610) 461 75. Closed Sunday.* On a terrace in a small street parallel to Odós Kapodistríou. Simple, fresh food and generous portions: *sofrito, pastitsad,* and a tasty andouillette *(gargouma).* Popular with locals and lively in the evenings, with a well-known local singer performing.

Taverna O. Boúlis – *Lákones. Open daily Apr-Oct.* ☎ *(26630) 494 29.* Simple taverna serving generous portions of freshly prepared dishes indoors or outside on a terrace: *tzatzíki, keftédes* (rissoles), *saganáki* (fried cheese in breadcrumbs), delicious chicken and perfectly barbecued meats.

Taverna Lagoon – *Ágios Spirídonas. Open May-Oct.* ☎ *(26630) 983 33.* A large beachfront terrace serving up excellent fresh-fish kebabs and grilled fish dishes. Fine views of the nearby Albanian coast.

Taverna Kouloúra – *Kouloúra, northeast side of the island.* ☎ *(26630) 912 53. Closed late Oct-early April.* An attractive terrace overlooking the peaceful harbour. Delicious fish specialities. Pleasant welcome and ambience.

The Venetian Well – *Corfu Town, Platía Kremastí* – ☎ *(26610) 44 761 – closed Sun.* Overlooking a small, flower-filled square, this has to be the most attractive restaurant terrace in Corfu. Refined menu, an excellent combination of Greek and Italian gastronomy. Delicious swordfish kebabs with walnut ... ideal for a romantic dinner. Booking essential.

WHERE TO STAY

Hotel Bella Venezia – *Corfu Town, 4 Odós N Zambélli* – ☎ *(26610) 46 500 – www.bellavenezia.com – 31rm.* A charming hotel with smart Italianate decoration (coffered ceilings, some rooms with tester beds) occupying an attractive 19C residence with a pleasant planted terrace.

Hotel Golden Fox – *Lákones, to the northwest of Corfu Town. –* ☎ *(26630) 49 101/2, www.corfugoldenfox.com – 10 apartments – open May-Oct.* This white-painted hotel overlooking Paleokastrítsa has comfortable apartments with kitchenettes and balconies (superb views). Book in advance. Restaurant offers vegetarian dishes. A very pleasant ambience.

Hotel Neféli – *Dafníla, northwest of Corfu Town. –* ☎ *(26610) 91 033, www.hotelnefeli.com – 45rm.* A charming ochre and white neo-Classical hotel set among olive trees. Spacious rooms with balconies overlooking the sea or the hills. Close to the beach, good value.

Levant Hotel – *Pélekas, west of Corfu Town* – ☎ *(26610) 94 230, fax (26610) 94 115, www.levant-hotel.com – 25rm.* On the hillside behind 'Sunset' village. A charming hotel occupying a beautifully presented neo-Classical villa. Warm welcome, good restaurant, romantic, cool rooms and fantastic views. Beaches 3km/2mi away, golf and riding 4km/2.5mi away. Four-bed rooms to accommodate families.

Hotel Cavalieri – *Corfu Town, Odós Kapoditríou 4 –* ☎ *(26610) 39 041, www.cavalieri-hotel.com – 50rm.*

The most luxurious establishment in the Old Town, occupying a 17C building decorated in Anglo-Venetian style. Splendid sea view, panoramic bar.
Érmones Golf Hotel – *Ermones, west of Corfu Town – ☎ (26610) 94 045/942 26, www.hotels-corfu.gr/ermones-golf-hotel – 41rm.* Two attractively decorated buildings laid out around a pleasant swimming pool. Big rooms with balconies and sea views, just up from the beach.
Menigos Hotel – *Glifáda, west of Corfu Town – ☎ (26610) 95 074, – 163 apartments.* Large bungalows built on terraces above the beach, some with big gardens. All are different, furnished and well equipped; balconies with sea views. Small swimming pool, supermarket, snack bar, and tennis courts available at nearby hotel.

TAKING A BREAK

In Corfu-Town, stop in at **Ta Olympia**, *(open daily 7am-2am)* with grand woodwork and Art-Deco furnishings. Also stop at **Arte Cafe** *(garden of the Palace of St. Michael and St. George, daily 9am-1pm)*, a lovely terrace amid cypress and jasmine is a good place to sample salads or cold dishes.

Phototravellers/MICHELIN
Fruit stall in the Old Town

Hotel Cavalieri – *Corfu Town, 4 Odós Kapodistríou*, to the south of the seafront in the direction of Garítsa Bay. The panoramic sixth floor terrace has splendid views over the town and the sea (especially striking at dusk). Open from 6pm; dress code (no shorts).
Nightclubs – All the trendy techno-music clubs are located in Corfu Town's northern suburb of Mandoúki, beyond the new port. Some are worth a visit for their ambitious decor, particularly the extravagant **Apocalypsi**.

France, Russia and Turkey all vied for control until 1818, when the Ionian Islands were granted independent status as a British protectorate. In 1863, the islands were ceded to Greece.
In the late 19C, Corfu became a playground for Europe's aristocracy, most notably Empress Elisabeth of Austria. Her fine residence (the Achilleion) is open to visitors.

Touring

The Beaches of Corfu

These are numerous and magnificent, but very busy in summer, the majority of them disappearing under parasols and sun loungers. Watersports are very popular. Those listed below are some of the island's finest; they are marked on the map and appear here in clockwise order starting from Corfu Town.

- **Benítses**: a popular tourist beach facing the coast of Epiros.
- **Vitaládes**: a long strip of sand at the foot of a cliff.
- **Ágios Geórgios**: sandy beach with compacted, rock-like dunes.
- **Paramóna**: west-facing beach below the attractive village of Ágios Matthéos.
- **Ágios Górdis**: 5km/3mi-long beach.
- **Pélekas**: below the village of the same name,and surrounded by rocks.
- **Mirtidiótissa**: This inaccessible little beach lies in an attractive bay.
- **Paleokastrítsa**: Numerous beautiful coves but very busy *(see below)*.
- **Ágios Geórgios**: Shares the same name as a beach to the south.
- **Arílas, Ágios Stéfanos**: Windy beaches set among rocks and green hillsides.

- **Perouládes**: Narrow strip of sand dominated by grey and ochre cliffs.
- **Sidári**: Many coves in a beautiful rocky setting.
- **Ágios Spirídonas**: Facing nearby Albania, a wild and striking beach.
- **Ípsos, Dassiá**: Big resorts with fine beaches.

Visit

Kérkira★★ (Corfu Town)

The old town of Corfu, between two huge citadels, has narrow streets, tiled roofs and cypress trees,evocative of Italy. There is also a significant British influence, most notable around the Spianáda, which is the hub of activity in Corfu Town *(see below)*.

Palace of St Michael and St George

Open daily 8.30am-7.30pm (3pm in winter). 3€. ☎(22610) 304 43.

Built in 1819 as the British High Commissioner's official residence, the palace features a fresco cycle depicting the *Odyssey*; a the throne room and banqueting hall. Today it houses the **Museum of Asiatic Art**★ containing urns, bronzes, rare lacquers, ceramics, engravings and Japanese screens; also beautiful 17C and 18C icons.

From the seafront head left around the palace; this leads into an attractive parade of old houses, looking northwards out to sea and the shores of Albania and Epiros.

Old Prefecture (Palaiá Nomarhía)

A 19C building typical of the architectural style of the British Protectorate.

Byzantine Museum (Vizandinó Moussio)

Open Tue-Sun 8.30am-3pm. 2€ (combined ticket with Asiatic and Archaeological Museums). ☎ (26610) 383 13. In the Church of Panagía Antivouniotissa.

A very fine collection of 16C and 17C icons.

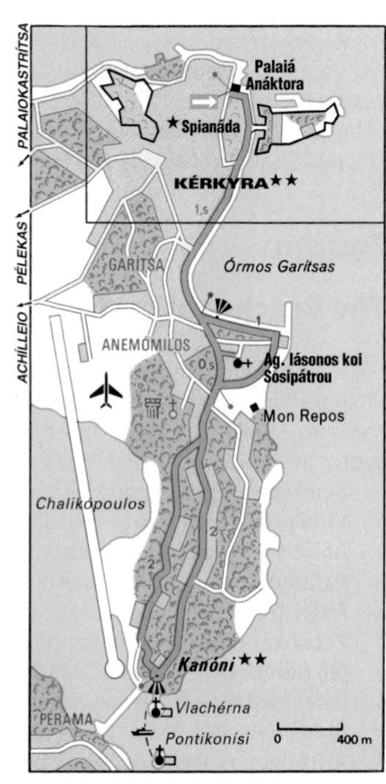

Panagía Spileótissa

Built on the seafront, this imposing Renaissance features some fine icons (16-18C).

Odós Donzelót, lined with fine houses, leads down to the square and quayside of the old port.

New Fort (Néo Froúrio)

Open 9am-10pm. 2€. ☎(22610) 273 30.

Built on a hillside in the 16 and 17C, the Neo Frourio is on an impressive scale.

Paleá Póli★ (Old Town)

This district has enormous charm: narrow streets, little paved squares, elegant church façades and high arcaded houses.

Follow Odós Solomou, then the shopping street Odós Nikifórou Theotokí, at the top of which is the 14C Church of Ágios Andónios (inside is a fine 18C baroque iconostasis). Turn left halfway along this street.

Ágios Spiridónas

This 16C church is dedicated to St Spiridon, a 4C Cypriot bishop who became the patron saint of Corfu. A chapel houses the silver coffin containing the mummified body of the saint. It is solemnly paraded round the town on the Orthodox feasts of Palm Sunday, Holy Saturday, 11 August and the first Sunday in November.

Panagía ton Xénon

Southeast of St Spiridon's Church is a charming little square flanked by the Church of Our Lady of Strangers, featuring a fine decorated ceiling.

Ágios Ioánnis Pródromos

This church has a pink façade and a fine marble iconostasis.

Town Hall

In Platía Dimaríhou, this 17C building, formerly the theatre, is decorated with carved medallions and is one of the finest Venetian monuments of Corfu.
Return towards the seafront, passing the remarkable Ricci House, a fine Venetian residence.

Spianáda★

Once an open space for drilling soldiers, the Spianáda (or Platía) is liberally adorned with commemorative monuments and statues. Very busy in the evenings. To the south are fine **views**★ of the old citadel, the sea and the coast of Epiros.

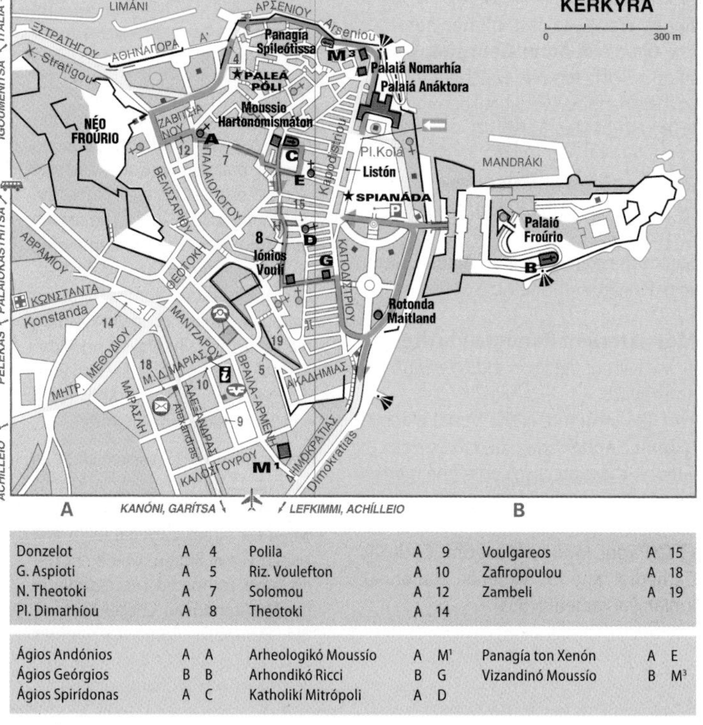

Donzelot	A	4	Polila	A	9	Voulgareos	A	15
G. Aspioti	A	5	Riz. Voulefton	A	10	Zafiropoulou	A	18
N. Theotoki	A	7	Solomou	A	12	Zambeli	A	19
Pl. Dimarhíou	A	8	Theotoki	A	14			

Ágios Andónios	A	A	Arheologikó Moussío	A	M¹	Panagía ton Xenón	A	E
Ágios Geórgios	B	B	Arhondikó Ricci	B	G	Vizandinó Moussío	B	M³
Ágios Spirídonas	A	C	Katholikí Mitrópoli	A	D			

Phototravellers/MICHELIN

Ágios Stéfanos beach

The west side of the Spianáda is lined by the '**Liston**', an arcaded terrace housing restaurants and bookshops; it was inspired by the rue de Rivoli in Paris.

The Spianáda also incorporates the Corfu **cricket pitch**. The game arrived here during the British Protectorate and Corfiots have played it with enthusiasm ever since.

Paleó Froúrio

Open daily 8am-7pm in summer, 8.30am-3pm in winter. 4€ (combined ticket with Archaeological, Byzantine and Asiatic museums: 8€). ☎ (26610) 483 10.

Separated from the Spianáda by a canal, the **Ancient Citadel** is sited on a rocky promontory. By the Middle Ages fortifications were already established here.

The Church of **Ágios Geórgios**, resembling a Doric temple, was built in 1830, and the barracks (Venetian) dominate the little port of Mandráki.

Archaeological Museum★

Open Tue-Sun 8.30am-3pm. 3€. ☎ (26610) 306 80.

Star of the collection is an Archaic **pediment**★★ from the Temple of Artemis.

Monastery of Panagía Platitéra

To the west of the town, Odós Polihroníou Konstandá.

This 19C structure is the burial place of Ioánnis Kapodístrias, first President of Greece; there are also some fine **icons**★ here.

Paper Money Museum; Catholic Cathedral (fine 15C Venetian Madonna); Ionian Parliament (1855).

Cricket in Greece

The first game of cricket in Greece was played on Corfu in April 1823 between officers of the Royal Navy and officers of the garrison, who were stationed there under the British Protectorate of the Ionian Islands (1814-63). Twelve years later there were two Corfiot teams to challenge the British visitors. Two clubs survived after the British left.

After the Second World War, amateur teams began scheduling regular matches in Corfu and the Anglo-Corfiot Cricket Association was founded in 1970-71. The season runs from April or May, depending on the weather, to the end of October. During those months there is a daily game; matches against visiting teams are usually played on Monday, Wednesday, Saturday and Sunday between 3pm and 8pm (2pm and 7pm in April and October).

There are now 15 cricket clubs in Greece: 13 on Corfu, one in Athens and one in Thessaloníki. Since 1966, when the Greek national team first visited Great Britain, Greek cricketers have competed successfully in the Mediterranean Cricket Festival, the European Clubs Champions Cup, European Nations Cup and European Indoor Championship.

Excursions

The South of the Island★★

Around 100km/63mi; allow one day.
Less mountainous than the north, this part of Corfu features many beaches, some excellent panoramic viewpoints and the Achilleion, Empress Sisi's villa.

Walk to Kanóni★★

4km/2.5mi south of Corfu Town.
Follow the attractive curve of Garítsa Bay as far as the suburb of Anemómilos, where the villas are surrounded by gardens. From here, there is a fine **view**★★ over the bay, the Ancient Citadel and the coasts of Albania and Epiros.
Bear right into Odós Iássonou Sossípatrou which leads to a 12C Byzantine church, **Ágios Iássonas-Sossípatros** *(open daily 9am-3pm; no charge)*. In the narthex are four fine 17C icons.
The road, which is narrow and congested, skirts the villa known as **Mon Repos** *(open 8am-7pm; no charge)* surrounded by a park and standing on the site of the Ancient acropolis of Corcyra. Prince Philip, Duke of Edinburgh, was born there in 1921.
Kanóni is one of Corfu's best known landmarks. From the gun emplacement there is a **view**★★ down onto the Monastery of Vlahérna (17C) and beyond it to the circular Mouse Island (Pondikoníssi), which also has a monastery. Vlahérna is accessible on foot, and Pondikoníssi by boat from Vlahérna.

Ahílio(Achilleio)★★

12km/7mi south of Corfu Town. Open daily, 8am-7pm. 6€. ☎(26610)562 10.
An imposing neo-Classical villa, the **Achilleion** was built in 1890 for Empress **Elisabeth of Austria**, who in 1898 was assassinated by an Italian anarchist. It is dedicated to Achilles, hero of the *Iliad*. Its large rooms are decorated with frescoes and Ancient motifs, and there are many items associated with the Empress on view.
The Italian terraced gardens are adorned with statues including *The Dying Achilles* (1884) by the German sculptor Herter, and a huge bronze of *Achilles the Victor*.
From the upper terrace extend views of the island and of the Albanian coast.

Benítses

13km/8mi south of Corfu Town.
Typical fishing village and seaside resort. There is also the head of an aqueduct built by the British to supply water to Corfu Town.

Pélekas★★

13km/8mi west of Corfu Town.
Stop to admire the superb **panoramic view**★★ of the centre of the island.

The North of the Island★★

Paleokastrítsa★★

25km/16mi northwest of Corfu Town.
This very popular seaside resort is located in a magnificent **bay**★★ at the foot of a steep hillside. The ochre rocks of the coastline are broken up into half a dozen sandy creeks, one of which provides a harbour.
The road runs to the end of the promontory where the monastery of Paleokastrítsa was founded in the 13C; the present buildings date from the 18C. *Open daily Apr-Oct 7am-1pm, 3-8pm; appropriate attire provided.*

▶ *Head back along the Corfu town road; turn left towards Lákones.*

A terrace beyond the village of **Lákones** *(sign 'Parking')* provides an extraordinary **view**★★ of the many rocky inlets in Paleokastrítsa Bay.

▶ *Continue towards Kríni.*

Before entering the village bear left into a narrow road to Angelókastro, which leads to a hamlet and then to a restaurant. Leave the car here and take the path to the ruins of **Angelókastro** *(1hr there and back on foot),* a 13C Byzantine fortress, from which stretch splendid **views**★★ of the coast.

Ágios Geórgios Beach

North of Paleokastrítsa.

In a rocky bay, this sandy beach is one of the island's finest.

Sidári★★

39km/24mi north of Corfu Town.

This little resort at the northern end of the island is on a stretch of coast unusual for its curious **rock formations**★★. The sea has caused erosion, creating rocky inlets, some with little beaches, islets and promontories resembling piles of ruins and caves and caverns where the sea rushes in.

Kassiópi★

38km/24mi north of Corfu Town.

This charming fishing port and resort is approached by a spectacular **corniche road**★ which goes to Koloúra. Remarkable views of the Albanian coast.

Spartílas★

26km/16mi north of Corfu Town.

The road loops its way up through the olive groves, providing fine views of the island scenery and the Epiros coast.

Pandokrátor Monastery

34km/21mi north of Corfu Town. Open daily Apr-Oct 7am-12.30pm, 2.30-8pm. Appropriate attire provided.

On the island's highest point, the monastery has a marvellous **view**★ over desert-like, almost lunar, plateaux to one side; sea, coastline and Albanian lakes to the other.

Ípsos (Ypsos)★

17km/11mi north of Corfu Town.

This pleasant resort is situated on the edge of a huge sandy bay that is ideal for all watersports: bathing, sailing, water-skiing etc.

Órmos Gouvión

9km/5.5mi north of Corfu Town.

Sheltered and gently curving, Gouviá Bay is very popular.

Excursions

Paxós★

Lying to the south of Corfu, this quiet island is the smallest (25km²/10sq mi) in the Ionian archipelago. Popular but not teeming, it is renowned for its olive oil, and its mountainous slopes are covered by olive groves. Its three small ports have retained their character, and its pebble beaches are never crowded, even in high summer.

Paxós Address Book

For coin categories, see the Legend on the cover flap.

GETTING ABOUT

By boat – Flying Dolphins offers hydrofoil service from Corfu Town (3/day summer, 1/day winter); the same hydrofoil sometimes runs to Igoumenítsa. There is a daily ferry service (passengers and cars) from Corfu (1/day summer). A passenger-only boat runs between Gáïos and Párga (1/day). There is a ferry and bus link between Gáïos and Athens (3/week). Hours vary, so consult a travel agency or the harbour police, ☎ *(26620) 32 259.*

WHERE TO EAT

Taverna Basílis – *Logós.* ☎ *(26620) 300 62.* In a pretty yellow house with stone floors. Fresh fish, lobster and mussels served on the waterfront terrace.

WHERE TO STAY

Private rooms are available in Gáïos, Logós and Láka. Booking is essential; prices are high in season. Everything closes from October to April.

Hotel Paxos Beach *– 1km/0.6mi from Gáïos –* ☎ *(26620) 32 211, www.paxosbeachhotel.gr – 42rm.* A peaceful hotel of stone bungalows set among trees by a private beach. Bright, clean rooms with rattan furniture. Reservations essential. Mini golf and games area.

Gáïos

With beautiful houses, a carefree atmosphere, and yachts dotting the bay, Gáïos is reminiscent of Venice. The bay is protected by two tiny islands: **Ágios Nikólaos**, a nature reserve with the ruins of a Venetian chateau; and Moní Panagía, crowned with a small monastery, *(reached by boat; only open on 15 August).*

Longos

A small village, with a small port and pleasant tavernas.

Laka

Situated at the far end of the island, this charming little port features authentic tavernas and a small-scale aquarium. *Open Jul-Aug, 10am-2pm, 7pm-10.30pm. 3€.*

Antípaxos★

South of Paxós; access by boat (2hrs) from Gáïos. Departs 10am, 11am and noon; returns at 5.30pm and 6.30pm; information available near the port.

The **boat trip**★★ to Antipaxos offers a marvelous chance to see Paxos' magnificent setting: pebbly beaches, cliffs, rocky outcrops, marine caves and arches carved out by the waves.

Given over to vineyards and market gardening, Antípaxos is Paxós's garden. There are also some fine sandy **beaches**★.

KÍTHIRA★★

KYTHERA – Κυθηρα

POPULATION 3 000

284KM²/114SQ MI – MICHELIN MAP 737 H 13 – IONIAN ISLANDS.

Mythical home of Aphrodite, goddess of love, Kythera presents two differing faces. Its northern landscape is composed of heath and pine woods; in the south there are wild gorges full of myrtles. Villages on Kythera have the striking whitewashed walls which are the norm in the nearby Cyclades.

- **Orient Yourself:** Kythera lies just off Cape Malea (Ákri Maléas). There are three ports: Agía Pelagía (to the north), Diakófti (northeast) and Kapsáli (south).
- **Don't Miss:** The ruins at Milopotamos and Paleohóra; Agía Sofía cave.
- **Organizing Your Time:** It's best to have a car here; plan 3-4 days to visit.

A Bit of History

The cult of Aphrodite, goddess of love, seems to have arrived on Kythera with the Phoenicians, who came here to collect the murex, a shellfish which yields a purple dye. Several temples to Aphrodite were built, but almost nothing remains. Kythera has been a rich source of inspiration for numerous artists and poets, including Watteau and Baudelaire. To the south, in the waters off the island of **Antikythera**, an Ancient wreck was discovered in 1900; the ship contained the famous Ephebe of Antikythera (4C BC), now in the Athens Museum.

Touring

Beaches★★

The best of Kythera's many beaches are marked on the map; popular with families are Kapsáli, near Hóra, and the beaches around Agía Pelagía to the northwest.
The fine red-sand beach at Firí Amos *(southwest of the island, not accessible by car)* is for naturists.
On the east coast, the beaches at Kalsadi, Avlémonas and Diakófti are attractive; the west-coast beaches are much less accessible and therefore less crowded.

M. Guillochon/MICHELIN

Pretty backstreet, Hóra

Visit

Hóra (or Kythera Town)★★

The capital of the island occupies a very beautiful **site**★★ overlooking a magnificent natural harbour on the south coast. The bright white walls of its houses show a Cycladic influence which combines with the ochre colours of Venetian architecture. The 16C Venetian citadel is sited on a rocky peak with a panoramic view of the town and the twin bays of Kapsáli. There are four Byzantine churches, a former aristocratic residence and numerous cannons. The small **Archaeological Museum** (Arheologikó Moussío) has examples of Minoan and Mycenaean finds from the island, including a pitcher, an Archaic lion and a dog's head. *Closed for restoration at press time.*

Address Book

For coin categories, see the Legend on the cover flap.

GETTING ABOUT

BY BOAT

It is sensible (and obligatory in summer) to book cars onto ferries in advance. Ferry service to Diakófti from Nauplion (1/day; more on weekends and in season). There is also intermittent service from Gíthio, on the east coast of Máni (frequency and timetable vary).

BY AIR

Service to Athens (1/day); the airport is 15km/9mi northeast of the capital.

WHERE TO EAT

Taverna Salonikios – ☎ *(27360) 317 05*. Family atmosphere, delicious and healthful traditional cuisine.

Panaretos – *Potamós, in the main square* – ☎ *(07360) 342 90*. An open-air restaurant offering local cuisine, such as *loukánika* (sausages) and excellent oriental pastries.

Zephiros – *Diakófti, opposite the hydrofoil port* - ☎ *(27360) 342 90*. Right on the beach, looking out over a blue sea, this taverna serves Greek fare and grilled-fish dishes.

Hydragogío – *Kapsáli* ☎ *(27360) 310 65*. With a good view over the harbour, this is the best taverna in Kapsáli; tables sit in the shade of a vine-covered arbour. The young proprietors create lively and inventive dishes, with tasty honey doughnuts to finish off the meal. Arrive before 8.30pm to ensure a table.

WHERE TO STAY

Hotel Margarita – *Hóra, in an alley leading to the right off the main street* – ☎ *(27360) 317 11* – *12rms.* – ☕. A 19C house, renovated to create a charming hotel in the heart of the capital. Breakfast on one of two peaceful terraces overlooking the countryside.

Ta Sfentónia – *Pitsinádes* – ☎ *(27360) 33 570, annie@ath.forthnet.gr* – *4 studios*. Spacious and cool studios with kitchen facilities in two magnificently restored old houses decorated with old tools and implements. The private terraces look out over peaceful countryside, and the owner, Anna, is very hospitable.

Pitsinades – ☎ *(27360) 338 77* – *6rms* – *open Apr-Oct*. Lovely rooms with vaulted ceilings in a charming old house. Rooms (2 with kitchenettes) open onto a common patio.

TAKING A BREAK

Ouzerí Selana – *Potamós, on a terrace in the main square*. Shaded by large pine trees, this is the best place to enjoy an ouzo and grilled octopus with the locals.

Amir Ali – *Karavás*. Café-bar near the rushing river.

EVENTS AND FESTIVALS

12 May: Feast day of the Monastery of Ágios Theódoros.

In early August, there are two festivals with singing, dancing and feasting: the wine festival at Mitáta, and the Portokália (orange tree) festival at Karavás.

15 Aug: Potamós festival.

20 Sep: Feast of Agía Pelagía.

Kapsáli★

To the east lie two bays separated by a rocky promontory. The little port of Kapsáli, which becomes busy in the evenings, is a popular yacht mooring.

Monastery of Ágios Ioánnis

North of Hóra, in the direction of Livádi.
This 16C monastery sits atop a cliff overlooking pine woods.

Livádi

South island.
This former retreat for 19C British administrators includes the Church of Ágios Andréas (12C) and Kythera's largest bridge, which was built by the British and has 13 bays.

Poúrko

South island.
This village features the church of Ágios Dimítrios, decorated with 12C frescoes.

Milopótamos

West island. Not without charm, this village has neo-Classical houses with ornate balconies. A little to the west lies the site of **Káto Hóra**★★, a ruined town dating to Byzantine and Venetian times with a gateway surmounted by the lion of St Mark.

Cave of Agía Sofía★★

West island. Open Tue-Sun, 10am-5pm. Guided tours (hard hats and lamps). 3€.
Chambers within this cave were used as chapels (fresco decoration and flooring). There are also galleries with stalactites, stalagmites and underground lakes.

Avlémonas

East coast.
This fishing village has a Venetian citadel at its harbour mouth.

Diakófti

East coast.
From this town (modern port and good sandy beach), a road leads to the abandoned **Monastery of Agía Moní**★ (1840), occupying a splendid site.

Potamós

North island.
The most commercially active town on the island, Potamós reveals a pleasant main square and little streets lined with attractive neo-Classical houses. Less than 1km/0.6mi to the south is the white monastery of Ágios Theódoros; the medieval church has a whitewashed façade and a fine painted wooden iconostasis.

Ruins of Paleohóra★★

North island; access by a poorly maintained road.
In a spectacular mountain cirque above the Langáda Gorge lie the ruins of the Byzantine capital (12C). The peaceful community came to a catastrophic end in 1536 when the pirate Barbarossa sacked the town and massacred the inhabitants.

Karavás

North island.
On a steep slope, this little village with its fast-running stream is located in the greenest part of the island. A little farther north is the Moudari lighthouse. From here on a clear day, it is possible to see the Máni peninsula, some 20km/13mi away.

ITHÁKI★

ITHACA – Ιθακη

POPULATION 3 100

96KM²/38SQ MI – MICHELIN MAP 737 C 8 – IONIAN ISLANDS. SEE ALSO MAP P 398.

Lying close to Cephallonia but a little removed from the tourist mainstream, Ithaca, is made up of two mountain massifs connected by an isthmus. The steep west coast contrasts with the eastern shoreline, which is less rugged and more welcoming. The island corresponds to descriptions in Homer's *Odyssey*: mountains rising out of the sea, pleasant seascapes, and welcoming coves. Excavations have identified the places where Odysseus, his father Laertes, his wife Penelope and their son Telemachos lived. Nothing of ancient Ithaca remains today. *www.ithacagreece.com, www.ithakiholidays.com.*

Visit

Vathí (Itháki)

The port and resort town of Itháki, widely known as Vathí, occupies a charming site at the head of a deep and narrow inlet; the green slopes on either side are covered with smart white houses built after the 1953 earthquake. There are several fine **beaches** nearby, some accessible only by boats which operate from the harbour. Make a quick stop at the **Museum of Folk Art and the Sea** (*open Tue-Sat 10am-2pm, 5-9pm; 1.50€)* to see some reconstructed interiors; the **Archaeological Museum** (*open Tue-Sun 8.30am-3pm; no charge)* displays Ancient ceramics.

Address Book

For coin categories, see the Legend on the cover flap.

GETTING ABOUT

By boat – Ferry service from Patra: (2/day, 1 to Aetos, 1 to Vathí). From Cephallonia: Sami to Aetos (5/day); Sami to Vathí (2/day); Fiskardo to Frikes (1/day). From Leukas: Vasiliki or Nidri to Fikes via Fiskardo (1/day). Timetables vary over the course of the year; inquire at travel agencies or at the harbourmaster's office in Vathí ☎ *(26740) 329 09.*

WHERE TO EAT

Taverna Kalnakis – *Vathí, Platia Polixetion.* Popular with locals, this taverna serves generours portions of traditional Greek dishes.

Restaurant Calipso – *Kióni, large terrace on the harbour. Open May-Oct.* A gourmet experience. The creator of the Ionian paté (three cheeses, cream, raw and smoked ham), which is widely, though poorly, imitated elsewhere. Fresh fish, artichoke soufflé and a delicious lamb pie *(kleftiko)*. The best restaurant on the island.

Restaurant Pementzo – *Fríkes, on the harbour.* ☎*(26740) 317 19.* Good-quality local cuisine.

WHERE TO STAY

Hotel Mentor – *Vathí* – ☎ *(26740) 32 433/33 033 – www.hotelmentor.gr – 36rm.* Situated near the harbour, this white and cream painted hotel has rooms in pink and white with balconies overlooking the sea. Clean bathrooms. Breakfast available *(5€).*

Hotel Nostos – *Fríkes outskirts –* ☎ *(26740) 31 644 (31 476 out of season) – www.hotelnostos-ithaki.gr – 31rm.* This large cream-coloured hotel with red shutters has bright and spacious rooms with balconies. Family atmosphere and good restaurant. Swimming pool. Breakfast available *(5€).*

Phototravellers/MICHELIN

Kióni harbour

Stavrós

The village is reached from Vathí by a **road**★★ built high on the cliff face providing fine views; it is the starting point for two walks.

Pelikáta

30min on foot there and back.

Excavations here have uncovered Mycenaean remains. There are also good views over the island. The small **Pelikáta Archaeological Museum** *(1km/0.6mi from Stavrós, on the Fríkes road)* displays figurines, ceramics, statuettes, vases and oil lamps dating from the Mycenaean period. *Open Tue-Sat, 9.30am-3pm. No charge.*

Pólis Bay

1hr 30min on foot there and back.

A path leads down to this charming bay (pebble beach) where the port is thought to have been in Odysseus' day; in the cave sanctuary of Loizos *(closed)* on the north side of the bay, numerous Mycenaean artifacts have been found.

Fríkes

This little port with its clear waters is charming; old windmills, tavernas and houses line the quayside, the slopes of the mountain behind covered by olive groves.

Kióni★

Close to a number of ruined windmills and far from the tourist routes, this serene little harbour iies at the foot of three hills.

Ithaca on foot★★

The island is ideal for keen walkers; detailed itinerary maps are available in Fríkes.

LEFKÁDA★

LEUKAS – Λευκαδα

POPULATION 24 000

305KM²/122SQ MI – MICHELIN MAP 737 C 8 – IONIAN ISLANDS.

Leukas is a mountainous island (high point: Mount Eláti at 1 158m/3 799ft) linked to the mainland by a narrow strip of land and, since 1987, by a bridge. The island has several fertile valleys where wheat, olives and citrus fruit are cultivated. Its villages, white cliffs and vast beaches are very beautiful. It retains a fair number of its old houses with wooden balconies. *www.lefkas.net.*

Visit

Leukas Town and the Lagoon

Lefkáda (Leukas Town)

This peaceful port town appears Venetian thanks to its paved streets lined by low houses. The Church of **Ágios Minás**, at the end of the main street, has a very fine ceiling painted in the middle of the 18C.

There are several small museums: the **Ethnographic Museum** *(closed for renovation)*, the **Phonograph Museum** *(open in the evenings)*, and most importantly the **Archaeological Museum** *(open daily 8.30am-3pm, no charge)*; terracotta wares, statuettes, archaic milling tools, and Hellenistic funerary stelae, displayed in a recently renovated environment.

Fairly shallow, the **lagoon** (only 1-2m/4-6ft deep) is used for fish farming and salt extraction. Drive around the north branch to enjoy beaches, windmills, and stunning view of Leukas Town.

Faneroméni Monastery *(3km/2mi southwest)* also provides **views** of Leukas Town and the lagoon.

Santa Maura Fort

Constructed on a narrow island, this old fort (14C) was originally surrounded by water. Inside the curtain wall are traces of the town of Santa Maura. From the ramparts there is an attractive view of Leukas Town and the lagoon. On the mainland opposite stands Grivas Castle, built during the War of Independence.

H. Champollion/MICHELIN

Santa Maura Fort

Tour of the Island★★

Around 100km/63mi – allow one day to include sightseeing.
The road from Leukas Town skirts the west side of the lagoon, with a view across to Fort St George (17C). It then follows the east coast of the island facing Etolía. On reaching Nidrí turn left to visit the harbour.

Address Book

For coin categories, see the Legend on the cover flap.

GETTING ABOUT

BY BUS
There are four Athens-Leukas services a day, and four or five a day to Préveza and Áktio airport.

BY AIR
There is a daily flight from Athens to Préveza (bus or taxi from there).

BY BOAT
There are daily ferry services from Leukas Town to Fiskárdo (Cephallonia) and Fríkes (Ithaca). From Vassilikí and Nidri, daily ferry service to Fríkes and Písso Aetós (Ithaca), Fiskárdo and Sámi (Cephallonia). Timetables are subject to change so check at the port.

WHERE TO EAT

Taverna Romantica – *Leukas Town, 11 Odós Mitropóleos – ☏ (26450) 222 35 – open 8.30am-1am.* This popular family taverna serves good local cuisine (fish, *pastítsio* and *maridópita*, a sort of pizza with fried fish). Live music in the evenings.

Restaurant Iónion – *Nidrí, at the end of the harbour – ☏ (26450) 930 94.* Good local cuisine accompanied by dry local wines; courteous service and a quiet pergola terrace.

Taverna Leftéris – *Ágios Nikítas, in the main street. – ☏ (26450) 974 95 – open May-Oct.* Excellent freshly prepared dishes served on a large airy terrace. Specialities include fish, spaghetti with prawns; friendly welcome.

Taverna Stéllios – *Vassilikí – ☏ (26450) 315 81 - open May-Oct.* Attractive, shady waterside terrace, the ideal spot for grilled fish.

Light House Tavern – *Leukas Town, 14 Odós Philarmonikí – ☏ (26450) 251 17 – open Apr-Oct.* Excellent food: grilled dishes, fresh fish, and simple freshly prepared starters. The tables are laid out under a pretty ivy-covered arbour, steps from the open-air theatre.

WHERE TO STAY

Katina's Place – *Vassilíki – ☏ (26450) 312 62 - 5rms.* Simple, comfortable rooms in one of the town's oldest houses; bathrooms on each floor. Striking views, warm welcome. Next door, studios with balconies available ().

Hotel Santa Maura – *Leukas Town, near Platía Ágios Spirídonas – ☏ (26450) 21 308 – 18rm –* ☕. This renovated hotel in the town centre occupies a historic yellow residence. Cool rooms, some of which overlook the garden. Friendly welcome and reasonable rates (discounts for stays over three days).

Hotel Athos – *Nidrí – ☏ (26450) 92 384, athos@otenet.gr – 43rm.* A white hotel at the end of the harbour. Cool rooms with balconies, housed in several different buildings. Jacuzzi; evening entertainment and excursions to the islands of Skorpiós and Meganíssi. Family atmosphere. Booking essential.

Hotel Nefeli – *Agios Nikitas, near the beach. ☏ (26450) 974 00 – www.nefelihotel.gr - 20rms. Open May-Oct.* Charming hotel with green shutters; bright, cool rooms, some with sea views. Impeccably clean hotel, friendly welcome.

EVENTS AND FESTIVALS

From June to August: **Festival of Music, Arts and Literature** in Leukas Town.
Last 2 weeks of August: **International Folk Dancing Festival**.

Nidrí Bay★

The main resort of the island, attractive Nidrí is very popular with tourists and the waterfront teems with people by evening. The **bay**★ sheltered by a screen of little tree-covered islands, is an enchanting sight.

Departing from Nidrí, boat trips skirt the bayand its islands: Madourí, Spárti, Meganíssi and Skorpiós (formerly the home of shipping magnate **Aristotle Onassis**, who was married on the island to Jacqueline Kennedy in 1968).

3km/2mi west of Nidrí, a path leads up to two refreshing waterfalls on the mountainside.

Vlihó Bay

All around this deep, narrow-mouthed bay are vertiginous views down onto the sea. The village of the same name is well known for its attractive fishing port.

Póros

Picturesque inlet below a village sitting on an olive grove-covered hillside.

Vassilikí★

Charming village on the edge of a fertile plain *(beach)*. There are boat trips from Vassilikí to the famous **Leukas Leap**★, a cliff high above sea level *(lighthouse)* from which the poetess Sappho, deceived in love, is supposed to have jumped to her death in the 6C BC. The headland (Ákri Doukáto) bears traces of a Temple to Apollo.

Viewed from the sea, the site is very impressive, and the view towards Cephallonia and Ithaca is also memorable (the same view can be seen from the Corfu-Patras ferry). The headland is also accessible by a poorly maintained road and then by a track from Komilió, about 10km/mi north of Vassilikí.

West Coast★

White cliffs and lovely beaches, especially in the north; **Porto Katsiki**★, Egremni, Gialos, Kathisma, Milos, Pefkoulia. Nice views from here of Mount Elati.

The Mountain★

To the south of Leukas Town, a road to the right leads to Kariá, a charming village hidden on an olive-grove and cypress-covered mountainside. The road offers fine **views**★ as it winds over empty high plateaux.

ZÁKINTHOS★

ZAKYNTHOS – Ζακυνθοζ

POPULATION 35 000

406KM²/162SQ MI – MICHELIN MAP 737 C-D 9-10 – IONIAN ISLANDS.

Despite being shaken by earthquakes, Zakynthos is praised for its gentle climate, luxuriant flora, fertile soil and fine sandy beaches (the one in Shipwreck Bay is the most famous in Greece). The island rises in the west in a chain of limestone peaks, but levels out to the east in a fertile plain producing olives, citrus fruit and wine grapes. Protected sea turtles nest on several of the island's beaches.
www.zanteweb.gr.

A Bit of History

From 1489 to 1797 Zakynthos belonged to Venice. When Crete fell to the Turks in 1669 many artists moved here and contributed to the Ionian School of painting, which combines the Byzantine tradition and the Venetian Renaissance. Local architecture was also marked by the Venetian influence. In the late 18C and early 19C Zakynthos became a breeding ground for poets, whose work was a blend of the Hellenic and Italian cultures, among them **Ugo Foscolo** (1778-1827); and **Dionysios Solomós** (1798-1857), author of the Greek national anthem.

Address Book

For coin categories, see the Legend on the cover flap.

GETTING ABOUT

BY BOAT

Ferry service from Kilíni (8/day in season, 5/day winter). Ferry service (2/day) from Pessáda on Cephallonia, arriving at Ágios Nikólaos at the northern end of the island. From here, taxis are the only transport to the capital.

BY AIR

There is a daily flight from Athens to the island (airport south of Zakynthos Town on the Lithakiá road; bus and taxi service from there) ☏ *(26950) 283 22.*

WHERE TO EAT

Arékia – *Zakynthos Town, north side of town – ☏ (26950) 263 46.* A small roadside taverna with terrace opposite overlooking the sea. Very popular with locals but little frequented by tourists. Good, simple Greek cuisine and singers performing *arékia* (traditional ballads).

Venetziana – *Zakynthos Town, Platía Ágios Márcos.* Lamb *kléftiko*, cooked in paper with tomatoes and potatoes. Friendly, professional service and a pleasant atmosphere.

To Pósto – *Límni Kerí, on entering the village – ☏ (26950) 262 43.* Dining under the trees in a pleasant garden. The á la carte menu features traditional Greek dishes. Open evenings only.

Amos – *Ágios Nikólas Beach – ☏ (26950) 350 00.* Under a huge straw canopy, this bar is a pleasant spot for a meal or a drink, with a good selection of music (Greek, international, jazz).

WHERE TO STAY

Geórgios Zourídis – *Zakynthos Town, 30 Odós L. Karrer – ☏ (26950) 44 691 – 14rm.* Look for the 'Rooms to let' sign on the façade. The ground floor has a pleasant split-level lounge area. Upstairs, the bright, comfortable and spacious rooms (two with air-conditioning) all have kitchen facilities. Excellent value. Open all year; no breakfast.

Christina's Appts – *Zakynthos Town, near village entrance – ☏ (26950) 354 74 – 6rms, 4 studiios.* Charming little building with comfortable appartments, prettily appointed with garden-style furniture and balconies. No breakfast.

Seaside – *Límni Kerí, on the harbour – ☏ (26950) 228 27, mobile 69 37 25 01 58 – Four apartments for 3-5 persons, and four studios for 2 persons.* A truly charming place to stay. Olympia, an English-speaking artist, welcomes guests to this renovated property with spacious, clean rooms with terraces. Unbeatable price, especially in winter *(open on request).*

Villa Fínikes ('Phoenix') – *Límni Kerí, set back from the harbour – ☏ (26950) 265 13 – www.villa-phoenix.com – Ten apartments.* A real haven of tranquillity; the studios are set in a well-tended garden planted with olive trees. Spacious, well equipped and very quiet; all with terraces overlooking the countryside. Booking essential.

TAKING A BREAK

Rock Café – *Límni Kerí, on the harbour; next to the Seaside apartments.* A stylish modern building in stone and wood which has been tastefully furnished. The terrace is the ideal spot for an iced coffee, an ouzo or a fresh orange juice. Good local and international music.

Logós Café Bar – *among pine trees on the Vassilikós-Ágios Nikólaos road.* Disco which opens every night at 10pm.

Touring

The Sea and Beaches★★

The beaches of Zakynthos are among the best in the eastern Mediterranean. Those listed below are some of the island's finest; they are marked on the map and appear here in clockwise order starting from Zakynthos Town. Other resort beaches dot the east coastal plain (salt marshes, orchards) between Alikés and Zakynthos Town.

Banana Beach★

East coast. This long strip of sand is bordered by dunes, rocks and pine trees.

Pláka

East coast. Neighbouring the above beach, and before the rocks of Cape Ágios Nikólaos.

Pórto Róma

East coast. An attractive inlet with low cliffs; a good taverna here and lovely views.

Gérakas★

South coast. A vast crescent of sand, part of which is covered by sunbeds; the beach is bordered by curious tufa rocks.

Dafni

South coast.
This wild beach is a longtime nesting site for endangered loggerhead turtles.

Cape Kerí★★

West coast. Ideal place to watch the sun set against the backdrop of the tall cliffs. To the south lie the twin reefs of the Mizíthres, two slivers of white stone.

Shipwreck Bay★★★

West coast. Probably Greece's most famous natural landmark acquired its nickname after the *Panayótis* was wrecked here over 20 years ago. A viewing platform has been built (signposted 'Shipwreck'), from where the **view**★★★ is breathtaking. *The only way to reach this idyllic spot is by boat from Pórto Vrómi (5km/3mi to the south), Límni Kerí, Kokínou or Zakynthos Town.*

Shipwreck Bay

Cape Skinári★★

Beyond Korithi, Cape Skinári has stunning views towards Cephallonia.

Kokínou

East coast. From this tiny harbour, boats depart for the famous **blue caves**★, a fine series of arches gouged out of the cliffs. Refracted light turns the sea turquoise.

Makrís Gialós

East coast. A charming beach among white rocks.

Alikés

East coast. This resort with its fine sandy beach has excellent views of Cephallonia.

Boat trips★★★

In addition to the excursions mentioned above leaving from Pórto Vrómi and Kokínou, the following are recommended.

Tour of the island★★★

Around 20€ (prices vary from one boat to another). Choose one of the smaller vessels, like the Dias, from opposite the Pilot J agency in Zakynthos Town.

The trips head north and round Cape Skinári before the impressive **cliffs**★★★ of the west coast come into view, interspersed here and there by delightful beaches.

Marathoníssi★

There are boats from Límni Kerí, at the southern end of the island, which take sightseers to the nearby sea caves *(2hr, departures on the hour every hour from 9am to 6pm, 15€)* and to the island of Marathoníssi.

Visit

Zakynthos Town★

One of the most picturesque towns in the Adriatic, Zakynthos Town was rebuilt in the Venetian style after 1953 with pretty churches, palaces and arcaded squares.

Strata Marina

Near the ferry port, this seafront promenade is very popular.

Platía Dhionísios Solomós

At the palm-shaded main square, you can visit the **Museum of Byzantine Art** *(open Tue-Sun 8am-2.30pm; 3€)* with its collection of icons and religious art.

Kiría ton Angélon

Renaissance-style facade; the interior features a sumptuous 17C iconostasis.

Kástro★

Open Tue-Sun 8am-2.30pm (7pm in summer). 3€.

The old Venetian citadel set on a hill survived the earthquake and provides an extended **view**★★ of the town, the bay and the Peloponnese coast.

THE NORTHERN AEGEAN ISLANDS

For the purposes of this guide, the islands of the northern Aegean (with the exception of the Cyclades) have been grouped together. Administratively, however, Thássos and Samothrace are part of the eastern Macedonia and Thrace region. Chios, Icarus, Lesbos, Lemnos, Sámos and adjacent small islands form the Northern Aegean Islands region. On the very frontier between East and West, each island is its own little world, with unique landscapes and histories. The two nearby islands situated towards the Dardanelles form part of Turkey.

Address Book

GETTING ABOUT

The islands are served by ferries from various mainland ports, most importantly Kavála (not far from Thássos), Alexandroúpoli (north of Samothrace) and from Piraeus via the Cyclades. The remoteness of some islands can make the crossing very long and it is preferable to fly. In high season there is a link between Chios and Turkey (boats from Cesme, near Izmir).

Numerous airports link the islands to the rest of Greece, most notably Athens and Thessaloníki. Chios, Lesbos, Lemnos, Sámos and Icarus all have airports.

WHERE TO STAY

See the Address Book sections of each island's entry. It is wise to book accommodation in advance to save time during your trip. Ask to be met at the ferry; most Greeks are happy to do this.

HÍOS★

CHIOS – Χιοζ

POPULATION 23 779

842KM²/337SQ MI – MICHELIN MAP 737 N 8 – NORTHERN AEGEAN ISLANDS.

Homer's birthplace is dominated by volcanic mountains of volcanic origin, the highest of which, Mount Pelinéo, reaches 1 297m/4 255ft. Aromatic resin from the lenits or mastic treen is used to make alcoholic drinks, chewing gum and sweets. Chios has lovely beaches, an unspoilt local culture, and fine Byzantine art and history. *Chios Town, Odós Kanari, corner of Odós Roïdou ☎ (22710) 44 389. Open Mon-Fri 7am-2.30pm, 6-10pm, Sat-Sun 9am-1pm, 6-10pm (in season); Mon-Fri 7am-2.30pm (offseason).*

A Bit of History

Mediterranean maritime trading centre – Situated on major shipping routes, Chios played a major role in contact between East and West from Antiquity to the 19C and enjoyed its first cultural and economic heyday in the 6C. The Persian invasion in 493 BC brought an end to the island's prosperity. After centuries of decline, it resumed its pivotal role during the Venetian period (12C). The port handled commodities from throughout the Mediterranean, especially the local mastic, and alum from Anatolia, which was essential to the dyeing process and exported mainly to Bruges.

The Turkish occupation of Chios did not damage the island's trade. In the 19C Chiot's merchant fleet rivalled those of Hydra, Spetsae and neighbouring Psará.

Chios Massacres – At the beginning of the War of Independence, in 1822, the island rose against the Turks, but the revolt failed and the Turks exacted a terrible vengeance: thousands of Christians were massacred or enslaved. This cruel punishment aroused intense emotion in Western Europe, particularly in France: Delacroix's famous painting *The Massacres in Chios*, Alfred de Vigny's poem *Helena*, and Victor Hugo's verses *The Greek Child* were inspired by it. Chios finally became part of Greece in 1912.

Visit

Híos Town★ (Chios Town)

This small harbour town facing the Turkish coast retains a certain charm. Cafés and restaurants border the lively and colourful **port**★. Behind the business area parallel

Address Book

For coin categories, see the Legend on the cover flap.

GETTING ABOUT

By boat – Ferry service from **Piraeus**, *(2/day)*, Mitilini *(2-3/day)*, Sámos *(3/wk)*, Limnos *(5-6/wk)*, and Rhodes via Kalimnos and Kos *(1/wk)*. Also ferry service to Cesme in Turkey *(daily; purchase tickets the day before travel, passport required)*.
By air – The airport is 4km/2.5mi from Chios Town. There are several flights a day to Athens, and several per week to Mitilini, Limnos, Rhodes and Samos.

WHERE TO EAT

Iakovos Plytas– *Chios Town, 20 Odós Georgiou) – ☎(22710) 238 58.* Lovely restaurant serving carefully prepared Greek dishes; reasonable prices.
Byzantio – *Chios Town, market district, Odós Rali – ☎(22710) 410 35.* This restaurant always has several daily specials. The cuisine is tasty and served in a characteristic local setting.
Restaurant Perivoli – *Kambos, a little out of Chios Town – ☎(22710) 319 73.* In the gardens of the pleasant hotel of the same name (see below). Try the veal in wine, or the *psaronefri* (pork).
O Zikos – *Volissos, at the harbor – ☎(22710) 220 40.* The ideal spot for sampling seafood: mussels, lobster pasta, swordfish, etc.

WHERE TO STAY

Chios Rooms – *Chios Town, at the harbour – ☎(22710) 201 98, www.chiosrooms.gr – 10rm.* Charming old building; half the rooms have en suite facilities and several have balconies.
Alex Rooms – *Chios Town, 29 Odós Livanou, near the harbour – ☎ and fax (22710) 26 054 – 7rm. Shared bathrooms.* The owner is a very cordial retired sea captain, and all guests are treated as family. Sober decoration in the comfortable rooms; attractive terrace which is a good meeting place.
Perivoli – *See 'Where to Eat' – ☎ (22710) 31 513, fax (22710) 32 042 – 12rm.* A fine building in typical island style. Try to book one of the four larger rooms with high ceilings, which are comfortable even in high summer. Bus stop close by.
Kyriaki House – *Volissos; follow the Artemis Apartments" sign – ☎(22740 219 41 – 2apts.* Two comfortable studios; magnificent terrace with sea views.
Volissos Travel – *Volissos, various houses in the upper part of the village – ☎ (22710) 21 421, fax (22710) 21 521.* Historic stone houses offering accommodation, all two-storey with kitchen downstairs and bedrooms above. Simple, tasteful interiors.

EVENTS AND FESTIVITIES

Volissos – The village hosts a rather unusual Easter tradition: a fireworks "battle" between the two main churches.
Pirgi – **15 August**, annual village festival.

to the quayside is **Platía Vounáki**, the town centre; on the north side of the square is a charming **Turkish fountain**★ (1768) decorated with floral low reliefs.
Near the port, stop in at the **Archaeological Museum**, *(Odós Mihalou, near the University of the Aegean; open Jul-Oct: Tue-Sun 8am-5pm; Nov-Jun 8.30am-3pm; 2€)* to see objects recovered from the island's archaeological sites.

Kástro (Citadel)

North of the harbour and of Platía Vounáki.
The formerly elegant old town is still surrounded on three sides by ramparts built in the 14C. Today it is a quiet area, somewhat run-down. Inside the main gate on the right is the dark basement room of the keep, formerly used as a dungeon.

To Palatákia (Small Palace)

Opposite the Kástro gate. Open Tue-Sun, 9am-2.30pm. 2€.
This 15C mansion houses a small collection of Byzantine art; a fine mosaic (5C AD) found in the modern town and Byzantine and post-Byzantine icons and frescoes.
Nearby is the **Fort Museum** (*same opening times and charges as To Palatákia)* which displays artillery pieces, most notably French cannons.
To the left as you exit lies the tiny old **Turkish Cemetery**.

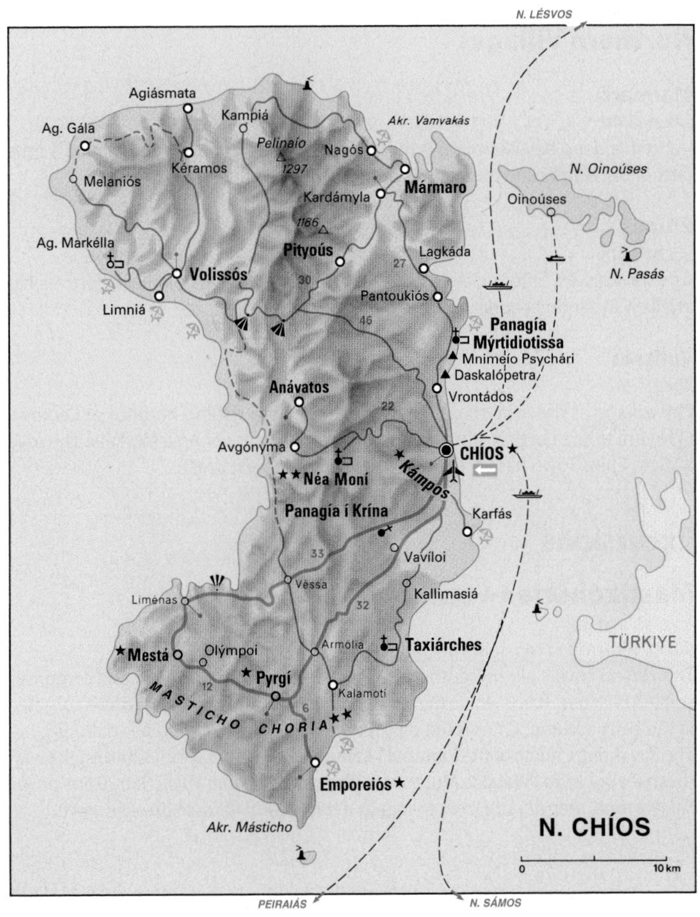

Odós Frourio

This road runs through the kástro district and up a bare hill from where there are fine **views**★ over the town and the sea. Clearly visible is the rooftop of the old Turkish Baths; four terracotta domes dotted with small holes and overrun with greenery.

Koraïs Library and Argentis Museum★

Junction of Odós Koraïs and Odós Argendis near the cathedral. Open Mon-Thu 8am-2pm, Fri 8am-2pm and 5-7.30pm, Sat 8am-12.30pm. No charge to enter the hall, 3€ for the galleries. ☎(22710) 442 46.
100 000 books collected by the writer **Adamántios Koraïs**, a small **Ethnographic Museum** and collection of **portraits** of the Argentis family.

The Kámbos Plain★

A trip to the Mastikohória (see below) can be extended to take in this area.
From the 15C to the 19C some 200 houses **(arhondiká)** and mansions were built in this fertile plain by wealthy merchants for use as summer residences. The 10 or so that survive evoke a bygone age.
Houses occasionally open to the public include the neo-Classical **Zigomalas House,** which has a fine courtyard with pebble decoration *(beginning of the road, about 800m/0.5mi after the bridge over the River Parthenis); and* the well-preserved **Argenti House** *(about 5km/3mi farther in a parallel road to the west, Odós Argentis);*

Northern Villages

Mármaro

27km/17mi.
Lying in a deep bay, Mármaro is the harbour for neighbouring Kardámila. A little farther on, **Nagós** and its environs boast the island's finest **beaches**★★.

Pitioús

28km/18mi.
As with Volissós, Pitioús claims to be Homer's birthplace. Its medieval fortress has a yellow Byzantine church with a red dome.

Volissós

46km/29mi.
This village at the foot of a medieval fortress has a fishing harbour at Lemnos. 6km/4mi to the north is a fine **beach** by the Monastery of Agía Markéla. The road back to Chios Town has vertiginous **views**★ of the west coast.

Excursions

Mastikohória★★ (Mastic Villages)

90km/56mi round trip, south of Chios Town.
This region covers all the southern part of the island from Armólia and comprises some 20 villages. This is where the **lentis** grows; the shrub's resin (**mastic**) is collected in the early autumn. Chios is the only place where the resin solidifies naturally.
The Byzantine Church of the **Panagía i Krina** (12C or 13C) may be visited on the way; (frescoes are in To Palatákia Museum in Chios). *Access from Vavíli, 1km/0.6mi on the Sklaviá road, then about 15min on foot by a track (right) through an olive grove.*

P. Jausserand/MICHELIN

Typical architecture, Pirgí

Pirgí★

A tower dominates the medieval village, although the walls have been razed. The geometric *sgraffito* decoration of the houses and churches is an unusual feature; the technique known as *xistá* or *skalistrá* is still in use today.
A covered passage northeast of the square leads to the Church of the **Holy Apostles** (Ágii Apostóli, c 1200) with its typically Byzantine exterior. The interior is decorated with frescoes (1665). The 17C Church of the Dormition in the square contains fine carved furnishings.

Emboriós★

6km/3.5mi south of Pirgí.
A small square bordered by a few houses gives onto the sea. To the south of the port, a path leads to two black pebble **beaches**★★ tucked away under volcanic cliffs.

Mestá★

Beyond the medieval village of Olímbi.
It is pleasant to stroll through the old lanes and vaulted passages. The church and the main square have replaced a defensive tower. Farther along the old Byzantine **Taxiarchs Church** (Paliós Taxiárhis) contains a beautifully carved iconostasis (18C).
Return to Chios Town via Liménas, Mestá's port, and the Véssa road, which offers at the start extensive **views**★ of the barren and jagged west coast.

The Centre of the Island★★

50km/31mi round trip, west of Chios Town.
A superb panoramic road climbs the foothills of Mount Épos to the Monastery of Néa Moní, which stands in a wooded valley guarded by cypress trees.

Néa Moní Monastery★★

Open dawn to dusk; closed from 1-4pm. No charge.
Declared a Unesco World Heritage Site in 1990, this is one of the most important buildings of the Byzantine era and was founded on the spot where a miraculous icon of the Virgin had been found. It was built in the 11C and is the work of architects and painters from Constantinople. The **exterior** is protected by a layer of plaster.
The octagonal church is the best surviving architectural example of its age. Its large triple-domed **exonarthex** was originally faced in red marble painted with post-Byzantine frescoes; only the Last Judgement on the south wall remains.

The austere figures and expressive features of the brightly coloured 11C **mosaics★** in the narthex and the nave show great unity of style. The tall dome of the nave and the mosaic of the Pantocrator were restored in 1900.

Anávatos

Perched on a rocky spur, the village was probably built to defend the east coast against the Turks. Today it is deserted and a delight for lovers of solitude.
There is a fine **view★** of the west coast from **Avgónima**.

IKARÍA

ICARUS – Ικαρια

POPULATION 5 392

267KM²/107SQ MI – MICHELIN MAP 737 N 10 – NORTHERN AEGEAN ISLANDS.

This island close to the Dodecanese and the shores of Turkey rises to 1 037m/3 465ft (Mount Athéras). According to myth, Icarus drowned near the island's shores when the sun melted his wax wings after he had escaped the Labyrinth with his father, Daidalos (see Knossós). Grapes cultivated here produce a red wine mentioned by Homer.

Visit

Ágios Kírikos and surrounding area

This small fishing town has typical two-story houses around its port. A bit farther west along the coast lies **Thérma Lefkádas**, a resort famous for its hot springs. Farther still lies the stunning **Evangelistria Monastery** (17C) near Xylosirtis.

Northern coast★

With its hilly terrain and cool climate, the northern coast holds more interest for the visitor. The majority of the island's beaches are found here; they are quite small in size, with a couple of exceptions mentioned below.

Address Book

For coin categories, see the Legend on the cover flap.

GETTING ABOUT

By boat – Ferry service from **Piraeus**, *(3/wk, usually Mon, Thu, Fri)*. Some boats dock at Ágios Kírikos (south coast) or Évdilos (north coast). In summer, ferries link the island to Pátmos, Páros, Chios, Léros, Kos and Kálimnos.

WHERE TO EAT AND STAY

Taverna – *Karavostamo*. This large, pleasant restaurant with tasty cooking and a friendly proprietor.

Hotel Akti – *Ágios Kírikos, opposite the harbour* – ☎ *(22750) 23 905*. This simple hotel occupies a house perched on a rock above the island's main port. Clean, presentable rooms. Fine sea view from the terrace.

Hotel Karras – *Ágios Kírikos* – ☎ *(22750) 22 494*. This quiet and simple hotel is not far from the port.

Rooms Spanos – *Évdilos* – ☎ *(22750) 31 220*. These simple rooms all have their own bathroom.

The surfaced road from Ágios Kírikos goes through the pleasant village of **Karavostamo**, dominated by a splendid Byzantine chapel, Ágioi Pantes, and arrives at **Évdilos** with its small port. Beyond, an unsurfaced road leads to **Kampos**; its tiny archaeological museum houses objects found at the Ancient site of Oinoe.
In **Pigi**, there is a lovely monastery; its frescoes recall those at Mount Áthos.
After Kampos, head towards the loveliest part of the island, which stretches beyond **Armenistís**. Nearby are the two large beaches of **Messachit** and **Livadi**.
Near the adorable village of **Christos Raches**, enjoy splendid views of the coast.

LÉSVOS or MITILÍNI★

LESBOS – Λεσβοζ

POPULATION 27 247

1 633KM²/653SQ MI – MICHELIN MAP 737 N 6 – NORTHERN AEGEAN ISLANDS.

Close to Turkey's Anatolian coast, Lesbos is renowned for its beautiful villages, its countless beaches, its mountainous and wooded landscapes, and its huge gulfs. Sometimes called Mitilíni, the name of its capital, Lesbos has a large population; its size makes it the third largest island in Greece after Crete and Euboia. The fertile soil supports over 11 million olive trees, the island's most important crop. There are several distilleries producing the best *ouzo* **in Greece; spas, and a flourishing tourist sector.** *EOT, 6 Odós Aristarcho, near the harbour, ☎(22510) 425 11. Open Mon-Fri 9am-2pm. EOT, street leading to Molivos harbour, ☎(22530) 713 47. Open May-Oct 9am-3pm. www.mithymna.gr*

A Bit of History

A poetess renowned the world over – Artist, genius and free spirit, **Sappho** is the most reknowned figure of Lesbos. Her poetic works were highly reputed in Antiquity. The poetess is said to have run a 'moisopolon domos' in Mitilíni, a school of art and poetry devoted to the praise of muses. Whether it was odes, hymns or songs, all of Sappho's verses spoke of love and beauty in a style that particularly touched female sensitivity. She committed suicide in Leukas.

Festivals – Religious festivals are celebrated on Lesbos with great enthusiasm and sometimes incorporate very Ancient elements such as ritual sacrifice (only tolerated by the Church).
The feast of St Michael the Archangel, patron saint of the island, is celebrated on the third weekend after Easter at **Mandamádos** *(34km/21mi northwest of Mitilíni)*. During the festivites, several animals are sacrificed and spectators mark their foreheads with the blood to protect themselves from illness. Worshippers throng the monastery to kiss a very old terracotta icon of the Archangel Michael.
A similar celebration takes place the last week in May near the town of **Agía Paraskeví**. After a colorful procession, a bull is sacrificed on Saturday evening and on Sunday, after the service and the distribution of the meat, there is horse racing.
The Assumption of the Virgin on 15 August is celebrated in Pétra and **Agiássos**.

Visit

Mitilíni★

The island capital is on the east coast facing Anatolia. The district on the isthmus between the two harbours, which was the centre of town during the Turkish occupation, has retained some fine houses, the remains of a mosque and the cathedral, which contains a very fine post-Byzantine iconostasis. There are two small museums: the **Byzantine Museum** (*open May-Oct Tue-Sun 10am-1pm; 2€; (22510) 289 16)* housing precious icons from the 13C to the 17C; and the **Archaeological Museum** (*open Tue-Sun 8.30am-1pm (7pm in summer); no charge)* with fine ceramics, Greek sculpture and Roman mosaics.

House of Lesbos (Lesviakó Spíti)

Collections of art and popular traditions; adjacent small museum.

Kástro

Open Tue-Sun 8.30am-5pm (7pm in summer). 2€.

The castle (rebuilt 14C) stands on a promontory projecting seawards beyond the town and overlooking the two harbours. Note above the gate the arms of the Palaiologos emperors of Byzantium, the horseshoe of the Gatteluzzi and Arabic inscriptions.

Hellenistic Theatre

Open Tue-Sun, 8am-3pm (7pm in summer). No charge.

Northwest of the old district lie the remains of a Hellenistic theatre; most of the terraces have disappeared. The size of the theatre (it seated 15 000 spectators) indicates the cultural importance of Lesbos in Antiquity. From the upper terraces there is a fine view of the old town, the castle and the Turkish coast.

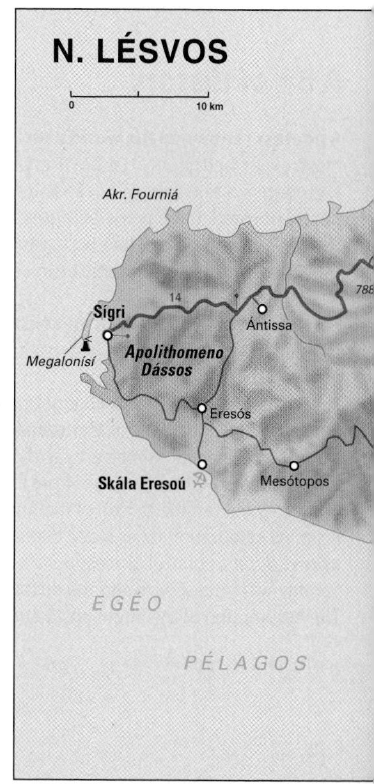

Around Mitilíni

Thermí

11km/7mi. Loutropóli Thermís is a popular spa, its curative waters were reknowned even in Antiquity. South of Thermí and west of the village of Mópia are traces of an impressive **Roman aqueduct**. There are traces of another near the village of Lámbou Míli on the road to Kaloní.

Variá

4km/2.5mi. The **Theophilos Museum** presents 86 works by the famous naïve painter Theophilos (1873-1934) who was born in Variá; the paintings are gaily coloured representations of popular scenes or incidents in Greek history. On the same site, under the olive trees, stands the **Teriade Museum,** which contains a rich library and engravings and lithographs by Chagall, Picasso,

Fernand Léger, Matisse and Giacometti. There are also paintings by Iánis Tsarouchis and other works by Theophilos.

South of the Island

Agiássos

25km/16mi. The wooded lower slopes of the highest peak on the island (Mount Olympos, 968m/3 235ft) frame this charming unspoilt town.

Plomári

42km/26mi. Plomári is famous throughout Greece for the high quality of its anised liqueur (ouzo). Tucked in a hollow in the cliff face, it is scarcely visible from a distance. The modern seafront provides cafés, restaurants, and a tiny beach. East of the town extends a shingle beach, **Ágios Issídoros**, which is very popular.

Vaterá

52km/32mi. This is the most beautiful beach on the island. There are traces of palaeo-Christian basilicas on the Fokás headland and to the east of the village.

West of the Island

Eressós and Skála Eressoú

90km/56mi. Skála Eressoú, which is the port for the larger village of Eressós, attracts many holidaymakers to its long sandy **beach★**. **Ancient Eressós**, on a hill to the

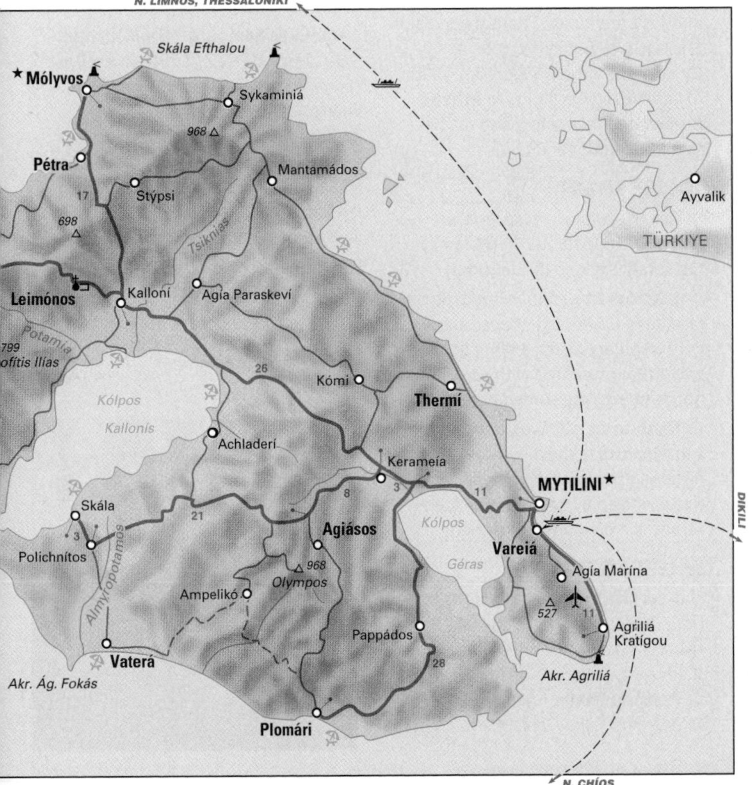

east of the village, is thought to be the birthplace of Sappho; there are two palaeo-Christian basilicas (mosaics) and the ruins of a Genoese and a Turkish tower.

Petrified forest (Apolithoména Déndra)

Open mid-Jun-mid-Oct: daily 8am-8pm. Rest of the year: daily 8.30am-4.30pm. 2€. (22530) 544 34, www.petrifiedforest.gr.

Between Sígri and Eressós there is a petrified forest of fossilised trees that were buried in volcanic ash millions of years ago. The trees reach up to 10m/33ft in height and the trunks measure about 8m/26ft round the bole. The most accessible trees are to be found on the south side of the Ándissa to Sígri road (about 7km/4mi from Ándissa). The **views**★★ from the highest point of the 'forest' are stunning.

Limónos Monastery

43km/27mi. Open year-round, dawn to dusk.

Just beyond Kaloní on the Sígri road stand the impressive buildings of Lesbos's chief monastery. The 40 monks, whose social and educational work extends throughout the island, maintain a Museum of Religious and Popular Art.

Address Book

For coin categories, see the Legend on the cover flap.

GETTING ABOUT

By boat – Ferry service to **Piraeus** *(daily in summer)*; and neighbouring islands, notably Lemnos, Sámos and Rhodes *(several/wk)*. There are occasional services to Turkey.

By air – The airport is 8km/5mi south of Mitilíni; regular flights to **Athens** *(several/day in summer)*; also to Thessaloníki, Lemnos and Chios.

WHERE TO EAT

Avero – *Mitilini, at the historic harbour. (22510) 221 80.* Family restaurant since 1925...delicious!

Matzourana – *Mitilini, Odós Komninaki, 69485 804 63. open evenings.* Contemporary bistro serving up inventive dishes presented with care. Try the honey beef or the stuffed peppers.

Panorama – *Mólivos, opposite the entrance to the citadel.* Typically Greek dishes and pastries which will delight those who enjoy good, simple food, served in a pleasant atmosphere.

WHERE TO STAY

New Life Rooms – *Mitilíni, near Odós Ermoú – (22510) 234 00 – 9rm.* Tastefully decorated guesthouse; shady garden to the side for relaxing.

Pension Thalia – *Mitilini, east of Odós Ermoú – 3rm, 1apt.* In an older part of own, house at the end of a barred street; small garden.

Alkaios – *16 Odós Alkaio, west of the historic harbour – (22510) 477 37/69455 070 89 – 18rm.* Villa surrounded by orange trees; handsome architecture; comfortable rooms.

Molivos Camping – *Efthalou road – (22530) 711 69/710 79, www.molivos-camping.com – 88 sites. May-Oct.* Shady sites; clean common areas.

Paradise – *Molivos, village entrance – (22530) 717 78/69454 032 36 – 6apts.* Simple, clean studios with views of the kastro and the village.

Nassos – *Molivos, up the main street from the tourist office – (22530) 712 32, www.nassosguest.com – 7rm, 1 apt. Mar-Dec.* Charming, rustic home, simply decorated; several rooms with private bath. Reserve in summer.

Phototravellers/MICHELIN

Phototravellers/MICHELIN

Frescoes, Ágios Nikólaos

Mólivos (Míthimna)★

64km/40mi. Picturesque little town favoured by artists; pebble beach and fishing port. The handsome houses, painted in pastel shades, climb the steep slope towards an impressive Byzantine-Genoese castle *(open Tue-Sun 8am-2.30pm; 2€)*, which offers views of the town and the coast.

A radioactive spring (46.8°C/124°F) beyond the beach at Eftaloú *(3km/2mi east of Míthimna)* is captured in a covered bath before warming the sea water off the shingle beach *(open daily 10am-2pm, 3-7pm; 5€)*.

Pétra

60km/37mi. The rock, which gives the village its name, is crowned by the Church of the Virgin (**Panagía Glikofiloússa**), which contains some remarkable icons. At the centre of the village stands the **Vareldzidéna House** (Arhondikó Vareldzidéna); the salon on the first floor is decorated with delicate paintings of the towns and fleet of the Ottoman Empire. St Nicholas' Church (**Ágios Nikólaos**) contains 15C frescoes.

Sígri

95km/59mi. This fishing village (crayfish a speciality) nestles in a little bay, guarded by a ruined Turkish fort and protected from the open sea by an island, Nissiópi.

LÍMNOS★

LEMNOS – Λημνοζ

POPULATION 18 104

477KM²/191SQ MI – MICHELIN MAP 737 L 5 – NORTHERN AEGEAN ISLANDS.

Situated midway between Mount Athos and the coast of Asia Minor, near the mouth of the Dardanelles, the volcanic island of Lemnos has an astonishing variety of landscapes. Historical sites are in fertile plains to the east; the barren mountain chains with cultivated valleys to the west form a rugged coastline indented with bays and sandy coves. The main resort is the capital Mírina, with its Genoese citadel. The distance separating the island from the rest of Greece makes this a destination little frequented by tourists. *In the waiting room at the ferry landing. Open in season daily 8am-2.30, 6-10pm. www.lemnos-island.com*

A Bit of History

Pocked with volcanoes and sulphurous springs, Lemnos was the mythological home of **Hephaïstos** (Vulcan), who landed here when was cast off Mount Olympos by his angry father Zeus. Afterwards, the god of fire lived on the island and toiled at his forges (the Lemnos volcanoes), and instructed the islanders in the art of metalworking.

Visit

Mírina★

Quiet and pleasant, the island's capital has a charming fishing harbour in a bay to the south. Beyond the harbour is the Turkish Beach (Toúrkikos Gialós) and to the north lie the fine sandy 'Greek' beach (Roméïkos Gialós, where there is a small **Archaeological Museum** (*open Tue-Sun 8.30am-3pm; 2€*), and Rihá Nerá (a low tide) beach. Also worth a visit is the **Kástro**★ *(no charge)*. The climb to the fortress gates affords good views of the harbour and the south side of the bay. The foundations of an Ancient wall are the only traces of a Temple to Artemis and a town which stood on the jagged headland. Beyond the gates, a track on the left leads to the top of the south wall. From this spot and from the tip of the headland there are splendid **views**★★★, especially at sunset, of Kástro Bay, the indented west coast, and on the horizon Mount Athos rising from the sea.

Káspakas Bay★★ (Ormos Káspaka)

11km/6.5mi north of Mírina.

After Cape Pétassos the road skirts the Avlónas coast (bays and coves). The vast **bay**★★ with Cape Kalógeri at the far side comes into view before the village of **Káspakas**★ nestling on the mountainside. Beyond the village a byroad runs down to the beach and hamlet of Ágios Ioánis. There are fine sandy beaches north of the bay.

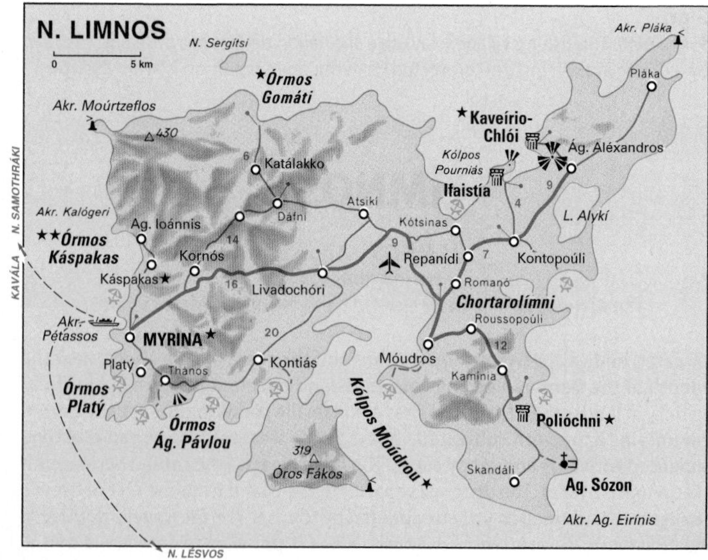

Platí and Ágios Pávlos Bays

About 15km/9mi south of Mírina.

A large sandy beach stretches below the mountain village of **Platí**. To the south of the village, just after Thános, lies the vast Ágios Pávlos Bay.

Moúdros Bay★ (Kólpos Moúdro)

20km/12mi northeast of Mírina.

This immense bay is one of the most important natural anchorages in the Aegean. There are numerous, virtually deserted little villages, notably **Fanaraki**. From the village of **Kalithéa**, to the south of Livadohóri, there are fine views. To the east of Moúdros Bay is the Commonwealth War Cemetery dating from the Dardanelles campaign.

Polióhni★

37km/23mi northeast of Mírina.

A 4C BC village with oval huts was replaced in the 3C BC by a fortified town built in four stages *(indicated in blue, green, red and yellow on the site)*. According to archaeologists, the earliest city (c 2800-2550 BC) is more ancient than Troy in Anatolia. Finds from the later 'yellow' period (2200-2100 BC) include human skeletons, pottery and gold jewellery. Settlement on a more modest scale continued until about 1275 BC,

Address Book

For coin categories, see the Legend on the cover flap.

GETTING THERE

By air – The airport is located in the middle of the island, 22km/14mi from Flights from **Athens** *(3/day)*, Lesbos, Rhodes *(4-5/wk)*, Chios, Samos *(1/wk)*.
By boat – Ferry service to **Piraeus** *(1-2/wk)*, Lavrio *(2-3/wk)*, Lesbos, Chios *(5-6/wk)*, Samos *(2/wk)*, Kalimnos, Kos and Rhodes *(1/wk)*.

WHERE TO EAT

Plátanos – *Mírina, Odós Karatza. ☎(22540) 220 70.* Typical Greek spot; very popular. Dishes may be selected directly from the kitchen; no fish, but tasty meat in sauces, pasta, vegetables.
Gláros – *Mírina, at the fishing harbour. ☎(22540) 222 20. Mid-Apr-Nov.* Incomparable setting; Fresh *dorade*, sardines and mackerel.

WHERE TO STAY

O Stokali – *Mirina, lane behind north bay – 8 apts.* Simple studios in a handsome building; quiet street near the beach.
Poseidon – *Mírina, at the end of Roméikos Gialós Beach – ☎ (22540) 24 821/69449 196 64 – 20 apts.* A comfortable and well-run hotel, located in a quiet setting on the edge of town. The airy rooms have fridges and balconies; warm welcome.
Apollo Pavilion – *Odós Garofalidi, behind the cinema – ☎(22540) 237 12, www.apollopavilion.com – 11 apts.* Unabashedly kitschy decor; beautiful terrace; attentive service. Some rooms for 5 persons (good value).
Sunset – *Agios Yannis, above the main street – ☎(22450) 615 55/615 93, www.sunsetapartments.gr – 14 apts. Jun-Sept.* Magnificent views of beach, cliffs and hills. Several studios.
Petradi – *Thanos, on the beach – ☎(22540 299 05, www.petradi.gr – 12 apts. May-Sept.* Clean studios with sunset-facing balconies, isolated at the end of the beach.

TAKING A BREAK

Karagkiozis – *Mirina, on Romeikos Gialos beach.* Local watering hole: one room with DJ, one quiet lounge, one charming terrace. Choice of whiskies.

SHOPPING

Culinary treats to take home: **retsina**, **fig jam**, thyme-scented **honey**, Kalambaki (a local **white wine**).

Ph. Longin/MICHELIN

The Kástro

probably just before the Trojan War. There are scant remains, but the streets, wells, rectangular houses and wall sections are well presented and explained.
To the south is the Monastery of **Ágios Sózon**, situated amid sand dunes.

Ifestía (Hephaistia)

36km/22mi northeast. Open Tue-Sun 8.30am-3pm. No charge.
Hephaistia was inhabited in the pre-Hellenic era and was Lemnos's principal city in the Classical period. It was destroyed by a landslide.
The **site**★ was particularly well chosen on a little promontory jutting out to sea. A sign shows the site of an agora with a shrine above and a small theatre below. From the hilltop above the sanctuary the **view** extends over Pourniás Bay and Kavírio-Hlói.

Kavírio-Hlói★ (Sanctuary of the Kabeiroi)

41km/26mi north of Mírina. Open Tue-Sun 8.30am-3pm. No charge.
As on the island of Samothrace, the **Kabeiroi,** the mysterious gods of the Underworld, were venerated during the Hellenistic period with huge nocturnal ceremonies. Before the sanctuary climb up to the top of a hill *(indicated by a white column on the left)* to enjoy a magnificent **panorama**★★ over Pourniás Bay.
The ruined Kabeirion in its lonely majestic **site**★ overlooking Pourniás Bay dates from a later period. Eleven columns of a vast Hellenistic *telestrion* (where the mysteries were enacted) remain on the upper terrace. The earliest section of the sanctuary (8C-7C BC) on the lower level included a temple, a portico and a telestrion.

SÁMOS★

Σαμοζ

POPULATION 6 236

477KM²/191SQ MI – MICHELIN MAP 737 O 10 – NORTHERN AEGEAN ISLANDS.

A narrow strait separates Sámos from the Turkish coast. The island's beaches, coves and indented coastline, together with its interesting archaeological remains make Sámos a pleasant resort for a prolonged stay; excursions to Ephesus (Efes) in Turkey are an added attraction. On Sámos itself the Temple of Hera is one of the most ancient in all Greece. *Alley behind Platía Pithagóra, north of the square. (22730) 28 530. Another office in Pithagório. www.samos-gr, www.pythagorion.net*

A Bit of History

In the Archaic period the island flourished, reaching its apogee in the middle of the 6C BC under the rule of **Polycrates.** The enlightened tyrant caused construction of a long mole to protect the port, and an underground aqueduct, one of the wonders of the Ancient world. Sámos retained its prosperity until the Roman period.

Famous sons of Ancient Samos include the mathematician **Pythagoras** (6C BC), the sculptor **Pythagoras** (5C BC), the philosopher **Epicurus** (4C BC) and the astronomer **Aristarchos** (3C BC), who anticipated Copernicus and Galileo in discovering that the earth revolves round the sun.

Under the Byzantine Empire, Sámos fell into decline. The Venetians occupied it several times. When the island fell to the Turks in 1475, the population emigrated to Chios and Lesbos.

In 1821 Sámos took an active part in the national liberation movement. The Turkish fleet was sunk in 1824 near Pithagório. Despite being excluded from the new Greek State under the 1830 London Accord, Sámos was reunited with Greece in March 1913.

Address Book

For coin categories, see the Legend on the cover flap.

GETTING THERE

By boat – Most ferries arrive at Sámos Town. Ferris link **Sámos** to **Piraeus** *(daily)*, Syros *((6/wk)*, Mikonos *(4/wk)*, Chios *(3/wk)*, Limnos, Mitilini, Naxos, Paros *(2/wk)*, Rhodes and Kos *(1/wk)*. Also service to **Pithagório** from Kalimnos, Pátmos *(3/wk)*, **Piraeus** *(daily)* and, in season, to Rhodes and Kos.

By air –The airport is located 4km/2.5mi from Pithagório; there are several flights a day to **Athens**, and several a week to Mitilini, Limnos, Rhodes and Chios.

WHERE TO EAT

Notos – *Pithagório, on the beach near the Kastro – ☎(22730) 623 51.* *May-Oct.* Salads, souvlaki served on a pleasant terrace on the beach.

El Coral – *Pithagório, at he harbour – ☎(22730) 611 93.* Meat-based specialities (pork, lamb) dressed with sauces according to your preference.

Next – *Sámos Town, on the bay – ☎(22730) 277 19.* Italian cuisine, devoured by a youthful clientele.

To Ostraki – *Sámos-Town, on the bay – ☎(22730) 270 70.* Wide variety of excellent fish and seafood.

WHERE TO STAY

Pension Déspina – *Pithagória, in the museum square – ☎ (22730) 61 677, – 3rm, 6 apts.* Clean, bright rooms; studios overlooking the square or a verdant courtyard.

Pension Daphné – *Pithagória, to the left of the museum – ☎ (22730) 61 529 – 5rm.* Some rooms have balconies overlooking the attractive square.

Paris – *Pithagória, coast road – ☎(22730) 953 97/694 72/083 00 – 7apts.* *May-Oct.*Diminutive guest-house just steps from the sea. Rooms with balconies

Dreams – *Sámos Town, 9 Odós Areos (north of Pithagorio Square) – ☎(22730) 243 50 – 11rm.* At the top of a staircase overlooking the bay; clean, high-ceilinged rooms.

Mirini Hotel – *Sámos Town, up from the landing stage – ☎ (22730) 28 452, – 34rm. May-Oct.* Well-presented rooms; dramatic views from the balconies over the rocky coastline.

Aeolis Hotel – *Sámos Town, on the harbour – ☎ (22730) 28 904, www.aeolis.gr – 50rm.* The town's best hotel in this category, well kept and stylish.

Visit

Sámos Town★

The island capital occupies an attractive **site**★★ in the Bay of Vathí (meaning deep). The lower (and newer) town is the business and administrative centre. In Platiá Pithagória a great marble lion symbolizes the people's bravery during the liberation movement. The **Municipal Gardens**★ set back from the quayside are the town's most attractive spot. The only beach is at Gangos, 1km/0.6mi from the jetty. In the **Archaeological Museum**★ (*open Tue-Sun 8.30am-3pm; 3€; (22730) 520 55*)there is a remarkable collection of artefacts from the Heraion and from Ancient Sámos, including a marble *kouros* and fine bronzes. You can also visit the small **Paleontology Museum** (*open Apr-Oct: Tue-Sat 9am-2pm, Sun 10am-2pm; 3€*) with its collection of fossils; some are 10 million years old.

Áno Vathí

The old town (Áno Vathí – the upper town) spreads up the hillside behind the port. Walk up Odós Smirnis to explore the picturesque streets lined with Turkish corbelled houses. **Ágios Gianákis**, a lovely Byzantine church dedicated to St John and St Theodore, nestles in a hollow on the hillside to the east.

Zoodóhos Pigí Monastery

8km/5mi east. Open daily except Fri, 10am-1pm and 3-8pm. No charge.
Founded in 1755, the **Monastery of the Source of Life** crowns a wooded hill on the Prasso headland. The church columns are probably from Ancient Miletus in Asia Minor. Extensive **views**★★ of the Turkish coastline.
On the way back, in Kamára, turn left into a small road leading to the village of **Agía Zóni**. The monastery (1695) contains late-17C frescoes and an iconostasis (1801).

Psilí Amos

12km/8mi east. The attractive beach of Psilí Amos ('fine sand') looks out towards Turkey's Cape Mycale. The narrowest point between Greece and Turkey (1 300m/1 430yd) is 1km/0.6mi east of here.

Driving Tour

Tour of the Island

Around 140km/88mi. Allow a full day. The route covers the north and south coasts, the Temple of Hera, and Pithagório.

North Coast★

Kokári

This fishing village and a lively resort boast a nice harbour and pebbly beach to the west. The road then overlooks the beaches of Lemonákia and **Tsamodoú** and continues to Avlákia for a splendid **view**★★ of Cape Kótsikas and of Kokári and its promontory.

Vourliótes★

Beyond Avlákia bear left for 4km/2.5mi.

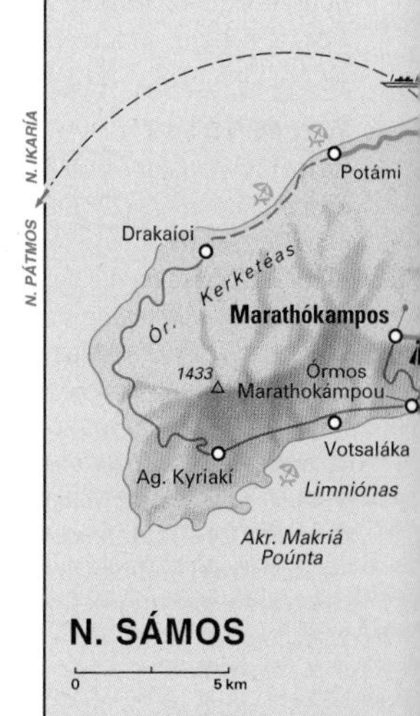

A wine-growing village with traditional houses. Continue 2km/1.25mi to the southeast to reach **Vrondianí Monastery** (1566); it is the oldest on the island.
The road winds through vineyards, affording **views**★★ of the island's coastline.

The Wines of Sámos

According to legend it was Dionysos, god of wine and vines, who offered the island some amazing plants along with some advice on viticulture. Today the wine from Sámos is known the world over. A fine quality Muscat, it can be drunk as an aperitif or with dessert. The island also produces other quality white and rosé wines

Aïdónia Gorge★

Turn left after the bridge at Platanákia and drive through the valley of the fast-flowing Aïdónia River; the occasional song of nightingales – *aïdónia* – breaks the silence. The road climbs to the village of **Manolátes** overlooking the Aïdónia Gorge.

Karlovássi

Paleó Karlovássi overlooks the harbour area and its churches and old houses. The 11C **Church of the Transfiguration** (Metamorfóssis), its dome resting on four Ancient columns, nestles near the beach at Potámi.
Head south across the island, passing through mountainous country.

The South★

Take the road leading to Marathókambos.

Marathókambos

The harbour, Órmos Marathókambou, is also a resort (large beach and excursions by boat to Samiopoúla and Pátmos). Numerous fine beaches in the area.

Return to the main road and head towards Pithagório (right).

At first the road affords lovely **views**★ over Marathókambos Bay, then cuts through the forest to the villages of **Pírgos** and **Koumaradéi**; at the latter, bear right.

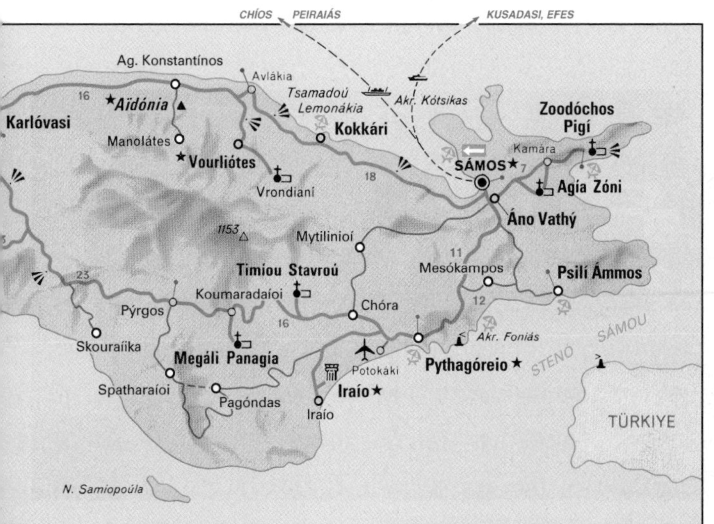

Megáli Panagía

Founded in 1586 in a wooded valley, the Monastery of the Great Virgin was rebuilt in the 18C after a fire. It was again damaged by fire in 1988.

▶ *Return to the main road. After 5km/3mi turn left to the Monastery of Timíou Stavroú.*

Timíou Stavroú

Open daily 9am-noon, 5pm-sunset. No charge.

The Monastery of the Holy Cross, was founded in the 16C after an icon of the Crucifixion was found on the spot.

The circular road passes through **Hóra**, the island's capital in the Middle Ages; 3km/1.8mi farther on turn right towards the ruins of the Temple of Hera.

Iréo★ (Heraion)

Open Tue-Sun, 8.30am-3pm. 3€. ☎(22730) 952 77.

Facing the sea are the meagre ruins of the celebrated Shrine of Hera, wife of Zeus. Several shrines have been built on this spot from the Bronze Age to the end of the Roman Empire; it is the earliest known Greek temple.

Walk past the foundations of the enormous **Temple of Hera** (6C BC). The gigantic scale of the building (twice the size of the Parthenon) can be deduced from the single standing column, although it is only half its original height of 20m/65ft. . Note the three headless **korai**★ (originals in the Archaeological Museum in Sámos Town). Farther to the left are traces of a **Christian basilica** built in the 5C or 6C. Beyond a paved street lie the remains of the **altar** dedicated to Hera. Beyond is the **Sacred Way**, which linked the sanctuary with the town of Sámos.

Pithagório★

This popular port was renamed in 1955 in honour of the mathematician and philosopher **Pythagoras**, born on Sámos. Two beaches, and Potokáki Beach *(west)*.

Logothetis Castle

Built in the early 19C, its tower soars above the town. There are extensive **views**★ to Cape Mycale in Turkey, Agathoníssi Island (south) and Cape Foniás (east).

Efpalínio★ (Eupalinos's Aqueduct)

1.5km/1mi north of Pithagório. Under restoration at press time. ☎(22730) 628 11.

H. Champollion/MICHELIN

Pithagório Roman baths

According to Herodotus, the historian and geographer (5C BC), the aqueduct hewn through the mountain was one of the wonders of his time. It provided Sámos with fresh water from the Agiádes stream on the other side of the mountain.

Ancient wall

One of the best preserved sections of the Ancient circuit wall rises about 100m/328ft west of the tunnel entrance. Other sections can be seen by the side of the road to the west, and above the road to Sámos Town on leaving Pithagório to the east.

Panagía Spilianís

Access by a road that climbs from the theatre. Open from dawn to dusk. No charge.
The Monastery of the Virgin of the Grotto derives its name from a vast cave where the oracle Phylo made prophecies in Antiquity. Outstanding view of the Pithagório Plain, Cape Fonis, and Agathoníssi Island and Cape Mycale in Turkey on the horizon.

Thérma (Roman baths)

To the west of Pithagório. Open Tue-Sun, 8am-2.45pm. No charge.
The Romans converted a large Hellenistic gymnasium into baths. A Roman basilica was replaced by a palaeo-Christian basilica (5C AD), then a Byzantine baptistery.

SAMOTHRÁKI

SAMOTHRACE – Σαμοθρακι

POPULATION 677

178KM²/71SQ MI – MICHELIN MAP 737 M 3-4 – NORTHERN AEGEAN ISLANDS.

Samothrace is a wild island, rarely visited for lack of safe harbours, but there are interesting traces of the past. Mount Fengári rises to 1 611m/5 285ft.

Visit

Ruins of the Sanctuary of the Great Gods★

Open daily 8am-7.30pm. 3€. Museum: closed Mon. (25510) 414 74.
The sanctuary, in a ravine above Paleópoli, was dedicated to two mysterious subterranean divinities known as the **Kabeiroi**.
The Anaktoron, the Hall of Princes (1C BC), was built of polygonal masonry and used for initiation ceremonies. The **Arsinoeion**, the largest rotunda in Greece, dates from about 285 BC. A rectangular precinct (temenos) whose foundations date from the 4C BC contained an allegorical statue of Desire by the great sculptor Skopas. The **Hieron**, a 4C BC temple with a Doric doorway and an apse, was used for sacrifices. Near the theatre, of which little remains, was the Victory Fountain, set in a rocky niche and decorated with the famed **Winged Victory of Samothrace**, a masterpiece of Hellenistic art (3C BC), now in the Louvre in Paris. It was discovered here in 1863; the hand was not recovered until 1950.
The Ptolemaion was erected by the ruler of Egypt, Ptolemy Philadelphos (280-264 BC) as a monumental gateway to the sanctuary.
In the **museum**, models depict the main buildings in the Sanctuary of the Great Gods. Sculptures include a headless statue of Victory from the Hieron and a bust (5C BC) of **Tiresias**, the seer who was blinded by Athena.

THÁSSOS★★

Θασσοζ

POPULATION 3 130

380KM²/152SQ MI – MICHELIN MAP 737 K 3 – NORTHERN AEGEAN ISLANDS.

Lying just off the coast of eastern Macedonia, Thássos is a wooded island, mountainous and beautiful. The island was famed in Antiquity for its gold and marble. In addition to its mountains and archaeological treasures, Thássos has golden beaches which attract holidaymakers seeking silence and space. *www.thassos.gr*

- **Orient Yourself:** Northernmost Greek island, Thássos lies 20km from Kávala.
- **Don't Miss:** Splendid coastline (see by boat or car); ruins of Thássos.
- **Organizing Your Time:** Plan a four-day visit.
- **Also See:** Kávala, Thrace.

A Bit of History

In Antiquity, particularly from the 7C to the 5C BC, Thássos was of considerable economic importance because of its exports of oil and wine, of white marble and of gold and silver; the metal was used to mint money throughout the Mediterranean.

Address Book

For coin categories, see the Legend on the cover flap.

GETTING ABOUT

By boat – Ferries from Kavála to Skála Prínos *(8/day)*. In summer, link from Keramotí to Liménas every hour. Hydrofoil service *(4/day, 6 in summer)* between Liménas and Kavála. Timetables at the harbourmaster's office.

WHERE TO EAT

Takis – *Odós Polignotou Vagi*. International and Greek cuisine.

Restaurant Vigli – *Northern end of Golden Beach*. Superbly situated; the menu includes *meze*, grilled dishes, pizzas and seafood.

Taverna Theagénis – *Skála Potamiás, near the little harbour*. Greek cuisine and seafood.

Christos – *Ágios Geórgios*. A pleasant little fish restaurant under a pergola.

Pachys – *Pahís Beach*. Shady terrace near the beach; excellent fish.

WHERE TO STAY

Hotel Vicky – *Liménas – ☎ (25930) 22 314 – 21rm*. Bright, comfortable rooms in a small three-storey building. Most rooms have kitchen facilities; a good place to stay.

Hotel Victoria – *Liménas, Odós K. Dimitriádou, by the Hotel Mironi – ☎ (25930) 23 256 – 11rm*. A small building with spacious rooms, equipped with fridges. Breakfast not included.

Timoleon Hotel – *Liménas, on the harbour, near the bus stop – ☎ (25930) 22 117 – 30rm*. A large building, comfortable rooms with balconies overlooking the harbour. Bus service to Isteri beach.

Hotel Mironi – *Liménas, Odós K. Dimitriádou – ☎ (25930) 23 256 – 10rm*. A huge marble lobby leads to large, spotlessly clean rooms (with fridges).

Dionysos – *Golden Beach, ☎(25930) 618 22 – 33rm*. Simple, bright, comfortable rooms; lovely views.

TAKING A BREAK

Anonymous Café – *Liménas, Odós 18 Oktovriou*. Eclectic selection of music.

In the 15C Thássos was occupied for a period by the Genoese, who set up a trading post under the Gatteluzzi, the lords of Lesbos and Samothrace.
Interest in Thássos was renewed in 1971 when oil was discovered offshore.

Tour

Liménas★ (Thássos Town)

The traces of the Ancient Greek civilisation are spread over a vast area enclosed within a marble wall (5C BC); a few of the gates are decorated with low-relief carvings.

Agorá

The agora was not far from the harbour. Surrounded by porticoes and studded with monuments, it was linked to the neighbouring shrines by the **Ambassadors' Passage**, which was decorated with low-relief sculptures.Remains of three porticoes frame the agora; within the open space lie the remains of a *thólos*, an altar dedicated to the deified Theagenes, a Thassian athlete who had been victorious in the Olympic Games, and some round stone benches (exedrae).

Eastern ramparts and the acropolis★

2hr on foot there and back.
Starting behind the long Turkish building overlooking the caique harbour, the path runs inside the ramparts, then climbs above the **Ancient port**; the outline of the old jetties can be traced beneath the water. A little way offshore lies the islet of Thassopoúla. After passing the remains of a 5C palaeo-Christian **basilica** set on a promontory, the path climbs up by the wall, which is superbly constructed in places with polygonal blocks. Halfway along is the theatre; it was built in the Hellenistic period but remodelled by the Romans as an arena for wild-animal fights.
The **acropolis**★ comprises three peaks in a line separated by two narrow saddles. On the first peak stood a Sanctuary to Pythian Apollo, which was converted into a fortress. The second peak boasted a Temple to Athena: the 5C foundations are still visible. At the base of the third is a small rock sanctuary dedicated to Pan; from the peak there are beautiful **views**★★ of Thássos and the Aegean Sea as far as Samothrace..
In the **museum** *(open 15 Jun-15 Sept: Tue-Sun 9am-7pm (rest of the year 9am-3pm; 2€; (25930) 221 80)* you'll find various objects from the excavations: note the ivory **lion's head**★.

Driving Tours

Tour of the Island★★

Around 80km/50mi round trip heading clockwise from Liménas.
Those seeking something other than archaeology can discover the island's splendid coastline. There is a good road that hugs the coast, remaining fairly close to the shore. It passes inlets and beaches, crosses tiny coastal basins or cuts into the cliff face.

Panagía

Leaving Liménas in a southeasterly direction the road first climbs to Panagía, the ancient capital of the island; the picturesque houses have balconies and schist roofs.

Alikía

On the south coast, this village is built at an attractive site on the neck of a peninsula consisting entirely of marble quarries, which seem to have been abandoned only yesterday. There was an Ancient city here, proved by the remains of a double sanctuary; the edge of the hill bears traces of two palaeo-Christian basilicas.

Limenária

To the southwest, this is a fishing village and a lively summer resort with some good beaches nearby.

Along the west coast the road passes many fishing villages and there are fine views of the Macedonian coast. If there is time make a detour to Mariés *(29km/18mi there and back)*, a pretty village which is close to Mount Ipsári, the island's highest point.

Boat Trips★★

The *Eros* and the *Zorbas* offers day-long circuit trips of the island, stopping at some of the most beautiful spots to allow swimming and fishing (*departs Liménas around 9.45am and returns around 5.45pm*).

The *Angetour*, based in the old port at Liménas, offers sea-fishing trips.

THE SARONIC GULF ISLANDS

POPULATION 47 000 (ALMOST HALF ON SALAMIS)
340KM²/131SQ MI.

These five easily accessible islands (Aigina, Hydra, Póros, Salamis and Spetsae) are sometimes called the Argo-Saronic Islands because of their proximity to the Argolid. Greeks regard them as a little paradise just off the mainland coast. Aigina has become the favoured place for Athenians seeking relaxation; Póros and Spetsae attract a more prosperous crowd.

- **Orient Yourself:** Aigina and Salamis are close to Athens, while Hydra, Póros and Spetsae are nearer to the Peloponnese. All are easily reached by boat, principally from Piraeus. Cars are forbidden on Hydra and Spetsae (except taxis).
- **Organizing Your Time:** The islands make a good day trip.
- **Also See:** Epidauros coast, on the mainland.

ÉGINA★

AIGINA – Αιγινα
POPULATION 11 639
83KM²/32SQ MI – MICHELIN MAP 737 I 10 – ATTICA.

The isle of Aigina comprises a series of volcanic heights culminating in Mount Zeus, now known as Mount Profítis Ilías. In the Archaic era (7C-6C BC) Aigina was a powerful maritime state that rivalled Athens, but was eventually eclipsed by its powerful neighbour. Today, it is a leafy suburb of the Greek capital and a popular weekend escape from the big city noise and heat. The tasty pistachio nut is grown in huge quantities on the coastal plains.

Visit

Temple of Aféa★★

Near Agía Marína (connections to Piraeus). Open 8.15am-7pm. €4 (includes museum) (22970) 322 52. Organise your visit around the rather inconvenient opening times at the museum (9-9.15am, 11-11.15am, noon-12.15pm, 1-1.15pm).

This Doric temple is one of the best preserved in Greece. It stands on a magnificent **site**★★ on the summit of a wooded hill overlooking the Bay of Agía Marína, the rocky coastline, Athens, Salamis and the Peloponnese *(north and west)*.

Dedicated to Aphaia, a local divinity, the temple (5C BC) has 22 monolithic limestone columns. Its pediments of sculpted marble, known as the Aigina Marbles, were bought in 1812 by Prince Ludwig of Bavaria, and displayed in Munich.

Within the temple the position of the naos is clearly visible. To the south lie traces of an entrance gate *(propylaia)* and priests' lodgings.

To the west of the temple, there is a small **Museum** which attempts to reconstruct the second Temple of Aphaia (destroyed by fire in 510 BC) using original fragments, most notably the polychrome façade.

Paleohóra★

In the centre of the island, halfway between the Temple of Aphaia and Aigina Town.

Paleohóra was the capital of the island under the Venetians and the Turks. It was abandoned early in the 19C; the houses (once numbering 400) are gone but the cathedral, a basilical building, and the churches and chapels have been restored; some are adorned with interesting frescoes and iconostases. The Venetian castle on the hilltop provides a good view of Mount Zeus and the northwest coastline.

Aigina Town

Western end of the island.

The town enjoyed a brief moment of glory during the struggle for independence from 1827 to 1829, when it was the capital of the new Greek state. **Kapodístrias** set up his government here and Greece's first national money was minted, bearing a phoenix, symbol of rebirth.

Pink-and-white houses cluster around the little harbour overlooked by a charming chapel dedicated to **St Nicholas**, the patron saint of sailors. From the harbour, there is a magnificent **view**★★ over to the islets in the Saronic Gulf and the Peloponnese. The shops along the waterfront sell the local specialities: pottery, pistachio nuts and marzipan. Some of the boats sell fish, fruit and vegetables.

Temple of Apollo

North of Aigina Town. Open Tue-Sun, 8.30am-3pm. 3€ (includes museum).

On **Cape Kolóna** stands a fluted column crowned with a capital, once part of a Temple to Apollo erected in the 5C BC; **excavations** have uncovered the remains of a theatre and a stadium, as well as a prehistoric dwelling. A small **Archaeological Museum**, laid out along the lines of a Classical villa, displays items found on the island, including funerary stelae and sculpture from the Temple of Aphaia (museum).

From the beach nearby one can see remains of the quays of the Ancient harbour below the surface of the sea.

Pérdika

10km/6mi south of Aigina Town.

Address Book

For coin categories, see the Legend on the cover flap.

GETTING THERE

By boat – Many ferry companies offer daily service to Piraeus, Méthana, Póros, Hydra and Spetsae. Ferries also run to the Cyclades in Jul-Aug. Daily shuttles link Aigina Town and Agia Marina.

WHERE TO EAT

Areti – *Aigina Town, opposite the Hotel Plaza.* This seafront spot serves specialities of fish caught the same day.

Argyris – *Messagrós, road out of the village.* Popular with locals, this taverna serves the freshest grilled fish, and a tasty local retsina. Try the spinach pie.

Kostas – *Álones, south of Agía Marína.* Under a shady pergola, this taverna (like its neighbour Takis) serves authentic Greek fare in a village atmosphere. Good *meze* and fish specialities.

WHERE TO STAY

Hotel Plaza – *Aigina Town, left of the landing – ☎ and fax (22970) 25 600, plazainaegina@yahoo.co.uk – 37rm.* One of a group of three hotels; rooms all across the price range (the cheapest are among the island's least expensive.

Nafsika Hotel Bungalows – *Aigina Town, 55 odos Kazantzaki, north of the port – ☎ (22970) 223 33 – open mid-Apr-mid-Oct– 34rm.* Bougainvillea-draped bungalows, almost invisible from the road, attract lovers of nature and peace. A popular spot; best to reserve.

FESTIVALS

9 Nov: Agios Nektarios Festival.

This charming fishing harbour affords a good view of Moní Island. Excursions by boat can be made to the island (old monastery, beach) in summer. There are two fine beaches between Aigina Town and Pérdika: Faros and Marathonas.

Mount Zeus

4hr round trip from Marathonas Beach.

The highest point on the island (532m/1 745ft); there are vestiges here of Ancient structures, most notably an extraordinary set of steps. From here on a clear day it is possible to see Póros, the mountains of the Peloponnese, the isthmus of Corinth, Salamis, the Athens conurbation and the coast as far as Cape Sounion.

North coast

There are numerous beaches and pleasant inlets looking out towards Salamis and the mainland. The **view** of sprawling Athens is impressive.

ÍDRA★★

HYDRA – Υδρα

POPULATION 6 000

86KM²/34SQ MI – MICHELIN MAP 737 I 11 – ATTICA.

The Gulf of Hydra separates the island from the Peloponnese. From the 15C it was one of the most important ports in Greece. Today Hydra is a popular tourist destination. *On the quay, at the Manessi Hotel.*

- **Orient Yourself:** Ferry service from Piraeus and Ermióni. Vehicular traffic is prohibited here.
- **Don't Miss:** Hydra Town, charming and scenic.
- **Organizing Your Time:** A good choice for a day trip.
- **Also See:**Póros

A Bit of History

It seems that Hydra was once greener and more abundantly supplied with water than it is now (hence its name). Pine forests once covered the slopes, and gardens

B. Kaufmann/MICHELIN

Hydra harbour and town

flourished with water channelled from huge underground cisterns. Gradually the surface water grew rarer, the forests were over-exploited for shipbuilding and the cultivated terraces were abandoned. Since 1960 water has been imported from the mainland by tanker.

Visit

Hydra Town★★

The little port of Hydra, which is packed with yachts in the season, occupies an extraordinary **site**★★★, hidden in a rounded inlet and bordered by old houses which fan out up the rocky hillside like seats in a theatre. Lively crowds stroll the **quayside**★★, past cafés, tavernas, restaurants and cake shops.
Near the port, the **Museum of Historical Archives** *(open Jul-Aug Tue-Sun 9am-4.30pm, 7.30-9.30pm; Sep-Jun Tue-Sun 9am-4.30pm; 3€)* traces Hydra's maritime history.

Monastery of the Assumption

A large clock tower marks the entrance to this monastery, built in 1643, and restored in the 18C after earthquake damage. Its two marble courtyards form a tranquil

Address Book

For coin categories, see the Legend on the cover flap.

GETTING THERE

By boat – Ferries run every hour from Piraeus; hydrofoil service from Zéa; also ferry services to Ermióni on the Peloponnese coast. Service to to the Cyclades in Jul-Aug.
Daily water taxis link the beaches.

WHERE TO EAT

To Steki – *Hydra Town, Odós Miaoúli.* This taverna offers meals including ouzo and dessert at reasonable prices. Very busy in the evenings.

Gitonikon – *Hydra Town, behind and to the right of Xerí Eliá taverna.* This restaurant on two floors (with terrace) serves forth carefully prepared dishes of the freshest ingredients. Great value.

Xerí Eliá (Douskos) – *Hydra Town, in the centre.* In a pretty square of white houses,with tables set out under two old trees. Try the stuffed squid with wine straight from the barrel, accompanied by Greek music.

Mertazani Zoi – *Near Mandráki.* An unpretentious restaurant where the tomatoes come fresh from the vegetable garden and the fish from the sea just below.

Bratsera – *Hydra Town, in the hotel of the same name.* The best restaurant in town with magnificent decor. Traditional dishes as well as international cuisine (*tabbouleh*, Caesar salad) and a good selection of pasta.

WHERE TO STAY

Hotel Nefeli – *Hydra Town,at the top of the town. – ☎ (22980) 53 297 – 10rm.* If you have much luggage, use the services of a donkey. Simple rooms arranged tastefully. Lovely view of the town from room 15.

Miramare – *Mandráki – ☎ (22980) 52 300, www.miramare-hotel.net – 28rm.* Cool bungalows with terraces and fridges on the edge of Mandráki Beach, five minutes by boat from the centre of town (service until 3am). Various watersports and chidren's pool; island tours in the hotel boat.

Miranda – *Hydra Town, Odós Miaoúli – ☎ (22980) 52 230 – 14rm* – . This fine historic residence retains its shady courtyard garden and its museum-like decor (coffered ceilings).

Orloff – *Hydra Town, near public gardens – ☎ (22980) 52 564 and in Athens (210) 52 26 152, www.orloff.gr – 9rm.* This 18C mansion's discreet exterior will appeal to lovers of authentic architecture; gracious welcome.

haven. In the basilica (nave and two aisles) there is a fine marble iconostasis and a gilt icon of the martyr Constantine the Hydriot. Note also the chandeliers decorated with ex-votos featuring ships.
At the exit of the church, a stairway leads to the small **Byzantine Museum** (*open Tue-Sun 10am-5pm, 2€; ☎ 22980 54071*); collection of liturgical objects, icons.

Belvedere

To the west of the port, a shady promenade offers a good view of the island of Dokós and the mainland. Cannons from the 19C guard the entry to the bay.

Upper town★★

Cool and quiet, the upper town offers impressive views over the port below.
The area's **ship owners' houses**★ were mostly built in the 19C, often in imitation of Venetian palaces (loggias, internal courtyards). Many of these noble residences have remained in the same families. Three on the west side of the harbor are worth noting: the Voúlgaris House *(far end of the waterfront)*, the Tombázis House *(farther up)*, now a School of Fine Arts, and the Koundouriótis House *(halfway up the hillside)*.

Around Hydra★

Monasteries of Profítis Ilías (Prophet Elijah) and Agía Efpraxía (St Euphrasia)

2hr on foot there and back by Odós Miaoúli and the valley.
These two convents, one for men, the other for women, were built near a pine forest. There are; fine **views**★ of Hydra, the coast and the other Saronic Gulf Islands.

Kamínia

45min on foot there and back following the harbour quay round to the west.
Beyond the fort the coast path continues to Kamínia, a quiet fishing hamlet with a shingle beach.

Vlichós

West of Hydra, beyond Kamínia.
The red pebble beach contrasts with the immaculate white of the houses.

Mólos Bay

West of Hydra, beyond Vlichós.
Yachts at anchor in this wide bay make for an attractive scene.

Cape Bísti

West of Hydra.
This wild spot is accessible by boat or on foot and is a good place for a swim.

Mandráki

1hr on foot there and back or by taxi-boat or caique.
Follow the quayside round to the east past the Merchant Navy Captains' School, which occupies an old ship owner's house. The road continues to Mandráki Bay *(sandy beach)*, former site of the 19C shipyards. Most of the Hydriot fleet, used to anchor in the bay. The **sandy beach** here is very pleasant.

PÓROS★★

Ποροζ

POPULATION 3 605

33KM²/13SQ MI – MICHELIN MAP 737 I 10 – ATTICA.

Poros' pleasant climate and verdant landscape make it an agreable place to visit. A canal divides the island in two: the major part, called Kalavría, is a limestone ridge; the other half is a volcanic islet called Sfería, is home to Póros Town, the main port.

- **Orient Yourself:** A mere few hundred metres separate the island from the Peloponnese; excursions from the Argolid Peninsula are an easy hop.
- **Organizing Your Time:** Stay a few days, alternating beach time with visits to nearby historic sites (Nafplio, Epidaurus, Corinth, Tirinth, Mycenae).

Walking Tour

Arriving by boat one has enchanting **views**★★★ of the bay, the little white town and of the green shores of the mainland. From **Galatás** on the mainland, there are also great views of Póros Town reflected in the calm waters of the strait.

Address Book

For coin categories, see the Legend on the cover flap.

GETTING THERE

By boat – Many ferry and hydrofoil services to Piraeus, Méthana and Galatás (from where a car ferry operates all day). If you plan to just visit Póros Town, leave your car in the parking lot at Galatás and take the shuttle.

WHERE TO STAY

Manessi – *Póros Town, almost directly opposite the ferry dock – ☎ (22980) 22 273 – 15rm.* An elegant building with a white and blue façade and a pleasantly old-fashioned interior.

Seven Brothers – *Póros Town, near the shuttle landing. ☎ (22980) 34 12 – www.7brothers.gr.* Pretty, modern hotel; some rooms have balconies.

Póros Hotel – *Neório Bay – ☎ (22980) 22 216 or in Athens (210) 94 00 580, porosimage@hit360.com – 100rm –* ☕. A recently renovated complex with large, bright rooms; good views over the harbour. Private beach. Open mid-Apr-late Oct.

Sirene – *Monastiri Bay – ☎ (22980) 22 741 to 743.* This luxury hotel stands on a cliff between the road and the sea. Attractive rooms (the best overlook the sea), restaurant, dance hall, private beach, two swimming pools. Open mid-Apr-mid-Oct.

TAKING A BREAK

Poseidon Music Club – *Between Póros Town and the Temple of Poseidon.* Great views over the harbour and Galatás; bar with pool open in summer with concerts of Greek and international music.

EVENTS AND FESTIVALS

Summer watersports week (regattas).

H. Champollion/MICHELIN

Póros Town★

The white cuboid houses mount the slopes of the promontory towards a blue painted bell tower; from the top there is a **view★★** of the town, and the busy strait.

A stroll along the quay opens up a picturesque view of Galatás. In the typical fishermen's district *(east)* the cafés and tavernas are decorated with naïve paintings. The old arsenal *(west)* now houses a naval school. The small **Archaeological Museum**, *(Platiá Alexis Korizis; >open 8.30am-3pm, weekends 9.30am-2.30pm, closed Mon, 2€)* displays architectural fragments and statuettes dating from 4C-3C BC.

Kalavría★

A magnificent forest of covers this part of the island on the other side of an isthmus. The road climbs to the ruins of a **Sanctuary to Poseidon (Naós Possidóna)** *(open Tue-Sun, 8am-2.30pm; no charge)* dating from the 6C BC; only the outline remains, but it is on a superb site overlooking the island and the Saronic Gulf.

From the temple follow the road downhill to the **Zoodóhos Pigí Monastery★**, a white building set in a valley refreshed by many springs. The cloisters with their noble cypress trees are open to the public *(open 9am-4pm winter, 9am-9pm summer; no charge)*.

Beaches

There are several pleasant sandy beaches: Mikro, Megalo Neorio and Askeli.

SALAMÍNA

SALAMIS – Σαλαμινα

POPULATION 23 000

96KM2/38SQ MI – MICHELIN MAP 737 I 9 – ATTICA.

Fringing the Bay of Eleusis, Salamis is the closest island to Athens and the largest in the Saronic Gulf. Easily accessible, it is very popular with Athenians. Its name is inextricably linked with one of the greatest sea battles in history.

The Battle of Salamis

Having occupied Athens and Attica in the Second Persian War, the Persian fleet gathered in the Saronic Gulf as the Persian King Xerxes looked on from shore. A large number of Persian ships engaged the Greeks in the narrow straits off Pérama, but were unable to maneuver in such a small space. The Greek *triremes*, fitted with bronze prows, rammed the enemy vessels. The engagement is described by Aeschylus, an eyewitness, in his play *The Persians* (472 BC), and by the historian Herodotus.

GETTING THERE

By boat – Numerous ferries to the mainland (Piraeus, Pérama and Mégara). Between Pérama and Paliouka, there is a service every 15min by day and every hour by night.

WHERE TO EAT

Various tavernas in **Salamis** (Koulouri) and **Selinia**.

WHERE TO STAY

It's best to stay in **Athens** and come for the day. Those wishing to stay on the island will find the best accommodation in **Selinia**.

Visit

The island is largely a weekenders' suburb, composed of second homes belonging to Athenians. The resort of **Selinia** to the east is quite busy. The south of the island is more mountainous and offers fine views of Aigina and the Peloponnese coast.

Monastery of Faneroméni

Western end of the island, 1.5km/1mi from the arrivals dock for the Mégara ferry.
Built in the 17C, the church here has some fine 18C frescoes (Last Judgement). The Virgin is said to have appeared here, and the monastery attracts many pilgrims.

SPÉTSES★★

SPETSAE – Σπετσεζ

POPULATION 3 500

22KM²/9SQ MI – MICHELIN MAP 737 H 11 – ATTICA.

Popular with the Athenian middle class, many of whom own houses here, Spetsae is an attractive island bathed in a gentle light and scented with jasmine. There is only one town, which stretches along the coast facing the Argolid Peninsula. The rest of Spetsae is given over to a vast forest of Aleppo pines.
Like its rival, Hydra, Spetsae grew rich through trading in the Mediterranean during the 18C and 19C. When the War of Independence began in 1821, the islanders converted merchant vessels into powerful warships, and played an active role in the conflict, destroying the enemy admiral's flagship.

- **Orient Yourself:** Spetsae lies just 3km/1.9mi from the Peloponnese coast. No cars are allowed on the island.
- **Don't Miss:** Bouboulina's house.
- **Organizing Your Time:** A good day trip destination.

A Bit of History

Born in a Turkish prison in 1771, Lascarína Pinótzis (called Bouboulina) was married twice; first to a Spetsiot sea captain (killed when his ship was sunk by pirates), and then to another sailor (also killed by pirates).

Chabrol B./MICHELIN

Horse and carriage at Spetsae port

Her husbands' deaths made Bouboulína the owner of shipyards and a fleet of brigs and schooners. She took part in naval engagements between 1821 and 1824, leading her crews in person. A national heroine, she died violently in a family dispute in 1825.

Touring

Kaiki Beach

1km/0.6mi west of Dapia.

Near the Anárgyros-Orgialénios College, this beach is busy but attractive.

Órmos Zogeriás★★ (Zogeriá Bay)

Take the coast road northwest (5hr on foot there and back; 2hr by bicycle there and back). There are also boats from Dápia.

The road climbs through forests of Aleppo pines until it reaches the huge bay at Zogeriá, a beautiful **site**★★ facing north up the Bay of Nauplion.

Agía Marína Beach

This attractive beach is to the south of the old harbour.

Address Book

For coin categories, see the Legend on the cover flap.

GETTING THERE

By boat – Spetsae is 1hr10min from Athens by hydrofoil. There are also plenty of ferries to Kósta on the Argolid mainland. There are moorings for pleasure craft and yachts in the old harbour and at Portocheli and Tolo.

WHERE TO EAT

Orloff – *Halfway between Dápia and the old harbour.* A trendy spot; views over the water. Good choice of *meze*, and pricier fish dishes.

Mourayo – *Far end of the old harbour.* Peaceful restaurant with terrace overlooking the sea. Quality cuisine: fish à la Spétses and French dishes. Greek music and piano bar until 2am.

Tassos Taverna – *Ágioi Anárgiri Beach, western part of the island.* Good choice for oven-baked dishes. Try the lamb or *moussaka*.

Patralis – *beyond the Posidonion Hotel.* Excellent fish restaurant, refined atmosphere. Terrific views over the Argolid coast.

WHERE TO STAY

Armata – *Dápia. From the port take Odós Santou, the left into a small square – ☎ (22980) 72 683 – 14rm.* An authentic Spetsiot house with pleasant rooms giving onto a garden; breakfast by the pool. Good value and charm too.

Posidonion – *On the seafront to the right of Dápia – ☎ (22980) 72 208 – 43rm and 3 suites.* The atmosphere of the Roaring Twenties lingers in this palatial establishment; marble staircase, high-ceilinged rooms and a huge shaded terrace. Charming.

TAKING A BREAK

Figaro – A pleasant disco in the old harbour.

Papagayo – For dinner or cocktails. Band on Friday, Saturday and Sunday.

Politis – *Not far from the Papagayo.* Don't miss the almond cakes here.

EVENTS AND FESTIVALS

26 July: Traditional festival at the Church of Agía Paraskeví, on the beach of the same name.

2-8 September: commemoration of the victory of the Spetsiot ship owners over the Turks, with dancing, singing and fireworks (on the Saturday).

Ágioi Anárgiri Beach★

13km/8mi west of the town (bus from Agía Marína).
Magnificent beach bordered by pine trees and scrubland.

Walking Tour

Spetsae Town★★

Spetsae consists of two districts round the harbour, Dápia and Paleó Limáni, as well as the upper town, Kastéli. It has become a fashionable destination and is particularly popular with the British.

Dápia★

The modern port is a lively place. The waterfront is lined with shops and restaurants;, but the nearby alleys, with their ship owners' houses, are quiet. It is pleasant to stroll past the ship owners' and sailors' houses set in their gardens (note the thresholds decorated with pebble mosaics). You can visit **Bouboulina's House** *(open daily 9.45am-7.30pm; guided tour only, 4€)*, now a house museum; or the **Maison Mexis** *(open Tue-Sun 8am-2.30pm; 3€)* for a glimpse of the fabulous interior decor of a ship owners house.

Upper Town (Kastéli)★

The upper town above Dápia was fortified by the Venetians in the 16C. The largest church, **Agía Triáda** (Holy Trinity), contains a beautiful carved-wood iconostasis.

West of the port, the waterfront is bordered by a pleasant **residental quarter** with lovely villas. The **Hotel Posidonion** (1914) overlooking the sea has a magnificent façade flanked by two towers. Also note the former **Anargirios-Orgialenios** School (now a conference centre), for boys of the Greek aristocracy.

Paleó Limáni★

The old port is composed of many inlets filled with the vestiges of 18C marine facilities. This quarter is less developed than Dápia and has some pleasant restaurants.

St Nicholas' Monastery (Ágios Nikólaos)

Not far from the old port is the bell tower of the island's cathedral. The war memorial with two cannons marks the place where the first flag of independence was flown in 1821. The dimly lit church interior contains a fine wood iconostasis.

Walk to the lighthouse★

Located on a promontory to the east of the town. The walk along the seafront *(30min there and back)* is pleasant; along the way is the Chapel of Panagia Armata, erected to commemorate the destruction of the Turkish admiral's flagship on 8 September 1822, (large painting of the event). From the lighthouse there is a fine view of Spetsae and the Peloponnese coast.

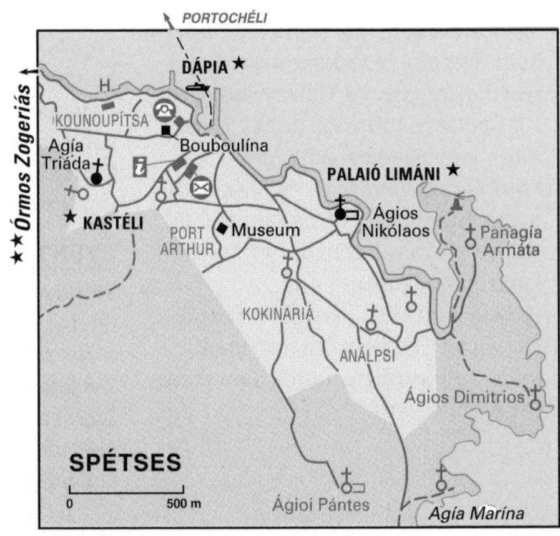

THE SPORÁDES★★

POPULATION 16 000 – 470KM²/188SQ MI.

These four islands – Skiáthos, Skópelos, Alónissos and Skíros – lie close to the mainland and are invaded each summer by tourists drawn to their beaches, their icon-filled monasteries, their little fishing ports, and their villages of shady alleys. Skiáthos is the nearest to the mainland and the most visited; Skíros, set apart somewhat from the other islands, is the most secretive. *Sporádes* means 'scattered', a fitting name for these islands and their many associated islets.

- **Orient Yourself:** Ferries run year-round from Vólos and Kimi; there are also links to Lemnos and Thessaloníki. There's air service from Skiáthos and Skíros to Athens and some European cities.

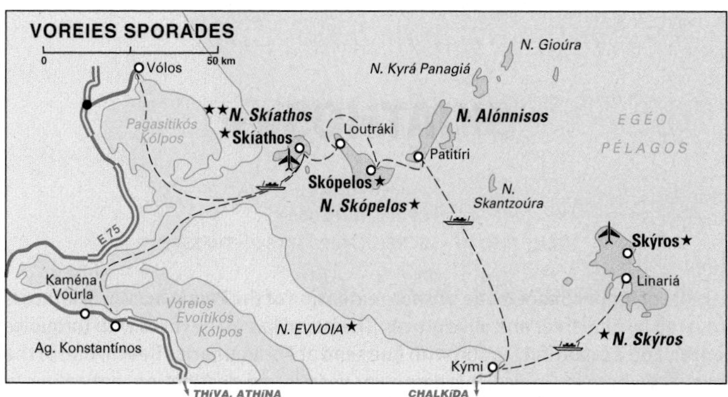

ALÓNISSOS

Αλονισσοζ

POPULATION 3 000

65KM²/26SQ MI – MICHELIN MAP 737 J 6 – THESSALY.

This northernmost island of the Sporádes has a rugged topography of pine-covered hillsides, and pebble or sand beaches. Curiously undiscovered, it is in a rich wildlife reserve for endangered monk seals and dolphins.

Visit

Patitíri

The principal port and capital of the island, Patitíri is a large modern town. It is located in a bay dominated by promontory covered by pine trees and a few hotels. At the **Folklore Museum** *(open daily 11am-7pm)* tools and other objects of daily life offer a peek at life in centuries past.

Alónissos★

Perched on a hill, this is a charming village of white and blue houses with tile or slate roofs. From the top of the village there is a fine view over the sea.

Beaches
Several beaches are accessible from Alónissos, including Megálo Mourtiá, Mikro Mourtiá *(45min walk)*, Marpoúnda and Vtysítsa *(35min walk)*. Farther north, there are numerous (mostly pebble) beaches which can be reached by boat or on foot. Those seeking a sandy beach should try Hrysi Miliá. At the northern end of the road is the pebble beach at Gérakas.

Walks★
The island offers a great deal to keen walkers. The Anavasi 1:40 000 map *(available from travel agencies in Patitíri)* shows the main footpaths.

National Marine Park★
Kids *Boat trips from Patitíri (the* Kassandra*) leave daily at 11am, returning at 5.30pm.* The sea to the north of the island, where there are a number of islets, is a protected area. Here it is possible to see endangered monk seals, Audouin's gulls, shags and dolphins ... a worthwhile trip.

SKIÁTHOS★★

Σκιαθοζ

POPULATION 5 000

50KM²/20SQ MI – MICHELIN MAP 737 I 6-7 – THESSALY.

Like its neighbor Skopelos an offshore extension of the Pelion massif, Skiáthos is covered by pine trees and olive groves. The island has many coves with turquoise water, and a beautiful lagoon with fine sand at Koukounariés Beach, one of the best anywhere in Greece. It is a popular year-round destination, appealing to those seeking its tranquillity, swimming, boat trips and nightlife. *Tiny wood structure to the left of the ferry landing.*

- **Orient Yourself:** Ferries run year-round from Vólos.
- **Don't Miss:** Skiáthos Town; the island's stunning beaches.

Touring

Beaches
Renowned for their fine sand and crystal-clear water, the beaches of Skiáthos are the island's main attraction. There are around 60 to choose from; most get busy in summer. The quietest are on the north coast (Lalia, Nikotsára, Xánemo) and are accessible by boat.

At the southwest end of the island, **Bananá Beach** is pleasant. Tiny Hidden Beach lies at the foot of a heather-covered hill. Mandráki is a glorious carpet of fine sand. The most famous and busiest is **Koukounariés Beach**★★ on a pine-fringed lagoon that seems more Polynesian than Greek (protected area).

Walks★
The best way to see the island is on foot.

Kástro★
North coast; access by boat (1hr 30min) or on foot (4hr round trip) from Skiáthos Town. The path passes two monasteries – **Evangelístria** (a beautiful iconostasis of carved wood in the church) and **Ágios Harálambos** – before reaching the ruins of the

medieval fortress (Kástro). It stood on a promontory, accessible only by a drawbridge. Two of its houses (which numbered 300) are well preserved; Christchurch contains a 17C carved wooden iconostasis.

Monastery of Panagía Kounístra★

3hr round trip from Fteliá; also accessible by car. This walk provides superb views of the island. From the monastery, the **view**★ takes in the entire coastline.

Walking Tour

Skiáthos Town★

Skiáthos is the capital of the island; a charming place, its white houses with red roofs scale two hillsides. Its two harbours are separated by a pine-covered islet (Boúrdzi). Although quiet in winter, it gets extremely busy in summer. There are many bars, restaurants and shops, making for very lively evenings.

SKÓPELOS★

Σκοπελοζ

POPULATION 5 000

97KM²/39SQ MI – MICHELIN MAP 737 I 6 – THESSALY.

The most densely inhabited of the Sporades and also the most fertile, this orchard island is covered by pine trees, olive groves, almond trees and plum trees; the fruit of the latter makes excellent prunes when dried. The island has many churches and chapels, as well as several monasteries dating from the 17 and 18C. Tourists love its coves with sandy beaches and emerald waters. *At the port.* ☎ *(24240) 24567.*

Visit

Skópelos Town★

This attractive hillside settlement, set deep in a wide bay, is protected by a sea wall. Pleasantly shaded by the plane trees and flanked by houses with tiled roofs and little chapels, the alleyways make for a lovely stroll.

The medieval **fortress** (Kástro) contained many houses and religious buildings. St Athanasius's Chapel was built in the 9C on the foundations of an Ancient temple, and contains a sumptuous polychrome iconostasis. From the top of the ruins there is a fine view of Skópelos Town, the island and the Sporades archipelago.

Glóssa★

This large town to the north of the island has an unspoilt authenticity, with its old church, its white houses and its network of alleyways. A road leads down to **Loutráki**, its port, where there are a number of pleasant restaurants.

Mount Paloúki★

Like a lesser Mount Athos, this is an important monastic site. The summit is a superb viewpoint over the island and beyond.

Evangelístria Convent

Open daily, 8am-1pm and 5-8pm. Donation.

A nun will show visitors the iconostasis and the stunning views over the island.

Ph. Longin/MICHELIN

Metamórfossi Monastery

Metamórfossi Monastery

Open daily, 8am-1.30pm and 5-8.30pm. Donation.
This dates from the 16C and has a church in its attractive courtyard.

Pródromos Convent

Open daily, 8am-1pm and 5-8pm. Donation.
This convent is cut off from the outside world and also has a church; superb view.

The coast★

There are many attractive beaches, some pebble, others sand. The finest are on the south and west coasts. **Miliá**, on the west coast, is probably the most popular.
A pleasant coast **road**★ runs south from Loutráki.

SKÍROS★

Σκυροζ

POPULATION 2 900

223KM²/89SQ MI – MICHELIN MAP 737 K 7 – CENTRAL GREECE.

Facing Euboia, Skíros is the largest of the Sporades. It is composed of two mountainous outcrops connected by an isthmus, and has a wilder character than the other islands in the archipelago. The southern part, called Vounó ('mountain'), provides grazing for half-wild goats and sheep, and small native horses. The northern part, Méri, is farmed or planted with pine trees. All round the coast are deserted coves with turquoise waters and beautiful seascapes.

Visit

Hóra (Skíros Town)★

The main town, Hóra, has tiny white cuboid houses, more typical of the Cyclades. It is a pleasure to stroll through the network of narrow alleyways and steps, which pass under arches and open into courtyards. The interior of a house may be viewed at no 992 of the **Agora** (narrow pedestrian street with shops).
On a bastion on the northeast edge of the town stands a statue in memory of **Rupert Brooke** (1887-1915). The poet's grave lies in a valley on the southern shore of the island in Trís Boúkes Bay *(1hr by road from Hóra or by boat from Linariá).*

Address Book

For coin categories, see the Legend on the cover flap.

GETTING ABOUT

BY BOAT

The port is at Linariá on the west coast. There are two ferries to Kími (Euboia) a day. Hydrofoil service *(June-Sep)* links the island to Alónissos, Skópelos, Skiáthos, Vólos and Thessaloníki.

BY AIR

The airport is at the northern end of the island; service to Athens in summer.

WHERE TO EAT

Taverna Metopo – *main street.* Tasty, varied cuisine (lasagne, fresh vegetables, lentil soup), quick service and a shady terrace.

WHERE TO STAY

Domátia Anna Kiriazi – *Hóra, above the agora, fork left and then head up to the museums on the right* – *(22220) 91 574*. Charming traditional house with, fireplace, ceramics and terrace.

Nefeli – *Hóra, outskirts of town* – *(22220) 91 964/920 63 – 23rm.* Apartments and rooms in an attractive building with fireplaces and antiques. The bar is very pleasant.

Hotel Hydroussa – *Magazía, beach north of Hóra* – *(22220) 92 063 to 65 – 22rm.* The main hotel on the beach. Balconies with sea views.

EVENTS AND FESTIVALS

Festivals – In February don't miss the famous **Skiros Carnival**, an amazing mix of pagan rites. In the first three weeks of August, **Faltaïts Festival** (theatre, music, dance); details available from the Folklore Museum *(shows around 9pm; tickets 4-5€).*

At the **Faltaïts Museum of Folk Arts** *(open summer 10am-2pm, 6-9pm; winter 10am-6pm; 2€; (22220) 911 50)* you can see local crafts, both modern and traditional. Helladic and Roman period artifacts are on view at the **Archaeological Museum** *(open Tue-Sun 8.30am-3pm; 2€; (22220) 913 27).*

Kástro

Closed for restoration.

The Venetian fortress was built on the old acropolis where Achilles is supposed to have been brought up disguised as a girl. There is an unusual **view**★★ over Hóra. Adjacent to the kástro is the monastery of Ágios Nikólaos with its 10C church, perched on a rocky outcrop above the town.

The Northern Peninsula (Méri)★

This part of the island has numerous beaches: Magaziá and Mólos (just north of Hóra); Kyrá Panagiá and Atsítsa (west coast); and Ágios Fókas, near a pine forest (southwest coast).

There are also three ports: Péfkos, Ahérounes and Linariá (where the ferries dock). On a hill above Péfkos is the Chapel of Ágios Pandeleímonos, from where there is an excellent **view**★ of the island.

The Southern Peninsula (Vounó)★

Beyond the little resort of Kalamítsa and the beach at Kolibádas Bay, the road traverses a desert landscape and passes some beautiful **cliffs**★★ bordering a gulf, across which are scattered numerous islets.

A

ATHENS 111

H

I

J

K

L

N

O

P

W, X, Y

Z

ACCOMMODATIONS

RESTAURANTS

MAPS AND PLANS

LIST OF MAPS

THEMATIC MAPS

TOWN PLANS

PLANS OF MONUMENTS AND ARCHAEOLOGICAL SITES

TOURING MAPS

COMPANION PUBLICATIONS

From our range of products we recommend the following:

MICHELIN MAP 737

– on a scale of 1:700 000, the whole Greek road network, islands and mainland (including Crete), with names indicated both in Greek letters and their Latin transcription.

TRAVELLING TO GREECE:

- **Michelin Road Atlas Europe**

– with an index of place names, 73 town and city plans.

Internet users can access personalised route plans, Michelin maps and town plans, and addresses of hotels and restaurants featured in the *Michelin Guide Europe* through the website at:

www.ViaMichelin.com

Legend

Selected monuments and sights

- Tour - Departure point
- Catholic church
- Protestant church, other temple
- Synagogue - Mosque
- Building
- Statue, small building
- Calvary, wayside cross
- Fountain
- Rampart - Tower - Gate
- Château, castle, historic house
- Ruins
- Dam
- Factory, power plant
- Fort
- Cave
- Troglodyte dwelling
- Prehistoric site
- Viewing table
- Viewpoint
- Other place of interest

Sports and recreation

- Racecourse
- Skating rink
- Outdoor, indoor swimming pool
- Multiplex Cinema
- Marina, sailing centre
- Trail refuge hut
- Cable cars, gondolas
- Funicular, rack railway
- Tourist train
- Recreation area, park
- Theme, amusement park
- Wildlife park, zoo
- Gardens, park, arboretum
- Bird sanctuary, aviary
- Walking tour, footpath
- Of special interest to children

Special symbols

- Metro
- Olympic Airways
- ΕΛΠΑ ELPA — Greek Automobile-Club
- Ancient site
- Ancient theatre
- Christian cemetery
- Muslim cemetery
- Monastery
- Beach
- Olympic sites 2004

Abbreviations

H	Town hall
M	Museum
T	Theatre

Highly recommended ★★★

Recommended ★★

Interesting ★

Additional symbols

	Tourist information
	Motorway or other primary route
	Junction: complete, limited
	Pedestrian street
	Unsuitable for traffic, street subject to restrictions
	Steps – Footpath
	Train station – Auto-train station
S.N.C.F.	Coach (bus) station
	Tram
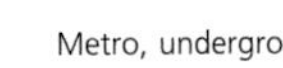	Metro, underground
	Park-and-Ride
	Access for the disabled
	Post office
	Telephone
	Covered market
	Barracks
	Drawbridge
	Quarry
	Mine
B F	Car ferry (river or lake)
	Ferry service: cars and passengers
	Foot passengers only
③	Access route number common to Michelin maps and town plans
Bert (R.)...	Main shopping street
AZ B	Map co-ordinates

Hotels and restaurants

Hotels- price categories:

	Provinces	Large cities
⊖	<40 €	<60 €
⊖⊖	40 to 65 €	60 to 90 €
⊖⊖⊖	65 to 100 €	90 to 130 €
⊖⊖⊖⊖	>100 €	>130 €

Restaurants- price categories:

	Provinces	Large cities
⊖	<14€	<16€
⊖⊖	14 to 25 €	16 to 30 €
⊖⊖⊖	25 to 40 €	30 to 50 €
⊖⊖⊖⊖	>40 €	>50 €

20 rooms: Number of rooms

	No credit cards accepted
P	Reserved parking for hotel patrons
	Swimming Pool
	Air conditioning
	Rooms accessible to persons of reduced mobility

The prices correspond to the higher rates of the tourist season

NOTES

NOTES

Michelin Maps and Guides
One Parkway South – Greenville, SC 29615 USA
☎ 800-423-0485
www.MichelinTravel.com
michelin.guides@us.michelin.com

Manufacture française des pneumatiques Michelin

Société en commandite par actions au capital de 304 000 000 EUR
Place des Carmes-Déchaux – 63000 Clermont-Ferrand (France)
R.C.S. Clermont-Fd B 855 200 507

Dépot légal mars 2007 – ISSN 0763-1383
Printed: June 2007
Printed and bound in Germany